THIRD EDITION

ESSENTIAL READINGS IN URBAN PLANNING

*AICP is a registered trademark of the American Planning Association (APA) and the APA's Institute. Neither the APA nor AICP are affiliated with Planetizen or this book.

Edited by Emily Talen

Produced by **PLANETIZEN** Press

Bassim Hamadeh, CEO and Publisher
Carrie Montoya, Manager, Revisions and Author Care
Kaela Martin, Project Editor
Christian Berk, Production Editor
Jess Estrella, Senior Graphic Designer
Michael Skinner, Senior Licensing Specialist
Natalie Piccotti, Director of Marketing
Kassie Graves, Vice President of Editorial
Jamie Giganti, Director of Academic Publishing

Copyright © 2020 by Cognella, Inc. All rights reserved. No part of this publication may be reprinted, reproduced, transmitted, or utilized in any form or by any electronic, mechanical, or other means, now known or hereafter invented, including photocopying, microfilming, and recording, or in any information retrieval system without the written permission of Cognella, Inc. For inquiries regarding permissions, translations, foreign rights, audio rights, and any other forms of reproduction, please contact the Cognella Licensing Department at rights@cognella.com.

Permission to reprint all selections granted to Cognella by the publishers for this individual course reader. Please don't photocopy—to do so would be a violation of copyright law.

Trademark Notice: Product or corporate names may be trademarks or registered trademarks, and are used only for identification and explanation without intent to infringe.

Cover image copyright © 2013 Depositphotos/polina21.

Printed in the United States of America.

CONTENTS

INTRODUCTION ... V

LOCAL PLANNING: CONTEMPORARY PRINCIPLES AND PRACTICE ... 1

> The Value of Planning
> > By Frederick C. Collignon, Alexander Garvin, Patricia E. Salkin, and Jerold S. Kayden

PLANNING AND URBAN DESIGN STANDARDS ... 33

> By American Planning Association

LAND USE AND THE CONSTITUTION ... 143

> Introduction and the Constitutional Analysis Tree
> > By the American Planning Association

LAND USE PLANNING AND DEVELOPMENT REGULATION LAW ... 159

> Comprehensive Plans and the Planning Process
>
> Land Use Controls: History, Sources of Power and Purposes
> > By Julian Conrad Jurgensmeyer, Thomas E. Roberts, Patricia E. Salkin, and Ryan Max Rowberry

PLANNING THEORY FOR PRACTITIONERS ... 207

> Centralized Rationality: The Planner as Applied Scientist
> > By Michael Brooks

URBAN LAND USE PLANNING ... 233

> Framing The Land Use Planning Process
> > By Philip R. Berke, David R. Godschalk and Edward J. Kaise

THE HIGH COST OF FREE PARKING ... 257

> Putting the Cost of Free Parking in Perspective
> > By Donald C. Shoup

THE PLANNER'S USE OF INFORMATION ... 273

> Survey Methods
> > By Nancy Nishikawa; ed. Hemalata Dandekar
>
> Information from Secondary Sources
> > By Maria Yen and Grace York; ed. Hemalata Dandekar

THE LIVING LANDSCAPE 289
Introduction
By Frederick Steiner

DESIGN WITH NATURE 315
The Metropolitan Region
By Ian L. McHarg

GROWING COOLER: EVIDENCE ON URBAN DEVELOPMENT AND CLIMATE CHANGE 325
Policy and Program Recommendations
By Reid Ewing, Keith Bartholomew, Steve Winkleman, Jerry Walters, and Don Chen

ENVIRONMENTAL PLANNING HANDBOOK FOR SUSTAINABLE COMMUNITIES AND REGIONS 349
Taking Stock of the Environment and Creating Environmental Plans
By Tom Daniels

PLANNING FOR COMMUNITY RESILIENCE 387
What Is Resilience?
By Jamie Hicks Masterson et al.

SITE PLANNING: INTERNATIONAL PRACTICE 405
Infrastructure Systems
By Gary Hack

HAZARD MITIGATION AND PREPAREDNESS 419
Preparedness, Hazard Mitigation, and Climate Change Adaptation: An Overview
By Anna K. Schwab, Dylan Sandler, and David J. Brower

THE TRANSPORTATION PLANNING HANDBOOK 439
The Transportation Planning Process
By Michael D. Meyer

Transportation System Characteristics & Urban Travel Characteristics
By Michael D. Meyer

THE ETHICAL PLANNER 477
Interpretations and Conclusions
By Jerry Weitz

INTRODUCTION

Urban planning, as a field, deals with a vast variety of issues and specializations. In their everyday work, planners consider the demands of infrastructure, transportation engineering, construction, architecture, affordable housing requirements, and historic preservation. Because of this broad scope, it is essential to obtain a solid grounding in the core competencies and theories of planning from the beginning—and to return to them throughout one's career.

The American Institute of Certified Planners (AICP*) is the American Planning Association's professional institute, providing recognized national leadership in the certification of professional planners, ethics, professional development, planning education, and the standards of planning practice. To become a certified planner, APA members must meet certain education and experience requirements and pass a written examination.

For over a decade, Planetizen has provided the best independent training to planners seeking AICP certification, helping many thousands of planners on their journey to improve their professional career and the communities they serve.

As part of our training program, we have assembled readings that are recommended by the American Planning Association and some which, in our opinion, represent the key knowledge necessary to become a certified planner. Whether or not you are currently seeking certification, this collection will give you a firm grounding in the essential theories and practice of urban planning.

The certification exam (and these readings) covers the following broad areas:

- Functional Areas of Practice
- Plan Making and Implementation
- Spatial Areas of Practice
- Fundamental Planning Knowledge
- Areas of Practice
- Ethics

You'll learn about significant historical decisions and theories that continue to impact cities today.

You'll learn cutting edge practices in collecting and analyzing data to make rational, informed planning decisions. Planners work in increasingly holistic and interdisciplinary professional roles. With this book, you'll learn new thinking about how best to collaborate with the many intersecting fields of planning. And, of course, you'll learn best practices and theories behind the complicated task of engaging with the public and delivering outcomes that reflect the desires of the community.

With the creation of the volume, we are indebted to our colleague, Emily Talen, PhD, FAICP, who has carefully curated these readings and who teaches Planetizen's AICP preparation class. Dr. Talen is Professor of Urbanism at the University of Chicago. Her research is devoted to urban design and urbanism, especially the relationship between the built environment and social equity. Her books include *New Urbanism and American Planning, Design for Diversity, Urban Design Reclaimed,* and *City Rules.* She is the recipient of a Guggenheim Fellowship (2014–15) and is a Fellow of the American Institute of Certified Planners.

We welcome you to the Planetizen community and hope you enjoy this selection of readings. We are confident that throughout your career you will have occasion to return to these pages to refresh your memory, guide your practice, and inspire your actions.

—Planetizen Editorial Staff

LOCAL PLANNING: CONTEMPORARY PRINCIPLES AND PRACTICE

CHAPTER 3: *The Value of Planning*

BY FREDERICK C. COLLIGNON, ALEXANDER GARVIN, PATRICIA E. SALKIN, AND JEROLD S. KAYDEN

Frederick C. Collignon

No time is more exciting and challenging than the present for metropolitan communities. In 2006, the population of the United States reached 300 million, and it is expected to pass 400 million well before 2050.[1] In most metropolitan areas, the rate at which land is being consumed is greater than the rate of population growth. While urban areas in the North and Midwest are losing population and employment, those in the West and South-where there are fewer geographical (and, in some cases, regulatory) constraints on growth are gaining residents. Major changes are occurring in where people are choosing to live and work: suburbs and exurban areas are capturing more and more residents and jobs at the same time that downtowns are becoming more attractive.

The makeup of the U.S. population is changing as well. As of 2006, the country was home to 37.5 million immigrants, accounting for 12.5 percent of the total U.S. population more than at any time since the 1920s.[2] Americans are living longer, and in many different kinds of households. In general, we are more highly educated, but there are widening disparities in income. These and other social, economic,

---

Frederick C. Collignon, Alexander Garvin, Patricia E. Salkin, Jerold S. Kayden, "The Value of Planning," *Local Planning: Contemporary Principles and Practice,ed. Gary Hack*, et al., pp. 23-46. Copyright © 2009 by International City/County Management Association (ICMA). Reprinted with permission.

and demographic changes are greatly affecting the amount of land we occupy; our ability to conserve open space; how much we travel and by what means; and our need for infrastructure, housing, and a wide range of public services, from parks and schools to libraries, community centers, and facilities for senior citizens.

Every day, news headlines highlight urban problems: sprawl, congestion, a shortage of affordable housing, decaying infrastructure, not-in-my-backyard conflicts, environmental risk, and many more. These conditions cry out for communities to think about their futures: to engage in planning. Communities must plan for future growth and development, plot investments in capital projects, administer zoning and subdivision regulations, and budget to pay for improvements.

Although most communities develop their plans through extensive citizen participation, few of your neighbors, co-workers, or friends are likely to know exactly what local planning is. They may have run up against a zoning ordinance when they tried to remodel, attended a public meeting about a nearby project, or voted on a bond issue for community improvements. But they probably do not have a broad understanding of how planning touches their lives or of why communities plan.

There is a simple answer: communities plan in order to make informed choices about the future—that is, to create and maintain places where people want to live, work, and conduct business. Specifically, communities use planning to

Communities plan in order to make informed choices about the future— that is, to create and maintain places where people want to live, work, and conduct business.

- Anticipate contingencies, such as shifts in the policies of higher levels of government; prepare for potential shocks, such as a natural or technological disaster; and take advantage of opportunities, such as an influx of high-tech companies
- Promote growth while protecting valued aspects of the current built and natural environments
- Coordinate the long-term investments and actions that will be needed to achieve the agreed-upon goals
- Coordinate land use regulation, transportation, utilities, and other governmental functions and services
- Balance and integrate public and private sector activities
- Resolve conflicts between different areas within the community and between neighboring communities
- Ensure that local policies are in step with those of state, regional, and federal entities
- Fairly distribute both the benefits and burdens of growth, and protect the interests of those who have the fewest resources
- Assess previous planning efforts, identify errors or weaknesses, and change direction as needed
- Document collective agreements about the future of the community, outline strategies for achieving them, and set forth individual and governmental actions that will be required to implement those strategies.

Given the complexity of these tasks, it is clear that a well-planned community does not result from disparate, unrelated efforts, but from the collective and coordinated actions of many individuals and organizations over time. Every well-planned place has a cadre of planners: people who help shape and advance community aspirations by working with elected officials, government agencies, businesses, civic groups, neighborhood associations, and nonprofit organizations. These planners may work in the public, private, or nonprofit sectors. They may be professional planners employed by local government or consulting firms; citizens appointed to planning commissions; or advocates working for special-interest groups. Whatever their background or affiliation, these planners understand growth, development, and design, and they know how to engage in serious discussion about planning issues. They have the skills help resolve conflicts, and to assist with the collective decision making that is the basis of a well-planned community.

It is important to note that planning does not solely benefit the community at large: it also benefits individuals and entities. In fact, it is because plans are derived from individual interests that residents, businesses, and nonprofit organizations choose to actively engage in planning.

In the case of residents, the importance of various community features will differ depending on age, income, education, profession, and cultural background. Residents' needs and expectations also shift over time: for example, concerns about obesity are strengthening the demand for walkable streets; an aging population, with a higher prevalence of disability, is increasing the need for more accessible streets and buildings; and the use of cell phones is requiring new communications infrastructure. Nonetheless, most citizens want

- Adequate and affordable housing, with sufficient choice to meet a wide range of preferences
- A good transportation system that provides easy access to work, school, and other destinations

A well-planned community does not result from disparate, unrelated efforts, but from the collective and coordinated actions of many Individuals and organizations over time.

- Good schools-and, to ensure the community's continuing competitiveness, opportunities for lifelong learning
- Public services at acceptable levels of quality and cost
- A healthy and well-maintained environment that is safe from crime, clean and well maintained, and adequately prepared to cope with natural or technological hazards
- Protection of property values-which, for most families, are the largest components of wealth
- Good architecture, urban design, and natural amenities
- Diverse and accessible cultural, retail, sports, and recreational opportunities
- Institutions and services to meet the needs of the most vulnerable members of the population.
- A healthy business climate that will attract and sustain economic growth.

In some cases, differences in preferences may spark conflict. For example, a community may be split over whether to develop an abandoned industrial waterfront site as a community recreational amenity or as an upscale residential and retail center. Similarly, some segments of a community may support the development of low-priced retail as a means of creating jobs and increasing business tax revenues, while others may believe that such projects will lead to disorderly growth and threaten the traditional character of the community. Planning provides a way to address such conflicts and help keep the community focused on its larger goals.

Businesses have other planning concerns. Businesses are highly diverse: some create products and services for a local market, and others compete nationally or globally. While each kind of business has its particular needs, businesses generally want a favorable business climate that offers

- Cheap, safe, and convenient access to viable markets
- Good transportation for freight and consumers (although technology is changing the nature of transportation demands)
- Access to a labor pool with appropriate skills
- The opportunity to be part of a "business cluster"—a geographic concentration of related businesses that includes suppliers, financial and accounting services, and other specialized facilities and services that will foster business expansion and efficiency
- Affordable rents, taxes, fees, and regulatory requirements
- Reliable public services
- Attractive environments for employees and customers.

Employers in the nonprofit sector—cultural and faith-based institutions; nonprofit organizations that provide services or play advocacy roles; educational institutions; medical facilities; local, state, and federal agencies: and public authorities, such as port and airport authorities, utility districts, and transportation authorities—also want good transportation access, a skilled labor pool, a safe and attractive environment, good public services, and a predictable future to secure their long-term investment in buildings and property. While some of these entities are not subject to the same regulations that pertain to the private sector, it is essential to include them in planning endeavors: as residents and businesses become more and more footloose, institutions are increasingly likely to serve as anchors for a community.

In sum, planning confers important benefits on individuals, and on the various entities—public, private, and nonprofit—that make up a community. Planning helps communities sustain their desirability as places to be.

FOCUS ON

PLANNERS AS LEADERS

Alex Garvin

Planners are in the change business. A planner's work should be judged by the quality and depth of its influence on people's lives.

Many marvelous planners were not trained as professional planners, and many planners with professional training have had little influence on their surroundings. The difference between the two is the sometimes mysterious quality of leadership. To understand the role of leadership in planning, it may be instructive to look at some historical examples of how planners have helped bring about change.

THE POLITICAL AND ECONOMIC CONTEXT OF PLANNING

Planning in the United States is based on two operative factors: a pluralistic, representative democracy and a well-regulated freemarket economy. In practical terms, this means that American elected officials make decisions based in large part on what they believe the voters will support. In keeping with the American economic system, most construction occurs on private property, in response to private market demand, and is tenanted by private citizens and organizations. Developers try to anticipate demand by building in places where people would like to live, work, or shop. When they are successful, they make a profit—their reward for the financial risk.

Of course, this is a somewhat idealized view of how American towns and cities are built, and there are exceptions, both benign (economic incentives) and not (corruption). But by and large, more than those of any other nation in the world, the American political and economic systems are designed to be responsive to individual choice. Moreover, both systems are intentionally kept highly fragmented. On the political level, power is divided between national, state, and local governments and between the executive, legislative, and judicial branches. In the economic realm, the government encourages competition, preventing monopolies and prosecuting cartels that grant any one entity too much control. Within either the political or the economic system, a variety of constituencies may face off. Such carefully bounded conflicts are intended to provide checks on the power of any one actor. Of course, the government also intervenes to enforce laws, to coordinate, to regulate, and to create projects for the public good.

Baron Haussmann, the great nineteenth-century planner of Paris, succeeded in imposing a plan only because he had the support of Emperor Napoleon III, who had helped design it. Even with the emperor's support, however, Haussmann faced fierce opposition every step of the way and was eventually forced to resign. In America, this sort of planning is impossible. In New York, Robert Moses, so often depicted as an autocratic power broker, accomplished what he did, not through raw power but through compromise, political acumen, savvy, opportunism, and sheer energy-and even then, he accomplished only a small part of what he had set out to build.

IMPLEMENTING BURNHAM'S PLAN FOR CHICAGO

To understand American planning, one must first make a distinction between planning and making a plan. Too many planners believe that the end result of planning is a static plan. But planning is a fluid and dynamic process: cities are constantly changing, often in unexpected ways, and planning must continuously respond to new realities. The best planning anticipates these new realities and shapes the changes in a way that benefits the public, while making the most efficient possible use of resources. When considered closely, even famous plans turn out to be more about process than about achieving a fixed goal. Daniel Burnham's 1909 *Plan of Chicago*, for example, was originally intended as a plan for every part of the city. However, much of what Burnham proposed—grand axial boulevards and civic centers—was initially discarded as impractical. Although many of the projects recommended in the plan were eventually implemented, transforming the city and triggering billions of dollars in private investment, implementing the changes took years of advocacy and political effort. In other words, some aspects of the plan were enacted only when they proved politically and economically feasible. As Burnham himself said, "When particular

Planning is a fluid and dynamic process: cities are constantly changing, often in unexpected ways, and planning must continuously respond to new realities.

portions of the plan shall be taken up for execution, wider knowledge, longer experience, or a change in local conditions may suggest a better solution."[1]

Burnham's proposal to construct a bridge across the Chicago River at Michigan Avenue and to widen Pine Street, which was to be renamed North Michigan Avenue and transformed into a wide boulevard, illustrates just how complicated the planning process is and just how many people need to be involved (see Figure 1a). Burnham didn't invent the idea for the bridge; Chicagoans had been proposing similar projects since the early 1880s. In 1896, Burnham had proposed a tunnel under the Chicago River to connect Michigan Avenue and Pine Street. In 1905, a committee of the city council voted to build a bridge to achieve the same end. Both of these plans died.

In 1906, the Merchants Club (a business association that, in 1907, merged into the Commercial Club) sponsored Daniel Burnham and Edward Bennett to prepare a plan for Chicago, Burnham had been a member of Chicago's political and business establishment for more than two decades. His reputation as a planner had been enhanced by his work on the 1893 World's Columbian Exposition in Chicago and by his subsequent plans for Cleveland, San Francisco, and Manila. Burnham's firm spent three years producing the *Plan of Chicago*, which included proposals for a Michigan Avenue bridge and for North Michigan Avenue (Figure 1b). To carry out the plan, the city established the City Plan Commission—which, under the leadership of businessman Charles Wacker, published booklets, sponsored presentations, and lobbied in favor of the plan.

The published plan faced opposition from property owners along Pine Street, who did not want their buildings condemned to make way for the widened avenue. Meanwhile, Chicago's business and political elites organized political support for the Michigan Avenue proposals. In 1913, the Chicago city council authorized the condemnation of property along Pine Street,

Figure 1a. The Rush Street Bridge, Chicago (circa 1890), one block west of Michigan Avenue, accommodated only one lane of traffic in each direction.

Source: Courtesy of the Chicago Historical Society

Figure 1b. The Burnham and Bennett Plan of Chicago envisioned a straightened two-level riverfront with a new Michigan Avenue Bridge.

Source: Daniel Burnham and Edward Bennett. *Plan of Chicago* (1909)

and the issuance of a bond to cover both the cost of the property and the construction of the new bridge and boulevard. The city began condemning the property in 1916 and spent the next two years fighting off a series of lawsuits by outraged property owners, most of whom wanted more money for their property. It was not until 1918 that the city completed the property acquisition and began demolition and construction. By 1920, the bridge and the new boulevard were complete (Figure 1c).

The city began to rebuild North Michigan Avenue even before the bridge was complete. This work was shaped, in large part, by Chicago's 1923 zoning ordinance, which allowed buildings along the avenue to rise to 264 feet along their street wall, and permitted towers set back from the street to rise higher still. During the 1920s, the combination of zoning and pent-up demand created an enormous building boom. As a result, North Michigan Avenue was transformed from a narrow thoroughfare lined by warehouses and small shops into the Magnificent Mile—a stretch of skyscraper office buildings, department stores, elegant hotels, and high-end shops. The building boom continued through the decades; today, North Michigan Avenue is the premiere shopping, residential, and business address in Chicago (Figure 1d).

Thus, it took nearly forty years-from the 1880s to 1920—of planning, advocacy, elections, court battles, political jockeying, and construction before the plan for a bridge and boulevard could move from conception to reality. And it took decades more for developers, lenders, architects, and builders to recreate the avenue and construct new buildings with new uses. Ultimately, what emerged bore little resemblance to the watercolor renderings illustrating Burnham's original plan. Although Burnham was an essential figure and his plan the essential document in the process, the planning and implementation of this single improvement engaged thousands of people: bankers, politicians, real estate speculators,

Figure 1c. By the late 1920s, the new bridge and widened North Michigan Avenue had already begun to spark massive private development.

Source: Courtesy of the Chicago Historical Society

Figure 1d. By the start of the twenty-first century, North Michigan Avenue had become the city's primiere retail and office district.

Source: Alexander Garvin

judges, lawyers, developers, civic organizations, architects, and voters.

BUILDING PUBLIC CONSTITUENCIES

The length of the planning process in Chicago, and the large number of people involved, reflect the nature of the political process. It took time to develop a constituency to support the idea, to organize and lobby for the improvements, to foster the political will to face down property owners and other local interests that opposed the new bridge, and to build support for the taxes and bonds required to pay for the improvements. A variety of interest groups contributed to the process and eventually agreed on a physical design that met the functional, physical, political, financial, and aesthetic requirements of all the participants. Forty years is a long time to build a bridge and widen a street—but, by the end of the process, thousands of entities and individuals had had their say, and every legal requirement had been fulfilled. The final result perfectly met Chicago's needs—and transformed the city.

Those involved fell into roughly three categories: private interests (such as property owners and real estate developers); public officials (such as the mayors who supported the project): and private organizations (such as the Commercial Club) that lobbied in the name of the public good. Yet it cannot be said that everyone involved was a planner and that the plan was simply the handiwork of thousands. Burnham's work really was essential to the outcome.

PLANNERS AS INTEGRATORS OF IDEAS

What made Burnham unique and extraordinary was his ability to look beyond competing interests and single functions to integrate a variety of interests, functions, and Influences and so create a compelling-and transformative—vision. Successful planners are integrators: they know how to address a variety of needs, satisfy a variety of interests, develop a comprehensive vision, and imagine how the effects of a project will spill over, transforming the surrounding area or the city as whole.

Integrative visions are not always successful at first. After the Great Fire in 1666, the architect Christopher Wren produced a plan for the reconstruction of London, but it was never implemented. In 1956, the architect Victor Gruen—one of the most influential planners of the twentieth century and inventor of the modern enclosed shopping mall—proposed a plan for Fort Worth, Texas: *A Greater Fort Worth Tomorrow* (Figure 2). Apart from the idea of a ring road surrounding the central business district, the plan was not implemented.

Frederick Law Olmsted, the greatest planner of the nineteenth century and perhaps America's greatest planner ever, was the quintessential integrative thinker. Through his designs for Manhattan's Central Park and Boston's Emerald Necklace; his plans for Riverside, a suburb in Illinois, and for Sudbrook, a suburb in Maryland; his reports on Yosemite and Niagara Falls; and his hundreds of lectures, articles, and park proposals, Olmsted did more to reshape the American

Figure 2. Victor Gruen's 1956 plan for Fort Worth advocates a pedestrian environment, with underground services and multilevel garages, all accessible from an expressway loop encircling the downtown.

Source: Victor Gruen, *A Greater Fort Worth Tomorrow* (1956)

landscape than any other individual. His parks reorganized the ways that cities worked, attracting new development and connecting the rest of the city through parkways. His suburbs created a new model for civilized living (see Figure 3). In short, Olmsted saw city, suburb, and the natural environment as an integrated whole, and his work reflected the fullness and complexity of that vision.

The twentieth century saw the rise of large public bureaucracies and a resulting demand for public administrators capable of thinking in integrative ways. None was more talented than Robert Moses, who once said, "Our watchword should be that we found our city a wilderness of stone and steel, crowded and inaccessible, and that we opened it to light and air, planted with the green of parks and the laughter of playgrounds, and carved out wide spokes of rims for parkways and expressways to make the city and country one." This philosophy guided Moses for decades. Holding as many as a dozen public positions at once, he laid out highways and parkways that were lined and punctuated by parks; demolished slums to build new housing projects permeated by light and air; constructed playgrounds and parks throughout the city; and created Lincoln Center and New York's first genuine convention center. In fact, he remade New York in a manner that was nothing short of astonishing. At the same time, he embodied all the flaws and risks of public bureaucracy: lack of political accountability, disregard for local concerns, and rigidity in the face of opposition. Although Moses found the word *planning* repugnant, his combination of vision, practicality, entrepreneurship, and ability made him a planner of the highest order (see Figure 4).

For-profit developers can also bring an integrated vision to their work. In planning the new town of Columbia, Maryland, the developer James Rouse assembled a team of expert advisers—leading thinkers in education, sociology, government, health, psychology, family life, planning, and more—to help him create the ideal environment. Conceived as an alternative to the "formless places without order, beauty, or reason" that Rouse saw being "splattered

Figure 3. Frederick Law Olmsted's plan for Riverside, Illinois, created a tree-lined public realm that became a model for suburban design.

Source: Alexander Garvin

Figure 4. Brooklyn's Shore Parkway is typical of the way that Robert Moses combined financing for roads, bridges, and parkland to pay for a much improved quality of life.

Source: Alexander Garvin

across the landscape,"[4] Columbia was carefully designed as a collection of small neighborhoods, each with their own community facilities. Each group of neighborhoods supported a village with its own shopping facilities and houses of worship, and the villages, in turn, supported a town center with office space and a shopping mall. All this was set in a landscape of generous parks, verdant woods, and lovely public spaces (Figure 5). Columbia was integrative planning at its best: a fully realized vision of ideal suburban life. Unfortunately for Rouse, however, it was a financial failure: the lenders foreclosed on the Rouse Company and later had to write off millions of dollars in losses.

One recent development in cities has been the rise of public-private partnerships, entities that link the government's powers to the private sector's entrepreneurial skills and relative freedom from constraints. Opportunities for such partnerships have given rise to a new generation of civic entrepreneurs who are particularly skilled at creating business improvement districts (BIDs). In the hands of a talented leader such as Paul Levy, executive director of Philadelphia's Center City District, a BID can become a planning tool capable of transforming a downtown. In 2006, the Center City BID had a budget of more than $14 million devoted to sanitation, security, and marketing for the district. But the BID has also worked with the Philadelphia police department on new law enforcement practices; has helped establish a community court to deal promptly with quality-of-life offenses; has worked to create

Figure 5. At Columbia, Maryland, James Rouse demonstrated that private developers, without government assistance, could provide a model of integrated planning.

Source: Alexander Garvin

opportunities for the homeless; releases a constant stream of market research on the downtown housing, retail, and office markets; and lobbies for policies and projects that will strengthen the competitiveness of downtown. The result has been a total transformation of the Center City District: it is cleaner, safer, more congenial, and more vibrant. Levy—and other talented leaders of BIDs, such as Daniel Biederman of New York's Bryant Park Restoration Corporation and 34th Street Partnership—have demonstrated that a gifted manager can develop a comprehensive view of the issues and opportunities within a district and integrate them into a vision that transforms a part of the city.

PROFESSIONAL PLANNERS

Professional planning was born in the early decades of the twentieth century; it arose from the need to coordinate chaotic urban growth—for example, to ensure that the infrastructure could support the new populations flooding into cities—and to create visions that would guide future development. In 1914, the Newark Plan Commission hired Harland Bartholomew as its secretary and engineer, making him the first full-time municipal planning employee in the United States. Bartholomew later became the primary planner for St. Louis, and his firm, Harland Bartholomew and Associates, became one of the country's most active and influential planning firms.

Bartholomew came to the job from an engineering background, and he approached his job from an engineer's perspective. Armed with statistics on demographics, economics, traffic, growth trends, and more, Bartholomew and his colleagues undertook elaborate studies and developed projections to determine how a city would grow and what changes to infrastructure and regulations would make that growth possible.

Bartholomew called his approach "scientific"; others used the phrase "the City Efficient" to refer to his work—contrasting it, perhaps simplistically with the City Beautiful movement associated with Burnham and his followers. But no matter what the name, the idea was to provide the rational, coordinated planning that cities needed in order to grow.

Bartholomew was particularly effective in implementing his recommendations because he recognized that plans not only had to be conceived, but also had to be implemented. When his firm undertook planning for a city or town, it sent a staff member to live in that place, full-time, for three years. The staff member worked closely with local government agencies and with a citizens' advisory committee, discussing proposals and helping to generate political support. The final recommendations came complete with price tags and a strategy for funding the improvements. Bartholomew's employees were so successful that when they finished, the jurisdictions they had worked for often hired them away from him.

In the wake of Bartholomew's work-and thanks in large part to his efforts—the role of professional planner became an accepted part of the municipal landscape, and it remains so to this day. Every major city has a planning department under the leadership of a planning director. In some cases, the planning department provides a platform for visionary and integrative leadership.

Edmund Bacon, executive director of Philadelphia's City Planning Commission from 1949 to 1970, raised the role of professional planner to a new level of visibility. Educated as an architect, Bacon first worked as a housing advocate and later joined a group of young Philadelphia reformers (known as the Young Turks) who were determined to bring an end to the corrupt Republican machine and drag Philadelphia into the modern era. Bacon, a Philadelphia native, later said, "In 1940 or 1941, I made a vow that come hell or high water. I would make Philadelphia as good as I could."[5]

One of Bacon's first planning efforts was helping to organize the Better Philadelphia Exhibition of 1947. Mounted in space donated by Gimbel's department store, the exhibition used three-dimensional models, accompanied by text, to present Philadelphians with a compelling vision of the future of their city. The models showed Philadelphia as it existed at the time, but it had parts that could be flipped over to show what each section of the city could become. From 1949 to 1970, Bacon led the most sophisticated planning process in the nation, creating highly visible changes that included demolishing the Broad Street Station and railroad viaduct (known locally as the Chinese Wall) and replacing it with the shops and offices of Penn Center (Figures 6 and 7); expanding the shopping district by constructing the Market East shopping complex; and, in perhaps his most extraordinary achievement, renewing Society Hill, which became the most desirable neighborhood in Philadelphia.

PLANNERS AS SKILLED GENERALISTS

In the brochure for the Better Philadelphia Exhibition, Edmund Bacon wrote that the purpose of the exhibition was "to gain the confidence of a public made cynical by utopian futuramas and the inertia of local politicians."[6] This assertion—that the role of the planner is to look out for the public interest—is an ideal prescription for modern planners, whether they come from the planning profession or not. Planners must balance public and private interests, general and local concerns. They must also prove their value to society by advancing feasible projects of import—and then ensuring that those projects are completed.

Perhaps more important, planners must be entrepreneurs. Their objective must be to create and shape change. That means looking for opportunities to do things differently, taking

Figure 6. Trains used to enter Philadelphia on an elevated viaduct, dripping soot and making a terrible racket as they made their way into the old Broad Street Station. Property owners avoided building anywhere near this rail viaduct, known locally as the "Chinese Wall."

Source: Courtesy of the Chicago Historical Society

note of shifts in society or in markets, and taking the initiative to create a new reality rather than being swept along by events.

Over the past century, society has become vastly more complex. Every field of knowledge has advanced in leaps and bounds as our research methods have improved, our technologies have advanced, and we systematically amass new data and new knowledge. The result is a society of incredibly talented and well-informed specialists. The planning field alone includes experts in architecture, civil engineering, transportation, public safety, public health, finance, law, and more.

One unfortunate consequence of specialization, however, is a fragmented approach to examining issues and making decisions. Take, for example, an ordinary city street. The design, placement, and construction of the roadway and sidewalk are determined by the transportation department, which is focused on keeping traffic moving smoothly. The gutters are controlled by the agency that is responsible for sewers. The water pipes are installed by the water department. The fire department wants to be sure its trucks can get through. The police are concerned about public safety. The sanitation department wants to be sure it can pick up the garbage. The transit authority needs places for its buses to park; in a large city, there may be a subway underneath. And this list doesn't even mention

Figure 7. As a result of Edmund Bacon's efforts, the "Chinese Wall" was demolished and replaced by Penn Center, which triggered massive private investment on Market Street.

Source: Alexander Garvin

the private property that fronts the street, which is of concern to landlords, retailers, tenants, and other parties.

What society needs in planning, and elsewhere, is not more specialists; it needs skilled generalists. Planners must be able to grasp many viewpoints and ways of understanding the world, and knit them together. This does not require being an expert in every field; that would be impossible. But it does require the ability to understand the fundamental issues in a variety of fields, and the relationships between them. Planners must be able to speak the language of architects, bankers, engineers, public servants, politicians, and citizens. They must be fluent in the language of finance, market analysis, politics, design, and more. They must be able to divine what is feasible and what is not. They must be effective communicators- able to write clearly, speak effectively, and convey ideas through images. Finally, planners must be diplomats, able to forge compromises among disparate groups.

Drawing on all these skills, a planner must be able to create a compelling vision that captures the public imagination. This is what Burnham meant when he said,

> Make no little plans; they have no magic to stir men's blood and will not be realized. Make big plans; aim high in hope and work, remembering that a noble, logical diagram once recorded will never die, but long after

What society needs in planning, and elsewhere, is not more specialists; it needs skilled generalists.

we are gone will be a living thing, asserting itself with ever growing insistency.[7]

Bacon expressed the same idea slightly differently: "Create a figure that is so overpowering that people forget alternatives."[8] Burnham, Bacon, and Olmsted all understood the power of a great figure. Bartholomew, for all his talents, never did. It is the planner's greatest weapon.

FOCUS ON

THE AUTHORITY TO PLAN

Patricia E. Salkin

Planning is perhaps the single most important function of local government in the United States. Residents depend on local government officials to ensure, through planning, the sustainability of their neighborhoods and communities. As is noted in the statutes of New York State, "Significant decisions and actions affecting the immediate and long-range protection, enhancement, growth and development of the state and its communities are made by local governments."[9] This responsibility calls for the development and coordination of various types of plans—including, but not limited to, comprehensive land use plans, master plans, capital improvement plans, emergency plans, and transportation plans.

Local planning authority comes from a variety of federal, state, local, and regional sources. While the focus in this article is on municipal authority to develop a comprehensive land use plan—which is the central planning function for municipalities—a multitude of other plans are authorized, and sometimes required, by various levels of government. Unfortunately, these plans are not always coordinated with the comprehensive plan. For example, although the state and federal governments require plans to address hazards such as hurricanes, flooding, earthquakes, and wildfires, the effectiveness of such plans often hinges on their being synchronized with local land use plans and zoning.[10] The lack of mandated intra—and intergovernmental plan coordination is perhaps the greatest weakness of local planning in the United States.

THE STANDARD CITY PLANNING ENABLING ACT

Local governments' authority to shape their growth and development originated in the 1920s, when various states adopted enabling legislation for planning. Most followed the guidance offered in the Standard City Planning Enabling Act (SCPEA), which was developed by the U.S. Department of Commerce in 1928. Written by prominent leaders in the planning field—including Cincinnati zoning lawyer Alfred Bettman and Edward M. Bassett, the author of the New York City zoning ordinance—the SCPEA covered six main subjects:

- The organization and power of the planning commission, which was tasked with preparing and adopting a master plan[11]
- The content of the master plan
- The adoption of a master street plan by the governing body

- The approval, by the planning commission, of all public improvements
- Control of the private subdivision of land
- The establishment of a regional planning commission and a regional plan[12]

Under the model set forth in the SCPEA, local planning was dominated not by elected officials but by appointed officials—who, it was felt, would be better able to evaluate planning issues from a nonpartisan perspective.[13] The SCPEA remains a strong influence, and many state enabling acts are still based on this model.[14]

STATE GOVERNMENTS ADOPT PLANNING

Today, according to the American Planning Association, ten states make local planning optional: twenty-five states make it conditionally mandatory (i.e., local governments are required to develop a plan only if they choose to create a planning commission); and fifteen states make it mandatory.[15]

The content of the comprehensive plan and the level of detail at which the subjects are addressed vary considerably. Some state statutes provide no guidance or mandates, while others are more prescriptive. New York law, for example, suggests a wide range of elements that may be included in a comprehensive plan; California law requires every municipality to create a general plan that includes, at a minimum, the following elements: land use, circulation, housing, conservation, open space, noise, and safety.[16] A few states, such as Oregon, require local land use plans to be consistent with the state plan and policies.[17]

LEGAL SIGNIFICANCE OF THE COMPREHENSIVE PLAN

One of the SCPEA's most significant influences was its endorsement of optional rather than mandatory planning.[18] The notion that planning is optional led, in turn, to the controversial view that planning, or the adoption of a comprehensive plan, is not necessarily a prerequisite to the adoption of zoning laws-a view that has been confirmed by the majority of state courts.[19] Nonetheless, it is common practice for zoning and other land use controls to be consistent with the comprehensive plan. Thus, the plan is the foundation for the legal actions that are designed to implement the goals set forth within it.

Some states, including Arizona, California, Delaware, Florida, Kentucky, New Jersey, and Oregon, mandate consistency between zoning regulations and the comprehensive plan.[20] Because of the legal significance of the plan, some state statutes and case law specify that the adoption and amendment of the comprehensive plan is a legislative rather than an administrative function. The modern trend is for courts to view the comprehensive plan as either a significant factor or the governing principle in land use regulation.[21] Because the comprehensive plan is central to land use control, it is essential for local governments to exercise their authority to develop comprehensive plans, to ensure that other local and regional plans reflect the goals and principles of the comprehensive plans, and to design their comprehensive plans to take into account the relationships between their jurisdictions and neighboring local governments.

NATIONAL EFFORTS TO REFORM PLANNING LAW

Over the years, several groups have promoted updating the model planning legislation to accommodate contemporary concerns. In the 1970s, the American Law Institute produced *A Model Land Development Code*, but the code had little practical impact because most state officials, planners, and associated professionals were preoccupied with the new environmental statutes and regulations of the era.[22] Regrettably, they failed to see the connections between land use law and environmental law, perhaps because these areas of the law arose at different times and were designed to address different—and apparently unrelated—problems.[23]

In 2002, the American Planning Association set out to modernize the SCPEA and issued the two-volume *Growing Smart Legislative Guidebook: Model Statutes for Planning and the Management of Change*. The result of a seven-year study, the model statutes were designed to

- Bring certainty and efficiency to the development approval process
- Promote planning through a mix of "carrots" and "sticks"
- Ensure that citizens who would be affected by planning decisions were given the opportunity for early involvement in the planning process
- Address the interrelationships between employment, housing, fiscal health, transportation, environment, and social equity
- Offer governments a range of planning tools to manage growth and change
- Link the timing, location, and intensity of development with planned or existing infrastructure
- Help local governments monitor the ongoing performance of planning systems.[24]

The guidebook recommends that state enabling statutes reflect a three-tiered approach to the elements of local comprehensive plans: some should be mandatory, others should be mandatory with an opt-out alternative, and still others should be optional. (See the

---

TREATMENT OF LOCAL COMPREHENSIVE PLAN ELEMENTS IN MODEL STATUTES

Mandatory
Issues and opportunities
Land use
Transportation
Community facilities
Housing
Program implementation

Mandatory with opt-out alternative
Economic development
Critical and sensitive areas
Natural hazards

Optional
Agriculture, forest, and scenic preservation
Human services
Community design
Historic preservation
Subplans

Source: Stuart Meck. ed. *Growing Smart Legislative Guidebook: Model Statutes for Planning and the Management of Change* (Chicago: American Planning Association. 2002), 7–61.

accompanying sidebar for a list of elements in each category.) The guidebook also calls for local governments that are preparing plans to consider issues, opportunities, and needs associated with the larger region.[25]

REGIONAL PLANNING

As it has become increasingly clear that the impacts of local land use decisions know no political boundaries, local governments have begun to engage in voluntary intergovernmental cooperation in the area of land use planning. Most states grant broad statutory authority to local governments to cooperate with neighboring communities; joint comprehensive plans are among the results of such cooperation. It is increasingly common for local comprehensive plans to include statements acknowledging that the municipality exists as part of a larger region, and for local land use decisions to reflect this perspective.

While publicly authorized regional planning agencies have existed since the early decades of the twentieth century, they have proliferated in the past several decades. The federal and state governments have promoted regional planning agencies (e.g., the Tahoe Regional Planning Agency, the Adirondack Park Agency, and the New Jersey Pinelands Commission) by granting them limited authority to plan for the protection and preservation of natural or environmentally significant resources, or to review specific local and state actions. (Metropolitan planning organizations, for example, are the federally recognized review bodies for transportation planning.) In other cases, regional planning agencies have been established by statute or otherwise authorized to provide extralocal perspectives on trends and resources in a multijurisdictional region. Depending on the legislation establishing these regional planning entities, they may or may not have the authority to develop binding land use plans for their areas of jurisdiction.

ENABLING, NOT LIMITING

In most cases, the design of a comprehensive plan is limited only by the creativity of local officials and their political will. Federal and state mandates and enabling legislation for planning can provide guiding principles, a broad outline of plans, and sometimes fiscal incentives; ultimately, however, it is the community itself that must determine how to become, and to remain, the kind of place it wishes to be.

FOCUS ON

PROPERTY RIGHTS, PLANNING, AND THE PUBLIC INTEREST

Jerold S. Kayden

"After all, if a policeman must know the Constitution, then why not a planner?"[26] Posed in a dissenting opinion issued in 1981 by U.S. Supreme Court Justice William J. Brennan, this rhetorical question warned planners to learn what the Constitution has to say about property rights, planning, and the public interest. Like many foundational texts, however, the Constitution is hardly a model of clarity: broad phrases, many of which are subject to interpretation, establish basic principles. References to property are sparse. The term *private property* is mentioned only once—in the Fifth Amendment's just compensation clause, which states that "private property" shall not "be taken for public use, without just compensation."[27] The word *property* alone, without the modifier *private*, appears twice, in the Fifth and Fourteenth Amendments, which guarantee that government shall not deprive persons of "life, liberty, or property, without due process of law."[28] Hardly self-defining, *private property* and *property* have gained meaning through a long skein of opinions issued by the U.S. Supreme Court.

Since the beginning of the twentieth century, the Court has issued thirty-eight opinions that collectively define its interpretation of the Constitution with respect to property rights, planning, and the public interest. In none of these opinions does the Court expressly define private property as such; direct definitions have come from state common and statutory law and from seminal legal texts written by renowned jurisprudential scholars. These sources have seen property as a set of rights—or, metaphorically, as a bundle of sticks representing, individually, the rights to use and transfer property, and the right to exclude others from it.[29]

Notwithstanding Sir William Blackstone's muscular evocation of an owner's "sole and despotic dominion" over this thing called property,[30] property rights have never been conceived as absolute and unlimited. Most often, the common law of nuisance (*sic utere tuo ut alienum non iaedes*, translated as "use your own property in such a manner as not to injure that of another"), developed and applied by common-law judges, has for centuries limited what owners could do with their sticks.[31]

THE INTERPLAY BETWEEN PROPERTY RIGHTS AND REGULATION

The true definition of property arises from the interplay between property and government regulation. In the United States, that interplay began with the creation and elaboration of the modern regulatory state. During the first decades of the twentieth century, a fast-growing, rapidly industrializing nation found itself beleaguered by incompatible, cheek-by-jowl land uses and found salvation in scientific city planning solutions. As systematic legislative approaches to land use control supplanted case-by-case application of nuisance law, the Supreme Court emerged as [he crucial arbiter of how much government intervention was constitutionally acceptable. Testing new techniques such as zoning against the enduring principles of the Constitution, the Court developed a stance that tolerated significant interference with property rights, especially when those rights involved a change from an existing use to a higher and better use.

The 1915 *Hadacheck v. Sebastian* opinion is a classic example of this stance.[32] J. C. Hadacheck was thrown into jail for operating a brickyard in Los Angeles in violation of a local ordinance. He claimed that his eight-acre tract, used for brick making, was worth $800,000, whereas if it were used for residential or any other purpose (and he claimed that there were no purposes other than brick making to which it could be put), if would be worth $60,000. Although C. E. Sebastian, the Los Angeles chief of police, did not dispute Hadacheck's contention that the property would lose value if put to any other use, he denied that the ordinance as applied would "'entirely deprive Hadacheck of his property and the use thereof.'"[33] In language so sweeping that it still causes constitutional land use law experts to catch their breath, the Court heartily endorsed the government's exercise of the so-called police power, which gives it the authority to protect the health, safety, morals, and general welfare of society:

> It is to be remembered that we are dealing with one of the most essential powers of government,—one that is the least limitable. It may, indeed, seem harsh in its exercise, usually is on some individual, but the imperative necessity for its existence precludes any limitation upon it when not

exerted arbitrarily. ... There must be progress, and if in its march private interests are in the way, they must yield to the good of the community.

The logical result of [Hadacheck's] contention would seem to be that a city could not be formed or enlarged against the resistance of an occupant of the ground, and that if it grows at all it can only grow as the environment of the occupations that are usually banished to the purlieus.[34]

During the 1920s, the Court issued eight opinions that, taken together, approved new methods of government restriction on private property while drawing the line at extreme deprivations. Two opinions, *Pennsylvania Coal Co. v. Mahon*[35] and *Village of Euclid v. Ambler Realty Co.*,[36] stand out. The *Pennsylvania Coal* decision is best known for Justice Oliver Wendell Holmes's declaration that "if regulation goes too far it will be recognized as a taking.'"[37] The case addressed a state statute, known as the Kohler Act, which forbade coal companies from conducting subsurface mining in ways that caused houses located on the surface to subside, even where the coal company had expressly retained the subsurface rights at the time that it had sold the surface rights to the homeowner. Because the Kohler Act made it "commercially impracticable" to mine the coal, the Court concluded that the law had "very nearly the same effect for constitutional purposes as appropriating or destroying" the property right to mine the coal.[38] In such an extreme case, in which the property interest was effectively destroyed, the Court found an unconstitutional taking, even as it recognized the nature of the balancing act:

Government hardly could go on if, to some extent, values incident to property could not be diminished without paying for every such change in the general law. As long recognized, some values are enjoyed under an implied limitation, and must yield to the police power. But obviously the implied limitation must have its limits, or the contract and due process clauses are gone. One fact for consideration in determining such limits is the extent of the diminution. When it reaches a certain magnitude, in most if not in all cases, there must be an exercise of eminent domain and compensation to sustain the act.[39]

On its own, *Pennsylvania Coal* might be read as undermining *Hadacheck*'s ample endorsement of government regulation—a view that was, in fact, vigorously expressed by Justice Louis Brandeis in his dissent. Read in the context of other 1920s opinions, however, *Pennsylvania Coal* may be better understood as declaring an outer limit—the complete destruction of a property interest-to *Hadacheck*'s otherwise expansive dictum.

Four years later, in *Village of Euclid v. Ambler Realty Co.*, the Court decisively affirmed the constitutionality of comprehensive zoning. Ambler Realty owned sixty-eight acres in Euclid, Ohio, and wanted to develop the tract for industrial uses—which, it claimed, would yield a value of $10,000 per acre, versus $2,500 or less per acre if used for residential purposes, as called for by Euclid's zoning regulations. In its general exposition, *Euclid* sounded like *Hadacheck*—only more so:

Building zone laws are of modern origin. They began in this country about twenty-five years ago. Until recent years, urban life was comparatively simple; but with the great increase and concentration of population, problems have developed, and constantly are developing, which require, and will continue to require, additional restrictions in respect of the use and occupation of private lands in urban communities. Regulations, the wisdom, necessity and validity of which, as applied to existing conditions, are so apparent that they are now uniformly sustained, a century ago, or even half a century ago, probably would have been rejected as arbitrary and oppressive. Such regulations are sustained, under the complex conditions of our day, for reasons analogous to those which justify traffic regulations, which, before the advent of automobiles and rapid transit street railways, would have been condemned as fatally arbitrary and unreasonable. And in this there is no inconsistency, for, while the meaning of constitutional guaranties never varies, the scope of their application must expand or contract to meet the new and different conditions which are constantly coming within the field of their operation. In a changing world, it is impossible that it should be otherwise. But although a degree of elasticity is thus imparted, not to the *meaning*, but to the *application* of constitutional principles, statutes and ordinances, which, after giving due weight to the new conditions, are found clearly not to conform to the Constitution, of course, must fall.[40]

Reviewing the heart of the Euclid ordinance exclusion of business, industry, and, most controversially, apartment houses from single-family residential districts—the Court accepted the village's planning justifications as "sufficiently cogent to preclude us from saying, as it must be said before the ordinance can be declared unconstitutional, that such provisions are clearly arbitrary and unreasonable, having no substantial relation to the public health, safety, morals, or general welfare"[41] The Court did not insist upon irrefutable arguments to buttress the regulatory action, and reminded all that if the validity of the legislation is "fairly debatable," the legislative judgment should prevail.

Zoning—a manifestation of Progressive Era enthusiasm for scientific solutions to social problems, and the object of popular support from a coalition of business groups and professional organizations—entered the body politic.[42] At least with respect to this category of regulatory enthusiasm, the Supreme Court deferred to pragmatic problem solving, reserving its disapproval only for extreme cases. A somewhat more cynical explanation is that the justices of the time did not view land use regulation as a threat to private property but as a potential means of increasing its value. *Euclid*, for example, can easily be read as a decision supporting the property rights of the homeowners whose properties surrounded the Ambler parcel—and who had apparently been able to persuade local officials to prohibit the incursion of industry and multifamily housing into their neighborhood. The Court's thinly veiled—and, through today's lenses, unsettling—disgust for "parasitic" apartment buildings makes this reading all the more persuasive.[43]

Important cases in land use law

CASE	HOLDING
Welch v. Swasey, 214 U.S. 91 (1909)	Upheld height limits
Murphy v. California, 225 U.S. 623 (1912)	Upheld a prohibition on billiard halls
Reinman v. Little Rock, 237 U.S. 171 (1915)	Upheld a ban on livery stables
Hadacheck v. Sebastian, 239 U.S. 394 (1915)	Upheld a ban on brick manufacturing
Cusack Co. v. City of Chicago, 242 U.S. 526 (1917)	Upheld a billboard ordinance
Pierce Oil Corp. v. City of Hope, 248 U.S. 498 (1919)	Upheld an ordinance prohibiting oil storage within 300 feet of dwellings
Perley v. State of North Carolina, 249 U.S. 510 (1919)	Upheld a requirement preventing removal or burning of waste timber
Wall v. Midland Carbon Co., 254 U.S. 300 (1920)	Upheld a ban on carbon manufacturing
Block v. Hirsh, 256 U.S. 135 (1921)	Upheld rent control
Pennsylvania Coal Co. v. Mahon, 260 U.S. 393 (1922)	Overturned a ban on subsurface mining
Village of Euclid v. Ambler Realty Co., 272 U.S. 365 (1926)	Upheld comprehensive zoning
Zahn v. Board of Public Works, 274 U.S. 325 (1927)	Upheld a residential zoning restriction
Corieb v. Fox, 274 U.S. 603 (1927)	Upheld rules on building setbacks
Miller v. Schoene, 276 U.S. 272 (1928)	Upheld a decision requiring trees to be destroyed in order to save other trees
Nectow v. City of Cambridge, 277 U.S. 183 (1928)	Overturned a zoning provision as applied
Berman v. Parker, 348 U.S. 26 (1954)	Upheld the exercise of the power of eminent domain
Goldblatt v. Town of Hempstead, 369 U.S. 590 (1962)	Upheld an ordinance regulating gravel mining
Penn Central Transportation Co. v. New York City, 438 U.S. 104 (1978)	Upheld a historic preservation ordinance
Kaiser Aetna v. United States, 444 U.S. 164 (1979)	Overturned an attempt to impose the right of public access to a dredged pond
Agins v. City of Tiburón, 447 U.S. 255 (1980)	Upheld a zoning ordinance that restricted density
San Diego Gas & Electric Co. v. City of San Diego, 450 U.S. 621 (1981)	A dissent by Justice Brennan in favor of compensation if regulation effects a taking
Loretto v. Teleprompter Manhattan CATV Corp., 458 U.S. 419 (1982)	Held that a regulation authorizing permanent physical occupation is an automatic taking
Williamson County Regional Planning Comm'n v. Hamilton Bank, 473 U.S. 172 (1985)	Held that owners must seek a final decision about permitted development from the government before going to court and must seek compensation remedies from the state, if available
MacDonald, Sommer & Frates v. County of Yolo, 447 U.S. 340 (1986)	Held that owners must seek a final decision about permitted development from government before going to court
Keystone Bituminous Coal Ass'n v. DeBenedictis. 480 U.S. 470 (1987)	Upheld a restriction on coal mining

(Continued)

Important cases in land use law (*Continued*)

CASE	HOLDING
First English Evangelical Lutheran Church v. County of Los Angeles, 482 U.S. 304 (1987)	Held that compensation must be paid for the period of time that a regulation effects a taking
Nollan v. California Coastal Commission, 483 U.S. 825 (1987)	Held that a taking occurs when there is no essential nexus between a development condition and the purpose behind it
Pennell w City of San Jose, 485 U.S. 1 (1988)	Upheld a rent control provision
Preseault v. ICC. 494 U.S. 1 (1990)	Held that an owner's takings challenge of a federal rails-to-trails statute was premature
Yee v. City of Escondido, 503 U.S. 519 1992)	Held that a rent control ordinance for mobile homes did not effect a physical taking
Lucas v. South Carolina Coastal Council, 505 U.S. 1003 (1992)	Held that denial of all economic use is usually a taking
Dolan v. City of Tigard, 512 U.S. 374 (1994)	Held that there must be a rough proportionality between a government-imposed condition on proposed development and the impact of that development
Suiturn v. Tahoe Regional Planning Agency, 520 U.S. 725 (1997)	Held that an owner's takings claim was ripe
City of Monterey v. Del Monte Dunes, Ltd., 526 U.S. 687 (1999)	Upheld a takings judgment in which a jury had considered whether denial of development permission was reasonably related to legitimate government purposes
Palazzolo v. Rhode Island, 533 U.S. 606 (2001)	Held that the existence of a regulation at the time an owner acquires property does not preclude a subsequent takings claim
Tahoe-Sierra Preservation Council v. Tahoe Regional Planning Agency, 535 U.S. 302 (2002)	Upheld a moratorium
Lingle v. Chevron U.S.A. Inc., 544 U.S. 528 (2005)	Limited the application of reasonable relationship analyses to physical invasion circumstances
Kelo v. City of New London, 545 U.S. 469 (2005)	Upheld government exercise of eminent domain for economic development purposes

REJOINING THE DEBATE

It would be many decades before the Supreme Court would resume a frenetic engagement with property rights, planning, and government regulation. The reemergence of the Court's interest in property rights began in 1978 and followed upon society's emerging ambivalence about growth. That ambivalence had three roots: environmentalism, dissatisfaction with the by-products of growth, and concern about rapid change. The environmental movement had hit full stride by the late 1960s, spawning national interest in goals such as clean air, clean water, and the protection of endangered species.[44] That interest propelled the enactment of federal, state, and local legislation regulating the use of environmentally sensitive lands. By the 1970s, a swamp that would have been a terrific location for a subdivision in the l9S0s had metamorphosed into a wetland that needed protection from dredging and filling.

It was in the burgeoning suburbs that the disadvantages of growth were felt most strongly. Increased traffic congestion, crowded classrooms, and vanishing open space fomented calls for growth controls that sometimes capped outright the annual number of housing units to be developed[45] or that tied building approval to the availability of adequate infrastructure.[46] Through the introduction of subdivision exactions and impact fees, the costs of constructing the infrastructure needed to serve growth were shifted to new, rather than existing, development.[47]

Change itself appeared to be destabilizing. Historic buildings and neighborhoods, once seen as candidates for urban renewal's bulldozer or as teardown opportunities for more profitable development, were now seen as social and economic assets. Historic preservation laws prohibited owners from altering or demolishing landmarks and historic neighborhoods without first seeking permission from locally appointed commissions.

This expanded regulatory regime of environmental laws, growth controls, and historic preservation ordinances placed new pressures on private property rights. The conceptual evolution that relabeled a swamp as a wetland left the owner with the identical physical parcel but with greatly reduced development opportunities. The landowner whose property was ready to be developed for housing had to absorb or pass on to subsequent buyers the costs associated with the provision of roads and water and sewer facilities. The owner of a newly designated landmark building still owned the building, but would no longer enjoy an unfettered ability to alter or demolish it in search of greater profit.

Not surprisingly, the change from progrowth to ambivalent-about-growth attitudes, and the

The reemergence of the Court's interest in property rights began in 1978 and followed upon society's emerging ambivalence about growth.

resulting application of heightened regulatory restrictions, led to opposition from individuals and groups that were financially, politically, or intellectually sympathetic to expansive private property rights. Starting in the early 1980s, the protection of private property gained traction as a political, economic, and legal imperative.

Special-interest groups, riding under the banner of "wise use," among others, appeared.[48] *The Wall Street Journal* editorialized on behalf of aggrieved property owners. Legal scholars provided deeper intellectual content—as well as cover—for the growing property rights movement.[49] Private lawyers and conservative legal organizations searched for opportunities to bring lawsuits that were designed to expand constitutional protection for private property under the Fifth Amendment's just compensation clause.[50]

The Court's vigorous reentry into the property rights arena—which consisted of twenty-one opinions between 1978 and 2005-obviously demonstrated interest but failed to produce paradigm-shifting pronouncements. Beginning in 1987, a steady parade of cases ruled in favor of specific property owners;[51] nevertheless, the justices not only passed up repeated opportunities to dramatically expand the reach of private property, but also continued to affirm government's power to greatly restrict private property. Cautious, case-by-case judgment prevailed over sweeping, bright-line rules. Frustrated property-rights advocates ultimately turned to federal and state legislatures for relief that was not forthcoming from the Court.[52]

The gold standard for the case-by-case approach was Justice William Brennan's 1978 regulatory takings magnum opus, *Penn Central Transportation Company v. New York City*.[53] In that case, New York City's landmarks preservation commission had awarded landmark status to Grand Central Terminal, a 1913 Beaux-Arts masterpiece. Penn Central, the owner of the terminal, wanted to build a skyscraper above the terminal or to replace it entirely but was denied permission by the commission. The commission's refusal prevented the company from realizing millions of dollars in annual lease revenue.

In its six-to-three decision favoring the city, the Court accepted the base position articulated in *Pennsylvania Coal*—that a regulation could go too far—and elaborated on it; henceforth, Brennan said, judges would consider factors such as the character of the governmental action and the economic impact of the regulation (particularly its effect on the owner's distinct, investment-backed expectations). The Court provided no generic guidance as to how such factors should be weighed against one another. In the specific factual setting of *Penn Central*, because the owner had earned a reasonable return on its primary expectation-ownership of the terminal itself—and might be able to transfer the newly unusable development rights above the terminal to adjacent properties, the Court concluded that there was no taking.

How did *Penn Central* change the definition of private property? The short answer is, very little. The opinion recapitulated the core constitutional conclusion introduced in the early twentieth century: in order to further public interests, government can significantly restrict private property rights. Consistent with the 1920s cases, *Penn Central* considered the most malleable aspect of private property to be its financial value, especially when such value is speculative rather than firmly grounded. Newly ascertained public goals, such as preservation of historic buildings and neighborhoods, would be no more troubling to the Court than the newly ascertained goals served by zoning when it emerged in the 1920s.

What about the celebrated cases of the 1980s and 1990s that seemed at first to burnish property rights? In the 1992 case of *Lucas v. South Carolina Coastal Council*[54] for example, the Court announced that when regulations go so far as to deny an owner all economically viable, beneficial, productive, or feasible use of property-that is, when there is a 100 percent diminution in value-then the owner has in all likelihood suffered a regulatory taking. But how many examples of a 100 percent wipeout would one encounter in real life? And even in the case of such a draconian outcome, the Court equivocated: if the background principles of a state's prevailing property or nuisance laws would have already prevented the owner from doing what the new law prohibits, such background principles would insulate the new law from unconstitutionality. On the factual record before it, the Court could not declare that David Lucas, the appellant, had suffered a taking, and Lucas had to seek relief in subsequent state judicial proceedings.

The Court's decision five years earlier in *Nollan v. California Coastal Commission*,[55] which held that a regulation that does not "substantially advance" legitimate state interests constitutes a regulatory taking, seemed at first to suggest heightened Judicial scrutiny of local planning activities. In that case, the coastal commission had made approval for construction of a new house on the California coast conditional on the owners' agreement to allow the public to walk up and down their beach. What made the Court's constitutional pronouncement especially ominous was the suggestion, in a footnote to the opinion, that the phrase "substantially advance" meant something more than "rationally advance" or "reasonably advance"—implying that government land use regulations might now be subject to some form of intensified judicial review. Heightened scrutiny had previously been reserved for cases involving government discrimination against minorities or infringements upon fundamental constitutional rights. If heightened scrutiny truly applied, it would disrupt the traditional presumption of validity that had protected land use regulation since the days of *Euclid*.

Nollan's seed, however, never bore much fruit. In the 1994 case of *Dolan v. City of Tigard*,[56] in which government approval of a hardware-store expansion had been made conditional on the owner's agreement to provide public access to a floodplain and a pedestrian/bicycle pathway, the Court appeared to limit the Nollan analysis to cases involving "a requirement that [the owner] deed portions of the property to the city."[57] Eleven years later, in *Lingle v. Chevron U.S.A. Inc.*,[58] the Court definitively limited the *Nollan/Dolan* analysis to regulatory impositions that authorized physical invasions of private property.

Even the so-called compensation remedies cases failed to create a significantly more favorable climate for property rights. After a long warm-up, with four attempts to reach the issue—including a table-setting dissent by Justice Brennan in *San Diego Gas & Electric Co. v. City of San Diego* (1981[59]—the Court definitively held, in First *English Evangelical Lutheran Church v. County of Los Angeles*,[60] that if a regulation effects a taking, the owners are entitled to compensation for the period of time that the regulation

Beginning in 1987, a steady parade of cases ruled in favor of specific property owners; nevertheless, the Justices not only passed up repeated opportunities to dramatically expand the protected domain, but also continued to affirm government's power to greatly restrict private property.

unconstitutionally took their property. Although this remedy could indeed have a chilling effect on government regulators, the high bar for proving a taking and thus getting to the remedy should preserve the confidence to pursue local planning efforts.[61]

Two twenty-first-century cases suggest that the Court will continue to give wide berth to local planning, even when it interferes substantially with the exercise of individual property rights. In *Tahoe-Sierra Preservation Council v. Tahoe Regional Planning Agency*,[62] the Court held that a thirty-two-month moratorium temporarily denying a landowner all economically viable use of land is not an automatic taking under relevant precedents. Although the decision surely pleased local governments that use moratoria to achieve governmental ends, the highlight was its rhetorical positioning. Justice John Paul Stevens, the Court's most reliable vote in favor of land use planning, wrote the majority opinion. He observed that "moratoria ... are used widely among land use planners" and cited favorably the "consensus in the planning community" supporting moratoria as "an essential tool of successful development."[63] The process of planning takes time and effort, and keeping development in its place while planning occurs is a reasonable imposition on property owners.

Land use regulations, Stevens noted, are "ubiquitous," usually "impact property values in some tangential way," and would become "a luxury few governments could afford" if a finding of regulatory taking were automatically applied.[64] *Tahoe-Sierra*, in short, was a rude awakening for anyone who thought that the Court's pendulum swung in one direction.

Kelo v. City of New London[65] was another rhetorical, as well as pragmatic, affirmation of planning powers in the face of property. The court's controversial, five-to-four majority opinion, again authored by Justice Stevens, cited the virtues of comprehensive, thorough, and careful planning for economic development purposes as sufficient justification for a city to exercise the power of eminent domain. Although the outcry following that opinion was sharp and sustained-the notion that the government could take a nonblighted single-family house, against the owner's will, to further so-called higher and better land uses was hard for the public to swallow-the majority found that this exercise of power advanced a public use, as is required by the just compensation clause.

FUTURE JURISPRUDENCE

If the past is truly prologue, then the Supreme Court's roughly 100-year record of engagement with property rights, planning, and the public interest reveals an evolutionary, rather than a revolutionary, pattern.

The self regulating, nonjudicial interplay between political and private market forces took precedence, and the Court reserved its disdain only for extreme cases. Owners continued to enjoy their property rights, subject to limitations crafted by planners seeking to protect the public interest. Because owners accepted the modern view that land rights no longer extended uninterrupted from the center of the Earth to the moon, and because government regulators largely recognized that tacking as close as possible to the line dividing constitutional from unconstitutional would not yield a politically, or even judicially, sustainable outcome over the long haul, the Court's need to intervene was practically mitigated.

Future environmental, economic, social, and technological challenges will place novel pressures on the relationship between private property and public needs. The question is whether such pressures will escape satisfactory solutions outside of the courtroom, forcing the Court to play a more prominent role in defining the nature and extent of private property. Given the record of the twentieth and early twenty-first centuries, there is little to suggest that the Court will make a different contribution in the coming years. In all likelihood, the nature and extent of private property will continue to be determined, first and foremost, by political forces rather than by the courts, in concert with private market forces.

NOTES

1. U.S. Census Bureau, "Projected Population of the United Slates, by Race and Hispanic Origin: 2000 to 2050." Table 1a, census.gov/ipc/www/usinterimproi/natprojtab01a.pdf (accessed April 13, 2008).
2. U.S. Census Bureau, 2006 American Community Survey: Data Profile Highlights, factfinder.census.gov/home/saff/main.html?_lang=en (accessed April 12, 2008); Migration Policy Institute, MPI Data Hub, "Size of the Foreign-Born Population and Foreign Born as a Percentage of the Total Population, for the United States:1850 to 2006," migrationinformation.org/datahub/charts/final.fb.shtml (accessed April 12, 2008).

3. Daniel H. Burnham and Edward H. Bennett, *Plan of Chicago* (Chicago: Commercial Club of Chicago, 1909), 2, encyclopedia.chicagohistory.org/pages/10417.html (accessed March 24, 2008).

4. From a statement by James W. Rouse before a committee of Congress in support of the New Communities Section, Title II of the Housing Bill for 1966, as cited in Morton Hoppenfeld, *The Columbia Process: The Potential for New Towns* (Letchworth Hertfordshire, England: Garden City Press Limited, 1971), 3.

5. Edmund Bacon, interview with author, August 20, 1998.

6. Edmund Bacon, phone conversation with author, October 5, 2001.

7. Despite the fact that there is no known source for this quotation, it was quoted in a 1918 Christmas card from Wilis Polk to Edward Bennett as a statement Daniel Burnham made in 1907, and it has always been attributed to Burnham.

8. Edmund Bacon, interview with author, November 22. 1998.

9. See New York Town Law, § 272-a, dos.state.ny.us/lgss/townlaw.html#272a (accessed April 21, 2008).

10. Patricia E. Salkin, "Effective Disaster Mitigation Depends upon Well-Coordinated Local Land Use Planning and Zoning." *Real Estate Law Journal* 34 (Summer 20051:108.

11. It should be noted that in some contexts (and depending on the age of the document), the terms "comprehensive plan," "master plan." and "general plan" are used interchangeably.

12. U.S. Department of Commerce, *A Standard City Planning Enabling Act* (Washington, D.C.: Government Printing Office, 1928), planning.org/growingsmart/pdf/CPEnablingAct1928.pdf (accessed April 20, 2008); see The Value of Planning also Ruth Knack, Stuart Meck, and Israel Stollman, "The Real Story behind the Standard Zoning and Planning Acts of the 1920s," *Land Use Law & Zoning Digest* 48 (February 1996): 4, planning.org/growingsmart/enablingacts.htm (accessed April 20, 2008).

13. Stuart Meck, ed., *Growing Smart Legislative Guidebook: Model Statutes for Planning and the Management of Change* (Chicago: American Planning Association, 2002), 7–11.

14. Rodney L. Cobb, "Toward Modern Statutes: A Survey of State Laws on Local Land-Use Planning," in *Modernizing State Planning Statutes: The Growing Smart Working Papers,* vol. 2 (Chicago: American Planning Association, 1998), 21.

15. Ibid., 23.

16. See New York Town Law, § 272-a, and California Government Code, § 65300, et seq.; see also Daniel J. Curtin and Cecily Talbert. *Curtin's California Land Use and Planning Law*, 27th ed. (Point Arena. Calif.: Solano Press. 2007), chap. 2.

17. Oregon Revised Statutes, § 197.250. For a discussion of the Oregon system of land use planning and control, see Edward J. Sullivan, "Oregon Blazes a Trail," in *State & Regional Comprehensive Planning: Implementing New Methods for Growth Management*, ed. Peter A. Buchsbaum and Larry J. Smith (Chicago: American Bar Association, 1993).

18. Daniel R. Mandelker. *Land Use Law*. 5th ed. (Lexis/Nexis, 2003).

19. Stuart Meck, "The Legislative Requirement That Zoning and Land Use Controls Be Consistent with an Independently Adopted Local Comprehensive Plan: A Model Statute," *Washington University Journal of Law & Policy* 3 (2000): 295, 305.

20. Mandelker. *Land Use Law*, § 3.16.

21. Edward J. Sullivan, "The Evolving Role o! the Comprehensive Plan." *Urban Lawyer* 32 (2000):

813, and Edward J. Sullivan, "Comprehensive Planning," *Urban Lawyer* 36 (2004): 541.

22. American Law Institute. *A Model Land Development Code: Complete Text and Commentary* (Philadelphia. Pa.: American Law Institute. 1976).

23. See, generally, Patricia Salkin, "The Next Generation of Planning and Zoning Enabling Acts Is on the Horizon: 2002 Growing Smart Legislative Guidebook Is a Must Read for Land Use Practitioners," *Real Estate Law Journal* 30 (2002): 353.

24. Meck, *Growing Smart Legislative Guidebook.*

25. Ibid., 7–62.

26. *San Diego Gas & Electric Co. v. City of San Diego.* 450 U.S. 621, 661 n.26 (1981), dissenting opinion of Justice Brennan.

27. U.S. Constitution, Fifth Amendment.

28. U.S. Constitution, Fifth and Fourteenth Amendments.

29. Over the course of centuries, private property has been conceptualized by legal scholars as a physical thing (Sir William Blackstone's view) or as a divisible set of legal relationships (W. N. Hohfeld's view), although such conceptions have, more recently, received criticism. See, for example, Michael A. Heller, "Three Faces of Private Property," *Oregon Law Review* 79, no. 2 (2000): 417, 429–431, law.uoregon.edu/org/olr/archives/79/79o1r417.pdf (accessed April 21, 2008).

30. 2 William Blackstone, *Commentaries.*

31. One could almost refer to nuisance law as part and parcel of foundational property law, as Justice Antonin Scaha himself virtually did in his 1992 *Lucas v. South Carolina Coastal Council* opinion.

32. *Hadacheck v. Sebastian.* 239 U.S. 394 (1915).

33. Ibid., 408.

34. Ibid., 410.

35. *Pennsylvania Coal Co. v. Mahon.* 260 U.S. 393 (1922).

36. *Village of Euclid v. Ambler Realty* Co., 272 U.S. 365 (1926).

37. *Pennsylvania Coal,* 415.

38. Ibid., 414.

39. Ibid., 413.

40. *Village of Euclid.* 386–387.

41. Ibid., 395.

42. See Charles M. Haar and Michael Allan Wolf. "Euclid Lives: The Survival of Progressive Jurisprudence," *Harvard Law Review* 115, no. 8 (2002): 2158, 2182–2184,

43. The Court noted. "With particular reference to apartment houses, it is pointed out that the development of detached house sections is greatly retarded by the coming of apartment houses, which has sometimes resulted in destroying the entire section for private house purposes: that in such sections very often the apartment house is a mere parasite, constructed in order to take advantage of the open spaces and attractive surroundings created by the residential character of the district." See *Village of Euclid.* 365.

44. See Jerold S. Kayden, "National Land-Use Planning in America: Something Whose Time Has Never Come." *Washington University Journal ol Law & Policy* 3(2000): 445. 461, discussing clean air and water.

45. *Construction Industry Assoc. v. City of Petaluma,* 522 F.2d 897 (9th Cir. 1975), *cert. denied,* 424 U.S. 934 (1976).

46. *Golden v. Planning Board of Ramapo,* 30 N.Y.2d 359, 334 N.Y.S.2d 138, 285 N.E.2d 291, *appeal dismissed,* 409 U.S. 1003 (1972).

47. See Alan Altshuler and José Gómez-Ibáñez, *Regulation for Revenue: The Political Economy of Land Use Exactions* (Washington, D.C.: Brookings Institution Press, 1993), 16–46.

48. See John Echeverria and Raymond Booth Eby, eds., *Let the People Judge: Wise Use and the Private Property Rights Movement* (Washington, D.C.: Island Press, 1995).
49. See, for example, Richard A. Epstein, *Takings: Private Property and the Power of Eminent Domain* (Cambridge: Harvard University Press, 1985).
50. California attorney Michael Berger, who argued the *First English, Preseault,* and *Tahoe-Sierra cases,* has been the top litigator in Supreme Court cases addressing private property rights; the California-based Pacific Legal Foundation is active as primary or *amicus curiae* counsel in many regulatory takings cases.
51. *First English Evangelical Lutheran Church v. County of Los Angeles*, 482 U.S. 304 (1987); *Nollan v. California Coastal Commission*, 483 U.S. 825 (1987); *Lucas v. South Carolina Coastal Council*, 505 U.S. 1003 (1992); *Dolan v. City of Tigard*, 512 U.S. 374 (1994); *Suitum v. Tahoe Regional Planning Agency*, 520 U.S. 725 (1997); *City of Monterey v. Del Monte Dunes, Ltd.*, 526 U.S. 687 (1999); *Palazzolo v. Rhode Island*, 533 U.S. 606 (2001).
52. See Jerold S. Kayden, "Hunting for Quarks: Constitutional Takings, Property Rights, and Government Regulation," *Washington University Journal of Urban and Contemporary Law* 50 (1996): 125, 138–139.
53. *Penn Central Transportation Co. v. New York City*, 438 U.S. 104 (1978).
54. *Lucas v. South Carolina Coastal Council*, 505 U.S. 1003 (1992).
55. *Nollan v. California Coastal Commission*, 483 U.S. 825 (1987).
56. *Dolan v. City of Tigard*, 512 U.S. 374 (1994).
57. Ibid., 385.
58. *Lingle v. Chevron U.S.A. Inc.*, 544 U.S. 528 (2005).
59. *San Diego Gas & Electric Co. v. City of San Diego*, 450 U.S. 621, 636 (1981), dissenting opinion of Justice Brennan.
60. *First English Evangelical Lutheran Church v. County of Los Angeles*, 482 U.S. 304 (1987).
61. See Daniel Pollak, *Have the U.S. Supreme Court's 5th Amendment Takings Decisions Changed Land Use Planning in California?* CRB-00-004 (Sacramento: California Research Bureau, March 2000), for a discussion of the results of a survey of local officials.
62. *Tahoe-Sierra Preservation Council v. Tahoe Regional Planning Agency*, 535 U.S. 302 (2002).
63. Ibid., 337–338.
64. Ibid., 324.
65. *Kelo v. City of New London*, 545 U.S. 469 (2005).

PLANNING AND URBAN DESIGN STANDARDS

PART 1: *Plans and Plan Making*
PART 2: *Environmental Planning and Management*

BY AMERICAN PLANNING ASSOCIATION

PART I: PLANS AND PLAN MAKING

COMPREHENSIVE PLANS

The comprehensive plan is the adopted official statement of a local government's legislative body for future development and conservation. It sets forth goals; analyzes existing conditions and trends; describes and illustrates a vision for the physical, social, and economic characteristics of the community in the years ahead; and outlines policies and guidelines intended to implement that vision.

Comprehensive plans address a broad range of interrelated topics in a unified way. A comprehensive plan identifies and analyzes the important relationships among the economy, transportation, community facilities and services, housing, the environment, land use, human services, and other community components. It does so on a communitywide basis and in the context of a wider region. A comprehensive plan addresses the long-range future of a community, using a time horizon up to 20 years or more. The most important function of a comprehensive plan is to provide valuable guidance to those in the public and private sector as decisions are made affecting the future quality of life of existing and future

American Planning Association, "Types of Plans," *Planning and Urban Design Standards*, pp. 6-58. Copyright © 2006 by John Wiley & Sons, Inc. Reprinted with permission.

residents and the natural and built environments in which they live, work, and play.

All states have enabling legislation that either allow, or require, local governments to adopt comprehensive plans. In some states, the enabling legislation refers to them as general plans (California, Maryland, and Arizona, for example), or master plans (Colorado). Most state-enabling legislation describes generally what should be included in a comprehensive plan. However, several states, including Oregon and Florida, detail the content of plans through administrative rules promulgated by a state agency.

REASONS TO PREPARE A COMPREHENSIVE PLAN

Local governments prepare comprehensive plans for a number of reasons, which are described in the following subsections.

View the "Big Picture"

The local comprehensive planning process provides a chance to look broadly at programs on housing, economic development, public infrastructure and services, environmental protection, and natural and human-made hazards, and how they relate to one another. A local comprehensive plan represents a "big picture" of the community related to trends and interests in the broader region and in the state in which the local government is located.

Coordinate Local Decision Making

Local comprehensive planning results in the adoption of a series of goals and policies that should guide the local government in its daily decisions. For instance, the plan should be referred to for decisions about locating, financing, and sequencing public improvements, devising and administering regulations such as zoning and subdivision controls, and redevelopment. In so doing, the plan provides a way to coordinate the actions of many different agencies within local government.

Give Guidance to Landowners and Developers

In making its decisions, the private sector can turn to a well-prepared comprehensive plan to get some sense of where the community is headed in terms of the physical, social, economic, and transportation future. Because comprehensive planning results in a statement of how local government intends to use public investment and land development controls, the plan can affect the decisions of private landowners.

Establish a Sound Basis in Fact for Decisions

A plan, through required information gathering and analysis, improves the factual basis for land-use decisions. Using the physical plan as a tool to inform and guide these decisions establishes a baseline for public policies. The plan thus provides a measure of consistency to governmental action, limiting the potential for arbitrariness.

Involve a Broad Array of Interests in a Discussion about the Long-Range Future

Local comprehensive planning involves the active participation of local elected and appointed officials, line departments of local government, citizens, the business community, nongovernmental organizations, and faith-based groups in a discussion about the community's major physical, environmental, social, or economic development problems and opportunities. The plan gives these varied interests an opportunity to clarify their ideas, better envisioning the community they are trying to create.

Build an Informed Constituency

The plan preparation process, with its related workshops, surveys, meetings, and public hearings, permits two-way communication between citizens and planners and officials regarding a vision of the community and how that vision is to be achieved. In this respect, the plan is a blueprint reflecting shared community values at specific points in time. This process creates an informed constituency that can be involved in planning initiatives, review of proposals for plan consistency, and collaborative implementation of the plan.

PLAN ELEMENTS

The scope and content of state planning legislation varies widely from state to state with respect to its treatment of the comprehensive plan. The American Planning Association has developed model state planning legislation in its *Growing Smart℠ Legislative Guidebook* (2002).

Required and Optional Elements

The guidebook suggests a series of required elements and optional elements. Required elements include:

- Land use
- Transportation
- Community facilities (includes utilities and parks and open space)
- Housing
- Economic development
- Critical and sensitive areas
- Natural hazards
- Agricultural lands

Optional elements addressing urban design, public safety, and cultural resources, for instance, may also be included. Moreover, the suggested functional elements are not intended to be rigid and inflexible. Participants in the plan process should tailor the format and content of the comprehensive plan to the specific needs and characteristics of their community.

According to the guidebook, comprehensive plans should include two "bookend" items: an issues and opportunities element at the beginning in order to set the stage for the preparation of other elements, and an implementation program at the end that proposes measures, assigns estimated costs (if feasible), and assigns responsibility for carrying out proposed measures of the plan. The level of detail in the implementation program will vary depending on whether such actions will be addressed in specific functional plans.

Issues and Opportunities Element

The issues and opportunities element articulates the values and needs of citizens and other affected interests about what the community should become. The local government then interprets and uses those values and needs as a basis and foundation for its planning efforts.

An issues and opportunities element should contain seven items:

- A vision or goals and objectives statement
- A description of existing conditions and characteristics
- Analyses of internal and external trends and forces
- A description of opportunities, problems, advantages, and disadvantages
- A narrative describing the public participation process
- The legal authority or mandate for the plan
- A narrative describing the connection to all the other plan elements

Vision or Goals and Objectives Statement

This statement is a formal description of what the community wants to become. It may consist solely of broad communitywide goals, may be enhanced by the addition of measurable objectives for each of the goals, or may be accompanied by a narrative or illustration that sets a vision of the community at the end of the plan period.

Existing Conditions and Characteristics Description

This description creates a profile of the community, including relevant demographic data, pertinent historical information, existing plans, regulatory framework, and other information that broadly informs the plan. Existing conditions information specific to a plan element may be included in that element's within the plan.

Trends and Forces Description

This description of major trends and forces is what the local government considered when creating the vision statement and considers the effect of changes forecast for the surrounding region during the planning period.

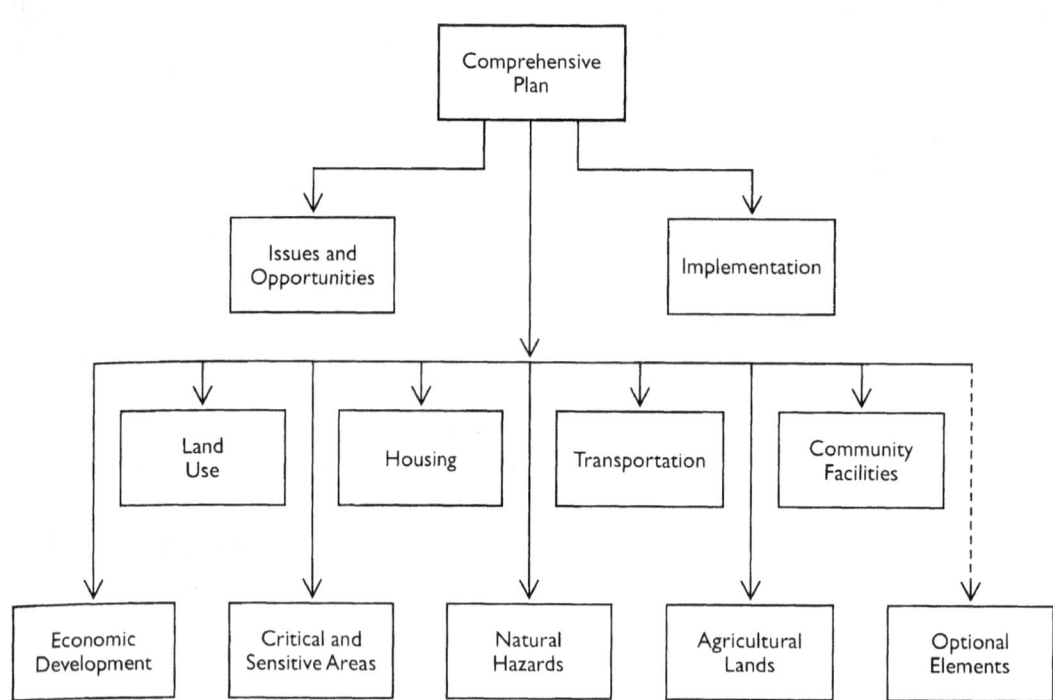

Comprehensive Plan Elements
Source: American Planning Association.

PLANNING AND URBAN DESIGN STANDARDS

SAMPLE VISION STATEMENT: OAKLAND, CALIFORNIA

The Vision for Oakland

In the year 2015, Oakland will be a safe, healthy, and vital city offering a high quality of life through:

- a dynamic economy that taps into Oakland's great economic potential and capitalizes on its physical and cultural assets;
- clean and attractive neighborhoods rich in character and diversity, each with its own distinctive identity, yet well integrated into a cohesive urban fabric;
- a diverse and vibrant downtown with around-the-clock activity;
- an active and accessible waterfront that is linked to downtown and the neighborhoods, and that promotes Oakland's position as a leading United States port and a primary regional and international airport;
- an efficient transportation system that serves the needs of all its citizens and that promotes Oakland's primacy as a transportation hub connecting the Bay Area with the Pacific Rim and the rest of the United States; and
- awareness and enjoyment of Oakland's magnificent physical setting—hills, views, water, estuary—in every district and neighborhood.

Opportunities, Problems, Advantages, and Disadvantages

The plan should include a statement of the major opportunities, problems, advantages, and disadvantages for growth and decline affecting the local government, including specific areas within its jurisdiction. This is often referred to as a *SWOT analysis*—a description of strengths, weaknesses, opportunities, and threats.

Public Participation

This summary of the public participation procedures describes how the public was involved in developing the comprehensive plan.

Legal Authority or Mandate

This brief statement describes the local government's legal authority for preparing the plan. It may include a reference to applicable state legislation or a municipal charter. Summaries of past planning activities may be included here (if not included in existing conditions discussion).

Connection to Other Elements

The implications of the local government's vision on other required and/or optional elements of the local comprehensive plan, including the potential changes in implementation measures, should be described in this concluding section.

The Land-Use Element

The land-use element shows the general distribution, location, and characteristics of current and future land uses and urban form. In the past, comprehensive plans included color-coded maps showing exclusive land-use categories, such as residential, commercial, industrial, institutional, community facilities, open space, recreational, and agricultural uses.

Many communities today use sophisticated land-use and land-cover inventories and mapping techniques, employing Geographic Information Systems (GIS) and new land-use and land-cover classification systems. These new systems are better able to accommodate the multidimensional realities of urban form, such as mixed-use and time-of-day/seasonal-use changes. Form and character are increasingly being used as important components of land-use planning, integrating the many separate components into an integrated land-use form.

One example of a process that can be used to create such multidimensional mapping is the system of Land-Based Classification Standards (LBCS), developed by the American Planning Association (APA). This system creates a current land-use map using a number of data sources, including orbital and suborbital remotely sensed data, tax assessor records, U.S. Geological Survey quadrangle maps, soils maps, and other county or state mapping data, which are field checked on the ground.

Future Land-Use Map

Future land uses and their intensity and density are shown on a future land-use map. The land-use allocations shown on the map must be supported by land-use projections linked to population and economic forecasts for the surrounding region and tied to the assumptions in a regional plan, if one exists. Such coordination ensures that the plan is realistic. The assumptions used in the land-use forecasts, typically in terms of net density, intensity, other standards or ratios, or other spatial requirements or physical determinants, are a fundamental part of the land-use element. This element must also show lands that have development constraints, such as natural hazards.

Land-Use Projections

The land-use element should envision all land-use needs for a 20-year period (or the chosen time frame for the plan), and all these needs should be designated on the future land-use plan map. If this is not done, the local government may have problems carrying out the plan. For example, if the local government receives applications for zoning changes to accommodate uses the plan recognizes as needed, the locations where these changes are requested are consistent with what is shown on the land-use plan map.

The Transportation Element

The modern transportation element commonly addresses traffic circulation, transit, bicycle routes, ports, airports, railways, recreation routes, pedestrian movement, and parking. The exact content of a transportation element differs from community to community depending on the transportation context of the community and region. Proposals for transportation facilities occur against a backdrop of federally required transportation planning at the state and regional levels.

The transportation element considers existing and committed facilities, and evaluates them against a set of service levels or performance standards to determine whether they will adequately serve future needs. Of the various transportation facilities, the traffic circulation component is the most common, and a major thoroughfare plan is an essential part of this. It contains the general locations and extent of existing and proposed streets and highways by type, function, and character of improvement.

Street Performance

In determining street performance and adequacy, planners are employing other approaches in addition to or instead of level-of-service standards that more fairly measure a street's performance in moving pedestrians, bikes, buses, trolleys, and light rail, and for driving retail trade, in addition to moving cars. This is especially true for urban centers, where several modes of travel share the public realm across the entire right-of-way, including adjacent privately owned "public" spaces. Urban design plans for the entire streetscape of key thoroughfares can augment the transportation element. In addition, it is becoming increasingly common for the traffic circulation component of a comprehensive plan to include a street connectivity analysis. The degree to which streets connect with each other affects pedestrian movement and traffic dispersal.

Thoroughfare Plan

The thoroughfare plan, which includes a plan map, is used as a framework for roadway rehabilitation, improvement, and signalization. It is a way of identifying general alignments for future circulation facilities, either as part of new private development or as new projects undertaken by local government. Other transportation modes should receive comparable review and analysis, with an emphasis on needs and systems of the particular jurisdiction and on meeting environmental standards and objectives for the community and region. Typically, surface and structured parking, bikeways, and pedestrian ways should also be covered in the transportation element.

Transit

A transit component takes into consideration bus and light rail facilities, water-based transit (if applicable), and intermodal facilities that allow transportation users to transfer from one mode to another. The types and capacities of future transit service should be linked to work commute and nonwork commute demands as well as to the applicable policies and regulations of the jurisdiction and its region.

The Transportation/Land-Use Relationship

The relationship between transportation and land use is better understood today and has become a dominant theme in the transportation element. For instance, where transit exists or is proposed, opportunities for transit-oriented development should be included; where increased densities are essential, transit services might need to be improved or introduced. This would also be covered in the land-use element.

The Community Facilities Element

The term "community facilities" includes the physical manifestations of governmental or quasi-governmental services on behalf of the public. These include buildings, equipment, land, interests in land, such as easements, and whole systems of activities. The community facilities element requires the local government to inventory and assess the condition and adequacy of existing facilities, and to propose a range of facilities that will support the land-use element's development pattern.

The element may include facilities operated by public agencies and those owned and operated by for-profit and not-for-profit private enterprises for the benefit of the community, such as privately owned water and gas facilities, or museums. Some community facilities have a direct impact on where development will occur and at what scale—water and sewer lines, water supply, and wastewater treatment facilities, for example. Other community facilities may address immediate consequences of development. For example, a stormwater management system handles changes in the runoff characteristics of land as a consequence of development.

Still other facilities are necessary for the public health, safety, and welfare, but are more supportive in nature. Examples in this category would include police and fire facilities, general governmental buildings, and elementary and secondary schools. A final group includes those facilities that contribute to the cultural life or physical and mental health and personal growth of a local government's residents. These include hospitals, clinics, libraries, and arts centers.

Operation by Other Public Agencies

Some community facilities may be operated by public agencies other than the local government. Such agencies may serve areas not coterminous with the local government's boundaries. Independent school districts, library districts, and water utilities are good examples. In some large communities, these agencies may have their own internal planning capabilities. In others, the local planning agency will need to assist or coordinate with the agency or even directly serve as its planner.

Parks, Open Space, and Cultural Resources

A community facilities element may include a parks and open-space component. Alternatively, parks and open space may be addressed in a separate element. The community facilities element will inventory existing parks by type of facility and may evaluate the condition of parks in terms of the population they are expected to serve and the functions they are intended to carry out. To determine whether additional parkland should be purchased, population forecasts are often used in connection with population-based needs criteria (such as a requirement of so many acres of a certain type of park within a certain distance from residents). Other criteria used to determine parkland need may include parkland as a percentage of land cover or a residents proximity to a park.

Open-space preservation may sometimes be addressed alone or in connection with critical and sensitive areas protection and agricultural and forest preservation. Here the emphasis is on the ecological, scenic, and economic functions that open space provides. The element may also identify tracts of open land with historic or cultural significance, such as a battlefield. The element will distinguish between publicly held land, land held in private ownership subject to conservation easements or other restrictions, and privately owned parcels subject to development.

The Housing Element

The housing element assesses local housing conditions and projects future housing needs by housing type and price to ensure that a wide variety of housing structure types, occupancy types, and prices (for rent or purchase) are available for a community's existing and future residents. There may currently be a need for rental units for large families or the disabled, or a disproportionate amount of income may be paid for rental properties, for example. Because demand for housing does not necessarily correspond with jurisdictional boundaries and the location of employment, a housing element provides for housing needs in the context of the region in which the local government is located. In some states, such as California, New Hampshire, and New Jersey, there may be state-level or regional housing plans that identify regional needs for affordable housing, and the local housing element must take these needs into account as part of a "fair-share" requirement.

Jobs/Housing Balance

The housing element can examine the relationship between where jobs are or will be located and where housing is or will be available. The jobs/housing balance is the ratio between the expected creation of jobs in a region or local government and the need for housing expressed as the number of housing units. The higher the jobs/housing ratio, the more jobs the region or local government is generating relative to housing. A high ratio may indicate to a community that it is not meeting the housing needs (in terms of either affordability or actual physical units) of people working in the community.

Housing Stock

The housing element typically identifies measures used to maintain a good inventory of quality housing stock, such as rehabilitation efforts, code enforcement, technical assistance to homeowners, and loan and grant programs. It will also identify barriers to producing and rehabilitating housing, including affordable housing. These barriers may include lack of adequate sites zoned for housing, complicated approval processes for building and other development permits, high permit fees, and excessive exactions or public improvement requirements.

The Economic Development Element

An economic development element describes the local government's role in the region's economy; identifies categories or particular types of commercial, industrial, and institutional uses desired by the local government; and specifies suitable sites with supporting facilities for business and industry. It has one or more of the following purposes:

- Job creation and retention
- Increases in real wages (e.g., economic prosperity)
- Stabilization or increase of the local tax base
- Job diversification (making the community less dependent on a few employers)

A number of factors typically prompt a local economic development program. They include loss or attraction of a major employer, competition from surrounding communities or nearby states, the belief that economic development yields a higher quality of life, the desire to provide employment for existing residents who would otherwise leave the area, economic stagnation or decline in a community or part of it, or the need for new tax revenues.

An economic development element typically begins with an analysis of job composition and growth or decline by industry sector on a national, statewide, or regional basis, including an identification of categories of commercial, industrial, and institutional activities that could reasonably be expected to locate within the jurisdiction. It will also examine existing labor force characteristics and future labor force requirements of existing and potential commercial and industrial enterprises and institutions in the state and the region in which the local government is located. It will include assessments of the jurisdiction's and the region's access to transportation to markets for its goods and services, and its natural, technological, educational, and human resources. Often, an economic development element will have targets for growth, which may be defined as number of jobs or wages, or in terms of targeted industries and their land use, transportation, and labor force requirements.

The local government may also survey owners or operators of commercial and industrial enterprises, and inventory commercial, industrial, and institutional lands within the jurisdiction that are vacant or significantly underused. An economic development element may also address organizational issues, including the creation of entities, such as nonprofit organizations, that could carry out economic development activities.

The Critical and Sensitive Areas Element

Some comprehensive plans address the protection of critical and sensitive areas. These areas include land and water bodies that provide habitat for plants and wildlife, such as wetlands, riparian corridors, and floodplains; serve as groundwater recharge areas for aquifers; and areas with steep slopes that are easily eroded or unstable, for example. They also can include visually, culturally, and historically sensitive areas. By identifying such areas, the local government can safeguard them through regulation, incentives, purchase of land or interests in land, modification of public and private development projects, or other measures.

The Natural Hazards Element

Natural hazards elements document the physical characteristics, magnitude, severity, frequency, causative factors, and geographic extent of all natural hazards. Hazards include flooding; seismic activity; wildfires; wind-related hazards such as tornadoes, coastal storms, winter storms, and hurricanes; and landslides or subsidence resulting from the instability of geological features.

A natural hazards element characterizes the hazard; maps its extent, if possible; assesses the community's vulnerability; and develops an appropriate set of mitigation measures, which may include land-use policies and building code requirements. The natural hazards element may also determine the adequacy of existing transportation facilities and public buildings to accommodate disaster response and early recovery needs such as evacuation and emergency shelter. Since most communities have more than one type of hazard, planners should consider addressing them jointly through a multihazards approach.

The Agriculture Element

Some comprehensive plans contain agriculture and forest preservation elements. This element focuses on the value of agriculture and forestlands to the local economy, although it can also include open space, habitat, and scenic preservation. For such an element, the local government typically inventories agriculture and forestland, and ranks the land using a variety of approaches, such as the U.S. Department of Agriculture's Land Evaluation and Site Assessment (LESA) system. It then identifies conflicts between the use of such lands and other proposed uses as contained in other comprehensive plan elements.

For example, if an area were to be preserved for agricultural purposes, but the community facilities element proposed a sewer trunk line to the area, that would be a conflict, which if not corrected would result in development pressure to the future agricultural area. Implementation measures might include agricultural use valuation coupled with extremely large lot requirements (40 acres or more), transfer of development rights, purchase of development rights, conservation easements, marketing programs to promote the viability of local agricultural land, and programs for agricultural-based tourism.

IMPLEMENTATION

A local comprehensive plan must contain an implementation program to ensure that the proposals advanced in the plan are realized. Sometimes referred to as an "action plan," the implementation program includes a list of specific public or private actions organized by their scheduled execution date—short-term (1 to 3 years), medium-term (4 to 10 years), and long-term (11 to 20 years) actions. Typical actions include capital projects, changes to land development regulations and incentives, new programs or procedures, financing initiatives, and similar measures. Each listed action should assign responsibility for the task and include an estimate of cost and a source of funding.

Some communities produce comprehensive plans that are more broadly based and policy-driven. These plans will require a less detailed implementation program. The individual functional plans produced as a result of the comprehensive plan address the assignment of costs or specific tasks.

REFERENCE

Meck, Stuart (gen. ed.). 2002. *Growing Smart^{sm} Legislative Guidebook: Model Statutes for Planning and Management of Change*, 2 vols. Chicago: American Planning Association.

See also:
Critical and Sensitive Areas Plans
Economic Development Plans
Housing Plans
Mapping
Parks and Open-Space Plans
Participation
Plan Making
Projections and Demand Analysis
Regional Plans
Transportation Plans
Urban Design Plans

URBAN DESIGN PLANS

Urban design is the discipline between planning and architecture. It gives three-dimensional physical form to policies described in a comprehensive plan. It focuses on design of the public realm, which is created by both public spaces and the buildings that define them. Urban design views these spaces holistically and is concerned with bringing together the different disciplines responsible for the components of cities into a unified vision. Compared to comprehensive plans, urban design plans generally have a short time horizon and are typically area or project specific.

Key elements of an urban design plan include the plan itself, the preparation of design guidelines for buildings, the design of the public realm—the open space, streets, sidewalks, and plazas between and around buildings—and the "public interest" issues of buildings. These include massing, placement, and sun, shadow, and wind issues.

Urban design plans are prepared for various areas, including downtowns, waterfronts, campuses, corridors, neighborhoods, mixed-use developments, and special districts. Issues to be considered include existing development, proposed development, utility infrastructure, streets framework, open space framework, environmental framework, and sustainable development principles. Urban design plans require interdisciplinary collaboration among urban designers, architects, landscape architects, planners, civil and environmental engineers, and market analysts. The central role of the urban designer is to serve as the one who can often integrate the work of a diverse range of specialists.

REASONS TO PREPARE AN URBAN DESIGN PLAN

An urban design plan must respond to the circumstances under which the project will be conducted, including the goals of the sponsors of the plan, the political or social climate in the community, and financial and marketing realities. Below are a few examples of reasons to prepare an urban design plan.

Forging Visions

Urban designers are often asked to provide a vision for communities to attract investment and coordinate many disparate and even discordant interests. By providing such a vision, urban designers can bring individual efforts together to create a whole that is greater than the sum of its parts. Creating such a vision needs to be a public process, to cultivate widespread enthusiasm for the vision and build a "bandwagon" of support.

Devising Strategies

In addition to an overall vision, an urban design plan must also include a strategic implementation plan, with both short- and long-range initiatives. To keep the momentum going, it is also important to assign specific tasks or projects to groups conducting implementation.

Creating Good Locations

Many projects begin with sites that are compromised or deteriorated. An urban design plan illustrates how a site is linked to surrounding strengths, and it can show how the site can become a great location.

Marketing Sites or Areas

Urban design plans often work to transform an area, creating a new image for an area once overlooked or blighted. Urban design documents, illustrations, and publicity around the process all become part of the overall marketing effort to attract development and residents.

Forming "Treaties"

Urban design plans are sometimes born as a result of a conflict; for example, a proposed redevelopment project may result in displacing existing businesses or residents. An urban design document can serve as a "treaty," to bring about a truce among warring parties. By focusing on the issues, presenting thoughtful analysis, and urging parties to come forward with their concerns and ideas, urban designers can use an urban design plan to help resolve problems in a non-confrontational way.

THE URBAN DESIGN PLANNING PROCESS

An urban design planning process has much in common with a comprehensive planning process; both include basic elements such as data collection and analysis, public participation, and involvement of other disciplines. However, urban design differs in the use of three-dimensional design tools to explore alternatives and communicate ideas. Below are the essential attributes of an urban design planning process.

Public Outreach

Because urban design plans usually involve multiple stakeholders, public participation in the planning process is essential. A representative steering committee is one mechanism to ensure involvement of a cross section of interests. Among the various public outreach techniques used are focus groups and public meetings. Input from the public informs the urban design team about assets, liabilities, and visions for the project area.

Involvement of Major Stakeholders

In addition to the public outreach process, one-on-one meetings with key representatives of the major stakeholders, such as elected officials, community leaders, and major institutions, are

PLANNING AND URBAN DESIGN STANDARDS

important for both sides—the urban design team gains insight into the stakeholders concerns and goals, and the major stakeholders develop confidence in the team and the planning process.

Multi-Disciplinary Team

Urban design is a collaborative process involving urban designers, architects, planners, and landscape architects. However, other disciplines are usually required, such as transportation planners and engineers, civil and environmental engineers, residential and commercial market analysts, construction cost consultants, and public/private finance consultants. When such a team has been assembled, the individual consultants should be coordinated so that their expertise permeates the planning process from beginning to end.

Focus on Implementation

Urban design projects are often complicated plans with multiple projects and participants. Implementation can be difficult, even when

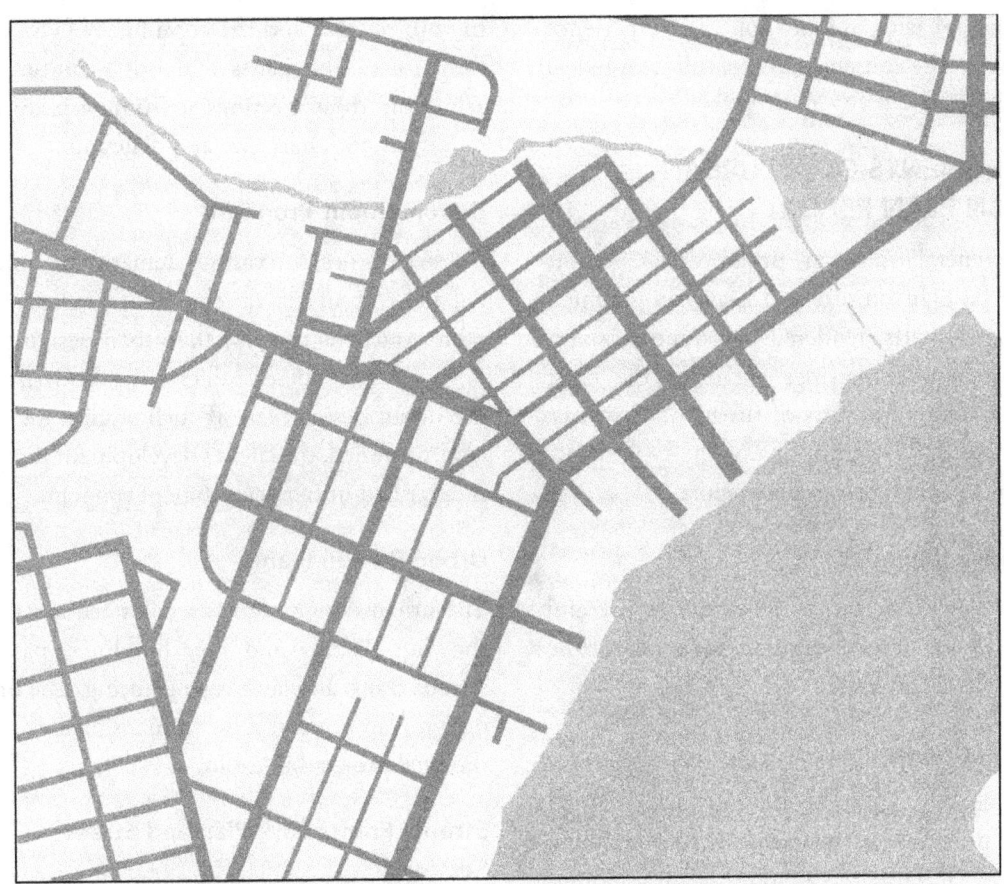

Features such as waterways and adjacent land features influence street grid orientation.

Existing Street Patterns
Source: Urban Design Associates.

all the forces are aligned properly. The process should begin with implementation in mind. Develop a plan that is tied to the realities of receiving funding, obtaining approval, and getting the project built.

Design as a Tool for Decision-Making

By exploring alternatives—the "what ifs" of a site or district—the design process allows for speculation, brainstorming, and innovative thinking. Alternatives can be tested against various factors, including physical constraints, regulatory controls, the market, overall costs and benefits, economic feasibility, property valuation, phasing, public input, and experience elsewhere. The consensus vision will then reflect those realities.

COMPONENTS OF AN URBAN DESIGN PLAN REPORT

As a general rule, an urban design report should be light on text and heavy on graphics. Diagrams, charts, rendered plans and sections, and perspective drawings are often the most effective communicators of the plan's elements. Below are brief descriptions of the typical sections of an urban design plan report.

Executive Summary

Key images from the body of the report and summary text can convey the "big ideas" of the plan in just a few pages.

Existing Conditions

Assemble all existing conditions data related to the project area, including streets, building coverage, land use, topography, vacant buildings and land, and environmental constraints. This information is documented in the report as the existing conditions "portrait" of the area.

Analysis Drawings

Analysis drawings can be some of the most influential materials of an urban design initiative. Creating these drawings involves professional review of existing conditions data and mapping, to translate this information into findings that will influence the plan. More information on analysis drawings can be found in *The Urban Design Handbook* (2003).

Summary of Issues

During the planning process, involve citizens and stakeholders in focus groups and public meetings to learn about the strengths and weaknesses of the project area and the community's vision for the future. The issues and opportunities that arise from these meetings are summarized in the report, in both narrative and diagrams.

Development Program

Market studies, forecasting demand for residential and commercial development, are frequently done concurrently with the urban design planning process. These studies are summarized in the urban design plan. If such studies were not commissioned, the client's development program is described in the development program.

Urban Design Plan

The urban design plan is a color rendered plan showing existing and new buildings, parking, streets, trails, and landscape planting. The urban design plan presents a two-dimensional vision of the final project build-out.

Streets Framework Plan and Street Sections

The streets framework plan identifies existing and new streets. It includes cross sections of streets indicating sidewalks, parking, travel lanes, and medians.

Open Space Framework Plan

The open space framework plan illustrates parks; trails; "green streets," which are streets designated for enhanced landscape planting and pedestrian amenities; plazas; public space; and the connections between them.

Perspective Drawings

Three-dimensional perspective drawings are essential in conveying the sense of place of an urban design plan. Often the general public cannot easily interpret plan drawings; however, eye level and bird's eye view perspectives are often more readily understandable.

Design Guidelines

Urban design plan reports often contain a section on design guidelines, including massing, height, building setbacks, architectural style, parking, streetscapes, signage, materials, and sustainable design.

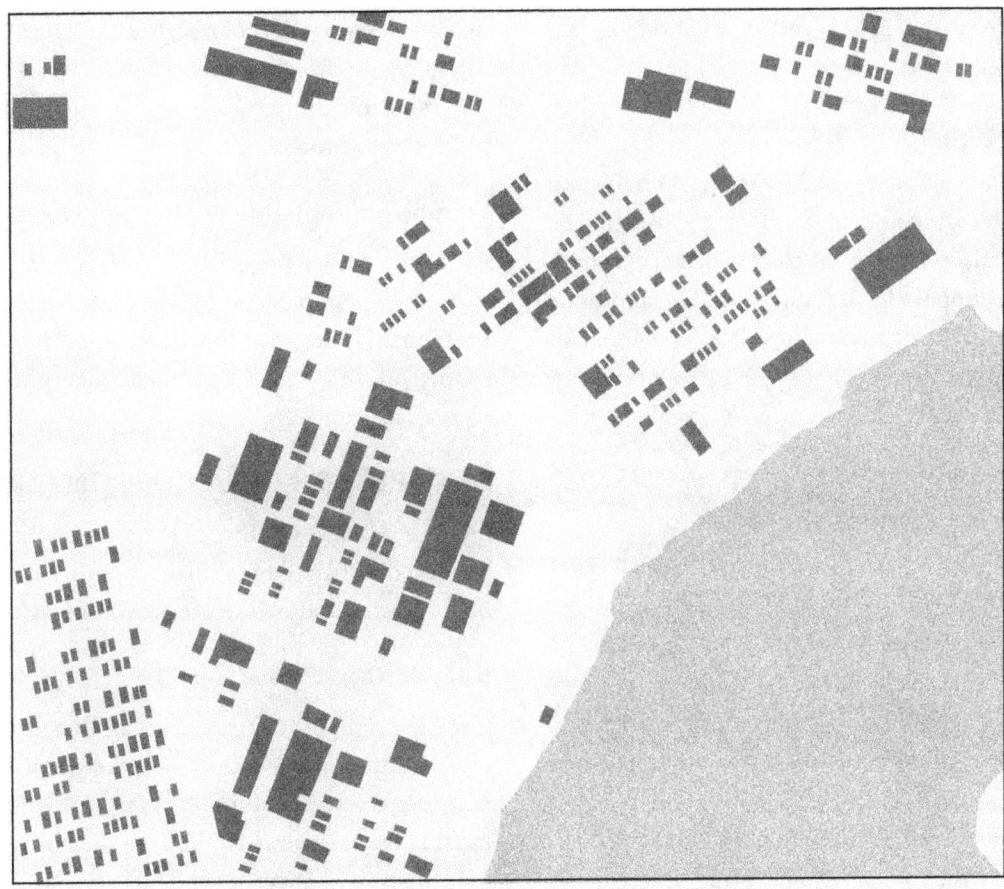

Block patterns of an area, presented here as a figure ground map, show the building coverage of a site.

Building Coverage
Source: Urban Design Associates.

Implementation and Phasing Plan

The implementation section details the mechanisms to make the plan a reality. Among the tools typically included are public and private partnerships, funding sources, regulatory issues, conceptual budgets, and a phasing plan with early action and long-range projects described.

THE ROLE OF URBAN DESIGN IN IMPLEMENTATION

By translating general planning policies into three-dimensional form, urban design makes the connection between planning and architecture, this makes it possible to test the feasibility of projects through a variety of mechanisms, described below.

Public Support

If the community perceives the various images and three-dimensional form of a development to be consistent with its goals and policies, then gaining support for the various public approvals needed for the development will be strengthened. Developing the urban design for a project in an open public forum helps to facilitate this outcome.

Zoning Enforcement and Regulatory Approvals

Use vivid and explicit representations of the proposed development to assist the various agencies responsible for zoning enforcement and regulatory approvals to support implementation. In many communities there are a number of agencies, with different mindsets, involved in administering the approval and implementation process. The urban design plan, especially if developed in a process that engaged the approval agencies as a group, can provide a common framework within which governmental decisions can be made.

Investment and Finance

Urban designs are often developed to a level of detail sufficient to determine the amount of space being built and to develop conceptual cost estimates for buildings and public improvements. Therefore, the economic feasibility and fiscal impact of developments can be effectively evaluated.

Marketing

A project's feasibility is directly related to the effectiveness of its marketing program. The character and quality of its address is one factor in how successfully a development can capture the market potential of an area. The products of an urban design project are often used in marketing programs to communicate the new image of the place and to promote the development.

Framework for Implementing Agencies

An urban design project often serves as a "road map" for the implementing agencies. It becomes a standard reference for developing budgets, setting priorities, funding projects, and granting regulatory approvals.

EXAMPLES OF URBAN DESIGN PLANS

Described below are three of the most commonly produced urban design plans: neighborhoods, down-towns, and mixed-use developments.

Neighborhood Plans

On the neighborhood scale, urban design plans often address the location and design of infill housing, new parks, and community institutions; main street revitalization; housing rehabilitation guidelines; and street reconfiguration. Sponsors of neighborhood plans include cities, community development organizations, foundations, and private developers.

PLANNING AND URBAN DESIGN STANDARDS

The street framework is upgraded to follow the patterns that the existing street patterns, building coverage, and open space framework define for the place.

Street Framework
Source: Urban Design Associates.

Downtown Plans

Downtown urban design plans are usually part of a larger economic development strategy focused on attracting jobs, residents, and visitors to a downtown. The development scale is relatively dense and multistory, which requires sensitive treatment of the public realm for pedestrians. Topics covered in downtown urban design plans include mixed-use buildings, historic preservation, adaptive reuse, height and density, setbacks, views, parking strategies, transit corridors and nodes, streetscapes, waterfronts, street networks, highway access, redevelopment policies, zoning overlays, incentive districts, new stadiums and convention centers, and entertainment and cultural districts.

Cities, downtown organizations, business improvement districts, and regional agencies all may sponsor downtown urban design plans.

Mixed-Use Developments

Mixed-use developments are typically one-owner, site-specific projects. Among the various types are infill projects in downtowns, Brownfield

ESSENTIAL READINGS IN URBAN PLANNING

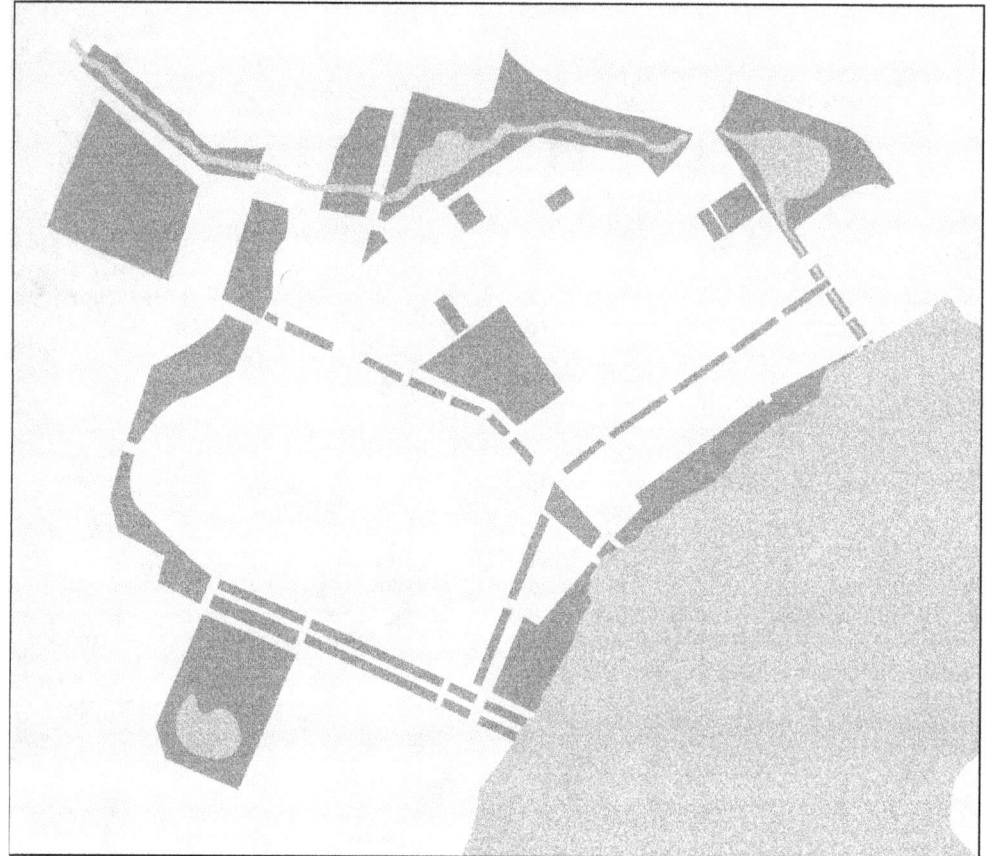

The open space of a site shows the green network that helps define a place.

Open Space Framework
Source: Urban Design Associates.

reclamation projects, lifestyle centers (also called specialty retail centers), and office/technology developments. Office, retail, and housing are among the typical uses in mixed-use developments. Project sizes can range widely, from a few acres to hundreds of acres. A central goal is to develop a pedestrian-friendly place to live, work, and play. Sponsors of mixed-use developments are often private developers, redevelopment agencies, and large institutions, such as universities and medical centers.

KEY AND EMERGING ISSUES
Housing Density

As the smart growth movement and rising housing costs have become determining forces in residential planning and development, density has emerged as a major issue. While there is still the great American desire for the single family home and the cul-de-sac subdivision, regulatory controls and environmental restrictions have begun to limit available land for such development. Smaller lot sizes, attached housing, and multi-family housing have become contentious issues in many communities. Urban design planning processes can help test different residential densities in the context of a holistic solution that includes housing, amenities, and place making.

Recognizing the Value of Urban Design

Urban design is a strong strategic planning tool. However, many cities and developers approach development on a project-by-project basis, often in isolation from adjacent uses and without a comprehensive view of all the forces impacting or impacted by the project. While urban design plans are not always regarded as essential pre-development projects, experience in the field has demonstrated that the new ideas and approaches that emerge from an urban design planning process can add significant value to a development and appreciably ease and shorten the public approval process.

Urban Design Education

Because of the three-dimensional building design and the physical transformation of the public realm aspect of urban design practice, an urban designer should have an architecture degree. Ideally, an urban designer has either received a master of architecture degree in urban design or has completed an internship in an urban design firm.

RESOURCE

Urban Design Associates. 2003. *The Urban Design Handbook: Techniques and Working Methods.* New York: W.W. Norton and Co.

See also:
Places and Placemaking
Viewshed Protection

REGIONAL PLANS

Regional plans cover geographic areas transcending the boundaries of individual governmental units but sharing common characteristics that may be social, economic, political, cultural, natural-resource-based, or defined by transportation. They often serve as the skeleton or framework for local government plans and special district plans, supplying unifying assumptions, forecasts, and strategies. The information that follows is adapted from the American Planning Association's *Growing Smart^{SM} Legislative Guidebook* (2002).

DEFINING THE REGION

The following factors may define a region:

- Geographic and topographic features, especially watersheds
- Political boundaries, especially county boundaries
- Transportation patterns, especially those related to the journey to work
- Region-serving facilities, such as hospitals, airports, trail terminals, and wastewater treatment plants
- Interrelated social, economic, and environmental problems
- Population distribution
- Existing intergovernmental relationships, usually expressed in the form of written agreements
- Metropolitan area or urbanized area boundaries as identified by the U.S. Census Bureau
- Boundaries of existing regional or multijurisdictional planning or service provision organizations, such as regional sewer districts

REGIONAL FUNCTIONAL PLANS

Regional planning agencies may prepare regional functional plans to cover specific topics such as parks and open space, bikeways, water, sanitary sewerage and sewage treatment, water supply and distribution, solid waste management, airports, libraries, communications, and others. For example, a regional sewer plan is a device used to ensure that disputes can be resolved over which jurisdiction will provide sewers and sewage treatment facilities to developing areas. The most typical regional functional plan is a regional transportation plan; see Transportation Plans in this chapter for more information.

The Regional Housing Plan

A number of states, including California and New Hampshire, require the preparation of regional housing plans. In general, regional planning agencies prepare these plans to assess present and prospective need for housing at the regional level, particularly affordable housing. Typically, they establish numerical housing goals to be included in local government plans.

In New Jersey, regional housing planning is the responsibility of a state agency, the Council on Affordable Housing, which prepares "fair-share" housing allocations for affordable housing for each local government. Under New Jersey law, local governments then have an obligation to identify sites for affordable housing and take necessary steps to remove barriers in order to provide a realistic opportunity that such housing can be built or rehabilitated.

THE REGIONAL COMPREHENSIVE PLAN

The regional comprehensive plan is intended to address facilities or resources that affect more than one jurisdiction and to provide economic, population, and land-use forecasts to guide local planning, so that local plans and planning decisions are made with a set of common assumptions. Consequently, a regional comprehensive plan will propose a more schematic pattern of development than provided in a local comprehensive plan.

For example, in a regional comprehensive plan, the land-use pattern is generally simple, demarcating land into urban and rural, with a general indication of a hierarchy of activity centers. Such centers may be targets for more intensive residential, office, commercial, and industrial developments, supported by transit, that are intended to serve a substantial portion of the region. Here, the intent is to use the regional plan as an device to direct both public and private investment to ensure that such development occurs.

Both public agencies and private organizations may prepare regional plans. Indeed, private groups prepared the first true regional plans, one in 1909 for the Chicago area and a second in 1929 for the New York City area. The Chicago plan was the work of planners Daniel Burnham and Edward Bennett, with funding by the Commercial Club. The Committee for the Regional Plan of New York and Its Environs, a private group whose efforts were funded by the Russell Sage Foundation, produced a multivolume regional plan for the New York metropolitan area, beginning in 1929.

Regional Comprehensive Plan Elements
Typical Plan Elements

State statutes usually define which elements are required in a regional comprehensive plan. The following list is for guidance only; to determine which elements are required, consult state legislation.

- A narrative of planning assumptions, and their relationship to state and local plans
- Population trends and projections
- Regional economy
- Existing land use
- A transportation system overview
- Regional housing trends and needs
- Community facilities and services
- Natural features and cultural assets
- Agricultural lands
- Natural hazards
- Regional density study
- Public involvement
- Urban growth areas
- Regional growth policy statements
- Implementation recommendations

Urban Growth Areas

Some regional plans delineate urban growth areas, which are land areas sufficient to accommodate population and economic growth for a certain period, typically 20 years, and which will be supported by urban-level services. The purpose of an urban growth area is to ensure a compact and contiguous development pattern that can be efficiently served by public services while preserving open space, agricultural land, and environmentally sensitive areas not suitable for intensive development.

Special Resource Areas

A regional comprehensive plan also identifies special resources areas, such as farmland, aquifers, and major wetlands. It may propose strategies for a particular watershed or basin to ensure that groundwater and watercourses are protected as supplies of potable water. The plan can also include actions to protect areas of biodiversity. Depending on the nature of the region, it may also identify the general location of natural hazard areas, such as earthquake zones or areas prone to wildfires.

Regional Facilities

The plan may contain proposals for new or upgraded regional facilities, such as multimodal transportation centers, new highways, transit, airports, hospitals, and regional parks or open space systems that link together. Functional plan elements may examine details of such proposals,

---

SAMPLE TABLE OF CONTENTS: THE METROPOLIS PLAN: CHOICES FOR THE CHICAGO REGION

Introduction: The Metropolis Plan
    Purpose of The Metropolis Plan
    Building The Metropolis Plan

The Metropolis Plan: Key Themes
    Opportunities Close to Home: Housing Choices for All
    Regional Cities and Centers
    A Robust Transportation System
    Great Streets
    Nature's Metropolis

Implementing the Metropolis Plan
    How We Got Here
    Getting from Here to There

Source: Chicago Metropolis 2020. 2003

such as road widening, highway safety improvements, and operational changes to mass transit systems, or the exact locations of regional wastewater facilities and major trunk lines.

Descriptive and Analytical Studies

In order to prepare a regional comprehensive plan, the regional planning authority or other suitable authority must undertake a series of descriptive and analytical studies. Such studies may cover the following topics:

- The economy of the region, which may include amount, type, general location, and distribution of commerce and industry within the region; the location of regional employment centers; and trends and projection of economic activity, both in terms of income growth and changes in the number and composition of jobs
- Population and population distribution within the region, as well as its local governments, including projections and analyses by age, education level, income, employment, or similar characteristics
- Natural resources, including air, water, forests and other vegetation, and minerals
- Amount, type, quality, affordability, and geographic distribution of housing among local governments in the region correlated with projected job and population change
- Identification of features of significant statewide or regional architectural, scenic, cultural, historic, or architectural interest, as well as scenic corridors and viewsheds
- Amount, type, location, and quality of agricultural lands
- Amount, type, intensity or density, general location of industrial, commercial, residential, and other land uses, and projections of changes in land use, correlated with projected job and population change

MAP COMPONENTS

The regional comprehensive plan provides a visual representation of the plan's objectives. The components of the map may include the following:

- Location of urban growth area boundaries
- Existing and proposed transportation facilities
- Other public facilities and utilities of extrajurisdictional or regionwide significance
- Potential areas of critical state concern (such as areas of significant biodiversity, scenic beauty, historic significance, or archaeological value, or areas around major facilities, such as military bases, airports, or national or state parks)
- Natural hazard areas
- Urban and rural growth centers
- Any other matters of regional significance that can be graphically represented.

THE IMPLEMENTATION PROGRAM

A long-range implementation program for the regional comprehensive plan may include the following components.

An Implementation Schedule

The implementation program may include a schedule of development for proposed transportation and other public facilities and utilities of extrajurisdictional or regionwide significance. The schedule may include a description of the proposed public facility or utility, an identification of the governmental unit to be responsible for the facility or utility, the year(s) the facility or utility is proposed for construction or installation, an estimate of costs, and sources of public and private revenue for covering such costs.

Development Criteria

The program may include development criteria for use in local government and special district plans. Performance benchmarks may be defined to measure the achievement of the regional comprehensive plan by local governments and special districts.

Monitoring and Evaluation

A statement may be included to describe the criteria and procedures the agency creating the plan will use in monitoring and evaluating the plan's implementation by local governments, special districts, and the state.

Coordination

There may also be a statement of measures describing the ways in which state and/or local programs may best be coordinated to promote the goals and policies of the regional comprehensive plan

Legislative Changes

The program may also include proposals for changes in state laws to achieve regional objectives, such as regional tax-base sharing or procedures to review large-scale developments with multijurisdictional impacts or to consolidate existing planning organizations to improve services and coordination. Regional planning agencies may also propose inter jurisdictional agreements to clarify responsibility for the provision of urban services.

REFERENCES

Burnham, Daniel H., and Edward H. Bennett. [1909] 1970. *Plan of Chicago.* Reprint, New York: DaCapo Press.

Chicago Metropolis 2020. 2003. *The Metropolis Plan: Choices for the Chicago Region.* Chicago: Chicago Metropolis 2020.

Committee for the Regional Plan of New York and Its Environs. 1929. *The Regional Plan of New York and Its Environs. The Graphic Plan.* Vol. 1. New York: The Committee.

Meek, Stuart (gen. ed). 2002. *Growing Smart^{SM} Legislative Guidebook; Model Statutes for Planning and Management of Change.* 2 vols. Chicago: American Planning Association.

See also:
Housing Plans
Population Projections
Regions
Transportation Plans
Watersheds

NEIGHBORHOOD PLANS

A neighborhood plan focuses on a specific geographic area of a local jurisdiction that typically includes substantial residential development, associated commercial uses, and institutional services such as recreation and education. Many of the same topics covered in a local comprehensive plan are covered in a neighborhood plan.

REASONS TO PREPARE A NEIGHBORHOOD PLAN

The neighborhood plan is intended to provide more detailed goals, policies, and guidelines than those in the local comprehensive plan. Neighborhood plans often emphasize potential partnerships among government agencies, community groups, school boards, and the private sector—partnerships that can act to achieve neighborhood goals. These plans are often developed through highly collaborative processes involving citizens, business, nongovernmental organizations (NGOs), and the local government of the neighborhood.

Neighborhood plans describe land-use patterns in more detail than do comprehensive plans. They may even approach the specificity required for amendments to a zoning district map or street classification system. These descriptions and maps can be used for greenfield or developing areas in a manner similar to that used in sector or specific plans, an approach used in Florida and California.

These plans also often propose a program of implementation shorter in duration than is proposed in a comprehensive plan. For an established neighborhood, the plan may emphasize issues that can be addressed in one to two years. They may include actions to be taken by the local government, other governmental agencies, school boards, nonprofit organizations, or for-profit groups. In many respects, this reflects the nature of the neighborhood planning process itself, which often focuses on visible and politicized problems that can be resolved quickly, such as trash cleanup, park improvements, or specific code enforcement issues. For newer neighborhoods, the plan's content may be more far-reaching and functional.

Neighborhood planning succeeds when the process is cyclical, small successes are emphasized, and the issue of identifying neighborhood leaders and legitimacy is addressed at the onset.

PLAN ELEMENTS

The American Planning Association conducted research in the mid-1990s that identified more than 36 elements in neighborhood plans. This group of elements, which appeared in various combinations, suggests a realm of possibilities for a particular neighborhood plan. While no definitive recommendation can be made about which specific elements a neighborhood plan should contain, the plan's content should result from a process that assesses the neighborhood's specific needs, resources, and ideals.

While there is no definitive list of required elements for neighborhood plans, certain elements appear to be common and essential. They can be grouped into five categories, based on their relative purpose and sequence in the planning process:

- *General housekeeping:* Organizational items that make the plan readable and usable, and serve to encourage further involvement in the planning process
- *Planning process validation:* Elements that demonstrate the legitimacy of the research and consensus-building processes that led to the development of the plan
- *Neighborhood establishment:* Elements that serve to create a community image or identity distinct from the jurisdiction as a whole
- Functional elements: Substantive items that may vary widely from plan to plan (e.g., safety element, housing element)
- *Implementation Framework:* The goals, programs, actions, or schedules used to implement the plan

General Housekeeping

The elements in this category are used to create a clear, usable plan document. Because neighborhood residents may not be familiar with planning, this element is particularly important to include. More information on this element is covered in the Plan Making section of this book.

Planning Process Validation

Stakeholder participation is critical at the neighborhood planning level. Planning information must be accessible and comprehensible to all involved parties. Certain information should be made public throughout the planning process. In addition, placing some of that information directly in the plan allows other citizens to participate in the planning process more intelligently at a later time. This makes the plan a working reference document and validates the process that culminated in the plan.

The Neighborhood Organizational Structure and Planning Process

An important part of plan validation is how the planning process is initiated and carried out. Flow charts are often used to illustrate the sequence of events. This section may also reference the ordinance that adopts the plan, the community feedback that supported it, or the background information about why the process was initiated. Many jurisdictions require a formal neighborhood organization to be in place as a condition for planning assistance or plan adoption. Neighborhood leadership should be made clear in a plan or at least emerge out of the planning process. A legitimate, publicly accessible power structure gives the neighborhood-city relationship credibility, encourages neighbors to act responsibly with public resources, and facilitates a leadership development mechanism within the community.

The Mission/Purpose Statement

The mission/purpose statement establishes the importance of the neighborhood planning process. It should convey, that the process is all-inclusive and in accordance with policies set forth in the jurisdiction's comprehensive plan, if one exists. The statement can also be linked to the municipal code or city charter.

The Participation Proclamation

This section documents the participation process as it actually happened for the plan. It should be located at the beginning of the plan, setting the stage for the policies and recommendations that follow. Local ownership of the planning process must be evident. Both positive and negative feedback is important to include. Meeting minutes, survey, results, or local newspaper articles can document feedback.

Needs Assessment

A needs assessment for services and facilities is a fundamental component of neighborhood planning, especially when it identifies underserved neighborhood groups. Needs assessments can measure social services, physical conditions, commercial resources, and cultural amenities. When assessing needs, it is important to take stock of existing community resources. Evaluating the positive aspects of a neighborhood can reveal unexpected opportunities for dealing with the negatives.

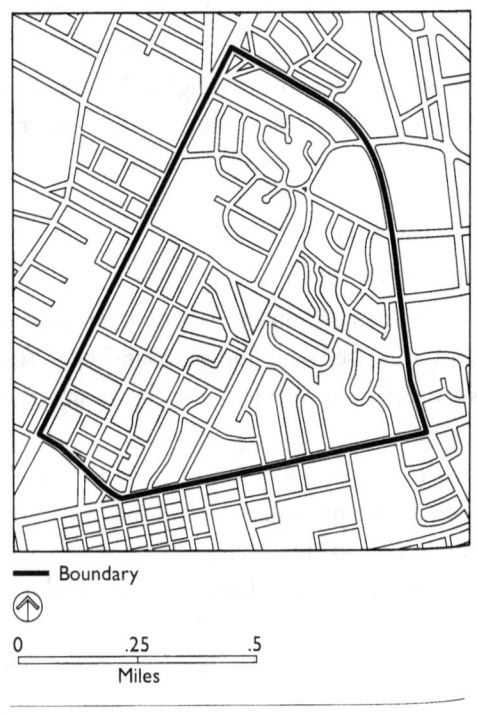

Neighborhood Boundary Delineation

Source: Adapted from Upper Boggy Creek Neighborhood Plan, City of Austin, TX, 2002.

Defining the Neighborhood

In addition to securing the future, neighborhood plans fortify the present by defining the neighborhood.

Boundary Delineation

The neighborhood and the city departments should agree to, or at least accommodate, each party's perception of neighborhood boundaries. Boundary identification should involve representatives from the community, pertinent city departments, and, if possible, social service providers. One method of determining boundaries is to have participants draw lines on maps to define their own boundaries. Combining the maps can reveal the most common perception of the area that constitutes the neighborhood. The walkable distances to key community services, such as elementary schools, public transportation, local grocers, and health care resources, often define neighborhood boundaries. Neighborhood definition is also sometimes related to historic district designation.

The Functional Elements

Most neighborhood plans address functional elements, such as housing, safety, land use, and recreation as separate topics. Plans may treat these topics from start to finish, beginning with a description of existing conditions and concluding with recommendations, or they may simply list policy recommendations and the implementation strategies for those recommendations. Some neighborhood plans have required that elements be consistent with those in the community's comprehensive plan or, sometimes, with the regional plan. These might include density targets or impact and mitigation requirements for new development.

Residential

Residential development policies can include promoting owner-occupied housing or rental housing, code enforcement, and amending zoning and other land-use controls to encourage more housing development and vacant property rehabilitation. Issues pertaining to private property maintenance, housing stock, affordability and demand, building conditions, safety, property values, infill, abandonment, and design standards can also be included.

Transportation/Circulation/Pedestrian Access

Transportation elements in neighborhood plans often identify specific circulation problems at intersections and street corners. Plans can include recommendations for improving sidewalks, reducing vehicles or vehicle speed, creating bicycle lanes, and improving access to transit. Transportation elements and policies should promote the connection and flow of all transportation forms to serve people of all ages and abilities.

Land Use/Zoning

Current land-use patterns and zoning classifications are frequently presented in neighborhood plans, often as part of a needs assessment. To help residents understand the information, land-use and zoning data should be provided simply and clearly. Growth projections and areas where growth is expected to happen should be identified.

Infrastructure/Utilities

Infrastructure quality is important to neighborhood residents and businesses. It is also perhaps the least controllable aspect of neighborhood development, particularly where city officials have not been involved in the neighborhood planning process. Public works departments and private utility companies are not always directly responsive to neighborhoods because their agendas are usually tied to citywide capital improvement programs rather than to

PLANNING AND URBAN DESIGN STANDARDS

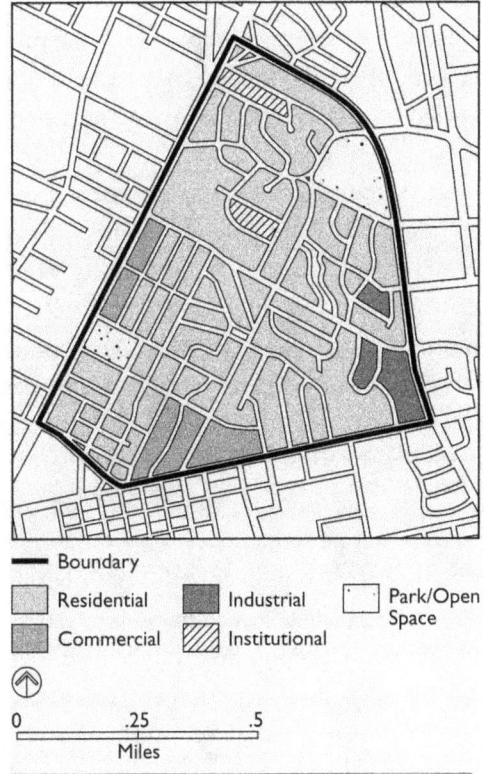

Generalized Neighborhood Land-Use Map

Source: Adapted from Upper Boggy Creek Neighborhood Plan, City of Austin, TX, 2002.

each neighborhoods planning process. Plans may include actions such as petitioning public works departments and the city council as a method of obtaining needed infrastructure improvements.

Implementation Framework

Once a neighborhood plan has evaluated the existing conditions, the needs assessment, and the community's desires for the future, generally the plan frames a set of goals and objectives. An implementation program sometimes follows the goals and objectives.

Goals, Objectives, and Other Resolutions

The goals and objectives of the neighborhood plan represent the community's vision and values. They may be presented as vision statements or policy recommendations.

Implementation Program

The schedule for achieving goals and objectives must be set, commitments must be made, and responsibility for actually accomplishing them has to be assigned. Neighborhood plans should include an implementation element, either woven into the functional plan elements or at the end of the document, shown as a chart or matrix.

Funding

City capital improvements funds, special assessments, transportation funds, tax increment funds, community development block grant (CDBG) funds, special state or federal program grants (such as historic preservation or urban forestry), donations, fund-raisers, private investors, and community development loans are viable funding sources to use in the implementation of neighborhood plans.

See also:
Neighborhoods
Participation
Plan Making

TRANSPORTATION PLANS

Effective transportation systems are central to maintaining the productivity, health, and safety of communities and regions. A transportation plan guides the investment in, and timing of, improvements to the transportation network to meet community mobility, accessibility, safety, economic, and quality-of-life needs.

REASONS TO PREPARE A TRANSPORTATION PLAN

Transportation plans are typically prepared to address the following items in a systematic, coordinated, and comprehensive manner:

- Management of existing systems
- Maintenance of previous investment
- Realignment of existing services
- Introduction of new services
- Construction of new facilities
- Identification of ways to finance system maintenance and improvements

The process of preparing various transportation plans gives government agencies, elected officials, and the public the opportunity to assess the adequacy of the existing system and to plan to meet future needs while maintaining local and regional transportation systems in good condition. The outcome of the process should be a transportation plan that defines existing problems and issues, predicts future deficiencies and problems, defines solutions, and identifies where to find the resources needed to manage and implement plan recommendations.

The goals of a particular transportation plan are usually determined by comparing existing transportation system performance to projected future demands and by considering the particular social, economic, and environmental circumstances of the community. Given the importance of effective transportation systems to the health and vitality of a community, transportation plans often provide a "blueprint" for future development and redevelopment in support of regional and comprehensive land-use plans.

TRANSPORTATION PLANNING ROLES AND RESPONSIBILITIES

The development of a successful transportation plan requires the insights of those entities responsible for various components of the transportation system, working in concert with those who will use and be affected by the transportation service and improvements, to develop solutions responsive to diverse considerations. Those responsible for plan development must create an effective forum for evaluating system deficiencies, assessing alternatives, and selecting the most effective course of action. Development of some plans is a highly structured process, complete with formal committees. Others are less structured and rely more heavily on exiting committees or informal communication networks to solicit participation.

Whether structured or informal, because transportation plans affect so many interests and a wide range of people, broad and meaningful participation in plan development is essential. The development stage of transportation planning should include representatives from the following constituencies:

- U.S. Department of Transportation
- State departments of transportation
- Metropolitan planning organizations
- Local governments
- Public transit providers
- Resource and regulatory agencies
- Citizens and communities

U.S. Department of Transportation

The modal administrations of the U.S. Department of Transportation, including the Federal Highway Administration, the Federal Transit Administration, and the Federal Railroad Administration, administer, grant, and oversee funds for the planning, development, implementation, and operation of transportation services and infrastructure. In transportation planning efforts funded by the federal government, such as corridor plans, direct involvement of the federal agency is advisable during key decision points, at a minimum. In the development of a local transportation plan where there is no clear federal interest, there may be no involvement of the federal government, or the involvement might be limited to consultation regarding the availability and applicability of federal programs and funding.

State Departments of Transportation

Through their departments of transportation, states are responsible for the construction, maintenance, and operation of designated state highways. As part of this responsibility, state departments of transportation (DOTs) are responsible for provision and administration of funds for construction, maintenance, and operation of transportation facilities and services. State DOTs are also responsible for leading the preparation of statewide plans. Like metropolitan planning organizations (MPOs), they may have responsibility in the development and maintenance of regional travel demand forecasting models. State DOTs provide technical assistance and support to a wide range of transportation plans. They are the repositories for much of the data required to assess existing transportation systems.

Metropolitan Planning Organizations

The federal government charges MPOs to prepare metropolitan area long-range plans for urbanized areas. In some instances, MPOs will also lead the preparation of corridor plans. In addition, MPOs are often in charge of developing and maintaining the regional travel demand forecasting models used as a basis to support many transportation planning functions, including the development of employment and population forecasts and administration and disbursement of transportation funds. Consequently, in addition to their leadership role in preparing metropolitan regional long-range transportation plans, MPOs also provide technical assistance in support of other transportation planning efforts.

Local Governments

Local governments play a major role in constructing, operating, and maintaining surface transportation networks, often including transit service and roadways. Consequently, their involvement in the development of transportation plans is essential. In some cases, such as for a local transportation plan, the city, county, or town public works departments or transportation divisions might take the lead in preparing the transportation plan or the transportation element of a comprehensive plan. For other plan types, such as metropolitan area long-range transportation plans, local governments might provide technical support and knowledge specific to their jurisdictions. In either case, the insights of those engaged in the day-to-day operations of the system are an invaluable asset to any plan. In addition, since local government might be charged with implementing particular recommendations of the plans, it is essential that there be consensus for action and an understanding of the basic needs and technical analysis supporting the action.

Public Transit Providers

With respect to public transportation services, the role and responsibilities of public transit providers is similar to that described for local governments. However, because transit providers may not have a dedicated funding source for operations and may be dependent upon local governments for funding, early consultation regarding the availability of resources is even more critical.

Resource and Regulatory Agencies

Transportation plan recommendations can affect a broad range of natural and social resources. Consequently, early involvement of resource and regulatory agencies in transportation plan development can help identify constraints that could potentially prohibit implementation of future projects because of regulatory requirements, schedule impacts, or financial requirements.

Citizens and Communities

Citizens and communities are an important resource in the development of transportation plans, as both the "customers" of the system and those who might be affected by proposed changes. Statewide plans, metropolitan area long-range transportation plans, and corridor plans specifically require public involvement to inform plan development. Involvement should range from the average resident to neighborhood or civic associations, community leaders, and business community representation, such as chambers of commerce. For larger transportation plans, it is advisable to establish a formal citizens advisory group.

TYPES OF TRANSPORTATION PLANS

Transportation plans vary widely in approach, content, and scope as determined by geographic coverage, scale, and time frame. There are four basic types of transportation plans:

- Statewide transportation plans
- Metropolitan area long-range transportation plans
- Local transportation plans
- Corridor plans

Statewide Transportation Plans

Statewide transportation plans, which are prepared by state DOTs, provide the basis for coordinating data collection and analyses to support planning, programming, and project development decisions. A basic requirement of plan development is coordination with the public and other entities with jurisdiction. The extent of coordination required with other transportation planning entities in developing the plan is based on the scale and complexity of many issues, including transportation problems: safety concerns; and land use, employment, economic, environmental, and housing and community development objectives within the state. The plans typically reference, summarize, or contain information about the availability of financial and other resources needed to implement the plan, although state plans, unlike metropolitan area long-range transportation plans, are not required to determine the likely availability of funding and the sources of funding to carry out the plan. State plans are evaluated on a regular basis and updated periodically to reflect changing statewide priorities and needs.

Statewide plans are intermodal in nature. They address passenger, goods, and freight movement for a minimum 20-year planning horizon. These plans are federally mandated to consider the following issues:

- Economic vitality
- Safety and security
- Accessibility and mobility
- Environmental quality
- Quality of life
- System connectivity
- System efficiency
- System preservation

In addition, state DOTs are all obligated to consider the opinions of elected officials representing local governments and the concerns of Native American tribal governments and federal land management agencies that have jurisdiction over land within the boundaries of the state. The plan is coordinated with adjacent states and counties and, where appropriate, international borders. It is conducted in a manner consistent with the metropolitan area planning process conducted by MPOs. By federal mandate, statewide plans are coordinated with air quality planning, and provide for appropriate conformity analyses as required by the Clean Air Act.

Metropolitan Area Long-Range Transportation Plans

Metropolitan area long-range transportation plans focus on evaluating alternative transportation and land-use scenarios to identify major travel corridors, assess potential problems, and provide a basis for planning and programming major improvements. These plans cover multiple jurisdictions and are therefore "regional" in emphasis. Prepared under the direction of a federally designated MPO, they typically cover a 20-year planning horizon. Under federal requirements, the adopted plans must be "fiscally constrained." In other words, the plan must demonstrate the likely availability of funding sources needed to implement proposed programs and projects.

Local Transportation Plans

Local transportation plans are prepared either as stand-alone documents or as an element of a comprehensive plan. Local governments or regional transit providers typically prepare these plans, but they are coordinated closely with MPOs and state DOTs. The plans provide the basis for the programming and implementation of local transportation actions. They address small-scale improvements and projects requiring major capital investments. The typical plan consists of an inventory of existing facilities and a description of existing conditions, an assessment of system deficiencies, a projection of future needs, a description of the proposed plan, discussion of cost implications, and a summary of actions required for plan implementation. These plans usually address some short-range early action items (1 to 5 years), some midrange actions (5 to 10 years), and longer-term activities in a 20-year time horizon. In addition, the land-use implications of the plan are addressed. As with the other plans discussed, public and agency coordination during plan development is essential to successful plan implementation.

Corridor Plans

Corridor plans that focus on transportation are prepared for high-priority areas showing signs of congestion or predicted for significant future travel volume, or for transportation facilities of historical or natural significance. The entity responsible for implementing the improvements most frequently prepares these plans; therefore, state DOTs and transit providers often undertake them, although MPOs, local governments. and resource agencies such as the National Park Service also conduct such studies. Coordination of corridor plans with the general public is required, as well as with federal, state, and local agencies with an interest in the plan's outcome. Corridor plans usually have a 20-year planning horizon. The degree of federal or state DOT participation is often governed by the proposed funding for the plan's implementation.

Corridor plans involve the definition of the corridor to be studied, along with a clear presentation of the problem to be solved, both of which form the basis of the purpose and need for action. Consideration of a wide range of alternative means to solve the identified transportation

ESSENTIAL READINGS IN URBAN PLANNING

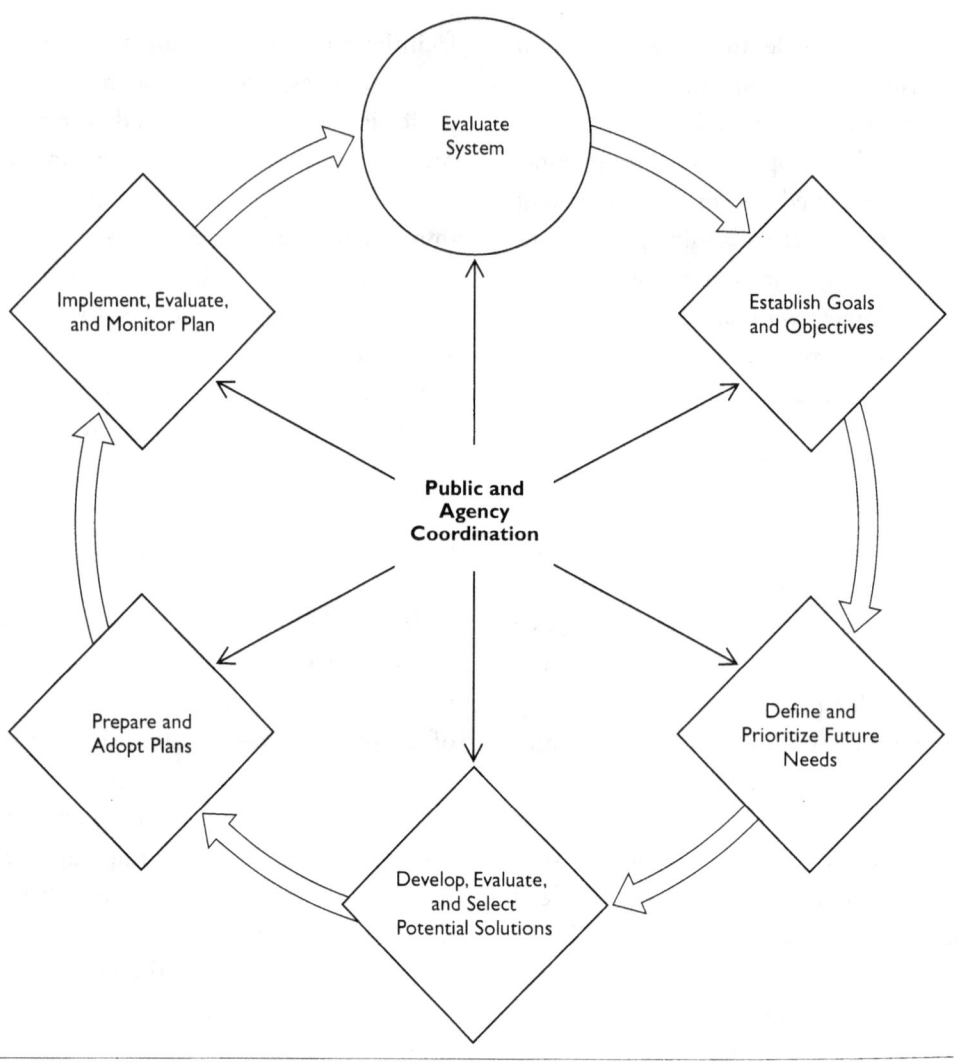

Transportation Plan Development Cycle
Source: Diana C. Mendes, AICP.

problem or resource management objectives should be at the core of plan development. These alternatives can involve different levels of investment or different types of corridor improvements. They are systematically evaluated using a set of stakeholder-developed evaluation criteria. These criteria typically include land use, environmental effects, community concerns, cost, capacity, and effectiveness. The analysis results are shared and discussed publicly prior to making a decision on a preferred course of action. The final plan document summarizes both the planning process and the results, explaining how the decision was made, and the actions necessary to implement the plan and recommended improvements.

PLAN COMPONENTS

Transportation plans should include the following elements:

- An overview of the planning process
- A description of existing conditions (transportation network and land use)
- A forecast of future conditions (transportation network and land use)
- A summary of transportation needs
- Goals and objectives
- An assessment of transportation system capacity
- A series of alternative scenarios for future and proposed improvements
- A description of cost implications and funding sources
- Guidelines for implementation and performance monitoring
- A program for ensuring public involvement

TRANSPORTATION PLAN DEVELOPMENT

There are six basic steps in the development of a transportation plan:

1. Evaluate system capacity, deficiencies, and needs.
2. Establish goals and objectives.
3. Define and prioritize future needs.
4. Develop, evaluate, and select potential solutions.
5. Prepare and adopt the plan, including public review and comment.
6. Implement, monitor, and evaluate plan performance.

The development of responsive and effective plans is predicated on the active involvement of the public and appropriate federal, state, and local agencies in transportation decision making at each step of transportation plan development.

Evaluate System Capacity, Deficiencies, and Need

Evaluation of the current system begins with an inventory of the existing facilities and services and their capacity, including the roadway network, transit systems, freight systems, as well as the interrelationships to air and waterborne transportation. This evaluation should establish where the transportation network is performing well and where deficiencies currently exist or are predicted to exist in terms of accessibility, mobility, and efficiency relative to community aspirations. Both quantitative and qualitative measures, including evaluation of population and employment characteristics, land-use trends, travel markets and patterns, and user surveys, are often used in the plans to describe the transportation problems to be solved and to establish a need for action.

Establish Goals and Objectives

The goals and objectives, which are developed in response to the analysis of system capacity, deficiencies, and needs, form the foundation upon which different alternative transportation scenarios and investments are evaluated during plan development. The goals and objectives vary and are dependent upon context (rural, suburban, and urban), trends in population and employment, and planning horizon (short term or long term). Transportation plans are increasingly becoming more context-sensitive, incorporating more goals related to land-use compatibility, economic considerations, energy, environmental management, and community quality. Criteria by which the performance of different potential actions can be measured against these goals and objectives should be

ESSENTIAL READINGS IN URBAN PLANNING

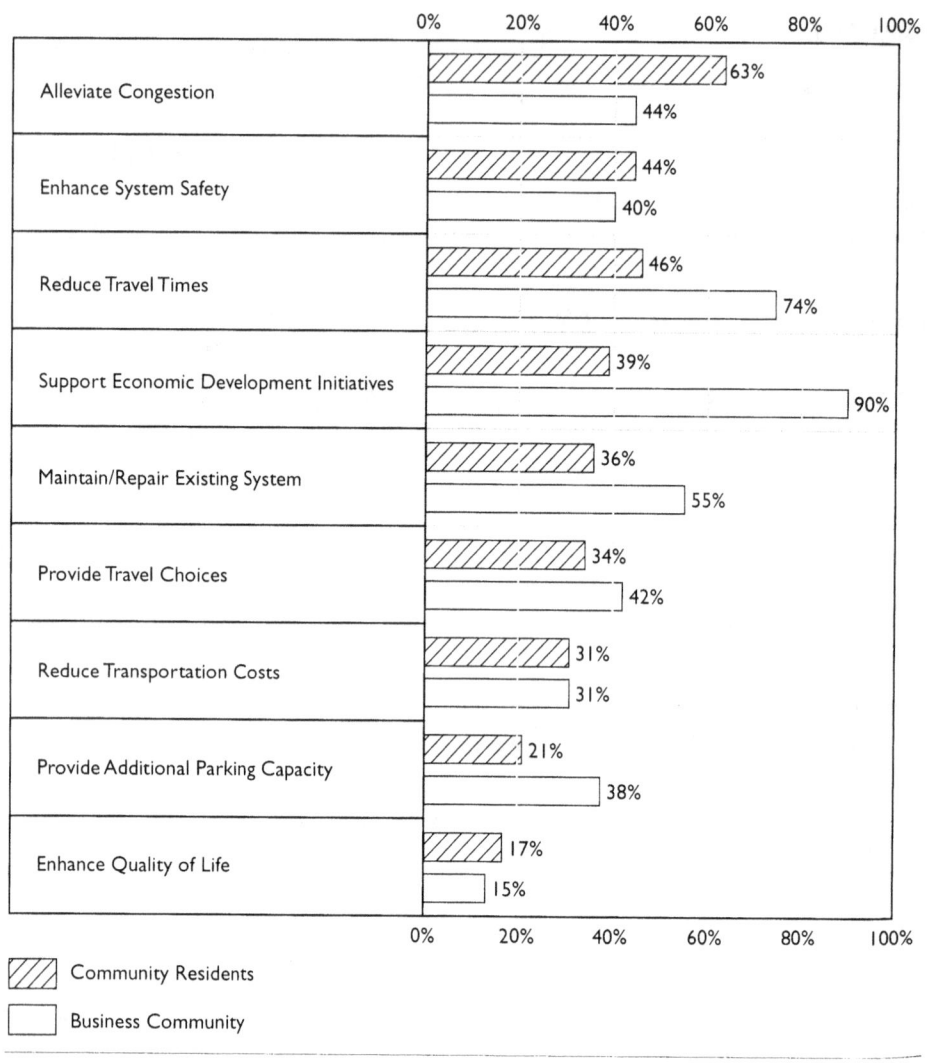

Transportation Goals by Participant Preference
Source: Diana C. Mendes, AICP.

clearly articulated to facilitate public understanding of the decision-making process.

Define and Rank Future Needs

Once planners have established the plan's goals and objectives, the next step involves defining and ranking future needs. This analysis uses the information gained during the initial system evaluation in combination with population and employment projections, regional and local land-use plans, and the results of public and agency coordination.

Transportation Models

Planners employ transportation models to conduct regional travel demand forecasting and to simulate

PLANNING AND URBAN DESIGN STANDARDS

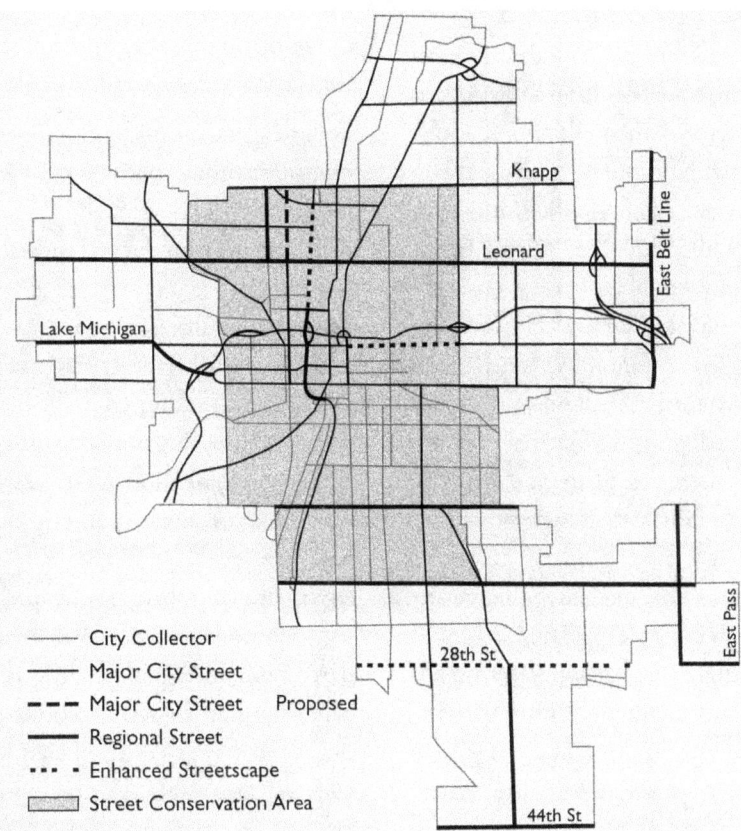

Transportation Framework Plan: Streets

Source: Adapted from City of Grand Rapids. Michigan, 2002, Plan for Grand Rapids.

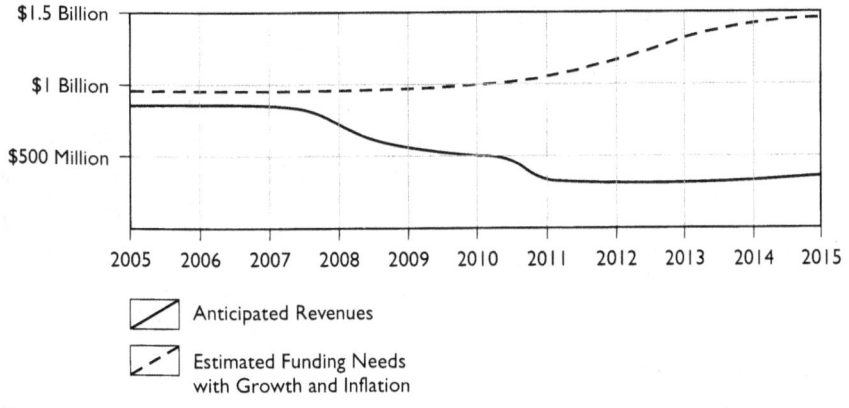

Needs Versus Funding for Transportation Infrastructure

Source: Diana C. Mendes, AICP

traffic impacts to assess and evaluate the capacity of existing and future transportation networks to accommodate projected demand. Regional models are focused on the large-scale "macro," travel movements in aggregate, while traffic simulation is focused on the smaller-scale, or "micro" travel movements on an individual basis.

The regional travel demand forecasting models are developed, maintained, and operated by MPOs and state DOTs, and can vary in size and scope dependent upon the area they are designed to serve. These regional models characterize the transportation systems) networks, as well as the demand for the system in terms of its users, travel patterns, and how changes to the system might affect demand. These regional models provide insights about where trips are generated and attracted, how trips are distributed, the likely choice of modes, and the routes to be traveled in order to predict the future volume of use.

In cases when regional models either are not available or may not be appropriate, such as when small changes in the transportation network need to be analyzed for a specific site, traffic simulation models are used. Traffic simulation models can be valuable not only in determining future conditions and level of service, but also in identifying appropriate mitigation measures such as changes in signal timing or additional street improvements to address degradation of capacity. A number of software packages are commercially available, and the models are typically developed and applied by the project sponsor on a case-by-case basis to address specific project needs. Irrespective of the type of modeling tools and processes applied, priorities should be based upon the results of the technical analysis, overlaid with the opinions of the public and agencies participating in plan development.

Develop, Evaluate, and Select Potential Solutions

Following a clear understanding of and agreement on priorities, alternative scenarios or solutions can be defined and developed. These scenarios consist of adjustments to the transportation system based on changes to services or investments in new programs or infrastructure. While planners may evaluate each of the transportation modes (e.g., rail, air, auto) addressed in the plan independently, the results of this initial assessment can be used ultimately to develop and to test potential combinations of investment among different modes to best meet needs.

It is during this iterative process that alternative solutions can be evaluated and compared based upon their performance and effectiveness in achieving stated goals and objectives and meeting needs. To assist elected officials, community leaders, and the public in making decisions among alternatives, planners need to explain and document the potential benefits and impacts, and the trade-offs of each alternative. They need to pay special attention to which populations benefit from a particular set of actions versus which may experience adverse impacts to anticipate support for and resistance to the plan.

Prepare and Adopt the Plan

The plan should document the public decision-making process and provide the technical rationale for its conclusions. It should also describe future implementation of proposed programs and improvements, including a clear delineation of action to be taken, the sequencing of improvements, responsibility for implementation, and cost.

A brief executive summary of the plan should be prepared for the public. Because transportation plans can be quite technical, the summary should be written for the lay reader. Adoption of the plan should follow a public review process that includes a number of public outreach activities, including formal hearings. During the project review process, it may be necessary to revise the plan. Particular attention should be paid to the financial element of the plan in terms of cost, revenues, shortfalls, and options for using current and potential new sources.

Implement, Monitor, and Evaluate Plan Performance

Plan implementation requires clear direction on responsibilities, schedule, and funding. Successful plan implementation also depends on ongoing monitoring and performance evaluation. This systematic, regular assessment of the effectiveness of implemented actions should provide the foundation for the evaluation phase of the next planning cycle. The performance measures should be the same as or a subset of the evaluation criteria used to assess and select the adopted plan.

See also:
Air Quality
Comprehensive Plans
Environmental Impact Assessment
Federal Legislation
Participation
Transportation

HOUSING PLANS

More than 70 years ago planning pioneer Patrick Abercrombie (1933) wrote. "The subject of housing enters into planning continuously, whether under the heading of density, of the living conditions of the population, of slum clearance or suburban growth." Those same issues remain central to the planning process today. To address them, jurisdictions with the authority to prepare and implement housing plans are increasingly likely to prepare and adopt housing plans or housing strategies, either as a part of their comprehensive plan, or as a separate freestanding document.

REASONS TO PREPARE A HOUSING PLAN

Municipalities have many different reasons for preparing housing plans.

To Address Legal Requirements

Some states require a housing plan as part of the municipal comprehensive plan or master plan. Washington State, for example, mandates a housing element, which must "make adequate provision for existing and projected needs of all economic segments of the community." (Laws of State of Washington, RCW 36.70A.070(2)). Other states, including California and New Jersey, require that the municipality address its fair share of regional housing need, as defined by a state or regional agency. Municipalities that receive HUD Community Development Block Grant or HOME funds must prepare a Consolidated Plan, which delineates the municipality's overall housing needs and strategy and shows how their federal funds will be used.

To Address Affordable Housing Needs

Even with no formal legal requirement, many municipalities undertake housing plans when they recognize that rising housing costs or loss of existing housing units is making the community unaffordable to many of its present and prospective residents. As described in the Cary, North Carolina, affordable housing plan, when the town realized that the "escalating price of housing was excluding many people from living within the city limits ... including Town staff, policemen, teachers, retail clerks, and service people," it adopted an affordable housing plan, which included a detailed action-oriented "affordable housing tool kit."

To Encourage Economic and Social Integration, and to Build Stronger Neighborhoods

Affluent suburbs may develop affordable housing plans to ensure that less affluent people can continue to live in, or move into, the community. At the same time, many older urban centers—for example, Baltimore and Norfolk—have begun to develop housing strategies designed to expand their economic diversity by attracting middle- and upper-income residents into their neighborhoods and downtowns. Such strategies can be citywide or can focus on creating economic diversity in a specific neighborhood, such as Fall Creek Place in Indianapolis. HUD's HOPE VI and Homeownership Zone programs have funded effective neighborhood-oriented housing strategies.

FORMS OF MUNICIPAL HOUSING PLANS

The form that a municipal housing plan takes flows from the reason it is being prepared. Where a housing element is part of a comprehensive plan, its features will usually be spelled out in the state planning statute. These typically include inventories, need assessments, and goal statements, as well as action plans. The New Jersey Fair Housing Act describes the contents of a fair-share plan, including "a consideration of the lands that are most appropriate for construction of low and moderate income housing and of the existing structures most appropriate for conversion to, or rehabilitation for, low and moderate income housing ..." (New Jersey Statutes 52:27D-310(f)). Washington State requires each city or county to identify "sufficient land for housing, including but not limited to government-assisted housing, housing for low-income families, manufactured housing, multifamily housing, and group homes and foster care facilities."

A municipality is driven to prepare a plan for internal reasons, such as the need for more affordable housing, but the scope of the plan may vary widely. Recognizing that housing needs far exceeded the community's ability to address them, the Stamford, Connecticut, Affordable Housing Strategy concentrated on a detailed strategy to assemble land and financial resources for affordable housing.

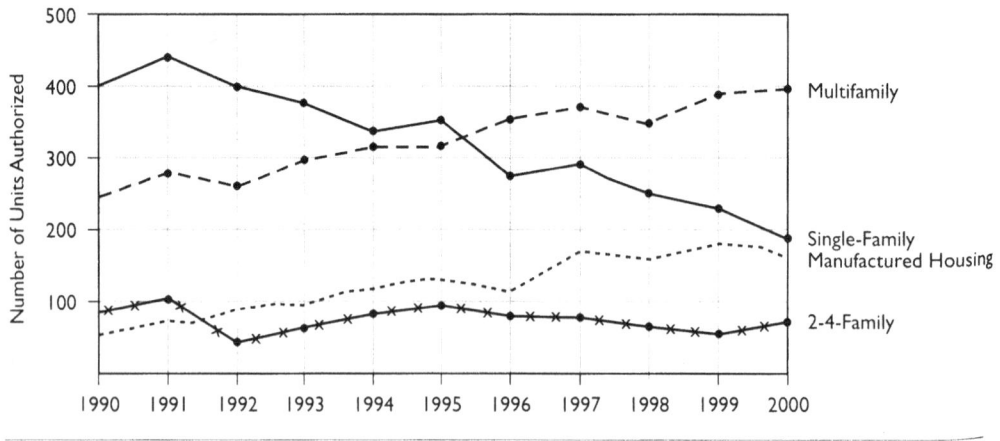

Housing Production Trends by Type, 1990–2000

Source: Alan Mallach.

Housing strategies in communities seeking to attract middle- and upper-income residents tend to focus much more on the real estate *market,* rather than on housing *needs.* These plans may include identifying potential target markets, such as empty-nesters or young professionals, focusing on how to attract them into the city's housing market, whether by developing new housing oriented to their preferences or by highlighting particular features of the city's existing housing stock.

A housing plan is fundamentally a *strategic action* plan, which emphasizes those parts of the housing market unlikely to be adequately reached by the private market unaided by public intervention. The assessment of conditions and analysis of trends is not an end in itself but should be designed to lead to specific strategies and programs designed to achieve the community's housing goals.

MUNICIPAL HOUSING PLAN ELEMENTS

Although housing plans vary widely, a series of elements are common to most plans. As noted, in some cases, state law will mandate that certain elements be included, while in others local officials and community stakeholders must determine which are most relevant to local concerns.

An Inventory of Existing Conditions and Trends

In order to understand existing housing conditions in the municipality, most plans begin with an inventory, including the distribution of housing in the community by cost and by type (for example, single-family, two-family, or multi-family housing), for both owner-occupied and rental housing. It should also identify specialized housing types, such as manufactured housing or single-room occupancy (SRO) housing. It should both provide a profile of current housing conditions and analyze trends to determine how those conditions are changing—increases in house prices, for example, or movement from ownership or rental, or vice versa, in the housing stock.

Regional conditions and trends should also be presented, to show how the municipality relates to the larger regional context. Job growth trends, important as an indicator of potential housing needs, should also be measured. Information on substandard or abandoned housing should be included where sound data is available. Census data should be used as a starting point, but, particularly as the end of each decade approaches, it must be supplemented by other data sources. A property information system, as has been developed in many cities (e.g., Los Angeles or Minneapolis), can be used to identify buildings at risk of abandonment by tracking code violations, tax arrearages, and crime complaints.

Housing Need Analysis

Most housing plans are designed to focus primarily on affordable housing. Affordable housing is defined differently in different jurisdictions. In New Jersey, it refers to households earning no more than 80 percent of the regional median income, while elsewhere it may include households earning as much as 120 percent of regional median or as little as 50 percent. At present, households earning less than 50 percent of regional median income are most likely to have deficient housing conditions and are least likely to see their housing needs addressed by the private market.

The housing plan should attempt to quantify housing needs wherever possible, using census data to identify the number of households living in overcrowded housing or suffering undue cost burdens in the community. Where feasible, a community survey should be used to identify households living in substandard housing. The

ESSENTIAL READINGS IN URBAN PLANNING

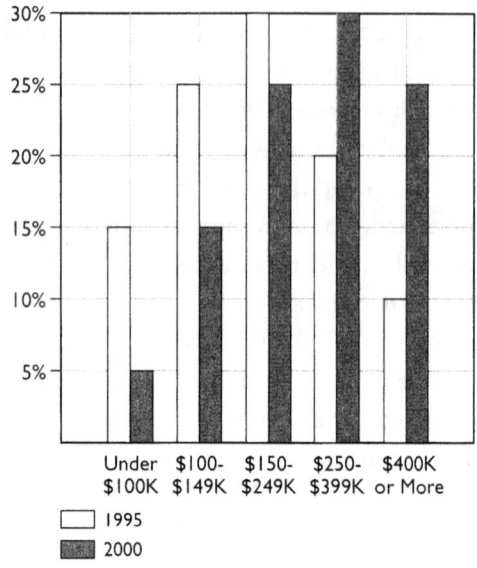

Distribution of House Sale Prices, 1995 and 2000
Source: Alan Mallach.

sum of these needs is often referred to as the community's present, or indigenous, housing need.

Prospective affordable housing needs are those of low- and moderate-income households who should have the opportunity to move into the community in the future. This is where the fair-share principle becomes most relevant since, by definition, a substantial percentage of all new households are low and moderate income. Since "low and moderate income" is defined relative to regional median income rather than as a set dollar amount, it will represent a consistent share of all households over time, with the share depending on where the cutoff is placed. Where low and moderate income is defined as 80 percent of regional median, roughly 40 percent of all households will fall below that line. Where it is defined as 50 percent of regional median, it will include roughly 25 percent of all households. (See table.) A fair-share plan, or regional fair-share allocation, identifies the share of the region's household growth that should appropriately be accommodated within the municipality and defines how housing for those households will be provided.

See *Housing Needs Assessment* elsewhere in this book for more detail on conducting such a study.

Market Analysis

Understanding the workings of the housing market, at the regional level and within the municipality—and in large municipalities, within individual neighborhoods—is a critical step toward framing effective, achievable goals and strategies, and determining realistic targets. Enacting a successful inclusionary program, for example. requires an understanding of how the market will respond to incentives, such as density bonuses, or the extent to which market prices will support internal subsidies. In an older city, the market analysis may be used to identify those households that may be attracted to redeveloping neighborhoods or downtown loft districts.

Goals and Targets

A strategic plan must be grounded in a body of clear goals and, to the extent feasible, realizable targets. Goals should be well focused, such as those in Denver's 1999 housing plan, listed here:

- Reduce the regulatory costs of housing.
- Expand the resources available for housing programs and services.
- Preserve the existing housing stock.
- Address the needs of low-income and special-needs populations.
- Attract and retain middle-income families.
- Undertake housing efforts to support economic development strategies.

Each of these goals is expressed in a way that can easily be translated into specific strategies and action programs.

Distribution of Households and Rental Units by Income and Affordability

CATEGORY	MAXIMUM INCOME	MAXIMUM AFFORDABLE RENT	PERCENT OF ALL HOUSEHOLDS IN COUNTY	PERCENT OF RENTAL UNITS AT/BELOW AFFORDABLE RENT
Low income (<50% of median)	$25,000	$625/month	25%	3%
Moderate income (<80% of median)	$40,000	$1,000/month	40%	32%
Middle income (<120% of median)	$60,000	$1,500/month	60%	74%
Countywide Median Income	$50,000			
Countywide Median Rent		$1,200/month		

Source: Alan Mallach.

Strategy Analysis

A vast number of potential housing strategies are available. Before settling on the specific strategies to pursue, a valuable part of the planning process is to conduct a strategy analysis to evaluate the available options to determine which are most likely to respond effectively to the community's conditions. The strategy analysis should look at removing impediments and establishing affirmative steps to reach affordable or other housing goals. Systems—including barriers created by the town's own regulations and administrative procedures—that affect the affordability or availability of housing should be examined, as should the means and resources the town can use to affirmatively promote its housing goals. Each strategy should be assessed with respect to its potential impact if implemented and the relative ease or difficulty of implementing the strategy.

Implementation Plan

The worth of a housing plan ultimately depends on its implementation. The implementation plan should begin with a description of the strategies and programs the town has selected to carry its goals forward. It should follow with specific information about how each strategy will be carried out, including:

- the financial resources that will be assembled;
- the sites, buildings, or target areas that will be the focus of the strategy;
- the design and planning standards to be followed;
- the key players or participants in implementing the strategy;
- identification of entities responsible for implementing each part of the strategy; and
- specific targets and timetables for each strategy or program.

The implementation plan should be *specific*. It should identify both specific areas to be rezoned and the specific standards that will ensure that the sites will be used as intended. It should include an assessment of the municipal, state, federal and private funds realistically available to carry out the plan.

Some productive implementation strategies municipalities use include:

- rezoning of areas for higher density;
- inclusionary zoning;
- creating infill opportunities;
- creating opportunities for specialized housing types, such as accessory apartments, SRO housing, or group homes;
- incentives for housing preservation and rehabilitation, including adaptive reuse projects;
- assembly strategies and land banking;
- removing regulatory barriers, including creating simpler and expedited approval procedures;
- financial assistance to developers of affordable housing; and
- housing trust funds.

Some housing strategies can be carried out within the existing stricture of town or city government, but others will entail new responsibilities and may require new managerial entities or partnerships to carry them out. Partnerships with community development corporations, developers, employers, and others are critical. Few, if any, towns or cities are capable of implementing a housing strategy without strong private sector partners.

KEY AND EMERGING ISSUES

Housing is a complex, multidimensional subject, both in itself and in its relationship to other planning and development issues. Changes in economic conditions and housing needs, as well as new thinking about how best to plan towns and cities, have led to the emergence of a series of important issues, many arising from smart growth principles, that a community's housing plan should address.

Integrating Housing with other Planning Activities

As planning moves away from a history of separated uses and disconnected plans to a more holistic view of a community, the importance of linking housing with other uses and other planning processes has become apparent. The recognition of the advantages of mixed-use development, in which housing and nonresidential uses complement each other, as well as recognition of the links between housing and open-space or major community facilities, such as schools, are important considerations for building stronger, healthier communities. The creation of transit-oriented development, for example, which combines housing and other uses around transit hubs, is but one of many such available strategies.

Housing and Jobs

The extent to which a community provides housing opportunities for a diverse workforce is not just a matter of creating a more balanced community; it is essential for the community's economic vitality. Housing plans should not only evaluate the community's economic base and job growth as a basis for planning future housing, but should also actively explore opportunities for direct linkages between major employers and workforce housing strategies.

Preservation

Housing plans are not only about what should be built in the future, but also about how to preserve what already exists. Housing strategies are a key element in preserving the fabric of existing neighborhoods and historic areas, particularly with respect to affordable housing. As the loss of the affordable housing stock, either through disinvestment or through price appreciation, becomes a critical issue in many communities, housing strategies must incorporate activities to preserve that stock as well as produce new affordable housing.

Downtown and Neighborhood Revitalization

Housing development grounded in market-building strategies has turned out to be one of the most powerful tools available to urban centers to spur reinvestment and revitalization in their downtowns and older residential neighborhoods. Cities such as Cleveland and Baltimore have reinvented their down-towns by drawing upon the regional pool of young professionals and empty-nesters, while attracting a diverse body of home buyers to buy and rehabilitate homes in the city's neighborhoods. Strategies designed to maximize private sector reinvestment and revitalization activities are important parts of the housing plans of the many cities and towns seeking to rebuild.

Resolving Conflicts over Affordable Housing

Certainly, any development is potentially controversial, but few areas are as likely to trigger conflict as affordable housing. Despite widespread public support for meeting housing needs in general, a specific affordable housing proposal will often become a lightning rod for a variety of community concerns. Indeed, even the term "affordable housing" can become a matter of contention, prompting some advocates to refer to their efforts as "workforce housing" or "affordable home-ownership." The framers of an affordable housing plan must recognize the reality and depth of community concerns, and incorporate into the planning process a method for building support and, to the extent possible, consensus around the plan's specific strategies, beginning well before the plans are finalized.

REFERENCE

Abercrombie, Patrick. 1933. *Town and Country Planning*. New York, NY: Henry Holt & Co.

See also:
Federal Legislation
Housing Needs Assessment
Neighborhoods
Residential Types

ECONOMIC DEVELOPMENT PLANS

An economic development plan guides a local or regional effort to stimulate economic growth and to preserve existing jobs. Economic development may also be aimed at ensuring increases in real wages, stabilization or increase of the local tax base, and job diversification—making the community or region less dependent on a few employers and thus insulating it from economic downturns in specific industries.

In most places economic development has broadened from job creation and retention and provision of land and infrastructure for business to promotion of prosperity and quality of life—the idea that with economic growth should come broader societal wellbeing. Thus, economic development is increasingly linked with education, culture, affordable housing, and preservation of the environment.

REASONS TO PREPARE AN ECONOMIC DEVELOPMENT PLAN

A number of factors typically prompt a local or regional economic planning effort. They include the following:

- Loss of a major employer or the attraction of a new employer
- Competition from surrounding communities or regions
- Belief that the community should take an active role in promoting itself
- A desire to provide employment for existing residents
- Economic stagnation or decline in a community, or part of it
- Need for new tax revenues, especially to finance the concurrent costs of residential growth

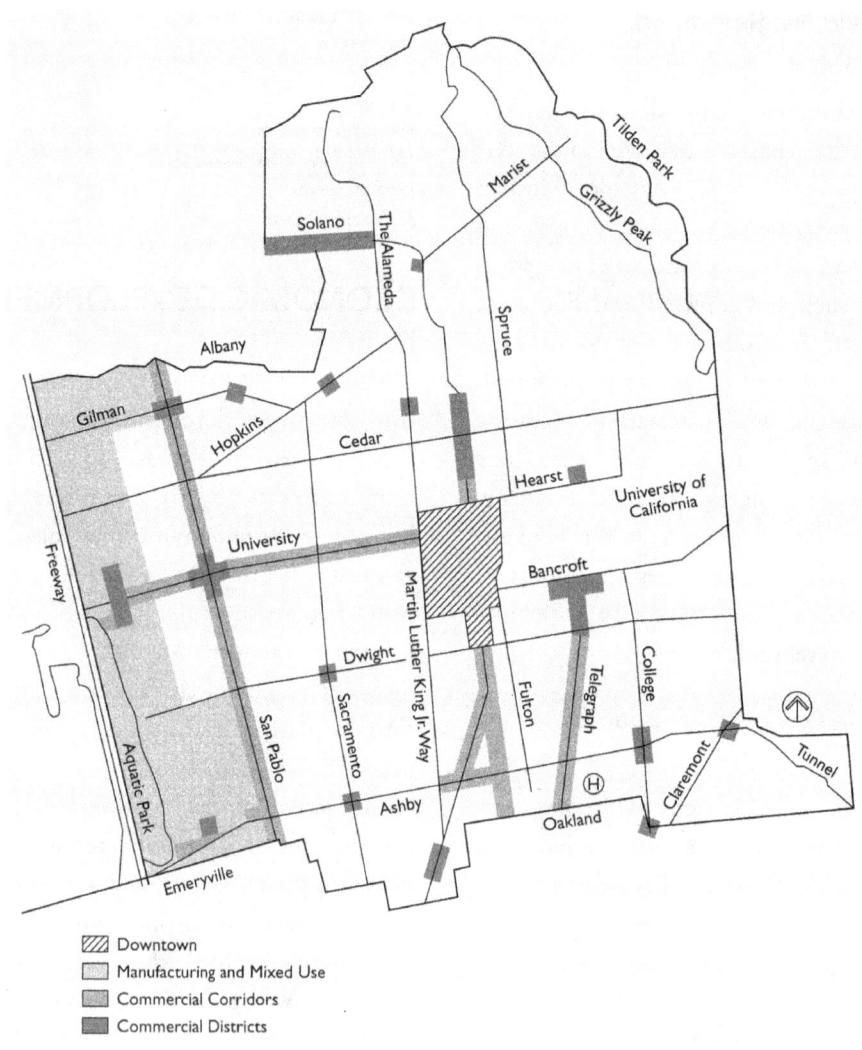

Commercial and Industrial Employment Areas, Berkeley, California
Source: Berkeley, California, General Plan, 2003.

Economic development efforts may also simply reflect an innate entrepreneurial spirit, a desire to experiment and to grow.

APPROACHES TO THE PLAN

All economic development plans should include a series of background studies intended to identify the strengths and weaknesses of the community or the region and make some assessments about the type and extent of desired economic growth. If the analysis is for a community, the larger frame of reference should be the region. If the analysis is for the region, the state or a substantial subregion of it should be the context. Trends that dominate the larger unit of analysis will in some way affect the subunit.

The planners preparing the plan should seek out or conduct background studies of a number of economic factors, especially the following:

- Economic base and shift-and-share analyses
- Job composition and growth or decline by industry sector on a national, statewide, or regional basis
- Tax structure of the community
- Existing labor force characteristics and future labor force requirements of existing and potential commercial and industrial enterprises in the state or region
- Locational characteristics of the community or region from the standpoint of access to markets for its goods and services
- Patterns of private investment or disinvestments
- Commercial, industrial, and institutional lands within the community that are vacant, significantly unused, or environmentally contaminated
- Projected employment growth by industrial sector for the state or region
- Regulations and permitting procedures imposed by the local government on commercial and industrial enterprises and their effects on the costs of doing business
- Existing businesses
- Quality of life and lifestyle

PLAN COMPONENTS

An economic development plan will use these background studies and data to draw inferences about the strengths and weaknesses of the regional economy of which the community- is part. From that analysis the local government can begin to define goals, policies, and guidelines for economic development. This analysis should, at a minimum, reveal the following:

- The community's role and responsibilities in the region's economy
- Categories or particular types of commercial, industrial, and institutional uses desired by the community
- The adequate number of sites of suitable sizes, types, and locations for such uses
- The community facilities that should be included in the community facilities element of the local comprehensive plan to support the economic development plan

The economic development plan may also include goals, policies, and guidelines to maintain existing categories, types, or levels of commercial. industrial, and institutional uses.

RELATED ACTIONS

Housing for Employees

Providing housing to accommodate new employees is an important part of economic development. The economic development plan must be closely coordinated with the housing

Economic Development Strategies: Direct Business Assistance—Projects

PROJECTS	LOCATION FACTOR ADDRESSED	PROS	CONS
Land or building purchase and assembly	• Land availability and cost	• Puts ownership of key property in hands of public job-creating authority. • Overcomes fragmented ownership and scarcity of large developable sites.	• Risk of holding undesirable property • Expensive
Industrial park creation	• Land availability and cost • Access to markets	• Prepares land for development. • Designed for multiple users and many jobs.	• Land can remain vacant and underused while waiting for desired firms.
Business accelerator (incubator)	• Land availability and cost • Workforce • Business formation	• Focuses on job creation. • Nurtures companies of the future.	• High initial costs for space and program management. • Need to have management expertise to provide technical assistance. • Small businesses do not lead to employment and tax base growth immediately.

Evaluation of the pros and cons of a discrete set of strategies and the locational factors they address as a way of sorting through actions for an economic development plan.

Source: ECONorthwest, Eugene, Oregon, 2003.

plan and its implementation to provide reasonable opportunities for new employees to obtain housing. If that is not done, the local government will effectively export the need for housing and its associated costs to other nearby communities. The local government should take aggressive steps to ensure that sufficient housing is available for the expected or desired type of businesses and job growth.

Public/Private Coordination

In some cases, the economic development plan will involve the orchestration of a number of public and private actors to bring about economic change in a certain part of the local jurisdiction. For example, a community may decide to attract conventions. Thus, a convention and tourism authority may need to be established and funded, a convention center built, hotels and restaurants enticed to locate nearby, and transportation improvements of various types (some the responsibility of the state, others of the county) built.

IMPLEMENTATION

Implementation of the goals and objectives of an economic development plan can involve several actions:

- Setting aside or making available, through clearance and land assembly, land for business and industry through zoning, environmental remediation of contaminated sites, urban renewal, and other techniques for land assembly
- Underwriting risks though grants, loans, and tax abatement

Excerpt from Washington County, Utah, Strategic Plan

I. RETAIN AND EXPAND BUSINESS			
GOALS	MEASURE OF SUCCESS	CRITICAL STRATEGIES	IMPLEMENTATION AGENT
Retain and expand existing businesses with the County that are consistent with the core economic values.	Employment in existing County businesses will expand by 5% per year.	I.I Facilitate incentive program for existing businesses equivalent to what is offered to new businesses.	[Omitted]
		1.2 Increase the education and training opportunities of the existing workforce to prepare employees to better meet customer needs.	
		1.3 Provide an outreach effort to directly contact and assist existing businesses.	
		1.4 Develop and provide financing packages to assist in financing growth of existing businesses.	
		1.5 Facilitate conflict resolution between businesses and government.	

A series of goals and strategies that Washington County Utah, has established for ensuring the retention and expansion of local businesses.
Source: Washington County, Utah, 2003.

- Providing amenities and infrastructure through a variety of capital investments
- Creating an ongoing economic development financing, attraction, and promotion entity
- Focusing attention on other quality-of-life factors such as colleges and universities, local schools, and environmental, recreational, and cultural amenities
- Attracting "creatives"—painters, writers, sculptors, musicians—to encourage a diverse cultural scene
- Establishing a joint economic development zone
- Instituting job training and placement
- Refining local, regional, or state permitting procedures and regulations to make them friendlier to business
- Establishing programs that monitor the needs of existing businesses and institutions, to ensure their retention
- Adopting design guidelines for commercial, industrial, and institutional areas

Implementing actions or strategies will be scheduled, with responsibility assigned to different actors or institutions, and costs estimated. An economic development plan should assume the private sector may need to take certain actions, either on its own or through formal public-private partnerships. Moreover, such a plan may contain measurable benchmarks in terms of job growth or retention, desired levels of private investment, and changes in real wages.

See also:
Housing Plans

Selected Goals and Benchmarks in the Washington County, Utah, Strategic Economic Development Plan

GOALS	MEASURE OF SUCCESS
Diversify and strengthen our economy and increase our wage scale by attracting value-added business.	Locate 750 new value-added jobs within the next five years. Increase the per capita wage of the county to the level of the Utah State average.
Develop improved industrial sites, which are affordable and attractive to new and expanding value-added businesses.	Monitor the industrial market to ensure that at least 100,000 square feet of industrial high cube inventory is available.
Encourage the construction of spec buildings for use by value-added companies.	Maintain sufficient fully developed land and available building space to service existing and new value-added business.
Expand existing infrastructure to maintain and improve service levels.	Increase private and public funding for key infrastructure and services by 25% over the next five years.
Increase the county's economic development capability such that it fully utilizes the strengths and resources of both the public and private sectors.	Fully fund economic development organization with sufficient cash reserves.
Increase the advanced degree, technical, and professional skills training provided 'within the county through Dixie State College of Utah and Dixie Applied Technology Center.	Annually increase the number of courses available for advanced technical skills training.

Benchmarks that Washington County has set for monitoring success for the plan's goals.

Source: Washington County, Utah, 2003.

PARKS AND OPEN-SPACE PLANS

A parks and open-space plan outlines a systematic approach to providing parks and recreation services to a community. Parks and open-space resources within a community include environmental, recreational, scenic, cultural, historic, and urban design elements. Planning for parks and open space takes place at national, state, and local levels.

REASONS TO PREPARE A PARKS AND OPEN-SPACE PLAN

Jan Gehl (1987), the Danish urbanist and architect, states. "The proper hierarchy of planning is life, space, and buildings, not buildings, space, life." Therefore, communities need to plan for open spaces that provide a multitude of public functions before development occurs. These functions are numerous and may include:

- protection of natural resources and biodiversity;
- creation of places for recreation;
- support for economic development opportunities;
- development of neighborhood gathering places;
- promotion of public health benefits;
- creation of civic and cultural infrastructure; and
- shaping patterns of development through open spaces.

APPROACHES TO THE PLAN

Many forms of park and open-space systems exist. Some communities have an interconnected system, linked by green corridors, while others have a disconnected system scattered throughout the neighborhoods of a community. Communities that are largely built out have new parks and open-space opportunities created primarily from redevelopment; communities with available land should concentrate on identifying and protecting park space in areas *before* development occurs.

Whatever the park system configuration, park and open-space plans are influenced by the following factors:

- Agency or departmental mandate and mission
- Parks and open-space definition
- Park classifications
- Parks standards
- Development and management policies

Agency or Departmental Mandate and Mission

The organization with authority over parks planning may need to meet the statutory requirements for the plan's contents. The mission should be reaffirmed at the beginning of the planning process and explicitly stated in the beginning of the plan document.

Definition of Parks and Open Space

Communities often have different definitions of what constitutes a park. The definition may list specific resources, such as plazas, greenways, and even cemeteries. Some communities may use a broader approach, defining open space as "any land that is free of residential, institutional, commercial, or industrial use"; and others may restrict the definition to include only conservation areas protected by law. Planners should define terms at the outset because they will influence demand and supply inventories.

Park Classifications

A park classification system is a way of creating order to and providing a common language for the park and open-space system. Park types are often arranged by service area, size, population served, and typical facilities. Park classifications may also address functions, such as serving recreation, social gathering, and green infrastructure functions.

Parks Standards

To quantify their demand for park space and facilities, in addition to a variety of public participation activities, many communities use a set of national park standards developed in the 1970s and 1980s by the National Recreation and Park Association (NRPA). However, in 1996, NRPA replaced those standards with a locally determined set of facility guidelines, following its publication, *Park, Recreation, Open Space and Greenway Guidelines*. Communities should complete a level-of-service (LOS) study to quantify the number of necessary recreational facilities to meet specific community needs as well as the minimum acreage to support those facilities. The LOS study and the standards that it produces are important tools in projecting the effect of residential growth on necessary facilities and space. This study is critical for both sound park planning and for addressing the rational nexus test in mandatory dedication and impact fee programs should there be legal challenge to those programs.

That said, LOS and assessment studies results reflect only the recreational facility function of the park spaces. They do not include other functions, such as resource conservation, cultural enrichment, or urban design. And though no

LOS formula currently exists for those functions, it is important that a plan address them.

Policies

Both development and management policies can shape the park and open-space plan. For instance, if the department normally pursues nongovernmental organization partnerships for service delivery, the plan inventories and implementation strategies should reflect that.

PLAN COMPONENTS

The majority of parks and open-space plans include the following elements. Consult applicable statutes and agency mandates to determine required plan components.

Goals and Objectives

Typical expressions of parks and open space goals and objectives consider the following:

- *Quantity*: Targeting a total percentage of the jurisdiction's acreage to be set aside for parks, or protecting a total percentage of the land in any new development as open space
- *Proximity*: Locating a park within a certain number of blocks of every resident, or providing a facility within a specific driving time of every resident
- *Accessibility*: Assuring that parks are located to be physically accessible by foot, bicycle, or public transit, and visually accessible for the greater public
- *Distribution*: Arranging park locations to ensure balanced service across geographic areas
- *Equity*: Providing facilities and programs evenly across socioeconomic populations
- *Environmental protection*: Assuring the protection of specific natural resources
- *Coordination*: Combining park objectives with other functional or jurisdictional plans
- *Balance*: Offering a mix of places and activities throughout the system
- *Shaping*: Identifying ways that the open space will promote or contain growth
- *Sustainability*: Determining physical and financial methods to support the park and open-space system
- *Urban design*: Addressing the way the park or space relates to the structures around it
- *Connections*: Identifying places and ways to link parklands and associated resources

Legal Requirements

The plan should include aS review of laws that might be applicable to the lands or facilities included in the plan. These typically include:

- federal: state, and local environmental protection regulations:
- federal, state, and local parkland preservation regulations;
- historic buildings and landscapes regulations; and
- the Americans with Disabilities Act (ADA) regulations

Supply Inventory

A park and open-space plan contains a set of inventories related to the park plan elements and functions. This includes a list of park sites, their size, the facilities and equipment at each site, the function each site serves, site photos, and an assessment of the condition of the site. In addition to sites typically considered part of the parks inventory, the following may be included:

- Endangered species habitats
- School sites with playgrounds
- Public and private golf courses

PLANNING AND URBAN DESIGN STANDARDS

- Waterways and floodplains
- Vacant lots
- Trails
- Private recreational facilities (e.g., ice rinks, tennis clubs)
- Bike lanes on highways
- Historical sites
- Cemeteries
- Gravel mines
- Private campgrounds
- Scenic viewsheds
- Country clubs
- Boulevards
- Parks in concurrent and adjacent jurisdictions (including county, state, and national)
- Industrial park open space

Demand Assessment

Most demand assessments are a combination of general data, such as demographic trends or

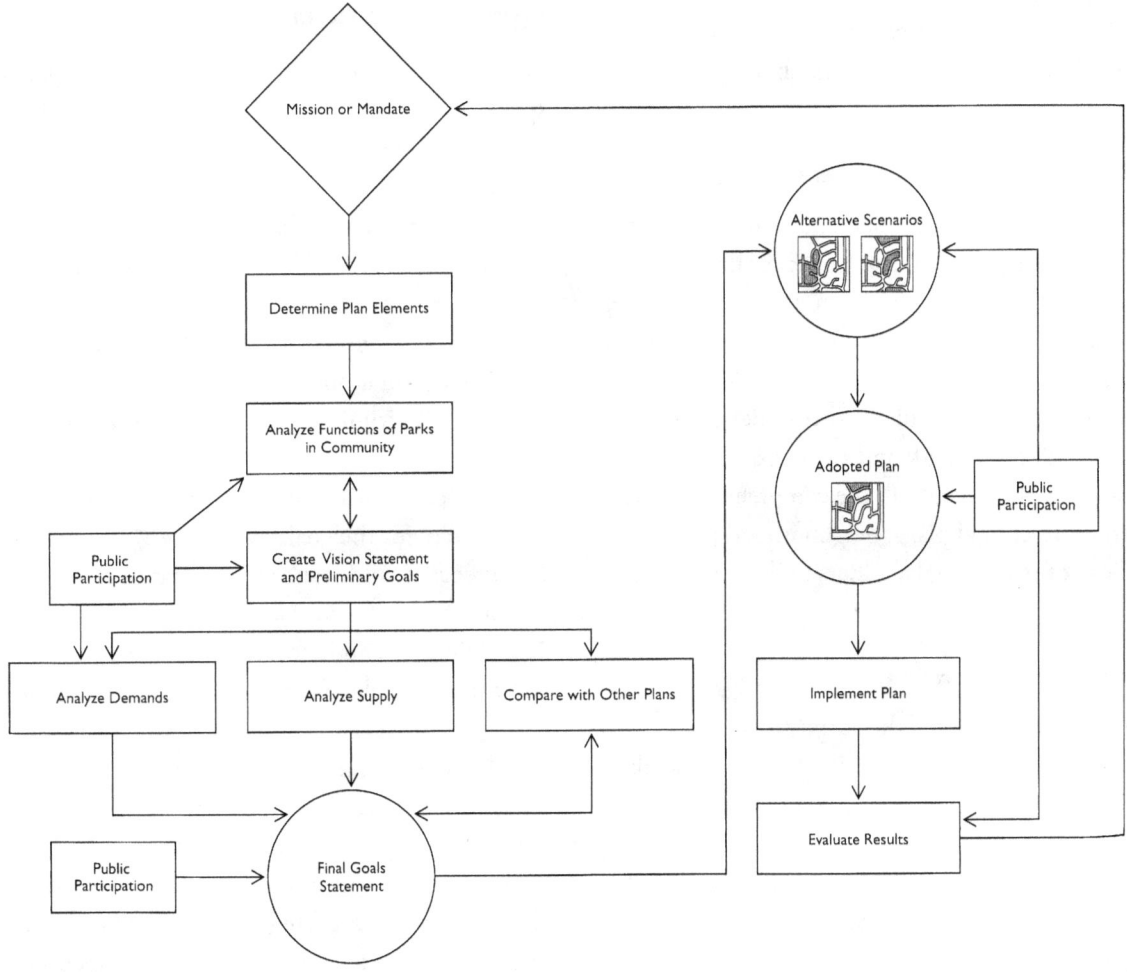

Park Planning Flowchart
Source: Mary Eysenbach.

physiographic resources, and specific community information gleaned from public participation mechanisms. The needs assessment for parks and open spaces can be initially organized by function:

- Recreation function
- Conservation function
- Community shaping function
- Additional functions. such as public health, economic development, and green infrastructure.

See Parks, Recreation, and Open-Space Needs Assessment elsewhere in this book for more detail.

Surpluses and Deficiencies Analysis

A comparison of the demand and supply data yields a surpluses and deficiencies analysis. The results may be expressed in terms of acreage, facilities, or other forms dictated by the various functions of the system.

The analysis should also consider how other plans affect the park and open-space plan goals Planners should consult the comprehensive plan, other functional plans, neighborhood plans, and those of partner stakeholders to determine those effects.

Alternatives and Draft Plan

After completion of the surpluses and deficiencies analysis, planners should generate a number of plan alternatives to correct the deficiencies identified by the analysis. The scenarios should address the creation of new park areas, the renovation of existing park areas, the linking together of parks, and the required connections to other plans to achieve park and open-space goals.

Following further review and revision, the adopted plan should include:

- a prioritized list of land protection areas (future parks, green infrastructure);
- a prioritized list of improvements for existing park areas,
- a prioritized list of opportunities for linkages;
- a list of site selection and acquisition criteria;
- the identification of opportunities for integration with other plans and processes; and
- a map summarizing these items.

IMPLEMENTATION

For each objective in the plan, a park and open-space plan should have an implementation strategy that takes the following actions.

1. Identify what will be accomplished.
2. Identify the party responsible for accomplishing the goal.
3. Identify any partners involved in implementation.
4. Establish timing or phasing for achieving the goal.
5. Set cost estimates and identify funding sources for the goal.
6. Prepare maintenance and operational impact statements for new land or facilities.
7. Define methods for evaluating success and set a schedule for conducting the evaluation.

The parks and recreation plan should be updated at a regular time interval, preferably every five years. Although that frequency may outpace the schedule for the comprehensive plan, the need for identifying and preserving parks and open space is an urgent business, especially in rapidly urbanizing areas.

PLANNING AND URBAN DESIGN STANDARDS

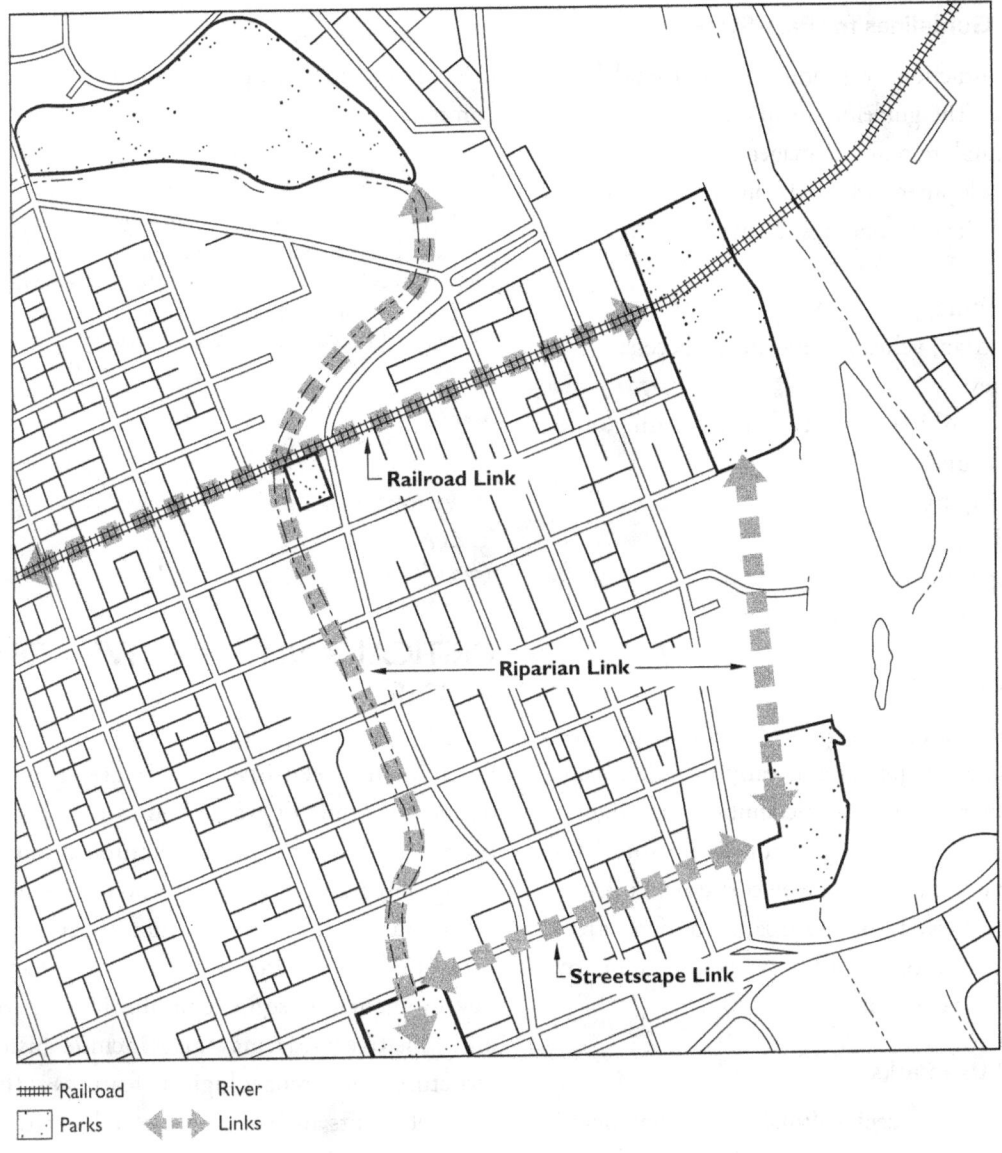

Open-space connections can be created with a variety of linear corridors.

Open-Space Connections

Source: Mary Eysenbach.

EMERGING ISSUES

Green Infrastructure

Green infrastructure is a green space network of natural ecosystem functions. Instead of investing in man-made "gray" infrastructure, some communities are using their existing system or creating new parks as way to manage stormwater, reduce the urban heat island effect, and create wildlife habitat.

85

Design Guidelines for Park Systems

Some jurisdictions are producing design guidelines for parks. The guidelines help create an aesthetic and natural resource management standard for park development while visually connecting the park with its surroundings. They may address:

- park siting;
- pedestrian, vehicular, and transit access;
- utilities;
- site furnishings such as fencing, seating, and playground equipment;
- landscaping;
- building materials;
- signage; and
- environmental sustainability.

Linkages

Much like the park and parkway systems designed in the late nineteenth and early twentieth centuries, there is growing recognition that a good parks system is one where individual park nodes are connected by linear green corridors. Linkages may be achieved through riparian buffers, street design, transit paths, utility rights-of-way, or any other linear corridor.

Special Use Parks

A number of recent cultural and technological trends have created new demands on today's park systems. These can include dog parks, skateboard parks, off-road vehicle (ORV) parks, mountain bike trails, water trails, parks designed to meet the needs of an aging population, and wireless technology availability in parks. Planners should conduct specific research to determine the planning needs of these types of parks and park functions.

Partnerships

An increasing number of communities are working with other governmental agencies, nonprofit agencies, and even private providers to create interconnected parks systems within their communities.

REFERENCES

Gehl, Jan. 1987. *Lift Between Buildings: Using Public Space.* New York: Van Nostrand Reinhold.

Mertes, James D., and James R. Hall. 1996. *Park, Recreation, Open Space and Greenway Guidelines.* Washington, DC: National Recreation and Park Association.

See also:
Parks and Open-Space Plans

Parks. Recreation, and Open-Space Needs Assessment
Types of Parks

CRITICAL AND SENSITIVE AREAS PLANS

Critical and sensitive areas are generally defined as lands or water bodies that provide protection to or habitat for natural resources, living and nonliving, or are themselves natural resources that require identification and protection from inappropriate or excessive development. In some communities, critical and sensitive areas may also include historic structures or archaeological features. These latter elements are often protected by state and federal regulations.

REASONS TO PREPARE A CRITICAL AND SENSITIVE AREAS PLAN

When acting to protect critical and sensitive areas, planners often have to make choices as to which resources should be protected and to what degree. These choices often include deeming some natural resources more or less "critical" and "sensitive" than others. The process of preparing a critical and sensitive areas plan or an element for a comprehensive plan provides a framework for identifying the resources, determining what will be protected, and identifying mechanisms for protecting them.

PLAN COMPONENTS

The components of critical and sensitive areas plans typically include the following:

- Descriptions of the identified critical and sensitive resource areas
- GIS maps of critical and sensitive resource areas, based on field surveys
- An analysis of the carrying capacity of the resources identified or, if not known, mechanisms for determining the carrying capacity of each resource
- A description of the public involvement used to determine which resources are critical and sensitive and the level of degradation deemed acceptable for each
- Policies to protect the resources
- Implementation strategies

APPROACHES TO THE PLAN

Whether you are preparing an element of a comprehensive plan or a separate plan, the same overall process applies, namely:

1. identify the resources;
2. evaluate their value:
3. determine their carrying capacity;
4. map the location of resources;
5. create policy to protect the resources; and
6. identify regulatory and nonregulatory tools to implement the plan and help ensure protection.

Identification of Resources

The first step in the analysis of critical and sensitive areas is the identification of these resources. APA's *Growing Smarts*^{SM} *Legislative Guidebook* identifies the following as resources that should be considered:

- Aquifers
- Watersheds
- Wellhead protection areas
- Inland and coastal wetlands
- Other wildlife habitats, including animals, birds, fish, and plants, along with habitats for federal- and state-listed endangered and threatened species
- Hillsides and steep slopes
- Any other areas considered to be critical or sensitive areas, including built resources such as historic structures, and, where relevant, the open spaces that accompany these built resources

Federal, state, and local government agencies, nonprofit organizations, and the private sector preparing development applications for public review have also created sources that can be used to identify critical and sensitive areas.

For example, the U.S. Environmental Protection Agency (U.S. EPA) has mapped major aquifer systems throughout the nation. State agencies have mapped significant wildlife habitats and wellhead protection areas throughout their respective states. Local governments have often mapped wetlands, watersheds, and historic structures throughout their corporate boundaries. Developers seeking permits from federal, state, and local agencies often provide these agencies with details relating to critical and sensitive areas in pursuit of development permits.

Evaluation

After planners have identified these resources, they often evaluate the critical and sensitive areas according to the value they have to the community. There are three types of value:

- *Utility value:* How the resource is used by the community
- *Economic value:* How much dollar value the resource provides
- *Aesthetic value:* How the resource is valued for its qualitative importance, notwithstanding its economic value

For example, aquifers provide a utility value—drinking water for the community (if that is the drinking water source); an economic value—the price imposed by the water utility on water usage; and an aesthetic value—providing recharge to wetlands, surface water bodies, or coastal embayments (if a coastal community).

This placement of value on a resource, which may be difficult in some circumstances—how do you "value" a wildlife habitat?—nevertheless is an important step to undertake in determining what should be protected.

The protection of critical and sensitive areas has additional, obvious (albeit not always quantifiable) benefits. For instance, the regulations prohibiting construction within floodplains can benefit landowners by minimizing threats of flooding to real property; regulations limiting impervious coverage within watersheds can protect waters used for shellfishing; and regulations limiting the clear-cutting of forested kinds can also protect abutting properties from erosion.

Carrying Capacity

Carrying capacity analysis determines the point at which a resource's function will be reduced to an unacceptable level. (A resource's carrying capacity is often also referred to as its "assimilative capacity.") Establishing the carrying capacity of a resource requires an objective analysis. The goal is to establish the point at which the resource ceases to function as nature "intended" or the point at which the resource be used as intended by the community (its utility value is undermined).

Carrying capacity analysis provides a factual basis for a community's comprehensive plan provisions that promote resource protection. In other words, through this analysis the community gives itself a rational and logical basis for the adoption of management controls designed to limit development to the assimilative capacity of a resource.

Federal and state environmental protection agencies (e.g., U.S. EPA and state counterparts), the P.S. Geological Survey, state and local universities, and nongovernmental environmental organizations are all reliable sources of information for completing a carrying capacity analysis.

Thresholds

Identifying carrying capacity first requires establishing thresholds for the resource (e.g., a coastal water body's assimilative capacity for nitrogen) and, second, the carrying capacity of the specific resource (e.g., the carrying capacity of the specific water body in California or Maine).

General Resource Thresholds. The federal government regulates many critical resources, and local governments can use these regulations as a basis for determining the resources carrying capacity. For example, the federal Clean Air Act establishes maximum pollutant levels for air quality; the Safe Drinking Water Act establishes maximum contaminant levels for drinking water quality; and the Clean Water Act establishes maximum contaminant levels for coastal water quality. Similar thresholds are defined in state law.

SAMPLE CARRYING CAPACITY THRESHOLD ASSESSMENT

Nitrogen is a common water pollutant that can degrade water resources significantly. A carrying capacity threshold assessment can be used to determine the amount of nitrogen a water body can assimilate, thereby establishing a water quality standard. Data needed for this assessment include the surface area, volume, and flushing, rate of the water body. A sample calculation follows:

$$L = \text{Critical loading rate (lbs/yr)} = (TN \times V \times f)/454{,}000 \text{ mg/lb}$$

where:

A = Area
d = Water depth (mean low water, or MLW)
r = Average tidal range
V = Bay volume at mean tide = $(A)(d + r/2)$
f = Flushing rate (time per year)
TN = Total nitrogen standard or threshold (mg/m /R).

The equation can also be rearranged to calculate what the loading will be under a given development scenario:

$$TN \text{ (mg/m/yr)} = (L \times 454{,}000 \text{ mg/lb})/(V \times f).$$

Specific Resource Thresholds. Federal and state carrying capacity thresholds define the point at which the carrying capacity of the air, land, or water resources is threatened. They do not establish *if* the particular air, land, or water resource in the community will reach or exceed its assimilative capacity. A specific calculation for the specific resource at issue needs to be determined.

For example, while the quality of coastal water bodies begin to decline as nitrogen inputs increase—a result of the acceleration of the natural aging process (eutrophication)—the carrying capacity of such a water body in California can vary greatly compared to a coastal water body in Maine. This variation is a result of differences in water and air temperature, flushing cycles, depth of water, extent of the respective watersheds, and the presence of other contaminants in the water.

Maps

Planners should identify critical and sensitive areas on maps. Map makers should prepare these maps as overlays so that all resource areas can be identified individually (e.g., separate maps for watersheds, well head protection areas, wetlands resources, and historic structures) and cumulatively (by overlaying the separate maps) as the aggregate critical and sensitive areas. Maps should be based on field surveys and prepared with a geographic information system (GIS). While there is no required scale for the maps, it is strongly recommended that the scale chosen be practical and useful. For example, a scale of 1 inch = 100 feet is far more useful than a scale of 1 inch = 2,000 feet, but will require a greater level of precision and cost more.

Policies

The plan should contain a statement of the local government's goals, policies, and guidelines with respect to the protection of critical and sensitive areas. This portion of the plan may also include a map or maps showing the areas to be protected.

IMPLEMENTATION
Regulatory Tools

Zoning, subdivision controls, health regulations, and wetland regulations can all be used to protect critical and sensitive areas. Traditional regulatory tools include adopting overlay zoning districts for critical areas, requiring permits for uses that may negatively affect critical resource areas, adopting appropriate setbacks from resource areas, and employing related regulatory controls on private property. More innovative regulatory tools include transfer of development rights, impact fees, development agreements, and mandates that development not exceed defined carrying capacity thresholds set for critical and sensitive resource areas.

Nonregulatory Tools

Nonregulatory tools include fee and less-than-fee acquisition of critical and sensitive resource areas; public education programs, to inform the general public about the importance of the resources; and related programs, such as citizen monitoring of water and air resources and consistent attendance at local municipal board meetings to act as "watchdogs" and advocates for critical and sensitive resource areas. Nonregulatory tools have the advantage of avoiding the regulation of private property and the attendant potential negative political and legal consequences.

A community's capital improvement program provides an additional nonregulatory means to protect critical and sensitive resource areas. The outlay of local dollars to expand public water, sewer, and road access is a catalyst to new growth, and often conflicts with preserving these areas. Public improvements should not be built in critical and sensitive areas. The capital improvements plan and the comprehensive plan should both address such restrictions.

REFERENCE

Neck, Stuart ed. 2002. *Growing Smarr*^{SM} *Legislative Guidebook: Model Statutes for Planning and Management of Change*, 2 vols. Chicago: American Planning Association.

See also:
Environmental Planning and Management

PARTICIPATION

ROLE OF PARTICIPATION

Community participation is the involvement of people in the creation and management of their built and natural environments. Its strength is that it cuts across traditional professional boundaries and cultures. The activity of community participation is based on the principle that the built and natural environments work better if citizens are active and involved in its creation and management instead of being treated as passive consumers (Sanoff 2000).

The main purposes of participation are:

- to involve citizens in planning and design decision-making processes and, as a result, make it more likely they will work within established systems when seeking solutions to problems;
- to provide citizens with a voice in planning and decision making in order to improve plans, decisions, service delivery, and overall quality of the environment; and
- to promote a sense of community by bringing together people who share common goals.

Participation should be active and directed; those who become involved should experience a sense of achievement. Traditional planning procedures should be reexamined to ensure that participation achieves more than simply affirmation of the designer's or planner's intentions.

CHARACTERISTICS OF PARTICIPATION

Although any given participation process does not automatically ensure success, it can be claimed that the process will minimize failure. Four essential characteristics of participation can be identified:

- Participation is inherently good.
- It is a source of wisdom and information about local conditions, needs, and attitudes, and thus improves the effectiveness of decision making.
- It is an inclusive and pluralistic approach by which fundamental human needs are fulfilled and user values reflected.
- It is a means of defending the interests of groups of people and of individuals, and a tool for satisfying their needs, which are often ignored and dominated by large organizations, institutions, and their bureaucracies.

Experiences in the participation process show that the main source of user satisfaction is not the degree to which a person's needs have been met, but the feeling of having influenced the decisions.

CATEGORIES OF PARTICIPATION

Participation can be classified into four categories, or "experiences," with the goal of achieving agreement about what the future should bring (Burns 1979):

- *Awareness.* This experience involves discovering or rediscovering the realities of a given situation so that everyone who takes part in the process speaks the same language, which is based on their experiences in the field where change is proposed.
- *Perception.* This entails going from awareness of the situation to understanding it and its physical, social, cultural, and economic ramifications. It means sharing with each other so that the understanding, goals, and expectations of all participants become resources for planning and design.
- *Decision making.* This experience concentrates on working from awareness and perception to a plan for the situation under consideration. Here participants propose plans, based on their priorities, for professionals to use as resources to synthesize alternative and final plans.
- *Implementation.* Many community-based planning processes stop with awareness, perception, and decision making. This can have significant detrimental effects on a project because it ends people's responsibilities when the "how-to, where-to, when-to, and who-will-do-it" must be added to what people

want and how it will look. People must stay involved throughout the processes and take responsibility with their professionals to see that there are results (Hurwitz 1975).

DETERMINATION OF GOALS AND OBJECTIVES

The planning that accompanies the design of any participation program should first include a determination of participation goals and objectives. Participation goals will differ from time to time and from issue to issue. In addition, participation is likely to be perceived differently depending on the type of issue, people involved, and political setting in which it takes place. If differences in expectations and perception are not identified at the outset, and realistic goals are not made clear, the expectations of those involved in the participation program will likely not be met, and people will become disenchanted.

Related to this, to address participation effectively, the task should conceptualize what the objective is for involving citizens. For example, is the participation intended to:

- generate ideas?:
- identify attitudes?:
- disseminate information?:
- resolve some identified conflict?:
- measure opinions?:
- review a proposal?: or
- provide a forum to express general feelings?

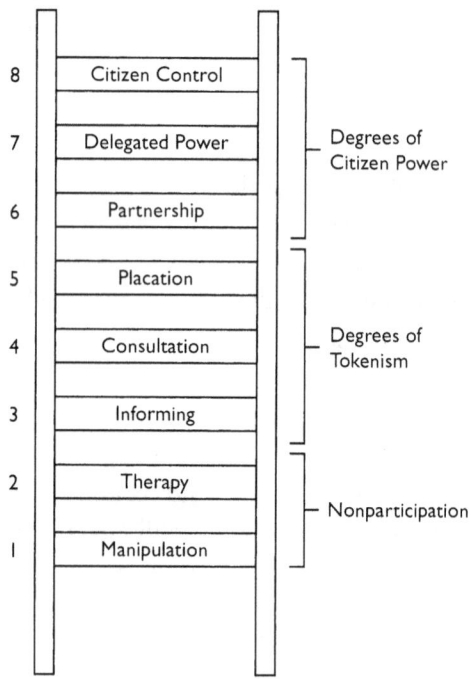

The ladder of citizen participation presents a typology of eight levels of participation. Each rung of the ladder corresponds to the degree to which stakeholders had power in determining the outcome. The gradations represented go from nonparticipation to token participation to various degrees of citizen power. While the ladder was conceived in the context of federal programs of the late 1960s, planners and urban designers today still should strive to ensure that they are working near the top of the ladder in their public participation activities.

Ladder of Citizen Participation

Source: Reprinted with permission from Journal of the American Planning Association, copyright July 1969 by the American Planning Association, Suite 1600, 122 South Michigan Avenue. Chicago, IL 60603-6107.

PLANNING FOR PARTICIPATION

Once planners have identified the overall goals and objectives for the participation process, planning for participation requires the following steps (Rosner 1978):

- Identify the individuals or groups that should be involved in the participation activity being planned.
- Decide where in the process the participants should be involved, from development to implementation to evaluation.
- Articulate the participation objectives in relation to all participants who will be involved.
- Identify and match alternative participation methods to objectives in terms of the resources available.

- Select an appropriate method to be used to achieve specific objectives.
- Implement chosen participation activities.
- Evaluate the implemented methods to see to what extent they achieved the desired goals and objectives.

THEORY AND PRACTICE

The theories and practices of participation can be synthesized into the following five statements:

There is no "best" solution to design and planning problem.

Each problem can have a number of solutions, based traditionally on two sets of criteria:

- *Facts.* The empirical data concerning material strengths, economics, building codes, and so forth
- *Attitudes.* Interpretation of the facts, the state of the art in any particular area, traditional and customary approaches, and value judgments.

"Expert" decisions are not necessarily better than "lay" decisions.

Given the facts with which to make decisions, citizens can examine the available alternatives and choose among them. In a participation process, planners and designers should work along with citizens to identify possible alternatives, discuss consequences of various alternatives, and state opinions about the alternatives (not decide among them).

A planning task can be made transparent.

Professionals often consider alternatives that are frameworks in their minds. They should be presented for users to discuss. After understanding the components of planning decisions and exploring alternatives, citizens in effect can generate their own plan rather than react to one provided for them. The product is more likely to succeed because it is more responsive to the needs of the people who will use it.

All individuals and interest groups should come together in an open forum.

In this setting, people can openly express their opinions, make necessary compromises, and arrive at decisions acceptable to all concerned. By involving as many interests as possible, the product is strengthened by the wealth of input. In turn, learning more about itself strengthens the citizens' group.

The process is continuous and ever changing.

The product is not the end of the process. It must be managed, reevaluated, and adapted to changing needs. Those most directly involved with the product, the users, are best able to assume those tasks.

The professional's role is to facilitate the citizen group's ability to reach decisions through an easily understood process. Most often this will take the form of making people aware of alternatives. This role also includes helping people develop their resources in ways that will benefit themselves and others.

INDICATORS OF THE VALUE OF PARTICIPATION

A review of the public involvement literature, conducted by Lach and Hixson (1998), revealed that participants valued such issues as public acceptability, accessibility, good decision

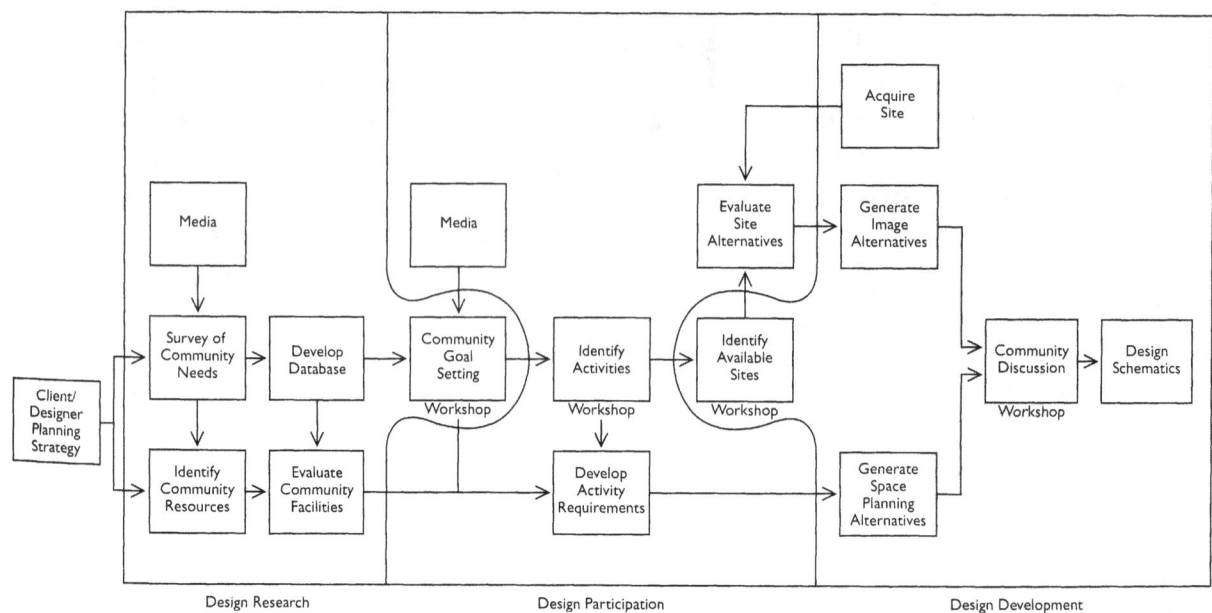

Design Research, Participation, and Development Process
Source: Henry Sancti.

making, education and learning, time commitments, and trust. To identify value and cost indicators of public involvement, they conducted interviews with people who had been involved in participatory projects. Combining the literature review, interviews, and expert judgment, they identified these key indicators of the value of participation:

- Opening the process to stakeholders
- Diversity of viewpoints
- Meaningful participation
- Integrating stakeholder concerns
- Information exchange
- Saving time
- Saving and avoiding costs
- Enhanced project acceptability
- Mutual learning
- Mutual respect

Lach and Hixson also developed direct and indirect cost indicators of the public involvement effort. Certain costs can be linked to traditional accounting practice, such as preparation and participation time, facilities, materials, and services. Other indirect costs, such as participants' time commitment, lack of opportunity to participate in other projects, and heavy emotional demands on participation, cannot be easily measured. The intent of their research was to develop prototype indicators to be tested in ongoing and completed public involvement programs. Results from project participants indicated that the positive aspects of their involvement were twofold: (1) a diversity of viewpoints in the participation process was valuable; (2) project savings occurred in the form of saving and of avoiding costs.

Informing a large audience about proposals, generating interest, or securing approval can take the form of a community meeting, also referred to as a public hearing or a public forum. Public meetings allow community leaders to present project information at any time during the process. The tight structure of such meetings does not, however, permit ample time for discussion. Although referred to as community participation, only the most aggressive personalities tend to participate and often dominate the discussion (Creighton 1994). Public reactions in open meetings are often taken by a vote through a show of hands. The key to making community design work effectively is to incorporate a range of techniques for enabling professionals and citizens to creatively collaborate, where voting is replaced by consensus decision making.

A wide range of techniques is available to designers and planners. Some of these techniques have become standard for use in participatory processes, such as interactive group decision-making techniques that take place in workshops. At the same time, designers and planners have effectively used field techniques, such as questionnaires, interviewing, focus groups, and group mapping, to acquire information. In general, many of the techniques facilitate citizens' awareness of environmental situations and help activate their creative thinking. The techniques can be classified as *awareness methods, group interaction methods,* and *indirect methods.*

REFERENCES

Arnstein, Sherry R. 1969. "A Ladder of Citizen Participation." *Journal of the American Institute of Planners.* 35, no. 4:216–224.

Burns, J. 1979. *Connections: Ways to Discover and Realize Community Potentials.* New York: McGraw-Hill.

Creighton, J.L. 1994. *In Citizens in Community Decision Making: A Guidebook.* Washington, DC: Program for Community Problem Solving.

Hurwitz, J.G. 1975. "Participatory Planning in an Urban Neighborhood. Soulard, St. Louis, MO: A Case Study." *DMG Journal.* 9, no. 4:348–357.

Lich, D., and P. Hixson. 1996. "Developing Indicators to Measure Values and Costs of Public Involvement Activities." *Interact: The Journal of Public Participation.* 2, no. 1:51–63.

Rosner, J. 1978. "Matching Method to Purpose: The Challenges of Planning Citizen Participation Activities." In *Citizen Participation in Amelia,* edited by S. Langton. New York: Lexington Books.

Sanoff, Henry. 2000. *Community Participation Methods in Design and Planning.* Hoboken, NJ John Wiley & Sons, Inc.

See also:
Plan Making

STAKEHOLDER IDENTIFICATION

Stakeholder is a term commonly used in planning and public policy. A stakeholder is defined as someone with a "stake," or interest, in the issues being addressed. In practice, this means anyone could be a stakeholder because a resident, taxpayer. and concerned citizen could all have an interest. Because the distinction between the public and stakeholders can be confusing, it is important to consider why stakeholders should be involved, and how they should be selected. People who convene a collaborative planning effort—conveners—need to plan this step carefully.

CATEGORIES OF STAKEHOLDERS

Stakeholders can be broadly classified into four categories. First, there are people who are representative of a certain sector of society. This sector may be a broad category, such as farmers or homeowners, or it may be a specific category, such as "Orchard Street residents" and park users. These stakeholders usually speak for themselves. Conveners choose them because their views may be "typical" of other people in their sector or because they have personal knowledge. However, because these people cannot be asked to speak on behalf of people they do not formally represent, the involvement of this category of stakeholder is not a substitute for public involvement.

Second, there are individuals who represent organized interests, which can range from an informally organized neighborhood coalition to a formally organized nonprofit interest group. Such an individual is expected to represent the views of the organization. However, this requires the person to confer with others in his or her organization. This is often referred to as the "two-table" problem because the individual may have to negotiate at the stakeholder table and the decision-making table within his or her organization.

Third, there are those who represent government organizations, such as city departments and state agencies. They must also work with both the stakeholder process and their organization's process, but they tend to operate under more specific administrative rules and policies. Individuals higher in the organization may have more discretion, but they also tend to have more demands on their schedule.

Finally, there are elected officials who are formally voted upon as representatives. Their elected position gives them a unique status because they are accountable to the public for their decisions. However, like staff in government organizations, they often have many demands on their time. Furthermore, members of local government councils and legislatures cannot speak for the entire legislative body.

LIST OF POTENTIAL STAKEHOLDERS
SECTORS OF SOCIETY

People living adjacent to a proposed activity
Neighborhood residents
Residents
Landowners
Renters
Minorities
Users (park users, boaters, etc.)
Neighborhood business owners

INTEREST GROUPS

Chamber of commerce
Environmental groups
Racial or ethnic groups
Industry organizations
Religious organizations
Civic groups
Social groups (Kiwanis, Optimists)
Neighborhood associations

AGENCIES

Special districts (water, sewer, park, etc.)
School districts
Planning commission members
Local government (city manager, department head, staff)
Council of government
State agencies
Federal agencies

ELECTED OFFICIALS

City and county councilors
Mayors
School board members
State representatives and senators

REASONS FOR SELECTING STAKEHOLDERS

Before starting a stakeholder selection process, a convener needs to consider the reasons for selecting stakeholders, to determine the potential pool of participants.

Jurisdiction over an Issue

One common reason is to include people or organizations that have jurisdiction over an issue. This includes organizations with the power

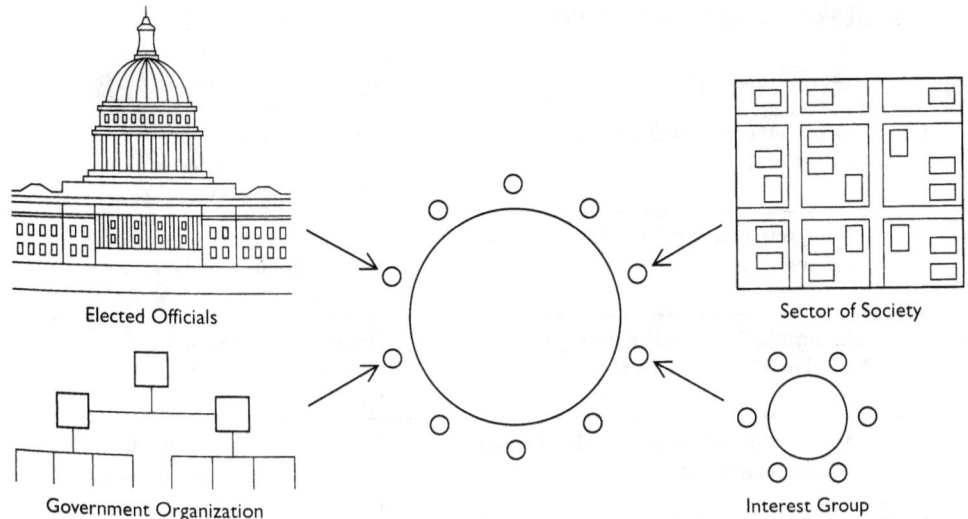

Types of Stakeholders
Source: Richard Margerum.

to make decisions as well as individuals with the power to veto decisions. For example, an open-space plan that involves city land, county parks, and state forests should include a representative from each jurisdiction.

Particular Information or Knowledge Base

Another reason for selecting a stakeholder is because he or she has information or knowledge that will lead to a comprehensive understanding of a problem or issue. A group composed of people with different training, different data, and different perspectives can develop a much more complete picture of an issue than if they each considered the issue individually. For example, information about watershed health may be spread among a range of different state agencies, local governments, and landowners.

Party to an Actual or Potential Conflict

A stakeholder process offers an informal and flexible forum for bringing participants together to try to resolve their differences. For example, a city proposal to annex land could involve county officials, landowners, and local residents in an effort to come to a mutually agreeable solution.

Connected to Community Networks

A fourth reason for choosing a stakeholder is because he or she is connected to community networks. Such people are important because of their informal networks of influence and the respect that they garner in the community. For example, an influential landowner who participates in an ecosystem management process could help convince other landowners to help protect critical habitat.

DETERMINING GROUP SIZE

Because a collaborative planning process may need stakeholders for many of the reasons listed above, the list of potential stakeholders could be lengthy. There are different views about the

Reasons for Stakeholder Involvement

REASON	DESCRIPTION	EXAMPLES OF STAKEHOLDERS
Jurisdiction	An organization or individual has jurisdiction over an issue.	Local government State and federal agencies Private landowner
Information	An organization or individual has information and knowledge.	Technical experts People with first-hand knowledge Agencies with data
Conflict	An organization or individual is party to an actual or potential conflict.	People with legal standing Existing parties to a dispute Decision makers
Networks	An individual is connected in the community or has local influence.	People involved in community groups People in social groups and clubs Long-term residents

optimum size of a stakeholder group. Some facilitators argue that groups should not be larger than 10 to 12, but some multiparty collaboration processes have successfully involved 20 or 30 stakeholders.

One way to reduce this number is to consider additional personal criteria in the selection process:

- Does the person work well in groups?
- Is the person interested in being involved?
- Does the person have the time to participate?
- Will the person help provide gender, racial, or ethnic balance?
- Does the person have additional skills that will help the group?

A process involving a large number of stakeholders may need to be broken into smaller groups. This increases the complexity of the process and increases the need for communication between groups, but it may be appropriate for large, complex, or controversial issues.

Some of the common categories include the following:

- Steering committee (to make the primary decisions)
- Technical advisory committee (to respond to technical questions)
- Citizens advisory committee (to provide broader public access)
- Geographic-based committees (to obtain input from different parts of a region)

Specific Selection Strategies

With these background issues in mind, a convener will have a better idea of the types of stakeholders to involve in a collaborative process. The next step is to determine the specific strategy for choosing a group of stakeholders. The perception of how the stakeholders are chosen can be just as important as who is chosen.

Collaborative processes that involve organizations add an additional level of complexity to the selection process. Some organizations want to appoint their own representatives, rather than have an external party choose one. In this case, the convener may simply designate a seat at the stakeholder table to a specific organization. This strategy may also be used to ensure that certain types of organizations are represented. For example, a group may have stakeholder slots designated for an environmental interest group, an industry organization, and a landowner.

Convener-Picked

There is no one correct way to select stakeholders, but different strategies are better suited for certain situations than others. One approach is for the convener to handpick the participants. This approach tends to work well if the convener is viewed as being neutral and if it is relatively clear who should be selected. It is an efficient strategy that also allows the convener to add other criteria for selection, such as group composition, group skills, and working relationships. That said, there will be some bias in this process because it will be defined by the knowledge of the convener.

Selection Committee

Another approach is to use a selection committee to choose the stakeholders. This approach tends to work well if the issues are politically charged or involve conflict. Each step of the collaboration process will be scrutinized. Any concerns about bias in stakeholder selection could lead people to question the decisions of the group. As with the handpicked approach, a committee can also incorporate additional criteria into the selection process. The primary disadvantages to this process relate to the additional time, resources, and participants required.

Self-Nomination

A third approach is to form a committee through self-nomination. This approach works well when the composition of the committee is not critical and when it is important to involve motivated stakeholders. Self-nomination is often linked to a public participation process. People are mailed newsletters, surveyed, or invited to public meetings; those who are interested are invited to participate in a stakeholder group. There is less opportunity or potential perception for bias with

Stakeholder Selection Strategies

STRATEGY	POSSIBLE ADVANTAGES	POSSIBLE DISADVANTAGES
Convener-picked	Compatible personalities Can meet expertise needs	Perception of bias Limited range of participants
Selection committee	Diverse committee can reduce bias Can choose for expertise and personalities	More time-consuming Requires additional participants
Self-nominating	Motivated participants Open process	Representation problems May only attract strongly opinionated
Snowball	Flexible Allows participants to expand with issues	Initial participants have more power Later participants may have concerns about earlier decisions

this process; however, the resulting group may lack diversity, may not include key stakeholders, or may, overrepresent certain interests or organizations.

Snowball

A final strategy for stakeholder selection is the "snowball" strategy. This is an important strategy for all stakeholder selection efforts, regardless of how it is initially established. The strategy involves asking those involved, Who is not at the table that should be? As the list of people expands, the new people are asked the same question, until a full set of participants is involved. This can improve the breadth of participants and ensure that stakeholder membership is adjusted as new issues arise. The disadvantage of this process is that stakeholders coming late to the process may have less ability to influence outcomes and therefore may be less inclined to support the effort. Furthermore, if not done carefully, it could lead to an ever-expanding list of stakeholders.

See also:
Plan Making
Types of Plans

SURVEYS

Planners looking to make good decisions need solid, reliable information. The survey is a widely accepted tool for gathering information from the people involved in any planning action. Good-quality surveys are doable even for the novice. The basic concepts and steps needed to plan and execute a survey are introduced here.

The particular advantages of the survey are that it allows planners to obtain quantitative results, to anticipate and address many of the sources of error before the data are collected, and ultimately to generalize findings from a relatively small number of respondents (the sample) to a larger group (the population). With increasing emphasis on representative citizen participation, surveys offer a useful method both to reach a broad public and to gather input from people who typically are not consulted on planning issues.

REASONS TO USE A SURVEY

Consider a survey when the data needed are not available from secondary sources. The existing data may be outdated and no longer reflect current conditions or may describe a geography that does not coincide with your needs, such as state-level data that cannot be disaggregated into local units.

Surveys are conducted to find out the characteristics, behaviors, opinions, and knowledge of a particular population. Before embarking on a survey, clearly establish your objectives. Determine who is to be sampled and what you want to learn about the sample. Your questionnaire should flow directly from your information objectives.

TYPES OF SURVEYS

At the core of all surveys is either a questionnaire or an interview—these are the instruments for gathering information.

Questionnaires

Questionnaires are self-administered instruments. They generally enable respondents to complete the survey at their convenience and to proceed at their own pace. Respondents often have a greater sense of anonymity, which leads to greater honesty. Respondents can also verify their responses against other records and documents.

	INTERVIEWER-ADMINISTERED		SELF-ADMINISTERED	
	FACE-TO-FACE	TELEPHONE	MAIL	WEB-BASED
Resource Constraints				
Inadequate Sampling Frame (e.g., Incomplete Mailing List or Directory)	++	++	--	--
Quick Turnaround to Complete Survey	--	++	--	++
Limited Skilled Staff	--	--	++	++
Limited Budget	--	+	++	++
Special Needs				
Multiple Languages	-	-	+	++
Maps or Other Visual Materials	++	--	++	++
Complex Instructions or Need to Follow Precise Order	++	++	--	+
Need to Probe, Explain Unclear Questions	++	++	--	--
Some Items Require Additional Research	-	--	++	++
Anonymity Needed for Sensitive Responses	--	++	+	++
Respondent Characteristics				
Large Sample Size	--	-	++	++
Geographically Dispersed	--	+	++	++
Survey Must Be Conducted at Specific Location	++	--	--	--
Target Population is Difficult to Contact	++	-	-	--

The matrix compares four major survey methods under varying conditions of re*source* constraints, survey needs, and respondent characteristics.

Selecting a Survey Method

Reprinted with permission from The Planner's Use of Information, *2nd Edition, copyright 2003 by the American Planning Association, Suite I 600, I 22 South Michigan Avenue, Chicago, IL 60603–6 107.*

Interviews

Interviews involve human interaction, even though it is scripted to some degree. In an interview, respondents can ask for clarification, thereby reducing the potential for error. The interviewer can control the sequence of questions by following a skip pattern according to previous responses—a feature now possible with self-administered, computerized questionnaires. Depending on the study objectives, a skilled interviewer can also pursue certain subjects by using probes and follow-up questions. In a face-to-face situation, interviewers have the advantage of being able to observe nonverbal cues. To a lesser degree, even telephone interviewers can detect and respond to changes in the respondent's tone of voice and speech.

MODES OF DISTRIBUTION

Surveys are further differentiated by their modes of distribution. They cover the entire range of communication technologies currently in use—face-to-face (both intercept/"street corner" interviews and in-depth interviews), posted mail, fax, telephone, email, and the Web—and combinations of these modes. The most appropriate survey method will depend on your resources, survey objectives, and characteristics of the sample. Increasingly, survey software is being used to gather data, reaching survey takers through email. The advantages of this approach include drawing upon an existing database of survey recipients and quickly creating reports, graphs, and tables from the data.

POPULATION SELECTION AND SIZE

Sampling

Sampling refers to a plan for randomly choosing a sample. Determining the correct sample size used to be one of the most daunting steps in survey preparation. Today this challenge is easily met by going online and typing "sample size calculator" or "random sample calculator" into a search engine. Several Web sites provide a utility that allows you to find out instantly how many people you need to survey. All require you to establish three parameters: population size, error level, and confidence level.

- *Population size* refers to the total number of people within the study area. For any given level of accuracy, the larger the population, the smaller the sample needed (percentage of people to be surveyed).
- *Error level* (or margin of error) is expressed as "plus or minus times percentage points- and refers to the difference between the estimated value (derived from the sample) and the true value (from the population).
- *Confidence level* is also expressed as a percentage and refers to the number of times similar results are expected if the study were replicated 100 times.

Error and confidence go hand in hand. Say a survey found that 59 percent of households in the city own one or more bicycles. If the survey were designed with an error level of ±3 percentage points and a 95 percent confidence level, it would mean that household bicycle ownership rates could actually range from 56 percent to 62 percent, and this finding would occur 95 out of 100 times if the survey were conducted over and over. If your survey does not have an acceptable level of confidence, it will be difficult to know what to make of the results.

In a city with a population of 50,000, the following sample sizes are needed:

CONFIDENCE LEVEL	MARGIN OF ERROR ± 3 %	MARGIN OF ERROR ± 5 %
90 percent	745	271
95 percent	1,045	381
99 percent	1,778	655

Response Rate

Sample size refers to the number of completed surveys. Therefore, the actual number of surveys distributed must be adjusted to account for the response rate—a function of contact (reaching respondents at viable addresses or working phone numbers) and cooperation (getting people to complete the survey). The formula to calculate the total number of surveys that must be distributed is:

Sample ÷ response rate = total surveys to be distributed

Therefore, if one estimates a 20 percent response rate for a mail survey with a sample size of 381, One would need to send out 1,905 questionnaires. However, if there are indications that a higher estimate of a 40 percent response rate is warranted, one could reduce the mailing to 953 questionnaires.

Some of the common techniques to improve cooperation include:

- sending out prenotification letters, then following the questionnaire with reminder cards:
- developing persuasive introductory language;
- ensuring that the questionnaire is attractive and easy to complete; and
- training interviewers for more effective "first contact."

Response rates are an important and challenging component of surveys. That said, noncontact and noncooperation should not seriously affect data quality to the extent that they occur randomly (Langer 2003). Addressing sources of bias is still paramount.

ALTERNATIVE SAMPLING DESIGNS

In addition to simple random sampling, planners should be familiar with two alternative sampling designs: stratified sample and clustered sample.

Stratified Sample

In a stratified sample, the population is divided into subgroups (strata) before sampling. For example, if the survey is about a city's bike paths and it is known that households with school-aged children are more likely to own bicycles, one might select separate samples for households with school-aged children and those without. Each subgroup is a separate sample, and the respective sample sizes would reflect the subgroup's size relative to the overall population. Within subgroups, individuals are selected at random.

Clustered Sample

In a clustered sample, the population is divided into smaller geographic units (clusters), such as neighborhood within a city or blocks within a district. The sample consists of a random selection of clusters and all individuals within those clusters are surveyed.

TIPS FOR SUCCESSFUL DATA COLLECTION

The survey is a way of creating an area-specific, customized database. Even a hurriedly put-together survey can fill a critical information gap. Designed properly, the survey can be a rigorous tool. The following tips can maximize your data-gathering efforts:

- Start with a brief, compelling introduction that clearly states the purpose of your study and its potential value to the respondent.
- Use plain language that is easy to understand; avoid jargon and acronyms.
- Organize questions in logical groups; provide transitions when shifting topics.
- Ask important questions first, profile questions last.
- Proofread to eliminate typographic and grammatical errors; make the layout crisp and legible.
- Include graphics (maps, plans, diagrams, renderings, and photos), as appropriate.
- Keep the survey short and simple.
- Pretest with a few people (ideally representing a cross section of the sample), then debrief and ask for candid feedback.

DESIGNING A QUESTIONNAIRE

Researchers have several options in designing a questionnaire, primarily in constructing and sequencing items. Two basic categories of questions are the closed- versus open-ended inquiries.

Close-Ended Questions

In close-ended questions, respondents are asked to select from a list provided by the researcher, with instructions either to select a single answer (one that "best fits") or multiple answers (all that apply). A variation of the closed-ended question is one that asks respondents to evaluate on a scale or rank in order of preference, such as one of the following:

- *Rating scale* is an ordinal measurement of degree, which asks respondents to indicate a position between opposite word pairs (e.g., noisy-quiet or frequently-never, etc.).
- *Liked scale* asks respondents to indicate the extent to which they agree with a statement (e.g., strongly agree, agree, disagree, strongly disagree, don't know).
- *Numerical scale* asks respondents to correlate their position to a numerical rating (e.g., satisfaction level rated on a scale of 1 to 5, with 1 being least satisfied and 5 being most satisfied).

In close-ended questions, the choices do not have to be words. Many planning-oriented issues are amenable to choices presented in drawings, plans, and photos. Another possibility is to ask respondents to indicate their preferences by allocating a "theoretical budget—$1 and $100 are easiest to work with.

Open-Ended Questions

Open-ended questions give respondents an opportunity for self-expression and spontaneity that can lead researchers to new insights. Their disadvantage is that they can be difficult to summarize without postcoding. A compromise is to offer a list of what are expected to be the most popular choices, based on prior knowledge of the subject, then include an "Other" category that allows respondents to provide answers outside the predetermined categories.

The importance of sequencing questionnaire items in a clear, logical order should not be overlooked. Respondents are more likely to find an instrument credible if it is readily apparent that questions are relevant to the overall purpose of the study and are connected in a way that makes sense. The most basic patterns are the *funnel sequence,* which begins with the most general question and works down to detailed points, and the *inverted funnel sequence* which begins with specific questions and then moves to more general issues. Transitional questions, brief explanations, or headings can be inserted to signal a change of topic or to show how the new topic relates to what had been asked previously.

ADDITIONAL CONSIDERATIONS

Despite the tremendous usefulness of surveys for researchers, they are not met with the same level of enthusiasm among the survey-taking public. Many factors have contributed to the survey's diminished reputation; however, it is possible to avoid further tarnish by observing a few common-sense practices. Foremost, respect the privacy of respondents. Do not release names and addresses of respondents. Codes are typically assigned to questionnaires, in which case, secure the name-to-code assignments. Results can be reported confidentially by tabulating data so that individual responses cannot be singled out. And, whenever possible, provide respondents with a copy of your findings—prompt feedback will demonstrate how the study has contributed to a better understanding of important community issues.

REFERENCES

Dandekar, Hemalata C. 2003. *Planner's Use of Information.* 2nd ed. Chicago: Planners Press.

Linger, Gary. 2003. "About Response Rates: Some Unresolved Questions." *Public Perspective,* May, June, 16–18. www.ropercenter.uconn.edu. pub-per. pdf. pp143c. pdf

PLANNING AND URBAN DESIGN STANDARDS

See also:
Analysis Techniques
Plan Making

COMMUNITY VISIONING

Community visioning offers local communities new ways to think about and plan for the long-term future. The visioning process was inspired in part by the concept of "anticipatory democracy," an approach to governance that blends futures research, grassroots public participation, and long-range strategic planning.

Visioning has caught on quickly around the country in communities undergoing rapid growth and development as well as those experiencing economic decline. As an adjunct to traditional community planning, visioning promotes greater awareness of societal change and deepened citizen involvement. It also gives communities a stronger sense of control over their destinies.

WHAT IS VISIONING?

In the simplest terms, visioning is a planning process through which a community creates a shared vision for its future and begins to make it a reality. Such a vision provides an overlay for other community plans, policies, and decisions, as well as a guide to actions in the wider community. While a significant number of communities employing a wide range of approaches and techniques have undertaken community visioning, the most successful efforts seem to share these five key characteristics:

- *Understanding the whole community.* The visioning process promotes an understanding of the whole community and the full range of issues shaping its future. It also attempts to engage the participation of the entire community and its key stakeholder groups.
- *Reflecting core community values.* The visioning process seeks to identify the community's core values—those deeply held community beliefs

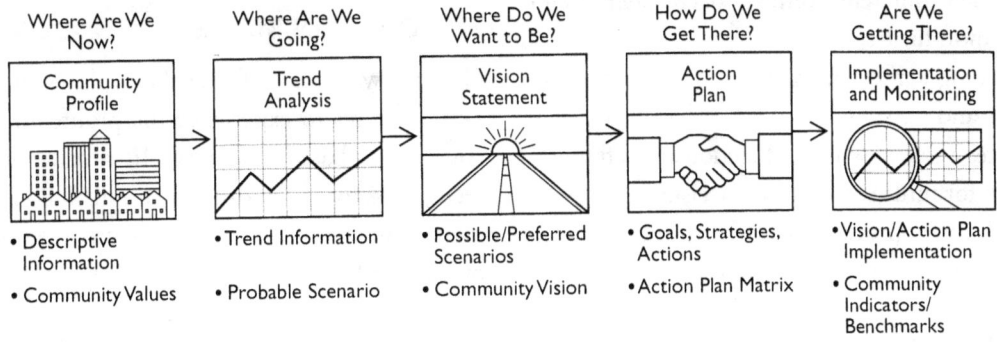

The New Oregon Model
Source: Steven Ames Planning

and ideals shared by its members. Such values inform the idealistic nature of the community's vision.
- *Addressing emerging trends and issues.* The visioning process explores the emerging trends driving the community's future and the strategic issues they portend. Addressing such trends promotes greater foresight, adding rigor and realism to the community's vision.
- *Envisioning a preferred future.* The visioning process produces a statement articulating the community's preferred future. The vision statement represents the community's desired "destination"—a shared image of where it would like to be in the long-term future.
- *Promoting local action.* The visioning process also produces a strategic action plan. The action plan serves as the community's "road map": to move it in the direction of its vision in the near-term future.

BENEFITS OF VISIONING

For communities that successfully engage in visioning, the process offers clear benefits. Visioning:

- brings community members together in a uniquely different context to consider their common future;
- encourages the community to explore new ideas and possibilities;
- creates a shared sense of direction and a framework for future community decisions; and
- produces a process that results in concrete goals and strategies for action

Additionally, there can be second-order benefits that may not be immediately apparent in undertaking the process, such as:

- enriching public involvement by expanding the terms and scope of civic engagement;
- fostering new leadership in citizens who have not been previously active in public life;
- promoting active partnerships among government, business, civic, and nonprofit organizations; and
- strengthening community cohesion and "social capital."

In other words, engaging in the *process* of visioning can be as rewarding as its *products*.

Finally, there can be significant visioning benefits for the function of planning itself. For example, strong consensus on community goals can provide an informed and supportive context for the development of other plans and policies. This, in turn, can facilitate and even streamline public involvement.

At the same time, visioning can place new demands on planning. It stretches the traditional role of planners, calling upon new skills and competencies. It demands increased levels of dialogue and trust with the public. Ultimately, to the degree that visioning extends beyond the traditional domain of planning, it requires more effective cross-sector communication and collaboration.

THE OREGON MODEL

Oregon was one of the first places in the United States to experience the proliferation of community-based visioning. In a state widely recognized for its land-use planning and growth management policies, visioning was seen as an overlay for local land-use plans and a tool to help communities manage change.

Based on Oregon's early community visioning successes and similar state-level efforts, the Oregon Model represents a comprehensive approach to visioning that has since gained widespread acceptance around the country. The model is framed by four simple questions, which collectively form the basis of the visioning process:

1. Where are we now?
2. Where are we going?
3. Where do we want to be?
4. How do we get there?

Answering each question implies a discrete step in the process, with different activities, outcomes, and products. Step one involves profiling the present community's current conditions and core values. Step two involves analyzing emerging trends and their probable impact on the community's future. Step three is geared to the creation of a vision, and step four involves developing an action plan.

Some communities have added a fifth step promoting action plan implementation:

5. Are we getting there?

This addition to the Oregon Model responds to criticism that the visioning process does not always produce real results. The fifth step may also incorporate the development of indicators or benchmarks to monitor and measure the community's success in achieving its vision over time.

Visioning is designed to be iterative and ongoing. Benchmarking provides an important feedback loop for the eventual update of the community's vision and action plan. The action plan, having a much shorter planning horizon than its companion vision, requires more frequent updates.

Applying the Model

The Oregon Model is a flexible approach that can be adapted to a wide variety of settings and can be scaled up or down depending on the nature of the community, its needs, and its resources. The key to its success is to shape the process to fit the place.

Establishing a vision framework—timeframe, overall focus, and specific focus areas—provides a strategic starting point. Most communities set their vision timeframe at 20 to 25 years into the future. They also adopt a broad overall focus, encompassing the full spectrum of community concerns. Focus areas may range beyond traditional planning to encompass such topics as education, arts and culture, health, and public safety. Building on this framework, the design of every visioning process will vary widely.

As a relatively new approach to planning, community visioning can have a steep learning curve; it may employ nontraditional planning techniques such as "environmental scanning" or alternative scenarios. Managing diverse stakeholder groups or alleviating public skepticism regarding the process can prove daunting. Midprocess course corrections are necessary."

Fortunately, none of these challenges are insurmountable. Moreover, the ability of visioning to provide strategic input for such perennial planning concerns as growth management, urban design, transportation, housing, community development, and sustainability justifies the up-front investment. Indeed, planners often use the outcomes of visioning to frame and legitimize other major planning initiatives.

Involving the Public in Visioning

True to visioning's roots in anticipatory democracy, public involvement is a critical element of the visioning process. Engaging the public is essential in creating a shared community vision and action plan, as well as in promoting their eventual achievement. This implies an inclusive, participatory process capable of forging broad public consensus on key community goals.

To some planners, such a dialogue may seem increasingly difficult in today's society, given the

> ## SUCCESSFUL COMMUNITY VISIONING
>
> Visioning works when:
>
> - The community is concerned about its future and is eager for dialogue.
> - The process is well designed, managed, and adequately resourced.
> - Key community institutions and opinion leaders are involved in the process.
> - Elected officials and city managers are supportive of the process.
> - The public is authentically engaged in the process.
>
> Visioning doesn't work when:
>
> - The community is too polarized to engage in a civil dialogue.
> - The process is poorly designed or managed or inadequately resourced.
> - Key community institutions or opinion leaders are not involved in the process.
> - Elected officials or city managers are unsupportive of the process.
> - There is no follow-through in implementing the vision and action plan.

numerous urgent issues on the public agenda, shrinking local government budgets, the busy lives of citizens, and the ever-present distractions of the media and pop culture. For these reasons, public out-reach and strong "branding" of the visioning process are absolutely critical to successful public involvement.

Fortunately, for many people, there remains a fundamental appeal in talking about the future of their community. The reason is probably the abiding importance of "place." People relate to and care about where they live; it's one of the fundamental ways through which we continue to connect as human beings.

There is also an array of tools and techniques to stimulate and facilitate the visioning dialogue. These include participatory techniques, such as public workshops and open houses, as well as more representative techniques, such as citizen task forces, scientific surveys, and focus groups. The former help ensure broad public input, allow for open dialogue, and promote public awareness; the latter help capture diverse viewpoints, promote in-depth discussions, and facilitate the development of specific visioning products.

Additionally, computer-mediated communications are increasingly integral to the visioning process. While "electronic town meetings" have yet to realize their original promise, other tools have stepped in to fill the gap. Visioning today would be inconceivable without the Internet, search engines, and community Web sites, with their respective capacities for disseminating and gathering information. Graphical computer simulations have also increased our ability to actually *see* aspects of preferred—or not-so-preferred—futures.

Undoubtedly, evolving forms of electronic communication will continue to add new dimensions to community visioning, just as the process itself continues to evolve as an integral part of community planning.

See also:
Places and Place Making
Public Meetings
Surveys
Visualization

CHARRETTES

A charrette involves a multidisciplinary team of professionals developing all elements of a plan. The team works closely with stakeholders through a series of feedback loops, during which alternative concepts are developed, reviewed by stakeholders, and revised accordingly. The charrette is a sophisticated process that best serves controversial and complicated urban design and planning problems. Its capacity to bring all the decision makers together for a discrete amount of time to create a solution makes it one of the most powerful techniques in a planner's toolkit.

Charrettes are not a substitute for a standard planning process, which is executed over several months. They are conducted to address specific problematic situations and should complement the overall planning process. The charrette process works best for situations such as:

- high-stakes projects;
- volatile yet workable political environments;
- complex design problems; and
- projects that include imminent development.

The combination of the sophistication of the process with the complexity of the situations in which it is most often used means charrette practitioners *must* be well trained.

DYNAMIC PLANNING

A charrette is the central event of a larger process that the National Charrette Institute calls *Dynamic Planning*, a multiday, collaborative planning and design effort with the goal of arriving at a comprehensive, feasible plan.

Dynamic Planning has three governing values:

- Anyone affected by the project has the right to provide input with potential impact on the outcome.
- Each participant has a unique contribution that is heard and respected.
- Many hands make the best plans.

BENEFITS OF THE CHARRETTE PROCESS

The benefits of the charrette process are numerous. When done correctly, the charrette promotes trust between citizens and government through meaningful public involvement and education. It fosters a shared community vision by turning opposition into support. It continuously strives for the creation of a feasible plan, which increases the likelihood of the project getting built by gaining broad support from citizens, professionals, and staff. Identifying the stakeholders early and often, and encouraging public participation creates a better plan through diverse input and involvement. Finally, the charrette makes economic sense. Because all parties are collaborating from the start, no voice is overlooked, which allows the project to avoid costly rework. Also, the charrette allows for fewer and more highly productive work sessions, making it less time-consuming than traditional processes.

THE NINE STRATEGIES OF THE CHARRETTE PROCESS

The term "charrette" is overused and often misused. Although "charrette" refers specifically to a holistic plan to bring transformative change to a neighborhood, some use the word to refer to an afternoon meeting or a marathon planning workshop. The following nine strategies are what differentiate a charrette from other planning processes.

1. *Work collaboratively.* All interested parties must be involved from the beginning. Having contributed to the planning, participants are in a position both to understand and to support a project's rationale.
2. *Design cross-functionally.* A multidisciplinary team method results in decisions that are realistic every step of the way. The cross-functional process eliminates the need for rework because the design work continually reflects the wisdom of each specialty.
3. *Compress work sessions.* The charrette itself, usually lasting two to seven days, is a series of meetings and design sessions that would traditionally take months to complete. This time compression facilitates creative problem solving by accelerating decision making and reducing unconstructive negotiation tactics. It also encourages people to abandon their usual working patterns and "think outside of the box."
4. *Communicate in short feedback loops.* During the charrette, design ideas are created based upon a public vision and presented within hours for further review, critique, and refinement. Regular stakeholder input and reviews quickly build trust in the process and foster true understanding and support of the product.
5. *Study the details and the whole.* Lasting agreement is based on a fully informed dialogue, which can be accomplished only by looking at the details and the big picture concurrently. Studies at these two scales also inform each other and reduce the likelihood that a fatal flaw will be overlooked in the plan.
6. *Produce a feasible plan.* The charrette differs from other workshops in its expressed goal to create a feasible plan. In other words, every decision point must be fully informed, especially by the legal, financial, and engineering disciplines.
7. *Use design to achieve a shared vision and create holistic solutions.* Design is a powerful tool for establishing a shared vision. Drawings illustrate the complexity of the problem and can be used to resolve conflict by proposing previously unexplored solutions that represent win-win outcomes.
8. *Include a multiday Charrette.* Most charrettes require between two and seven days, allowing for three feedback loops. The more difficult the problem is, the longer the charrette should be.
9. *Hold the charrette on site.* Working on site fosters the design team's understanding of local values and traditions, and provides the necessary easy access to stakeholders and information. Therefore, the studio should be located in a place where it is easily accessible to all stakeholders and where the designers have quick access to the project site.

THE THREE PHASES OF DYNAMIC PLANNING

As discussed above, the charrette is the central element of a larger comprehensive process called Dynamic Planning. There are three phases in Dynamic Planning: *research, education, and charrette preparation; the charrette; and plan*

PLANNING AND URBAN DESIGN STANDARDS

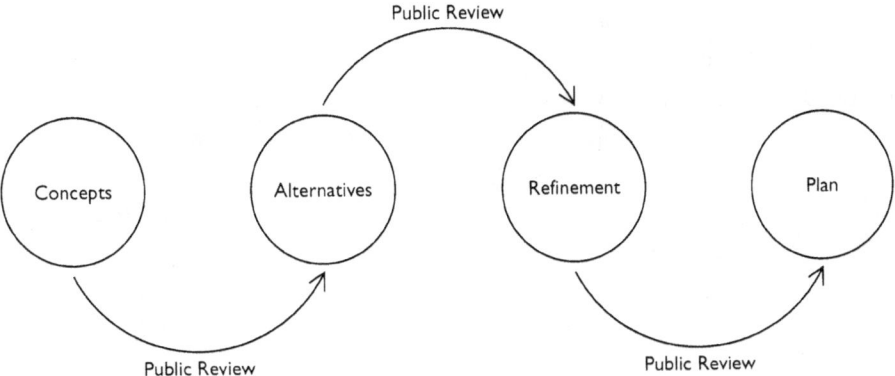

Charrette Feedback Loops

Source: National Charrette Institute, 2003.

implementation. The most common cause of project failure is not a poorly run charrette; rather, it is usually due to incomplete preparation and/or inadequate follow-through during the implementation phase.

Research, Education, and Charrette Preparation

During this phase, all the necessary base information is gathered and all the necessary people are identified and engaged. A complexity analysis

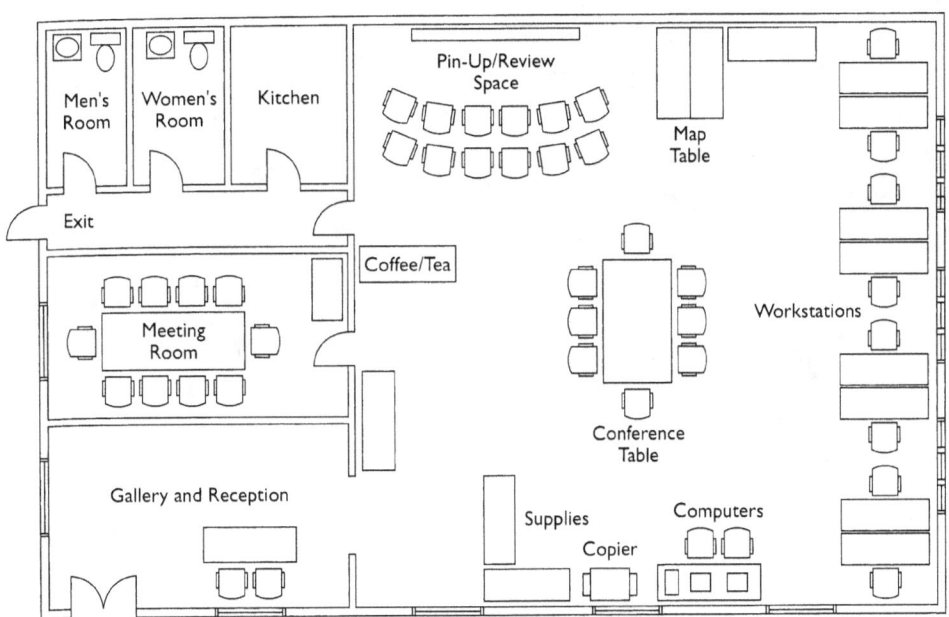

Charrette Studio Layout

Source: National Charrette Institute, 2003.

111

of the project is completed, so that the charrette manager can decide how much time is needed for the charrette. During this time initial stakeholder meetings are held and feasibility studies are completed. Finally, the charrette logistics are arranged. The studio setup is planned, the design team is formed, and the charrette is scheduled step by step. This step can typically take around four months.

The Charrette

The charrette brings all the right people and all the right information to a series of highly focused and productive work sessions. Before the first public meeting is held, the design team takes a tour of the area and holds meetings with key stakeholder groups. The first public meeting is held to determine the direction in which the public would like to take their community. Based on public input, gathered through a number of different participatory methods employed during the first public meeting, the design team begins to work on the development of alternative concepts. The next evening, another public meeting is held to display the alternative concepts and gather another round of public feedback. After this second public meeting, the design team meets to discuss the best way to synthesize the different concepts into one preferred plan. This new plan is then presented to the public in an open house. Following the open house, the preferred plan is developed further, and the design is refined. Additional stakeholder input is gathered. The preferred plan is then presented to the public again during the final charrette public meeting.

Plan Implementation

Dynamic Planning does not end with the charrette. It is critical that the preferred plan undergo further feasibility testing and public review. Each team member is in charge of his or her element of the charrette plan and performs feasibility tests and then refines the element as necessary. These revisions to the plan are then presented to the public again, usually about a month after the charrette. The final product of the Dynamic Planning process is a full set of documents that represent the complete record of the Dynamic Planning and charrette processes, including records of the meetings, who was involved, and the evolution of the plan.

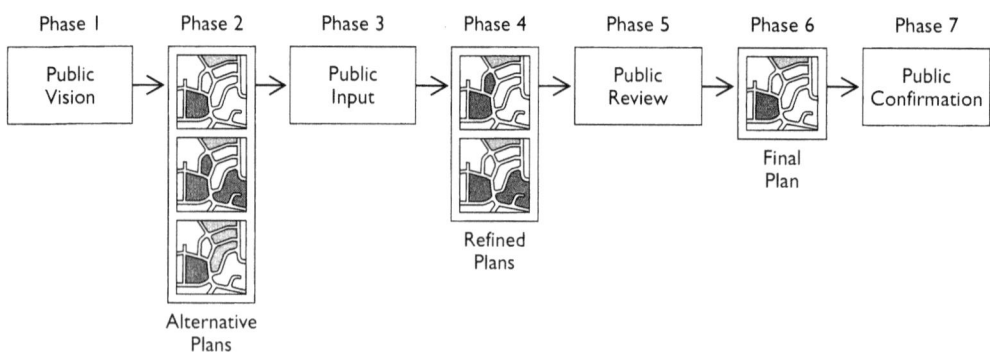

Charrette Work Cycle

Source: National Charrette Institute, 2003.

WHERE CHARRETTES SUCCEED

The key to a successful charrette is in its preparation. Because a successful charrette requires all the right people and all the right information, most mistakes are made by not identifying and involving the right people early and throughout the process and/or not planning enough time to produce the documents necessary for implementation. The importance of stakeholder reviews and soliciting public feedback cannot be overemphasized.

NEXT EVOLUTION OF CHARRETTES

Traditionally, charrettes have been "high-touch," relying on low-tech elements, such as hand drawings. High-tech modeling tools are increasingly being incorporated into traditionally high-touch charrettes. They include keypad polling, environmental impact analysis programs, and vision scenario development. These tools are helping to increase public involvement, execute design, and perform feasibility analysis. As high-tech tools are refined, they will provide the design team with an increased capability to give quick feedback during a charrette.

See also:
Visualization

PUBLIC MEETINGS

Public meetings are among the most common forms of citizen participation for planners and urban designers. They can be used to ascertain public opinion generally or to reach consensus on a recommended action. When they are successful, it is due to careful planning and follow-through. Well-organized and executed public meetings can be valuable opportunities for planners to provide information on important issues to the citizenry and obtain meaningful input.

There are three primary purposes for holding a public meeting: share information, seek advice, or solve problems. Though any issue can be the subject of this form of public dialogue, planners most frequently deal with matters such as zoning, comprehensive planning, parks and open space, environmental protection, and transportation. The meetings themselves may take a variety of forms. They differ substantially from public hearings, which generally follow formal rules and procedures. In fact, it can be said that governmental bodies usually are required to hold public hearings, whereas they have a choice about whether and how to hold public meetings.

At an effective public meeting, planners can enlist citizens as partners or at the least give them important information. By listening and responding respectfully, they can help diffuse opposition and build trust and confidence. The most successful public meetings are designed and executed very carefully, with attention paid to myriad details and nothing left to chance.

THE PURPOSE OF A PUBLIC MEETING

Before developing the agenda or any other part of the public meeting, the first matter to be agreed upon is its purpose: Is the meeting being convened primarily to share information, to seek advice, or to solve problems? Once that is decided, planners then should choose the appropriate structure and organization that best carries out this objective. To avoid misunderstandings, it is important that all notices indicate clearly the nature of the meeting and the expected outcomes. This also should be emphasized during introductory remarks. For example, citizens can be upset if they come to a public meeting ready to vote on options or alternatives, only to find that the purpose of the gathering is only to ask for their opinions.

Informational Meetings

Informational meetings are held to convey information or data to the public and to receive their comments. Public hearings are the most common, but not the only, form of informational meetings. At public hearings, staff presents information to the decision makers or hearing officers, followed by testimony from citizens, all within strict constraints. Other informational meetings are more informal, with planners making reports to neighborhood, civic, or other interested groups, and then answering questions. Although time for short presentations from the attendees may be permitted, prolonged dialogue and interaction are discouraged.

Advisory Meetings

While advisory public meetings also provide information, the public is given meaningful opportunities at these meetings to interact with staff or decision makers. Similar to the structure of informational meetings, advisory meetings begin with a presentation of basic information, possibly followed by a summary of the advantages and disadvantages of various alternatives. After the presentations at an advisory meeting, however, the public engages in an open but structured dialogue.

Workshops

The most common form of dialogue session is the workshop, where 8 to 10 participants discuss issues pertinent to the subject, led by a facilitator. Notes are taken, with the assurance that feedback from the attendees will be shared with the decision makers. No promises are made that the results from the workshop will be the final decision; the only assurances given are that decision makers will consider citizen concerns in their final deliberations.

Open House

Another form of advisory meeting becoming popular among planners is the community open house. While informational or advisory meetings should be no more than three hours long, an open house is typically longer, from 3:00 to 8:00 p.m., for example. A busy public appreciates the flexible hours. For example, seniors or others may prefer not being out after dark, and working people can drop by on the way home or after supper.

To hold an open house requires a large room that can hold many people milling about, such as a school gymnasium or cafeteria, senior or community center, or church basement. As people enter, they are given information packets that include a small map or room layout, agenda, and background materials. Well-placed signs mark the different areas of activity or stations. Planners and others who can answer questions and engage people in a dialogue about a particular segment of the issue staff each station. For example, if the open house is being held about a draft comprehensive plan, the people at the various stations can address elements of the plan, such as transportation, parks, and housing. Speakers may provide formal presentations in a screened-off part of the room at specific times. Citizens are encouraged to stay as long as they like, moving at their own pace between stations and other informational displays. Short written questionnaires give attendees additional opportunities to comment and express their opinions. This open format, with staff and decision makers committed to listening and actively engaging the public, can generate much community goodwill as well as provide valuable information.

Problem-Solving Meetings

The purpose of the third, and least common, form of public meeting is to solve problems. In

PLANNING AND URBAN DESIGN STANDARDS

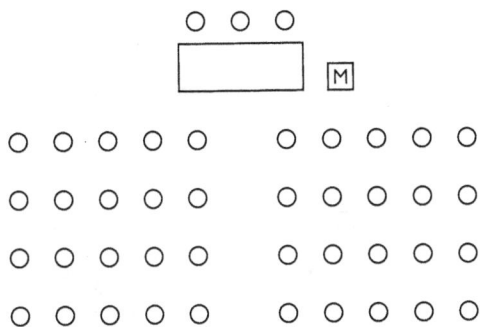

With this arrangement, all eyes are on the speaker. There is minimal interaction with the audience, typically limited to questions and answers. To be heard, one must generally go to the front.

Typical Informational Seating Arrangement

Reprinted with permission from Successful Public Meetings, copyright 2000 by the American Planning Association, Suite 1600, 122 South Michigan Avenue, Chicago, IL 60603–6107.

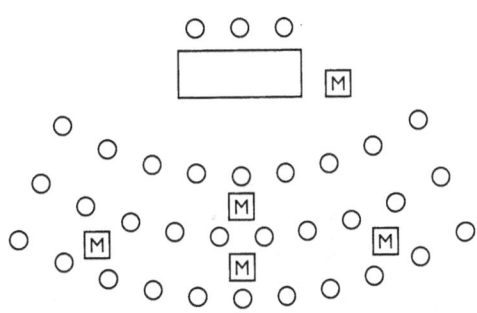

The curved shape of the arrangement creates fewer perceived barriers between the speakers and the audience. It also allows the audience to have views of each other. The placement of microphones invites questions and comments.

Improved Informational Seating Arrangement

Reprinted with permission from Successful Public Meetings, copyright 2000 by the American Planning Association, Suite 1600, 122 South Michigan Avenue, Chicago, IL 6060:–6107.

this case, the results of citizen input will directly influence the decision-making process. The workshop format discussed above, consisting of a presentation of technical material followed by facilitated discussion, is also a useful technique for problem-solving meetings. However, in this case, the public is asked to reach conclusions or make recommendations. If there are more than a dozen attendees, people should be divided into small discussion units. Group consensus or agreement is more likely to emerge if participants are randomly dispersed at small discussion tables. This will produce results more reflective of the group process than of any particular advocate or dissenter. The successful problem-solving meeting requires an informed citizenry, skilled discussion leaders following an agenda with specific questions and discussion topics, well-trained recorders, and decision makers who commit themselves to following the results.

UNDERREPRESENTED POPULATIONS

In an increasingly diverse society, planners should be sensitive about how to involve people who may not generally come to public meetings. One successful technique is to contact representatives of minority, non-English speaking, or other underrepresented communities to ask them to help you reach their constituents, friends, and neighbors. Take their advice seriously. They may suggest several approaches, such as:

- advertising in local newspapers or radio stations;
- printing notices in languages other than English;
- using interpreters at meetings;
- providing child care; and
- meeting at unconventional times, such as weekends;

ESSENTIAL READINGS IN URBAN PLANNING

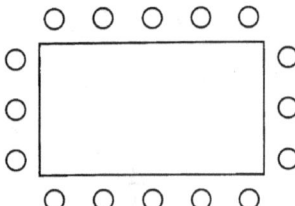

The rectangular table is typical for conference room meetings. It encourages face-to-face interaction, but those on the ends may talk more and receive more attention. Substituting an oval or round table allows participants to see each other easily.

Boardroom Seating Arrangement

Reprinted with permission from Neighborhood Planning, *copyright 1990 by the American Planning Association, Suite 1600, 122 South Michigan Avenue, Chicago, IL 60603–6107.*

This arrangement is similar to the improved informational seating arrangement. It allows for interaction when a circle arrangement is not possible. A main speaker may have to turn to view certain audience members.

Theater Seating Arrangement

Reprinted with permission from Neighborhood Planning, *copyright 1990 by the American Planning Association, Suite 1600, 122 South Michigan Avenue, Chicago, IL 60603–6107.*

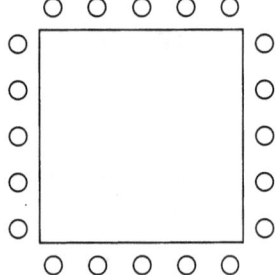

(with or without table)

This arrangement is similar to the boardroom seating arrangement. It makes the role of "leader" less obvious. Corners may be "dead" areas, however.

Closed-Square Seating Arrangement

Reprinted with permission from Neighborhood Planning, *copyright 1990 by the American Planning Association, Suite 1600, 122 South Michigan Avenue, Chicago, IL 60603–6107.*

When a circle is not possible, a semicircle gives most of the same advantages. Use an even number of rows, as the odd, middle row is often left vacant.

Semicircle Seating Arrangement

Reprinted with permission from Neighborhood Planning, *copyright 1990 by the American Planning Association, Suite 1600, 122 South Michigan Avenue, Chicago, IL 60603–6107.*

PLANNING AND URBAN DESIGN STANDARDS

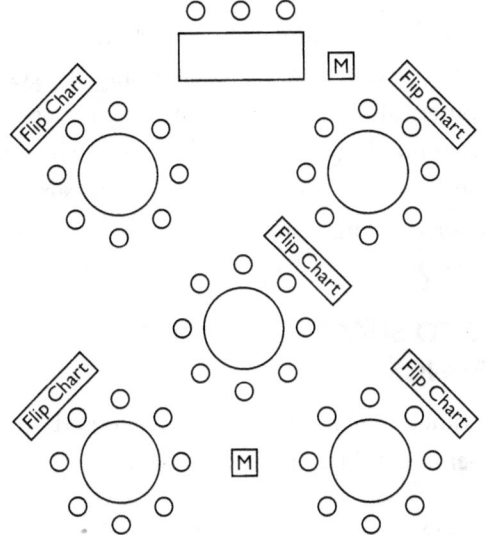

Several smaller tables allow for small-group interaction. Flip charts and microphones allow for breakout exercises and reporting back to the group.

Workshop Seating Arrangement

Reprinted with permission from Neighborhood Planning, *copyright 1990 by the American Planning Association, Suite 1600, 122 South Michigan Avenue, Chicago, IL 60603–6107.*

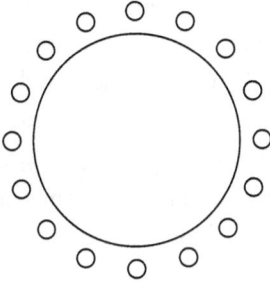

A circle arrangement allows everyone to see everything and creates a more equal setting. Including a table allows participants to take notes.

Circle Seating Arrangement

Reprinted with permission from Neighborhood Planning, *copyright 1990 by the American Planning Association, Suite 1600, 122 South Michigan Avenue, Chicago, IL 60603–6107.*

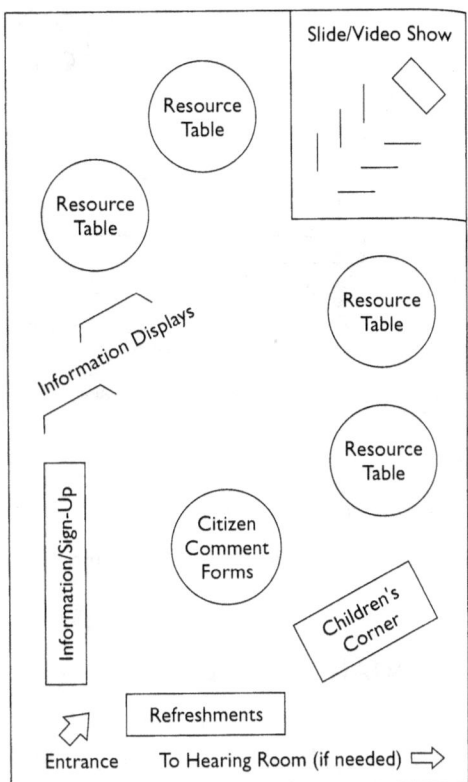

The community fair arrangement allows for many informal opportunities to receive information, discuss issues, and give opinions.

Community Fair Arrangement

Reprinted with permission from Neighborhood Planning, *copyright 1990 by the American Planning Association, Suite 1600, 122 South Michigan Avenue, Chicago, IL 60603–6107.*

ESSENTIAL READINGS IN URBAN PLANNING

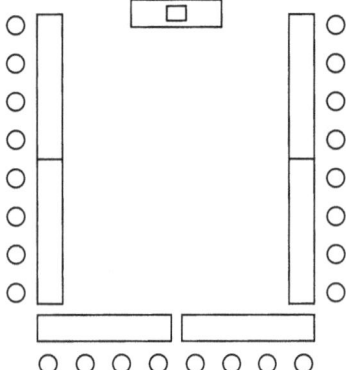

This room arrangement is commonly used for group meetings. The "U" allows a speaker to move around within the group. However, it creates open space between participants. Moving the tables closer together encourages interaction across the "U."

U-Shape Seating Arrangement

Source: © 1995 David Knox Productions, Inc.

PRESENTATION SKILLS

In deciding the amount and kind of information to provide at all public meetings, consider the needs of your audience. What do they need or want to know in order to be conversant with the subject and provide useful feedback? By asking this question and answering it honestly, planners will avoid making the common mistake of writing technical papers instead of simple handouts or speaking in jargon or language well beyond citizens' understanding. Recognize also that not all good planners are good presenters. Some professionals relate well to people at informal neighborhood meetings but are not able to speak to a great number in a big hall. Others have just the opposite skills. Either obtain training to increase your abilities in different settings or recognize your limitations and deploy the people best able to handle specific situations.

Likewise, remember that one type of presentation does not fit all situations. While computer presentations are popular with planners and designers, they can backfire if clone poorly, using too many words and confusing images. Computers also are prone to malfunction so it is important always to have a backup, such as a written handout. With some audiences, simple charts or drawings may be more effective than flashy graphics.

KEYS TO SUCCESSFUL PUBLIC MEETINGS

Successful public meetings are characterized by a number of considerations:

- Set aside sufficient time and resources to plan each event, agreeing first on the basic purpose and primary audience.
- Choose the best format to meet your objectives.
- Provide notice well in advance and in the language(s) understood by your target audiences.
- Hold the meeting at a time and in a place convenient to the people you want to attend.
- Agree on roles and responsibilities for hosts, presenters, discussion leaders, and recorders.
- Develop clear, appropriate, and readable written materials and graphics.
- Be well prepared so that you can deal with any last-minute crises or challenges.

See also:
Public Hearings

PUBLIC HEARINGS

The law requires that most public agencies and elected bodies hold public hearings before making important decisions. These hearings follow specific rules and procedures legally prescribed by state statutes and local ordinances. Generally, public hearings are held near the end of the planning and development process, just before

PLANNING AND URBAN DESIGN STANDARDS

the authority in charge votes about or decides the final disposition of the matter at hand. Notification of the hearing is sent to those parties legally required to receive them or inserted in advertisements in the local newspaper.

The hearing body usually sits on a raised dais with staff close by. The public is seated auditorium-style. Public comments are limited, and they may be recorded on audio or videotape, or by professional stenographers.

Planners participate as staff or consultants, reporting to the hearing holy and answering questions. Public testimony follows. To maintain a sense of fairness, proponents and opponents may be given alternate turns to speak. Decision makers listen and rarely ask questions. If an issue is contentious, the hearing may go on for hours.

THE ELEMENTS OF A GOOD PUBLIC HEARING

Planners, who must follow the legally prescribed rules for public hearings, can ensure that the hearings achieve their desired ends (receiving and documenting comments from the public about the nature of the matter at hand). Beyond that, however, they should also ensure that the actions they take meet the letter of the law, the spirit of the law, and the standards for effective and fair planning. The following sections offer some guidelines for effective public hearings. These actions should constitute a standard for the way in which public hearings are arranged and conducted.

Notification and Other Informational Materials

1. Write all notices in plain language, with translations as needed for non-English-speaking people. Disseminate as widely as your budget will allow, using community newspapers, Web pages, and other electronic means of communicating. If legal text is required, have it accompany the plainly written notice.

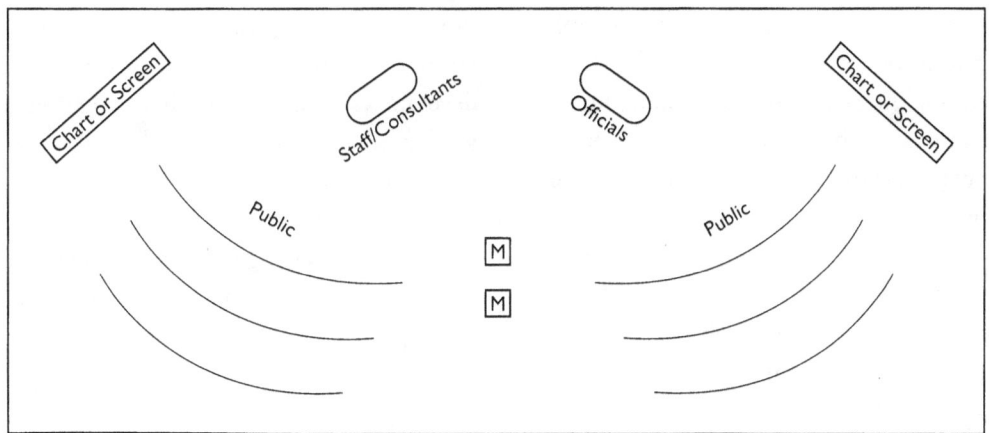

Hearing room arrangements should have public officials and staff seated at the same level as the audience. More than one screen often is provided for presentations, and they are positioned so the public and the officials can see them. Several microphones should be placed strategically so citizens have easy access.

Hearing Arrangement

Source: Elaine Cogan.

2. Hand out written agendas and summaries so attendees can follow along with the presentations. Make sure to have a sufficient quantity for all, and arrange to duplicate extras if needed.
3. Present technical material in as nontechnical a manner as possible. Remember that the public and some of the decision makers are not likely to be as well versed on the subject as the planners.

Room Arrangements

1. Hold the hearing in a room where all can see and hear with ease. If the dais is a fixed platform, set up chairs and tables for the public officials and staff at the same level as the audience.
2. Arrange charts or screens for slides or video presentations so the public as well as the officials can see them. If the room is large, position several screens so that everyone can see.
3. Have a sufficient number of working microphones for presenters, hearing personnel, and the public, and place them strategically to give citizens easy access.
4. Combine the hearing with an "open house" or similar opportunity for the public to receive and provide information in a more informal setting.

Interaction and Involvement

1. Station one or two staff at the door to greet the public, give them the handouts, and show them to empty seats. It is especially important to make latecomers welcome.
2. Have a sign-in sheet for all who want to comment, and call upon them in order.
3. Divide a long agenda into manageable portions. Instead of programming all the technical reports at one time, seek public comments after each section or portion under consideration. This decreases the likelihood that large groups of angry or restless people will remain throughout, as most will leave after the matters in which they are interested have been discussed.
4. Announce beforehand and throughout if the public's comments are being recorded.
5. Provide alternative ways to give public testimony. Deploy a stenographer in another room to take down, verbatim, comments; have a tape recorder and staff person available; or hand out written comment forms.

See also:
Public Meetings

COMPUTER-BASED PUBLIC PARTICIPATION

Planners are increasingly recognizing the potential of computer-based participation as a key element in developing appropriate and effective solutions to community design and planning problems. As computer and Internet technology becomes more mainstream. Planners should develop ways to harness these technologies to work more effectively with the public.

Computerized tools represent a paradigm shift in the planning and design process that may fundamentally change the way planners communicate ideas to the public. These computer-based participation tools presently consist of the following:

- *Electronic sketchboard.* This simulates traditional pen and paper sketching and provides additional capabilities of layering, tracing, and coloring.
- *Geographic information systems (GIS).* Use of GIS represents a move from a paper map to

"USER-FRIENDLY" NOTIFICATION FORM

The key elements of a successful public hearing notification are:

- Clear statement of purpose is included at the top of the notice.
- Purpose of the meeting and the public action being taken are described in plain language.
- Date, time, and location of the public hearing are included near the top of the notice.
- Potential financial implications of the project, of interest to citizens, are included.
- Ways that citizens can provide comments, at the hearing or in other ways, are provided.
- More detailed contact information is included.
- Legal references, if needed, are cited at the end of the notice.

The user-friendly version of a notification form follows.

Proposal to Change Use of Residential Property to Allow Senior or Community Center
Thomas McIntire, living at 2900 Elm Street, is asking the city to rezone his property from residential rise (RS-2) to PS-1, to allow construction of a senior or community center.

The city's Planning and Zoning Commission may either allow or deny this request and is holding two public hearings to obtain citizen comments. Both hearings will be held in the third-floor city hall auditorium. February 28 and March 9, at 6:30 p.m.

If the property is approved as proposed, it will be used by a nonprofit corporation, which will not pay property taxes. The remaining property taxpayers in the city will be required to make up the difference. The current property taxes paid by the owner are approximately $1,500 per year.

All citizens who own property within 400 feet of this property are invited to testify in person or write to the Department of Planning and Zoning before midnight of the second hearing, March 9. Any other interested parties also may speak at the hearing or write a letter.

For more information, contact Hortense Allen, project planner, Department of Planning and Zoning, City Hall, Room 725, or call Ms. Allen at 811-555-5050.

Please refer to accompanying map for specific site information. The legal petition for this case is on file as =1789222 PB and =5589107 PB

= = = = =

Source: Elaine Cogan. 2000.

a digital one empowered with spatial analysis. navigation.

- *Imaging Software.* This Software provides new ways of editing, manipulating, and animating traditional photographs.
- *Virtual reality (VR).* VR represents a move from 3-D physical models to digital ones that provide participants a degree of freedom in "experiencing" proposed projects before construction.
- *Urban simulation.* Building on virtual reality, urban simulation shows simulations of dynamic changes of the environment, including seasons, weather, landscape, pollution, and movement of people and automobile.
- *Hypermedia.* Also called *multimedia,* this is a new computerized environment that integrates multiple media, such as maps, photographs, videos, and sounds on a stand-alone PC.
- *Internet.* The Internet can provide a virtual setting of traditional same-place and same-time participation that integrates multiple tools, such as GIS, drawings, photographs, and virtual reality.

ADVANTAGES OF COMPUTERIZED TOOLS

Represent Contextual Data

Computerized tools can illustrate abstract concepts, such as environmental impacts, in a way that would be impossible with traditional tools, such as paper, photographs, or physical models. For example, with GIS, one can layer maps derived from different data on top of one another, query the database that is the source of the map information to highlight correlations between data, and visualize those correlations through the use of patterns and colors on the maps. Such tools also allow the user to extrude data into 3-D models and to simulate a fly- and walk-through experience. In a planning process that employs GIS, hypermedia, and virtual reality, average citizens are granted unprecedented access to a rich array of data presented in an easy-to-understand format. Computerized tools may enhance the public's interaction in the decision-making process because the tools provide so much more specific information that can be provided on the spot, thus enabling the public to explore alternatives quickly and with more competence.

Selective Display of Information

One key advantage of computerized tools is that they provide the capacity to selectively display information. When working on paper, even a relatively small amount of information can quickly become overwhelming and appear cluttered. The amount of detail displayed in computerized programs can be adjusted interactively as the scale is changed. Also, participants

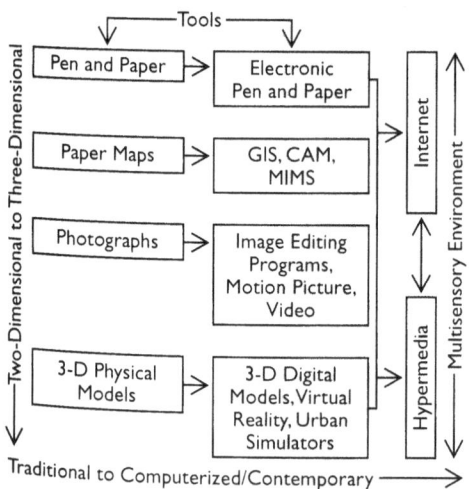

The Progression from Traditional to Computerized Visualization Tools

Source: KheirAl-Kodmany, 2004.

can easily overlay data by turning layers on and off as needed. In systems that incorporate hypermedia, different types of information can be queried and complex information displayed simply. Different types of data, such as sound, movies, animations, maps, and texts, can also be used selectively to enrich the study and analysis.

However, in a complex computerized data environment, citizens may not be able to freely participate because they will need "expert" assistance to manipulate data.

Geographic Scale

Another clear advantage of computerized tools is the ability to navigate geographic scale. With traditional tools, multiple maps are needed for each geographic scale: region, city, community, neighborhood, and individual lots. Computerized mapping allows for zooming in on a region, city, neighborhood, or even a specific house on a single map. As a result, computerized tools may increase interactivity, accessibility, and selectivity of information concerning issues at various geographic scales and therefore enhance discussion about contextual and spatial issues.

CONCERNS ABOUT COMPUTER-BASED PARTICIPATION

Believability

One drawback of computerized tools is that the images can be so realistic and persuasive that they mislead people. It has been found that computer visualization can lead to false conclusions by the public. Some critics have suggested that the use of impressive video and graphics will cause decisions to be made on the strength of visual images alone. Further, with the capability of creating very concrete, realistic images, there is the danger that audiences may see a generated image as constituting reality.

The more realistic the maps and images appear, the more danger there is they will be accepted as "truthful."

Similarly, computerized images can erroneously appear to be value-neutral. Just as these tools can be used to create compelling representations of future urban development, they can create compelling misrepresentations as well. Computer visualization must combat this by explicitly demonstrating the accuracy of the data being used and by providing accessibility to metadata (Ohermeyer 1998).

Affordability

The hardware and software needed for computer visualization require a large capital outlay: thus the question of whether to implement advanced visualization technology often comes down to a question of resources. Depending on the scale of implementation and the richness of the data, these systems can vary widely in development and maintenance costs. Low-tech tools can provide an alternative when it is necessary to respond to a tight timeline or cost control that are a reality in many local planning arenas (Pietsch 2000).

Engagement

A prime consideration in any public participation-planning scheme is how well the tools engage the targeted participants. In general, traditional noncomputerized public participation methods are more participatory, experiential, and interactive. They provide more social interaction among participants. These approaches are particularly effective when the audience involves varied interest groups and stakeholders with opposing interests. They are also useful for conflict resolution when face-to-face interaction is needed to facilitate discussions. Practical experience asserts that the added value of real-time social interaction among neighbors, while using a physical simulation game, for example, surpasses computer simulations even when they have user-friendly computer interfaces. Computerized methods lose their advantages when people have to "work" the computer. Findings indicate that traditional methods of manipulating physical objects facilitate comprehension and retention more than working on a computer screen (Moughtin 2003).

Access to Institutions

In public participation, whether computerized or traditional, access to institutions and people remains the most challenging issue. Are citizens willing to participate? What are the motivating factors and incentives? Will their participation be taken seriously? Will their opinions make a difference in the decision-making process and ultimate outcome? How open are the planning processes? Are the powerful players willing to open up and allow others to participate through information sharing? Institutional challenges may continue regardless of technological advancement.

The foremost advantage of computerized participation is access to accurate representation and presentation of complex contextual information. That said, while computerized tools usually impress participants and help them attain a comprehensive understanding of the spatial relationships, these tools often fall short in allowing the participants to design and alter the representation; computerized tools must do a better job of allowing the public to "get their hands on" something. The real need is not to force a choice between the social benefits of low-tech methods and the efficiency and power of high-tech methods; rather, we need tools that support the integration of real worlds and virtual worlds by providing users with the flexibility to move along the continuum.

REFERENCES

Moughtin, J.C., Rafael Cuesta, Christine Sarris, and Paola Signoretta. 2003. *Urban Design: Methods and Techniques.* 2nd ed. Oxford: Elsevier Press.

Obermeyer, Nancy J. 1998. "The Evolution of Public Participation GIS." *Cartography and Geographic Information Systems.* 25, no. 2:65–66.

Pietsch, Susan M. 2000. "Computer Visualization in the Design Control of Urban Environments: A Literature Review." *Environment and Planning It: Planning and Design,* 27, no. 4:521–536.

See also:
Charrettes
Geographic Information Systems
Visualization

PART II: ENVIRONMENTAL PLANNING AND MANAGEMENT

ENVIRONMENTAL MANAGEMENT OVERVIEW

ENVIRONMENTAL PLANNING CONSIDERATIONS

"Environment" refers to our surroundings. Its meaning is closely related to two other terms used in planning and urban design, "ecology" and "landscape." Ecology involves the study of the reciprocal relationships of all organisms to each other and to their biological and physical environments. Landscapes comprise the sum of natural and cultural elements seen in a single view. When we add "planning" to each of these terms, the combined term refers to developing future options for our surroundings, for the

PLANNING AND URBAN DESIGN STANDARDS

interrelationships among biological and physical processes, and for the visual manifestation of those relationships.

Because our surroundings contain physical, biological, and built elements, environmental planning involves using knowledge about those elements to provide options for decision making. The typical components that need to be considered include physical phenomena, such as air, climate, rocks, terrain, and water; biological elements, such as plants and animals; and the built environment, which encompasses buildings, streets, yards, and parks. Soils are an especially important element because they occur at the interface between physical and biological processes. Some surroundings may appear natural, such as farmlands, but are actually part of the built environment.

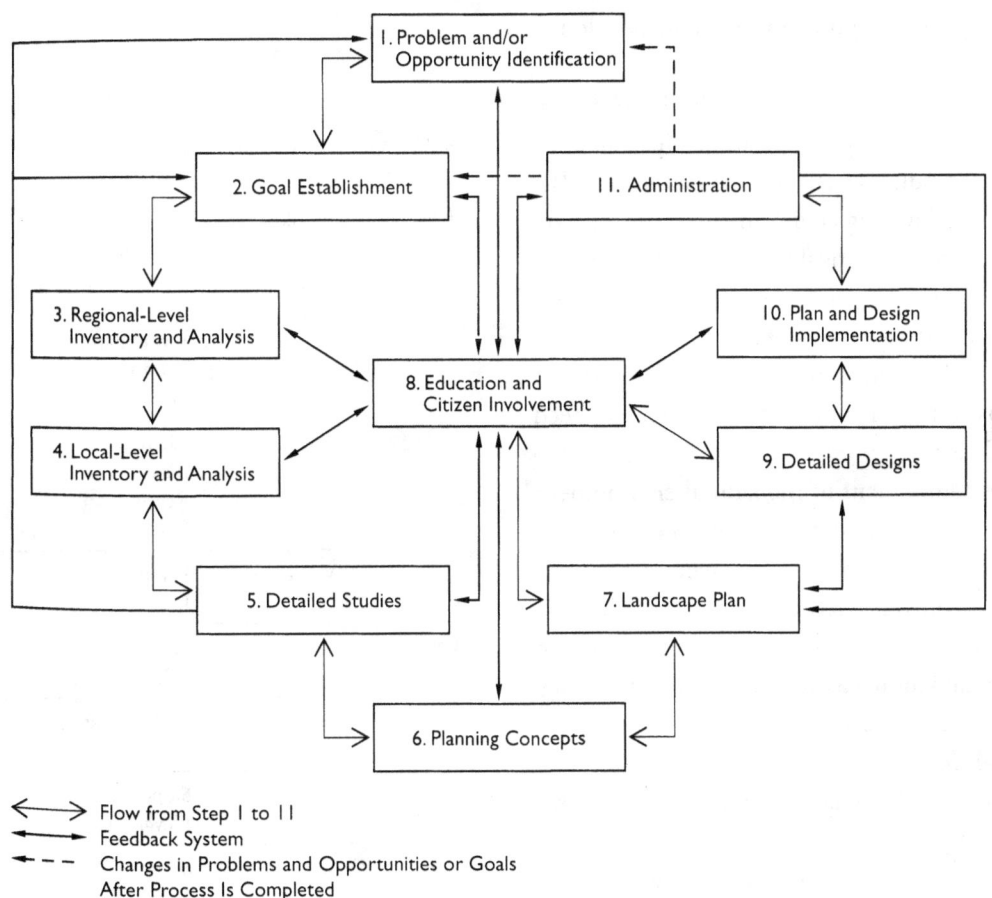

Ecological Planning Model

Source: Steiner 2000.

COMPONENTS OF THE ENVIRONMENT

The elements and processes involved in environmental planning are complex, hence the ordering of various components is important. Planning theorist Ian McHarg suggested a layer-cake model for such ordering. In this approach, time and ecology were used as organizing devices. Older environmental layers were used to understand younger phenomena. For example, regional climatic and geology processes result in specific physiographic, groundwater, and surface water characteristics. These physical processes create the parent material for soils, which allow specific plants to grow. Animals and people use these plants to live.

These layers can be overlaid in order to understand ecological relationships and to determine suitable land-use possibilities. The concept of layering environmental information provides the theoretical underpinnings for geographic information systems (GIS). Planners and urban designers use GIS maps to explore relationships and patterns, and to determine the possibility of suitability with greater speed and efficiency.

The components of the natural environment can be viewed as both sources and sinks for human activity. The environment is a source when it provides resources for people, such as productive soils, drinking water, clean air, timber, and minerals for energy and building. Environments are sinks when they are used as disposals for our wastes.

Natural environments can also pose hazards to human health, safety, and welfare. Some hazards, such as floods, are relatively easy to forecast, while others are more difficult to predict, such as earthquakes, hurricanes, and tornadoes. Even though difficult to predict, areas susceptible to earthquakes, hurricanes, and tornadoes are well defined by geologists and climatologists. As a result, emergency plans can be prepared and building modifications can be made to minimize the loss of life and property. Even well-defined areas might change as a result of human activities, shifting hazard areas or creating new ones, such as when new built-up areas change flooding regimes or when developments move into woodlands, thereby increasing wildfire potential. Certain hazards are quite cataclysmic, such as the eruption of a volcano. Others may occur more gradually but also result in deleterious consequences, such as soil erosion.

Layer-Cake Model

HUMAN	People	Community Needs Economics Community Organization Demographics Land Uses Human History
BIOTIC	Wildlife	Mammals Birds Reptiles Fishes
	Vegetation	Habitats Plant Types
ABIOTIC	Soils	Soil Erosion Soil Drainage
	Hydrology	Surface Water Groundwater
	Physiography	Slope Elevation
	Geology	Surficial Geology Bedrock Geology
	Climate	Microclimate Macroclimate

Source: Steiner 2000.

THE LEGAL BASIS FOR ENVIRONMENTAL PLANNING

With the passage of the National Environmental Policy Act (NEPA) in late 1969, the U.S. Congress put into motion the machinery for protecting the environment. NEPA required all federal agencies to "initiate and utilize ecological information in the planning and development of resource oriented projects." Furthermore, agencies were required to use "a systematic, interdisciplinary approach which will insure the integrated use of the natural and the social sciences and environmental design arts in planning and in decision making which may have an impact on [the human] environment." NEPA instructs all federal agencies to include an impact statement as part of future reports or recommendations on actions significantly affecting the quality of the human environment.

Several states and many other nations adopted similar environmental protection measures. So many environmentally oriented laws were enacted during the 1970s that it was dubbed the "environmental decade." These laws sought to protect water quality and quantity, clean air, coastal zones, floodplains, wetlands, historical areas, rare and endangered animal and plant species, and prime agricultural lands. The laws originating from the 1970s to the present provide the basis for environmental planning in the United States and other nations.

In the United States, environmental planning laws rely on three general approaches: *regulatory, financial incentives,* and *voluntary.* Regulatory approaches control activities that result in environmental degradation. For example, the amount of pollution that can be dumped by a factory into a water body can be regulated. If the factory managers fail to comply with regulatory limits or standards, they can be fined or forced to close operations. Financial incentives can involve direct grants, such as providing funds to purchase lands for wildlife habitat conservation, or tax benefits, such as reductions in taxes for dedicating property for conservation. Voluntary activities can be encouraged through environmental education designed to convince an individual to do the right thing, such as not to litter. Voluntary programs also involve nonprofit organizations engaged in conservation. cleanup, and protection activities.

Federal environmental laws significantly influence regional and community planning. For instance, the federal Clean Air Act requires the regional control of ozone, carbon monoxide, nitrogen dioxide, sulfur dioxide, lead, and particulate matter. These pollutants have serious health and welfare consequences. If an air quality control region fails to comply with federal air quality standards, then state and local transportation funding and plans can be affected. Federal flood control laws provide another example. Federal law requires local governments to adopt flood zones in order for buildings to qualify for federal flood insurance. Without such floodplain zoning, it becomes extremely difficult to build in a flood-prone area.

Environmental laws encompass many similar issues to air quality and flood protection that planners and urban designers need to address on a regular basis. This approach to environmental planning has a strong rule-making orientation. As planning educator Paul Niebanck (1993) noted, "Rules are everywhere and seem to cover everything: rules for disaggregating an issue; rules for selecting priorities; rules for measuring impacts; substantive rules; procedural rules; rules for discourse; rules for appeal; and so on." Critics observe that this approach contains a strong reliance on analysis that might lead to "analysis paralysis."

Environmentally Sensitive Area Classification System

CLASS	SUBCLASS
Ecologically critical areas	Natural wildlife habitat areas Natural ecological areas Scientific areas
Perceptually and culturally critical areas	Scenic areas Wilderness recreation areas Historic, archaeological, and cultural areas
Resource-production critical areas	Agricultural lands Water quality areas Mineral extraction areas
Natural-hazard critical areas	Flood-prone areas Fire hazard areas Geologic hazard areas Air pollution areas

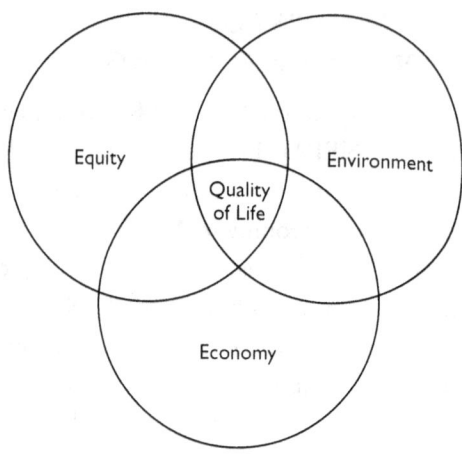

Three-E Diagram

Source: From A Region at Risk by Robert D. Yam and Tony Hiss, Copyright © 1996 by Regional Plan Association. Reproduced with permission of Island Press, Washington, D.C.

A contrary approach to environmental planning is based in *place making*. Whereas rule making has a strong legal and scientific orientation, place making has a stronger grounding in the environmental design arts. To achieve its maximum potential, environmental planning first needs rules to prevent harmful actions and to direct positive changes, and then creative interventions that result in healthier, more sustainable places.

A guiding principle for both rule making and place making is: first, do no harm. Understanding environmentally sensitive or critical areas is useful in preventing harmful actions. Environmentally sensitive areas can be defined as places vulnerable to negative environmental impact. These could include areas such as unstable soils, steep slopes, floodplains, wetlands, and vulnerable habitat. Areas can be defined as ecologically critical, perceptually and culturally critical, resource-production critical, and natural-hazard critical. On the local level, such an area may be used as a basis for a zoning district or an overlay zone that employs regulations specifically designed to protect that district.

SUSTAINABLE DEVELOPMENT

An emerging issue in environmental planning is sustainable development; that is, development that meets the needs of the present without compromising the ability of future generations to meet their own needs. Advocates of sustainable development argue that environmental concerns need to be balanced with social equity and economics. The intersection of these three Es—equity, economics, and environment—is suggested to be where the quality of human life can be best obtained. Some planners include a fourth E. In the case of Burlington, Vermont, it is education; for others, it is ethics. In urban design, it might be esthetics because of the visual relationship of built form to equity, environmental, and economic concerns.

The concept that we should leave the planet a better place for subsequent generations provides one ethical argument for environmental planning. And there are other ethical and practical reasons:

- We depend on the environment for our survival, so we better take good care of it.
- We are not the only species on the planet, and we have a responsibility to protect the habitats of other creatures.
- We can reduce costs and enhance benefits by using resources effectively and through environmental protection.
- We will improve our health by ensuring that air, water, and soils are not polluted.

REFERENCES

McHarg, Ian. 1969. *Design with Nature*. Garden City, NY: Natural History Press. Inc.

Niebanck, Paul. 1993. "The Shape of Environmental Planning Education." *Environment and Planning B: Planning and Design* 20:511–518.

Steiner, Frederick. 2000. *The Living Landscape: An Ecological Approach to Landscape Planning*. 2nd ed. New York:McGraw Hill.

Yaro, Robert and Tony Hiss. 1996. *Region at Risk: The Third Regional Plan for the New York-New Jersey-Connecticut Metropolitan Area*. Washington, DC: Island Press.

AIR

AIR QUALITY

National Ambient Air Quality Standards Criteria Pollutants

Air quality in the United States is measured by whether region is in compliance with the National Ambient Air Quality Standards (NAAQS) for the six criteria area pollutants initially designated in the Clear Air Act Amendments of 1970: carbon monoxide, lead, nitrogen oxides, particulate matter, ozone, and sulfur dioxide.

Carbon Monoxide

Poisonous to humans, carbon monoxide (CO) is a colorless, odorless gas. Approximately 90 percent of it in the atmosphere is a by-product of vehicle emissions from internal combustion engines. Fatal in large enough doses where ventilation is lacking, carbon monoxide reduces the ability of the body's circulatory system to deliver oxygen. CO emissions increase when conditions are poor for combustion; thus, the highest CO levels tend to occur when the weather is very cold or at high elevations where there is less oxygen in the air to burn the fuel.

Lead

Lead (Pb) is a heavy metal. In the past, it came primarily from automotive emissions as an airborne pollutant, but since lead was phased out of U.S. fuels starting in 1973, atmospheric lead has been greatly reduced. Instead, stationary sources, such as lead smelters, peeling paint, and the production of storage batteries, have become the main sources. Lead poisoning of the bloodstream can result in development disabilities among children as well as cause cancer and neurological damage. In some urban areas, lead remains an issue due to remaining lead-based paint on older structures and past lead deposits in soils along highway corridors.

Nitrogen Oxides

Nitrogen oxides are a group of highly reactive gases that contain nitrogen and oxygen in varying amounts. Nitrogen dioxide (NO_2), the most common, can often be seen as a reddish-brown layer over many urban areas. It is a main ingredient in smog. When combined with water vapor, it forms nitric acid, which as precipitation is known as acid rain. Nitrogen oxides form when oxygen and nitrogen in the air react with each other during combustion. Primary sources are motor vehicles, electric utilities, and other industrial, commercial, and residential sources that burn fuels.

Particulate Matter

Particulates are microscopic particles that comprise dust, soot, smoke, and other airborne debris. PM-10 refers to particulate matter no more than 10 micro-meters in diameter. PM-2.5 is particulate matter less than 2.5 microns in diameter and is referred to as PM-fine. Sources for particulate matter include smokestacks, fireplaces, open fires, blown dust on dirt roads, various manufacturing plants, and almost all motor vehicles. Particulates produce haze, reducing visibility. Health threats include various respiratory ailments and nose and throat irritation. Particulates are a particular threat to those with existing respiratory ailments such as asthma.

Ozone

One of the most familiar criteria pollutants is ozone (O_3). Ground-level ozone is also commonly known as smog. This is different from stratospheric-level ozone, also known as the ozone layer, which serves to protect the planet from ultraviolet radiation from the sun. At ground level, ozone is produced by a combination of pollutants. Sources include cars, smokestacks, and various volatile organic chemicals from paints, solvents, and other industrial materials. The process of smog formation is accelerated by certain weather factors, such as heat and temperature inversions (where warm air is trapped near the ground instead of rising).

Sulfur Dioxide

Like nitrogen dioxide, sulfur dioxide (SO_2) is a component of acid precipitation when sulfur dioxide combines with airborne water vapor. The resulting mix can, over time, erode stone, metal, rubber, and plastic materials and structures. Sources include coal-fired electric generating plants, paper and metal factories, and gasoline-powered vehicles. Sulfur dioxide as a gas can also harm lungs and destroy plants by inhibiting photosynthesis.

AIR QUALITY STANDARDS

Criteria air pollutants are regulated based on health-based criteria (science-based guidelines), which are used as the basis for setting permissible levels. For each of these pollutants, the U.S. Environmental Protection Agency (U.S. EPA) has established primary standards to protect health and secondary standards to prevent environmental and property damage.

Attainment and Nonattainment Areas

An attainment area is a geographic area whose air has been determined through monitoring and modeling to have criteria pollutant levels below the primary standard. A nonattainment area is one whose air exceeds the primary standard for one or more criteria pollutants.

In the *Green Book,* maintained by the U.S. EPA's Office of Air and Radiation, Air Quality Planning and Standards Division, there are current data about areas of the United States that are in nonattainment for which criteria pollutants and the criteria behind current NAAQS standards. This publication also provides data on the areas of the country where air pollution levels persistently exceed the national ambient air quality standards.

Of the six criteria pollutants, ozone has been particularly important to monitor because it is the main component of smog and contributes to lung damage and respiratory problems.

Location of Nonattainment Areas for Criteria Pollutants, 2002

Source: U.S. EPA 2002.

Air Quality Index

The Air Quality Index (AQI) also provides information on pollution concentrations for the six criteria pollutants. State and local agencies use the AQI for reporting daily air quality to the public. The AQI may be found in national print and broadcast media. It also serves as a basis for community-based programs that encourage the public to take action to reduce air pollution on days when levels are projected to be of concern.

AQI values for each of the pollutants are based on the concentration of that pollutant. The index is "normalized" across each pollutant so that, generally, an index value of 100 is set at the level of the short-term, health-based standard for that pollutant. The higher the index value, the greater the level of air pollution and health risk. The U.S. EPA has established six general AQI categories corresponding to different levels of health concern and index value ranges:

Good (0–50): Air quality is considered satisfactory. Air pollution poses little or no risk.

Moderate (51–100): Air quality is acceptable; however, for some pollutants, there may be a moderate health concern for a very small number of individuals. For example, people who are unusually sensitive to ozone may experience respiratory symptoms.

Unhealthy for Sensitive Groups (101–150): Certain groups of people may be particularly sensitive to the harmful effects of certain air pollutants, but the general public is not likely to be affected. For example, people with respiratory disease are at greater risk from exposure to ozone, while people with respiratory disease or heart disease are at greater risk from particulate matter.

Unhealthy (151–200): Everyone may begin to experience health effects. Members of sensitive groups may experience more serious health effects.

Very Unhealthy (201–300): Air quality in this range triggers a health alert, meaning everyone may: experience more serious health effects.

Hazardous (over 300): Air quality in this range triggers health warnings of emergency conditions. The entire population is more likely to be affected.

TOXIC AIR POLLUTANTS

The 1990 Clean Air Act Amendments established a list of 189 toxic air pollutants for which the U.S. EPA must establish categories of sources for their release, such as auto body shops or coal-burning electric generation plants. The difference between these 189 toxic air pollutants and criteria pollutants is that the latter were targeted because they are the most common pollutants, while many of the toxic air pollutants are specific to certain industrial processes, such as various types of chemical plants, and thus are not common. They may still pose important public health issues, in particular local areas affected by sources emitting such hazardous air pollutants.

SOURCES OF AIR POLLUTION

Mobile Sources

Motor vehicles, engines, and equipment that moves or that can be moved from place to place, including cars, trucks, buses, earth-moving equipment, lawn and garden power tools, ships, railroad locomotives, and airplanes, are considered mobile sources of air pollutants.

Stationary Sources

Stationary sources include any place or object from which pollutants are released that does not move around. Stationary sources can be further defined as point, biogenic, and area sources. Point sources include factories and electric power plants; biogenic sources include trees and vegetation, gas seeps, and microbial activity; area sources consist of smaller stationary sources, such as dry cleaners and degreasing operations.

PLANNING ISSUES

Planning decisions routinely affect air quality in metropolitan areas. Traffic patterns resulting from the routing of highways and the development of transit systems that help to relieve congestion affect air quality by influencing the level of vehicle emissions. Decisions about the location and permitting of various stationary sources, such as industrial plants, also affect air quality. Increasing vegetative and forest cover through land-use regulations, incentives, and other means may help to mitigate regional air pollution problems.

More broadly, urban form dictates the shape of many transportation and other decisions that can affect air quality. The Washington State Department of Ecology has identified five characteristics of urban form that help reduce driving distances, increase use of alternative modes of

PLANNING AND URBAN DESIGN STANDARDS

transportation, and, as a result, positively influence air quality:

- Increasing neighborhood, development, or regional density
- Incorporating different land uses within a development or neighborhood
- Locating transit near high-density locations
- Encouraging pedestrian-friendly designs
- Centralizing or clustering activities within a metropolitan area and in relation to transit development

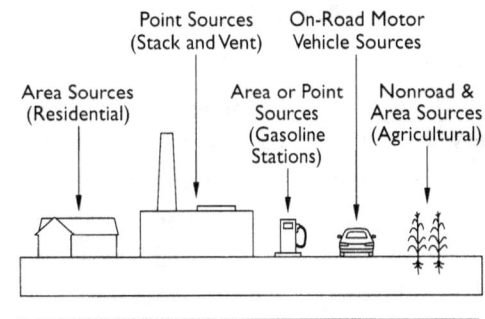

Types of Air Pollution Emission Sources
Source: U.S, EPA 2004.

Metropolitan Planning Organizations

Metropolitan planning organizations (MPOs) are responsible for planning transportation projects meant to maintain their region's air quality or move toward attainment of federal air quality standards over time. There are 341 MPOs, and each has to develop a transportation plan containing three elements:

> **Regional Transportation Plan (RTP):** RTPs have a 20-year planning horizon, and must Be consistent with the state transportation plan and the state air quality improvement plan.

> **Transportation Improvement Plan (TIP):** TIPs, which are updated at varying intervals, depending upon state requirements (typically between two to three years and for varying planning horizons (typically six to seven years), must also be consistent with the state transportation plan and air quality plan. These plans include specific techniques and implementation actions to address air quality.

> **Individual Transportation Projects:** Individual transportation projects include specific projects to be undertaken, such as roads, rail lines, and bus routes. To be considered for federal funding, these projects must be consistent with the state transportation plan, TIP, and air quality improvement plan. They also have to be listed in both the RTP and TIP.

State Implementation Plans

The U.S. EPA also requires states to submit State Implementation Plans (SIPS). These plans describe a state's strategy for achieving and maintaining the National Ambient Air Quality Standards. States with areas that do not meet the standards are required by the Clean Air Act to develop a written SIP outlining the steps they will take to reduce air pollution.

The purpose of a SIP is to ensure the implementation of programs that will reduce emissions. State environmental agencies prepare and submit a proposed SIP to the U.S. EPA that describes their plan, outlines air pollution reduction programs, contains projections of emission reductions from these programs, and commits to implement and enforce these programs. The SIP must also explain how funding and resources will be provided, and it must provide supporting technical information.

TOXICS RELEASE INVENTORY

An urban area's industrial base has potential impacts on local air quality. The Toxics Release Inventory (TRI) is a publicly available U.S. EPA database containing information on toxic chemical releases and other waste management activities reported annually by certain industry groups and federal facilities. This information is also available at the state and local levels.

REFERENCES

U.S. Environmental Protection Agency. Office of Air and Radiation, Air Quality Planning and Standards Division. *Green Book Nonattainment Areas for Criteria Pollutants.* http://www.epa.gov/oar/oaqps/greenbk/

Washington State Department of Ecology. 2003. *Focus on Linking Land Use Air Quality, and Transportation Planning.*

See also:
Air Sheds
Federal Legislation
Transportation Plans

AIR SHEDS

An air shed is a specified volume of air with similarities in climate, weather, and topography. Typically, it also shares issues of development, planning, or problems of air quality related to emissions, meteorology, and terrain. Air sheds are dynamic in geographic extent and volume: the volume of air that constitutes an air shed for any given period greatly depends on emissions, local/regional meteorology, and accepted regulations of health related to pollutants of concern to the community located within the air shed.

An air basin is often defined as a large land area containing one or more individually distinctive air sheds that generally has within it similar meteorological and geographical conditions. To the extent possible, an air basin is also defined along political boundary lines, including both the source and receptor areas of pollutants. For example, California is divided into 13 air basins, which contain many smaller individual air sheds.

In many ways, an air shed is similar to a watershed. It contains a "fluid." which in this case is the atmosphere; its geographical extent may be confined to a specific area; it may contain air contaminants concentrated more frequently in lower elevations due to inversions and air drainage: and, without major external weather effects from outside the air shed, it may be well identified through the analysis of digital terrain mapping, vertical profiling of the atmosphere, and local emission inventories.

However, unlike water, air can move upvalley or upslope in the terrain and spill into another nearby topographic basin. As a result, air shed dimensions and boundaries may be highly variable geographically and over time of day, year, and from year to year.

CONDITIONS WITHIN AN AIR SHED

The vertical mixing potential of air over a day varies considerably. As the sun heats the Earth's surface and causes air to rise over an increasing volume of air above the surface, the volume of air carrying pollutants expands accordingly. This expanded volume may cause the pollutants to be diffused over a larger zone than may occur at night when the Earth cools, the lower atmosphere contracts, inversions set in, and more local diffusion or confinement of pollutants occurs over a smaller zone both vertically and horizontally. Thus, the air shed relative to a particular pollutant may expand and contract even within a day's time.

Movement of air within an air shed is often characterized from weather stations with the aid of wind "roses," which describe the frequency of

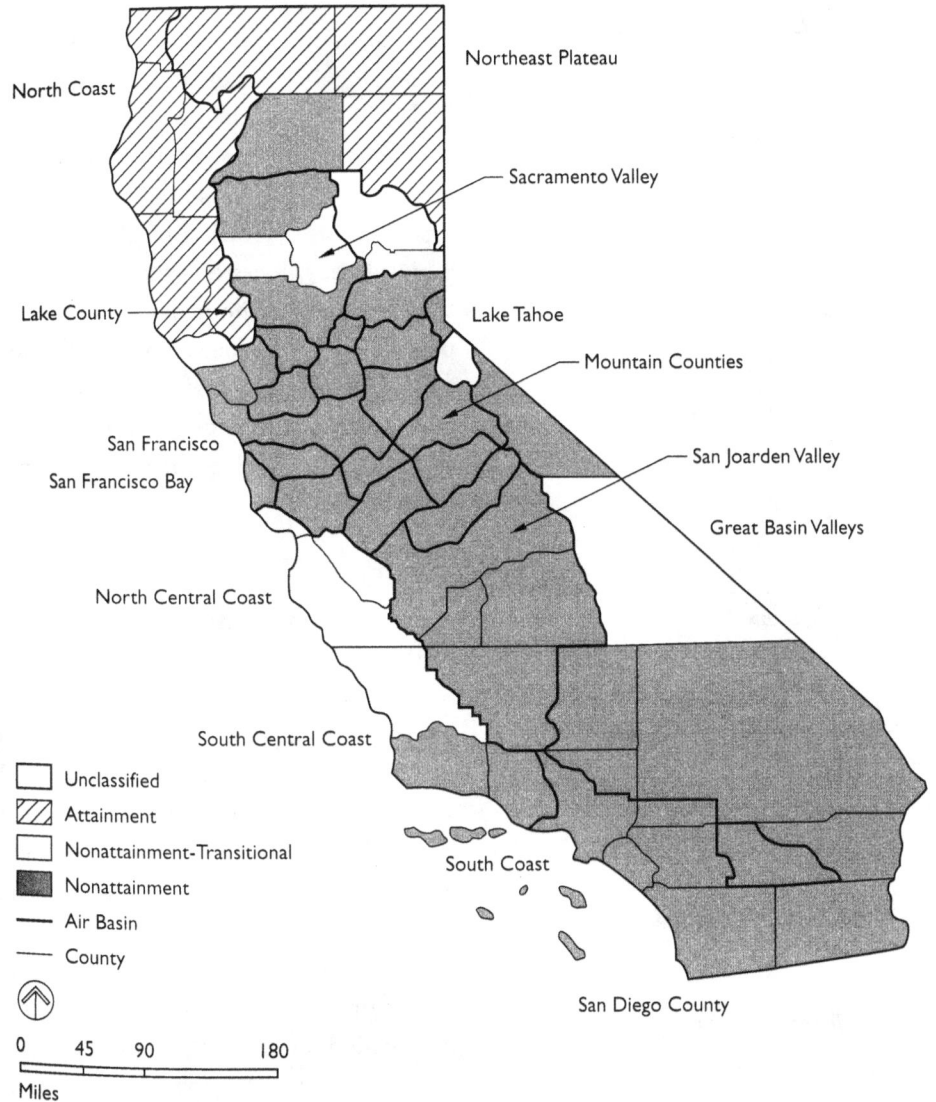

The area designations for ambient air quality standards are a combination of local air sheds and political boundaries.

Area Designations for California Ambient Air Quality Standards for Ozone
Source: California Air Resources Board.

wind direction at any location for any time of day or year and the speeds associated with those directions.

Air shed analysts keep close tabs on the vertical mixing potential by using air-sampling devices to measure the vertical dimension of the atmosphere, which includes factors such as temperature, wind velocity, wind speed, humidity, and pressure. Models and monitoring systems are used to predict diffusion and concentration, and to monitor air quality.

ESSENTIAL READINGS IN URBAN PLANNING

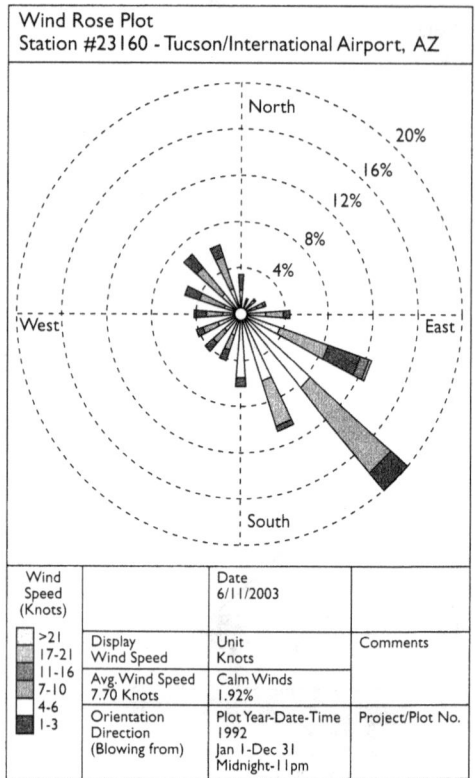

Sample Wind Rose, Tucson, Arizona

Source: U.S. Department of Energy 2003.

SCALE OF AN AIR SHED

The penultimate air shed is the entire three-dimensional spherical shell of air surrounding the Earth. It is essential to analyze this dimension to facilitate the understanding and mitigation of gases, such as carbon dioxide (CO_2), major continental emissions of sulfur dioxide (SO_2), diffusion into the upper atmosphere of chlorofluorocarbons (CFCs) that affect global ozone (O_3), and massive emissions of particulates from continents to oceans or to other continents from dust emissions and industrialization processes. These global-to-regional interconnections must be kept in mind when addressing certain environmental problems, such as how long-range transport of pollutants might explain local pollutant events. Modeling of global and regional atmospheric processes over geographical areas larger than the immediate confines of any particular air shed may be required. These scales and levels of air sheds/air basins are common across countries, hence protocols for modeling these processes, such as the Kyoto Protocol, have to be developed at high governmental levels.

AIR TRAJECTORY ANALYSIS

Although at first glance an area demarked initially by terrain characteristics (e.g., a small valley) may provide a definition of an air shed, on a regional-to-local scale, a planner or analyst may also have to consider external forces that can affect the local area, thus often accepting an expanded view of the local air shed in air quality assessments. One way this is done is with an "air trajectory analysis," whereby the analyst tries to determine where the air and its concentrations of various pollutants came from over many clays preceding an important period of concern about pollutant levels exceeding a standard or a series of such excesses.

An excellent example is the air trajectory pollution climatology of the Lake Champlain Basin of eastern Canada and the United States. The local air shed does not necessarily have fixed geographical boundaries. In fact, those boundaries can vary over the seasons and years. The local air shed also may be characterized by upwind meteorology, meaning that it can suffer pollution from regional sources that affect the basin downwind. Thus, regional air sheds of varying sizes are determined for SO_2, volatile organic compounds (VOCs), and nitrogen oxide (NOx) emissions, based on probabilities of occurrence, in a more holistic view

PLANNING AND URBAN DESIGN STANDARDS

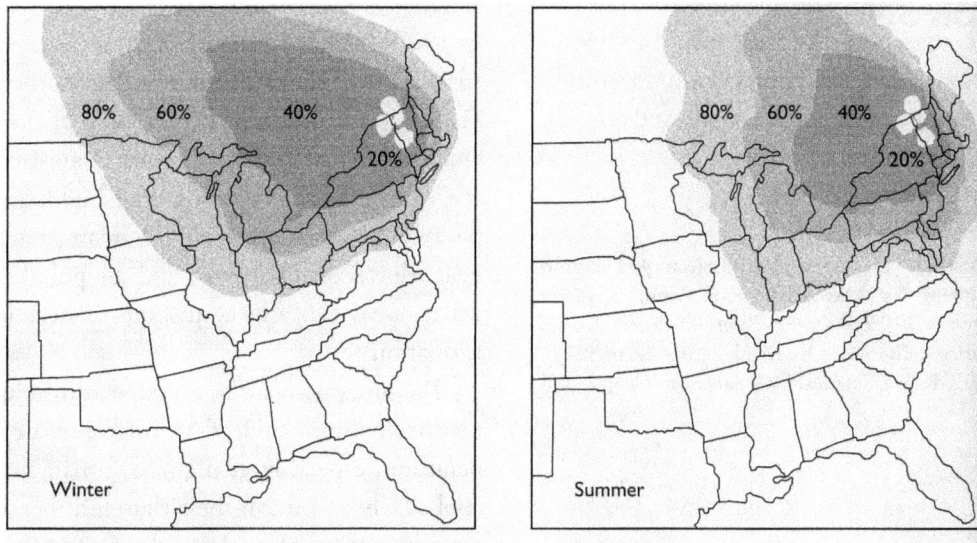

Regional air sheds are based on air trajectory climatology analysis of variations in upwind meteorology and emissions of various selected pollutants. Local data should be collected and analyzed to define local air sheds.

Seasonal Variations in Probabilistic Lake Champlain, New York, Air Shed

Reprinted courtesy of *American Geophysical Union.*

of regional-to-local variability of source regions, emissions. and regional-to-local meteorology.

PLANNING AND AIR SHEDS

When considering a particular air shed, planners, air quality analysts, and policy makers, among others, often face many methodological, scientific, and managerial issues, which typically require the formation of local alliances or stakeholder affiliations in order to fully comprehend them. For example, Our Airshed is a partnership covering approximately 2,700 square miles (4.500 square kilometers), including various communities and a park, near Edmonton, Alberta. Such alliances assist in developing management plans, focusing on problems, and ultimately identifying possible air quality and sustainability solutions.

From the planning perspective, considerations often range from producing fast-track fixes to preventing deleterious possibilities of air quality in a proactive way so as to carefully address the future quality of life and health of the populace. The focus must become the "nonattainment" area, other critical parts of the area, or the whole air shed. Environmentally related management plans for communities and regions are multifaceted, often comprising many issues that have to be considered together to produce solutions, such as factors related to biological, land resource, recreation, water, and, certainly, air resources. Each of these areas is challenging, and conflicts often arise among planners in attempting to find solutions.

In addressing air issues, each area plan should attempt to identify those of local and regional concern that affect health, while considering, to as great a degree as possible, the larger regional issues, such as greenhouse gas impacts on the local region and long-range transport of pollutants that affect the local area. These plans must also develop an appreciation for future development scenarios in the region and account for them in the plan.

REFERENCE

Poirot. Rich, et al. 1999. "Air Trajectory Pollution Climatology for Lake Champlain Basin," in *Lake Champlain in Transition: From Research Toward Restoration.* Thomas O. Manley and Patricia L. Manley, eds. Washington, DC: American Geophysical Union.

See also:
Air Quality
Federal Legislation
Heat Islands

HEAT ISLANDS

Dark roofs and paving materials absorb more of the sun's rays than vegetation, causing both surface temperature and overall ambient air temperature in urban areas to rise. This phenomenon is called the *urban heat island effect.* Trees and other vegetation naturally process solar radiation and help reduce ambient air temperatures through evapotranspiration—when water absorbed by vegetation evaporates from leaves and surrounding soil, naturally cooling the surrounding air. When vegetation is removed and replaced by urban development, temperatures can increase noticeably. Areas of the United States with a hot, arid microclimate, such as Phoenix, Arizona, are particularly affected adversely by the heat island effect. Annual temperatures. rainfall, and wind regimes all are factors in urban heat island formation.

REASONS HEAT ISLAND OCCUR

Most urban building materials are watertight, so moisture is not readily available to dissipate the sun's heat through evaporation. Temperatures of unshaded, impermeable surfaces can reach up to 190°F (88°C) during the day, while vegetated surfaces with moist soil might reach only 70°F (18°C). Also, urban areas trap more of the sun's energy due to the use of dark materials and the canyonlike configurations of buildings and pavement. Anthropogenic (human-produced) heat, slower wind speeds, and air pollution in urban areas can also contribute to heat island formation.

The increased surface temperatures in the urban environment lead to increased air temperatures, especially at night, as urban surfaces cool slowly and warm the air around them. The warming effects of the heat island are most pronounced during calm, clear weather conditions, and are most conspicuous during summer and winter. In most communities, the negative effects of the summer heat island include increased discomfort, a rise in the incidence of human health problems, higher energy bills, and stress on vegetation. In contrast, in colder areas at higher latitudes and elevations, the winter warming effects of the heat island can be somewhat beneficial.

HEALTH AND COST IMPLICATIONS

Research by the Lawrence Berkeley National Laboratory (LBNL) in Berkeley, California, indicates that on summer days in Los Angeles, a one-degree Fahrenheit temperature increase boosts the risk of smog formation by 3 percent. Smog, or ground-level ozone (as opposed to the atmospheric ozone that protects the Earth from ultraviolet radiation) is an invisible pollutant that can permanently damage lungs. Chronic bronchitis, asthma, and other cardiopulmonary disorders may be caused or exacerbated by ground-level ozone.

There are also noticeable cost implications. The same one-degree increase in Los Angeles is estimated to increase the demand for cooling

PLANNING AND URBAN DESIGN STANDARDS

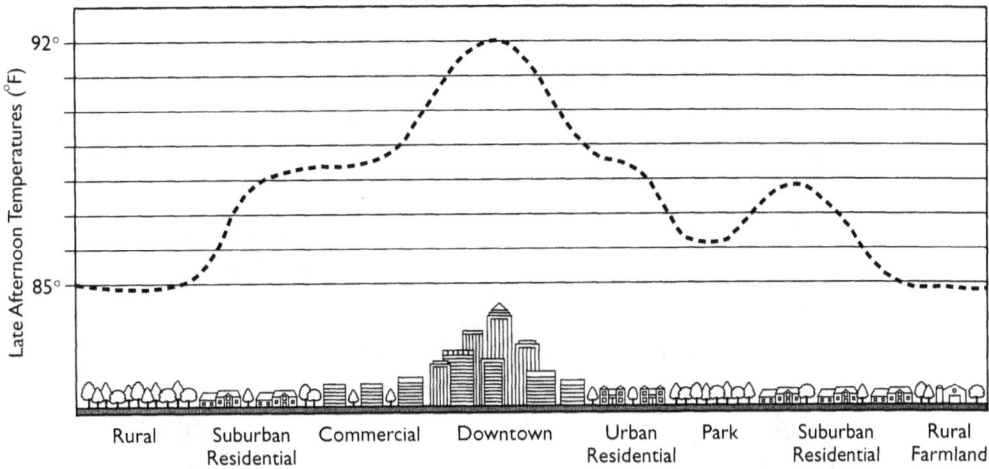

Urban Heat Island Profile

Source: U.S. EPA.

power by 2 percent, which translates to about $2–5 million worth of electricity every year over the entire city. In addition, metropolitan areas can lose federal transportation dollars if their states do not provide the U.S. Environmental Protection Agency (U.S. EPA) with an acceptable State Implementation Plan (SIP) to ensure compliance with U.S. EPA air quality standards for ozone.

LAND COVER ANALYSIS

To develop a heat island mitigation strategy, it is important to understand the relationship between land cover types and the formation of urban heat islands. Remote sensing data from satellites and aircraft can provide infrared images from which surface temperatures can be derived and associated with land cover and land-use classes.

In infrared images, warmer areas appear bright or white, and cooler areas appear dark, from gray to black. Brighter areas are often roofs and paved surfaces. Darker areas are primarily vegetation and highly reflective light roofs. Infrared satellite data at approximately 100-foot (30-meter) and coarser resolutions are available for all areas of the United States. By using these data, urban areas can be analyzed for hot spots in terms of their land cover or whatever elements exist on the land (e.g., forest, grass, concrete, asphalt, buildings and water). The spatial and temporal resolution of the imagery will influence the depth of possible analysis.

Based on a preliminary analysis of major land cover types in four cities—Atlanta, Georgia; Baton Rouge, Louisiana: Salt Lake City, Utah; and Sacramento, California—that were part of the joint NASA and U.S. EPA Urban Heat Island Pilot Project, conducted in 1998, surface temperatures by land cover type may be generalized from hottest to coldest, as follows:

- Dark roofs
- Roads and parking areas (dark asphalt is warmer than concrete, and aged asphalt is similar to concrete)
- Grass and other vegetation
- Forest
- Water

139

Planners, urban designers, urban foresters, and others can use remotely sensed data to identify hot spot areas and then develop appropriate urban heat island mitigation strategies.

MITIGATION STRATEGIES

Successful urban heat island mitigation strategies require community participation and acceptance. The identification of stakeholders and partners as early as possible will facilitate development and implementation of strategies.

As the connection between higher temperatures in urban areas and poor air quality continues to be realized, strategies such as using more reflective building materials and tree planting designs to reduce surface temperatures are becoming more popular. Continuing research indicates such strategies can improve air quality, promote energy savings, and produce the added benefit of increasing the livability of urban environments.

Local climate has a significant connection to the overall benefits that can be expected from urban heat island mitigation strategies. For example, areas with cooler mean temperatures and more cloudy days, as in the Pacific Northwest, would likely have less energy savings compared to the southwestern United States with its reduced cloud cover and rain and higher summertime temperatures. Also, the effect of sea breezes in dispersing pollutants may affect potential air quality benefits. Finally, trade-offs between roofing types and insulation may also be influenced by the local climate.

Reflective Roofs

When the sun shines on buildings with dark-colored roofs, most of the heat absorbed by the roof is transferred inside, which causes a number of adverse impacts: the demand for air conditioning increases; energy usage and costs are higher; and the roof materials deteriorate more rapidly. More than 90 percent of the roofs in the United States reach summer peak temperatures of 150°F (66° C) to 190°F (88° C). Materials commonly used in commercial property roofing include ethylene propylene diene monomer (EPDM), a type of rubber and asphalt and tar with a gravel base.

Roofs with these materials have been found to be hot spots of surface heating in all four cities studied in the Urban Heat Island Pilot Project. By putting a lighter-colored material on the roof, such as river rock, the roof becomes cooler, primarily because it is more reflective. The insulating capability depends upon the thermal conductivity of the rock material: that is, the amount of energy absorbed by the rock that is then conducted to the roof.

Depending on the slope of a building's roof, two categories of roofing materials are available for use. Low-sloped roofs, with slopes of 2:12 or less (less than 2 inches of rise over 12 inches of run), are most commonly found on commercial and industrial buildings and can be covered with cool roof coatings or single-ply materials. Many cool, low-slope products are available, primarily white; however, manufacturers are working toward providing highly reflective, colored products for low-slope roofs.

Sloped roofs with more than 2 inches of rise per 12 inches of run are found mostly on houses and small commercial buildings. They are generally covered with clay or concrete tiles, metal roofing, shingles, or shakes. Cool roof products available for sloped roofs are much more limited, which includes the majority of the residential market, where aesthetic considerations become more important as well. The U.S. EPA's Energy Star Program and the Cool Roof Rating Council are two sources of additional information on cool roofing products.

Green Roofs

Cooler roofs can also be achieved by innovative rooftop design, which can also provide aesthetically pleasing and functional places. One design alternative is the so-called green roof, a combination of vegetation, hydrology, and architecture. Originally conceived in Iceland, where sod roofs and walls have been used for centuries, modern green roof technology was developed more than 30 years ago in Germany, and today it is a popular approach throughout Europe. Such roofs consist of several layers of protective materials, including a waterproof membrane at the base, a root barrier, an optional insulation layer, drainage layers, a filter fabric for fine soils, the growing medium, and the plant material. These systems are not designed for the weight of people or trees. However, they can be installed on roofs with slopes up to 33 percent.

Rooftop Gardens

In contrast to green roofs, rooftop gardens are more elaborately designed landscapes intended for human interaction and are engineered to conform to heavier load requirements. The City of Chicago, for example, has installed a rooftop garden on top of City Hall. The city also has plans to install gardens on other city ward buildings and buildings along elevated public transit routes.

Trees and Shading

Planting trees to shield buildings from the sun's rays can reduce the amount of heat buildings absorb. Within 10 to 15 years—the time it takes a tree to grow to a significant size—strategically placed trees can reduce heating and cooling costs for a typical home or office by an average of 10 to 20 percent.

Trees and vegetation are most useful when planted in strategic locations around buildings. Researchers have found that planting deciduous species to the west and east is typically most effective for cooling buildings, especially if these trees shade windows and part of the building's roof. Planting deciduous trees to the south may reap the benefits of solar energy in the winter, when the sun is low in the sky, because these trees shed their leaves in winter, allowing sunlight and warmth through. Conversely, planting evergreen species to the north is one approach to impede winter winds (Nowak and Dwyer 2000).

Shading pavements in parking lots and streets is also an effective way to cool and beautify urban areas. Trees can be planted around the perimeters or in medians inside parking lots or along streets. Some communities have enacted ordinances requiring street and parking lot planting. Generally, increased shading will make urban areas more comfortable and healthy for people.

Additional benefits from trees include reductions in stormwater runoff, erosion, and urban noise.

Paving Materials

Roads, parking lots, and driveways paved with dark impervious materials contribute to the urban heat island effect. Most paved surfaces in an urban area are asphalt or concrete. While dark new asphalt has a lower reflectivity and higher surface temperature than new concrete, as both surfaces age, the differences in reflectivity become significantly smaller. Additives can also be used with either surface to increase reflectivity and give planners a range of potential heat island mitigation options.

One technique, Ultra-Thin Whitetopping, can be used on roads and parking lots to reduce maintenance costs and cool surfaces. This process removes the outer several inches of deteriorated asphalt and tops the remaining asphalt with a concrete mold 2 to 4 inches thick. Key design elements include adequate pavement thickness, concrete strength, drainage, and jointing.

Porous pavement, an alternative for parking areas, tennis courts, pool decks, greenhouse floors, and patios, both reduces runoff and cools surfaces. It allows airflow and moisture to penetrate the paved surface, producing a cooler surface than impervious paving materials. Porous pavements can consist of concrete, asphalt, open-celled stones, and gravel mixed to create an open-cell structure allowing for the passage of air and water. Water is allowed to filter through the concrete layer and recharge groundwater sources, thereby reducing runoff volume and velocity.

Development Patterns

A study by Stone and Rodgers (2001) focused on the relationship between residential development patterns and urban heat island formation in the Atlanta, Georgia, area. While acknowledging that further work must be done to establish the significance between urban design decisions and heat island formation in different climactic areas, the authors found for the Atlanta area that lower-density housing patterns contribute more radiant heat to surface heat island formation than higher-density development. The amount of land dedicated to residential lawns and landscape planting in areas of one-half- to three-acre lots emitted higher net thermal emissions than areas with one-eighth- to one-half-acre lots. Compact moderate to high-density new construction, along with area-based tree ordinances, are recommended as policy strategies to mitigate the effects of development on regional climate change.

REFERENCES

Nowak, D. J., and J. F. Dwyer. 2000. "Understanding the Benefits and Costs of Urban Forest Ecosystems." In *Handbook of Urban and Community Forestry in the Northeast*. J. E. Kuser, ed. New York: Kluwer Academic/Plenum Publishers.

Stone, Brian Jr., and Michael O. Rodgers. 2001. "Urban Form and Thermal Efficiency: How the Design of Cities Influences the Urban Heat Island Effect ..." *Journal of the American Planning Association.* 67, no. 2: 186–198.

See also:
Air Quality
Remote Sensing and Satellite Image Classification

LAND USE AND THE CONSTITUTION

INTRODUCTION AND THE CONSTITUTIONAL ANALYSIS TREE

BY THE AMERICAN PLANNING ASSOCIATION

SECTION 1:

PURPOSE

This handbook for planners was conceived by planners and lawyers in the summer of 1987 in the wake of the U.S. Supreme Court's important land use decisions in *Keystone, First English,* and *Nollan* which, incidentally, coincided with our country's bicentennial celebration of the U.S. Constitution. The book's purpose is to provide professional and citizen planners with a practical, usable guide to federal constitutional principles for land use planning practice. In short, it is a response to Justice Brennan's exhortation in *San Diego Gas and Electric Co. v. City of San Diego*, 450 U.S. 621, 655 n.26 (1981), (Brennan, J., dissenting) that planners as well as policemen should "know the Constitution." Some planners may not agree with Brennan's equation of the extent of policemen's and planners' responsibilities in the constitutional arena. However, there is no doubt that the Supreme Court's recent decisions have motivated planners to know the constitutional limits of the regulatory programs that they propound—to avoid what one planner described as "the feeling of walking backwards toward a cliff."

Why the focus on federal constitutional principles? After all, landowners' property interests are defined by state law, and the vast majority of land use court decisions concern questions of state law decided by state courts. There are four principal reasons. First, the supremacy clause, Article VI of the Constitution, states that there are certain minimum constitutional requirements that the states must observe. That clause, in effect, places a floor of constitutional limitations below which local governments may not go in their imposition of land use controls.

Second, land use decisions by local governments can raise federal constitutional questions based on the Fifth Amendment's just compensation (takings) clause made applicable to the states through the Fourteenth Amendment, and based on the due process and equal protection clauses of the Fourteenth Amendment itself. These federal constitutional provisions drawn from the Bill of Rights and the supremacy clause together establish the floor of federally protected rights. The constitutions of the individual states and court decisions interpreting them can always *expand* on individual rights. But the Constitution establishes the minimum floor of protection against the exercise of governmental power. It is that floor which this book endeavors to define in practical terms for planners (see illustration).

Third, consistent with the supremacy clause, the U.S. Supreme Court has now determined that if it can be proven that certain land use regulations effect a taking of property, then just compensation in the form of monetary damages is due to the property owner as a matter of law under the Fifth Amendment regardless of what the state law says. It is this newly enunciated principle that perhaps gives Justice Brennan's exhortation the most urgency.

Finally, the Supreme Court has said that the Civil Rights Act of 1871 [42 U.S.C. §1983] applies to the actions of local governments. This law does not give property owners any additional rights, but it does, by statute, give them an independent source of remedies, including injunctive relief, damages, and attorneys' fees. As applied to local governments this law potentially gives property owners the right to damages on proof of any deprivation of their rights under the Constitution, not just the taking clause.

For these reasons, planners are well served to have a book which dimensions the edges of each of the boards making up the floor of

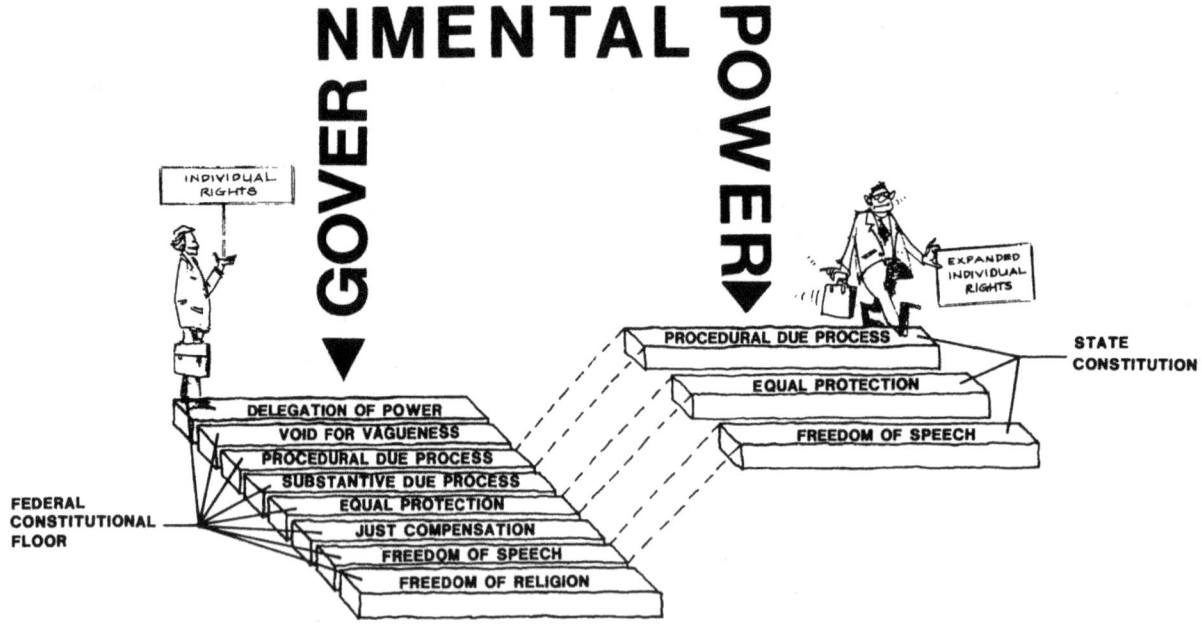

federal constitutional principles that apply to land use planning practice. At the same time, the book does not ignore state law, because it is important for planners to know that there are areas in which the state courts have established doctrines that either parallel the federal constitutional doctrines or largely supplant federal courts' pronouncements in a particular area. Indeed, throughout the book, particularly in the transcribed dialogue of the planners and lawyers who participated in a symposium in St. Louis to discuss the draft manuscript of the book, readers will note some marked differences in emphasis and interpretation among the symposium participants concerning federal and state legal principles. This is not surprising. It reflects the larger tension between the federal government and the states that was recognized by the original drafters of the U.S. Constitution and ultimately in the adoption of the Bill of Rights.

SECTION 4:

OVERVIEW OF LEGAL TERMS IN RELATION TO CONSTITUTIONAL PRINCIPLES

The constitutional principles are presented and discussed in the following order:

- Principle 1: Delegation of Power
- Principle 2: Void for Vagueness
- Principle 3: Procedural Due Process
- Principle 4: Substantive Due Process
- Principle 5: Equal Protection
- Principle 6: Just Compensation (the taking clause)
- Principle 7: Freedom of Speech
- Principle 8: Freedom of Religion

To the extent possible, these constitutional principles are organized and explained so as to reflect a sequence and interrelationship that will be useful to planners. In doing so, it is necessary to use certain legal terms, which, once understood, will greatly assist planners in understanding and discussing the constitutional principles and their application to typical land use planning problems. What follows is a brief overview of those legal terms as they relate to the constitutional principles presented in Part II.

4.01 LEGAL TERMS GENERALLY

[1] police power; [2] property interest; [3] entitlement; [4] vested right; [5] estoppel; [6] expectancy interest; [7] nuisance; [8] downzoning; [9] upzoning; [10] as applied challenge; [11] facial challenge.

Police power is a shorthand term for the legislative or policy-making power that resides in each state to establish laws and ordinances to preserve public order and tranquility and to promote the public health, safety, and morals and other aspects of the general welfare. The zoning of property derives from the state's police power. Generally, each state has delegated the power to zone property and exercise other land use controls to the local governments (counties, cities, villages, and towns) within their jurisdictions by means of specific zoning enabling legislation. Local governments may also have additional authority to regulate land use deriving from a more general delegation of the police power.

The application of zoning and other land use controls by local governments affects land, also known as real property, or more accurately, affects **property interests.** The term property interest, when referring to real property or land, is not synonymous with *title* to property, since legal title to real property is only one form of property interest. A property interest is merely a person's right to have the benefits of the particular type of interest the person holds in the property. For example, a person who holds legal title to a parcel of real property has the right to use the property, to exclude others from using it, and to sell the property for value. By contrast, a person whose property interest is the grant of an *easement* of access to certain property does not actually own the land across which the easement lies, but merely has the right to use the land described within the easement area for access to the property. Depending on the nature of the grant of the easement, the person who is given the easement may or may not have the right to exclude others from using the easement for the same purpose for which it was given. A permit is another form of property interest.

If an individual actually has a right to a particular property interest, that right is often referred to as an **entitlement.** In the land use context, a landowner is frequently said to have an entitlement to a property interest if his or her right has accrued or vested. A **vested right** to a property interest is a right which the law recognizes as having accrued to an individual by virtue of certain circumstances and that as a matter of constitutional law cannot be arbitrarily taken away from that individual. The theory of vested rights has particular application in cases where government makes zoning changes which affect development projects in progress. In such cases, a developer may argue that it has acquired a vested right in the prior zoning. The developer may also use the theory of **estopped** and argue that the government is estopped, or precluded by its own acts, from making the zoning change that affects the developer's property. Unlike the theory of vested rights, estoppel is based on the concept of equity or fairness. It requires proof that the landowner or developer made substantial expenditure in good faith reliance on some act of omission of the government. As a practical matter, the facts needed to prove a vested right or estoppel in a zoning case are identical, and the courts frequently use the terms *vested rights* and *estoppel* interchangeably.

If a right to a property interest is merely hoped for or not yet vested, it is frequently referred to as an **expectancy interest.** For example, a landowner can usually demonstrate an entitlement to a building permit on compliance with all the application requirements, because the administrative official authorized to approve building permits usually has no discretion to grant or deny a building permit if all the requirements for issuance are met. However, where the administrative official or body is delegated the authority with standards to exercise discretion in deciding whether or not to give a certain type of approval such as a variance, a landowner is said merely to have an expectancy interest in the variance.

The term **nuisance** refers to the use of one's property in a manner that seriously interferes with another's use or enjoyment of his or her property (a private nuisance) or is injurious to the community at large (a public nuisance). Unlike trespass to land, nuisance does not require a physical invasion of others' property. In a private nuisance case, the land use that is claimed to be a nuisance is usually adjacent or close to the plaintiff's property and the plaintiff seeks to prohibit the use by injunction and obtain damages for injury suffered. Zoning was originally based on concepts of nuisance and consisted of a comprehensive scheme for separating incompatible land uses into mapped zones or districts. Because of the adoption of zoning in most communities, private nuisance actions are used less frequently by landowners to resolve land use disputes. However, a land use permitted by a zoning ordinance may still be operated in such a way as to constitute a nuisance.

In the exercise of zoning under the police power, a local government may decide to change the zoning classification of certain property or reduce the permitted density. For example, a zoning classification may be changed from commercial to residential or from industrial to residential, or the density may be reduced from 30 units per acre to 10. This change in the zoning classification to a less intensive use or a lower density is referred to as **downzoning.** The reverse action is frequently referred to as **upzoning.** These terms can be misleading. In some parts of the country, they are sometimes used to mean the opposite from the definitions just given. Furthermore, a developer's view that the rezoning of a parcel of property constitutes a downzoning may be directly at odds with the perspective of the neighbors.

Regardless of what terminology is used, a property owner whose property is rezoned against his or her will, or a neighborhood which objects to a rezoning, may decide to bring suit in state or federal court claiming that way the zoning ordinance was applied to particular property was unconstitutional. In this type of legal challenge, termed an **as applied challenge,** the landowner or neighbor does not attack the constitutionality of the zoning ordinance itself; rather, they argue that while the ordinance may be constitutional in general terms, its application to the property under the specific facts of the case is unconstitutional. However, if the person suing believes that the zoning provisions themselves are inherently unconstitutional, that is, that the language of those provisions violates certain constitutional limitations, then that person may decide to challenge those zoning provisions in their entirety without reference to any specific case in which they have been applied. This type of legal challenge is referred to as a **facial challenge.** A challenge to a regulation on its face is also sometimes described as a challenge to the regulation per se.

4.02 LEGAL TERMS: PROCEDURAL DUE PROCESS

[1] due process; [2] separation of powers; [3] legislative decision-making; [4] ex parte contacts; [5] findings of fact; [6] administrative decision-making; [7] quasi-judicial decision-making; [8] adjudicative.

The term **due process** or, more accurately, due process of law, refers to the constitutional protections given to persons to ensure that laws are not unreasonable, arbitrary, or capricious. When such laws affect individuals' lives, liberty, and property, due process requires that they have sufficient notice and opportunity to be heard in an orderly proceeding suited to the nature of the matter at issue, whether a court of law or a zoning board of appeals. In a word, due process means fairness.

There are three terms which have particular application in the context of procedural due process—separation of powers, legislative decision-making, and quasi-judicial decision-making. The term **separation of powers** refers to the notion originally expressed by the Supreme Court in the late Nineteenth century that each branch of government must be limited to the powers appropriate to its functions. Through subsequent decisions, the term has come to encompass the concept that each branch is also dependent on the others to exercise their respective functions and that at least two branches of government must cooperate before governmental choices affecting individual rights can be put into effect.

Legislative power is the power of the legislative branch to make laws, that is, to establish public policy. The making of legislative decisions is generally not subject to the requirements of the due process clause. This means that **legislative decision-making** is relatively informal.

Members of the legislative body are not prevented from communicating with individuals outside the legislative chamber before making a decision. Such **ex parte contacts** outside of the hearing on a particular matter are permissible in legislative decision-making, and participants at a legislative hearing cannot challenge the information obtained through such contacts. In addition, in making legislative decisions, the legislative body, whether it is a state legislature, a county board of commissioners, or a city council, is not required to recite the facts it considered in reaching its decision. Such a requirement that a decision-making body make written **findings of fact** and demonstrate in writing that its decision is supported by those facts is a procedural requirement that the due process clause imposes on **administrative decision-making.**

Administrative decision-making concerns actions or decisions to carry out policies or purposes previously declared by the legislative body. At the federal level, by virtue of the doctrine of separation of powers, such decisions are viewed as falling within the governmental powers assigned to the executive branch and its departments. At the local level, where the separation of powers doctrine does not apply in the same fashion, such administrative decision-making is usually performed by boards or commissions established by the legislative body. These bodies are subject to procedural due process requirements which include holding formal hearings on matters for decision, avoiding *ex parte* contacts outside of hearings, providing the opportunity for cross examination on the evidence presented, and preparing written findings of fact and conclusions. Because administrative bodies must review and draw conclusions from facts presented with respect to a specific parcel of property under procedural requirements that are similar to those followed in a court of law, their actions are sometimes referred to as **quasi-judicial** or **adjudicative,** that is, judicial-type or adjudicating actions performed by individuals who are not judges. In some jurisdictions, notably Oregon, the courts have held that a decision by a local legislative body concerning the zoning of an individual parcel is a quasi-judicial rather than a legislative decision.

4.03 LEGAL TERMS: SUBSTANTIVE DUE PROCESS

[1] presumption of constitutionality; [2] fairly debatable rule; [3] arbitrary and capricious.

In addition to imposing procedural requirements on land use decision-making, the due process clause also imposes substantive requirements; for example, the requirement that land use controls further legitimate governmental purposes. When a land use regulation is challenged in court as not advancing a legitimate governmental purpose, the court usually will start its analysis of the regulation with a legal presumption, namely that the regulation in question is constitutional. This **presumption of constitutionality** means that the person challenging the regulation, or regulatory decision, has the burden—a heavy one—of presenting evidence sufficient to overcome the presumption in favor of the constitutionality of the regulation.

This presumption cannot be overcome if the evidence presented regarding the legitimate purpose of the regulation merely raises questions about which people could reasonably differ. This judicial rule is known as the **fairly debatable rule** or the reasonably debatable rule. When the evidence presented does not raise questions about which people could reasonably differ and indicates instead that the government's action was arbitrary, the court may invalidate the regulation on the ground that it is **arbitrary and**

capricious, meaning that the regulation has no substantial relation to the public health, safety, morals, or general welfare.

4.04 LEGAL TERMS: EQUAL PROTECTION

[1] equal protection; [2] suspect classification; [3] strict scrutiny.

Because land use regulation involves the classification of land uses through the drawing of zone lines and the imposition of use standards, such classifications can raise questions of **equal protection.** Equal protection is a shorthand way of referring to equal protection of the laws which, in general constitutional terms, refers to the right of all persons under like circumstances to enjoy equal protection and security in their life, their liberty, and their property and to bear no greater burdens than are imposed on others under like circumstances. Equal protection in the land use context means that there must be a legitimate governmental purpose for the classifications and use restrictions that are applied to properties; properties which are similarly situated must be treated similarly, unless there is a rational justification for their disparate treatment. In sum, equal protection means equal treatment.

Where a land use classification impinges on such constitutional rights as freedom of speech, freedom of association and privacy, and freedom from discrimination on the basis of race—all considered fundamental rights guaranteed under the First and Fourteenth Amendments to the Constitution—a court will term such classification a **suspect classification.** A suspect classification triggers a more rigorous form of judicial review called **strict scrutiny,** meaning that the court requires a precise showing by the proponents of the regulation that it is justified by a compelling governmental interest.

4.05 LEGAL TERMS: JUST COMPENSATION (TAKING CLAUSE)

[1] taking; [2] eminent domain; [3] regulatory taking; [4] just compensation; [5] inverse condemnation; [6] development exaction; [7] nexus; [6] average reciprocity of advantage.

Government appropriation of private land, either directly pursuant to a statute, or indirectly, through the restrictive effect of its regulations, is termed a **taking** of property. A taking of property by local government may occur directly through **eminent domain,** which is the power of government to condemn or take property for public use, an attribute of sovereignty. Or, it may occur indirectly through regulation. The latter is termed a **regulatory taking.** The Fifth Amendment limits the government's power by requiring that government pay **just compensation** when it takes private property under the eminent domain power or by regulation. The term *just compensation* means that the owner is entitled to the fair market value of the property which was taken. The owner is entitled to the value of the property to the owner—not the worth to the government—at the time of taking. Where government regulation has taken private property and the government has not exercised any formal eminent domain proceedings, a landowner may seek to recover the value of property taken by instituting a legal action known in most states as an action for **inverse condemnation.**

One form of regulation which raises taking issues is the **development exaction.** A development exaction is a contribution requirement in the form of land or money which government imposes on new development as a condition for development approval, usually in order to accommodate the need for capital facilities and services created by the new development.

In order to determine the constitutionality of a development exaction, a court will address various questions, including whether there is a sufficient demonstrated relationship or **nexus** between the burden imposed on the development and the need which the development is said to have created.

In determining whether a regulatory taking has occurred, the court will examine some, but not necessarily all, of the factors discussed in Part II, Section 6. Usually, however, the court will at least examine the degree of decline in property value in order to determine if the economic loss imposed by the regulation amounts to a taking. There are various economic loss theories. In a landmark opinion in *Pennsylvania Coal Company v. Mahon*, 260 U.S. 393 (1922), Justice Holmes labeled one of these theories **average reciprocity of advantage.** This phrase refers to the proposition that a land use restriction that burdens all land within a district may also benefit that land by virtue of the fact that all of the land is equally restricted. Thus a regulation which prohibits certain uses in a residential area has the reciprocal benefit of preventing all property subject to the regulation from being harmed by those uses. Where a court determines that this circumstance exists, it may conclude that there is no taking because the benefits conferred equal the burdens imposed.

4.06 LEGAL TERMS: FREEDOM OF SPEECH AND RELIGION

[1] overbreadth doctrine; [2] vagueness; [3] prior restraint.

Because freedom of speech and freedom of religion are fundamental rights guaranteed by the First Amendment, a principal area of inquiry when courts review regulations which may impinge on those rights, is whether the regulation sweeps so broadly that it encompasses subject matter or behavior that is constitutionally protected. That is the meaning of the **overbreadth doctrine.** This doctrine, while important in the application of other constitutional principles, has particular application to regulations challenged on first amendment grounds. In applying the overbreadth doctrine, a court examines the extent to which regulatory terms are vague. The term **vagueness** has particular legal significance; it is a concept, based on procedural due process concerns about adequate notice, which requires courts to invalidate a regulation that is so unclear or ambiguous that a person of normal intelligence will not be able to comprehend what the regulation forbids or permits.

One other possible effect of regulation which the Supreme Court has held to be particularly offensive to the free speech protections afforded by the First Amendment is **prior restraint.** In essence it means the preventing or forbidding of speech unless there is prior approval by a government official. Licensing requirements, when made part of land use regulatory schemes that apply to expressive activities, can potentially create prior restraints. The concept of vagueness and prior restraint are interrelated. Where a regulation is so unclear or ambiguous that a person does not know whether a particular type of expression is permitted, there is a strong likelihood that unregulated expression will be deterred, which effectively causes a voluntary prior restraint.

CONSTITUTIONAL ANALYSIS TREE

SECTION 1:

PURPOSE

The following outline provides planners with a form of constitutional decision tree for use in addressing the types of problem-solving areas presented in Part III of this book. The outline is not intended to be exhaustive of all issues that must be considered in preparing regulations addressing the specific problem-solving areas discussed. Rather, its purpose is to provide planners with a concise summary of the constitutional considerations discussed in Part III, which can be used in consultation with their legal counsel to identify possible constitutional issues in proposed land use regulations.

SECTION 2:

CONSTITUTIONAL ANALYSIS TREE

DISCRETIONARY PERMITTING

Delegation of Power	**Void for Vagueness**
[a] Is there clearly articulated legislative policy as to the general circumstances when a discretionary approval is appropriate?	[a] Are there meaningful standards that alert a reasonably intelligent applicant to the criteria by which his application will be judged?
[b] Does the decision-making body have unfettered authority to determine when and if a discretionary permit should be issued?	[b] Do the standards indicate the weight to be given to each of the criteria in making a discretionary decision?
	[c] Are the standards for the issuance of a discretionary permit sufficiently definite that a court can review an individual decision and determine whether the decision was arbitrary and capricious?

Procedural Due Process	**Substantive Due Process**
[a] Are there established procedures for the consideration of an application for a discretionary permit?	[a] Does the discretionary permitting process serve a valid public purpose?
[b] Do the procedures provide for a reasonable opportunity for the applicant to present material and information in support of his application?	[b] Is the relationship between the provisions authorizing a discretionary permit and the public health, safety and welfare apparent?
[c] If there is a public hearing, is notice of the hearing sufficient to alert affected persons of the hearing?	**Equal Protection**
[d] Do the procedures afford the applicant a reasonable opportunity to respond to staff or citizen input in regard to the application?	[a] Do the standards ensure that similarly situated persons will receive comparable treatment?
	[b] Are the standards such that any [classifications] are based on a reasonably logical and apparent basis?
	[c] Are the standards such that no suspect class of persons (e.g. minorities) are singled out for disparate treatment?

AESTHETIC REGULATION

Delegation of Power	**Substantive Due Process**
[a] Is there a clear grant of power from the state to the municipality authorizing it to regulate aesthetics?	[a] Does the design review ordinance serve a valid public purpose?
[b] Is there a clearly articulated legislative policy regarding the purpose for both citywide and building or district specific design standards?	[b] Is the relationship between the standards, embodied in the ordinance and the public health, safety, and welfare apparent?

[c] Is the discretion of the architectural review board clearly limited by standards contained in the ordinance? [d] Do the standards indicate the weight to be given to each of the criteria in making a design review decision?	**Equal Protection** [a] Do the standards ensure that similarly situated persons will receive comparable treatment? [b] Are the standards such that any classifications are based on a reasonably logical and apparent basis?
Procedural Due Process	**Just Compensation (Taking)**
[a] Are there established procedures for consideration of an application for design review? [b] Do the procedures provide for a reasonable opportunity for the applicant to present material and information in support of his application? [c] Do the procedures afford the applicant a reasonable opportunity to respond to staff or citizen input regarding the application? [d] Are applicants provided sufficient notice of the hearing on their application?	[a] Do the standards, as written and applied, allow property owners to retain a reasonable use of their property?

SPECIAL EXCEPTION

Delegation of Power	**Equal Protection**
[a] Is there clearly articulated legislative policy as to the general circumstances when a legislative approval is appropriate? [b] Does the decision-making body have unfettered authority to determine when and if a special use permit should be granted?	[a] Do the standards ensure that similarly situated persons will receive comparable treatment? [b] Are the standards such that any classifications are based on a reasonably logical and apparent basis?
Substantive Due Process	**Just Compensation (Taking)**
[a] Does the special use permitting process serve a valid public purpose? [b] Is the relationship between the provisions authorizing a special use permit and the public health, safety, and welfare apparent?	[a] Does the denial of the special exception requested still leave the property owner with a reasonable use of his property?

NEGOTIATED (REZONING) APPROVALS

Delegation of Power	**Substantive Due Process**
[a] Is there clearly articulated legislative policy as to the general circumstances when a rezoning of this sort is appropriate? [b] Does the decision-making body have unfettered authority to determine when and if a discretionary zoning should be adopted?	[a] Does the discretionary rezoning process serve a valid public purpose? [b] Is the relationship between the provisions authorizing a discretionary rezoning and the public health, safety, and welfare apparent?

Procedural Due Process	**Equal Protection**
[a] If quasi-judicial: Are there established procedures for the consideration of an application for a discretionary (negotiated) rezoning?	[a] Do the standards ensure that similarly situated persons will receive comparable treatment?
[b] If quasi-judicial: Do the procedures provide for a reasonable opportunity for the developer applicant to present material and information in support of his application?	[b] Are the standards such that any classifications are based on a reasonably logical and apparent basis?
[c] If quasi-judicial: If there is a public hearing, is notice of the hearing sufficient to alert affected persons of the hearing?	[c] Are the standards such that no suspect class of persons (e.g. minorities) are singled out for disparate treatment?
[d] If quasi-judicial: Do the procedures afford the applicant a reasonable opportunity to respond to staff or citizen input in regard to the application?	

PROHIBITION OF ADULT USES

Void for Vagueness	**Freedom of Speech**
[a] Are the definitions in the ordinance sufficiently specific to alert a reasonably intelligent individual as to which products and publications are the subject of the ordinance?	[a] Does the ordinance attempt to place a prior restraint on freedom of speech by defining certain products and publications as obscene and prohibiting their sale or exhibition?
[b] Are the definitions in the ordinance sufficiently definite that a court can review an individual decision and determine whether the decision was arbitrary and capricious?	[b] Does the ordinance attempt to exclude adult businesses rather than to regulate their location?

Equal Protection	**Substantive Due Process**
[a] Does the regulation discriminate between two or more similarly situated property owners?	[a] Does the regulation substantially advance public health safety and welfare?
	[b] Does the legislation itself identify the public interest to be served and are their studies, findings, etc. forming the basis of the means selected to promote that interest?

PROHIBITION OF PLACES OF WORSHIP

Substantive Due Process	**Equal Protection**
[a] Does the ordinance apply retroactively in addition to prospectively?	[a] Does the ordinance ensure that similarly situated religious institutions will receive comparable treatment?
[b] If the ordinance does apply retroactively, is there a strong public interest involved and is the owner of the subject property given a reasonable period of time to comply with the new standard?	[b] Are the provisions in the ordinance such that classifications are based on a reasonably logical and apparent basis?

Freedom of Religion

[a] If the ordinance totally excludes houses of worship from residential neighborhoods, is this permissible under state law?

[b] If the ordinance regulates religious activities for accepted planning reasons, do the benefits gained from the regulation greatly outweigh the burdens imposed on the religious activities?

[c] If the ordinance regulates secular activities conducted by the religious institution, does the ordinance comply with constitutional due process and equal protection standards?

PROHIBITION OF GROUP HOMES

Equal Protection

[a] Do the standards in the ordinance ensure that similarly situated persons will receive comparable treatment?

[b] Are the standards such that any classifications are based on a reasonably logical and apparent basis?

[c] Do the reasons stated by the city for denying a permit rest on neutral grounds or are they based on unjustifiable discrimination against the mentally ill?

DOWNZONING

Procedural Due Process	Substantive Due Process
[a] Did the property owner receive sufficient advance notice of the proposed rezoning?	[a] Does the downzoning serve a legitimate public purpose?
[b] Was the owner afforded a fair opportunity to be heard on the issue and evidence before the rezoning authority?	[b] Does the master plan support the downzoning?
	[c] Has the property been singled out and treated differently from similar adjacent or nearby properties?
	[d] Does the public record state valid land use reasons for the downzoning?

Equal Protection	Just Compensation (Taking)
[a] Do the standards ensure that similarly situated persons will receive comparable treatment?	[a] Does the downzoning substantially advance a legitimate governmental interest?
[b] Is the effect of the downzoning to zone out lower income people from the community?	[b] Does the downzoning take away all reasonable use of the property?
	[c] Is the owner's distinct, investment-backed expectations substantially destroyed?

PARCEL REZONING

Procedural Due Process	**Substantive Due Process**
[a] Under the applicable state law, is rezoning considered a legislative act or an administrative or quasi-judicial act?	[a] Is there a valid public purpose underlying the rezoning? Does the rezoning advance the public health, safety, welfare, and morals? is the link between the public objectives and the rezoning evident?
[b] Are there established procedures for rezoning and, if so, have they been followed?	[b] Is there a comprehensive plan? If so, does the rezoning conform to it? If the rezoning does not conform to the plan, have conditions in the area which would be affected by the rezoning changed materially since adoption of the plan?
[c] Is there a comprehensive plan? If so, does the rezoning conform to it, and have the planners participated in evaluation of the rezoning proposal in light of the plan?	[c] Would the uses allowed under the rezoning be harmonious with the current nearby uses? Is the area to be rezoned an island in the midst of another type of land use, or is it on a boundary between uses?

Equal Protection	
[a] Does the rezoning establish a classification of land which appears logical?	
[b] Are landowners whose land has similar characteristics treated similarly?	

	Just Compensation (Taking)
	[a] Does the rezoning "substantially advance" a "legitimate state interest? Is there a strong link between the effect of the rezoning and the public purpose to be served?
	[b] Would the rezoning so reduce the value of the parcel as to leave the owner with no reasonable economic use?
	[c] Is the rezoning likely to be temporary rather than permanent and, if so, what reduction in value would occur as a result of this temporary restriction?

INTERIM LAND USE CONTROLS

Procedural Due Process	**Substantive Due Process**
[a] Are there established procedures for the consideration of an application for a demolition permit?	[a] Does the ordinance serve a valid public purpose?
[b] Do the procedures provide for a reasonable opportunity for the applicant to present material and information in support of his application?	[b] Is the relationship between the provisions authorizing the moratorium and the public health, safety, and welfare apparent?
[c] If there is a public hearing, is notice of the hearing sufficient to alert affected persons of the hearing?	**Equal Protection**
	[a] Do the standards ensure that similarly situated persons will receive comparable treatment?
[d] Do the procedures afford the applicant a reasonable opportunity to respond to staff or citizen input in regard to the application?	[b] Are the standards such that any classifications are based on a reasonably logical and apparent basis?
	[c] Are the standards such that no suspect class of persons (e.g. racial minorities) are singled-out for disparate treatment?

Just Compensation (Taking)

[a] Does the interim regulation deny property owners an economically viable use of their property?

[b] Has the interim regulation which temporarily denies property owners of all economically viable use of their property been extended without justification?

RESOURCE PROTECTION

Substantive Due Process	Just Compensation (Taking)
[a] Does the city's action limiting density/use on the property bear some substantial relationship to the public health, safety, and welfare?	[a] Does the city's action leave the landowner with a physically possible use of his property?
[b] Does an explanation exist for why the city acted which can be said to "make any sense at all?"	[b] Is the physically possible use of the property economically feasible?
[c] Is the explanation for the city's action based on reliable, believable information?	[c] Is the developer's proposed use consistent with natural character of the site or does the developer's proposal require that the site be altered to accommodate the proposed use?

AMORTIZATION OF NONCONFORMING USE

Substantive Due Process

[a] Does the amortization provision serve a valid public purpose?

Just Compensation (Taking)	Equal Protection
[a] Is the amortization period of sufficient length to allow the owner of the nonconforming use to recoup his investment?	[a] Do the amortization provisions ensure that similarly situated persons will receive comparable treatment?
	[b] Are the differing amortization periods supported by a reasonable policy that can be supported by facts?

DEVELOPMENT EXACTIONS

Substantive Due Process	Equal Protection
[a] Does the regulation substantially advance public health, safety, and welfare?	[a] Do the standards ensure that similarly situated persons will receive comparable treatment?
[b] Does the legislation itself identify the public interest to be served and are there studies, findings, etc. forming the basis of the means selected to promote that interest?	[b] Are the standards such that any classifications are based on a reasonably logical and apparent basis?

Just Compensation

[a] Is there a demonstrable fit or "nexus" between the exaction imposed upon the property owner as a condition to granting a permit and the public need or burden created by the proposed development?

[b] Does the regulation substantially advance a legitimate state interest?

GROWTH PHASING

Void for Vagueness	**Substantive Due Process**

[a] Are there discernable standards in the regulation which
    [1] are rationally based and
    [2] adequately alert an applicant to the criteria to be used in applying the ordinance?
 	
[b] Are the standards utilized sufficiently definite so that decisions may be reviewed on the basis of the application of the standards to a given proposal?
	[a] Does the regulation substantially advance public health, safety, and welfare?
	
	[b] Does the legislation itself identify the public interest to be served, and are their studies, findings, etc. forming the basis of the means selected to promote that interest?

GROWTH PHASING

Equal Protection	**Just Compensation (Taking)**
[a] Does the regulation discriminate between two or more similarly situated people? [b] If so, does it discriminate between a member(s) of a "suspect class" and others? [c] If not, is the regulation rationally related to a legitimate public concern?	[a] Is the impact of the regulation on a landowner such that it either prevents any reasonable use of his property or denies a recognizable property right in the regulated parcel (e.g. the right to exclude others)? [b] If so, does the regulation substantially advance a legitimate state interest? If not, the regulation may result in a "taking". If "yes", no taking occurs *unless* the regulation nevertheless denies the owner all economically viable use of the property as a whole, in which event a compensable taking has probably occurred. [c] Does the regulation, as applied, destroy a "vested" property right under state law?

Equal Protection	
[d] If so, is there a compelling state interest justifying the disparate treatment?	

LAND USE PLANNING AND DEVELOPMENT REGULATION LAW

CHAPTER 2: *Comprehensive Plans and the Planning Process*
CHAPTER 3: *Land Use Controls: History, Sources of Power and Purposes*

BY JULIAN CONRAD JURGENSMEYER, THOMAS E. ROBERTS, PATRICIA E. SALKIN, AND RYAN MAX ROWBERRY

CHAPTER 2: COMPREHENSIVE PLANS AND THE PLANNING PROCESS

I. PLANNERS AND PLANNING

§ 2:1 THE PRACTICE OF PLANNING

There is no universally accepted definition of planning, nor is there a definition of "planner" which would be endorsed by all those who now practice urban planning. Currently, only one state, New Jersey,[1] as well as the Commonwealth of Puerto Rico,[2] have legislation concerned with defining or licensing the urban planner as a professional.[3] Nevertheless, those involved with urban planning would generally agree that the planner who deals with land use regulation has several principal characteristics.[4]

First, the planner has technical training at the undergraduate or graduate school level, often in one of the many university urban planning programs, or possibly in another discipline such as engineering, architecture or landscape architecture.

Second, the planner is future-oriented. The urban planner believes that by analyzing existing conditions, forecasting future trends, and establishing normative goals and policies, an optimum path for the development or redevelopment of a geographic area may be formulated.

Julian Conrad Jurgensmeyer, Thomas E. Roberts, Patricia E. Salkin, and Ryan Max Rowberry, "'Comprehensive Plans and the Planning Process' and 'Land Use Controls: History, Sources of Power, and Purposes,'" *Land Use Planning and the Development Regulation Law*, pp. 15-62. Copyright © 2018 by West Academic Publishing. Reprinted with permission.

This process usually results in a "plan." In addition, many urban planners perform independent projections, statistical analyses, studies of housing needs and conditions in blighted or underdeveloped areas, and draft municipal ordinances for zoning, aesthetic regulation, and environmental protection. These studies are often done in conjunction with the process of preparing a plan.

Third, the planner acts as a catalyst in the political process by which plans and land use regulations are developed, adopted, and implemented by a local government such as a county or city. This catalytic role arises from the planner's function as an analyst of conditions and trends in development or decline, and as a proponent of alternative means to guide the development, or redevelopment, of urban and rural areas. As the proponent of new regulations and of the plan, the planner exerts an influence through the legislative and administrative processes by which local governments plan for, and regulate, development.

Planners are most often employees of governmental agencies. According to a 2012 APA/AICP Survey:

> The typical (median) planner is 44 years old and has been in the planning field for 14 years. Almost all (95%) planners indicated at least one area of specialization, the most common being community development and redevelopment (51%), and land-use or code enforcement (45%). Other common areas of specialization include transportation planning (30%), environmental and natural resources planning (26%), economic planning and development (25%), urban design (22%), and sustainability (20%). 71% of planners work in public agencies and 22% in private consulting firms. 62% of planners report their principal place of employment is located in a city, another 21% indicated a suburb, 12% a small town, and 4% a rural area.[5]

The planning profession has been seeking recognition as a profession for several decades. Engineers, architects, and landscape architects are often found in planning positions, but many colleges and universities now offer bachelor, masters, and doctoral degrees in urban planning. Curricula in these academic programs range from a technical, design-oriented approach, termed "physical planning" by planning theorists, to a more policy-oriented approach at the opposite extreme. Considerable intermixing of the two disciplines in planning occurs in practice.

In an effort to foster professionalism, the American Institute of Certified Planners (the professional component of the American Planning Association)[6] administers an examination and certification program for urban planners. Passing the application and examination criteria entitles the planner to present himself as a "certified planner." Increasingly, government agencies seeking to fill positions request applicants with such certification. However, it has not yet become a thoroughly-established prerequisite for the practice of urban planning in either government or the private sector.

Thus, the planner may be educated in a field other than planning, and if so, is likely to be a licensed engineer, architect, or landscape architect. In truth, these professionals have not recently invaded the field of urban planning. Rather, the modern science of urban planning grew out of the efforts of individuals in these fields to design cities to accommodate the rapid growth that has consistently characterized the history of the United States. A debate continues to take place among these professions regarding their respective entitlements, and qualifications, to practice planning. Thus, when a state undertakes to regulate or register planners, litigation may ensue regarding the rights of other professionals to qualify as planners.[7]

A coming of age sign for the planning profession is the attention given by the United States Supreme Court in recent years. The attention, however, has not been benign. On several occasions, the Court has voiced concern over what it perceives as abusive treatment of property owners by planners acting for local government.[8] Exemplifying this is the rhetorical question posed by Justice Brennan in his *San Diego Gas & Electric Co. v. City of San Diego* dissent, that "[a]fter all if a policeman must know the Constitution, then why not a planner?"[9]

The consequence of this concern is that the Supreme Court and lower courts review the administration of land use regulatory programs with heightened scrutiny. This increases the likelihood that courts will find that municipalities have violated constitutional rights. When municipalities violate constitutional rights, planners, along with other government officials, may be held personally liable for money damages under federal law.[10]

The Court is not uniformly hostile to land use regulation; nor is it always skeptical of planners' motives. The Court has given wide latitude to government to enact laws protecting the environment, open space, and historic preservation.[11] Indeed, in *Dolan v. City of Tigard*, the Court acknowledged that "[c]ities have long engaged in the commendable task of land use planning, made necessary by increasing urbanization …,"[12] More recently, the Court took a strong pro-planning stance in regard to the use of moratoria in *Tahoe-Sierra Preservation Council, Inc. v. Tahoe Regional Planning Agency*.[13] Still, the overall thrust of the Supreme Court's cases since 1987 is that the actions of government, and its planners, are less likely to be given the benefit of the doubt, particularly in cases challenging the means chosen to achieve admittedly legitimate public ends. More than in the past, courts today require planners to support the reasonableness of regulations affecting private property.

II. ANTECEDENTS OF LOCAL GOVERNMENT PLANNING

§ 2:2 THE COLONIAL PLANNING ERA[14]

Town planning in the United States, from early colonial days, resembled the modern science of subdivision design. At this stage in the early development of the American city, the planning of frontier settlements was dominated principally by civil engineers and land surveyors. The seminal town plan during the colonial era was the plan for the new City of Philadelphia, commissioned by William Penn and drawn up in 1681.[15] A site between two rivers was selected, and a gridiron system of streets was devised. Open spaces in the central area of the city were set aside, and uniform building spacings and setbacks were prescribed. Penn's engineer, Thomas Holme, prepared this plan, which became the model for most early city plans prepared for other colonial-era towns and cities. The Philadelphia Plan thus left its gridiron-street imprint on many cities planned later.

Such early town plans were invariably drawn by surveyors and engineers, and so the man-made aspects of cities took the rectilinear forms preferred by those professions. A notable departure from this approach was the first plan for Washington, D.C., commissioned in 1791 by the new federal government, and prepared by engineer Pierre L'Enfant that year. This plan superimposed an impressive diagonal-street and radial—thoroughfare system upon a traditional gridiron street system, thus incorporating elements of French civil design. Today, L'Enfant's plan can still be seen in the broad, sweeping vistas that characterize the nation's capital.

The Philadelphia and Washington plans are only two well-known examples of early town planning. Many other plans were prepared, some taking a different, smaller-scale approach.[16] Most of these city plans were no more than early forms of land subdivision control, since they were usually maps showing street right-of-way lines, parcel boundaries, open spaces and water bodies. The towns themselves were often no larger than modern tract subdivisions, but they accommodated that era's primitive technology and simple, agrarian economy.

After the American Revolution, power became more centralized in state governments, with a corresponding loss of autonomy by cities. With the adoption of state constitutions, cities henceforth derived powers of self-government usually by an act of the state legislature delegating that power. Thus, without a delegation of specific powers to control land uses, municipalities, mere creatures of the state, could not exert broad, effective control over the use, and intensity of use, of private property. During this time, the reach of municipalities in regulating the use of land was largely confined to prevention of nuisances.[17] Land speculation became a new industry, and the practice of maximization of economic returns upon land investments made it difficult to implement the open space and civic design elements of city plans such as those for Philadelphia and the District of Columbia.

§ 2:3 THE SANITARY REFORM MOVEMENT

Along with the advent of widespread land speculation came the era of city-building. Factories were built in existing towns, attracting workers from abroad and from agrarian areas. Slowly, American cities became aware that urbanization might be a contributing factor to disease and poor sanitation. Because their growth had been unplanned (and perhaps unanticipated), no American cities had ever comprehensively addressed the problems of drainage and disposal of wastes. The typical American city, by the 1840's, was characterized by filth, stench and stagnant water in the streets, backyard privies, dampness, and the absence of sunlight in residential space. As a result, deadly diseases such as yellow fever, cholera, typhoid, typhus, scarlet fever and diphtheria were commonplace.[18] Backyards, gullies, and even public streets became repositories of all kinds of waste matter, and drainage ditches became choked with debris, including fecal matter and animal carcasses.

There was a remedy to this serious danger to the public health. English sanitary reformer Edwin Chadwick, commencing in 1842, began to champion the construction of "water-carriage sewerage systems." By use of an egg-shaped pipe, flushed with water, Chadwick learned, sewage and even the carcasses of animals could be carried away from homes and cities, and channeled into water bodies in which, presumably, they would disappear. The system required the construction of public potable water supply systems, and sewer lines to carry away wastes. Chadwick's ideas took root in the United States, during a brief period before the Civil War now referred to as the era of the Sanitary Reform Movement.

New York City opened its first public water piping system in 1842, recognizing early on the need to provide an adequate water supply system. Boston opened its first system in 1848. The delivery of water obviously led to the need to pipe it away again, laden with wastes. By 1865, New York City had constructed about 125 miles of sewerage pipelines; Boston completed about 100 miles of sewers by 1873.[19] These early systems were mostly unplanned, and constructed in response to pressures from landowners and political interest groups. Thus, a sort of incrementalist, project-by-project approach typified these early efforts at sanitation reforms.

Installation of sanitary sewers grew more widespread after the Civil War, and by 1875 sanitary engineering was firmly established as a profession in the United States. During this time period, there was also a virtual renaissance in the development of the design professions: in 1866, the American Institute of Architects was formed and in 1871 the engineering professions were first organized.[20] However, none of these professions engaged in comprehensive planning for the future, in the modern sense. The first major, comprehensive American effort to plan for future public health was spurred by the spread of a massive yellow-fever epidemic in the lower Mississippi River Valley in 1878. The epidemic killed over 5,000 people in Memphis, Tennessee, then a city of only 45,000.

In 1879, in response to the plague, Congress created a National Board of Health to advise state governments and to regulate quarantines. By 1880, the Board, at the request of Tennessee authorities, completed an exhaustive, unprecedented study of physical and structural conditions in the City of Memphis, a study that filled 96 volumes and made over 12,000 recommendations for improvements of a remedial nature on property in Memphis—principally nuisance abatements.

The recommendations also included major proposals for a new sanitary public water supply, a sewerage system, destruction of substandard buildings, enactment of a sanitary code for the entire city requiring elevation of buildings whose floors were less than two feet above the ground, repaving of many streets, ventilation of all city houses, and the appointment of a city sanitation officer to oversee all future sanitary work.

This scheme is regarded by modern observers as the first major example of the modern "comprehensive" approach to urban problems, although limited to the goals of prevention of disease and sanitation problems caused by unregulated growth of an urban area. The Memphis scheme did not address many concerns now regarded as properly within the purview of urban planning, such as planning vehicular circulation, districting of incompatible land uses, and recreation space planning. But it was a sign of things to come.

A prophetic expression of the broad approach the planner of urban areas must take was expressed during this era by at least one writer. Horace Bushnell, in his essay "City Plans," observed in 1864 that:

> Considering the immense importance of a right location, and a right planning for cities, no step should ever be taken by the parties concerned, without employing some person who is qualified by a special culture, to assist and direct. Our engineers are trained by a very different kind of service, and are partly disqualified for this by the habit of a study more strictly linear. ... The qualifications of surveyors are commonly more meagre still. ... We have cities for the new age that has come, adapted to its better conditions of use and ornament. So great an advantage ought not to be thrown away. We want, therefore, a city planning profession ...,[21]

§ 2:4 THE CITY BEAUTIFUL MOVEMENT

The consciousness of a new age, with new opportunities for civic improvement, was not limited to those who advocated sanitary reforms. With the increasing congestion of urbanizing areas came a growing awareness that aesthetics also plays a role in the evolution of urban form and function.

American cities grew rapidly during the 19th century. In 1840, the census showed only twelve American cities with populations of over 25,000 and of these only three had populations of over 100,000. But as industry grew, so grew American cities. By 1880, 77 cities had populations of over 25,000 and twenty cities had more than 100,000 residents. This rapid centralization of population in cities, where job opportunities were, led to an increased awareness of the need for civic beauty and amenities in America's unplanned urban areas.

The proponents of civic beauty would hardly have claimed the title, but their agitations for greater attention to aesthetics in city planning later became known as the City Beautiful Movement, the precursor to modern urban planning. The movement was really a groundswell, grass-roots concern with the physical appearance of towns and cities. Because they were largely the product of unrestrained private enterprise, towns across the United States were, before the advent of the 20th century, largely unattractive, muddy, cluttered clusters of buildings. Individual residences sported trash-strewn alleys and yards, and there was little monumental civic architecture. But if sanitary reform could be planned, many believed, so could aesthetics.

The origin of the City Beautiful Movement is commonly traced to the Chicago World's Fair of 1893, a massive celebration of technology, art and architecture in which Americans were first introduced *en masse* to classical design via the Columbian Exposition. The exposition was an array of neo-classical structures and sculpture forming part of the Chicago World's Fair. But the World's Fair exposition was only a symbol of a growing consciousness of the importance of the physical appearance of towns.

In villages and towns across the country, "village improvement associations," usually ad-hoc committees of townspeople, were being created during the 1890s. The village improvement associations championed street lighting, paving of dirt streets and sidewalks, the cleaning up of private yards and alleys, planting of public and private gardens, and setting aside of public, urban parks. By 1901, over 1,000 such improvement associations had sprung up across the United States, advocating both urban aesthetics and sanitation.[22]

The City Beautiful Movement, like the Sanitary Reform Movement, was oriented to physical improvements to rectify a perceived evil: the lack of order and cleanliness in American towns. Well-kept streets, beautiful parks, attractive private residences, fresh air and sanitary improvements became its hallmarks. Many of the village associations were persuaded to join the National League of Improvement Associations, which crusaded for these causes. Renamed the American League for Civic Improvement in 1901, the national association created advisory panels of experts in municipal art, sanitation, recreation and related concerns. To a great extent, the City Beautiful Movement reflected the ideals of the Progressive Era of reform in which it flourished. But it also planted the seeds for a more comprehensive view of the science of planning urban spaces.

City Beautiful proponents caused a great deal of municipal expenditure for civic architecture and municipal improvements. But the proponents of beautification did not necessarily espouse comprehensive regulation of land uses and development. In fact, there was a fear of governmental regulation, rooted in a fundamental aversion to the limitation of private enterprise by local government. As one early commentator observed:

> In America, it is the fear of restricting or injuring free and open competition that has made it so difficult for cities to exercise proper and efficient control over their development. The tendency therefore has been to promote those forms of civic improvement which can be carried out without interfering with vested interests. ...[23]

§ 2:5 THE ADVENT OF PLANNING COMMISSIONS

Proponents of the City Beautiful advocated the creation of citizens' advisory planning commissions, which were the precursors to modern local government planning commissions. The early advisory planning commissions were composed, usually, of locally-prominent merchants and professionals who had an interest in civic beautification, the construction of parks, and the financing of municipal outdoor art. Frequently, these early planning commissions engaged prominent architects and landscape architects to prepare advisory "plans" for civic improvement. These early plans by consultants were non-legal documents, principally maps and lists of suggestions for civic improvements. Several of the early advisory plans, however, attempted to achieve a comprehensiveness of scope that was similar to the modern local government comprehensive plan.[24]

The citizens' advisory planning commissions, in some instances, achieved the status of organs of municipal government. Hartford, Connecticut in 1907 created the first city planning commission. Milwaukee, Wisconsin initiated its city planning commission in 1908. In 1909, Chicago, Illinois appointed a 328-member city planning commission. These commissions, without powers conferred by statute or ordinance, could only recommend the plans they produced as guidelines for decision making by the local municipal legislative body.

In 1909, Chicago became the first city in the United States to voluntarily adopt, only as a non-legal, advisory document, a "comprehensive plan" for its future development. The plan was prepared by famed architect Daniel H. Burnham, who had been director of works for the Columbian Exposition at the 1893 Chicago World's Fair. Backed by wealthy commercial interests in Chicago, and with a budget of $85,000, Burnham prepared a long-range plan for the Chicago region more comprehensive in scope than any plan previously prepared for an American city.

The Chicago plan addressed transportation and recommended a system of regional highways extending far outside the city. It made suggestions for improvement of traffic circulation within the city limits, including the development of new collector streets and consolidation of regional railroad terminals. It recommended new city shipping docks, new parks and beaches on Lake Michigan, and construction of a new city civic center. While the plan was to remain principally advisory in nature, it was nonetheless adopted as the official General Plan of Chicago, by the city's advisory planning commission, in 1911. Ultimately, implementation of its recommendations depended upon the degree of political influence over city government exercised by the businessmen who were members of the Chicago Planning Commission.

§ 2:6 EARLY CONCEPTIONS OF THE CITY PLAN

In 1909, the First National Conference on City Planning and the Problems of Congestion was convened in Washington, D.C., and attended by many of the design professionals who were working, at that time, as consultants to advisory planning commissions across the United States.

At this conference, Frederick Law Olmsted, a prominent landscape architect and planning consultant, described the city plan as a compendium of all regulations on building, physical development, "districting" of land, health ordinances, and "police rules" for the use and development of land. Olmsted drew many of his ideas on plans from earlier experiments in town planning in Germany and Switzerland.[25]

In 1911, Olmsted, again addressing the National Conference on City Planning, said the plan was a forecast of the best path for development to take, which should be followed by the local legislative body in making land use and development-related decisions:

> We must cultivate in our minds and in the minds of the people the conception of the city plan as a device or piece of ... machinery for preparing, and keeping constantly up to date, a unified forecast and definition of all the important changes, additions, and extensions of the physical equipment and arrangement of the city which a sound judgment holds likely to become desirable and practicable in the course of time, so as to avoid as far as possible both ignorantly wasteful action and ... inaction in the control of the city's physical growth. It is a means by which those who become at any time responsible for decisions affecting the city's plan may be prevented from acting in ignorance of what their predecessors and their colleagues in other departments of city life have believed to be the reasonable contingencies.[26]

Olmsted's conception of the city plan was prophetic of today's plans, in focusing on the role of the plan as a rational, policy document by which development-related decisions by successive, elected city officials should be guided. Later, Alfred Bettman, a land use attorney from Cincinnati, reinforced the concept of the city plan as a master development guide for the city or town. Addressing the National Conference on City Planning in 1928, Bettman said:

> A city plan is a master design for the physical development of the territory of the city. It constitutes a plan of the division of land between public and private uses, specifying the general location and extent of new public improvements, grounds and structures ... and, in the case of private developments, the general distribution [of land areas] amongst various classes of uses, such as residential, business and industrial uses.[27]

III. RELATIONSHIP OF PLANNING AND ZONING

§ 2:7 THE PROMULGATION OF ZONING ORDINANCES

The comprehensive plan's emphasis on setting the distribution of classes of land uses caused some confusion by many local governments over the difference between comprehensive *plans* and comprehensive *zoning ordinances.* Unlike the plans adopted during this era, which were advisory documents of a policy nature, zoning ordinances were local ordinances establishing land-use districts for residential, commercial, industrial and agricultural activities, and usually prescribing standards within each district for building height and bulk, setbacks from lot lines, and density or intensity of the use of individual lots within each district. When faced with the choice of either preparing a comprehensive plan, followed by adoption of a zoning ordinance to implement the policies in the plan, or just preparing and adopting a "comprehensive zoning ordinance," most local governments opted for the latter alternative.

The first modern, comprehensive zoning ordinance was enacted by New York City in 1916. The ordinance classified land uses and created zones for these uses, depicted on zoning maps. The purposes of zoning were to segregate residential uses from more intensive uses of land, such as industrial, and thereby to provide safer, quieter areas for family life. By 1921, zoning had become fashionable: its advocates had persuaded almost half of the state legislatures to adopt zoning enabling acts, conferring upon municipalities the power to adopt and enforce zoning ordinances.

The popularity of zoning was given a boost by the preparation of a model zoning enabling act by the United States Department of Commerce. The Act, published in 1924, was entitled the Standard State Zoning Enabling Act.[28] It provided a ready-made model for legislatures to follow in delegating police power to municipalities to prepare, adopt, and administer zoning codes. The act authorized the appointment of zoning commissions by local governments, which would set district boundaries and regulations, hold a public hearing on the proposed zoning ordinance, and submit it to the city council for final hearings and enactment into law. Without such an enabling act, a municipal zoning ordinance was in danger of being invalidated as *ultra vires* if challenged in court.

By 1926, 564 cities and towns had adopted zoning ordinances, and several state courts had upheld zoning as a valid exercise of police powers delegated by states to their municipalities. In that year, the United States Supreme Court upheld the use of the police power to zone. In *Village of Euclid v. Ambler Realty* Co.,[29] the Court heard a challenge by an Ohio landowner of a "comprehensive zoning plan" adopted by the city council of Euclid, Ohio. The ordinance established districts for land use, and district regulations for building heights and minimum lot sizes. The ordinance, the Supreme Court held, did not violate due process, and bore a rational relationship to valid governmental interests in preventing congestion and in segregating incompatible land uses.

But the attractiveness of zoning to the general public was due principally to the fact that a new zoning ordinance tended to validate existing land use patterns by including them on the zoning map, and also provided the opportunity to over-zone for profitable industrial and business uses. The comprehensive zoning ordinance of the City of New York, the first such ordinance in the nation, set aside enough land in business and industrial zones to accommodate an eventual city population of some 340 million persons.[30] Hence, zoning appeared to be a welcome device for facilitating land speculation and validating the existing pattern of land uses.

§ 2:8 ZONING DISPLACES PLANNING

While "comprehensive zoning" proliferated, planning remained principally the province of advisory planning commissions. Few cities had created full-time planning staffs. By 1929, only 46 cities had an annual city planning budget of more than $5,000.[31] Most city plans were prepared by consultants, and typically addressed a half-dozen principal elements of city design:

1. A land use plan or zoning plan.
2. A plan for streets.
3. A plan for public transit.
4. An element addressing rail and water transportation.
5. A plan addressing parks and public recreation.
6. An element addressing civic art or civic appearance.[32]

These plans exerted an influence upon the drafters of the first model act for planning, the Standard City Planning Enabling Act of 1928. The earlier Standard State Zoning Enabling Act had made little mention of planning. However, the Standard City Planning Enabling Act, also prepared by the U.S. Department of Commerce, addressed only city planning. The Act enabled local governments to prepare plans for five principal urban concerns (streets, public grounds, public buildings, utilities, and zoning) via a municipally-appointed planning commission:

> **§ 6. General Powers and Duties**—It shall be the function and duty of the commission to make and adopt a master plan for the physical development of the municipality … [showing] the commission's recommendations for the development of said territory, including, among other things, the general location, character, and extent of streets, viaducts, subways, bridges, waterways, water fronts, boulevards, parkways, playgrounds, squares, parks, aviation fields, and other public ways … [and] the removal, relocation, widening, narrowing, vacating, abandonment, change of use or extension of any of the foregoing … as well as a zoning plan for the control of the height, area, bulk, location and use of buildings and premises. … The commission may from time to time amend, extend, or add to the plan.
>
> **§ 7. Purposes in View**—In the preparation of such plan the commission shall make careful and comprehensive surveys and studies of present conditions and future growth of the municipality. … The plan shall be made with the general purpose of guiding and accomplishing a coordinated, adjusted, and harmonious development of the municipality … as well as efficiency and economy in the process of development. …

Thus, the Standard City Planning Enabling Act envisioned a more comprehensive approach to regulating land uses and providing municipal services for future growth than zoning could attempt. Zones for land uses were to be only one concern in preparation of the plan, and efficient provision of utilities, transportation and other public services figured as prominently as land use districting.

The Act, however, contributed to the confusion over the differences between city plans and zoning ordinances, by stating that the plan should include a zoning element. As a result of this confusion and because of the growing interest in zoning, many communities prepared and adopted zoning ordinances without ever making the general, comprehensive plan upon which zoning was supposed to be based. This practice tended to divert attention from the future-oriented, general policies of city planning in favor of squabbles over the details which dominated individual zoning decisions and controversies.[33]

In addition, under the Act planning was not mandatory, but optional. While the Act implied that zoning was distinct from planning, it did not expressly state that zoning should be enacted in accordance with an existing comprehensive plan document. The Standard State Zoning Enabling Act did expressly state that zoning should be enacted "in accordance with a comprehensive plan,"[34] but in view of the fact that planning was optional under the Standard City Planning Enabling Act, most courts addressing this question have held that the plan with which zoning must be in accord could be found in the entirety of the zoning ordinance. A separate plan was generally not required.[35] However, a growing number of states are requiring their municipalities to prepare comprehensive plans with specific "elements" therein, and in a growing minority of these jurisdictions zoning ordinances and other land use regulations are required to be "in accordance with," or consistent with, policies and provisions of the comprehensive plan.[36]

The federal government has also supplied strong incentives to municipalities to prepare comprehensive plans. Under the Housing Act of 1949,[37] municipalities applying for federal financial assistance in slum clearance were required to prepare a comprehensive plan before funds would be provided. Later, Congress provided federal funds to municipalities to finance preparation of such plans, under the Housing Act of 1954.[38] As a result of both federal and state initiatives, many local governments across the nation now maintain planning departments and routinely prepare and revise comprehensive plans.

IV. THE PROCESS OF PLANNING COMPREHENSIVELY

§ 2:9 THE FUNCTION OF THE PLAN

Traditionally, land use regulations such as zoning and subdivision ordinances adopted by local governments were written and promulgated without reference to any prior comprehensive plan. However, in a growing number of states, the adoption of such regulatory ordinances in the absence of a general comprehensive plan may cast doubts upon the validity of the ordinances. The comprehensive plan, once viewed as primarily an advisory document to the local legislative body, is in many states becoming a legal, binding document as well as a prescription for future development patterns.

The plan serves as an overall set of goals, objectives, and policies to guide the local legislative body in its decision making in regard to the physical development of the community.[39] When particular regulatory decisions are made by the county commission or the city council, the comprehensive plan's policies, goals, and objectives may be invoked as the "rational basis" upon which local government exercises of the police power to zone must be based. Planners have encouraged the use of the comprehensive plan as a rational basis for land-use decisions, and, in an effort to promote planning as a new profession, have developed a theory of urban planning as a rational process of choice between different policy alternatives.[40]

As Professor Nelson has recently observed: "While pundits argue against even attempting to plan for the future, we must. It may not be so much the crafting of plans themselves but the process of planning that reveals the challenges and opportunities based on data collection, analysis, interpretation, and application as opportunities arise. … [P]lanning depends on what we know about such things as trends that can influence the future even though we cannot project future outcomes precisely. It is through planning that we can become prepared to seize opportunities."[41]

§ 2:10 THE RATIONAL PLANNING PROCESS

An overall definition of "comprehensive plan" has become necessary. The comprehensive plan is generally defined as an official public document preferably (but often not) adopted as law by the local government as a policy guide to decisions about the physical development of the community. Usually it sets forth, in a general way, using text and maps, how the leaders of local government want the community to develop in the future. The length of the future time period to be addressed by a comprehensive plan varies widely from locale to locale, and is often set by state legislation enabling or requiring local governments to plan.

The growing importance of the comprehensive plan in local land-use decisions prompted urban planning practitioners and theorists to develop a theory of planning as a "rational process." The rational, comprehensive planning process has four principal characteristics. First, it is *future-oriented,* establishing goals and objectives for future land use and development, which will be attained incrementally over time through regulations, individual decisions about zoning and rezoning, development approval or disapproval, and municipal expenditures for capital improvements such as road construction and the installation of municipal utilities.

Second, planning is *continuous,* in that the plan is intended not as a blueprint for future development which must be as carefully executed as the architect's design for a building or the engineer's plan for a sewer line, but rather as a set of policies which must be periodically reevaluated and amended to adjust to changing conditions. A plan that is written purely as a static blueprint for future development will rapidly become obsolete when circumstances change.

Third, the plan must be based upon a *determination of present and projected conditions* within the area covered by the plan. This requirement ensures that the plan is not simply a list of hoped-for civic improvements, as were many of the plans prepared during the era of the City Beautiful Movement. Substantial efforts have been made by public planning staffs, university planning departments, and planning consulting firms, to develop useful techniques for gathering data, analyzing existing conditions, and projecting future trends and conditions within the geographic area covered by a comprehensive plan. This body of methods, procedure and models is generally termed *planning methodology.*

Fourth, planning is *fair.* Traditional regulations used to control development patterns often give rise to practices that many would view as arbitrary, uncertain, and exclusionary.[42] Comprehensive planning on the state, regional, and local levels, however, advocates a "framework of collective, community-wide decision-making" so that landowners are treated fairly, exclusionary practices and tactics are resolved, and a greater amount of certainty is attached to the regulation of the use of land.[43]

Fifth, planning is *comprehensive.* In the past, architects, and engineers who became involved in solving urban problems, such as those attacked in the Sanitary Reform Movement, tended to identify one problem perceived to be solvable by one solution. Having targeted that problem, these early planners preferred to develop and advocate one solution, usually expressed as a static blueprint which, if fully implemented, would solve that problem. This problem-solution approach was the product of the project orientation that was typical of traditional civil engineering and architecture.

Planning theorists over the past several decades have observed that this approach has led to a phenomenon termed "disjointed incrementalism," in which successive governmental problems such as drainage, traffic circulation, or sewage treatment might be incrementally "solved" without reference to related concerns of local governments. For example, sewer systems in the era of the Sanitary Reform Movement were usually designed without reference to any overall plan for the optimum future locations, and densities, of different land uses to be served by them. Highways were often laid out without reference to any long-range plans for the types of land uses they were to serve in the future.

The recognition, starting after World War II, that the entire range of municipal land use, transportation, and growth problems were all interrelated, led to advocacy of comprehensive plans as a means of identifying the key problems in land use regulation, and recommending alternative solutions to these problems which were the product of a rational planning process. The courts have recognized this role of planning, in defining planning as concerned with:

> the physical development of the community and its environs in relation to its social and economic well-being for the fulfillment of the rightful common destiny, according to a "master plan" based on "careful and comprehensive surveys and studies of present conditions and the prospects of future growth of the municipality," and embodying scientific teachings and creative experience.[44]

The rational planning process essentially subsumes four discrete steps: *data gathering and analysis, setting of policies, plan implementation,* and *plan re-evaluation.* Rather than resulting in a final plan effective for all time, the process is instead reiterative over a period of years: re-evaluation of the plan starts the process over again, resulting in a new set of policies to be implemented, and the success of the new plan is again evaluated at a future date. Thus, the rational planning process is both reiterative and continuous.

During the first step of the process, the planner preparing the comprehensive plan performs research and analysis of a wide range of present and projected physical, economic, and sociological conditions of the municipality, aided by a wide variety of planning methodologies. Statistical surveying, population forecasting, mapping of existing conditions in land use, transportation, and environmentally-sensitive areas, mathematical modeling of economic trends, analysis of traffic flows on major highways, and techniques borrowed from other professions such as economics, geography, and engineering are some of the methods employed by planners in data gathering and analysis.

The data-gathering and analysis phase of the process usually results in the identification of present and potential future concerns in land use, transportation, environment, utilities, housing, and other areas to be addressed in the plan. Thus, following the first stage of the process, the planner may identify and prioritize a range of municipal problems and opportunities which should be addressed in the policy-formation stage of the planning process.

Analysis of the data then leads naturally to the second phase, setting of policies for the plan. In this phase, the planner ceases being a data gatherer, and assumes a policy formation role. Working closely with the planning commission and sometimes the local legislative body, the planner examines and proposes alternative means of solving or averting the problems identified in the first phase of the process. Through communication with the local legislative body and the planning commission (if one exists), the planner develops a set of policies, goals, and objectives which constitute the principal, future-oriented sections of the comprehensive plan. Thus, for example, the policies may include a provision that sewage-treatment services must be expanded to accommodate new development; that the legislative body should initiate a program to stimulate new economic development in the declining downtown; and that steps should be taken to prevent further flood-prone development in low-lying areas adjoining rivers and streams.

As a supplement to these general policies, or goals, of planning, the planner may suggest means of achieving these goals. In setting the goals and recommending alternative objectives, the planner may refer to standards and principles widely-accepted in the planning profession: that excessive use of septic tanks rather than public sewers tends to pollute groundwater; that decay of the central business district leads to devaluation of the tax base; that development in flood-prone areas is detrimental to public safety by exposing buildings and their occupants to flood hazards.

The mere statement of policies and objectives will not, in itself, ensure that action is taken. Thus, the third stage of the planning process, implementation of the plan, becomes the most important stage. Implementation involves three discrete steps: developing public support for the plan by means of various forms of citizen participation and a series of public hearings and media coverage; securing adoption of the plan, either as an advisory document (as in many states) or as a legally-binding ordinance (as in a growing number of states); and action by the legislative body to implement the policies and objectives. Not only is this one of the most important stages of the planning process, but it is also one of the most difficult goals for the planner to achieve. Planners often face harsh opposition to proposed changes in development patterns. As a result, it is helpful for the planner to clearly lay out the causal nexus between the implementation of the plan and positive outcomes for the community in order to gain popular support.

Upon adoption of the plan, the adopting agency espouses the policies and objectives of the plan as guidelines for daily decision-making. Thus, to return to our three examples of policies, the local legislative body will undertake revisions of the municipal zoning map to bring it into accordance with the land-use recommendations of the plan. Similarly, the governing body may prepare plans for expansion of sewers and construction of new roads to serve new development. The legislative body may appoint a downtown revitalization authority to oversee efforts to attract new businesses back into the central business district. The governing body may authorize the city attorney to draft a new flood-plain protection ordinance prohibiting careless construction of new buildings in low-lying areas adjoining streams and rivers.[45]

V. THE LEGAL STATUS OF THE COMPREHENSIVE PLAN

§ 2:11 PLANS AS OPTIONAL POLICY DOCUMENTS

The majority of the states whose legislation enables the preparation of comprehensive plans do not *require* local governments to prepare plans, and comprehensive plans in these states are principally land use policy documents without the force of law.[46] The justification frequently given for the lack of legal status is that urban planning has not yet proven itself capable of solving urban problems, and there is no consensus among the states over what elements of urban development plans should always address. Furthermore, some commentators believe that the comprehensive plan serves an important "visionary function," unlike the regulatory function of ordinances and statutes, and that to require the plan to be a painstakingly-drafted, regulatory document would prevent plans from being suggestive and boldly-innovative.[47]

The fact that plans are usually neither mandated by state laws nor given the force of law is traceable to the standard planning and zoning legislation promulgated by the United States Department of Commerce in the 1920s. The Standard State Zoning Enabling Act required that zoning regulations and zoning decisions be made "in accordance with the comprehensive plan," but failed to address the obvious question of what a comprehensive plan was. Later, the Standard City Planning Enabling Act of 1928, while boldly setting forth suggested "elements" of comprehensive plans, and the manner in which a city might prepare and adopt them, failed to strictly define the legal relationship between plans and zoning ordinances. In addition, plans were optional under the Standard City Planning Enabling Act.[48]

Many states adopted these acts verbatim or only in slightly-altered form. The task of defining the relationship between local zoning statutes and local comprehensive plans (if one existed at all) naturally fell to the courts. In the majority of states, since a separate plan was not required, courts considering challenges to zoning ordinances as not "in accordance with a comprehensive plan" looked to the overall land-use policies of the zoning ordinance, if an optional comprehensive plan did not exist.

The classic case taking this position is *Kozesnik v. Montgomery Township*.[49] The case arose before New Jersey enacted legislation requiring municipalities to prepare plans.[50] The existing zoning enabling legislation required zoning decisions to be "in accordance" with a plan, but the defendant township in the case had not prepared any plan. The state supreme court noted that New Jersey's zoning enabling legislation (like that of most states) predated the adoption of its planning enabling legislation. Inferring from this that the legislature could not have possibly required zoning to be in accordance with non-existent "plans," the court concluded that the plan with which zoning had to accord could "readily be revealed in ... the zoning ordinance ... and no more is required by the statute."[51] Thus, although it appears to be a somewhat circular reasoning process, the court was willing to measure individual zoning decisions—even those that altered the community's zoning maps—for their "accordance" with the master zoning code for the municipality, which included the maps. This amounted to no more than a process of "discovering" a comprehensive plan and policies for land use within the dictates of a zoning code.

This process, which has been followed by the majority of states,[52] does not always result in a validation of rezoning decisions when challenged. Indeed, it may be no more than a reflection of the general requirement, under substantive due process, that exercises of municipal police powers be reasonable. However, the majority position appears to be largely the result of the historical accident of zoning becoming a widespread practice before the advent of comprehensive planning. The result of this doctrine, however, has been to perpetuate the "optional" nature of comprehensive plans in most states, because zoning codes so often became the "comprehensive plan" against which individual rezoning decisions had to be measured for conformity.

In a variation on this position, the New York Superior Court in *Udell v. Haas* required that "accordance" between rezoning and the overall zoning plan be "rational" as well. Reviewing a challenge to a zoning decision regarding an individual lot of land, the court observed that:

> the comprehensive plan is the essence of zoning. Without it, there can be no rational allocation of land use. It is the insurance that the public welfare is being served and that zoning does not become nothing more than just a Gallup poll.[53]

§ 2:12 INCENTIVE BASED COMPREHENSIVE PLANNING

A recent development in some states which do not mandate comprehensive plans is to nonetheless strongly encourage their adoption by offering incentives to those local governments that do adopt them. The State of Georgia, for example, has employed a framework of planning that provides for certain incentives and disincentives designed to encourage the planning process.[54] Utilizing the funding incentives directed at them, nearly all of Georgia's counties have "voluntarily" adopted comprehensive plans.[55] Illinois, in 2002, adopted the Local Planning Technical Assistance Act to encourage its local governments through funding and other incentives "to engage in planning, regulatory, and development approaches that promote and encourage comprehensive planning."[56]

§ 2:13 PLANS AS MANDATORY POLICY DOCUMENTS

The traditional position, that individual zoning decisions could be compared to the general zoning code to determine whether they are "in accordance with a comprehensive plan," had a circularity of reasoning which did not make sense to planning advocates. Many urged reform of the planning enabling statutes so as to clarify the role and status of the comprehensive, or master, plan. Thus, Harvard Law School Professor Charles Haar wrote in 1955:

> While the statutory references [to planning by municipalities] are cast in large and hopeful terms, they assign no clear legal position to the plan. The legal impact of planning is significant only as it imports governmental control of physical development ... [and] no consistent pattern of interpretation of the effect of the plan on the real world has yet emerged in the legislation or judicial opinions. ... The requirement in the Zoning Enabling Act that the zoning ordinance shall be made "in accordance with a comprehensive plan" has apparently carried the courts no further than requiring that the ordinance be reasonable and impartial so as to satisfy the *constitutional* conditions for the exercise of a state's police power. ... Some acts do not even require the adoption of the master plan in order to exercise subdivision controls.[57]

Clearly, Haar said, the plan ought to have some legal significance, and it ought to be a separate document from zoning ordinances. The states that have adopted this approach, by requiring a separate comprehensive plan, have escaped from the confusion, caused by the standard planning and zoning acts, over the role of the comprehensive plan.[58] In these jurisdictions, a zoning challenge does not draw the court into a process of "discovering" a comprehensive plan inside a general zoning ordinance. As a result, in these states the comprehensive plan is the "constitution" for the jurisdiction's land use regulations.[59] The legal concept for implementing this recently accepted status for comprehensive plans in the "consistency" requirement.[60]

§ 2:14 THE CONSISTENCY REQUIREMENT

A. The Meaning of Consistency

In a broad sense, consistency refers to the relationship between planning and land use regulations. The concept can be traced back to the Standard State Zoning Enabling Act's (SZEA) requirement that zoning be "in accordance with a comprehensive plan."[61] Controversy regarding the term's precise meaning has existed for many years.[62] Much of this confusion stems from a difference in terminology used in the SZEA, referring to a comprehensive plan, and in the Standard City Planning Enabling Act (SPEA),[63] calling for a "master plan."[64] The SPEA provided for establishment of a local planning commission whose duty was to produce a master plan, to be used as a guide for orderly future development. The master plan was meant to serve as a substantive document, stating the goals of a locality to direct subsequent implementing legislation.[65] Because the SPEA's master plan was not considered binding, and because it has not traditionally been equated with the SZEA's comprehensive plan, implementation of the consistency mandate has been slow and controversial.

An unfortunate effect of this confusion has been a judicial tendency to interpret the "in accordance with" directive as meaning nothing more than that land use regulation ordinances be comprehensive or uniform in scope and coverage. Thus, many courts have looked to the zoning ordinance itself to fulfill the requirement and have regarded as sufficient elements of internal consistency and rationality within the ordinance. This is a fairly common judicial response to the consistency requirement in those jurisdictions which do not statutorily mandate consistency.[66]

The scope of the consistency doctrine today is wide, and a number of different forms of the requirement have evolved. As noted above, consistency refers to the relationship between a comprehensive plan and its implementing measures. Not only does this mean that the plan and regulations promulgated under it must be consistent, it also means, in a growing number of jurisdictions, that any development orders and permits issued must be consistent with the local plan.[67] From a practical standpoint, the plan—implementation form is probably the most important type of consistency. It is from this relation that the bulk of inconsistency challenges are mounted.[68]

Jurisdictions that statutorily mandate planning frequently also require that the individual elements of the plan be consistent with one another. As one commentator has noted:

> [i]nternal consistency refers to compatibility within the general plan—that is, dimensions of planning are to be addressed with cognizance of other dimensions. Where several separate plan elements are mandated, for example, integration of elements is required.[69]

Thus, internal consistency requires coordination between the various elements of a plan so that they can operate in an effective and comprehensive manner.

Still another form of consistency, appearing with greater frequency, is the type mandated between local, regional, state, and even federal[70] comprehensive plans. A number of state planning acts now require this form of consistency.[71] This has caused a certain amount of controversy as some regard it as an affront on local land use autonomy.[72] Although the purpose of this form of consistency is to assure that individual local and regional plans operate in a rational and coordinated manner, the effect has been to place even greater control over local land use policy in the hands of state government.[73]

The consistency doctrine did not exist at common law and is purely a creature of statute and case law.[74] Attempts to define the concept precisely have proven largely unsuccessful. As Professor DiMento notes:

[e]ven in those states where legislation has been passed to effect consistency, there is no generally accepted understanding of the term in affected local governments. This is certainly a common state of affairs in statutory interpretation; however, differences in terminology need to be addressed if other issues surrounding the legal effect of the comprehensive plan are to be resolved.

In California, for example, several attempts have been made to clarify the cryptic language in the consistency statutes. The major consistency mandate notes:

A zoning ordinance shall be consistent with a city or county general plan only if:

(i) The city or county has officially adopted such a plan, and
(ii) The various land uses authorized by the ordinance are compatible with the objectives, policies, general land uses and programs specified in such a plan.[75]

This definition is neither very helpful nor clear, as zoning deals with more than just uses.[76] If consistency is limited to uses—as the definition suggests—then an ordinance permitting greater density than the plan might not be within the scope of the requirement, and as such might not be regarded as inconsistent with the plan.[77]

The difficulty in defining consistency has undoubtedly been influenced by the use of similar terms; the "in accordance with" requirement of the SZEA, for example. Other synonymous terms include "substantially consistent with," "in conformity with," "in furtherance of," "closely attuned to," and "in basic harmony with" a comprehensive plan. None of these, however, has provided much in the way of progress toward an understanding of the term's meaning.

Another uncertain aspect of the doctrine concerns the phasing of consistency. Some jurisdictions might be willing to allow as consistent a less intensive use than the one contemplated by the plan on the theory that this type of development will lead toward achievement of the planned goal; for example, single family homes in an area with a plan designation approximating multifamily residential would be considered consistent. This holding zone approach reflects the planner's awareness of timing constraints, and recognizes the validity of interim development measures not inconsistent with the plan's long-term objectives.[78] Other jurisdictions might reject this as inconsistent, favoring instead a more literal one-to-one relationship between planning and zoning. A number of different approaches to the phasing problem have been suggested: i) requiring revision of the zoning ordinance to occur when the plan is adopted, ii) resolving the question through litigation on a case-by-case basis, iii) allowing a reasonable transition period, and iv) applying the comprehensive plan in a prospective manner only.[79]

Almost every zoning challenge contains an allegation that the contested action is inconsistent with some aspect of the comprehensive plan. Until recently, however, such challenges were seldom based solely on the grounds of inconsistency. In 1973, the Oregon Supreme Court in *Fasano v. Board of County Commissioners*[80] held that the state's planning act required that zoning ordinances and decisions be consistent with the adopted comprehensive plan. The court invalidated a rezoning which was determined to be inconsistent with the comprehensive plan. *Fasano* is seen by many as one of the earliest and strongest judicial endorsements of both consistency and comprehensive planning.[81]

Finally, an additional insight into the meaning of consistency can be gained by a consideration of some of the arguments for and against the doctrine. Proponents of consistency argue that the effectiveness of planning as a rational mechanism for allocating public resources will be weakened considerably by failure to mandate consistency. They additionally argue that planners can identify community objectives through a variety of means and present alternatives for rational and informed decisionmaking.[82] It has further been suggested that consistency helps prevent the taking challenge by putting landowners on notice well in advance as to what types of uses can be made of their property.[83] Thus proponents contend that only if consistency—the "missing link" between planning and zoning—is mandated can rational planning find any hope of successful implementation.

On the other hand, opponents of consistency argue forcefully that the doctrine creates more problems than it solves.[84] An interesting counter to one of the proponent's views is the argument that not only does mandatory consistency not prevent the taking challenge, it actually moves forward the point in time at which the taking occurs. Opponents suggest that if consistency really means that the plan controls, then planning is in reality regulatory, and such regulation results in "planning blight," potentially giving rise to claims of inverse condemnation.[85] They also contend that consistency does not prevent the spot zoning problem, but instead causes "spot planning."[86] Thus, rather than isolating planning from outside forces, consistency in reality subjects planning to the pressures of political and economic influence.[87]

The consistency debate continues today. Although only a relatively small number of states currently have legally enforceable consistency requirements,[88] it is significant that several of these—California, Florida and Oregon—are regarded as innovators in land use and environmental law and the American Planning Association's Growing Smart Legislative Guidebook recommends including the following consistency requirement in comprehensive plans:

> 8-104(1) Land development regulations and any amendments thereto, including amendments to the zoning map, and land use actions shall be consistent with the local comprehensive plan, provided that in the event the land development regulations become inconsistent with the local comprehensive plan by reason of amendment to the plan or adoption of a new plan, the regulation shall be amended within 6 months of the date of amendment or adoption so that they are consistent with the local comprehensive plan as amended.[89]

Uncertainty about its true meaning will undoubtedly continue to plague the concept, but a growing number of statutory and judicial interpretations should help make a practical understanding of the concept possible.

B. Judicial Enforcement of the Consistency Requirement

As a practical matter, the meaning of consistency is in large part determined by what action courts will take for failure to meet the mandate. Remedies available include a reprimand,[90] injunctive relief, development moratoria,[91] and invalidation of the zoning ordinances.[92] It is clear that the impact of consistency will be greatly blunted unless an effective set of judicially enforceable remedies exists.[93] Thus the statutory remedies available for failure to meet the mandate will play an important role in defining consistency in a given jurisdiction.

Thus far, the most dramatic instance of judicial "enforcement" of the consistency requirement occurred in Florida as a result of the construction of a residential development which was found to be inconsistent with Martin County's comprehensive plan.[94] Neighboring property owners challenged the county board's approval of an apartment development and sought injunctive relief and removal (i.e. destruction) of the newly constructed apartment complex. Although the developer prevailed in the circuit court, the District Court of Appeal ordered a trial de novo to determine the consistency issue.[95] The Circuit Court on trial de novo issued an injunction against further development and ordered demolition of the apartments even though the loss to the developer would be approximately $3,300,000, and the loss in market value to the adjoining property owner (plaintiff) was only $26,000. On re-appeal the District Court found the development inconsistent with the comprehensive plan and held that the lower court's order to destroy the apartments was an appropriate remedy.[96] The apartments were, in fact, demolished pursuant to the court order in September of 2002.[97]

C. Consistency and the Standard of Judicial Review

Courts in states with mandatory local comprehensive planning and legally enforceable consistency requirements have begun to reexamine the traditional rules and procedures by which land use decisions are reached and judicially reviewed. Traditionally, courts have viewed zoning decisions as legislative decisions, subject to deferential review under the fairly debatable rule.[98] However, there is growing judicial recognition that local government decision-makers are not always equivalent to state and national legislatures, particularly where local governments are statutorily required to apply the standards and policies of the local plan in reaching land use decisions.[99] Challenges to the consistency of those decisions with the comprehensive plan have prompted some courts to characterize certain local land use decisions as quasi-judicial, subject to greater judicial scrutiny than legislative decisions.

In *Board of County Commissioners of Brevard County v. Snyder*,[100] the Florida Supreme Court held that while comprehensive rezonings affecting a large portion of the public are legislative in nature, rezoning actions which entail application of general rules or policies to specific individuals, interests, or activities are quasi-judicial, and subject to strict scrutiny review. *Snyder* involved a landowner's request to rezone a one-half acre parcel in an area designated for residential use under the county's comprehensive plan. The parcel was zoned for single-family residences and the requested zoning classification would allow fifteen units per acre. While either classification was considered potentially consistent with the residential use designation under the comprehensive plan, the county denied the rezoning.

The court held that a landowner seeking to rezone property has the burden of proving the proposal is consistent with the comprehensive plan. Upon demonstrating such consistency, however, the landowner is not presumptively entitled to such use. Instead, the burden thereupon shifts to the local government to demonstrate that maintaining the existing zoning classification accomplishes a legitimate public purpose.[101]

In 1997, Florida courts shed further light on the distinction between planning and zoning explaining the scope of judicial review with respect to amendments of local comprehensive plans. In *Martin County v. Yusem*,[102] the Florida Supreme Court held that amendments to a comprehensive land use plan are legislative decisions subject to the fairly debatable standard of review. The court further held that the fairly debatable standard applied even when such plan amendments are being sought as part of a rezoning application in respect to only one piece of property. The court found that amendments to a comprehensive land use plan, like the adoption of the plan itself, result in formulation of policy, rather than application of policy, and, since amendments to comprehensive plans are legislative actions, the "fairly debatable" standard of review applies in these cases.

As future opinions illuminate the extent of quasi-judicial land use decision making, the courts seem likely to confront and clarify the procedural responsibilities of local governments in reaching such decisions. At present, these procedural requirements are not well-developed in state law.

§ 2:15 SMART GROWTH AND NEW URBANISM

The role of comprehensive plans—and indeed of planners themselves—has intensified in the first years of the twenty-first century as a result of the "smart growth" and "new urbanism" movements.[103] Without comprehensive and legally enforceable plans conceived and implemented by and through planning techniques and principles, neither movement could exist. In fact,

> *Smart growth means using comprehensive planning* to guide, design, develop, revitalize and build communities for all that have a unique sense of community and place, preserve and enhance valuable natural and cultural resources, equitably distribute the costs and benefits of development, expand the range of transportation, employment and housing choices in a fiscally responsive manner, value long range, regional considerations of sustainability over short term incremental geographically isolated actions; and promotes public health and healthy communities.[104]

New urbanism is equally dependent on comprehensive plans and planning principles to achieve urban reconfiguration.[105] The same is true in regard to many environmental protection projects.[106]

A related recent development in regard to comprehensive plans and the planning process is the in creasing importance of *regional comprehensive plans.*[107]

NOTES

1. N.J. Stat. Ann. §§ 45:14A–1 et seq.
2. P.R. Laws Ann. tit. 20, § 3501(e).
3. Michigan formerly had such a statute (M.C.L.A. 339.2309) until the law was repealed by P.A.2014, No. 154, § 1 on June 11, 2014.
4. For information on the profession and practice of planning, see generally The Practice of Local Government Planning (So and Getzels eds.1998); Hall, Urban and Regional Planning (4th ed. 2002); Cullingham, Planning in the USA: Policies, Issues, and Processes (2003); Levy, Contemporary Urban Planning (7th ed. 2005); Institutions and Planning (Ninaj Verma, ed.) (2007).
5. http://www.planning.org/salary/summary.htm.
6. See http://www.planning.org/aicp/.
7. See, e.g., *New Jersey Chapter, Am. Institute of Planners v. New Jersey State Bd. of Professional Planners,* 48 N.J. 581, 227 A.2d 313 (1967) (state statute licensing planners did not violate equal protection clause by exempting, from examination requirements, any licensed engineer, land surveyor or registered architect of New Jersey).

8. See *Lucas v. South Carolina Coastal Council*, 505 U.S. 1003, 112 S. Ct. 2886, 120 L. Ed. 2d 798 (1992) (beach set back law suspected as pressing "private property into some form of public service under the guise of mitigating serious public harm"). See also *Nollan v. California Coastal Com'n*, 483 U.S. 825, 107 S. Ct. 3141, 97 L. Ed. 2d 677 (1987) (beach easement program labeled "extortion"), discussed infra §§ 10:5 to 10:6.

9. *San Diego Gas & Elec. Co. v. City of San Diego*, 450 U.S. 621, 661, 101 S. Ct. 1287, 1309, 67 L. Ed. 2d 551 (1981). The point of the comment was that a monetary remedy was necessary to compel planners, as government officials, to abide by the Constitution. The Court subsequently decided that compensation was the mandatory remedy for a Fifth Amendment taking. See *First English Evangelical Lutheran Church of Glendale v. Los Angeles County, Cal.*, 482 U.S. 304, 107 S. Ct. 2378, 96 L. Ed. 2d 250 (1987).

10. See discussion infra § 10:9 and §§ 10:23 to 10:26.

11. See, e.g., *Wallach v. Town of Dryden*, 23 N.Y.3d 728, 2014 WL 2921399 (2014) (local governments have the power to regulate hydrofracking under their authority to enact zoning ordinances).

12. *Dolan v. City of Tigard*, 512 U.S. 374, 396, 114 S. Ct. 2309, 2322, 129 L. Ed. 2d 304 (1994).

13. *Tahoe-Sierra Preservation Council, Inc. v. Tahoe Regional Planning Agency*, 535 U.S. 302, 122 S. Ct. 1465, 152 L. Ed. 2d 517 (2002).

14. For discussions of land use regulation during the colonial period, see Hart, Land Use Law in the Early Republic and the Original Meaning of the Takings Clause, 94 Nw. U. L. Rev. 1099 (2000).

15. W. Goodman & E. Freund, Principles and Practice of Urban Planning 9–10 (1968).

16. W. Goodman & E. Freund, Principles and Practice of Urban Planning at 10–14.

17. See infra §§ 14:1 et seq., for discussion of land use regulation through nuisance law.

18. J. A. Peterson, The Impact of Sanitary Reform upon American Urban Planning, 1840–1890, in Introduction to Planning History in the United States 13–17 (D. Krueckeberg ed. 1983).

19. J. A. Peterson, The Impact of Sanitary Reform upon American Urban Planning, 1840–1890, in Introduction to Planning History in the United States at 19.

20. D. Krueckeberg, The Culture of Planning, Introduction to Planning History in the United States 13–17 (D. Krueckeberg ed. 1983).

21. H. Bushnell, Work and Play 196 (1864).

22. Introduction to Planning History in the United States 46–49 (D. Krueckeberg ed. 1983).

23. J. Nolen, New Ideals in the Planning of Cities, Towns and Villages 133–34 (1919).

24. J. Nolen, New Ideals in the Planning of Cities, Towns and Villages 133–34 (1919).

25. M. Scott, American City Planning Since 1890, at 97 (1969).

26. Proceedings of the Third National Conference on City Planning, Philadelphia, Pennsylvania, 1911, as reprinted in W. Goodman & E. Freund, Principles and Practice of Urban Planning 352 (1968).

27. Planning Problems of Town, City and Region: Papers and Discussions of the Twentieth National Conference on City Planning, reprinted in W. Goodman & E. Freund, Principles and Practice of Urban Planning at 352–53.

28. Issued in draft form in 1922 and first published in mimeographed form in 1923, the Act was revised and printed for the first time in 1924, and reprinted in 1926. By the time the final version was released in 1926, 43 states had enacted it.

29. *Village of Euclid, Ohio v. Ambler Realty Co.*, 272 U.S. 365, 47 S. Ct. 114, 71 L. Ed. 303 (1926). *Euclid* is discussed in depth in Ch. 3 and § 10:12 infra.
30. R. Walker, The Planning Function in Urban Government 11 (1941).
31. Principles and Practice of Urban Planning 23 (W. Goodman & E. Freund, eds. 1968).
32. M. Scott, American City Planning Since 1890, at 228 (1969). Compare the list of required elements for local government comprehensive plans in Florida's Local Government Comprehensive Planning and Land Development Regulation Act: capital improvements; intergovernmental coordination; future land use plans; traffic circulation; general sanitary sewer, solid waste, potable water, and natural ground water aquifer recharge; conservation; recreation and open space, housing; and coastal management (if coastal). Fla. Stat. Ann. § 163.3177.
33. Principles and Practice of Urban Planning (W. Goodman & E. Freund, eds. 1968) at 353.
34. A Standard State Zoning Enabling Act, § 3 (1926): *"Purposes in view.* Such regulations shall be made in accordance with a comprehensive plan. ..."
35. A minority of states requires that plans be enacted and that zoning he in accordance with comprehensive plans. For a detailed discussion of this trend, see § 2:13 infra.).
36. See § 2:14 infra; DeGrove, Planning Policy and Politics: Smart Growth and the States (2005). See also *Trail v. Terrapin Run, LLC*, 403 Md. 523, 943 A.2d 1192 (2008).
37. 42 U.S.C.A. §§ 1441 et seq.
38. 42 U.S.C.A. §§ 1450 to 1469(c).
39. See, generally, Principles and Practice of Urban Planning 349 (W. Goodman & E. Freund, eds. 1968).
40. For additional information on planning theory see generally Burchell and Sternlieb, Planning Theory in the 1980s (1978). For comprehensive planning, see generally, Branch, Comprehensive City Planning, Introduction & Explanation (1985); Kaiser, Godschalk, and Chapin, Urban Land Use Planning (4th ed. 1996); Nelson, Estimating Land Use and Facility Needs and Impacts (1998); Arthur C. Nelson & Robert E. Lang. The New Politics of Planning: How States and Local Governments are Coming to Common Ground on Reshaping America's Built Environment (2009); Arthur C. Nelson & Robert E. Lang, Megapolitan America: A New Vision for Understanding America's Metropolitan Geography (2011).
41. Nelson. The Mass Market for Suburban Low-Density Development is Over, 44 Urb. Law. 811, 819 (2012). See also Arthur C. Nelson, Reshaping Metropolitan America: Development Trends and Opportunities to 2030 (2013).
42. For a discussion of exclusionary practices, see infra §§ 6:1 et seq.
43. See American Planning Association Policy Guide on Smart Growth Planning Structure, Process, and Regulation, No. 7 (APA, 2002), available at https://www.planning.org/policy/guides/adopted/smartgrowth.htm.
44. *Angermeier v. Borough of Sea Girt*, 27 N.J. 298, 142 A.2d 624, 629 (1958).
45. This synopsis of the process represents a synthesis of current theories on the planning process. For a more detailed discussion, see F. Chapin & E. Kaiser, Urban Land Use Planning 68–104 (3d ed. 1979).
46. A slightly different approach to classifying states according to the status of comprehensive plans—or lack thereof—is found in the periodic review of comprehensive planning cases compiled by Edward J. Sullivan and published by the *Urban Lawyer:* 'These cases

fall into three major categories. The first category, the 'unitary view,' reflects what still may be the majority rule, i.e., that there is no requirement for a plan that is separate from the zoning regulations and that any existing plan has no legal effect. The second category gives the plan some significance as a factor, but not the exclusive or even the most significant one, in evaluating land use regulations and actions. The weight to be given to the plan varies from state to state and from case to case. Finally, the third category comprises those cases in which the plan is described as a quasi-constitutional document that governs the regulatory ordinances and actions of the local government implementing the plan." Sullivan, Recent Developments in Comprehensive Planning Law, 38 Urb. Law. 685, 686–87 (2006). See also Sullivan, Recent Developments in Comprehensive Planning Law, 43 Urb. Law. 823 (2011). Sullivan and Bragar, Recent Developments in Comprehensive Planning, 46 Urb. Law. 685, 702 (2014).

The American Planning Association's Growing Smart Legislative Guidebook: Model Statutes for Planning and the Management of Change (2002) offers state legislatures four choices: "(1) planning as an advisory function; (2) planning as activity to be encouraged through incentives; (3) planning as a mandatory activity necessary in order to exercise regulatory and related powers; and (4) mandated state-regional-local planning that is integrated both vertically and horizontally." See https://www.planning.org.policy/guides/adopted/smartgrowth.htm.

47. See DiMento, The Consistency Doctrine: Continuing Controversy, F. Strom, ed., 1982 Zoning and Planning Law Handbook 77.
48. See § 2:8 supra.
49. *Kozesnik v. Montgomery Tp.*, 24 N.J. 154, 131 A.2d 1 (1957).
50. N.J. Stat. Ann. § 40:55D–62 partially overruled *Kozesnik*, requiring elements of a formal plan and consistency unless set aside by a majority vote of the full membership of the governing body.
51. 24 N.J. at 166, 131 A.2d at 7. See also *Iowa Coal Min. Co., Inc. v. Monroe County*, 494 N.W.2d 664, 669 (Iowa 1993) (plan need not be reduced to writing and can be found in ordinance itself).
52. "[T]he view that the comprehensive plan is found in zoning ordinances and maps was once the majority view, very few states now adhere to that analysis." Sullivan and Bragar, Recent Developments in Comprehensive Planning, 46 Urb. Law. 685, 687 (2014). Examples of recent decisions still adopting this view include *Schulhof v. Zoning Bd. of Appeals of City of Norwalk*, 144 Conn. App. 446, 74 A.3d 442 (2013); *State ex rel. Phillips Supply Co. v. Cincinnati*, 2012-Ohio-6096, 985 N.E. 2d 257 (Ohio Ct. App. 1st Dist. Hamilton County 2012); *Apple Group Ltd. v. Granger Twp. Bd. of Zoning Appeals*, 2013-Ohio4259, 2013 WL 5437644 (Ohio Ct. App. 9th Dist. Medina County 2013), appeal allowed, 139 Ohio St. 3d 1404, 2014-Ohio-2245, 9 N.E.3d 1062 (2014) and judgment aff'd, 144 Ohio St. 3d 188, 2015-Ohio-2343, 41 N.E.3d 1185 (2015); *Parris v. City of Rapid City*, 2013 SD 51, 834 N.W.2d 850 (S.D. 2013).

See also Salkin, American Law of Zoning §§ 21.01 (5th ed.); but see *Forestview Homeowner's Ass'n, Inc. v. Cook County*, 18 Ill. App. 3d 230, 309 N.E.2d 763 (1st Dist. 1974) (holding that the presumption of validity usually accorded zoning is shifted or weakened in the absence of a comprehensive plan).
53. *Udell v. Haas,* 21 N.Y.2d 463, 469, 288 N.Y.S.2d 888, 893, 235 N.E.2d 897, 900 (1968). See also *Palatine Nat. Bank v. Village of Barrington,* 177 Ill.

54. See Ga. Code Ann. § 50-8-2(a)(18). See Weissman, Dillard & Skinner, Zoning and Land Use Law in Georgia, Ch. 8 (2013). The Supreme Court of Georgia recently reversed an inverse condemnation judgment for a landowner based on a special use permit requirement that required projects be not inconsistent with the comprehensive plan. *City of Suwanee v. Settles Bridge Farm, LLC*, 292 Ga. 434, 738 S.E.2d 597 (2013).

App. 3d 839, 127 Ill. Dec. 126, 532 N.E.2d 955 (2d Dist. 1988).

55. One of the incentives is the power to adopt certain impact fees. The Georgia system is described more fully infra § 9:1 ID.

56. 20 Ill. Comp. Stat. Ann. § 662/1.

57. Haar, The Master Plan: An Impermanent Constitution, 20 Law & Contemp. Probs. 353, 366 (1955) (emphasis in original). Professor Haar's position was adopted and his article quoted from by the Court of Appeals of New York in *Udell v. Haas*, 21 N.Y.2d 463, 288 N.Y.S.2d 888, 235 N.E.2d 897 (1968).

58. Those states, by statute or by court decision, include California, Delaware, Florida, Kentucky, Maine, Nebraska, Nevada, New Jersey, Oregon, South Dakota, and Vermont. See Sullivan and Pelham, Comprehensive Planning and Growth Management, 28 Urb. Law. 819 (1996).

59. "The plan is likened to a constitution for all future development. ..." *Machado v. Musgrove*, 519 So. 2d 629, 631 (Fla. 3d DCA 1987).

60. "The trend in case law for 2012–13 demonstrates increased respect for comprehensive planning, less tolerance for the view that zoning regulations are isolated from their planning roots and more emphasis on the role of planning when plans are amended or interpreted." Sullivan and Bragar, Recent Developments in Comprehensive Planning Law, 43 Urb. Law. 685, 702 (2014). See Stroud, A History and New Turns in Florida's Growth Management Reform, 45 J. Marshall L. Rev. 397 (2012), and, generally, Sullivan, Recent Developments in Comprehensive Planning Law, 43 Urb. Law. 823 (2011).

61. U.S. Dep't of Commerce, A Standard State Zoning Enabling Act § 3 (1926). See also supra § 2:11.

62. See, generally, Haar, In Accordance with a Comprehensive Plan, 68 Har. L. Rev. 1154, 1158 (1955).

63. U.S. Dep't of Commerce, Standard City Planning Enabling Act (1928).

64. An explanatory note to the SZEA indicated the comprehensive plan's purpose: "This will prevent haphazard or piecemeal zoning. No zoning should be done without such a comprehensive study." U.S. Dep't of Commerce, Standard City Planning Enabling Act (1928) § 3.

65. See J. DiMento, The Consistency Doctrine and the Limits of Planning, 9 n. 1 (1980). (Portions of this work are reproduced herein with the author's permission.).

66. See, generally, J. DiMento, J. DiMento, The Consistency Doctrine and the Limits of Planning, 9 n. 1 (1980).

67. See e.g. Cal. Gov't Code § 65567 mandating that development requiring a building permit, subdivision approval, or open space zoning be consistent with the local open space plan. Curtin & Talbert, Curtin's California Land Use and Planning Law 18 (26th ed. 2006). See, generally, the Florida Environmental Land and Water Management Act of 1972, Fla. Stat. Ann. ch. 380, in particular, § 380.04(1) (defining development) and § 380.06 (mandating local and regional review of developments of regional impact and requiring that such projects be consistent with state and local comprehensive plans before development approval).

68. See, generally, J. DiMento, J. DiMento, The Consistency Doctrine and the Limits of Planning, 9 n. 1 (1980).
69. Roddewig, Recent Developments in Land Use, Planning and Zoning, 21 Urb. Law. 769 (1989).
70. See e.g., The National Coastal Zone Management Act of 1972, 16 U.S.C.A. § 1456(c)(1), requiring that federal activity affecting coastal zones be consistent with state management programs. Section 1456(d) makes the act cut in both directions by requiring state and local coastal activities to be consistent with the federal plan as a prerequisite to receiving federal assistance.
71. See e.g. Cal. Gov't Code § 65567 mandating that development requiring a building permit, subdivision approval, or open space zoning be consistent with the local open space plan. Curtin & Talbert, Curtin's California Land Use and Planning Law 18 (26th ed. 2006). "Whether a development order is consistent with a comprehensive plan is determined by comparing what the order permits, not what the current holder intends to do under the order." *United States Sugar Corp. v. 1000 Friends of Florida,* 134 So. 3d 1052 (Fla. 4th DCA 2013). See, generally, the Florida Environmental Land and Water Management Act of 1972, Fla. Stat. Ann. Ch. 380, in particular, § 380.04(1) (defining development) and § 380.06 (mandating local and regional review of developments of regional impact and requiring that such projects be consistent with state and local comprehensive plans before development approval). See also Fla. Stat. Ann. § 163.3194(l)(b) (requiring consistency between land development regulations and the adopted comprehensive plan).
72. See, e.g., F. Bosselman & D. Callies, The Quiet Revolution in Land Use Controls (1971).
73. F. Bosselman & D. Callies, The Quiet Revolution in Land Use Controls (1971); Attkisson, Note: Putting a Stop to Sprawl: State Intervention as a Tool for Growth Management, 62 Vand. L. Rev. 979 (2009).
74. See e.g., *Fasano v. Board of County Com'rs of Washington County,* 264 Or. 574, 507 P.2d 23 (1973) (disapproved of by, *Neuberger v. City of Portland,* 288 Or. 585, 607 P.2d 722 (1980)).
75. Cal. Gov't Code § 65860(a). See J. DiMento, supra note 5, at 18.
76. See Hagman & DiMento, The Consistency Requirement in California, 30:6 Land Use L. & Zoning Dig. 5, 6 (1978); Curtin & Talbert, Curtin's California Land Use and Planning Law Ch. 2 (26th ed. 2006); Ziegler, Rathkopf's The Law of Zoning and Planning § 14:8 (4th ed.).
77. But see *Twain Harte Homeowners Assn. v. County of Tuolumne,* 138 Cal. App. 3d 664, 188 Cal. Rptr. 233, 254 (5th Dist. 1982), where the state planning act was held to require that population density be expressed numerically, and not merely in terms of uses (e.g., dwelling units per acre).
78. See J. DiMento, The Consistency Doctrine and the Limits of Planning (1980), at 22.
79. See J. DiMento, The Consistency Doctrine and the Limits of Planning, 9 n. 1 (1980), at 22.
80. *Fasano v. Board of County Com'rs of Washington County,* 264 Or. 574, 507 P.2d 23 (1973) (disapproved of by, *Neuberger v. City of Portland,* 288 Or. 585, 607 P.2d 722 (1980)) and (rejected by, *Quinn v. Town of Dodgeville,* 120 Wis. 2d 304, 354 N.W.2d 747 (Ct. App. 1984)) and (rejected by, *Hampton v. Richland County,* 292 S.C. 500, 357 S.E.2d 463 (Ct. App. 1987)).
81. The case is perhaps better known for the surprising approach it took in regard to judicial review of local land use decisions. See infra § 5:9.

82. See, generally, Long, Making Urban Policy Useful and Corrigible, 10 Urb. Aff. Q. 379 (1975). See also J. DiMento, The Consistency Doctrine and the Limits of Planning (1980), at 45.

83. See Housing for All Under Law: New Directions in Housing, Land Use and Planning Law, Report of the A.B.A. Advisory Comm'n on Housing and Urban Growth, 379 (Fishman ed. 1978).

84. See, generally, Tarlock, Consistency with Adopted Land Use Plans as a Standard of Judicial Review: The Case Against, 9 Urb. L. Ann. 69 (1975).

85. See, generally, DiMento, "But It's Only Planning": Planning and the Taking Issue in Land Development and Environmental Control Law, 1984 Zoning and Planning Law Handbook, ch. 5 (Clark Boardman 1984).

86. Spot planning occurs when instead of adhering to the existing plan designation, a locality allows both a comprehensive plan amendment and a zoning change to occur simultaneously without valid justification. Another definition was recently suggested in an article on Florida's new growth management legislation; spot planning, the practice of post-hoc consistency by amending plans or planning maps to coincide with or follow individual rezoning approvals. Davidson, Florida Restructures State and Local Growth Management Laws, 9:5 APA Planning & Law Div. Newsletter 7, 10 (Sept. 1985).

87. See, generally, J. DiMento, The Consistency Doctrine and the Limits of Planning (1980), ch. 3.

88. See e.g., Cal. Gov't Code § 65860; D.C. Code § 5-414 (1981); Fla. Stat. Ann. § 163.3194; Ky. Rev. Stat. Ann. § 100.213; Neb. Rev. Stat. § 23–114.03; N.J. Stat. Ann. § 40:55D–62; Or. Rev. Stat. § 197.010(1); Wash. Rev. Code Ann. § 36.70A.040.

89. American Planning Association, Growing Smart Legislative Guidebook (2002).

90. See J. DiMento, The Consistency Doctrine and the Limits of Planning (1980), at 24.

91. *Allen v. Flathead County*, 184 Mont. 58, 601 P.2d 399 (1979).

92. *Manley v. City of Maysville*, 528 S.W.2d 726 (Ky. 1975).

93. See J. DiMento, The Consistency Doctrine and the Limits of Planning (1980), at 23.

94. *Pinecrest Lakes, Inc. v. Shidel*, 795 So. 2d 191 (Fla. 4th DCA 2001).

95. *Poulos v. Martin County*, 700 So. 2d 163 (Fla. 1997).

96. The language of Judge Farmer indicates the strong role assigned by the court to the consistency requirement: "The statute says that an affected or aggrieved party may bring an action to enjoin an inconsistent development allowed by the County under its Comprehensive Plan. The statutory rule is that if you build it, and in court it later turns out as inconsistent, it will have to come down." 795 So. 2d 191 (2001).

97. For an analysis of the importance of the case to implementation of the consistency requirement in Florida, see Grosso, The Pinecrest Lakes Case: the Demolition Heard "Round the State" https://web.archive.org/web/20100610113048/http://www.nsulaw.nova.edu/faculty/documents/Pinecrest%20Analysis.pdf. See also, Land Planning: Demolition of Buildings Permitted, 31-MAR Real Est.L.Rep 2 (2002).

98. See infra § 5:9.

99. See *Fasano v. Board of County Com'rs of Washington County*, 264 Or. 574, 580 (1973); § 5:9 infra.

100. *Board of County Com'rs of Brevard County v. Snyder*, 627 So. 2d 469 (Fla. 1993).

101. Although the local government is not required to make findings of fact in denying the

application for rezoning, upon review the circuit court must be shown that there was competent substantial evidence presented to the local government to support its ruling. *Board of County Com'rs of Brevard County,* 627 So. 2d at 476.

102. *Martin County v. Yusem,* 690 So. 2d 1288 (Fla. 1997).

103. Both movements are discussed in detail infra § 9:1. See, generally, New Urbanism: Comprehensive Report and Best Practices Guide (2001); Codifying New Urbanism (APA Planning Advisory Service, Report No.526, 2004).

"[T]he mere existence of a comprehensive plan is not sufficient to create smarter growth. In fact, comprehensive plans sometimes favor sprawl by mandating single-use, low-density zoning and wide, automobile-oriented streets. Further, comprehensive plans are not necessary to achieve smarter growth. Although a comprehensive plan can encourage smart growth by allowing compact development, mixed use, and narrower streets, a reformed zoning code can also achieve these goals. A comprehensive plan can be useful insofar as it explains or consistently applies the policies behind a municipal zoning code—but this benefit applies to sprawl-oriented plans and codes as well as those that encourage smart growth." Lewyn, The [Somewhat] False Hope of Comprehensive Planning, 37 U. Haw. L. Rev. 39, 69 (2015).

104. American Planning Association Policy Guide on Smart Growth (adopted April 4, 2002 by Chapter Delegate Assembly and ratified April 15, 2002) [emphasis supplied]; Andres Duany et al., The Smart Growth Manual (2010).

105. See Charter of the New Urbanism (Michael Leccese and Kathleen McCormick, ed. 2000).

106. Nolon, An Environmental Understanding of the Local Land Use System, 45 Envtl. L. Rep. New & Analysis 10215 (Mar. 2015).

107. See infra § 9:5, Growth Management Through Regional Planning and Regulation. See also Arthur C. Nelson & Robert E. Lang, Megapolitan America: A New Vision for Understanding America's Metropolitan Geography (2011).

CHAPTER 3: LAND USE CONTROLS: HISTORY, SOURCES OF POWER AND PURPOSES

I. INTRODUCTION

§ 3:1 INTRODUCTORY NOTE

Public and private land use controls have a long history in Anglo/American law, dating back to at least Elizabethan times. Modern public controls, our emphasis in this book, date back to the early 20th century. While zoning, the division of land into areas according to use, building height and bulk, remains the core tool of land use control, its inability to deal with the explosion of land use development which began in the last quarter of the 20th century and gradual recognition of the environmental effects of intense development led to the adoption of new controls and significant changes in zoning itself. Though this chapter focuses primarily on zoning, other land use controls are covered in other chapters, such as the planning process, building codes, subdivision control law, and growth management systems. These are often so intertwined with zoning that drawing a clear division between them is difficult. Thus, much of what is said here relates not solely to zoning but to the land use control power in general.

Alternatives to zoning have been suggested over the years. The Model Land Development Code integrates zoning and subdivision controls and provides state oversight of local control of developments of regional impact. Drawbacks from the parochial effects of localism have prompted greater use of state and regional controls. Finally, and more fundamentally, use of the regulatory power to limit land use has been challenged. Some critics would simply, or essentially, omit government from the field, while others would zone using the power of eminent domain in combination with the police power.

II. THE HISTORY OF LAND USE CONTROLS

§ 3:2 PRE-20TH CENTURY

Land use regulations date back to colonial America, and earlier.[1] In the earliest days, colonists treated land as a community resource to be used in the public interest. For example, a 1632 Cambridge, Massachusetts ordinance provided that no buildings could be built in outlying areas until vacant spaces within the town were developed. Roofs had to be covered with slate or board rather than thatch. Heights of all buildings had to be the same. Lots were forfeited if not built on in six months. Finally, buildings could only be erected with the consent of the mayor.[2]

The Cambridge ordinance is typical of laws found throughout colonial America. Many restricted the location of dwellings, imposed affirmative obligations of use, compelled the fencing of agricultural land, required owners of wetlands to share the cost of drainage projects, and allowed the public to hunt on private land.[3] Over the following centuries, land use ordinances were enacted to deal with specific problems. For example, they excluded certain kinds of buildings and uses from particular areas of the city, such as wooden buildings, horse stables, and cemeteries, and imposed bulk requirements providing for setbacks and yards, and set height limits.

§ 3:3 COMPREHENSIVE ZONING

Zoning became prevalent in the 20th century.[4] New York City enacted the first comprehensive zoning ordinance in 1916. It was comprehensive in the sense that it classified uses and created zones for all uses, which zones were then mapped, and it included height and bulk controls. Four years after enactment, the ordinance was upheld in *Lincoln Trust Co. v. Williams Building Corporation*.[5]

Zoning proved enormously popular and spread rapidly. By the time the Supreme Court upheld its constitutionality in 1926 in *Village of Euclid v. Ambler Realty Co.*,[6] some 564 cities and towns had enacted zoning.[7] After the *Euclid* decision, so-called Euclidean or use zoning swept the country. The zoning was Euclidean in two senses—the kind of zoning adopted was similar to that used in the Village of Euclid—and the landscape was divided into a geometric pattern of use districts.

While the Euclidean origins of most present-day zoning ordinances can be recognized, there have been many changes. Most notably, they allow for a flexibility in the development approval process not present in early ordinances. Basic use zoning and the flexibility devices used today are discussed in Chapter 4.

§ 3:4 EARLY CONSTITUTIONAL HISTORY OF ZONING
A. Pre-Comprehensive Zoning Cases

The Supreme Court decided a number of land use cases on its way to sustaining comprehensive zoning. From 1885 to 1922, the Court upheld a San Francisco ordinance restricting the hours of operation of laundries in certain locations,[8] but invalidated another ordinance prohibiting laundries in wooden buildings unless permission was obtained from the Board of Supervisors, where it was applied exclusively against Chinese.[9] The Court upheld an ordinance designating certain areas of a city for prostitution,[10] a Massachusetts statute setting height limitations in Boston,[11] and an ordinance precluding further burials in existing cemeteries.[12] The Court also invalidated an ordinance allowing neighbors to establish setback lines,[13] upheld an ordinance excluding stables from a commercial district,[14] upheld a Los Angeles regulation that precluded the operation of an existing brickyard within an area zoned to exclude them,[15] upheld an ordinance prohibiting signs in residential neighborhoods unless neighbors consented,[16] held invalid race-based zoning,[17] upheld an ordinance that precluded the storage of oil and gasoline within 300 feet of a dwelling house,[18] and invalidated a state statute that banned underground coal mining where it would cause subsidence of homes.[19]

In sum, during this turn of the century era, the Court found that the police power was "one of the most essential powers of government-one that is the least limitable. * * * There must be progress, [said the Court,] and if in its march private interests are in the way, they must yield to the good of the community."[20] Regulations, however, did have a constitutional limit, and if they went "too far," they would be recognized as takings.[21]

B. Constitutional Parameters of Comprehensive Zoning: Euclid and Nectow

While the string of late nineteenth and early 20th century cases noted above demonstrated the Court's view that the police power could be used to impose significant limitations on land use, there was still some doubt as to the validity of a comprehensive land use control system. In the early 1920s, several state courts addressed the issue, and, though most had upheld comprehensive zoning, some found it invalid, generally on the basis that it interfered with the free market.[22]

In 1926, the Court handed down the seminal land use decision of *Village of Euclid v. Ambler Realty Co.*,[23] where against a facial attack it upheld the general validity of an ordinance that set use, height, and bulk restrictions for an entire town. Key to the case was the use of a deferential standard of judicial review of municipal zoning. Urbanization, said the Court, had brought a set of problems that justified governmental intervention to protect the public. While there could be differences of opinion on the separation of residential, commercial, and industrial use in specific situations, as a general proposition the separation of uses made sense. Furthermore, said the Court, if all that could be said of a law was that it was "fairly debatable, the legislative judgment must be allowed to control."[24]

The Court tempered the reach of *Euclid* two years later in *Nectow v. City of Cambridge*,[25] when it held a zoning ordinance invalid as applied to a particular parcel because it found that the public good was not promoted by the zoning classification. In the end, though, it was the deferential review of *Euclid* rather than the closer scrutiny of *Nectow* that created the climate that allowed comprehensive zoning to flourish.[26]

C. The Current Generation of Cases

After setting constitutional guidelines for zoning in the 1920s, for almost fifty years the Court did not address zoning issues. Since the early 1970s, however, the Court has acted on a wide array of land use and zoning controls under the First Amendment's speech clause, the Fifth Amendment's takings clause, the 14th

Amendment's due process and equal protection clauses, and the commerce clause. These developments are covered in detail in Chapter 10.

III. SOURCES OF POWER

§ 3:5 IN GENERAL

Public land use controls, including zoning, subdivision regulation, building codes and growth controls, are exercises of the police power. Though broad, this power to enact laws to promote the health, safety, morals, and general welfare is limited by the federal and state constitutions. State legislatures can delegate their power to regulate land use and by and large have done so. In the early years, almost complete power was delegated to local governments, but over the past few decades, a number of state legislatures have limited local rule and instituted statewide controls.

Among local governments, the delegated police power is distributed to municipal corporations—cities, villages and towns—and to counties. These terms generally are used interchangeably in this book to refer to any political subdivisions that have land use control power. Limited purpose governments, such as utility districts and school districts, are seldom given the power to zone or otherwise regulate land use.

Though the source of power to control land use in most states is by way of a zoning enabling act, the power may come from other sources. In a number of states, the state constitution provides for home rule to distribute state power to local governments. Home rule power is also sometimes granted by legislation. Land use control power can also be implied from a law generally authorizing the exercise of the police power by local government. Rarely, land use control power may also be based on a doctrine of inherent powers, meaning that the mere creation of a political subdivision confers power to do the kinds of things local governments need to do, such as zone.

Generally, the power to zone is delegated to the legislative bodies of local governments. When the source is the enabling act, the power is sometimes divided among legislative and administrative bodies, such as planning commissions and boards of adjustment.[27] In many states, the people retain the power of initiative and referendum and may use them to control land use.

Finally, many states have enabling acts establishing or authorizing land use control systems for special situations, such as airport zoning, flood plain zoning, historic districting, landmark preservation, or watershed management. The following sections cover these matters in more detail.

§ 3:6 STANDARD ZONING ENABLING ACT

The popularity of Euclidean zoning was aided significantly by the fact that there was a good model: the Standard State Zoning Enabling Act (SZEA). Released in 1924, the SZEA resulted from the work of an Advisory Committee appointed by Herbert Hoover, then Secretary of Commerce.[28] Few model or uniform laws have enjoyed such widespread adoption or influence. All 50 states eventually adopted enabling acts substantially patterned on the Standard Act. Many regard the Act as outdated and some commentators suggest radical reform, but the basic provisions still apply in many states.

The first three sections of the SZEA state the purposes of zoning and define its scope.[29]

> Section 1. Grant of Power.—For the purpose of promoting health, safety, morals, or the general welfare of the community, the legislative body of cities and incorporated villages is

hereby empowered to regulate and restrict the height, number of stories, and size of buildings and other structures, the percentage of lot that may be occupied, the size of yards, courts, and other open spaces, the density of population, and the location and use of buildings, structures, and land for trade, industry, residence, or other purposes.

Sec. 2. Districts.—For any or all of said purposes the local legislative body may divide the municipality into districts of such number, shape, and area as may be deemed best suited to carry out the purposes of this act; and within such districts it may regulate and restrict the erection, construction, reconstruction, alteration, repair, or use of buildings, structures, or land. All such regulations shall be uniform for each class or kind of buildings throughout each district, but the regulations in one district may differ from those in other districts.

Sec. 3. Purposes in View.—Such regulations shall be made in accordance with a comprehensive plan and designed to lessen congestion in the streets; to secure safety from fire, panic, and other dangers; to promote health and the general welfare; to provide adequate light and air; to prevent the overcrowding of land; to avoid undue concentration of population; to facilitate the adequate provision of transportation, water, sewerage, schools, parks, and other public requirements. Such regulations shall be made with reasonable consideration among other things, to the character of the district and its peculiar suitability for particular uses, and with *a* view to conserving the value of buildings and encouraging the most appropriate use of land throughout such municipality.

Subsequent sections provide a procedure for adopting zoning and making amendments, including provision for protest by neighbors. The Act calls for the establishment of a zoning or planning commission, which makes recommendations on zoning. The Act also permits the establishment of a Board of Adjustment to hear appeals from enforcement of the ordinance, to hear and decide special exceptions (i.e., special permits) and to grant variances. Finally, the Act contains provisions for enforcement of the regulations.

The American Planning Association, which began a "Growing Smart" Project in 1994 to update the standard planning and zoning enabling acts of the 1920s,[30] has a created the Growing Smart Legislative Guidebook with various model statutes.[31] The Association has published drafts of model smart growth codes covering such topics as mixed-use, town centers, affordable housing density bonuses, a unified development permit review process, transferable development rights, cluster development, and pedestrian overlay districts.[32] Despite the SZEA's shortcomings, many states still use it, although they have enacted piecemeal modifications over the years.

In addition to ultra vires challenges to zoning enactments that fall outside the scope of the enabling act,[33] zoning can also be held invalid if the procedures established by the enabling act are not followed.

§ 3:7 INHERENT AND IMPLIED POWERS

Local governments, as creatures of the state, lack inherent powers, and judicial construction of local powers granted by state legislatures generally has been tight.[34] With this history of limited construction of municipal powers, it is not surprising that the power to zone is usually not implied from typical legislation conferring general police power on a municipality.[35]

Dillon's Rule, which limited municipal powers, prevailed in state courts throughout the country from the mid-nineteenth to mid-20th century and is still used in a few states today.[36] The rule provides that "a municipal corporation possesses and can exercise the following powers and no others: first, those granted in express words; second, those necessarily or fairly implied in or incident to the powers expressly granted; third, those essential to the accomplishment of the declared objects and purposes of the corporation, not simply convenient, but indispensable."[37] While the "fairly implied" language would have lent itself to reading grants broadly, the courts treated Dillon's Rule to dictate narrow construction.

This narrow view of local authority has been relaxed by court giving a broad reading of state enabling acts,[38] and by the establishment of home rule authority.[39] Enabling acts themselves frequently authorize liberal interpretation. One statute provides, for example, that:

> It is the policy of the General Assembly that the cities of this State should have adequate authority to execute the powers, duties, privileges, and immunities conferred upon them by law. To this end, the provisions of this Chapter and of city charters shall be broadly construed and grants of power shall be construed to include any additional and supplementary powers that are reasonably necessary or expedient to carry them into execution and effect * * *.[40]

Though Dillon's Rule has been formally rejected in most states,[41] it still lurks behind the scenes to strike on occasion.[42] Applying the above statute, which expressly authorizes broad construction, the North Carolina supreme court invalidated a city's stormwater utility ordinance, finding that the city exceeded the grant of authority.[43]

§ 3:8 CHARTER

A charter is the basic document of a local government, akin to a constitution. The state legislature can confer power on a city in a charter, including zoning power.[44] Sometimes home rule powers[45] can be obtained only by adopting a charter, that is, the zoning enabling act governs unless there is a charter.

§ 3:9 HOME RULE

While local governments lack inherent powers, in many states a degree of independence exists by virtue of home rule powers conferred by state constitution or state statute.[46] Dillon's Rule does not apply to governmental units with home rule authority.[47] The courts of the various states are not in agreement as to whether home rule power authorized by state constitution or legislation is a source of zoning power.[48] In California and Ohio,[49] for example, power to make and enforce local regulations is interpreted as authorizing zoning, whereas in New York, the constitutional power of municipalities to enact local laws does not authorize zoning.[50]

Even where zoning power is authorized by home rule, it only applies to local matters not in conflict with state law.[51] Conflict with zoning enabling legislation is possible, particularly on procedural issues. Due to a great state interest in procedural uniformity, the latter typically controls. A state requirement that cities adopt plans has been held to be of such statewide concern that home rule cities must comply.[52] Local zoning measures often implicate substantial state interests. Thus, the Colorado Supreme Court rejected, as a home rule measure, an affordable housing mitigation ordinance that addressed a matter of mixed local and statewide concern.[53]

§ 3:10 INITIATIVE AND REFERENDUM

In a few states, the people can enact legislation through use of the initiative, and in many states, can revoke legislative acts by referendum.

The initiative and referendum are discussed in detail in Chapter 5.

§ 3:11 SPECIAL ENABLING ACTS

Authority for some kinds of zoning may be provided by a separate enabling act. Airport zoning and flood plain zoning, both of which were stimulated by federal legislation, are two examples. Enabling acts have also been amended, or special acts passed, to permit the creation of districts to preserve historic and architecturally significant areas.[54]

Peculiar aspects of airport operations have led to the passage in many states of specific airport zoning enabling legislation.[55] Airport zoning has also been encouraged by the federal government, which has helped fund airport construction provided that uses adjacent to the airport are so regulated as to preclude interference with airport operation.

A state's participation in the National Flood Insurance Program requires that certain regulatory measures be adopted to exclude or limit building on flood plains.[56] While some local governments implement these requirements through general zoning enabling legislation, a number of states have specific flood plain legislation.[57]

§ 3:12 GEOGRAPHICAL REACH

A. Extraterritorial Zoning

The Standard Zoning Enabling Act did not provide for extraterritorial zoning. The act also only empowered municipalities to zone. Counties were excluded, and without county power to zone, the fringes of city areas could be developed without zoning control. The power to zone eventually was extended to counties in most states, but extraterritorial concerns persisted.

Some states grant the power to zone extraterritorially.[58] Such power is frequently conferred only on larger cities and is limited in terms of miles from the city.[59] It may be permitted only where the county does not zone or where the county approves. In metropolitan areas, overlapping extraterritorial jurisdiction is usually solved by limiting power to points equidistant between the municipalities exercising the power. Regionalization of zoning in metropolitan areas remains a major problem, and the prospective loss of zoning power is one of the major reasons why municipalities in metropolitan areas resist metropolitan government. The extraterritorial impact of a local exclusionary ordinance is discussed in Chapter 6.

B. Annexation and Prezoning

If extraterritorial zoning power is lacking, problems can arise upon annexation. Previous zoning regulations usually terminate upon annexation, leaving the land unzoned.[60] While the area can now be zoned, uses inconsistent with the plan for the area may become vested in the time that it takes to implement new zoning.

The Standard Zoning Enabling Act created no mechanism for zoning territory in advance of annexation, and states have handled the problem in a variety of ways. In California, cities are permitted to prezone territory to be annexed so that the zoning ordinance takes effect immediately upon annexation.[61] A zoning ordinance also may be part of the annexation ordinance.[62] Interim zoning also has been used. In other states, statutes provide that upon annexation the area, if already zoned, will retain that classification for a period of time.[63] Ordinances sometimes provide that upon annexation the territory is automatically zoned to the most restrictive zone available under the zoning ordinance, pending reclassification.

IV. PURPOSES

§ 3:13 IN GENERAL

The purposes for which zoning may be enacted are as broad as the source of power from the state allows. Whether by enabling act or home rule, the power may extend to the full limits of the police power of the state, or it may be more limited.

Section 1 of the Standard Act broadly grants the power to zone to municipalities "for the purpose of promoting health, safety, morals, or the general welfare of the community." Section 3, set out above,[64] then lists various "purposes in view." Official commentary to the act observes that Section 1 "defined and limited the powers" conferred, while Section 3 "contain[ed] a direction from the [legislature] as to the purposes * * * [and] constitute[ed] the 'atmosphere' under which zoning [was] to be done."[65] The New York Court of Appeals has read Section 1 as merely providing the "constitutional predicate" for zoning, and not as conferring the full police power of the state. To be valid, a zoning ordinance must be authorized, expressly or implicitly, by Section 3.[66]

Zoning may be invalid because it is beyond the power conferred by the enabling act.[67] The general language of the SZEA has led some courts to judge ultra vires challenges by reference to a reasonableness test that is the same as that used to determine whether an act is beyond the police power. This finds support not only in the fact that Section 1 of the SZEA provides a grant of power in language that equals the full reach of the police power, but in the long list of "purposes in view" of Section 3. Additional leeway exists since most courts will imply powers that are fairly related, or incident, to powers expressly granted.[68]

Courts have upheld numerous ordinances that lack precise grounding in the "purposes in view" list. In *Golden v. Planning Board of Town of Ramapo*[69] the court found that an ordinance that limited growth based on the availability of public services and infrastructure for an 18 year period was within the Standard Act's language that permits zoning "to avoid undue concentration of population [and] to facilitate the adequate provision of transportation, water, sewerage, schools, [and] parks, * * *."[70] Single-use zoning covering an entire municipality has been upheld even though a narrow reading of the enabling act arguably requires multiple districts.[71] Conditional zoning has also been upheld despite the lack of express language authorizing such a technique.[72]

Where a zoning ordinance is unrelated to the achievement of land use objectives, it will be invalidated. For example, a moratorium imposed on cellular telephone antennas enacted for the health of a village's residents was found to be outside the enabling act where there was not a scintilla of evidence to support the claim of a health hazard.[73] Revocation of a permit to operate a nursing home to "quell community opposition"[74] or to prevent riots[75] also has been held outside the enabling act.

Regardless of the breadth of the delegated power, zoning for a particular purpose may be invalid because the exercise of power constitutes an act that is beyond the scope of the police power. For example, if zoning is exercised to lower the market value of property so that a governmental body can acquire it more cheaply by eminent domain, exercise of the power for that purpose would be unconstitutional.[76]

In the sections that follow, some of the purposes of zoning are considered in further detail. A particular zoning action often effectuates several purposes and the purposes often overlap.

§ 3:14 PRESERVATION OF PROPERTY VALUES

The preservation of property values is often cited as an important, if not primary, purpose of zoning. While preservation is not an explicitly stated purpose, the Standard Zoning Enabling Act does speak of "conserving values." While none would likely quarrel with the preservation of value as a legitimate factor in zoning, it cannot stand alone. Value is a consequence of action or inaction, and it is the action or inaction that matters. Nonetheless, some courts say that is an independent interest. In a leading case in the area of aesthetic controls, the Wisconsin Supreme Court stated that "[a]nything that tends to destroy property values of the inhabitants of the village necessarily adversely affects the prosperity, and therefore the general welfare, of the entire village,"[77] is within the reach of the zoning power. The court's statement goes too far, and fails to recognize that one must ask what it is that affects value, and whether the regulation of that activity or occurrence is valid. That which causes the value to go down might be a commercial use in a residential neighborhood or the building of an architecturally unusual structure. It also might be the fact that a controversial radio talk show host wants to move into the neighborhood or that a nonmainstream religious group wishes to establish a place of worship in a neighborhood where other religious uses are located. The former, but not the latter two, could be restricted.[78]

Courts ought not allow a goal to preserve property values to obscure an unarticulated illegitimate motive. The Michigan Supreme Court recognized this when it held that the "conservation of property values is not by itself made a proper sole objective for the exercise of police power under the statute."[79] The court proceeded to invalidate an ordinance specifying a minimum house size enacted solely to preserve the value of existing homes.

The mere fact that zoning depresses values of particular buildings or parcels does not render it invalid.[80] Similarly, the zoning of a parcel can be valid though the value of neighboring property is adversely affected by the zoning.[81] In any event, to the extent zoning is effective, the sum total of real property values in a city should be increased by orderly rather than haphazard development.

The "maintenance of property values" purpose is sometimes used to support zoning that preserves the property tax base and to justify controls designed to preserve or promote aesthetics, or historic or natural areas. These matters are discussed separately.[82]

§ 3:15 PRESERVATION OF CHARACTER AND AESTHETICS

The Standard Act indicates that the zoning should take into consideration the character of the district. "Character" is a vague and loaded term. It may refer to the physical appearance of an area to justify architectural or other aesthetic controls.[83] It also may be "code" language to reflect "snob zoning," to exclude housing for persons of low and moderate income. The validity of such exclusionary ordinances is explored in Chapter 6.

Some ordinances indicate that zoning is to stabilize neighborhoods. Though the phrase is not in the Standard Act, perhaps the "character" language implies that zoning should not upset the status quo. Neighbors unhappy with a proposed zoning change often argue that they have a right to have the zoning affecting them remain unchanged. They do not. While zoning should provide some stability, it is not a guarantee against change.[84]

The vagueness of the "character of a district" is apparent in zoning ordinances deemed to promote aesthetics, typically the regulation of signs and the imposition of architectural controls.[85]

§ 3:16 TRAFFIC SAFETY

The Standard Act provides that regulations should be made to lessen congestion in the streets and to facilitate adequate provision of transportation.[86] The location and dimension of streets are typically not controlled by zoning. However, there are several aspects of zoning related to traffic. This purpose is used to argue against nonresidential development in residential areas because of the danger to children in street crossing. The purpose is also effectuated by front yard and setback requirements, so that vision will not be impaired at street corners. Density controls, such as minimum lot sizes, can be used to lessen the amount of traffic generating activity.[87]

Off-street parking requirements are also justified to promote public safety and to maintain the traffic capacity of streets.[88] While generally held valid,[89] off-street parking requirements have been opposed because they add expense to construction and limit use of a lot for its primary purpose.[90] Subject to constitutional limitations,[91] municipalities may require the dedication of land for streets as a condition for the granting of development permission. Such dedications relate to the purpose of lessening congestion in the streets caused by the development.

Traffic relates to zoning in at least two other ways. First, a substantial increase in traffic along a street may be a change of condition making a rezoning of a residential area proper. Second, parking is a use of land which, when not on public streets or areas, is a use of land subject to zoning regulation.

§ 3:17 PUBLIC HEALTH

Over the years shifts occur in the conceptualization of the purposes sought to be accomplished by land use regulation. For example, "public health" has always been in the litany of police power purposes but for decades the implementation of regulations designed to protect public health were largely confined to measures such as limitation of uses in wooden building in order to reduce fire hazards or to regulate street design and location in order to encourage traffic safety. Today, thanks to the smart growth and new urbanism movements, public health is being interpreted to justify regulations designed to accomplish such goals as reduction of obesity and other sedentary life style grounded diseases by requiring—or at least encouraging—bike paths, neighborhood playgrounds, and mixed use friendly urban design to discourage automobile usage and encourage walking. This recent development is discussed in greater detail in Chapter 9.

§ 3:18 REGULATION OF COMPETITION

The regulation of competition is often said to be an improper purpose of zoning,[92] but care must be taken not to overstate the matter. In one case, when a city amended its zoning ordinance to allow new types of dry cleaners using particular solvents, it delayed the effective date of the ordinance to give existing businesses a chance to adjust to the new competition. Deeming the purpose improper, the court invalidated the portion of the ordinance that delayed the effective date of the new zoning.[93] Reasoning that zoning should not be used to create a monopoly, some courts also have held zoning invalid if it does not provide space for the establishment of future competitive businesses.[94] On the other hand, the mere act of districting has some effect on competition,[95] and the fact that the control of competition was a factor in the zoning of an area will not necessarily be fatal. An ordinance excluding small retailers from operating in a planned commercial zone in which large operations in the same retail business were allowed was held legitimate since its purpose was to preserve economic viability of the downtown business district, rather than to serve any impermissible private anticompetitive purpose.[96] We discuss potential federal antitrust liability in Chapter 10.

The big box phenomenon has led to the adoption of various anti-big box measures such as architectural controls, size limitations,[97] minimum wage and benefits' laws,[98] and exclusions. Unsurprisingly, adversely affected big box stores object to and often challenge such regulations. In *Wal-Mart Stores, Inc. v. City of Turlock*,[99] the anticompetitive effect of an ordinance banning discount superstores did not lead to its invalidation. The court found it was rationally related to the public welfare inasmuch as it was designed to protect against urban and suburban decay, increased traffic, and reduced air quality.[100]

If the exclusionary effect of an ordinance is incidental to an otherwise legitimate zoning purpose, it will be held valid.[101] The desire to achieve stability and balance in the provision of services is a legitimate goal, even though competition is suppressed.[102] Furthermore, a zoning ordinance enacted pursuant to a comprehensive plan is more likely to survive attack.[103]

The improper regulation of competition argument is often used to attack spacing requirements between such uses as gasoline stations and bars.[104] Similarly, spacing requirements may be upheld for gasoline stations on the grounds of an undesirable increase of traffic or fire hazards, or even on the ground that there are already a sufficient number of stations in the area to serve the public need.[105]

§ 3:19 FISCAL ZONING TO INCREASE TAX BASE

Fiscal zoning to increase the tax base, provide for employment, or otherwise plan the local economy has met with mixed reaction in the courts. In some states the enabling act provides that protecting or enhancing the tax base is a purpose of zoning.[106] In those states with the SZEA, which has no express provision regarding tax considerations, the purpose might be inferred from the "conserving values" clause.[107] A non-fiscal purpose also may be found to support zoning that is alleged to be fiscally motivated.[108]

A number of courts have recognized the desire to stimulate the local economy as a valid purpose of zoning. In one case, a court upheld a rezoning based on the county's findings that the result would lead to the employment of eighty-seven people from the community and would produce tax revenues constituting 25% of the city's budget.[109]

For many courts, the goal of increasing the tax base and providing employment opportunities is not fatal, but it cannot stand alone. There must be other legitimate reasons.[110] Some courts, however, roundly condemn fiscal zoning, declaring it to be "totally violative of all the basic principles of zoning."[111]

Fiscal considerations often explain the use of exclusionary zoning devices, such as minimum lot sizes. The validity of such measures is discussed in Chapter 6.

§ 3:20 PROMOTION OF MORALS

It is unusual for zoning ordinances to rely expressly on morals as a purpose, and the degree to which such a purpose is permissible is uncertain. Section 1 of the Standard Act provides that local government has the power to promote morals through zoning, but Section 3 does not list morals as an express purpose. Some early cases that authorized the banning of billboards did so on the barely credible rationale that immoral activities could be conducted behind them.[112] This presumably was a makeweight argument for courts that accepted, but were unwilling to acknowledge, the fact that aesthetics was the real purpose. This was necessary since aesthetics was once deemed an improper, or inadequate, purpose for which to exercise the police power.[113]

Some zoning ordinances provide that liquor stores and bars must be a certain distance from schools and churches. In one case, a town actually created an overlay "inebriate" district.[114] Other ordinances regulate the location of sexually oriented businesses. These are arguably based, at least in part, on a morals purpose, as well as directed at the secondary effects of such uses. Municipalities that regulate adult uses on "morals" grounds run some risk of running into First Amendment violations if the measure suppresses protected speech.[115]

§ 3:21 MANAGING GROWTH

The Standard Act makes no reference to timing and sequencing controls used today to manage growth. Enabling act problems can be encountered with respect to both short and long-term timing controls.

A. Short-Term Controls: Interim Zoning[116]

When an area is not zoned or is zoned but under comprehensive study for rezoning, a significant time delay may occur from the beginning of the planning process to the ultimate adoption of the zoning ordinance.[117] Meanwhile, developers can emasculate the proposed controls by developing in a manner inconsistent with the proposed ordinance. In order to prevent such development, legislative bodies use temporary or interim zoning to freeze or stringently limit land use. The need for speedy enactment of the interim control means that standard procedural safeguards of notice, hearing, referral to planning commissions and the like are usually not possible.

The SZEA did not provide for temporary or interim zoning. In earlier years, some courts invalidated interim zoning for lack of express authority.[118] Other courts, recognizing that proper zoning cannot be done quickly, found implied authority for interim ordinances and upheld it where the time delay was reasonable.[119] Several states now authorize interim zoning by special legislation.[120] The acts generally limit the period of time during which the interim ordinances are effective.

B. Long-Term Growth Management

As is true with the short-term problem of stopping development pending completion of a planning process, municipalities face long-term growth concerns. During the 1960s and 1970s, the objectives of land use control expanded to include consideration of a community's appearance, open space preservation and phased growth. At this time, zoning came under attack as being inflexible, as discouraging innovation, and inadequately dealing with environmental and housing affordability issues. New mechanisms were introduced to implement long-term growth management plans. For instance, in the leading case of *Golden v. Planning Board of Town of Ramapo*,[121] the New York Court of Appeals found that the state's enabling act, patterned after the SZEA, authorized controls on the timing and sequencing of development. A number of states specifically authorize growth management, which is covered in detail in Chapter 9.

§ 3:22 ZONING TO LOWER CONDEMNATION COSTS

Where zoning limits the use of land to fewer uses than those for which the market creates a demand, the value of the land is reduced. The effect of zoning on land is taken into account in determining just compensation in eminent domain proceedings.[122] If government yields to the temptation to use zoning to depress values to lower future condemnation costs, the zoning will be held invalid.[123] Since courts do not generally inquire into motives, the circumstances surrounding the zoning must be considered before concluding that the purpose of zoning was to lower values rather than some legitimate purpose. An improper purpose may be evidenced when land that is rezoned is coextensive with land to be condemned, as distinguished from zoning that affects a large number of landowners or is part of a comprehensive rezoning.[124]

Zoning and condemnation proceedings that are substantially concurrent may reveal an improper purpose. When a court suspects that zoning is being used to depress values, it may hold the zoning invalid on other grounds without giving the real basis for its decision. For example, if an "island" is rezoned for agricultural uses in an area the government intends to acquire as an airport, the court may hold it invalid spot zoning.

Official maps, which restrict the right to build in the pathway of planned streets, parks and other public sites, and setback provisions[125] imposed so that streets can be widened without the necessity of paying for buildings, are examples of other regulations that may limit costs of acquisition in some circumstances.[126]

V. ALTERNATIVES

§ 3:23 ALTERNATIVES TO EUCLIDEAN ZONING AND THE STANDARD ACT

The Standard Zoning Enabling Act (SZEA) remains the basic enabling act in many states, but it, and its planning counterpart, the Standard Planning Enabling Act, are criticized as outdated. Many shortcomings in zoning enabling laws have been cured or improved upon by piecemeal changes to the SZEA.[127] There have been efforts at more revolutionary change, some more successful than others. As noted earlier, some call for deregulation, preferring to allow land use to be determined by market forces, limited only by the common law of nuisance.[128] Other alternatives are explored in the following sections.

The American Planning Association began a "Growing Smart" Project in 1994 to update the standard planning and zoning enabling acts. This led to the creation of the Growing Smart Legislative Guidebook with various model statutes.[129] The Association has published drafts of model smart growth codes covering such topics as mixed-use development, town centers, affordable housing with density bonuses, a unified development permit review process, transferable development rights, cluster development, and pedestrian overlay districts.[130]

§ 3:24 THE MODEL LAND DEVELOPMENT CODE

A major effort to modernize the land development process at one fell swoop began in 1963 when the Ford Foundation financed an American Law Institute effort to develop a model code for land development. Completed in 1976,[131] the Model Land Development Code (MLDC) deals with the physical development of land, so as to maximize social and economic objectives.[132] The MLDC is based on the same assumptions underlying the Standard State Zoning Enabling Act, (SZEA) and its companion, the Standard City Planning Enabling Act (SPEA), which provides powers for planning, control of subdivisions, official maps and regional planning. These assumptions are, first, that government should control privately initiated development rather than be the primary development agency itself as it is in some countries, and, second, that local government should exercise most of the control.

Nevertheless, the MLDC offers significant changes to the land development process. The drafters thought that changes were needed since land use was being regulated by standard acts, "product[s] of the twenties, that notwithstanding a mass of encrustations failed to provide the necessary guidance"[133] to the legislators, administrators, planners, developers, judges, and lawyers involved in the process. Ad hoc rulings left parties unable to predict what would be allowed. The standard acts also were based on outdated views of lot by lot development that impeded growth. The drafters intended to deal with these weaknesses and to reverse parochial decisionmaking that disregarded regional concerns.

The MLDC integrates zoning and subdivision regulations under the concept of a development ordinance and streamlines the process of obtaining development permission. The most important definition in the MLDC is that of "development," which essentially is any material change in the appearance of a parcel of land or in its shape.[134]

Land development, not planning, is the focus of the act. The position of the drafters was that comprehensive planning was desirable, but was beyond the scope of the MLDC.[135] While the Code does not mandate planning, it encourages it by providing local governments with additional powers if a plan is adopted. Regulation of the state and regional effects of local development practices is a major component of the MLDC. In the more than twenty years that have passed since promulgation of the MLDC, there has been little in the way of direct adoption. Its greatest effect has been its approach to regional controls. Early on, Florida adopted Section 7 of the Model Code that deals with control over developments of regional impact and protection for areas of critical state concern.[136] A few other states have enacted provisions dealing with specific areas that use the MLDC approach.[137] The MLDC has also been influential as persuasive authority in several leading cases supporting growth management[138] and condemning exclusionary zoning.[139]

§ 3:25 WIPEOUT MITIGATION AND WINDFALL RECAPTURE

Police power controls impose losses and create gains that generally go unrecognized. In recent years there has been a spate of legislative proposals around the country to compensate landowners who suffer economic loss from land use controls.[140] While only a few have been enacted, the concern with the losses sustained persists and deters the adoption of new controls needed to protect the public welfare. A notable omission from these proposals, and usually absent from the debate, is the question of recapturing for the public the gains conferred on landowners by virtue of public improvements and government regulation. Recently, however, commentators have raised for consideration the equity of windfall recapture, often citing to the nineteenth century writings of Henry George, particularly his classic work Progress and Poverty, and to the late 20th century work of Donald Hagman.[141]

Land value capture has long been a significant source of funds for local governments in Latin America and Western Europe to use in meeting the infrastructure needs created by new development.

> Value Capture refers to the recovery by the public of the land value increments (unearned income ...) generated by the actions other than the landowner's direct investments. ... Although all such increments are essentially unearned income, value capture policies focus

primarily of the increment generated by public investments and administrative actions, such as granting permission for the development of specific land uses and densities. The objective is to draw on publicly generated land value increments to enable local administrations to improve the performance of land use management and to fund urban infrastructure and service provisions. The notion is that benefits provided by governments to private landowners should be shared fairly among all residents.[142]

The American Lincoln Institute of Land Policy has long advocated the consideration of land value capture and has recently reported several examples of its "catching on" in the United States.[143] Currently, however, it is primarily implemented in the form of impact fees and transferable development rights.[144]

Donald Hagman, coauthor of the precursor to this book,[145] was an ardent student and advocate of addressing the fairness of land use controls by systems of wipeout mitigation and windfall recapture. Hagman and Dean Misczynski published through the Planners Press of the American Planning Association a major collection of essays in 1978 entitled Windfalls for Wipeouts: Land Value Capture and Compensation that serves as a major resource in the area.

§ 3:26 ZONING BY SPECIAL ASSESSMENT FINANCED EMINENT DOMAIN (ZSAFED)

One windfalls and wipeouts technique goes by the name of zoning by special assessment financed eminent domain (ZSAFED). It was used in the early years of the 20th century when there were doubts about validity of zoning under the police power.[146] Under this system, when the right to develop was restricted causing an economic loss, compensation was paid. Money to pay those restricted came from assessments that were levied on land benefited by the restrictions. The practice was never widespread, and not surprisingly, when the Supreme Court held zoning via the police power valid under the constitution, its use faded quickly. There are vestiges of the practice. Some parts of Minneapolis and St. Paul, and of Kansas City, Missouri are still zoned by eminent domain.[147]

NOTES

1. *Tahoe-Sierra Preservation Council, Inc. v. Tahoe Regional Planning Agency,* 535 U.S. 302, 122 S. Ct. 1465, 1494, 152 L. Ed. 2d 517 (2002) (Rehnquist, C.J., dissenting).
2. The ordinance is reprinted in Gallagher, Report of Committee on Zoning and Planning, 18 NIMLO Mun. L. Rev. 373 (1955).
3. Hart, Colonial Land Use Law and Its Significance for Modern Takings Doctrine, 109 Harv. L. Rev. 1252 (1996).
4. For an in-depth analysis of the first 100 years of Zoning in the United States and suggestions for its future evolution, see John Nolon, Zoning's Centennial: A Complete Account of the Evolution of Zoning into a Robust System of Land Use Law—1916–2016, Zoning and Planning Law Report, Part I Oct. 2016. Part II Nov 2016, Part III Dec. 2016, Part IV Jan. 2017.
5. *Lincoln Trust Co. v. Williams Bldg. Corporation,* 229 N.Y 313, 128 N.E. 209 (1920).
6. *Village of Euclid, Ohio v. Ambler Realty Co.,* 272 U.S. 365, 47 S. Ct. 114, 71 L. Ed. 303 (1926).
7. See supra § 2:7.

8. *Barbier v. Connolly*, 113 U.S. 27, 5 S. Ct. 357, 28 L. Ed. 923 (1884); *Soon Hing v. Crowley*, 113 U.S. 703, 5 S. Ct. 730, 28 L. Ed. 1145 (1885).
9. *Yick Wo v. Hopkins*, 118 U.S. 356, 6 S. Ct. 1064, 30 L. Ed. 220 (1886).
10. *L'Hote v. City of New Orleans*, 177 U.S. 587, 20 S. Ct. 788, 44 L. Ed. 899 (1900).
11. *Welch v. Swasey*, 214 U.S. 91, 29 S. Ct. 567, 53 L. Ed. 923 (1909).
12. *Laurel Hill Cemetery v. City and County of San Francisco*, 216 U.S. 358, 30 S. Ct. 301, 54 L. Ed. 515 (1910).
13. *Eubank v. City of Richmond*, 226 U.S. 137, 33 S. Ct. 76, 57 L. Ed. 156 (1912).
14. *Reinman v. City of Little Rock*, 237 U.S. 171, 35 S. Ct. 511, 59 L. Ed. 900 (1915).
15. *Hadacheck v. Sebastian*, 239 U.S. 394, 36 S. Ct. 143, 60 L. Ed. 348 (1915).
16. *Thomas Cusack Co. v. City of Chicago*, 242 U.S. 526, 37 S. Ct. 190, 61 L. Ed. 472 (1917).
17. *Buchanan v. Warley*, 245 U.S. 60, 38 S. Ct. 16, 62 L. Ed. 149 (1917).
18. *Pierce Oil Corp. v. City of Hope*, 248 U.S. 498, 39 S. Ct. 172, 63 L. Ed. 381 (1919).
19. *Pennsylvania Coal Co. v. Mahon*, 260 U.S. 393, 43 S. Ct. 158, 67 L. Ed. 322 (1922).
20. *Hadacheck v. Sebastian*, 239 U.S. 394, 36 S. Ct. 143, 60 L. Ed. 348 (1915).
21. *Pennsylvania Coal Co. v. Mahon*, 260 U.S. 393, 415, 43 S. Ct. 158, 160, 67 L. Ed. 322 (1922). See infra §§ 10:1 et seq. for discussion of constitutional issues.
22. *Village of Euclid, Ohio v. Ambler Realty Co.*, 272 U.S. 365, 390, 47 S. Ct. 114, 119, 71 L. Ed. 303, (1926), discussing state court cases.
23. *Village of Euclid, Ohio v. Ambler Realty Co.*, 272 U.S. 365, 47 S. Ct. 114, 71 L. Ed. 303 (1926).
24. 272 US. at 388, 47 S. Ct. at 118.
25. *Nectow v. City of Cambridge*, 277 U.S. 183, 48 S. Ct. 447, 72 L. Ed. 842 (1928).
26. See discussion infra § 10:12.
27. Boards of Adjustment are frequently called Boards of Appeal.
28. See Edward M. Bassett, Zoning: The Laws, Administration, and Court Decisions During the First Twenty Years 28-29 (1940).
29. Dep't of Commerce (1926). The Act, with official commentary, is reprinted in full in 8 Zoning and Land Use Controls § 53.01[1] (P. Rohan and E. Kelly eds. 1997).
30. The Department of Commerce published the Standard City Planning Enabling Act in 1928.
31. The Guidebook provides commentary with legislative alternatives and suggestions for implementation. See http://www.planning.org/growingsmart/.
32. See http://www.planning.org/research/smartgrowth/.
33. See infra § 3:13.
34. See, generally, Sands, Libonati, and Martinez, Local Government Law § 4:01; Briffault, Our Localism: Part I-The Structure of Local Government Law, 90 Colum. L. Rev. 1 (1990).
35. *M.S.W., Inc. v. Board of Zoning Appeals of Marion County*, 29 Kan. App. 2d 139, 24 P.3d 175 (2001) (municipality has no inherent power to enact zoning laws).
36. *Lamar Co., LLC v. City of Richmond*, 287 Va. 348, 352, 756 S.E.2d 444, 446 (2014); *Hayenga v. City of Rockford*, 2014 IL App (2d) 131261, ¶ 15, 386 Ill. Dec. 732, 21 N.E.3d 495, 498 (App. Ct. 2d Dist. 2014) (non-home-rule city is governed by "Dillon's Rule"); *Schefer v. City Council of City of Falls Church*, 279 Va. 588, 691 S.E.2d 778, 780–81 (2010); *Arnwine v. Union County Bd. of Educ.*, 120 S.W.3d 804, 807 (Tenn. 2003).
37. John F. Dillon, Commentaries on the Law of Municipal Corporations, § 237 (5th ed.

38. *Almquist v. Town of Marshan*, 308 Minn. 52, 245 N.W.2d 819 (1976).

39. *Home Builders Ass'n of Lincoln v. City of Lincoln*, 271 Neb. 353, 711 N.W.2d 871 (2006) (Dillon's rule does not apply to a city operating under home rule charter.); *South Carolina State Ports Authority v. Jasper County*, 368 S.C. 388, 629 S.E.2d 624 (2006). See also § 3:9.

40. N.C. Gen. Stat. § 160A–4. Dillon's Rule does not apply to municipalities with home rule authority. *PPL Elec. Utilities Corp. v. City of Lancaster*, 125 A.3d 837 (Pa. Commw. Ct. 2015) (home rule municipality not constrained by Dillon's Rule); *Williams v. Town of Hilton Head Island, S.C.*, 311 S.C. 417, 422, 429 S.E.2d 802, 805 (1993) (Dillon's Rule abolished when home rule enacted). See § 3:9.

41. Briffault, Our Localism: Part I-The Structure of Local Government Law, 90 Colum. L. Rev. 1, 8 (1990). But see *Robert Ito Farm Inc. v. County of Maui*, 111 F. Supp. 3d 1088 (D. Haw. 2015) (Stating "majority of jurisdictions follow what is known as Dillon's Rule," hut citing no authority).

42. Spitzer, "Home Rule" vs. "Dillon's Rule" for Washington Cities, 38 Seattle U.L. Rev. 809-810 (2015) (bemoaning "the zombie-like reappearance of Dillon's Rule [explained in part] by appellate judges' insistence on picking and choosing from doctrines (including ostensibly dead doctrines) to support a case's outcome; and (3) a combination of doctrinal forgetfulness and carelessness.").

43. *State v. Jones*, 350 N.C. 822, 539 S.E.2d 639 (1999).

44. *Society Created to Reduce Urban Blight (SCRUB) v. Zoning Bd. of Adjustment of City of Philadelphia*, 729 A.2d 117 (Pa. Commw. Ct. 1999).

45. See infra § 3:9.

46. *Condominium Ass'n of Commonwealth Plaza v. City of Chicago*, 399 Ill. App. 3d 32, 338 Ill. Dec. 390, 924 N.E.2d 596 (2010).

47. See § 3:7. See also *PPL Elec. Utilities Corp. v. City of Lancaster*, 125 A. 3d 837 (Pa. Commw. Ct. 2015) (home rule municipality not constrained by Dillon's Rule); *Williams v. Town of Hilton Head Island, S.C.*, 31 S.C. 417, 422, 429 S.E.2d 802, 805 (1993) (Dillon's Rule abolished when home rule enacted).

48. Baker and Rodriguez, Constitutional Home Rule and Judicial Scrutiny, 86 Denv. U. L. Rev. 1337 (2009).

49. *Brougher v. Board of Public Works of City and County of San Francisco*, 205 Cal. 426, 271 P. 487 (1928).

50. See *DJL Restaurant Corp. v. City of New York*, 96 N.Y.2d 91, 725 N.Y.S.2d 622, 749 N.E.2d 186 (2001).

51. *Rispo Realty & Development Co. v. City of Parma*, 55 Ohio St. 3d 101, 564 N.E.2d 425 (1990).

52. *City of Los Angeles v. State of California*, 138 Cal. App. 3d 526, 187 Cal. Rptr. 893 (1982). But see *Moore v. City of Boulder*, 29 Colo. App. 248, 484 P.2d 134 (App. 1971) (low cost housing a matter of purely local concern).

53. *Town of Telluride v. Lot Thirty-Four Venture, L.L.C.*, 3 P.3d 30 (Colo. 2000).

54. See, e.g., Mass. Gen. Laws Ann. ch. 40C, § 2; Mo. Ann. Stat. § 89.040.

55. See e.g., Cal. Gov't Code §§ 50485 to 50485.14. See also infra § 4:29 for discussion on zoning for airports.

56. 42 U.S.C.A. §§ 4001 et seq. See infra § 11:10.

57. See, e.g., Ala. Code §§ 11–19–1 et seq.

58. Wis. Stat. § 62.23(7a). See *Village of DeForest v. County of Dane*, 211 Wis. 2d 804, 565 N.W.2d 296 (Ct. App. 1997).

59. See, e.g., Ark. Code Ann. § 14–56–413.
60. *Ben Lomond, Inc. v. City of Idaho Falls*, 92 Idaho 595, 448 P.2d 209 (1968).
61. Cal. Gov't Code § 65859.
62. *Beshore v. Town of Bel Air*, 237 Md. 398, 206 A.2d 678 (1965).
63. Ohio Rev. Code §§ 303.18, 519. 08.
64. See supra § 3:6.
65. SZEA, § 3, n. 21.
66. *Golden v. Planning Bd. of Town of Ramapo*, 30 N.Y.2d 359, 334 N.Y.S.2d 138, 285 N.E.2d 291 (1972).
67. An ordinance may be sustained under another source of power. See, e.g., *T.J.R. Holding Co., Inc. v. Alachua County*, 617 So. 2d 798 (Fla. 1st DCA 1993).
68. *Giger v. City of Omaha*, 232 Neb. 676, 442 N.W.2d 182, 193 (1989).
69. *Golden v. Planning Bd. of Town of Ramapo*, 30 N.Y.2d 359, 334 N.Y.S.2d 138, 285 N.E.2d 291 (1972).
70. SZEA § 3.
71. *Valley View Village v. Proffett*, 221 F.2d 412, 416 (6th Cir. 1955). See discussion infra § 6:9 for contrary authority.
72. *Giger v. City of Omaha*, 232 Neb. 676, 442 N.W.2d 182 (1989).
73. *Cellular Telephone Co. v. Village of Tarrytown*, 209 A.D.2d 57, 624 N.Y.S.2d 170 (1995).
74. *Belle Harbor Realty Corp. v. Kerr*, 35 N.Y.2d 507, 364 N.Y.S.2d 160, 323 N.E.2d 697 (1974).
75. *DeSena v. Guide*, 24 A.D.2d 165, 265 N.Y.S.2d 239 (1965).
76. See, e.g., *Robyns v. City of Dearborn*, 341 Mich. 495, 67 N.W.2d 718 (1954).
77. *State ex rel. Saveland Park Holding Corp. v. Wieland*, 269 Wis. 262, 69 N.W.2d 217, 224 (1955).
78. See infra §§ 10:12, 10:14, 10:14, and 10:18.
79. *Elizabeth Lake Estates v. Waterford Tp.*, 317 Mich. 359, 26 N.W.2d 788, 792 (1947).
80. *Parking Ass'n of Georgia, Inc. v. City of Atlanta, Ga.*, 264 Ga. 764, 450 S.E.2d 200 (1994).
81. *Fritts v. City of Ashland*, 348 S.W.2d 712 (Ky. 1961).
82. See infra §§ 12:1 et seq.
83. See infra §§ 12:1 et seq.
84. *Lamb v. City of Monroe*, 358 Mich. 136, 99 N.W.2d 566 (1959).
85. §§ 12:1 et seq. covers aesthetic and sign regulation in detail.
86. *Jarvis Acres, Inc. v. Zoning Commission of Town of East Hartford*, 163 Conn. 41, 301 A.2d 244 (1972).
87. *Flora Realty & Inv. Co. v. City of Ladue*, 362 Mo. 1025, 246 S.W.2d 771 (1952).
88. *Grace Baptist Church v. City of Oxford*, 81 N.C. App. 678, 345 S.E.2d 242 (1986).
89. *Stroud v. City of Aspen*, 188 Colo. 1, 532 P.2d 720 (1975).
90. See Zoning: Residential Off-Street Parking Requirements, 71 A.L.R.4th 529.
91. See infra § 9:8.
92. See, e.g., *Coleman v. Southwood Realty Co.*, 271 So. 2d 742 (Miss. 1973).
93. *Wyatt v. City of Pensacola*, 196 So. 2d 777 (Fla. 1st DCA 1967).
94. *In re White*, 195 Cal. 516, 234 P. 396 (1925).
95. *City of Columbia v. Omni Outdoor Advertising, Inc.*, 499 U.S. 365, 111 S. Ct. 1344, 113 L. Ed. 2d 382 (1991).
96. *Hernandez v. City of Hanford*, 41 Cal. 4th 279, 59 Cal. Rptr. 3d 442, 159 P.3d 33 (2007).
97. See infra § 4:13D., discussing big box retailers in the context of building size.
98. George Lefcoe, The Regulation of Superstores: The Legality of Zoning Ordinances Emerging from the Skirmishes Between Wal-Mart and the United Food and

98. Commercial Workers Union, 58 Ark. L. Rev. 833 (2006).
99. *Wal-Mart Stores, Inc. v. City of Turlock,* 138 Cal. App. 4th 273, 41 Cal. Rptr. 3d 420 (2006).
100. See also *In re Wal-Mart Stores, Inc.,* 167 Vt. 75, 702 A.2d 397 (1997); *Hernandez v. City of Hanford,* 2007 WL 1629830 (Cal. 2007).
101. See *In re Wal-Mart Stores, Inc.,* 167 Vt. 75, 702 A.2d 397 (1997).
102. *In re Wal-Mart Stores, Inc.,* 167 Vt. 75. The vast majority of states hold that one whose goal is to prevent competition with an existing business lacks standing to challenge a zoning action. *Earth Movers of Fairbanks, Inc. v. Fairbanks North Star Borough,* 865 P.2d 741, 744 (Alaska 1993) (collecting cases).
103. *Ensign Bickford Realty Corp. o. City Council,* 68 Cal. App. 3d 467, 137 Cal. Rptr. 304 (1977).
104. *Mazo v. City of Detroit,* 9 Mich. App. 354, 156 N.W.2d 155 (1968).
105. *Van Sicklen v. Browne,* 15 Cal. App. 3d 122, 92 Cal. Rptr. 786 (1971).
106. Utah Code Ann. § 10–9a–102.
107. See supra § 3:14.
108. *Putney v. Abington Tp.,* 176 Pa. Super. 463, 108 A.2d 134 (1954).
109. See *Watson v. Town Council of Town of Bernalillo,* 111 N.M. 374, 805 P.2d 641 (Ct. App. 1991).
110. *Griswold v. City of Homer,* 925 P.2d 1015, 1023 (Alaska 1996).
111. *Concerned Citizens for McHenry, Inc. v. City of McHenry,* 76 Ill. App. 3d 798, 395 N.E.2d 944, 950 (1979).
112. *St. Louis Gunning Advertisement Co. v. City of St. Louis,* 235 Mo. 99, 137 S.W. 929 (1911).
113. See infra §§ 12:1 et seq.
114. *Jachimek v. Superior Court In and For County of Maricopa,* 169 Ariz. 317, 819 P.2d 487 (1991).
115. See discussion infra § 10:18B.
116. See related discussion infra §§ 5:28 and 9:5.
117. See *Tahoe-Sierra Preservation Council, Inc. v. Tahoe Regional Planning Agency,* 535 U.S. 302, 122 S. Ct. 1465, 152 L. Ed. 2d 517 (2002).
118. *Alexander v. City of Minneapolis,* 267 Minn. 155, 125 N.W.2d 583 (1963); *State ex rel. Kramer v. Schwartz,* 336 Mo. 932, 82 S.W.2d 63 (1935).
119. *Miller v. Board of Public Works of City of Los Angeles,* 195 Cal. 477, 234 P. 381 (1925).
120. See, e.g., Colo. Rev. Stat. § 30-28-121; Utah Code Ann. § 10-9a-504.
121. *Golden v. Planning Bd. of Town of Ramapo,* 30 N.Y.2d 359, 334 N.Y.S.2d 138, 285 N.E.2d 291 (1972).
122. See infra § 16.12.
123. *U.S. v. 480.00 Acres of Land,* 557 F.3d 1297 (11th Cir. 2009).
124. *Kissinger v. City of Los Angeles,* 161 Cal. App. 2d 454, 327 P.2d 10 (1958).
125. See infra § 16:12.
126. Regarding official maps, see infra § 4:13.
127. See, e.g., Liebmann, The Modernization of Zoning: Enabling Act Revision as a Means to Reform, 23 Urb. Law. 1 (1991).
128. See supra § 3:1. See also Krasnowiecki, Abolish Zoning, 31 Syracuse L. Rev. 719 (1980).
129. The Guidebook provides commentary with legislative alternatives and suggestions for implementation. See http://www.planning.org/growingsmart/.
130. http://www.planning.org/research/smartgrowth/.
131. American Law Institute, A Model Land Development Code (1976).
132. Model Land Development Code, Art. 3, Commentary at 111–112.
133. Model Land Development Code, Foreword at x.
134. Model Land Development Code, § 1–202.

135. Model Land Development Code, Art. 3, Commentary at 114.
136. See Pelham, Regulating Developments of Regional Impact: Florida and the Model Land Development Code, 29 U. Fla. L. Rev. 789 (1977).
137. See the Cape Cod Commission Act, 1989 Mass. Acts 716, noted in Epstein, Where Yards Are Wide: Have Land Use Planning and Law Gone Astray?, 21 Wm. & Mary Envtl. L. & Pol'y Rev. 345, 379, n. 107 (1997).
138. *Golden v. Planning Bd. of Town of Ramapo*, 30 N.Y.2d 359, 334 N.Y.S.2d 138, 146, 285 N.E.2d 291, 297 n.6 (1972).
139. *Southern Burlington County N.A.A.C.P. v. Mount Laurel Tp.*, 67 N.J. 151, 210, 336 A.2d 713, 743 n.132 (1975); *Associated Home Builders etc., Inc. v. City of Livermore*, 18 Cal. 3d 582, 135 Cal. Rptr. 41, 65, 557 P.2d 473, 497 (1976).
140. See discussion of takings legislation infra § 10:11.
141. Williams, Recovering the Full Complexity of Our Traditions: New Developments in Property Theory, 46 J. Legal Educ. 596, 606 (1996); Byrne, Ten Arguments for the Abolition of the Regulatory Takings Doctrine, 22 Ecology L.Q. 89, 126–127, n. 240 (1995).
142. Martim, Smolka, Implementing Value Capture in Latin America: Policies and Tools for Urban Development 8 (2013).
143. "AT LINCOLN HOUSE," September 24, 2015, at p. 2. See https://perma.cc/SD3Q-EANR.
144. Julian Conrad Juergensmeyer, Developer Funding of Affordable and Work Force Housing Through Impact Fees and Land Value Recapture: A Comparison of American and Spanish Approaches, XLIX No. 297 REVISTA DERECHO Urbanistico y Media Ambiente 131 (April-May 2015).
145. Donald G. Hagman and Julian Conrad Juergensmeyer, Urban Planning and Land Development Law (2d ed. 1986).
146. Anderson, Zoning in Minnesota; Eminent Domain vs. Police Power, 16 Nat'l Mun. Rev. 624 (1927). See, generally, Validity and construction of "zoning with compensation" regulation, 41 A.L.R.3d 636.
147. Minn. Stat. Ann. §§ 462.12 to 462.17. *City of Kansas City v. Kindle,* 446 S.W.2d 807, 41 A.L.R.3d 620 (Mo. 1969) (upholding such zoning).

PLANNING THEORY FOR PRACTITIONERS

CENTRALIZED RATIONALITY: THE PLANNER AS APPLIED SCIENTIST

BY MICHAEL BROOKS

THE NATURE OF RATIONALITY

If, as noted earlier, planning theorists have indeed thoroughly discredited the notion of planning as an exercise in rationality, why spend time on that notion here? The answer rests in the fact that, the theorists' views notwithstanding, the rational model is still widely invoked in the world of planning practice. Ask a professional planner to describe how he or she carries out the planning process, and the odds are good that you will hear some version of the rational model. Ironically, planning schools often display a split personality on this matter—trashing rationality in the planning theory class, while continuing to teach it in all its glory in the methods and studio classes. Much like the creatures in horror movies, rationality is dead—but keeps showing up in public places. Despite its purported flaws, rationality is still the dominant paradigm in planning practice, and therefore continues to deserve careful scrutiny.

The origin of the idea that rationality is the essence of planning has been attributed to a number of sources. One of the most important, certainly, was the University of Chicago's graduate program in city planning, which enjoyed a brief but productive life shortly after World War II. That program, the first to emphasize the social science aspects of planning, was staffed by several people who had participated in the exciting national planning efforts of the Roosevelt

Michael Brooks, "Centralized Rationality: The Planner as Applied Scientist," *Planning Theory for Practitioners*, pp. 81-114, 117-118, 205-212. Copyright © 2002 by Taylor & Francis Group. Reprinted with permission.

administration in the 1930s; as those teachers and their students dispersed to other graduate schools of planning throughout the nation, the gospel of rationality was spread.[1]

The Chicago scholars relied heavily on the "rational man" of classical economic theory, who always behaves in such a manner as to maximize his utility or satisfaction. This group's focus on rationality was essentially an effort to apply the tenets of the scientific method to the urban community. These scholars were, above all, applied social scientists, and rationality was the major instrument they intended to employ in the creation of a more orderly, attractive, and just urban America.

Rationality is, of course, an ambiguous term, used in a variety of ways, and it is therefore necessary to clarify how the word will be used here. To begin with, a distinction is generally made between two types of rationality: *pure* (or objective) and *pragmatic* (subjective, qualified, bounded). Pure rationality is the mode of reasoning that would be employed if we had perfect knowledge of all the factors in a given situation. For the planner, given a set of objectives to be attained, pure rationality would imply the ability to conceive of all potential courses of action that might be followed in pursuit of those objectives; it would also imply the ability to predict with certainty all the consequences of each potential course of action. Rationality of this sort is, of course, an impossibility; pure rationality is an ideal, an abstraction that constitutes the logical end point on a conceptual continuum but has no counterpart in the real world.

Pragmatic rationality, on the other hand, is simply the form of reasoning that we employ in that real world as we apply foresight and intelligence in our attempts to solve our problems or shape our future. As Niraj Verma has pointed out, it is the "opposite of intuition," and is "associated with scientific method, structured decision making, and the use of methods and analytic techniques such as mathematical modeling and hypothesis testing."[2] Rationality of this sort is bounded by constraints of many kinds; we accept these, however, as inevitable features of the human condition. Throughout history men and women have labored mightily to expand the scope of the knowable and manageable. But however far the constraints may be pushed and stretched, in the last analysis they are still there. Pragmatic rationality, then, does not require that we have perfect knowledge, but only that we make good use of the knowledge available to us. For the planner, who is no more capable of pure rationality than is anyone else, a pragmatically rational decision is thus simply one in which alternatives and consequences are considered as fully as he or she is able to consider them, given the time and other resources readily available.[3]

The process of planning in a pragmatically rational manner has been described in a number of ways, and with a highly variable number of prescribed steps. One of the most detailed and enduring descriptions appeared in the appendix of a book written in 1955 by Martin Meyerson and Edward C. Banfield, but countless other formulations have been offered since that time.[4] Rather than attempt to review that literature, I will simply note that most of these formulations present one or another variation on the following theme.

(1) *Goals.* What do we want to accomplish?

(2) *Alternatives.* What courses of action are potentially available for accomplishing our goals?

(3) *Consequences.* What consequences, both positive and negative, might be expected to result from the major alternatives under consideration?

(4) Choice. In light of the above steps—and given the values that are most important to us—which alternative should we pursue?

(5) Implementation. Having settled on a course of action, how shall we carry it out?

(6) Evaluation. To what extent is our chosen course of action achieving the goals at which it is aimed?

Having conceded that we must settle for the pragmatic form of rationality does not, of course, resolve the problems that inevitably accompany attempts at rational decision-making. Are we certain that our goals are appropriate, unambiguous, and endorsed by all major stakeholders? Since it is likely that far more alternative courses of action are potentially available than we can possibly conjure up, how do we know which ones to select for further consideration? Similarly, since the consequences of any major action are virtually limitless, rippling outward as when a stone is thrown into water, how do we decide which possible consequences to subject to analysis, and what do we do about those often important consequences that simply cannot be foreseen? In planning, Ernest Alexander has argued, rationality "implies that a plan, a policy, or a strategy for action is based on valid assumptions, and includes all relevant information relating to the facts, theories, and concepts on which it is based."[5] But what basis do we have (other than the word of the analyst) for determining that the assumptions are indeed valid, and that no relevant information has been ignored?

By itself, the concept of pragmatic rationality is, unfortunately, devoid of behavior rules; it tells us to make the best of the situation at hand but does not tell us how to evaluate that situation, what constitutes "best" for what kinds of situations, or how to behave if the boundaries and constraints of the situation are less than clear.

(How often is a planner told that he or she has exactly ten days and $20,000 to generate six distinct alternatives?) I suggest that pragmatic rationality is potentially useful only when it is rendered operational—that is, when it is embodied in a planning model or strategy that comes equipped with a set of instructions. Many such models have been developed, all of them intended to reduce the degree of uncertainty that is inherent in efforts to apply pragmatic rationality to planning problems. Some of these models will be examined briefly later in this chapter.

First, however, let us examine some of the arguments of those who have questioned the very feasibility of rational planning because of basic human intellectual and psychological limitations. In their classic 1953 work, Robert Dahl and Charles Lindblom observed that the "number of alternatives man would need to consider in order to act rationally is very often far beyond his limited mental capacity."[6] This constraint led Herbert Simon to articulate what he termed the "principle of bounded rationality": *"The capacity of the human mind for formulating and solving complex problems is very small compared with the size of the problems whose solution is required for objectively rational behavior in the real world—or even for a reasonable approximation to such objective rationality."*[7]

It would be foolish to deny that our problems are sometimes larger than we can fully grasp; we have already referred to this phenomenon in noting the "wicked" nature of contemporary urban problems. But it gets worse. Our psychological impediments—our hang-ups—create a second set of constraints. Here the issue is not the bounded nature of our rationality but the irrational impulses that can undermine it. Dahl and Lindblom paraphrased the Freudian perspective on "man" as follows (note that the passage was written before the emergence of gender consciousness in schoolarly writing—though the result is a depiction with which many women might be inclined to agree):

> He is autistic; he distorts reality to suit inner needs and then makes his distorted picture of reality the premise of his actions. He is compulsive. He projects his own motives and reality views on others; represses powerful and urgent wants deep into the unconscious for fear of penalties from conscience or the responses of others, only to have his repressed wants unrecognizably displaced on other goals; acquires and displays exaggerated fears; colors the world with emotional tones of forgotten childhood; expresses hatreds and resentments coming from long-buried events; rationalizes all his actions; and throws a veil of hypocrisy and dishonesty not only over his outer behavior in order to deceive others but even over his innermost wishes in order to deceive himself.[8]

And we want this guy planning our city?

Most of us would prefer to consider this a description not of a normal person but of one who is highly neurotic. Alternatively, we might take comfort in the fact that this portrayal is somewhat outmoded in the light of more recent theories of human behavior. But who can deny that each of us does indeed view reality through our own unique lens? Who can claim never to have exhibited any of the traits just described?

While the problem is undoubtedly overstated in the quotation, there is little doubt that we do possess psychological traits that tend to work against our capacity for rationality. Consider, for example, the goals we hope to accomplish through rational action. Kenneth Arrow, among others, has noted that the individual's utility function (that is, one's rank ordering of goals) is highly variable, changing virtually from day to day.[9] Nor, for that matter, is it even possible for an individual to attain a consistent utility function: "in truth the individual is a congress of selves, each pursuing values to which the other selves may be indifferent or hostile—if, indeed, they are even aware of the pursuit."[10]

Despite these constraints, most of us do succeed in mustering sufficient rationality to function on a day-to-day basis—and often rather well at that. The purpose of these comments, then, has been simply—as Dahl and Lindblom put it—to "stand as a warning not to romanticize our capacity for rational social action."[11]

It might be argued that one of our chief strategies for overcoming our individual constraints is to join with others in organizations and institutions—which, on the face of it, would seem to have many advantages over the individual with respect to the potential for rationality. Because institutions serve as the repositories of knowledge inherited from their past members, their collective available knowledge is apt to be far greater than that of any individual member. Institutions are more likely than individuals to have systematic procedures for gathering information of relevance to their functions. They also tend to keep in check their members' more blatant psychological aberrations; irrational impulses are likely to be muted in the face of organizational norms for appropriate behavior.

I suspect that these advantages are real, but they do not necessarily overcome the difficulties with rationality that were mentioned earlier. If individuals must come to terms with their internally inconsistent utility functions, moreover, how much more difficult is it for institutions to reconcile the often divergent values of their members when large-scale public policy issues are at stake?

Banfield listed six "compelling reasons which militate against planning and rationality on the part of all organizations."[12] Briefly summarized, they are that (1) the future is too uncertain, and reliable predictions can rarely be made for more than five years ahead; (2) even if a course of action can be decided upon well in advance, it is often unwise to do so since this invites organized opposition; (3) there is little use in considering fundamentally different alternatives in most organizations because conditions usually preclude them from doing anything very different from what they are doing at present; (4) organizations are preoccupied with present rather than future effects, and are no more likely to postpone gratification than are individuals; (5) the goal of organizational maintenance—of "keeping the organization going for the sake of keeping it going"—is usually paramount; and (6) planning requires money and the time of chief executives, both of which are often considered to be more appropriately deployed elsewhere (in the resolution of current crises, for example). Banfield undoubtedly overstates some of these reasons in his effort to show that organizations neither behave rationally nor plan; for most of them we would have little difficulty coming up with examples that both illustrate and contradict his claims.

To be sure, both individuals and organizations possess a number of characteristics that constrain their ability to operate in a highly rational manner. However, these characteristics are not by themselves sufficient to discredit rationality. Numerous means have been suggested to circumvent those limitations, one of which is the creation of strategies or models that make "realistic" use of rationality.

RATIONALITY-BASED PLANNING STRATEGIES

As noted earlier, rationality alone—whether of the pure or pragmatic variety—is of little help in the planning process. Rationality becomes potentially useful only when it is embodied or packaged in operational models or strategies, complete with instruction kits. Many such models have blazed across the planning sky, only to vanish when "newer, better" approaches are introduced. In his book on strategic planning, John Bryson apologetically notes that leaders and managers "are likely to groan at the prospect of having yet another new management technique foisted upon them. They have seen cost-benefit analysis, planning-programming-budgeting systems, zero-base budgeting, management by objectives, Total Quality Management, reinvention, reengineering, and a host of other techniques trumpeted by a cadre of authors and management consultants."[13] To this list might be added statistical decisionmaking, game theory, operations research, and systems analysis, among others. In varying degrees, each of these techniques has attempted to harness the notion of rationality for application to real-world problem solving; each has had its day in the sun, only to be brushed aside by the next highly touted strategy.

Perhaps the purest expression of the rationality idea in planning was that manifested in the development, in the 1950s and 1960s, of large-scale computer-based models of land use and transportation. The Chicago Area Transportation Study and the Penn-Jersey Study were the most prominent examples; in each case, large sums of money were expended to develop computerized mathematical models that could predict the impact of alternative developments or of changes in a metropolitan area's land use and transportation systems.[14] The proponents of the models hoped that they would "revolutionize the practice of urban policy making" by providing the data needed to "forecast and control the future of cities."[15] It didn't work out that way, of course; Michael Wegener notes that nowhere in the world have such models "become a routine ingredient of metropolitan plan-making."[16] In his view, the modeling approach faded because of its close association with the broader notion of rational planning; as our confidence in rationality faded, so did the models.

It is likely, too, that the modelers were not keenly attuned to the political dimensions of their work. An article by Alan Black provides an informative description of the seven-year Chicago Area Transportation Study, offering it as an example of effective rational planning; after all, it "followed the rational model closely, completed the planning process, and published a plan."[17] Black characterizes rational planning as a ten-step process, and notes that nine of the ten steps were successfully carried out by the study's team. The only exception: implementation. Black acknowledges that the staff had little interest in this; they were highly skilled technicians, and not oriented to the hurly-burly of citizen participation, public hearings, and coalition building. It is hardly surprising, then, that little or no implementation occurred. Even Black, who participated in the study and was justifiably laudatory regarding its technical sophistication, concluded that it is "easier to carry out the rational planning process if the planning agency is autonomous and free from political interference. But if planners want to affect decisions, they may have to get involved in politics and sacrifice rationality to some degree."[18]

Despite their association with the much-maligned rational paradigm, large-scale models continue to be developed. Writing in 1994, Wegener noted the existence of "a small but tightly knit network of urban modelers dispersed across four continents."[19] He identified and described twenty modeling processes (seven in the United States, thirteen elsewhere) varying widely in their comprehensiveness and level of sophistication. He acknowledged, however, that these models tended to deal with a rather narrow spectrum of the problems confronting metropolitan areas, and he advocated the development of models that would be "more sensitive to issues of equity and of environmental sustainability."[20]

Although Wegener and other authors have documented the fact that highly sophisticated urban models are still being developed, these models continue to function primarily as the objects of research activity. While they certainly have value in that regard, it is nevertheless clear that they have made few inroads into the processes whereby urban policy decisions are made. Like the proponents of other rationality-based strategies, the modelers might hope that the quality, elegance, and technical competence of their models would somehow carry the day—but alas, decisions within the political system continue to be responsive to other, more traditional variables.

THE LATEST CONTENDER: STRATEGIC PLANNING

This examination of rationality-based planning models should not conclude without consideration of the one that is currently most prevalent—namely, strategic planning. I suspect that the popularity of strategic planning derives, at least in part, from its roots in the private sector; any plan labeled "strategic" seems to possess an aura of respectability not necessarily enjoyed by plans with other designations. After all, every corporation worth its salt has a strategic plan in place, and what is good for our corporations must be good for government as well—right?

Despite this popularity, there is little consensus on what it means to plan strategically;

strategic planning has been described in a variety of ways, with each author or short-course instructor presenting his or her own preferred version.[21] At the risk of overgeneralizing, however, I suggest that policy- or decision-making processes carried out under the rubric of strategic planning often contain at least the following elements:

(1) *A mission statement.* What is the organization's basic purpose, and who are its major stakeholders (those whose interests are affected in some manner by the organization's activities)?

(2) *A "SWOT" analysis.* This focuses on (a) the organization's internal strengths and weaknesses (the "SW" part)—what is the organization doing well, what not so well; and (b) the organization's external opportunities and threats (the "OT" part)—what is happening in the political, economic, social, and other environments that should be taken into account as the organization charts its future? (The resulting analysis is often referred to as an environmental scan.)

(3) *An analysis of specific issues that the organization needs to address.* These will vary from case to case.

(4) *The development of a detailed and compelling vision for the organization's future.*

(5) *The development of a set of action strategies for achieving that vision.*

How do these elements relate to the six steps of the rational planning process cited earlier? That list began with a determination of goals as the first step, and I view the first four strategic planning elements I have listed here simply as a refinement on the goal- formulation process. An organization will presumably develop more useful goals (a better-informed vision) if it has a clear sense of mission, has performed a competent SWOT analysis, and has carefully examined all the current issues that are central to its future.

The vision statement, then, *is* the goal statement, describing in detail what the organization hopes to achieve or create in the future. Strategies, of course, are the implementation component—the means of getting there.

While strategic plans can be developed for any time frame, the approach tends to be applied most frequently to relatively short term planning processes—those intended to guide actions over a three- to five-year period, say, rather than the ten- to twenty-year horizons often associated with comprehensive plans. Advocates of strategic planning tend to believe that their approach is more politically sensitive than are other models. Whether this is true depends, however, on how the political process is handled in those other models; strategic planning has no monopoly on political savvy, nor does it come equipped with a guarantee of successful outcomes.

Strategic planning is, in the final analysis, simply one more entry in the long line of rationality-based strategies that have been packaged for use by planners. With its built-in emphasis on political sensitivity (the political process is, in fact, one of the strategy's objects for rational analysis), it represents a considerable improvement over strategies that seem to suggest that a plan's inherent wisdom and sophistication are sufficient to carry the day politically. Strategic planning has indeed proved more durable than most rationality-based strategies. Bryson may be right in attributing this to its emphasis on politics,[22] though I suggest that its widespread use in the private sector has played an important role as well. But strategic planning still assumes that a central planner (or planning organization) manages a process in which a variety of phenomena are analyzed, with that analysis being used to formulate a set of strategies—in other words, a plan—for achieving desired outcomes. The concept of rationality may indeed be broadened here—to include, for example, analyses of political pressures and the preferences of various stakeholder groups—but strategic planning never completely departs from the centralized, rational camp. Accordingly, it cannot escape the fundamental problems that have bedeviled other styles of planning based on assumptions of rational behavior.

CURRENT STATUS OF THE RATIONALITY CONCEPT

Nigel Taylor suggests that the notion of planning as a rational process, coupled with the view of cities as systems that are amenable to scientifically engineered improvement, represented the "high water-mark of modernist optimism in the post-war era."[23] Clearly the emergence of a postmodern world view has shattered that optimism, and few authors today feel compelled to devote more than a paragraph or two to their rejection of rational planning. This book is an obvious exception, for reasons stated at the beginning of this chapter.

Perhaps the most compelling anti-rationality argument in recent years has been that advanced by Bent Flyvbjerg, in his fascinating case study of central city planning in Aalborg, Denmark. Flyvbjerg argues that power defines what constitutes knowledge and rationality; indeed, power ultimately defines "what counts as reality." Thus, rationality is embedded in power relationships—and is, in fact, one of the tools used by those in power to get what they want.[24] What emerges from his study "is a picture of technical expertise used as rationalization of policy, of rationality as the legitimation of power."[25] To the extent that Aalborg's planners attempted to rely on rational analysis and plan-making for their central city plan, Flyvbjerg charges, they played into the hands of those who possessed genuine power (identified, in this instance, as the Chamber of Industry and Commerce, which—contrary to the planners—wanted no restrictions on the movement of automobiles in the city's downtown) and who were therefore able to define what was ultimately perceived to be rational.

Flyvbjerg sees Aalborg's public planning failures as providing evidence of the "fundamental weakness of modernity."[26] His proposed solutions are not particularly satisfying; he concludes that we need to better understand the nature of power (a step to which his book makes a significant contribution), reject the notion of a rationality-based democracy as the major vehicle for solving our problems, and join with like-minded allies to work toward what is right.[27] In fairness, it must be noted that Flyvbjerg's primary intent was to describe and analyze a particular case, not to provide solutions to the problems he unearthed. Indeed, he is generally perceived to be one of the "dark side" planning theorists described in Chapter 2—a group more given to critical analysis than to proposals for amelioration.

While he has enriched the conceptual basis for the case against rationality, Flyvbjerg's bottom line is the same as that of numerous other authors—namely, that rational planning reflects a world view that is not in tune with the dynamics of contemporary society (and was perhaps *never* very effective). So: what happens when one of a profession's most fundamental assumptions turns out to be mired in quicksand?

In a 1984 article, Alexander identified several responses to what he termed "paradigm breakdown"—in this case, the discrediting of rationality. Some theorists, he observed, simply continued to write as though there were no problems with the concept; others acknowledged its limitations but made adjustments that, in their minds, "solved" these limitations; others abandoned rationality and attempted to replace it with ideological positions; and still others went in search of new paradigms that might fill the gap.[28]

More interesting than the responses of planning theorists, however, are those of practitioners. As noted at the beginning of this chapter, they are still inclined, when asked, to describe their plan-making and problem-solving activities in ways that sound suspiciously akin to the rational model. Why is this the case?

Several possible explanations have been offered. Howell Baum suggests that planners cling to rationality for psychological reasons; it provides a measure of insulation from "risky reality."[29] Thus if "community groups are hostile, if bosses put agency politics above rigorous analysis, if coworkers duplicitously do not share information, taking the rational view that planning is simply abstract analysis eliminates these concerns and the feelings they evoke."[30] Hey, I'm just a technician here; if things don't work out, it's because of politics—and that's none of my concern.

In addressing the same question—the persistence of allegiance to rationality in planning practice—Linda Dalton has suggested several alternative explanations, including that (1) planning has been institutionally identified with rationality so deeply, and for so long, as to render the relationship extremely difficult to terminate; (2) planning educators may reject rationality intellectually, but they continue to model it in their teaching and research—a point not lost on their students; and (3) rationality provides a "secure base for a profession that is potentially in trouble."[31] Implied in this last point is the notion that planners may find it politically useful, in some circumstances, to be perceived as dispassionate, analytical, value-neutral, rational actors rather than as skilled participants in the political process. All these forces are undoubtedly at work; all have contributed to the durability of a concept that was long ago declared dead by the profession's community of theorists.

Should we conclude, then, that the purported demise of rationality is a figment of out-of-touch planning theorists' imaginations, and that in reality it remains a useful paradigm for the practice of planning? Absolutely not. My fundamental problem with rationality is not that it is a modernist strategy in a postmodern world, as numerous theorists have alleged (although I would not quarrel with this contention). Rather, my concern is that reliance on rational models is dysfunctional because *decisions relevant to public planning are not generally made on the basis of rational planning processes.*[32] Indeed, the kinds of problems with which planners are typically involved, as well as the environments in which these problems are generally addressed, militate strongly against the use of rationality-based strategies.

Most public planning issues—and certainly all of them that we would consider major—generate outcomes that affect individuals and groups differentially. Some people win, some lose, and some win or lose more or less than others. Even in cases where a significant number of people are not directly affected by a particular outcome, many members of the community will have strong opinions about the rightness or wrongness of what is happening.

Virtually any major issue, then, has a number of stakeholders and is likely to feature a large measure of interest group involvement. This in turn guarantees that political processes will be paramount in shaping the outcomes. Sometimes these political processes include a subsidiary role for rational analysis and planning (though Flyvbjerg would suggest that when this occurs, planning and analysis may well have been co-opted by those in power); often, however, the political process ignores planning altogether. There is, in fact, a strong unwillingness on the part of many interest groups to concede to public agencies and officials the legitimacy and authority needed to make the decisions that most affect their well-being; this in turn leads to pressures for the decentralization of decision-making on key public policy issues.

These characteristics of the public planning arena undermine the usefulness of strategies and models based on rationality. Rationality-based planning works best when value conflicts have been resolved in advance, when the goal is one of optimization (that is, everybody gains) rather than redistribution, when political processes do not intervene in any major way, when decision-making authority is clear and fully legitimated by all in the community, and when decision-making is centralized in a single unit rather than diffused among many. In short, rationality-based planning works best with "tame" problems rather than with wicked ones—and public planners do not often find themselves tackling tame problems.

Reliance on rationality may, in fact, be highly damaging to the planning process because it contributes so readily to self-delusion. If we follow the tenets of rational planning, one might ask, aren't we simply doing what planning is all about—regardless of whether anything comes of our analyses and plans? An exercise I often give my students posits the existence of two firms, A and B. Firm A makes all the right planning moves—defining its mission, studying its competition, carefully analyzing the market for current and potential products, and formulating goals and strategies for its short-term future. Firm B, on the other hand, is run by a happy-go-lucky CEO who makes all decisions for the firm by flipping a coin. Let's say, for the sake of argument, that Firm A, despite its good planning behavior, goes down the tubes, while Firm B prospers and becomes an industry leader. The question is, which firm was the more rational?

My students almost always answer correctly—namely, that Firm A was the more rational because it behaved in a rational manner, while Firm B was not rational at all. This exercise illustrates the fact that "rational planning" means "planning conducted in a rational manner"; the focus is on the process, not on the results. Successful outcomes are not necessary for rational planning; it is enough that we planned rationally. But is this truly satisfactory? I don't think so. Public planning is about improving the quality of life in our communities, and we should not take comfort in methods that may soothe our psyches but have little real-world impact.

To summarize, there is a tension in our nation (and I suspect in most nations) between rational planning and the political system. Because they fail to deal with that tension, most rationality-based planning strategies will ultimately prove disappointing to the planner. What we need, then, are models or strategies that do a better job of taking the political process into account. Let us continue our search.

NOTES

1. Herbert J. Gans, *People and Plans: Essays on Urban Problems and Solutions* (New York: Basic Books, 1968), pp. 71–73.
2. Niraj Verma, "Pragmatic Rationality and Planning Theory," *Journal of Planning Education and Research,* Vol. 16, No. 1 (Fall 1996), p. 5.
3. For a related discussion, see Edward C. Banfield, "Ends and Means in Planning," *International Social Science Journal,* Vol. 11 (1959), p. 362.

4. Martin Meyerson and Edward G. Banfield, *Politics, Planning and the Public Interest* (Glencoe, Ill.: The Free Press, 1955).
5. Ernest R. Alexander, *Approaches to Planning: Introducing Current Planning Theories, Concepts, and Issues,* 2nd ed. (Philadelphia: Gordon and Breach, 1992), p. 40.
6. Robert A. Dahl and Charles E. Lindblom, *Politics, Economics, and Welfare: Planning and Politico-Economic Systems Resolved into Basic Social Processes* (New York: Harper & Row, 1953), p. 60.
7. Herbert A. Simon, *Models of Man* (New York: John Wiley & Sons, 1957), p. 198. Emphasis in the original.
8. Dahl and Lindblom, *Politics, Economics, and Welfare,* p. 60.
9. Kenneth J. Arrow, "Mathematical Models in the Social Sciences," in *The Policy Sciences,* ed. Daniel Lerner and Harold D. Lasswell (Stanford: Stanford University Press, 1951), p. 136.
10. Abraham Kaplan, "Some Limitations on Rationality," in *Nomos VII: Rational Decision,* ed. Carl J. Friedrich (New York: Atherton Press, 1964), p. 58.
11. Dahl and Lindblom, *Politics, Economics, and Welfare,* p. 60.
12. Banfield, "Ends and Means," pp. 365–367.
13. John M. Bryson, *Strategic Planning for Public and Nonprofit Organizations: A Guide to Strengthening and Sustaining Organizational Achievement,* rev. ed. (San Francisco: Jossey-Bass Publishers, 1995), p. 10.
14. For a useful overview of the modeling movement, see Michael Batty, "A Chronicle of Scientific Planning: The Anglo-American Modeling Experience," *Journal of the American Planning Association,* Vol. 60, No. 1 (Winter 1994), pp. 17–29.
15. Michael Wegener, "Operational Urban Models: State of the Art," *Journal of the American Planning Association,* Vol. 60, No. 1 (Winter 1994), p. 17.
16. Ibid.
17. Alan Black, "The Chicago Area Transportation Study: A Case Study of Rational Planning," *Journal of Planning Education and Research,* Vol. 10, No. 1 (Fall 1990), p. 27.
18. Ibid., p. 36.
19. Wegener, "Urban Models," p. 18.
20. Ibid., p. 26.
21. For works emphasizing the use of strategic planning by local government, see Bryson, *Strategic Planning;* John M. Bryson and William D. Roering, "Applying Private-Sector Strategic Planning in the Public Sector," *Journal of the American Planning Association,* Vol. 53, No. 1 (Winter 1987), pp. 9–22; and Jerome L. Kaufman and Harvey M. Jacobs, "A Public Planning Perspective on Strategic Planning," *Journal of the American Planning Association,* Vol. 53, No. 1 (Winter 1987), pp. 23–33.
22. Bryson, *Strategic Planning,* p. 10.
23. Nigel Taylor, *Urban Planning Theory Since 1945* (London: Sage Publications, 1998), p. 60.
24. Bent Flyvbjerg, *Rationality and Power: Democracy in Practice* (Chicago: University of Chicago Press, 1998), p. 27.
25. Ibid., p. 26.
26. Ibid., p. 234.
27. Ibid., pp. 234–236.
28. Ernest R. Alexander, "After Rationality, What? A Review of Responses to Paradigm Breakdown," *Journal of the American Planning Association,* Vol. 50, No. 1 (Winter 1984), pp. 62–69.
29. Howell S. Baum, "Why the Rational Paradigm Persists: Tales from the Field," *Journal of Planning Education and Research,* Vol. 15, No. 2 (Winter 1996), p. 133.

30. Ibid.
31. Linda C. Dalton, "Why the Rational Paradigm Persists: The Resistance of Professional Education and Practice to Alternative Forms of Planning," *Journal of Planning Education and Research*, Vol. 5, No. 3 (Spring 1986), pp. 147–153.
32. Howell Baum makes the same point in "Why the Paradigm Persists," p. 127.

CENTRALIZED NON-RATIONALITY: THE PLANNER CONFRONTS POLITICS

The planning strategies reviewed in this chapter were developed in response to the perceived shortcomings of rationality-based models. They acknowledge the impossibility of pure rationality in planning and decision-making, and use that fact as the point of departure for the development of models that take explicit account of our nonrational characteristics. The major similarity between the rationality-based models and those discussed in this chapter is their emphasis on planning as a centralized function—that is, a task performed by professionals working for (or advising) a central planning or policy-making agency. Beyond that, however, the differences are substantial. The models in this chapter are intended primarily to provide decision-makers with behavior rules that are realistic, in the sense that they take into account both the constraints on rationality and the nature of large-scale bureaucracies.

SIMON SAYS "SATISFICE"

I have already mentioned Herbert Simon's "principle of bounded rationality," which notes the relatively limited capacity of the human mind in comparison with the size of the problems we attempt to resolve. The result of this limitation, wrote Simon, is that we often *satisfice*—that is, settle for a course of action that is merely "good enough" for the purposes at hand.[1] One who satisfices, Simon added, "has no need of estimates of joint probability distributions, or of complete and consistent preference orderings of all possible alternatives of action."[2]

Simon's principal target was the "economic man" of classical economics, a person with no counterpart in the real world. Simon wanted to replace him with the more realistic "administrative man." Economic men maximize; administrative men "*satisfice* because they have not the wits to *maximize*."[3] Economic man strives to deal with the real world in its full complexity; administrative man perceives a highly simplified model of the real world, omitting consideration of all but its most relevant and crucial aspects.[4] Thus, for example, he never attempts to consider all the alternatives open to him but only those that seem most plausible.[5] Having constructed a simplified model of the real situation, Simon wrote, administrative man does behave rationally with respect to that model—which, however, is "not even approximately optimal with respect to the real world."[6]

Administrative man satisfices with regard to ends as well as means. If a goal proves too ambitious, he simply lowers it; if progress toward the goal exceeds expectations, he can then raise it again. In business, for example, rather than search for the course of action that will maximize profit, the satisficer begins with an idea of the profit that the business should generate, then simply adopts the first course of action that will satisfy that profit requirement. If no such course of action is readily discovered, the profit requirement will probably be revised downward, to be raised again later if circumstances permit.

In short, the search is for a course of action that is good enough rather than for one that is best.

While this point has been debated, it appears to me that Simon was more interested in describing how people actually make decisions than in prescribing how those decisions should be made; in other words, his theory was more positive than normative. Indeed, the satisficing idea would have serious shortcomings if its intentions were prescriptive. It fails, for example, to specify criteria for determining when we have an alternative that is "good enough." Do we take the first acceptable alternative that comes along, even if it means lowering our goals? Do we postpone lowering the goals until we have devoted X dollars, or Y days, to analysis? Clearly, the definition of a satisfactory solution will vary with the situation, and will depend on a number of factors—such as values, costs, and time—unique to each. It is one thing to observe, however correctly, that people tend to satisfice; it is quite another to tell them how to do it.

To be sure, all planners—along with, I suspect, everyone else—sometimes engage in decision-making behavior that might reasonably be described as satisficing. There is something about such behavior, however, that is antithetical to the planner's role. Public planning often requires outcomes that are more than merely "good enough." Indeed, planning based on satisficing would appear to be the exact opposite of the visionary spirit being advocated in this book (see Chapter 13). Yes, much planning reflects satisficing—but planning at its best transcends this approach.

INCREMENTALISM

Charles Lindblom's first major reference to incrementalism appeared in 1953 in a book that he coauthored with Robert A. Dahl.[7] By 1959 Lindblom had become sufficiently impressed with the explanatory powers of the concept of incrementalism to publish an article about it entitled, descriptively enough, "The Science of 'Muddling Through.'"[8] By this time he had decided that in addition to describing how people make their plans and decisions, incrementalism was in fact a very good way to do so; hence he offered it as both a positive and a normative theory. In that article he referred to his strategy as "the method of successive limited comparisons," which he contrasted favorably with the traditional "rational-comprehensive method."

In 1963 the strategy—now called "disjointed incrementalism"—was developed more fully in a book coauthored with David Braybrooke, a philosopher; this book provides a thorough exposition of the strategy for those interested in its theoretical rationale, minute details, and empirical illustrations.[9] Finally, in 1965 Lindblom published another book dealing largely with other issues but containing a concise and highly useful description—in a single, fifteen-page chapter—of the strategy's central features.[10] (I have long considered this a better description of the concept than the more frequently cited "Muddling Through" article.)

Like Simon, Lindblom was concerned about the divergence between the methods that planners and decision-makers claimed to use (that is, those based on rationality) and those that they actually used. Thus he devoted considerable attention to a systematic demolition of the "synoptic model," which is roughly akin to what I have been calling "pure rationality." In its place he proposed an approach that he believed to be more realistic. As Nigel Taylor observes, Lindblom "suggested that, in most situations, planning has to be piecemeal, incremental, opportunistic, and pragmatic, and that planners who did not or could not operate in these ways were generally ineffective. In short, Lindblom presented a model of the 'real world' planning as necessarily 'disjointed' and 'incremental,' not 'rational' and 'comprehensive.'"[11]

Lindblom listed several "adaptations" or "tactics" that decisionmakers use in order to cope with the realities of the policy-making environment. Briefly summarized, they are as follows:

(1) Decision-makers compare and evaluate increments only.[12] No attempt is made to analyze alternatives in great depth; on the contrary, they are considered only at the margins, where they differ from one another or from what is being done at present. This approach is, moreover, highly practical, since most political systems cannot tolerate more than incremental changes from the existing situation.

(2) Decision-makers consider only a restricted number of policy alternatives[13] They ignore those that entail more than incremental change or that lie outside the "familiar path of policy making."[14]

(3) Decision-makers consider only a restricted number of important consequences for any given policy alternative. They ignore, for a number of practical reasons, many other important consequences.[15]

(4) Decision-makers engage in "reconstructive analysis."[16] That is, ends are adjusted to means as well as vice versa; the problem is continuously redefined. In this way potentially impossible problems are rendered manageable.

(5) Decision-makers carry out their analyses and evaluations serially.[17] That is, they approach a problem through a series of attacks rather than a one-shot effort. Values or consequences omitted in one attack can thus be added later if their importance becomes apparent.

(6) Decision-makers have a remedial orientation.[18] Most planning, in other words, is geared to solving existing problems rather than to achieving desired future states. Certain general ideals (such as justice or economic growth) may be kept in mind, but in practice their importance will be minor compared to that of the problems that the decision-maker is endeavoring to solve.

Lindblom himself summarizes the process as follows:

> The decision-maker makes an incremental move in the desired direction and does not take upon himself the difficulties of finding a solution. He disregards many other possible moves because they are too costly (in time, energy, or money) to examine; and, for the move he makes, he does not trouble to find out (again, because it is too costly to do so) what all its consequences are. He assumes that to the extent that his move was a failure or was marked by unanticipated adverse consequences, someone's (perhaps even his) next move will attend to the resulting problem.[19]

The last sentence reflects one of the strategy's most interesting characteristics—namely, the idea that one's decisions need not always be right. Given the serial nature of public policy decision-making, if a particular decision turns sour, it can always be fixed in the next iteration. To his credit, Lindblom noted that a "great deal of damage" could occasionally occur before corrective steps are taken; this is unavoidable, however, since the only alternative is the unworkable rational approach. A major feature of the strategy, in fact, is that it is often better to let adverse consequences develop and deal with them as separate problems than to attempt to anticipate all such consequences in advance.[20]

CURRENT STATUS OF INCREMENTALISM

Much about the concept of incrementalism is intuitively appealing to practicing planners. It does seem to describe a great deal of the planning that goes on at the local level—and it provides a welcome rationalization for the fact that so much of that planning is being done in a way that can hardly be considered rational. While Lindblom was a public administrator rather than a planner, he made a significant contribution to planning thought by pointing out that rationality need not be the only conceptual basis for the planning process—that in fact it is possible to develop alternative strategies that pay greater attention to the political realities of planning practice. Given the overwhelming dominance of the rational paradigm in the 1950s and 1960s, it would be difficult to overestimate the importance of Lindblom's work in loosening that paradigm's stranglehold on the profession.

It should come as no surprise, however, that incrementalism has also been widely criticized. Among the most significant arguments are the following:

• Lindblom may have been correct in his description of the way in which many public planning decisions are made, but he offered little empirical evidence to support his assertions. The illustrative cases that he presented did indeed support his theory—but they were selected to do so, after all, and hardly reflected a representative sampling of planning situations. Each of us, certainly, can think of real-world policy or planning decisions that have not conformed to his description—that is, were not incremental. Rapid developments in health, electronic communications, recreation, and other fields come immediately to mind; the world is undoubtedly changing at a faster pace than was the case in the 1960s.

• A closely related problem is simply that there are many circumstances in which we would not want to settle for an incremental approach. It can hardly apply, for example, to situations where there is substantial public dissatisfaction with current policies; when new problems emerge (or old situations are redefined as problems), thus necessitating new approaches; when new organizations or programs are created to tackle previously unrecognized problems; when new methodologies or action policies become available because of technological or other breakthroughs; when elected officials are given mandates for major reform; or when disasters or crises render new approaches both feasible and essential. In short, incrementalism ignores the very processes of innovation through which societies often change and grow. Such situations may occur relatively infrequently, compared with more routine decision-making situations, but they are of fundamental importance—and incrementalism ignores them.

• Some analysts have claimed that incrementalism is politically conservative (a weakness or strength depending, of course, on one's political orientation) because it pays great respect to past traditions and institutions, viewing them as givens and thus leaving them essentially unchallenged. It is therefore a rather unattractive strategy for those interested in fundamental change or reform.

• It has also been suggested that incrementalism favors the powerful members of a society at the expense of those who are underrepresented and politically weak because decision-makers, in their quest for moves that are practical and feasible, will accommodate their decisions to those who are most capable of blocking implementation—namely, those with power.[21]

• On the other hand, incrementalism contains its own political risks because it tends to offer small solutions for large problems (opening fire hydrants to deal with neighborhood unrest; appointing commissions to study problems that merit immediate action; combating drugs by "just saying no"; dealing with the nation's urban school crisis by having cities endorse a list of goals, as in the first President Bush's America 2000 project; and so on).

• Some critics have also suggested that incrementalism discourages activities that, while closely associated with rationality, are nonetheless important to any community's planning process. Incrementalism is rather cavalier, for example, in its treatment of goals and in its attitude toward analysis; neither is seen to have much practical value.[22]

• While intended to be more prescriptive than Simon's satisficing concept, incrementalism is similarly devoid of behavior rules. How small is incremental? How many alternatives make up the restricted number that are to be considered, and by what criteria should they be identified? How do we determine which important consequences to consider and which to ignore? Indeed, as Yehezkel Dror has noted, "the very concept of 'incremental' change is vague, because the same change may be both 'incremental' and 'radical' in different systems and at different times."[23]

• Finally, the strategy is thoroughly inefficient when it comes to correcting a course of action that proves to be inappropriate. Incrementalism posits no formal evaluation mechanisms; it assumes that if actions go sour, others will point this out to decisionmakers, who will then make the necessary adjustments. This is, of course, a wildly rash assumption. Most readers of this book would have little difficulty generating a list of governmental programs that have been continued long beyond their useful life—and even long after beginning to have adverse effects—simply because no one noticed or had sufficient clout to change the situation. (William H. Whyte offered a good example in his case study of incentive zoning in New York City; initiated in 1961, the program operated for nearly twenty years before planners began to realize that its impact was precisely the opposite of that which had been intended.)[24] To rely on a process of "partisan adjustment" (Lindblom's term), of reaction to the corrective observations of the decision-makers' colleagues and professional rivals, is to rely on a process that has proven remarkably inept in dealing with the major problems confronting America's cities.

Incrementalism may indeed describe the way in which certain decisions (typically those that are relatively routine) are made, but it hardly presents a model to be emulated. The strategy applies to a relatively narrow range of planning situations, excluding those that might lead to large-scale change; it is deferential toward the existing social order, paying great respect to current power configurations; and it is inefficient in its approach to corrective action. One could argue, in fact, that incrementalism is not a planning strategy at all, but is more appropriately viewed as the antithesis of planning—that is, as the way in which decisions get made when, for one reason or another, planning is not possible.

Recognizing some of these drawbacks, Amitai Etzioni proposed a "mixed scanning" strategy, intended as a compromise between the rational and incremental approaches—supposedly containing the virtues of both and the defects of neither.[25] A key element in the mixed scanning strategy is its distinction between "contextuating" decisions and "bit" decisions. The former are the more fundamental policy-shaping decisions, tend to be made by those higher in an organization's hierarchy, and are more apt to be based on a careful analysis of the options. Bit decisions, on the other hand, focus more on implementation than on policy-making, tend to be made at lower levels, and are thus more apt to reflect the characteristics of incrementalism as described by Lindblom. In discussing the interplay between these two levels of decision-making, Etzioni accurately noted that policy occasionally results from an agglomeration of bit decisions—in other words, by default—rather than from top-down decision-making. To its credit, his model also provided a "set of instructions for the unimaginative decisionmaker," including strategies for assessing alternatives repeatedly until only one is left.

Mixed scanning is indeed an improvement on incrementalism; by distinguishing between contextuating policy decisions and bit implementation decisions, it acknowledges the rather obvious fact that some decisions are not incremental—and thus it applies, at least theoretically, to a broader range of decision situations. Like the rational model and incrementalism, however, mixed scanning assumes a centralized decision-making process. It leaves unresolved the identity of those who will participate in that process or the possibility of conflict among the values held by those participants (the strategy seems to assume a benevolent decision-maker with all the right values; but which values are indeed the right ones, and who is empowered to make this decision?). The centralized, top-down character of incrementalism and mixed scanning ultimately undermines their potential utility, just as it undermined that of the rationality-based models.[26]

Public planning occurs in an environment characterized by conflicting ideologies and values, vigorous competition for scarce resources, and vast differentials in power. These aspects of the environment are expressed through the political system, of which the planning process is inescapably a part. As interest groups vie with one another in the political system, therefore, they tend to view planning as simply another tool to be used in pursuit of their ends.

We planners, then, find ourselves squeezed on both sides. On the one hand, we lack a workable and widely acceptable definition of the public interest—which, if available, would at least let us enter the political fray with a keen sense of moral compass. On the other hand, interest groups press their claims upon us in such a way that even if we had all the intellectual and conceptual tools needed to "plan rationally in pursuit of the public interest," we would still be politically constrained from doing so.

This is but another way of describing the tension between planning and politics to which I referred in the previous chapter. If we did possess a model or strategy that would enable us to make decisions in accordance with a highly developed sense of the public interest (however defined), we would need sufficient centrality of position, legitimate authority, and freedom from political interference to carry out that strategy. These are, however, concessions that a capitalist democracy is unwilling to make to us.

Incrementalism and mixed scanning acknowledge the impact of political power on the planning process—but they cave in too easily, failing to search for ways in which the dynamics of the political system might be harnessed to good purpose. We can do better. A good starting point is an examination of models that view planning as a decentralized process. That is the task of the next two chapters.

NOTES

1. Herbert A. Simon, *Models of Man* (New York: John Wiley & Sons, 1957), p. 205.
2. Ibid.

3. Herbert A. Simon, *Administrative Behavior,* 2nd ed. (New York: The Macmillan Company, 1957), p. xxiv. Emphasis in the original.
4. Ibid., p. xxvi.
5. Ibid., p. 99.
6. Simon, *Models of Man,* p. 199.
7. Robert A. Dahl and Charles E. Lindblom, *Politics, Economics, and Welfare: Planning and Politico-Economic Systems Resolved into Basic Social Processes* (New York: Harper & Row, 1953), pp. 64–88.
8. Charles E. Lindblom, "The Science of 'Muddling Through,'" *Public Administration Review,* Vol. 19 (Spring 1959), pp. 79–88.
9. David Braybrooke and Charles E. Lindblom, *A Strategy of Decision: Policy Evaluation As a Social Process* (New York: The Free Press, 1963). Also useful in this regard is Michael T. Hayes, *Incrementalism and Public Policy* (New York: Longman, 1992).
10. Charles E. Lindblom, *The Intelligence of Democracy: Decision Making through Mutual Adjustment* (New York: The Free Press, 1965).
11. Nigel Taylor, *Urban Planning Theory Since 1945* (London: Sage Publications, 1998), p. 72.
12. Lindblom, *Intelligence of Democracy,* pp. 144–145.
13. Ibid., p. 145.
14. Ibid.
15. Ibid., pp. 145–146.
16. Ibid., pp. 146–147.
17. Ibid., p. 147.
18. Ibid., pp. 147–148.
19. Ibid., p. 148.
20. Ibid., pp. 148–151.
21. Amitai Etzioni, *The Active Society: A Theory of Societal and Political Processes* (New York: The Free Press, 1968), pp. 272–273.
22. For counterarguments to these and other critiques of incrementalism, see Andrew Weiss and Edward Woodhouse, "Reframing Incrementalism: A Constructive Response to the Critics," *Policy Sciences,* Vol. 25, No. 3 (August 1992), pp. 255–273.
23. Yehezkel Dror, *Public Policymaking Reexamined* (San Francisco: Chandler Publishing Company, 1968), p. 146.
24. William H. Whyte, *City: Rediscovering the Center* (New York: Doubleday, 1988), pp. 229–255.
25. See Amitai Etzioni, "Mixed Scanning: A 'Third' Approach to Decision-Making," *Public Administration Review,* Vol. 27 (December 1967), pp. 385–392; and Etzioni, *Active Society,* pp. 282–305.
26. An anonymous reviewer of a draft of this book took issue with this claim, arguing that both incrementalism and mixed scanning are "mainly decentralized, hence bottom up, sideways, and top down." I disagree. Both Lindblom and Etzioni were clear in their intentions; they were proposing strategies intended to improve the role performance of policy makers.

DECENTRALIZED RATIONALITY: THE PLANNER AS POLITICAL ACTIVIST

ADVOCACY PLANNING

The authors whose strategies will be considered in this and the following chapter place a high value on democratic process. This is not to say that the rationalists and the incrementalists are not similarly inclined. In their preoccupation with the intellectual task confronting the central decision-maker, however, they reflect an implicit assumption that the important decisions will indeed be made (or recommended) by duly authorized planners, administrators, bureaucrats, and elected officials, either directly or in an advisory capacity.

The strategies examined under the "decentralized" heading, on the other hand, generally assume that major decisions should be in the hands of the citizenry itself. The role of the professional planner, then, is to facilitate decision-making by the citizenry. As with the centralized strategies, I have divided the decentralized models into those that assume rational planning behavior and those that do not. The former category offers only one strategy to consider: advocacy planning.

The central themes of advocacy planning are widely known—namely, that many groups are not adequately represented in standard or customary planning practices; that to correct this situation, various interest groups should be able to put forward their own plans for public consideration; and that professional planning assistance should be made available to such interest groups to assist them in that process.

Advocacy planning emerged as a major movement in the urban planning profession during the 1960s and 1970s, a time of considerable turbulence in American society.[1] Large-scale migration processes, accompanied by widespread racial discrimination and residential segregation, had concentrated hundreds of thousands of low-income and minority citizens in central city neighborhoods, where social problems abounded. The failures of the federal urban renewal program (generally perceived to have done more harm than good), incidents of property-destroying neighborhood violence in several major cities, growing concerns over an unpopular war in Vietnam—these and other elements combined to destabilize the society and to create a sense of crisis in the American spirit. Those readers old enough to have lived through that time will remember it as a period of considerable turmoil. Clearly, the old ways of doing things were simply not working; new approaches were called for—in planning as much as in most other major social institutions and processes.

Many of us have had professional heroes during our careers, and one name has always headed my own list: Paul Davidoff, who introduced the concept of advocacy to the planning profession. As Barry Checkoway has noted, Davidoff

> was an unyielding force for justice and equity in planning. He viewed planning as a process to address a wide range of societal problems; to improve conditions for all people while emphasizing resources and opportunities for those lacking in both; and to expand representation and participation of traditionally excluded groups in the decisions that affect their lives. He challenged planners to promote participatory democracy and positive social change; to overcome poverty and racism as factors in society; and to reduce disparities between rich and poor, White and Black, men and women.[2]

Davidoff was a lawyer-turned-planner whose career featured a blend of university teaching and direct social action. He was one of the few planners ever to run for the U. S. Congress—an aspiration not supported, as it turned out, by the vast majority of voters in Westchester County. By the time of his premature death in 1984, Davidoff had fundamentally and permanently altered the ideology of the planning profession.

While hints are detectable in some of his earlier writings, the major statement of the concept of advocacy planning appeared in a 1965 article in the *Journal of the American Institute of Planners*—an article that has probably been read and cited by more planning students than any other single work.[3] In that article, Davidoff took strong exception to the supposed value neutrality of the urban planner; any decision to act, he said, must be based on someone's conception of desired objectives. Having decided what objectives to pursue, the planner should not only make explicit the values underlying his or her prescription for a course of action but should also *affirm* them—in other words, become an advocate for what is deemed proper.[4] The planner should be able to engage in the political process as an advocate "of the interests both of government and of such other groups, organizations, or individuals who are concerned with proposing policies for the future development of the community."[5] Thus the advocacy planner bypasses the lack of a universally agreed upon public interest by concentrating on the values of a subunit of the larger community (thereby pitching a tent squarely in John Rawls's camp rather than in that of the utilitarians).

For Davidoff, public planning decisions are the end product of competition in the political arena. Hence:

> The recommendation that city planners represent and plead the plans of many interest groups is founded upon the need to establish an effective urban democracy, one in which citizens may be able to play an active role in the process of deciding public policy. Appropriate policy in a democracy is determined through a process of political debate. *The right course of action is always a matter of choice, never of fact.*[6]

The major innovation needed, in Davidoff's view, was a process whereby "plural plans" would be prepared, rather than continuing to rely upon a "unitary plan" developed by a single agency. This was quite a revolutionary idea for a body of planners who, at the time, tended to see the development of a community's master plan as the ultimate expression of their professional expertise.

The advocacy planner would be responsible to a particular interest group in the community and would attempt to express that group's values and objectives in the plans that he or she produced. If these values and objectives were unclear, the planner should assist the group in clarifying them. The planner could certainly have his or her own ideas, of course, and might attempt to educate or persuade clients regarding the wisdom of certain policies or actions; in the last analysis, however, the client group's preferences must prevail. The planner might also "become engaged in expanding the size and scope" of the client organization—words suggesting participation in community organization and development activities.[7] Overall, however, the planner's primary role would be "to carry out the planning process for the organization and to argue persuasively in favor of its planning proposals."[8] Clearly, then, Davidoff's advocacy planning consisted of two major elements: technical assistance and representation.

In theory, at least, all major groups in the community should generate plans reflecting their interests. Davidoff wanted to see plans emerging from political parties; from protest organizations; and from special interest groups such as "chambers of commerce, real estate boards, labor organizations, pro- and anti-civil rights groups, and anti-poverty councils."⁹ In practice, however, most proponents of advocacy planning viewed it primarily as a vehicle for providing assistance to low-income and minority groups, these being the groups that Davidoff and other observers believed had been neglected—and even harmed—by past planning processes.

Not surprisingly, a sizable literature emerged in response to Davidoff's arguments, and many fine points were debated at conferences and in journals. For example, must the advocacy planner be employed directly by the client groups whose interests he or she is furthering? Marshall Kaplan, at that time a consultant whose firm frequently undertook advocacy-related projects, distinguished between "inside advocates," those employed by City Hall and linked to a *constituency* rather than to a *client,* and "outside advocates," those employed by the client group itself. While noting that the inside advocate has a particularly difficult task, he concluded that both have useful roles to play.[10]

Why have I categorized advocacy planning as a *rational* form of decentralized planning? At least so far as Davidoff's formulation is concerned, such a label is entirely appropriate. For he was suggesting a change not in what the planner *does,* but only *for whom he or she does it.* Davidoff's own conception of the planning process was spelled out in a 1962 article coauthored with Thomas A. Reiner.[11] The "choice theory" presented in that article is clearly one more version of the rational planning model, and it positions Davidoff squarely in the mainstream of the rational planning tradition. His argument was not that we should abandon rational planning, but that we should make its benefits available to those who have previously been excluded from the rational planning process.

Nor did Davidoff suggest that planners should necessarily take on new substantive concerns.

A specialization in social planning enjoyed brief popularity in the profession in the 1960s and early 1970s, instigated by the social problems of the era and fueled by the flow of federal funds for community action programs (focused on poverty) and the Model Cities programs (which attempted to better integrate social and physical planning for the amelioration of inner-city problems).[12] It is often assumed, because of his concern for social equity, that Davidoff played a key role in the social planning movement. This was not the case, however; he was, and remained, primarily a physical planner. Davidoff's advocacy planner would still prepare land use and site plans, zoning ordinances, and schedules for improvements in municipal facilities; he or she would do so, however, in a way that reflected the needs and priorities of a specific subgroup of the community.

In theory, then, the advocacy planner continued to plan in a pragmatically rational manner, but defined the client in far narrower terms than had the more traditional community-wide comprehensive planner. In so doing, by the way, the advocacy planner improved the likelihood that the client group's values—at least those relevant to the problem at hand—would be somewhat homogeneous, and thus more susceptible to rational treatment.

I must concede, however, that my categorization of advocacy as a form of rational planning breaks down when advocacy is examined as practiced rather than as presented in theory. Davidoff himself may have been loyal to the concept of rationality, but most of those who actually functioned as advocates were more likely to view a plan simply as one of many tools available to the advocate in the pursuit of what is right. The advocacy planning initiatives of the 1960s and 1970s were often transformed into social protests, community organizing efforts, and other forms of political activism, with relatively little emphasis on the development of plans *per se.*

Because, I suspect, of the extent to which it reflected the political concerns felt by many young men and women in the 1960s, advocacy planning was tremendously popular in graduate schools of planning at that time. Well into the 1970s, when I would ask a class of students how many of them wanted to become advocacy planners, virtually every hand would be raised. Ironically, however, the extent of advocacy planning practice was never consistent with the concept's impact on planning thought. In several cities that housed major schools of planning and architecture, groups of graduate students, faculty members, and recent graduates banded together to offer their services to low-income neighborhoods, often under the auspices of "community design centers" (the Architects' Renewal Committee, in Harlem; Boston's Urban Planning Aid; and San Francisco's Community Design Center were the best-known examples).[13] A few concerned professionals of more advanced years and experience contributed *pro bono* services to such groups. A handful of consulting firms declared themselves to be interested primarily in advocacy planning projects (at least as long as federal funds were available for such projects); an occasional planner, acting alone, gave up an agency job to work for low-income groups for little or no pay; and a fairly sizable number of planners working for city planning agencies, Model Cities programs, and community action programs came to satisfy themselves—if not those they served—that they were in fact advocacy planners working inside the system.

Overall, however, only a small number of planners—that is, people who continued to identify with the planning profession—played advocacy roles of the sort called for by Davidoff in his 1965 article. When the national mood shifted in the 1980s and federal funds for social programs dried up, advocacy planning lost what little financial support it had enjoyed in the previous two decades. Nor did the idea of plural plans ever take hold in American cities; political decisions continued to be made without them.

In 1971, the American Institute of Planners created the Advocate Planners' National Advisory Committee, which was charged with recommending steps that the AIP should take to further the practice of advocacy planning, and I was asked to chair the group. Three years later (and they were turbulent years indeed, with many viewpoints vying for preeminence), we issued our report, which called for (1) the creation of a national clearinghouse for information about advocacy planning projects, intended to enable those running such projects to benefit from each others' experiences; (2) technical assistance to local groups attempting to organize for and carry out advocacy projects; (3) several forms of assistance to planners who had lost their jobs because of advocacy activities; and (4) the appointment, by the AIP, of a director of advocacy planning to oversee all these activities. A director was indeed hired but the position was short-lived, and little came of the other recommendations; by that time—the mid-1970s—the idea of advocacy planning was receding in popularity.

Advocacy too, it seems, had developed feet of clay. Several practical reservations had been expressed along the way. For example, Roger Starr, a prominent housing official, argued that advocacy fosters conflict, whereas planners would do better to focus on building consensus;[14] and Richard Bolan warned that multiple plans could result in decision-making gridlock.[15] More important in bringing about the decline of advocacy planning, however, were two fundamental issues.

The first surfaced at a unique and memorable event—the First (and, as it turned out, the last) Annual Advocacy Planning Conference, held in New York City in 1970 under the sponsorship of Hunter College, where Paul Davidoff was a member of the planning faculty. Billed as an opportunity to share experiences in order to advance the practice of advocacy planning, the conference was attended by several hundred faculty members and students from throughout the nation—and by a number of grass-roots leaders of New York City neighborhood organizations. It quickly became apparent that the latter group was not happy with the concept of advocacy planning as Davidoff had conceived it.

The gathering was raucous and unruly from beginning to end. In the spirit of the times, few speakers—including Davidoff—were able to complete their talks without being hooted down; platforms were stormed, microphones were wrested from the hands of speakers, and their messages were decried as "colonialist bullshit." All in all, it was heady and exciting stuff (and, if I remember correctly, more than a little daunting) for the many young advocacy enthusiasts in attendance.

The message communicated by the stage-stormers, most of them affiliated with New York neighborhood groups, was approximately this: "Advocacy has become the plaything of white middle-class professionals who receive sizable salaries for their efforts. We don't need their help, and we resent their patronizing behavior. The money spent on advocacy would serve our needs much more directly if it were simply given to us; we are capable of developing our own plans and strategies, and we can certainly speak for ourselves. If you planners are really serious about doing something for the poor and minorities, go root out racism where it operates most virulently—in the affluent, segregated suburbs."

All those who attended the conference went home with a new perspective on advocacy planning; what had previously seemed principled and noble had instead been described as colonialist, elitist, self-serving, top-down, and repressive. Clearly some of the luster had been lost from the advocacy ideal. Indeed, it was not long after this conference that Davidoff resigned his teaching post at Hunter and created the Suburban Action Institute, for the purpose of combating housing discrimination in Westchester County.

The second issue was a growing concern that the advocacy concept might be politically naive—that in fact it seemed to offer little hope of affecting the ways in which political decisions are actually made. Assuming that a number of plans are produced to compete with one another in the political arena, but assuming also that the distribution of power in the community remains unchanged, why should decisions on planning issues differ from those made in the past? What new tribunal can be called upon to render verdicts more pleasing to the advocacy planners' clients? According to this view, interest groups will be better represented only when the balance of power shifts in their favor. (But if such shifts occurred, would the interest groups need a planner to represent them?) The principal point was simply that the services of an advocacy planner did not automatically endow a group with additional power, and that advocacy planning without an increase in power was probably a fruitless undertaking. (Offered as evidence of this point was the frequency with which advocacy projects began as technical assistance in research and planning, only to shift eventually to community organizing and social protest.) This was the view of advocacy planning that was reflected by most of the progressive theorists discussed in Chapter 3, who tended to see advocacy as typical of the naive thinking of liberal reformers and rejected the notion that advocacy planners could have any significant impact on the power relationships inherent in the capitalist state. Advocacy planners were certainly well-intentioned, said the progressives, but they simply didn't understand how capitalist society operates.

NOTES

1. Barry Checkoway, "Paul Davidoff and Advocacy Planning in Retrospect," *Journal of the American Planning Association*, Vol. 60, No. 2 (Spring 1994), p. 140.
2. Ibid., p. 139.
3. Paul Davidoff, "Advocacy and Pluralism in Planning," *Journal of the American Institute of Planners*, Vol. 31, No. 4 (November 1965), pp. 331–338.
4. Ibid., pp. 331–332.
5. Ibid., p. 332.
6. Ibid. Emphasis added.
7. Ibid., p. 333.
8. Ibid.
9. Ibid., p. 334.
10. Marshall Kaplan, "Advocacy and the Urban Poor," *Journal of the American Institute of Planners*, Vol. 35, No. 1 (March 1969), pp. 96–101.
11. Paul Davidoff and Thomas A. Reiner, "A Choice Theory of Planning," *Journal of the American Institute of Planners*, Vol. 28 (May 1962), pp. 103–115.
12. For an overview of that specialization, see Michael P. Brooks, *Social Planning and City Planning*, Planning Advisory Service Report No. 261 (Chicago: American Society of Planning Officials, September 1970).
13. For a description of these programs, see C. Richard Hatch, "Some Thoughts on Advocacy Planning," *The Architectural Forum*, Vol. 128 (June 1968), pp. 72–73,103,109.
14. Roger Starr, "Advocators or Planners?" *ASPO Newsletter*, Vol. 33 (December 1967), p. 137.
15. Richard S. Bolan, "Emerging Views of Planning," *Journal of the American Institute of Planners*, Vol. 33 (July 1967), p. 239.

REFERENCES

Alexander, Ernest R. "After Rationality, What? A Review of Responses to Paradigm Breakdown," *Journal of the American Planning Association*, Vol. 50, No. 1, Winter 1984.

———. *Approaches to Planning: Introducing Current Planning Theories, Concepts, and Issues,* 2nd ed., Philadelphia, Gordon and Breach, 1992.

Arrow, Kenneth J. "Mathematical Models in the Social Sciences," in *The Policy Sciences,* edited by Daniel Lerner and Harold D. Lasswell, Stanford, Stanford University Press, 1951.

Edward C. Banfield. "Ends and Means in Planning," *International Social Science Journal*, Vol. 11, 1959.

Batty, Michael. "A Chronicle of Scientific Planning: The Anglo-American Modeling Experience," *Journal of the American Planning Association*, Vol. 60, No. 1, Winter 1994.

———. "Why the Rational Paradigm Persists: Tales from the Field," *Journal of Planning Education and Research*, Vol. 15, No. 2, Winter 1996.

Black, Alan. "The Chicago Area Transportation Study: A Case Study of Rational Planning," *Journal of Planning Education and Research*, Vol. 10, No. 1, Fall 1990.

Bolan, Richard S. "Emerging Views of Planning," *Journal of the American Institute of Planners*, Vol. 33, July 1967.

Braybrooke, David, and Charles E. Lindblom. *A Strategy of Decision: Policy Evaluation as a Social Process,* New York, The Free Press, 1963.

———. *Social Planning and City Planning,* Chicago, American Society of Planning Officials, Planning Advisory Service Report No. 261, September 1970.

Bryson, John M. *Strategic Planning for Public and Nonprofit Organizations: A Guide to Strengthening and Sustaining Organizational Achievement,* rev. ed., San Francisco, Jossey-Bass Publishers, 1995.

Bryson, John M., and William D. Roering. "Applying Private-Sector Strategic Planning in the Public Sector," *Journal of the American Planning Association*, Vol. 53, No. 1, Winter 1987.

Checkoway, Barry. "Paul Davidoff and Advocacy Planning in Retrospect," *Journal of the*

American Planning Association, Vol. 60, No. 2, Spring 1994.

Dahl, Robert A., and Charles E. Lindblom. *Politics, Economics, and Welfare: Planning and Politico-Economic Systems Resolved into Basic Social Processes,* New York, Harper & Row, 1953.

Dalton, Linda C. "Why the Rational Paradigm Persists: The Resistance of Professional Education and Practice to Alternative Forms of Planning," *Journal of Planning Education and Research,* Vol. 5, No. 3, Spring 1986.

Davidoff, Paul. "Advocacy and Pluralism in Planning," *Journal of the American Institute of Planners,* Vol. 31, No. 4, November 1965.

Davidoff, Paul, and Thomas A. Reiner. "A Choice Theory of Planning," *Journal of the American Institute of Planners,* Vol. 28, May 1962.

Dror, Yehezkel. *Public Policymaking Reexamined,* San Francisco, Chandler Publishing Company, 1968.

Etzioni, Amitai. *The Active Society: A Theory of Societal and Political Processes,* New York, The Free Press, 1968.

———. "Mixed Scanning: A 'Third' Approach to Decision-Making," *Public Administration Review,* Vol. 27, December 1967.

Flyvbjerg, Bent. *Rationality and Power: Democracy in Practice,* Chicago, University of Chicago Press, 1998.

Gans, Herbert J. *People and Plans: Essays on Urban Problems and Solutions,* New York, Basic Books, 1968.

Hatch, C. Richard. "Some Thoughts on Advocacy Planning," *The Architectural Forum,* Vol. 128, June 1968.

Hayes, Michael T. *Incrementalism and Public Policy,* New York, Longman, 1992.

Kaplan, Abraham. "Some Limitations on Rationality," in *Nomos VII: Rational Decision,* edited by Carl J. Friedrich, New York, Atherton Press, 1964.

Kaplan, Marshall. "Advocacy and the Urban Poor," *Journal of the American Institute of Planners,* Vol. 35, No. 1, March 1969.

Kaufman, Jerome L., and Harvey M. Jacobs. "A Public Planning Perspective on Strategic Planning," *Journal of the American Planning Association,* Vol. 53, No. 1, Winter 1987.

Lindblom, Charles E. *The Intelligence of Democracy: Decision Making through Mutual Adjustment,* New York, The Free Press, 1965.

———. "The Science of 'Muddling Through," *Public Administration Review,* Vol. 19, Spring 1959.

Meyerson, Martin, and Edward G. Banfield. *Politics, Planning and the Public Interest,* Glencoe, Ill., The Free Press, 1955.

Simon, Herbert A. *Administrative Behavior,* 2nd ed., New York, The Macmillan Company, 1957.

———. *Models of Man,* New York, John Wiley & Sons, 1957.

Starr, Roger. "Advocators or Planners?" *ASPO Newsletter,* Vol. 33, December 1967.

———. *Urban Planning Theory Since 1945,* London, Sage Publications, 1998.

Verma, Niraj. "Pragmatic Rationality and Planning Theory," *Journal of Planning Education and Research,* Vol. 16, No. 1, Fall 1996.

Wegener, Michael. "Operational Urban Models: State of the Art," *Journal of the American Planning Association,* Vol. 60, No. 1, Winter 1994.

Weiss, Andrew, and Edward Woodhouse. "Reframing Incrementalism: A Constructive Response to the Critics," *Policy Sciences,* Vol. 25, No. 3, August 1992.

Whyte, William H. *City: Rediscovering the Center,* New York, Doubleday, 1988.

URBAN LAND USE PLANNING

FRAMING THE LAND USE PLANNING PROCESS

BY PHILIP R. BERKE, DAVID R. GODSCHALK AND EDWARD J. KAISE

You are asked to help your community to prepare a new land use plan. Your first task is to create a conceptual framework that will guide you and your community in preparing and implementing the plan. The framework should be designed based on the assumption that planning operates in a complex and turbulent decision-making arena that reflects a high-stakes game in which the players attempt to gain land use decisions that most benefit their own interests. The framework should guide your community in carrying out several tasks: 1) identify and account for the goals and values of interest groups with a stake in the land development process; 2) establish a land use planning program that integrates community-based information with a collaborative planning process to create consensus-based plans for a sustainable future; and 3) monitor and evaluate how well land development outcomes make progress toward sustainability. What are the key dimensions of this conceptual framework? What are the primary functions of a local planning program within the framework? What special capabilities will you need to perform these functions?

Local land use planning can be seen as a high-stakes game of competition over a community's or region's future land use pattern. To win the game from a narrow, interest-group perspective is to gain adoption of land use plans, development regulations, and development decisions that most benefit a particular group. Land use planners are central players and game managers in their role as stewards of the public interest. Effective planners act as mediators to resolve conflicts, coalition builders to achieve multigroup benefits, and advocates to advance the interests of underrepresented groups. They must be visionary thinkers who look beyond immediate concerns to the needs of future generations, and effective communicators of these visions of the future who inspire confidence in the reality of sustainable land use patterns. Planners must carefully watch and respond to the interests, actions, and alliances of other players. By not understanding every stage of the game, planners risk losing their credibility and authority as well as the broader public's stake in the community's future.

The purpose of this chapter is to illustrate the dynamic context of local land use planning, the functions of a planning program, and alternative visions that guide planning toward more sustainable and livable places. We first discuss the basic premises of the land use planning arena. We then present a conceptual framework of the elements of local land use planning. The framework consists of three conceptual dimensions: 1) land use values of stakeholders; 2) local land use planning programs that help communities fashion consensus-based visions and plans to achieve those visions; and 3) sustainable land use patterns. Finally, the chapter summarizes the core capabilities that planners need to effectively advance outcomes that balance the values of multiple stakeholder groups.

THE LAND USE PLANNING ARENA

The land use planning arena can be confusing and frustrating even to the experienced planner. Rather than an orderly and rational procedure of adopting land use plans derived from systematic studies aimed at the overall public interest, planning can appear to be an ad hoc process based on misleading perceptions about reality and narrow interest-group politics. Theories of ideal urban form, policy-intervention strategies, and statistical modeling techniques taught in planning school often carry less weight with elected officials than the self-serving demands of a crowd of angry speakers at a public hearing. Long-range projections may fail as guides to decision making in complex and constantly changing decision-making arenas. Planning interventions can reverberate through the system in ways that can only be partially traced, and interventions may not account for unanticipated changes in social, economic, and environmental conditions.

The *complexity and turbulence* of the land planning arena pose a challenging decision-making environment, but also offer the opportunity to build innovative and adaptive land planning programs. Rather than experiencing continuity and stability, the land planning arena is almost always in a state of change (Innes and Booher 1999). Static systems have little capacity to respond and change to adapt to new conditions. Dynamic organizations, on the other hand, are in a position to adapt. During times of change, planning programs can play a key role in coordinating complex interest-group activities and to pursue new visions.

The land use planning and decision-making arena can be conceived as a high-stakes *competition* over an area's future land use pattern. However, the process is tempered by the need for *cooperation*. Players are locked in a framework of interdependence in which they must gain agreement to achieve their goals. This requires that players participate in a multiparty consensus-building process, learning from feedback about prior successes and failures, and experimenting with new planning solutions and actions. Characterizing planning as a serious game of competition and cooperation helps to understand the dynamics of the process and to visualize opportunities for improving game outcomes.

Thus, the land use plan is a key tool to *coordinate* community land use and development activities. Planning is not simply a process, but is a process guided by a plan. The plan fulfills many needs. It serves the traditional functions of guiding urban infrastructure and setting parameters for zoning and other land use regulations on private and public property. It also serves newer purposes. The plan helps turn competitors into collaborators through involvement in its preparation. It records a series of agreements among the players about ways to deal with their different goals, serving as a community consensus-building tool. Around a well-written plan, diverse interests can negotiate and agree on policy. The plan also sets forth factually grounded graphic images of the future that can rally and unite stakeholders to act. Citizens and interest groups like to back a plan that lets them "see" solutions to problems (Neuman 1998).

In the land use game, planners are not only players, they are also game managers, providing information to ensure informed decision making, advocating cooperation among the players, transforming words and facts to a collective vision, and drafting plans and rules to guide the game to achieve the vision. Because of these responsibilities, planners have a unique position at the center of the land use game. They have inside information and privileged access to other players. Land use planners are expected to keep careful track of all stakeholders' interests, actions, and alliances.

They also must continuously aggregate, analyze, and monitor intelligence from the population/economy, land use, environment, and transportation/infrastructure information systems and make it useful for plan making through a community involvement and review process. To lose track of the game status is to risk losing planners' credibility as experts, their role as visionary thinkers, their authority as land use change managers, and their opportunities to facilitate cooperation among competing interests in building a better, more sustainable community.

In practice, the inherent conflicts and tensions in the land planning arena are moderated by the legal and governance systems—"the rules of the game." The rules turn conflict into regulated competition and collaboration. Constitutional provisions, laws, regulations, and planning powers protect overall public interests from the extremes of unregulated maximization of market values and overregulated maximization of social and environmental values. The planner must rely on legal and governance systems to balance conflicts among values, to help make difficult choices about community priorities, and to ensure fairness in land use decisions. The planner is both the drafter and enforcer of the game rules (in the form of plan goals and policies and development regulations) but is not the final arbitrator. That role is reserved for the elected officials of the community or the courts if the elected officials' decision is challenged. But the planner must understand the influences of legal and constitutional checks and balances on the powers of land use plans to achieve community goals.

VALUES, PLANNING, AND SUSTAINABLE COMMUNITIES

Relationships between land use values of stakeholders, their planning programs, and outcomes

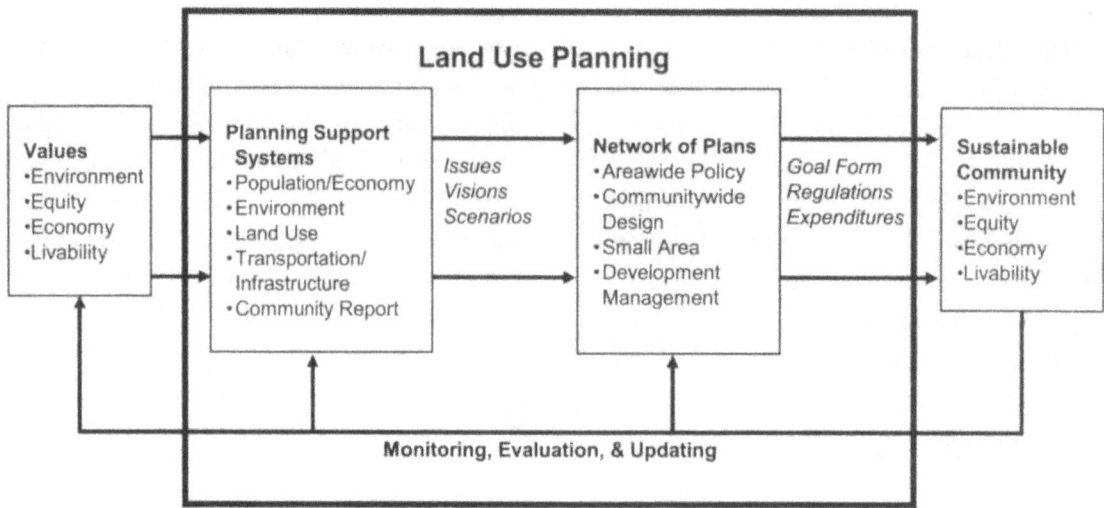

Figure 1. Conceptual framework of land use planning.

constitute the land use planning game. Figure 1 illustrates the conceptual framework of the land use planning game. This framework guides the organization and presentation of the content and format of the chapters in this book. The framework consists of three conceptual dimensions and the relationships among them.

Starting with outcomes, the goal is to seek *sustainable community land use* patterns that strike an appropriate balance among environmental, economic, social, and livability values. As will be discussed, there are alternative trends and visions that are advocated as the most preferable outcomes (i.e., conventional low-density development, Smart Growth and New Urbanism). The inputs to planning consist of interactions with stakeholder groups who view development through the lens of their *land use values* and seek to influence local planning decisions about future urban form and change to support their interests. The central dimension is the *land use planning program*, which serves to help communities identify existing and emerging issues; fashion visions, goals, and scenarios; create plans; adopt development management plans, regulations, and infrastructure expenditure programs; and monitor how well outcomes achieve plan goals.

In the remainder of this chapter we elaborate on a more complete definition of each dimension in the arena of land use planning. Under each dimension, we explore various prescriptions from theory and practice about how planning should be done and what planners should do. We conclude with a review of the pressures on planners and special capabilities that planners must develop to operate effectively within the land use game.

SUSTAINABLE COMMUNITIES: ALTERNATIVE TRENDS AND VISIONS

The local land use game is subject to continuous change in response to trends in land use, advances in technology that help planners to visualize current realities and invent possibilities, and the appearance of new and imaginative ideas about urban design. Trends affecting the play of the game at the beginning of the twenty-first century continue and extend those of the recent past. Conventional low-density development patterns (or sprawl) have dominated the landscape while concepts of sustainable development, Smart

Growth, and New Urbanism have emerged to counter the impacts of sprawl.

CONVENTIONAL LOW-DENSITY DEVELOPMENT

America's communities and metropolitan regions face multiple challenges, most of which are associated with sprawling, low-density development patterns caused by the outward expansion of suburban development on the urban fringe, and commercial strip development along highways leading into and out of cities and suburbs. The societal costs and benefits of conventional low-density development are subject to intense debate. Supporters maintain that this dominant pattern is shaped by deeply embedded cultural values that are reflected in strong desires for: 1) detached single-family homeownership; 2) spacious individual lots with a rural, bucolic appeal; 3) private automobile ownership, which provides personal freedom and mobility; and 4) communities free of poverty (Gordon and Richardson 1997). The positive effects of these features tend to accrue to the individual or household.

Critics point to the downside of conventional low-density development. In a comprehensive review of over 500 studies on the impacts of this land use pattern, Burchell et al. (1998) concluded that the negative effects of conventional development exceed the benefits, and that these effects tend to be distributed throughout an entire area. Negative effects of sprawl are most clearly evidenced by increased demand for land to accommodate each new increment of population growth. Figure 2 indicates that between 1982 and 1997 the percentage of increase in urban land dramatically outpaced the increase in population growth in all four regions of the country. These land consumption rates place intense pressure on environmentally sensitive lands and increase the costs of public infrastructure because lower densities require more linear feet of roads and sewer and water lines to service each lot (Burchell et al. 1998; Speir and Stephenson 2002). The increased spread between land uses also creates greater auto dependence. Between 1982 and 2000, auto passenger miles of travel increased 85 percent in metropolitan areas (Texas Transportation

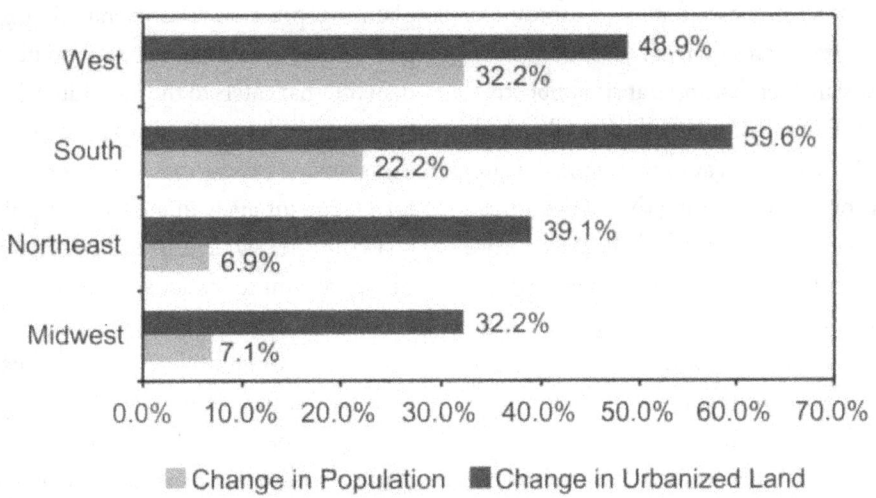

Figure 2. Between 1982 and 1997, the percentage of increase in urban land dramatically outpaced the increase in population growth in all four regions of the country.
Source: Fulton et al. 2001. Reproduced by permission from the Brookings Institution.

Institute 2002) and the average annual peak delay per road traveler grew from sixteen to sixty-two hours. Conventional low-density development has also been linked to the exacerbation of social inequities because some analysts believe that it drains fiscal and human resources from older core areas to the expanding suburban fringe (Downs 1994, 1999; Lucy and Phillips 2000).

Sprawl also has been linked to health concerns, as public health professionals have rediscovered the impacts of the built environment on physical activity. Physical inactivity has been shown to contribute to chronic disease, osteoporosis, poor mental health, and obesity (Frank, Engelke, and Schmid 2003, 1). Traditional low-density development patterns, with separated residential and commercial land uses, increased reliance on automobile travel, and a lack of adequate infrastructure for bicycling and walking, act as barriers or inhibitors to physical activity. Accumulating evidence suggests that transportation, land use, and urban design are related to people's decisions to be physically active.[1] Thus, transportation, land use, and urban design plans all can affect neighborhood factors that encourage physical activity. For example, researchers found significantly lower obesity rates for residents of more compact, denser, pedestrian-friendly, and transit-supportive areas of the Atlanta region (Frank, Engelke, and Schmid 2003, 185). In a nationwide study of the health effects of sprawl covering the 448 counties where 75 percent of Americans live, researchers found that people living in counties marked by sprawling development are likely to walk less, weigh more, and suffer from hypertension (high blood pressure) (McCann and Ewing 2003). The study's county sprawl index included six variables reflecting residential density and the connectivity of the street network.[2] Another nationwide study found that changes in the amount of land developed, holding population constant, were related to larger increases in obesity (Vandegrift and Yoked, 2004).

Land use planning in America has traditionally meant planning that supports this conventional low-density development process. The extended ribbons of commercial development along highways all follow standard zoning, as do big tracts of suburban housing each the same size on the same lots. The large-scale conversion of open landscapes to suburban developments often results from requirements of standard subdivision ordinances. The Chicago region's outward-spreading urban form reflects this pattern of change (see Sidebar 1 and Figures 3 and 1–4). As the two Landsat images in Figure 3 show, urban land has spread outward from the historic center over the twenty-five years between 1972 and 1997, replacing agricultural land. The plan notes that this territorial growth rate is far in excess of the rate of population growth, resulting in low-density sprawl and social segregation.

In an attempt to counter the outcomes of this development process, the *Chicago Metropolis 2020* plan offers a range of sustainability recommendations that depart from conventional land use planning practice. The overarching goal of this plan is not to simply accommodate the market demand that caters to the individual developer and homeowner, but to guide individual market decisions toward producing a more sustainable urban form. The intent is to ensure that public-interest goals are met while also realizing narrower aims. These recommendations span from improving education, workforce development, governance, and the inequitable living conditions associated with race and poverty to redeveloping and infilling within the city and older suburbs, maintaining quality built environments, and preserving valuable natural areas and working landscapes. In this case, zoning is viewed only as a mechanism, and, as the stakeholders in Chicago's metropolis have

SIDEBAR 1   CHICAGO METROPOLIS 2020

Rapid Expansion of Urban Form

The *Chicago Metropolis 2020* plan (Johnson 2001) for the Chicago metropolitan region analyzes social, economic, environmental, and livability aspects of regional development. The Chicago region's urban form is reflected in its land use pattern. Figure 3 shows that urban land has spread outward into the countryside from the historic center between 1972 and 1997. This spatial rate of expansion far exceeds the rate of population growth, resulting in low-density sprawl and social segregation. Although this spatial transformation has offered a number of benefits to households and businesses, it has also exacted serious costs. These costs include reduced viability of public transportation, reduced air quality, increased infrastructure costs, lessened sense of community, and loss of agricultural lands and environmentally important open space. Worst of all, the spatial transformation has resulted in poverty concentration and social segregation on a scale and to a degree unprecedented in history (Johnson 2001, 48).

1909 Burnham Plan and 2020 Regional Development Strategy

It is interesting to compare the *Metropolis 2020* plan with the famous 1909 Burnham *Plan of Chicago*. Both plans are sponsored by the Commercial Club of Chicago. Both seek to harness "two seemingly warring impulses: privatism and public control" (Miller 2001, ix). Both take a regional view of land use and transportation. The Burnham plan is best known for its twenty-mile-long lakefront park system and its radial and concentric boulevards, which are present-day landmarks. The Burnham plan, a businessman's vision of urban reform, turned out to be primarily about urban beautification, rather than housing and human services.

As Donald Miller (2001) points out in his preface, a strength of the *Metropolis 2020* plan is its attempt to connect job training, transportation, and housing policy. The *Metropolis 2020* plan "sees the entire Chicago region as an *interconnected* ecosystem and presages a return to the symbiotic relationship between city and suburb that existed in the age of the electric streetcar" (emphasis supplied). It "promises to narrow economic inequities and right the social balance in Chicago while keeping it a capitalist powerhouse" (Miller 2001, xvi). The 2020 plan proposes a metropolitan regional development strategy based on networked intermodal villages centered on transportation hubs and connected by continuous public greenways, as shown in Figure 4. In keeping with the Chicago ethic, the plan states that this strategy need not be imposed, but should develop naturally as opportunities are recognized and organized by local authorities, with facilitation and incentives provided by a regional coordinating council. Thus, the *Metropolis 2020* plan offers a regional vision, whose implementation depends on the extent to which the future network of local plans acknowledges, and seeks to implement, its goals.

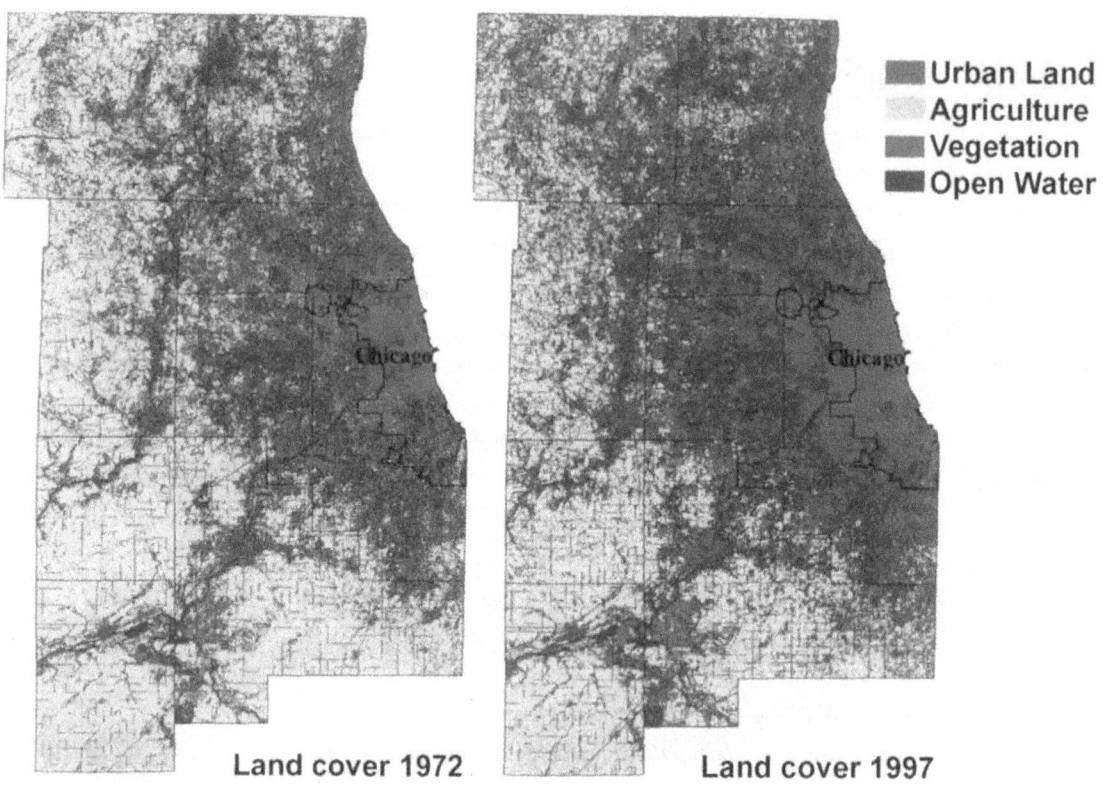

Figure 3. Urban land in Chicago has spread outward over the twenty-five years between 1972 and 1997, replacing agricultural land.

learned, it can be used to safeguard the environment, encourage neighborhoods with mixes of building types and housing affordable to a range of incomes, and require inner cities and older suburbs that are compact and walkable.

SUSTAINABLE DEVELOPMENT

The term "sustainable development" has generated popular appeal because it implies that the production and consumption of goods and services and the development of the built environment can be accomplished without degrading the natural environment. The 1987 report *Our Common Future* from the United Nations World Commission on Environment and Development (WCED) set forth the most widely used definition of the concept: "Sustainable development is development that meets the needs of the present generation without compromising the ability of future generations to meet their own needs" (43). The vision of sustainability has influenced the formulation of a generation of international, national, state, regional, and local plans and programs over the decade that followed the WCED report (Krizek and Power 1996; Lindsey 2003; Porter 2002). Table 1 illustrates a range of definitions of sustainability from U.S. planning and policy practice. Through diverse approaches to achieve sustainability, these definitions attempt to weave together various combinations of societal values referred to as the three *E*s (environment, economy, and equity) originally set forth by the WCED (Berke 2002). A fourth value, livability, has become prominent in planning practice

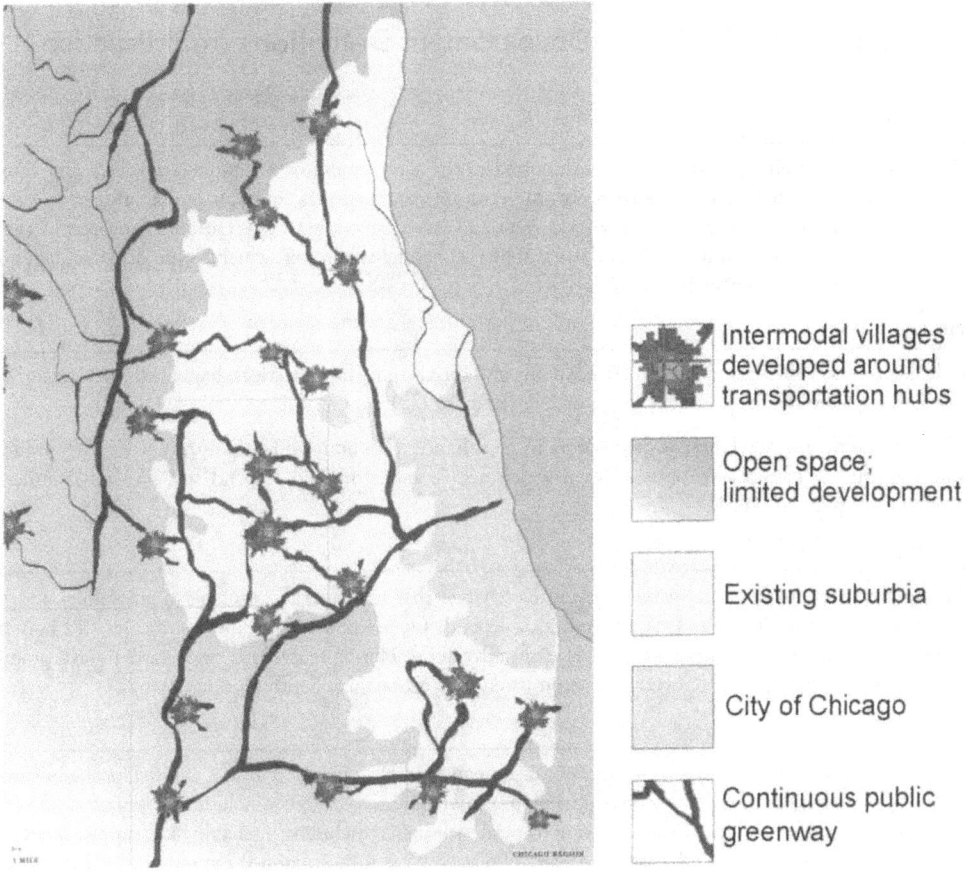

Figure 4. The strategy of networked intermodal villages need not be imposed but should develop naturally as opportunities are recognized and organized by local authorities. The Regional Coordinating Council facilitates and provides incentives.

involving the human interaction with the physical environment with a focus on making places that fit the needs and aspirations of residents. The definitions reflect work by planners and policy makers at the national, state, regional, and local levels in seeking to guide human settlement patterns in ways that balance the core values, and in the process exposing and tackling the inherent tensions among the values.

The central goal of sustainable development is intergenerational equity, which implies fairness to current and coming generations. That is, current and future generations must strive to achieve a decent standard of living for all people and live within the limits of natural systems. The concept of sustainable development is stimulating a rethinking of many facets of how we live, not the least of which is the conventional low-density suburban development pattern that has dominated growth in metropolitan and rural fringe areas since World War II. Defining the key elements of sustainable land use patterns for communities and regions depends on many actors, each with a definition of what is important.[3] For example, Berke and Manta-Conroy (2000) argue that land use plans should be developed based on six long-range sustainable development principles:

Table 1. Examples of Sustainable Development Definitions from Practice

National Policy

"Our vision is of a life-sustaining Earth. We are committed to the achievement of a dignified, peaceful, and equitable existence. A sustainable United States will have a growing economy that provides equitable opportunities for satisfying livelihoods and a safe, healthy, high quality of life for current and future generations. Our nation will protect its environment, its natural resource base, and the functions and viability of natural systems on which all life depends" (President's Council on Sustainable Development 1996, i).

State Planning Policies

"Sustainable development links the environment, economy and social equity into practices that benefit present and future generations" (North Carolina Environmental Resource Program 1997, 1).

"Sustainable development is development that maintains or enhances economic and community well-being while protecting and restoring the natural environment upon which people and economies depend" (Minnesota Planning and Environmental Quality Board 1998).

Regional Plan

Sustainable development involves "… achieving positive change that enhances the ecological, economic, and social systems upon which South Florida and its communities depend. Once implemented these strategies will bolster the regional economy, promote quality communities, secure healthy South Florida ecosystems, and assure todays' progress is not achieved at tomorrow's expense" (Governor's Commission for a Sustainable South Florida, 1996, 2).

Local Plans and Programs

"Sustainability includes: ecological integrity to satisfy basic human needs; economic security including local reinvestment, employment opportunities, local business ownership; empowerment and responsibility including respect and tolerance of diverse values and equal opportunity to participate; and social well-being, including a reliable food supply, housing and education, creative expression through the arts, and sense of place" (City of Burlington [Vermont] 1996, 2–3).

Sustainability is the "long-term cultural, economic, and environmental health and vitality" (City of Seattle [Washington] 1994, 4).

Sustainable development is "… the ability of [the] community to utilize its natural, human and technological resources to ensure that all members of present and future generations can attain high degrees of health and well-being, economic security, and a say in shaping their future while maintaining the integrity of the ecological systems on which all life and production depends" (City of Cambridge [Massachusetts] 1993, 30).

"Sustainability means using, developing, and protecting resources at a rate that enables people to meet their current needs while providing for the needs of future generations" (Multnomah County [Oregon] 2003, 1).

"As a community, we need to create the basis for a more sustainable way of life both locally and globally through the safeguarding and enhancing of our resources and by preventing harm to the natural environment and human health" (City of Santa Monica [California] 1995, 1).

- **Harmony with nature:** land use and development support ecosystem processes.
- **Livable built environment:** development enhances fit between people and urban form.
- **Place-based economy:** local economic activity operates within natural system limits and meets local needs.
- **Equity:** land use patterns provide equitable access to social and economic resources.
- **Polluters pay:** those who cause pollution bear its costs.
- **Responsible regionalism:** communities minimize harm to other jurisdictions in pursuit of local goals.

In an analysis of thirty high-quality local plans adopted between 1985 and 1995, Berke and Manta-Conroy (2000) discovered that plans do not take a balanced, holistic approach to guiding development and moving toward sustainability. Instead, they focus on creating more livable built environments, but have not branched out into nontraditional subject matter in the planning field involving a host of other sustainability goals (i.e., harmony with nature, place-based economy, equity, polluters pay, and responsible regionalism). These findings demonstrate the utility of the sustainability concept by revealing that new, expansive directions must be taken to fundamentally reform how planning practice approaches plan making.

Our primary interest in this book is to explain how land use planning can be applied to create human settlement patterns that promote sustainable outcomes in metropolitan regions, cities, towns, and villages. Two concepts prevalent in contemporary planning—Smart Growth and New Urbanism—are related to sustainable development and promote various aspects of sustainability, although they are not the same and do not substitute for sustainability.[4]

SMART GROWTH

Since the early 1990s, the concept of Smart Growth has been proposed as an alternative to conventional development (Porter 2002). Smart Growth programs seek to identify a common ground where communities explore ways to accommodate growth based on consensus on development decisions through inclusive and participatory processes. Smart Growth promotes compact, mixed-use development that encourages choice of travel mode (walking, cycling, transit, and autos) by coordinating transportation and land use, requires less open space, and gives priority to maintaining and revitalizing existing neighborhoods and business centers. State and local Smart Growth initiatives include incentives and requirements to direct public and private investment away from the creation of new infrastructure and development that spreads out from existing areas (Porter 1998).

The Smart Growth movement evolved from statewide growth management initiatives and drew its name from legislation and programs developed by the State of Maryland (see sidebar 2 and Figure 5). This program concentrates development through the designation of county-certified existing or planned development areas, and targets valued open spaces (e.g., prime agriculture lands, natural areas like forests, and aquifer recharge zones) for acquisition with state funds. Several other states have become active in mandating or encouraging communities to adopt Smart Growth as new programs have been developed in Delaware, Maryland, Oregon, Pennsylvania, Tennessee, and Washington (Godschalk 2000).

Although Smart Growth's central concern has been to reform state growth management legislation (Meck 2002), its concepts have also influenced local plans and been endorsed in the policy statements of professional- and business-interest groups, such as the American Planning Association, the International City County Management Association, the National Association of Homebuilders, and the Urban Land Institute. Its tenets are promoted by the Smart Growth Network (www.smartgrowth.org) and the Sustainable Communities Network (www.sustainable.org).

ESSENTIAL READINGS IN URBAN PLANNING

SIDEBAR 2 MARYLAND'S SMART GROWTH PROGRAM

Vision

Maryland's 1997 Smart Growth Areas Act was adopted to counter suburban sprawl. The core elements of the vision are: concentrate development in suitable areas; protect sensitive areas; and direct rural growth to existing villages to create or maintain compact urban forms.

Priority Funding Areas

The state provides funding for infrastructure to support growth only in state- and county-designated priority funding areas (PFAs). The county-certified PFAs are delineated on the basis that areas are suitable for planned growth, infrastructure is provided, and suitable areas are of adequate size to meet the demands of future development.

Counties must prepare plans that designate PFAs. Types of areas eligible for designation include: existing communities served by sewer and water; areas zoned for industry and employment; rural villages designated in local comprehensive plans; and areas that reflect a county's long-term policy for promoting orderly development and are planned to be served by sewer and water. To qualify for state funding, counties must also adopt a mix of incentives and regulations to promote development within the PFAs. Figure 5 illustrates the PFAs of Montgomery County, Maryland. The main core of PFAs represent the county's existing and planned growth corridor, and the smaller PFAs disconnected from the core are primarily rural villages.

Rural Legacy Program

The Rural Legacy Program provides funding and focus to identify and protect the most valuable farmland and natural resources outside the PFAs through the purchase of easements and development rights of landowners. The goal is to preserve 200,000 acres by 2001. In Montgomery County, these areas are located in the wedges of open space adjacent to the growth corridor of designated PFAs (see figure 1–5).

Related Programs

The Live Near Work Program offers employees a one-time payment toward the purchase of a house close to their places of work; the Job Creation Tax Credit Program offers reduced taxes to businesses that locate in PFAs; and the Voluntary Cleanup and Brownfields Program is designed to redevelop abandoned or underutilized sites.

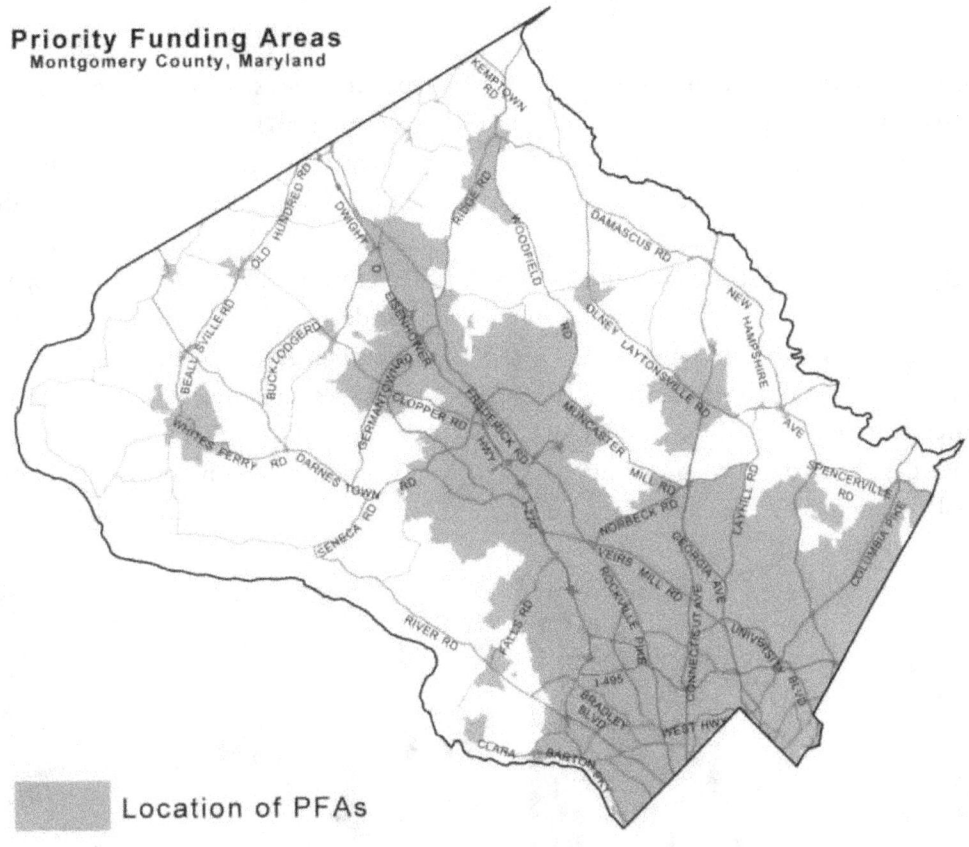

Figure 5. Priority funding areas in Montgomery County, Maryland.
Source: Maryland Department of Housing and Urban Development 2003.

NEW URBANISM

Compared to Smart Growth, New Urbanism is more architecturally prescriptive and detailed in specifying the physical layout of a community in which design, scale, land use mix, and street-network elements dominate (Calthorpe 1993; Calthorpe and Fulton 2001; Duany and Plater-Zyberk 1991; Duany, Plater-Zyberk, and Speck 2000). Its nonprofit organization—the Congress for the New Urbanism (CNU)—addresses the social cohesion and sense of place implications of urban design decisions. Members adopted a charter in 1996 (Leccese and McCormick 2000), which states:

We stand for the restoration of existing urban centers and towns within coherent metropolitan regions, the reconfiguration of sprawling suburbs into communities of real neighborhoods and diverse districts, the conservation of natural environments, and the preservation of our built legacy. We recognize that physical solutions by themselves will not solve social and economic problems, but neither can economic vitality, community stability, and environmental health be sustained without a coherent and supportive physical framework. (v)

The charter of the New Urbanism is basically a design manifesto that lays out twenty-seven principles for three scales of development (Calthorpe and Fulton 2001, 279–285): 1) region, metropolis, city, and town; 2) neighborhood, district, and corridor; and 3) block, street, and building. For example, the charter states that communities should be designed to create compact, mixed-use urban forms designed to foster close-knit social communities by enhancing civic interaction between public and private spaces, as well as to increase community legibility and sense of place (see Figure 6). Streets should be pedestrian (not auto) friendly and use a grid layout to shorten trip lengths, in contrast to the looped cul-de-sac pattern of conventional suburban developments (see Figure 7). Linkages are created among commercial, office, residential, and transit facilities; common community areas serve as spatial focal points; and

Figure 6. Streetscapes of the new urban development in Southern Village (left) and conventional development in Parkside (right) in Chapel Hill, North Carolina. New urban development shows narrower streets (twenty-six feet compared to thirty-two feet) and other features that lead to reduced imperviousness—smaller lots, shallower setbacks, and porches rather than driveways and garages. However, sidewalks are on both sides of the street for new urban development. Photos by Philip R. Berke 2002.

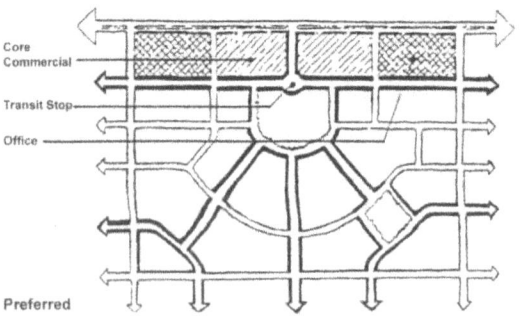 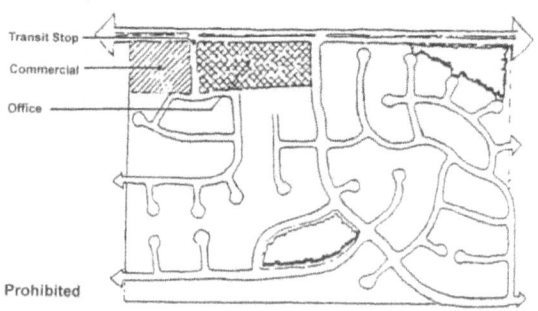

Figure 7. The preferred diagram shows a pedestrian-friendly layout that uses a grid layout to shorten trip lengths, in contrast to the looped cul-de-sac pattern of conventional suburban developments.
Source: Sacramento County Planning and Community Development Department 1990.

each community is designed at the half-mile-wide "village scale." These features are strongly reminiscent of the "neighborhood unit" approach to planning first popularized in the 1920s by the Regional Planning Association of America (Perry 1939).

Individual New Urban developments are conceived as fundamental building blocks of New Urbanism at the regional scale (Calthorpe and Fulton 2001; Duany and Talen 2002). They form an interconnected network of mixed-use, high-density nodes of development linked by transit corridors (see Figure 8). Within this network, regional open spaces create a landscape-scale commons and ecological identity that serve as parks, act as barriers to limit outward expansion of urban development, and protect farmlands and environmentally sensitive areas.

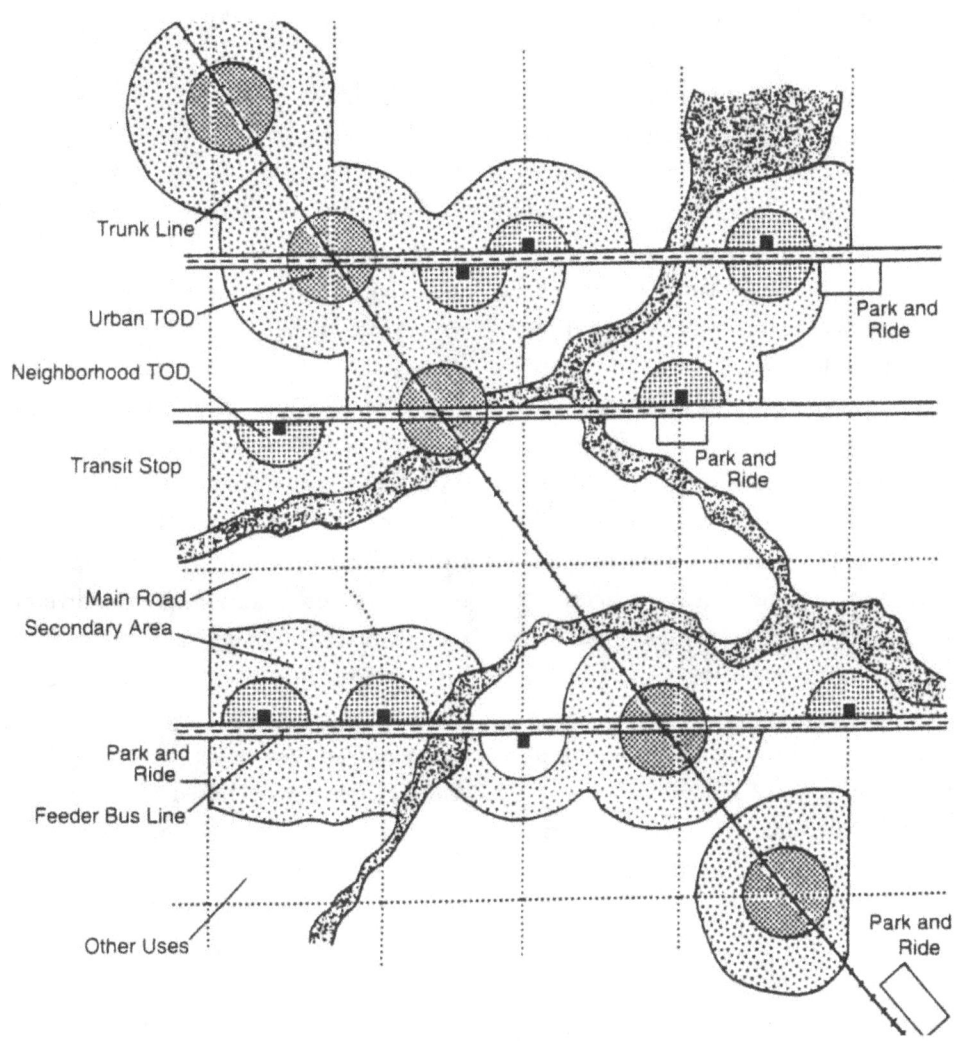

Figure 8. The Transportation-Oriented Development Concept. Each transit-oriented development (TOD) of 50–100 acres is a cluster of housing, retail space, offices, and civic uses centered on a transit station. TODs would be strung like beads along transit lines.
Source: Sacramento County Planning and Community Development Department 1990.

This New Urban version of regionalism builds on a long tradition of planning most ostensibly promulgated by British planners Patrick Geddes and Ebenezer Howard in the late nineteenth century and the Regional Planning Association of America in the 1920s (Wheeler 2002).

RELATIONSHIPS OF SMART GROWTH AND NEW URBANISM TO SUSTAINABLE DEVELOPMENT

Although Smart Growth and New Urbanism offer visionary alternatives of desired outcomes compared to the dominant pattern of conventional low-density development, there are questions about whether they fall short of the broader goals of sustainable development. Smart Growth specifies a macroscale community land use and infrastructure policy framework that is rooted more broadly in urban planning and public policy principles compared to New Urbanism, though it also includes urban design principles. However, Smart Growth does not offer a physical design image and layout of community form that is essential for guiding decisions about land use and urban development. The more detailed and site-specific design principles of New Urbanism take on many of the substantive policies of Smart Growth,[5] but only offer limited guidance and subsequent influence on the protection of environmentally sensitive areas, revitalization of inner cities and urbanized areas, and provision of affordable housing.

Given these limitations, a more holistic and integrated vision of community building is needed. The vision of sustainable development would extend Smart Growth and New Urban concepts to embrace natural systems, place-based economies, and social equity, as well as broader regional (and global) concerns. Under the sustainability vision, Smart Growth and New Urbanism would play an essential role as mid-range visions designed to guide communities toward long-range sustainable outcomes. Moreover, the vision of sustainability needs to be flexible and adaptable to meet the needs of diverse interest groups, fit in different contexts, and serve as a guide to consensus-based discourse and open communication in the planning process. (In chapter 2, we offer a more in-depth discussion of the management of land use change and provide a prism model of sustainability for guiding the plan-making process.) Tying such a vision into the land use planning arena demands several collaborative skills.

LAND USE VALUES

To be an effective player and manager in the land use game, the planner must understand the goals and values of other major players with a stake in game outcomes. The inputs to planning come from stakeholders who view development through the lens of their land use values (see Figure 1). Planners must seek opportunities to forge consensus among competing stakeholder groups to advance common interests and public purposes that are essential for building more sustainable communities. They must be able to track, identify, and clarify the diverging and complementary values among these groups. The composition of the groups and alliances among them can shift over time as consensus about how to resolve land use issues is achieved and new issues are raised (Jenkins-Smith and Sabatier 1994). As noted, there are several dominant stakeholder groups attempting to influence the direction of future urban growth and change, with each group giving the most weight to one of four sets of land use values: economic development, environmental protection, social equity, and livability. These values can be separate and competing or intermingled and supporting.

ECONOMIC DEVELOPMENT VALUES

Economic development values depict land as a commodity for the production, consumption, and distribution of products and services for profit. These values represent the engines of community building, adding value to the land through investment in industry, commercial structures, and residential buildings. From the perspective of these values, the most obvious measure of winnings in the land use game is the profit from the sale of land and buildings.

Logan and Motoloch (1987) explain how land development markets work by identifying three types of entrepreneurs who seek profit: serendipitous entrepreneurs who inadvertently gain wealth from land (inheritance); active entrepreneurs who depend on good forecasting skill and wise investments; and structural speculators who seek to structure markets by influencing political decision making about land use and infrastructure investment. The structural speculators tend to work in organized coalitions or "growth machines," and are the most important entrepreneur. Growth machines include bankers, lawyers, real estate agents, developers, and elected officials who work in concert to promote their development agenda. They scrutinize land policies, regulations, and plans for their impacts on the monetary values of the land. This group is sometimes joined by those who simply advocate the lessening of government intervention into the market as an ideological position.

These economic development investment interests are constrained by land planning and market demand. To succeed, their projects must pass both a government test and a market test. They must satisfy the intent of governmental plans and regulations adopted by the local elected representatives to obtain a development permit. They must satisfy the consumer's taste to sell and make a profit. They operate in a market of buyers and sellers that is influenced by public plans and service programs but are not driven by them. For this interest group, the driving forces are the growth of the population, the economy, and interest rates, which affect demand and capital availability.

Land use planning affects the development market by identifying land that is available or planned for development; by limiting the type, location, timing, and density of development that can take place; by programming the infrastructure to support development and allocating its costs between the public and private sectors; and by specifying the standards under which development proposals will be reviewed. These actions define the supply of suitable land for development. They have been described as "managing the market." Although that description is too extreme for most cases, it is clear that the active land planner is attempting to guide the process of land use change in accordance with community goals. In that sense, the land planner can be seen as both a "development manager" and a "manager of change."

ENVIRONMENTAL PROTECTION VALUES

Environmental protection values view the city as a consumer of resources and land and a producer of wastes. Environmental groups that take on these values range from those who seek to protect the environment for utilitarian purposes to those with a deep intrinsic value for nature. Often these groups are local chapters of such national advocacy groups as the Sierra Club, Ducks Unlimited, and the Isaac Walton League. They view land policies and plans through an ecological lens, seeking the protection of existing natural environmental features such as wetlands, streams, and forests. Sometimes they may form coalitions with neighborhood groups opposed to growth.

In practice, environmental values are often presented to the planner in the form of three perspectives: direct utility values, indirect utility values, and intrinsic values. *Direct utility values* ask the question "What good is it?" Many people value only the direct utility of nature for themselves. They use the powerful "product"-oriented argument for nature (e.g., board feet from forests, fish as a source of food). Under some circumstances, groups that take on these values might help raise public support for protecting certain parts of ecosystems, but they cannot be used to justify seemingly economically worthless life forms.

Indirect utility values focus on ecosystem services offered to human communities. They recognize the value of interdependent relationships within an ecosystem that are not taken into account by the direct utility values. Examples include soil generation and decomposition functions for food growth, and wetlands and beaver dams that offer flood mitigation and water pollutant filtering services. The indirect utility perspective helps justify the enactment of development controls like stream buffers to protect water quality and tree preservation to support wildlife and aesthetic beauty.

Intrinsic values counter the shortcomings of direct and indirect utilitarian arguments by emphasizing the deep, intrinsic appreciation for all life forms. In his 1948 classic book, *A Sand County Almanac,* Aldo Leopold maintains that human beings are part of larger communities or ecosystems, and that "conservation based solely on economic self-interest is hopelessly lopsided. It tends to ignore and thus eventually eliminate, many elements of the land community that lack commercial value, but that are essential to its healthy functioning. It assumes falsely that the economic parts of the biotic clock will function without the uneconomic parts" (Leopold 1948, 251). The Leopold perspective on land stewardship helped justify the passage of the federal Endangered Species Act in 1973 and international treaties to save whales and ban trade in ivory.

The connections between community land use and environmental quality will intensify as more scientific knowledge of environmental systems is accumulated and is translated into findings relevant for land use planning. As a result, environmental groups will be able to demand more sophisticated environmental quality monitoring, the setting of more precise performance standards, and the application of new land suitability and environmental impacts methods in the local land use planning process.

EQUITY VALUES

Social equity values depict the community as a location of conflict about the distribution of resources, services, and opportunities. Advocates of these values contend that land use patterns should recognize and improve the conditions of low-income and minority populations and not deprive them of basic levels of environmental health and human dignity. Equitable access to social and economic resources is essential for eradicating poverty and in accounting for the needs of the least advantaged. Advocates of environmental justice oppose the unfair siting of hazardous waste facilities, highway construction projects that cut through inner-city neighborhoods to link downtowns to wealthy suburbs, garbage dumps in minority communities, and discrimination in urban housing markets. They believe that the benefits and the burdens of a consuming society are not shared equitably. Too often the ability of the wealthy to prosper depends upon the restriction of other people's rights to communities that are clean, safe, and economically viable.

Feminist urban scholars (Spain 1992, 2001) assert a different set of social equity values in which gender is an organizing force equal to class and race. Gender does not lead to spatial segregation but to different urban forms within defined areas of class and ethnicity. In this view, conventional development patterns, oriented to male activity patterns, do not meet the needs for women's daily activities that involve waged, domestic labor, and child care. Separation of work places and residential areas under conventional development isolates women's space and lengthens travel times for work and household activities.

Scholars of nonconformist groups, including gay men, lesbians, and others, assert another perspective of social equity values in which sexuality can be a factor that explains community formation and land use change. Research has highlighted cultural and social reasons for nonconformist groups moving into and gentrifying urban neighborhoods that are equivalent to or more powerful than economic reasons. Castells (1997), Forsyth (2001), and Lauria and Knopp (1985), among others, maintain that forces driving gay and lesbian community formation are linked to group support, safety, and identify formation. Not all members of nonconformist groups, or even a majority, were determined to be high-income, middle-class professionals. Many people were only able to live in their neighborhoods because they were willing to make significant economic sacrifices.

Planners can gain important lessons about how the values of the increasingly influential nonconforming but traditionally marginalized groups affect land use change. Planners typically react to needs of conformist groups (e.g., providing housing for heterosexual families or dual heads of households), but have less experience with nonconformist ones. In light of an increasingly diverse population, the challenge for planners is to reconsider core values about family, culture, and community and to anticipate how urban forms should be adapted to meet emerging needs.

LIVABILITY VALUES

Livability values are expressed by those who react to land use change based on their social and community interests. Advocates of these values typically call for the preservation and enhancement of the social and physical amenities of communities that support desired activity patterns, safety, lifestyles, and aesthetic values. They scrutinize land policies and plans for the impacts on their quality of life while also keeping an eye on the impacts on the market value of their property. In the absence of an informed community consensus about future growth, those who give weight to these values may mobilize to block or modify development.

Neighborhood groups sometimes include those who seek to prevent any new development, or at least prevent adjacent development at densities higher than theirs. The stopping power of these groups often creates local gridlocks. Terms such as "not in my backyard" (NIMBY), "local unwanted land uses" (LULU), "build absolutely nothing anywhere near anyone" (BANANA), among others, have become symbolic of neighborhood livability values. Citizen-participation planner Randy Hester sums up the state of affairs in the neighborhood-preservation movement since the 1980s by arguing that contemporary public participation can be characterized as self-interested, short-sighted, segregated along class and racial lines, legally sophisticated, and fearful (1999, 19).

Although Hester's depiction is too extreme for most communities, local planning programs are well situated to break the barriers that create self-serving behavior. Planners can apply participatory urban design techniques to educate residents about urban forms that reflect the larger public interest necessary to help change the narrowly defined view of livability to a broader, more inclusive view. Planners can also work to develop communication and consensus-building strategies across neighborhood groups and create cooperation and bring about plans that promote mutual benefit.

COALITIONS OF LAND USE VALUES

In the land use planning arena, distinct alliances (or coalitions) of groups may form when their values overlap. These coalitions are often in conflict. Two traditional adversaries are the "anti-growth" versus "pro-growth" coalitions. The "antigrowth" coalition consists of neighborhood associations dominated by homeowners who share an interest in the preservation of the rural character of urbanizing areas and in limiting development to achieve those ends. Their interest in limiting development is shared by environmental groups who seek protection of the ecological integrity of the landscape. The "pro-growth" coalition includes developers, land owners, and the building industry who share an interest in profits from the development of land. Their interest in promoting development is shared by downtown businesses, suburban businesses, and the chamber of commerce, who believe that development will bring new people who, in turn, will become their customers, promote their economic prosperity, and, indirectly, promote the prosperity of the community.

A third alliance, the "social advocacy" coalition, is often an adversary to both the "anti-growth" and "pro-growth" coalitions. It consists of low-income groups and minority populations that share an interest in making the distribution of the benefits of a healthy living environment and economic development more equitable. Difficult issues must be tackled if conflicts associated with this coalition are to be resolved. A core issue for this coalition is how those at the bottom of society can find greater economic opportunity if environmental protection mandates diminish economic growth. Poor communities, for example, must frequently confront a no-win choice between economic survival and environmental quality when the only economic opportunities are landfills, waste incinerators, and polluting industrial plants that more affluent communities often oppose (Bryant 1995). In many cases, the poor communities consist mostly of minority populations, thus raising the specter that environmental racism is an integral feature of conflicts associated with the "social advocacy" coalition.

Planners must understand that the adversarial behavior assumption does not always hold. The relationships among diverse interest groups are often interdependent. For example, inner-city residents share an interest with suburban employers of low-wage workers in having frequent transit service and close location of transit stops. Their interest in promoting mass transit is shared by environmental advocacy groups who want transit to reduce dependency on automobiles that generate considerable air pollution. The competitive orientation within the land planning arena is thus tempered with the need for cooperation.

The task for planners in the land use game is to help communities build relationships by developing mutual trust and cooperation needed to improve overall game outcomes. To be acceptable and effective, land use plans must recognize and reconcile the pluralistic interests of other various stakeholder groups with those of markets. They must work to inspire and motivate groups to understand interdependencies and gain confidence in the reality of a common good or civic purpose. In *The Spirit of Community*, Amitai Etzioni speaks of building "social webs that bind individuals, who would otherwise be on their own, into groups of people who care for one another and who help maintain a civic, social, and moral order" (Etzioni 1993, 248). The "connectedness" within a place is the glue that binds social and natural communities. Planners should offer guidance to communities seeking to create and restore those elements of place that foster the social fabric of communities, including, for example: identifying buildings and natural landmarks of cultural importance to evoke a connection to the community's history; creating built environments that encourage spontaneous face-to-face interaction (e.g., pocket parks, pedestrian-oriented streets); encouraging public life in private places by encouraging spaces created by small businesses (e.g., sidewalk cafes, taverns, and bookstores), not just corporate theme spaces like shopping malls and Disneyland; and improving opportunities for community participation among all groups in planning for a sustainable future.

REFERENCES

Beatley, Timothy, and Kristy Manning. 1998. *The ecology of place: Planning for environment, economy, and community*. Washington, D.C.: Island Press.

Berke, Philip, and Maria Manta-Conroy. 2000. Are we planning for sustainable development? An evaluation of 30 comprehensive plans. *Journal of the American Planning Association* 66 (1): 21–33.

Berke, Philip. 2002. Does sustainable development offer a new direction for planning? Challenges for the twenty-first century. *Journal of Planning Literature* 17(1): 22–36.

Berke, Philip, Joseph McDonald, Nancy White, Michael Holmes, Kat Oury, and Rhonda Ryznar. 2003. Greening development for watershed protection: Does new urbanism make a difference? *Journal of the American Planning Association* 69 (4): 397–413.

Bryant, Bunyan, ed. 1995. *Environmental justice: Issues, policies and solutions*. Washington, D.C.: Island Press.

Burchell, Robert, George Lowenstein, William Dolphin, Catherine Galley, Anthony Downs, Samuel Seskin, Katherine Gray Still, and Terry Moore. 1998. *Costs of sprawl—2000*. Washington, D.C.: National Academy Press.

Calthorpe, Peter. 1993. *The next American metropolis: Ecology, community, and the American dream*. Princeton, N.J.: Princeton Architectural Press.

Calthorpe, Peter, and William Fulton. 2001. *The regional city*. Washington, D.C.: Island Press.

Castells, Manuel. 1997. *The power of identity*. Malden, Mass.: Blackwell.

City of Burlington. 1996. *Burlington municipal development plan*. Burlington, Vt.: Planning and Zoning.

City of Cambridge. 1993. *Toward a sustainable future: Cambridge growth policy document*. Cambridge, Mass.: Planning Board.

City of San Jose. 1994. *Focus on the future: San Jose 2020 General Plan*. San Jose, Calif.: Department of Planning, Building and Code Enforcement.

City of Santa Monica. 1995. *Santa Monica sustainable indicators program*. Santa Monica, Calif.: Planning Department.

City of Seattle. 1994. *The City of Seattle comprehensive plan: Toward a sustainable Seattle: A plan for managing growth 1994-2014*. Seattle, Wash.: Planning Department.

Donaghy, Kieran, and Lewis Hopkins. 2004. Particularist, non-positivist, and coherent theories of planning are possible ... and even desirable. Paper presented at the Association of Collegiate Schools of Planning conference, Portland, Oreg., October 22, 2004.

Downs, Anthony. 1994. *New visions of metropolitan America*. Washington, D.C.: Brookings Institution and Lincoln Institute of Land Policy.

Downs, Anthony. 1999. Some realities about sprawl and urban decline. *Housing Policy Debate* 14 (4): 955–74.

Duany, Andres, and Elizabeth Plater-Zyberk. 1991. *Towns and townmaking principles*. New York: Rizzoli Press.

Duany, Andres, Elizabeth Plater-Zyberk, and J. Speck. 2000. *Suburban nation: The rise of sprawl and the decline of the American dream*. New York: North Point Press.

Duany, Andres, and Emily Talen. 2002. Transect planning. *Journal of the American Planning Association* 68 (3): 245–66.

Etzioni, Amitai. 1993. *The spirit of community: Reinvention of American society*. New York: Touchstone.

Ewing, Reid, and Robert Cervero. 2001. Travel and the built environment. *Transportation and Research Record* 1780: 87–114.

Frank, Lawrence D., and Peter O. Engelke. 2001. The built environment and human activity patterns: Exploring the impacts of urban form on public health. *Journal of Planning Literature* 16 (2): 202–18.

Frank, Lawrence D., Peter O. Engelke, and Thomas L. Schmid. 2003. *Health and community design: The impact of the built environment on physical activity.* Washington, D.C.: Island Press.

Forsyth, Ann. 2001. Sexuality and space: Nonconformist populations and planning practice. *Journal of Planning Literature* 15 (3): 339–58.

Fulton, William, Rolf Pendall, Mai Nguyen, and Alice Harrison. 2001. *Who sprawls most? How growth patterns differ across the U.S.* Washington, D.C.: Survey Series, Brookings Institution.

Godschalk, David. 2000. Smart Growth around the nation. Popular *Government* 66 (1): 12–20.

Gordon, Peter, and Harry Richardson. 1997. Are compact cities a desirable planning goal? *Journal of the American Planning Association* 63 (1): 95–106.

Governor's Commission for a Sustainable South Florida. 1996. *Eastward ho! Revitalizing southeast Florida's urban core.* Hollywood, Fla.: Author.

Harvey, David. 1990. "Postmoderism in the city: Architecture and urban design. In *The condition of postmodernity*, 66–80. Oxford, England: Blackwell.

Hester, Randolph T. 1999. A refrain with a view. *Places: A Forum of Environmental Design* 12 (2): 12–25.

Hopkins, Lewis. 2001. *Urban development: The logic of making plans.* Washington, D.C.: Island Press.

Humpel, Nancy, Neville Owen, and Eva Leslie. 2002. Environmental factors associated with adults' participation in physical activity. *American Journal of Preventive Medicine* 22 (3): 188–99.

Innes, Judith, and David Booher. 1999. Consensus building and complex adaptive systems: A framework of revaluating collaborative planning. *Journal of the American Planning Association* 65 (4): 460–72.

Jenkins-Smith, Hank, and Paul Sabatier. 1994. Evaluating the advocacy coalition framework. *Journal of Public Policy* 14 (2): 175–203.

Johnson, Elmer W. 2001. *Chicago Metropolis 2020: The Chicago plan for the twenty-first century.* Chicago: University of Chicago Press.

Klosterman, Richard. 2000. The what if planning support systems. In *Planning support systems: Integrating geographic information systems, models, and visualization tools,* Richard Brail and Richard Klosterman, eds. Redlands, Calif.: ESRI Press.

Knapp, Gerrit, Chengri Deng, and Lewis Hopkins. 2001. Do plans matter? The effects of light rail plans on land values in station areas. *Journal of Planning Education and Research* 21 (1): 32–39.

Krizek, Kevin, and Joe Power. 1996. *A planners' guide to sustainable development.* Planning Advisory Service 467. Chicago: American Planning Association.

Laurence, Roderick, ed. 2000. *Sustaining human settlement: A challenge for the new millennium.* North Shields, UK: Urban International Press.

Lauria, Mickey, and Lawrence Knopp. 1985. Toward an analysis of the role of gay communities in the urban renaissance. *Urban Geography* 6: 152–69.

Lindsey, Greg. 2003. Sustainability and urban greenways: Indicators in Indianapolis. *Journal of the American Planning Association* 69 (2): 165–80.

Leopold, Aldo. 1948. *A Sand County almanac.* New York: Oxford University Press.

Logan, John, and Harvey Motoloch. 1987. *Urban fortunes: The political economy of place.* Berkeley: University of California Press.

Leccese, M., and K. McCormick. 2000. *Charter of the new urbanism.* New York: McGraw-Hill.

Lucy, William, and David Phillips. 2000. *Confronting suburban decline: Strategies and planning for metropolitan renewal.* Washington, D.C.: Island Press.

Maclaren, Virginia. 1996. Urban sustainability reporting. *Journal of the American Planning Association* 62 (2): 184–202.

Maryland Department of Housing and Urban Development. 2003. Smart Growth Program. Retrieved from www.dhcd.state.md.us/images, accessed June 21, 2004.

Maryland-National Capital Park and Planning Commission. 1993. General plan refinement of the goals and objectives for Montgomery County. Silver Springs, Md.: Author.

McCann, Barbara A., and Reid Ewing. 2003. *Measuring the health effects of sprawl: A national analysis of physical activity, obesity and chronic disease.* Washington, D.C.: Smart Growth America.

Meck, S. 2002. *Growing Smart legislative guidebook: Model statutes for planning and the management of change.* Chicago: American Planning Association.

Miller, Donald L. 2001. "Foreword." In *Chicago metropolis 2020: The Chicago plan for the twenty-first century,* Elmer W. Johnson. Chicago: University of Chicago Press.

Minnesota Planning and Environmental Quality Board. 1998. Mission statement. Retrieved from www.eqb.state.mn.us/SDI/index.html, accessed October 15, 2004.

Multinomah County. 2003. Sustainable community development program. Retrieved from www.co.multinomah.or.us, accessed October 15, 2004.

Nelson, Arthur, and Steven French. 2002. Plan quality and mitigating damage from natural disasters: A case study of the Northridge earthquake with planning policy considerations. *Journal of the American Planning Association* 68 (2): 194–207.

North Carolina Environmental Resource Program. 1997. *Guidelines for state level sustainable development.* Chapel Hill: Center for Policy Alternatives, University of North Carolina.

Neuman, Michael. 1996. Images as institution builders: Metropolitan planning in Madrid. *European Planning Studies* 4 (3): 293–310.

Neuman, Michael. 1998. Does planning need the plan? *Journal of the American Planning Association* 64 (2): 208–20.

Perry, Clarence. 1939. *Housing for the machine age.* New York: Russell Sage Foundation.

Porter, Douglas. 1998. *ULI on the future—Smart Growth: Economy, community, and environment.* Washington, D.C.: Urban Land Institute.

Porter, Douglas. 2002. *The practice of sustainable development.* Washington, D.C.: Urban Land Institute.

President's Council on Sustainable Development. 1996. *Sustainable America: A new consensus for prosperity, opportunity, and a healthy environment for the future.* Washington, D.C.: U.S. Government Printing Office.

Sacramento County Planning and Community Development Department. 1990. *Transit oriented development design guidelines.* Sacramento: Author (prepared by Calthorpe and Associates).

Saelens, Brian E., Jim F. Sallis, and Lawrence D. Frank. 2003. Environmental correlates of walking and cycling: Findings from the transportation, urban design, and planning literatures. *Annals of Behavioral Medicine* 25 (2): 80–91.

Smart Growth Communities Network. 2004. *Smart Growth online.* Retrieved from www.smartgrowth.org, accessed December 14, 2004.

Sustainable Communities Network. 2004. *Smart Growth.* Retrieved from www.sustainable.org, accessed December 14, 2004.

Spain, Daphne. 1992. *Gendered spaces.* Chapel Hill: University of North Carolina Press.

Spain, Daphne. 2001. *How women saved the city.* Minneapolis: University of Minnesota Press.

Speir, Cameron, and Kurt Stephenson. 2002. Does sprawl cost us all? Isolating the effect of housing patterns on public water and sewer costs. *Journal of the American Planning Association* 68 (1): 56–70.

Texas Transportation Institute. 2002. *2002 urban mobility study.* College Station, Tx.: Author.

Trost, Steward G., Neville Owen, Adrian E. Bauman, Jim F. Sallis, and W. Brown. 2002. Correlates of adults' participation in physical activity: Review and update. *Medicine Science and Sports Exercise* 34 (12): 1996–2001.

Vandegrift, Donald, and Tommer Yoked. 2004. Obesity rates, income, and suburban sprawl: An analysis of U.S. states. *Health and Place* 10(3), 221–29.

Wachs, Martin. 2001. Forecasting versus envisioning: A new window on the future. *Journal of the American Planning Association* 67 (1): 367–72.

Wheeler, Stephen. 2002. The new regionalism: Characteristics of an emerging movement. *Journal of the American Planning Association* 68 (3): 267–78.

World Commission on Environment and Development (WCED). 1987. *Our common future.* Oxford, England: Oxford University Press.

THE HIGH COST OF FREE PARKING

CHAPTER 7: *Putting the Cost of Free Parking in Perspective*

BY DONALD C. SHOUP

Instead of buildings set in a park, we now have buildings set in a parking lot.
—LEWIS MUMFORD

We can now put the cost of parking in perspective by comparing it with other costs of the transportation system. These comparisons show that "free" parking greatly reduces the driver's cost of vehicle travel and therefore seriously distorts individual travel choices toward cars.

TOTAL SUBSIDY FOR PARKING

For many land uses, the area devoted to parking exceeds the floor area of the building it serves. We have no trouble understanding that office buildings cost a lot of money, so it should not surprise anyone that the parking lots or structures (often bigger than the buildings they serve) also cost a lot. Furthermore, curb parking spaces usually line both sides of the adjacent streets. When we consider both curb spaces and off-street spaces

Donald C. Shoup, "Putting the Cost of Free Parking in Perspective," *The High Cost of Free Parking*, pp. 205-223. Copyright © 2011 by Taylor & Francis Group. Reprinted with permission.

in cities, the land and capital devoted to parking probably exceed that devoted to travel.

Mark Delucchi of the University of California, Davis, conducted what is by far the most comprehensive evaluation of the total cost of motor vehicle use in the U.S. He estimated both monetary costs (such as for vehicles, fuel, roads, and parking) and nonmonetary costs (such as for air and water pollution). Because inputs and assumptions for the estimates are uncertain, he presented both low and high estimates for each value. For the years 1990–1991, he estimated the annualized capital and operating cost of off-street parking at between $79 billion and $226 billion a year (see Table 18).[1]

Delucchi points out that most parking is not priced separately but is instead bundled with other goods and priced as a package. He estimated that drivers paid only $3 billion a year for parking, while the rest of the cost was bundled into the prices for goods, services, and housing. As a result, drivers paid somewhere between 4 percent ($3 billion ÷ $79 billion) and 1 percent ($3 billion ÷ $226 billion) of the total cost of parking. The other 96 to 99 percent of the cost of parking was hidden in higher prices for everything else.

Delucchi also estimated the annualized capital and operating cost of public roads (including the curb parking spaces) at between $98 billion and $177 billion, close to the estimated cost of parking spaces. If drivers paid only 4 percent of the cost of roads, most people would condemn this as outrageously unfair, but drivers pay at most 4 percent of the cost of off-street parking, and they complain loudly whenever its price increases.

Because Delucchi included the cost of curb parking in the cost of roads, the total cost of the parking supply (both off-street *and* on-street) is underestimated. Consider a 36-foot-wide residential street, with two 10-foot-wide travel lanes and two 8-foot-wide parking lanes: curb parking takes up 44 percent of the road space. Clearly, curb parking spaces account for a significant share of the total cost of roads, and an accurate estimate of the total subsidy for parking would take curb parking into account.[2] The U.S. Department of Commerce estimates that the total value of roads is 36 percent of the value of all state and local public infrastructure (which also includes schools, sewers, water supply, residential buildings, equipment, hospitals, and parks). Because curb parking occupies a substantial share of road space, it must be a substantial share of all state and local public infrastructure as well.[3] Since drivers do pay gasoline taxes while they are driving, but do not pay gasoline taxes while their cars are parked, curb spaces are subsidized far more than the travel lanes. Free curb parking may be the most costly subsidy American cities provide for most of their citizens.

Since drivers paid only $3 billion a year for parking in 1990–1991, the subsidy for off-street parking was between $76 billion and $223 billion a year. Because the U.S. gross domestic product was $6 trillion in 1991, the subsidy for off-street parking amounted to between 1.2 percent and 3.7 percent of the nation's economic output.[4] American cars and light trucks logged 2 trillion miles in 1990, so the off-street parking subsidy amounted to between 4¢ a mile (if the subsidy was $76 billion) and 11¢ a mile (if it was $223 billion).[5] In comparison, the average variable cost for gasoline, oil, maintenance, and tires for cars in 1990 was 8.4¢ a mile.[6] The subsidy for off-street parking was therefore somewhere between 48 percent and 131 percent of the drivers' cost for gasoline, oil, maintenance, and tires.

Delucchi's estimate refers to 1990–1991. Adjusted for inflation and the increase in the number of vehicles and off-street parking spaces since then, the total subsidy for off-street parking in 2002 was between $127 billion and $374 billion.[7] Because the U.S. gross domestic product had grown to $10.5 trillion in 2002, the subsidy for off-street parking as a share of the economy amounted to between 1.2 percent and 3.6 percent, almost exactly the same as in 1991. This subsidy is huge by any comparison. In 2002, the federal government spent $231 billion for Medicare and $349 billion for national defense.[8] National defense!! Can the subsidy for off-street parking be that big??? Well, why not? Since the 1950s, most American cities have required every new building to provide ample off-street parking. American households now have more cars than drivers, and their cars are parked 95 percent of the time. Because motorists rarely pay anything for parking, their cars live almost rent free. American cars and light trucks logged 2.6 trillion vehicle miles of travel in 2002, so the subsidy for *off-street* parking ranged between 5¢ a mile (if the subsidy was $127 billion) and 14¢ a mile (if it was $374 billion).[9] If we use the rule of thumb that increasing the gasoline tax by 1¢ a gallon increases gasoline tax revenues by about $1 billion a year, it would take an increase in the gasoline tax of between $1.27 and $3.74 a gallon to offset the subsidy for off-street parking.[10] Removing the subsidies for off-street parking would thus produce the same effect on travel as increasing the gasoline tax by between $1.27 and $3.74 a gallon. Because parking costs so much and motorists pay so little for it, the hidden subsidy is truly gigantic.

CAPITAL COST OF THE PARKING SUPPLY

The previous estimate referred to the *annual* cost of the parking supply. We can also estimate the *capital* cost of the parking supply, and the surprising result is that the cost of all parking spaces in the U.S. exceeds the value of all cars and may even exceed the value of all roads.

VALUE OF VEHICLES AND ROADS

The Department of Commerce has estimated the capital value of all fixed reproducible tangible wealth (i.e., excluding land value) in the U.S. for the years 1929 to 1997. Two categories of this estimate are the capital value of vehicles (all cars and trucks) and of roads (all streets and highways).[11] Table 2 shows the number of registered vehicles and the capital value of vehicles and roads for the years 1990 to 1997. The last row of the table shows that there were 208 million registered vehicles in 1997, and the Department of Commerce valued this vehicle stock at $1,144 billion. The average value per vehicle was therefore $5,507 ($1,114 billion ÷ 208 million). Although this value may seem low, the average age of all vehicles in 1995 was 8.3 years, and 62 percent of all vehicles were more than five years old.[12] The depreciation of the older vehicles explains the low average value of $5,507 per vehicle.

Table 1. Annual Capital and Operating Cost of Off-Street Parking Spaces ($billions per year in 1990–1991)

	LOW	HIGH
Bundled residential parking	$15	$41
Bundled nonresidential parking	$49	$162
Municipal and institutional parking	$12	$20
Priced parking	$3	$3
Total cost of parking	**$79**	**$226**
Total parking subsidy	**$76**	**$223**
Priced parking as % of total parking	4%	1%

Source: Delucchi (1997, Tables 1–5, 1–6, and 1–7).

ARE PARKING SPACES WORTH MORE THAN VEHICLES?

There are more parking spaces than vehicles because drivers must be able to park wherever they go, and many parking spaces are vacant much of the time. Cities typically require enough parking spaces to satisfy the *peak* demand for parking at every land use—at home, work, school, restaurants, shopping centers, movie theaters, and hundreds of other places—so that drivers can have convenient access to all addresses at all times. To see the result, think of what happens during the middle of the night when almost all vehicles are parked at home: almost all the spaces necessary to meet the peak demand for free parking at all other land uses are empty.

Cities require a specific number of parking spaces for every land use, but no city collects data on its total parking supply. As a result, no one knows the total number of parking spaces in the U.S. The eminent land-use planner Victor Gruen estimated that every car has at least one parking space at home and three or four waiting elsewhere to serve the same car.[13] To be conservative, suppose there is one parking space per car at home and only two elsewhere (at work, school, supermarkets, and so on), or only three parking spaces per vehicle.[14] Suppose we also make the conservative assumption that the average land and capital cost per parking space is only $4,000, an extremely low value given the evidence cited and calculated in Chapter 6. Given these two conservative assumptions, the value of the parking available per car is $12,000 (3 spaces per car x $4,000 per space), or more than twice the average value of a car ($5,507). If so, the total parking supply is worth more than twice the value of the total vehicle stock.

ARE PARKING SPACES WORTH MORE THAN ROADS?

We can use similar reasoning to compare the cost of parking spaces with the value of roads. The Department of Commerce estimated that the depreciated construction value of all roads (excluding land value) was $1,359 billion in 1997. With 208 million vehicles owned in 1997, roads were therefore worth $6,542 per vehicle. This value may seem low, but many rural roads are old and in poor condition, so their depreciated value can be quite low. If there are 3 parking spaces per vehicle and the average value of parking is $4,000 per space, the parking spaces would again be worth $12,000 per vehicle. If so, the parking supply is worth almost twice the value of all roads ($6,542 per vehicle).[15]

Finally, the total capital value of all vehicles *and* roads was $2.5 trillion in 1997, or $12,049 per vehicle (the last row of columns 7 and 8), about equal to the value of parking per vehicle. Because parking lanes occupy both sides of most urban streets, we should also attribute part of the cost of roads to parking rather than to vehicle movement. When both off-street *and* on-street parking spaces are taken into account, more infrastructure may be devoted to idle cars than to moving ones.

Another rough approximation suggests a huge disparity in what motorists pay for parking and what they pay for roads. Total receipts for public and private parking facilities in the U.S. were only $6.6 billion in 1997.[16] In comparison, motorists paid $90 billion for fuel taxes, vehicle taxes, and tolls in the same year.[17] Parking spaces may be worth more than all roads, but motorists paid only 7 percent as much for parking as they did for road-use taxes and tolls.[18]

Table 2. Capital Value of Vehicles and Roads in the United States, 1990–1997

YEAR	REGISTERED VEHICLES (MILLION)	CAPITAL VALUE OF VEHICLES		CAPITAL VALUE OF ROADS		CAPITAL VALUE OF VEHICLES AND ROADS	
		TOTAL ($BILLION)	PER VEHICLE ($/VEHICLE)	TOTAL ($BILLION)	PER VEHICLE ($/VEHICLE)	TOTAL ($BILLION)	PER VEHICLE ($/VEHICLE)
(1)	(2)	(3)	(4)=(3)/(2)	(5)	(6)=(5)/(2)	(7)=(3)+(5)	(8)=(7)/(2)
1990	189	$844	$4,473	$971	$5,144	$1,816	$9,616
1991	188	$856	$4,550	$994	$5,285	$1,850	$9,835
1992	190	$884	$4,645	$1,018	$5,349	$1,903	$9,994
1993	194	$927	$4,774	$1,059	$5,457	$1,986	$10,231
1994	198	$994	$5,018	$1,134	$5,724	$2,127	$10,742
1995	202	$1,055	$5,234	$1,218	$6,043	$2,273	$11,277
1996	206	$1,110	$5,380	$1,285	$6,224	$2,395	$11,605
1997	208	$1,144	$5,507	$1,359	$6,542	$2,503	$12,049

Sources: U.S. Department of Commerce (1998, Tables 3, 11, & 13), and Appendix H for number of vehicles.

Most analysts agree that construction of the interstate highway system greatly spurred the dominance of the automobile in urban transportation. Gasoline taxes financed the construction of these highways, so motorists did at least pay for them. Most analysts fail to notice, however, that parking takes up far more land than the interstate system does, costs far more, and is far more essential to automobile use, but motorists rarely pay anything for parking. Off-street parking requirements, far more than interstate highways, have spurred the dominance of the automobile in urban transportation.

NEW PARKING SPACES COMPARED WITH NEW CARS

Another way to put the cost of free parking in perspective is to compare it with the price of new cars. Column 2 of Table 3 shows the original (non-inflation-adjusted) cost per space added by the parking structures built at UCLA since 1961 (from column 8 of Table 1). Column 3 shows the average price of a new car purchased in the U.S. in the year the structure was built. Finally, column 4 shows the ratio between the average cost of a new parking space and the average price of a new car.[19] On average, a new parking space has cost 17 percent more than a new car. Drivers may not realize it, but many parking spaces cost more than the cars parked in them, especially because cars depreciate in value much faster than parking spaces do.[20] When we consider that many cars cost less than the parking spaces they occupy, and that many parking spaces are vacant much of the time, it is not surprising the parking supply is worth more than the vehicle stock.

Table 3. Cost of New Parking Spaces at UCLA Compared with the Price of New Cars

YEAR BUILT	COST PER PARKING SPACE	AVERAGE PRICE OF NEW CAR	SPACE COST AS % OF CAR PRICE
(1)	(2)	(3)	(4)=(2)/(3)
1961	$2,000	$2,841	70%
1963	$1,626	$2,968	55%
1964	$1,946	$2,954	66%
1966	$2,323	$3,070	76%
1967	$2,789	$3,216	87%
1969	$2,907	$3,557	82%
1977	$11,762	$5,814	202%
1980	$11,499	$7,574	152%
1983	$19,752	$10,606	186%
1990	$20,859	$15,042	139%
1990	$22,350	$15,042	149%
1991	$20,873	$15,475	135%
1995	$13,712	$17,959	76%
1998	$26,300	$20,364	129%
2002	$31,500	$21,440	147%
Average 1961–2002			117%
Average 1961–1969			73%
Average 1977–2002			146%

Sources: Column 2 is from Table 1, column 8. Column 3 is from Ward's Automotive Yearbook 2003 (page 270), and earlier editions.

The previous estimates have referred to the annual and capital costs of the total parking supply. We can also investigate the parking subsidies for individual trips. The next comparison shows that free parking at work subsidizes more than half of the average driver's variable cost of driving to work alone.

FREE PARKING COMPARED WITH THE COST OF DRIVING TO WORK

Nationwide, 95 percent of automobile commuters park free at work.[21] As a result, cities that base their parking requirements on the peak parking occupancy observed at existing worksites tend to require at least enough spaces to meet the *peak* demand for *free* parking. The resulting parking subsidies can be put in perspective by comparing the cost of providing free parking *at* work with the price that commuters pay for driving *to* work. For this comparison I will use an example based on the average distance for the journey to work in the U.S.

FREE PARKING REDUCES THE COST OF AUTOMOBILE COMMUTING BY 71 PERCENT

Consider an urban area where the cost of providing a structured parking space is $127 a month, as estimated in Chapter 6 (see row 1 of Table 4). If a commuter drives to work 22 days a month, it costs $5.77 per work day to provide a parking space at work ($127 ÷ 22 = $5.77). Because parking spaces provided for commuters usually serve only one car a day, a solo driver who parks free at work therefore receives a parking subsidy of $5.77 a day, which is greater than the round-trip transit fare for almost any commute trip (row 3).[22] As University of Pennsylvania professor of transportation Vukan Vuchic points out:

> With parking charges, car travel is more expensive than transit: Providing "free parking," however, creates a situation in which many commuters who select a mode on the basis of direct costs believe that they "save money" only by driving.

This confirms the experience of many cities that "free parking" is a major—often the most important—factor in the encouragement of car commuting. It may represent the dominant obstacle to diversion of trips from cars to transit or to any other mode.[23]

Now let's take this parking subsidy, express it in cents per mile traveled, and compare it with the other costs of commuting. The *2001 National Household Travel Survey* found that the average round-trip commute distance in the U.S. was 26.2 miles, so if the parking subsidy is $5.77 a day, it is 22¢ per mile driven to and from work (row 5).[24] In comparison, the average operating cost of an automobile (for gasoline, oil, maintenance, and tires) was 13.6¢ per mile in 2001 (row 6).[25] The subsidy for free parking at work is thus 62 percent greater than the cost of driving to and from work (22¢ ÷ 13.6¢).

The average solo commuter paid $3.20 a day for vehicle operating costs (row 7). The driver's total variable cost of automobile commuting (operating cost plus parking cost) was therefore $3.20 a day if the employer paid for parking or $8.97 a day if the driver paid for it (row 8). Free parking at work thus subsidized 64 percent of the total variable cost of automobile commuting. In an earlier study of commuters in Toronto, Canadian transportation economist David Gillen estimated that free parking at work subsidized 85 percent of the total variable cost of driving to work.[26]

If the variable cost of driving to work is $3.20 a day and the cost of parking is $5.77 a day, charging for parking at work increases the out-of-pocket cost of driving to work by 180 percent. This large increase occurs because the cost of parking is such a large share of the cost of commuting. The percentage increase is

Table 4. Parking Subsidies Compared with Commuting Costs

VARIABLE	MEASURE	SOURCE
1. Parking subsidy per month	$127 per month	Table 3
2. Working days per month	22 days	
3. Parking subsidy per day	$5.77 per day	$127/22 days
4. Average round-trip distance to work	26.2 miles	NHTS
5. Parking subsidy per mile driven	22¢ per mile	$5.77/26.2 miles
6. Average automobile operating cost per mile	13.6¢ per mile	Ward's
7. Automobile operating cost per day	$3.20 per day	26.2 miles x 13.6¢ per mile
8. Total variable trip cost per day	$8.97 per day	$5.77 + $3.20
9. Parking subsidy as share of variable trip cost	64 percent	$5.77/$8.97
10. Average fuel efficiency	20 miles per gallon	Ward's
11. Gasoline consumed per work trip	1.3 gallons	26.2 miles/20mpg
12. Gasoline tax equivalent of parking subsidy	$4.44 per gallon	$5.77/1.3 gallons
13. Average federal and state gasoline tax per gallon	37¢ per gallon	USDOT
14. Federal and state gasoline tax per mile	1.9¢ per mile	37¢/20 miles
15. Parking subsidy/ gasoline tax	12 (ratio)	22¢/1.9¢

Sources: Average trip distance is from the 2001 National Household Travel Survey (NHTS). Average variable operating cost (for gasoline, oil maintenance, tires) and fuel efficiency in 2001 are from Ward's Motor Vehicle Facts & Figures 2002. Average gasoline tax rate in 2001 is from U.S. Department of Transportation (2001, Table MF-121T).

smaller in countries where gasoline taxes are higher, but is still substantial. Belgian transportation economists Stef Proost and Kurt Van Dender estimated that charging for parking in central Brussels (where 70 percent of automobile commuters park free) would increase the commuters' costs of driving to work by 60 percent.[27]

FREE PARKING IS WORTH MORE THAN $4 PER GALLON OF GASOLINE

One way to understand how charging for parking could change commuter choices is to imagine another cost increase of equivalent value, such as a gasoline tax. In 2001 the average fuel efficiency of cars and light trucks was 20 miles per gallon (row 10), while the average round-trip commute distance by private vehicle was 26.2 miles, so the average commute consumed 1.3 gallons of gasoline a day (row 11).[28] If a commuter parks free in a space that costs $5.77 a day and burns 1.3 gallons of gasoline on the way to and from work, the parking subsidy is equivalent to $4.44 per gallon of gasoline (row 12). Removing the subsidy for workplace parking would thus have the same effect on commuting as increasing the gasoline tax by $4.44 a gallon! The existing gasoline tax rate of 37¢ a gallon (row 13) would have to increase by 1,100 percent merely to offset the subsidy provided by free parking.[29]

In the long run, charging for parking would increase the cost of driving to work by even more than a $4.44-per-gallon gasoline tax. In response to the gasoline tax, motorists would buy more fuel-efficient cars or work closer to home, and the fuel consumed per work trip would decrease, but improved fuel efficiency will not cut the cost of parking.[30] So long as a car needs to be parked, the driver will pay for it, and the disincentive to solo driving is unavoidable.

FREE PARKING IS WORTH 22¢ PER MILE DRIVEN TO WORK

For the average trip to work, free parking subsidizes the cost of a typical commute by 22¢ a mile (row 5). We can compare this subsidy with the cost paid per mile for the existing gas tax. The average combined federal-and-state gasoline tax in 2001 was 37¢ a gallon.[31] If fuel efficiency is 20 miles a gallon, the gas tax increases the cost of driving by 1.9¢ a mile (row 14). The subsidy per mile for parking *at* work is thus 12 times the gasoline tax per mile for driving *to* work (row 15). For shorter trips, of course, this ratio is even higher.

Other research also suggests that the cost of parking is higher than the cost of driving. In a study conducted for the Conservation Law Foundation, Apogee Research estimated that the cost of parking ranged from 25¢ per vehicle mile of travel (for all travel, not just commuting) in Boston and Cambridge to 11¢ per vehicle mile in the suburbs; because drivers usually parked free, they paid almost none of this cost.[32] The average cost of gasoline and oil was about 5¢ per vehicle mile, so the subsidy for parking was at least twice the fuel cost of driving.

To recapitulate, three comparisons show that free parking at work subsidizes a major cost of commuting by car. First, it reduces the out-of-pocket cost of driving by 64 percent. Second, it is equivalent to a subsidy of $4.44 per gallon of gasoline. And third, it subsidizes the cost of driving by 22¢ per mile, which is 12 times the gasoline tax per mile. Free parking is an offer that few commuters will refuse.

PARKING SUBSIDIES COMPARED WITH CONGESTION TOLLS

We can also compare how much parking subsidies reduce the cost of driving with how much congestion tolls would increase it. Most transportation economists agree that traffic congestion cannot be removed, or even significantly reduced, without charging a toll—such as the one that London introduced in 2003—for driving during peak hours. Economists argue that congestion stems from the government's failure to charge a higher price for driving during peak hours—an error of *omission*. But local governments impose minimum parking requirements to increase the supply and reduce the price of parking—an error of *commission*.

Michael Cameron and Kenneth Small independently estimated that a toll of 15¢ a mile (in 1990 dollars) would be necessary to achieve free flow during peak hours on Los Angeles highways.[33] Elizabeth Deakin and Greig Harvey estimated that the appropriate tolls on all congested roads in Los Angeles in 1991 would average 10¢ a mile.[34] Table 4 shows that free parking at work can *reduce* the cost of commuting by 22¢ a mile. Therefore, employer-paid parking reduces the cost of driving to work by more than the recommended congestion tolls would increase it.[35]

The average car is parked 95 percent of the time, so if most parking remains free, most drivers would pay congestion tolls only during the brief time they are traveling between two free parking spaces.[36] Parking charges complement congestion tolls, and Edward Calthrop, Stef Proost, and Kurt Van Dender showed that parking fees and congestion tolls combined would make transportation much more efficient than would either one alone. They used a simulation model of transportation in Brussels to analyze the effects of (1) charging fees for all parking in the Central Business District (CBD), (2) charging a congestion toll for all cars entering the CBD, and (3) charging both parking fees and a congestion toll.[37] They found that when parking fees and congestion tolls are introduced together, both the optimal parking fee and the optimal congestion toll are lower than when either one is introduced alone. But they also found that parking fees alone produced 96 percent of the benefit that parking fees and congestion tolls together would produce, while congestion tolls alone produced only 72 percent of this benefit. If a city had to choose either parking fees *or* congestion tolls, parking fees would produce higher benefits.

Two earlier comparisons of parking fees and congestion tolls yielded similar conclusions. In 1980, José Gómez-Ibáñez and Gary Fauth estimated that either a $1-a-day parking surcharge or a $1-a-day congestion fee on local streets in central Boston would about double the average traffic speed and would produce almost the same net transportation benefits.[38] In 1967, J. Michael Thomson estimated that parking fees in central London could produce about half the benefits of a peak-period congestion toll for all cars entering central London.[39] Thomson also estimated that half the total benefits of reduced congestion during the peak hours would accrue to bus passengers and operators because the reduced automobile congestion would increase bus speeds. At the time of the study, two-thirds of all the on-street parking spaces in central London were free.

Thomson estimated that the optimal congestion toll in 1967 would be £0.30 a day (£3.44 or $5.51 in 2003 prices) and would have increased the average peak-hour speed of traffic by 25 percent. In 2003 (35 years after Thomson's research), Transport for London introduced a congestion toll of £5 ($8) a day for entry into central London; during the first six months of the toll system, traffic into the zone declined by 16 percent, and the time spent either stationary or traveling less than 10 kilometers (6 miles) per hour declined by about 25 percent.[40] The

£5-a-day toll is modest compared to the price of curb parking in the congestion-charge zone (which ranged up to £4 an hour in 2004) and even more modest in comparison with the price of all-day commuter parking in London. Because 81 percent of automobile commuters to central London park free at work, market-priced parking should therefore produce even greater reductions in traffic congestion.[41]

Parking fees are sometimes recommended to reduce congestion. Although the basic problem is seen to be the absence of congestion tolls, parking fees are proposed as a way to compensate for the political reluctance to impose the tolls.[42] But this proposal neglects the political reluctance to charge parking fees that are high enough to pay even for the cost of the parking spaces themselves. Cities do not use parking fees to compensate for the lack of congestion tolls, but instead do just the opposite. Cities underprice parking and thereby make traffic congestion even worse. Many proposed transportation pricing policies—congestion tolls or higher fuel taxes—are intended to make driving more expensive, but actual parking policies make it cheaper.

Most transportation analysts seem to think about parking only as it relates to something else they are interested in, such as traffic congestion or air pollution. Few seem to worry that the parking itself is being managed so inefficiently.[43] Nevertheless, charging prices to allocate parking spaces efficiently will also reduce congestion, air pollution, and energy consumption. Charging for parking is simple, and it often means no more than ending an inappropriate subsidy. Because both congestion tolls and parking fees promote transportation efficiency, and because the technology needed to charge for parking is so much simpler than that needed to charge for driving in congested traffic, it makes sense to end parking subsidies *in* the CBD before charging tolls for trips *to* the CBD.

Traffic congestion discourages vehicle travel (including bus travel), while parking fees specifically discourage solo driving. Congestion increases the time it takes to get from place to place, but people can respond by adjusting their places of employment or residence. They may reduce the distance to work, perhaps, or choose to live and work in a less congested area, but they continue to drive to work alone, and the time it takes to get to work remains stable even as the average travel speed decreases.[44] By slowing bus travel, congestion may even shift some transit passengers to solo driving. In contrast, parking fees encourage car-pooling, walking, biking, or riding transit to work. These adjustments do reduce solo driving, which congestion does not.

SIMPLE ARITHMETIC

Another way to put free parking in perspective is to compare the cost of parking a car with the cost of driving it. In 2001, the average cost of operating a car (for gasoline, oil, maintenance, and tires) was 13.6¢ a mile, and the average car was driven 11,766 miles a year, so the total operating cost was $1,600 a year, or $4.38 a day.[45] If there were only three parking spaces per car, and if the average cost per space were only $1.46 a day, the average cost of parking a car would also be $4.38 a day. But because the average capital and operating cost of providing a parking space is surely more than $1.46 a day ($44 a month), the cost of parking exceeds the driver's cost of gasoline, oil, maintenance, and tires. Nevertheless, drivers pay for parking on only 1 percent of their trips. Total parking subsidies are thus probably higher than the total cost of operating all cars.

A final way to visualize the cost of free parking is to consider the total space needed to park all our cars. Suppose cars are packed closely together in a lot so each parking space is only 200 square feet, with no room to maneuver. If there are three parking spaces per vehicle, the area needed for parking is 600 square feet per vehicle. Because the U.S. had 230 million motor vehicles in 2002, the total parking area would be 4,950 square miles, about the size of Connecticut or larger than Delaware and Rhode Island combined.[46]

CONCLUSION: A GREAT PLANNING DISASTER

For any planning regulation, we should ask not only who will benefit from it, but also who will pay for it. With free parking, everyone seems to benefit, and no one seems to pay, so the cost of parking requirements has not been an issue for planners. But when we compare the cost of parking with other costs in the transportation system, we can see that the parking supply is probably worth more than all the motor vehicles in the U.S. Because drivers pay almost nothing to park, the subsidy is staggering, about the size of the Medicare or national defense budgets. In attempting to understand how these parking subsidies affect transportation and land use, we should follow the good advice of Deep Throat, who in an underground parking garage in 1972 reportedly told *Washington Post* writer Bob Woodward during his Watergate investigation, "Follow the money."

A cost of somewhere between $127 billion and $374 billion a year for off-street parking has been shifted into higher prices for everything else. This cost disappears from sight when drivers park free, but it does not cease to exist. Instead, free parking increases the demand for driving, which in turn increases the subsidy necessary to meet the peak parking demand. Minimum parking requirements are truly a great planning disaster—perhaps the greatest of all time.

CHAPTER 7 NOTES

1. Delucchi (1997, Tables 1.5, 1.6, and 1.7). Delucchi makes several conservative assumptions that tend to underestimate the cost of off-street parking. The lower bound of $79 billion a year is based on an estimate of 125 million nonresidential off-street parking spaces, and the upper bound of $226 billion a year is based on an estimate of 200 million spaces (Delucchi and Murphy 1998, Table 6.1). Because the U.S. had 189 million motor vehicles in 1990, this implies at most 1.06 nonresidential off-street parking spaces per vehicle. But using data based on off-street parking requirements for a variety of land uses, Murphy and Delucchi (1997, Table 1) estimate an upper bound of 895 million nonresidential off-street parking spaces in 1990, or 4.5 times more than the number of spaces used to calculate the upper bound of $226 billion a year for the subsidy for off-street parking. The huge uncertainty in calculating the cost of parking is perhaps explained by the ambiguity of how to count parking spaces. For example, many residents park in their driveways, so perhaps the driveways should be counted as parking spaces. On the other hand, residential garages not used for parking should not be counted as parking spaces. Many businesses were started in garages (the most famous being Reader's Digest, Walt Disney, Hewlett-Packard, Apple Computers, and Amazon.com). Buddy Holly and countless other musicians started out in garages, and some garage bands never leave their garages. Considering all the alternatives to parking cars in them, we should not count the cost of all residential garages as a cost of

parking, but we should also not underestimate the number of nonresidential parking spaces.

2. Because on-street parking spaces are so difficult to count, Delucchi included their cost in the cost of roads. Some researchers do not consider the cost of parking to be a part of the cost of automobile transportation at all. In his book on *Financing Transportation Networks,* for example, University of Minnesota transportation economist David Levinson (2002) estimates the cost of automobile transportation but excludes the costs of parking because "they are outside the strictly defined transportation sector," similar to U.S. defense costs that some people attribute to the defense of the Middle East oil-producing regions (Levinson 2002, 42–43). Excluding the cost of parking gives an incomplete account of the transportation system's total cost, to say the least.

3. U.S. Department of Commerce (1998). In 1997, the value of state and local roads and highways ($1.3 trillion) was 36 percent of the value of all state and local infrastructure ($3.7 trillion). Other infrastructure categories are a much smaller share of total infrastructure: educational buildings (18 percent), sewer systems (8 percent), water supply (5 percent), residential buildings (4 percent), equipment (4 percent), hospitals (3 percent), conservation and development (2 percent), and other (20 percent). These estimates exclude land value; because land value is a larger share of the total cost of roads than of the cost of other public infrastructure, including land value in the estimate would increase the share of total public infrastructure devoted to roads.

4. For the estimate of the U.S. gross domestic product, see Table B-1 in the *Economic Report of the President, 2004,* available online at www.gpoaccess.gov/eop/.

5. See *Ward's Automotive Yearbook 2003* (p. 269) for the total vehicle miles of travel in 1990.

6. See *World's Motor Vehicle Facts and Figures 2001* (p. 64) for the average variable cost of passenger cars in 1990.

7. Because there were 189 million motor vehicles in the U.S. in 1990, the parking subsidy was between $402 and $1,180 a year per vehicle. Adjusted for inflation to 2002, it was between $554 and $1,628 a year per vehicle. If there were only 3 parking spaces per vehicle, the parking subsidy per vehicle would thus be between $15 and $45 per parking space per month; these values are very low for the cost of a parking space in most cities, so even Delucchi's high estimate for the parking subsidy may be too low. Because parking requirements are intended to satisfy the peak demand for parking at every land use, it seems reasonable to assume that the off-street parking supply (and the total parking subsidy) increases in line with the number of cars. Some older cities were built before parking requirements were imposed, so the parking subsidy for new development probably exceeds the average parking subsidy for all development, and the total parking subsidy may therefore increase faster than the number of cars. Because the U.S. had 229,619,979 motor vehicles in 2002 (United States Department of Transportation 2002b, Table MV-1), Delucchi's estimates imply that the total parking subsidy was between $127 billion (if the subsidy was $554 per vehicle) and $374 billion (if the subsidy was $1,628 per vehicle).

8. See Tables B-70 and B-80 in the *Economic Report of the President 2003,* available online at www.gpoaccess.gov/usbudget/fy04/pdf/2003_erp.pdf.

9. See *Ward's Automotive Yearbook 2003* (p. 269) for the total vehicle miles of travel in 2002.

10. See Table 4. The average combined federal-and-state gasoline tax in 2001 was 37¢ a gallon. Because the average fuel efficiency was 20 miles a gallon, the gasoline tax increased the cost of driving by 1.9¢ a mile (37¢ ÷ 20). The subsidy for off-street parking is at least 2.6 times greater than the tax on gasoline (if the subsidy was 5¢ a mile) and may be 7.9 times greater (if the subsidy was 15¢ a mile).
11. The capital value of an asset is measured as the cumulated value of past gross investment in that asset minus the cumulated value of past depreciation. See Katz and Herman (1997) for the methodology for estimating the capital value of cars and roads. The values are expressed in current dollars for each year (i.e., they are not indexed for inflation).
12. Hu and Young (1999, Table 20).
13. Gruen (1973, 89). When Peter Newman and Jeffrey Kenworthy assembled their sourcebook of transportation statistics for cities, most cities were able to estimate the total number of parking spaces only in the Central Business District (CBD), and in some cases not even there. Newman and Kenworthy (1989, 31–32) report that the cities' parking data were almost always collected on an irregular basis by consultants in response to specific needs in specific areas.
14. Erik Verhoef (1996, 97) reports that in the Netherlands there are three parking spaces available for every car.
15. This estimated value in roads excludes the value of land. Therefore, the value of parking spaces must also exclude the value of land to make a valid comparison with the value of roads. The U.S. had 230 million motor vehicles and 4 million miles of roads in 2002, or about 58 cars per mile of road (U.S. Department of Transportation 2002b, Tables MV-1 and HM-20). If there are only three parking spaces per car, there are 174 parking spaces per mile of road or one parking space for every 30 feet of road.
16. The *1997 Economic Census* found that private parking lots and garages in the U.S. had total receipts of only $5.2 billion in 1997 (U.S. Census Bureau 1997). Parking lots and garages are code 81293 in the North American Industry Classification System. The U.S. Department of Transportation (2002a, Table 3-A) reported that the total receipts of all public parking facilities were $1.4 billion in 1997. The receipts of parking lots and garages overstate what drivers pay for parking because parking operators receive revenue that drivers don't pay if someone else pays it for them—as with validated and employer-paid parking.
17. Motorist payments for motor-fuel and motor-vehicle taxes and tolls were $90 billion in 1997. See U.S. Department of Transportation, Federal Highway Administration, Office of Highway Policy Information, *Highway Statistics 1998,* Table HDF, Disposition of Highway-User Revenues. Available online at www.fhwa.dot.gov/ohm/hs98page.htm.
18. Another comparison shows the size of parking subsidies, KPMG Peat Marwick (1990) estimated that in 1989 the annual capital plus operating cost of parking spaces provided free to automobile commuters in the U.S. amounted to $52.1 billion. The American Public Transit Association (1997) reported that in 1989 the federal, state, and local governments provided $8.7 billion in total operating subsidies for all public transportation in the U.S. Therefore, the parking subsidy for automobile work trips was six times the operating subsidy for all public transportation trips for all purposes.
19. Data for the average price of a new car are taken from the *Ward's Automotive Yearbook*

2000 (page 284) and from earlier editions of the same publication.

20. In the 1960s, the cost of a new parking space averaged 73 percent of the price of a new car. Parking spaces have remained the same (or become smaller) since the 1960s, while the quality of new cars has improved significantly, but a new parking space more than doubled in cost when compared with the price of a new car.
21. The *1995 Nationwide Personal Transportation Survey* found that 95 percent of all automobile commuters park free at work (U.S. Department of Transportation 1995a). The 2002 *National Household Travel Survey* did not ask commuters whether they paid for parking at work (U.S. Department of Transportation 2003a).
22. Some commuters will be absent from work, so more commuters can be offered parking than there are spaces. On the other hand, a parking system operates most efficiently with a vacancy rate of between 5 and 15 percent, so that drivers do not need to search the entire system for the last few available spaces. The absentee rate found in parking studies is usually between 5 and 15 percent, so these two factors are assumed to cancel each other.
23. Vuchic (1999, 77).
24. 2001 *National Household Travel Survey* (United States Department of Transportation 2003a).
25. *Ward's Motor Vehicle Facts & Figures 2002.*
26. In a study of commuters to the Toronto CBD, David Gillen (1977a) found that the average cost of parking at work was $1.56 a day and the average automobile variable cost (fuel, oil, tires) for driving to work was $0.28 a day. The total variable cost of a vehicle trip to work was thus $1.84 a day ($1.56 + $0.28), and free parking at work subsidized 85 percent of the total variable cost of driving to work ($1.56 ÷ $1.84).
27. Proost and Van Dender (2001, 401). Because vehicle operating costs are proportional to trip length, while the parking fee is independent of it, charging for parking produces even greater increases in the cost of driving for shorter trips. Charging for parking substantially increases the cost of driving to work because each commuter's car takes up a lot of space at work. A typical employment density in office buildings is four persons per 1,000 square feet, or 250 square feet of office space per employee. In comparison, parking lots and parking structures typically have about 330 square feet per space (half for the parked car, and half for the access aisles). Because a car parked at work typically occupies about a third more space than its driver does, charging for parking can substantially increase the cost of driving to work.
28. *Ward's Motor Vehicle Facts & Figures 2002.* The average fuel efficiency was calculated by dividing the total Vehicle Miles Travelled (VMT) for cars and light trucks by the total fuel consumption of cars and light trucks.
29. We are lucky our cars are not fueled by other common liquids such as Diet Snapple ($10 a gallon) or Evian water ($21 a gallon).
30. Richard Muth (1983) examined how the rapid rise in gasoline prices during the 1970s affected the cost of commuting. After correcting for general price inflation, the price of gasoline almost doubled between 1973 and 1980, but Muth estimated that the cost per mile for driving to work increased by only 5 percent. Two reasons explain this small increase in commuting cost. First petroleum costs were only about one-fifth of the cost of the 10-year average cost of operating an automobile (including gasoline, oil, depreciation,

repair and maintenance, replacement tires, accessories, sales tax, and taxes on gasoline and tires). Second, average car size declined and automobile fuel efficiency increased as a result of the gasoline price rise.

31. United States Department of Transportation (2001b, Table MF-121T). The federal tax was 18.4¢ per gallon, and weighted average of the state tax rates was 19.082 per gallon. The state tax rates ranged from 7.5¢ per gallon in Georgia to 29¢ per gallon in Rhode Island.

32. Apogee Research (1994, 99 and 109). Apogee estimated the sum of the costs for both residential and nonresidential parking spaces, not including the cost of on-street parking spaces. Apogee assumed that the capital cost of a residential garage was only $2,400 and that it would be depreciated over 80 years, so the estimate of residential parking cost seems conservative (Apogee Research 1994, 110).

33. PAS Report 532, *Parking Cash Out,* describes these congestion toll estimates by Michael Cameron (1991) and Kenneth Small (1992).

34. Deakin and Harvey (1996).

35. In response to a congestion toll, drivers would travel at off-peak hours, shift to untolled roads, or move closer to work, so the congestion toll per work trip would decrease. Therefore, charging for parking would in the long run increase the cost of driving to work by even more than would a congestion toll of 22¢ a mile.

36. See Appendix B for the evidence that drivers park free for 99 percent of their trips and that the average car is parked for 95 percent of the time.

37. "Pricing of parking and road use need to be simultaneously determined. As the level of parking fee becomes more efficient, or as the number of free parkers is reduced, so the level of optimally determined cordon charge falls. Additionally, by introducing a cordon charge, the level of the optimally determined parking fee falls" (Calthrop, Proost, and van Dender 2000, 64). Without parking fees, the optimal congestion toll was $3.70 per trip. With parking fees of $1.90 per trip (the estimated cost of providing parking spaces), the optimal congestion toll fell to $3.10 per trip. In the base case, they assumed that drivers park free for 70 percent of their trips. The cordon charges vary by time of day but parking fees do not. European Currency Units (ECU) are converted at an exchange rate of $1 = 1ECU.

38. Gómez-Ibáñez and Fauth (1980)

39. Thomson (1967). The optimal increase in the price of parking was £0.0375 an hour (£0.43 or $0.69 in 2003 prices), and it increased the average peak-hour speed of traffic by 14 percent. The optimal congestion toll was £0.30 a day (£3.44 or $5.51 in 2003 prices), and it increased the average peak-hour speed of traffic by 25 percent. Thomson did not model the effects of parking fees and a congestion toll. The 1967 prices are converted to their 2003 equivalents by the UK Retail Price Index and are converted at an exchange rate of £1 = $1.60. In 2003, Transport for London introduced a charge of £5 a day for entry into central London.

40. Transport for London (2003).

41. Baker (1987, 535) reports the results of a survey showing that 81 percent of commuters to central London park free at work.

42. For example, Glazer and Niskanen (1992, 124) say, "We thus do not address the role of parking fees in allocating more and less desirable parking spaces to users." They examine "the second-best solution: the optimal parking fees if the road-usage fee is too low." They do not examine what happens if the parking fee itself is too low to allocate spaces efficiently.

43. An exception is Eric Verhoef (1996, 112) who presents a sophisticated analysis of parking policies with two goals: "(1) optimizing the level of congestion on an urban road network and (2) optimizing the activity of parking itself." He concludes that parking fees are a first-best way to allocate scarce parking space but a second-best way to regulate other road transport externalities.

44. Gordon and Richardson (2001) explain how stable regional travel times can coexist with substantial increases in route congestion, and they present evidence showing that the average commuting time in the U.S. has not changed significantly since 1969 and perhaps has not changed since 1934.

45. *Ward's Automotive Yearbook 2003,* pp. 268–269. The total operating cost of driving a car is $1,600 a year (11,766 miles per year x 13.6¢ per mile), which is equivalent to $4.38 a day ($1,600 ÷ 365).

46. The area of 200 square feet per parking space is conservative because it does not include the area needed for access aisles in parking lots and garages. The total area needed for parking is 4,950 square miles (230 million vehicles x 600 square feet per vehicle ÷ 27,878,400 square feet per square mile). The land areas of Connecticut, Delaware, and Rhode Island are 4,845 square miles, 1,954 square miles, and 1,045 square miles, respectively.

THE PLANNER'S USE OF INFORMATION

CHAPTER 2: *Survey Methods* by Nancy Nishikawa
CHAPTER 3: *Information from Secondary Sources* by Maria Yen and Grace York

CHAPTER 2: SURVEY METHODS

Nancy Nishikawa

ALTERNATIVES TO THE SURVEY

OBSERVATIONS

One of the investigator's greatest fears is that their work will meet with resistance from the population being surveyed. In such an eventuality, *observation* provides an alternative data-gathering tool. For example, retail outlets in the CBD may refuse to be surveyed because they suspect competitors will learn about their business conditions. However, the investigator can still observe the activity of delivery vehicles or the number of employees and customers arriving and departing at various times. Like the survey methods, an observation schedule must be carefully designed to minimize inaccuracy and bias. The observation and recording of data can be aided with a list of required information that was devised before the field survey begins. In this way, the observer knows where to concentrate their attention when confronted with a barrage of sensual stimuli.

Every item must be fully recorded; reliance should never be placed on memory. Moreover, recorded information should distinguish between observations of actual occurrences

Nancy Nishikawa, "Survey Methods," *Planner's Use of Information*, ed. Hemalata Dandekar, pp. 73-78. Copyright © 2003 by Taylor & Francis Group. Reprinted with permission.

and interpretations. To resolve the problems of recording events simultaneously with their spontaneous occurrence, note-taking can be supplemented by use of a portable tape recorder.

KEY-INFORMANT TECHNIQUE

Anthropologists studying the structure and behavior of cultures have used the *key-informant technique* most extensively. It refers to an information-gathering method that taps the knowledge of a few people, usually through unstructured personal interviews. These people occupy positions or roles that allow them to communicate a broad, synthesized picture about a certain subject and/or a specialized picture of that topic. Use of key informants is appropriate when the objective is to obtain comprehensive or indepth information not expected from a sampling of the population. The low costs are also appealing.

Before using this method, the investigator must consider the qualifications of proposed key informants to decide whether each possesses the relevant information. Consideration should also be given to the sources of any biases the informant may have, possibly as a result of that unique role. This problem may be controlled somewhat by using multiple informants. In any case, the key-informant technique is not meant to take the place of survey data with its emphasis on unbiased estimates that can be projected to a more general population.

Key informants are especially valuable where there is a communication gap between the target study population and the researcher. Individuals are selected for their ability to bridge the gap by speaking the language of both sides. The interviews will often be held as a preliminary phase of a research project to see that the right problem, relevant issues and critical variables have been identified—similar to a pilot study.

FOCUS-GROUP INTERVIEWS

Much of the work on focus-group interviews has been in the area of market research. It involves a nondirective interview process that allows participants to comment, explain and share experiences and opinions. In part because of its popularity, the term "focus groups" has been attributed to different types of group interviews. However, the technique is actually quite distinctive. Krueger (1994) describes it as follows:

> *Focus groups have a rather narrow purpose for which they work particularly well—that is to determine the perceptions, feelings, and manner of thinking of consumers regarding products, services, or opportunities. Focus groups are not intended to develop consensus, to arrive at an agreeable plan, or to make decisions about which course of action to take.* (p. 19)

In particular, focus groups resemble brainstorming techniques that are similarly open and spontaneous; however, brainstorming sessions, as well as nominal groups and Delphic processes, are often used to solve particular problems. Focus-group discussions, on the other hand, are conducted without pressure or expectations of reaching a particular end point.

Focus groups typically involve six to 12 persons and are best conducted with participants who are similar to each other. A moderator or facilitator typically begins by pointing out the commonality shared by group members. They then stimulate discussion by posing a series of open-ended questions.

With several participants, a single person is not responsible for coming up with an answer or opinion. The group structure reduces the level of anxiety sometimes found in personal interview situations. It seeks to emulate a more real-life environment in which people interact, and listen to and mutually influence each other. The group format makes it possible for people to explore more thoroughly and reflectively the similarities and differences in their experiences. One person's comments may spark new ideas in another person, thus setting off a chain reaction and causing viewpoints to evolve.

At the same time, it is possible for the group dynamics to deteriorate. The facilitator must be skilled in handling dominant personalities, loudmouths and bullies who may intimidate or harass other participants. To balance out unevenness in individual sessions, the researcher should conduct interviews with several groups. Repetition also helps to identify trends and patterns by the frequency and consistency of comments.

On the whole, this method is relatively inexpensive and focus groups are fairly easy to organize. However, there are potential hurdles (e.g., in recruiting participants, particularly if the subject matter is not compelling, or finding a skilled moderator). Analyzing the results of the sessions may also present a challenge if the researcher is not familiar with qualitative data:

- How do you judge one person's comments against another's?
- What effect did the group's environment have on the statements made?
- Is it valid to take statements out of their context?

Focus-group research can provide useful information about human experiences not found in numbers and it is, therefore, an effective complement to quantitative studies. Focus groups held before a survey allow researchers to learn a target population's vocabulary and how it reasons. This is especially helpful in questionnaire development to avoid using unfamiliar terms, omitting important response choices, presenting questions in a seemingly illogical sequence or failing to ask critical questions. Focus groups held after a survey can help researchers interpret the results or formulate follow-up actions.

CONCLUSIONS

Despite the plethora of data stored in computer banks or in hard-copy files, planners will still rely on surveys as one of the basic methods for collecting information pertinent to their activities. This chapter has outlined the major components of survey research, some available options and factors to consider in putting together a project. It has been emphasized that the specific nature of a survey project will depend on the objectives being sought and the resources available for such an endeavor. Successful completion of a survey calls for adequate strategic planning, general attention to tactics and the ability to maneuver in midstream. The survey is a tool that will continue to serve diligent and creative planners well.

APPLICATIONS

1. The planning department in Middlesville is in the midst of revising a comprehensive revitalization plan for the CBD and surrounding neighborhoods. The city planners believe that adequate information is available on public needs and preferences. Assistant Planner, realizing that the planning process would benefit greatly from direct citizen participation, proposes that a survey be conducted. He even suggests a title for the

study: "Middlesville us Tomorrow: Toward the Year 2050."

   a. Draw up a list of objectives for such a survey. Begin by asking questions you would like the survey findings to answer. For example, you may want to investigate the relationship between a vital, high-density CBD and a high-quality urban lifestyle. Compare your list with that of one or two other persons and try to resolve any differences in survey objectives.

   b. Draw up a list of objectives that a neighborhood group called Citizens Against Towers (CAT) would adopt if it were to conduct a separate survey.

2. After consulting a sampling expert and weighing administrative costs, the city's planning committee for the survey decides on a mail-in questionnaire as most appropriate.

   a. Prepare a cover letter to send with each questionnaire. The primary objective of the letter is to encourage participation and thus minimize the nonresponse rate.

   b. CAT, an organization comprised of volunteers, feels that telephone interviewing is a more effective strategy. Write out an introduction—concise, yet engaging—that can be presented verbally.

3. At one point, the possibility of distributing the city's questionnaire as an insert in the only local paper was considered. What are the pros and cons of this approach? How would your assessment differ if newspaper officials informed you that the Sunday edition was delivered to 85% of the households in Middlesville? How would it differ if an address list were also supplied?

4. One alternative to surveys discussed in the chapter is the focus-group interview. To practice this technique, set up groups of six to eight people with one person as the moderator and another as the recorder. In half of the groups, members should read the same news account of a prominent local planning issue. In the other half, members should read an editorial or letters to the editor on the same issue. The moderator's role is to find out the range and intensity of opinions from group members and elicit suggestions about ways to address the issue. Spend about 15 minutes for this discussion. Follow with results of each groups' discussion by the recorders, then compare.

BIBLIOGRAPHY

Dillman, Don A. *Mail and Internet Surveys: The Tailored Design Method.* 2d ed. New York: John Wiley & Sons, Inc., 2000.

   The author, a noted authority and advocate of self-administered surveys, is credited with raising the status of mail surveys. Frequently plagued by low response rates, Dillman has developed a system of notification, contact and follow-up to maximize the data yield. Backed by more than 20 years of experience in the field, he discusses elements of his "tailored design method" in fine detail. This latest volume also includes a chapter on self-administered surveys using newer technologies, such as the Internet and interactive voice response.

Fowler, Jr., Floyd J. *Improving Survey Questions: Design and Evaluation.* Applied Social Research Methods Series, Vol. 38. Thousand Oaks, CA: Sage Publications, 1995.

> Questionnaire design lies at the heart of collecting the type of information needed. This book focuses on how to write good survey questions through choice of words and format It is a detailed yet practical how-to book, replete with examples for a wide range of situations.

Henry, Gary T. *Practical Sampling.* Applied Social Research Methods Series, Vol. 21. Thousand Oaks, CA: Sage Publications, 1990.

> Figuring out the sample size is still perceived as a major hurdle (or stumbling block) in many survey projects. This book helps to demystify the sampling issue. While statistical formulas and distribution curves are unavoidable, the author does not make them a focal point of the text. Explanations, supplemented by tables and flow charts, are dear and targeted to specific sampling questions. There is an excellent presentation of different sampling strategies and options.

Krueger, Richard A. *Focus Groups: A Practical Guide for Applied Research.* 2d ed. Thousand Oaks, CA: Sage Publications, 1994.

> In this compact and comprehensive textbook, equal attention is given to all aspects of the process of conducting focus groups—from logistics and recruiting participants, to moderating the sessions, to analyzing and reporting the results. Read Chapter 7, "Principles of Analyzing Focus Groups Results" first, because it highlights the qualitative and interpretive elements of this research method, as distinct from the surveys.

Lavrakas, Paul J. *Telephone Survey Methods: Sampling, Selection, and Supervision.* 2d ed. Applied Social Research Methods Series, Vol. 7. Thousand Oaks, CA: Sage Publications, 1993.

> This is an indispensable guide for anyone undertaking a telephone survey and the next best thing *to* on-the-job training. It is especially useful in helping to anticipate problems that might arise when the survey is executed and recommending ways of responding to problems that do.

Nesbary, Dale K. *Survey Research and the World Wide Web.* Boston: Allyn and Bacon, 2000.

> An early book on online survey research that is readily available and worth a quick look by readers who need a basic orientation. The author has conducted two interesting experiments pitting the Web-based survey against one administered by regular mail—with mixed results. Unfortunately, the definitive book on online survey and polling research is still to be written. The most productive tips are likely to come from the private sector where

online market research continues to develop in creative ways.

Rainie, Lee and Dan Packel. Pew Internet & American Life Project. "More Online, Doing More." Washington, DC: The Pew Internet & American Life Project, 2001 (www.pewinternet.org)

Rea, Louis M. and Richard A. Parker. *Designing and Conducting Survey Research: A Comprehensive Guide.* 2d ed. San Francisco: Jossey-Bass Publishers, 1997.

> Although the title of this book refers to designing and conducting surveys, a significant portion is devoted to analyzing and presenting the results. Where most texts on survey research end with data collection or construction of the database, this one extends into the data analysis phase, covering topics such as tests of significance and measures of association. There is also a brief, but useful, chapter on writing up the survey findings.

Salant, Priscilla and Don A. Dillman. *How To Conduct Your Own Survey.* New York: John Wiley & Sons, Inc., 1994.

This book has become a classic for novice survey researchers. It is the user-friendly version of Dillman's more academic textbook. A self-proclaimed nuts-and-bolts guide, the authors break down the survey process into discrete, do-able tasks, and provide illustrations and examples for virtually every step along the way. After reading this book, it's hard not to feel that anybody can do a survey.

CHAPTER 3: INFORMATION FROM SECONDARY SOURCES

Maria Yen and Grace York

It is a brave new world for planners, community groups and private citizens searching for reliable information that will lead to effective plans. While public sector agencies remain the primary gatherers and repositories of secondary source information, they are joined in the 21st century by private companies that can tailor a data search to a client's specific planning needs, and by not-for-profit groups that collect information for communities and populations previously overlooked by government agencies.

The expansion of the sources that collect planning data goes hand in hand with the democratization of access to this data. A private citizen can as easily gather information on a neighborhood from the U.S. Census Bureau as can the experienced planning professional, if they both have access to a computer and an Internet connection.

In this new world, secondary source information can be combined with new technologies for visual presentations that make data easier to grasp and applicable to real planning problems. Geographic Information System (GIS) mapping and analysis, computer animation and virtual reality programs are some of the tools planners can use to breathe life into dry statistics. These technologies, along with guidance on searching for and using secondary source materials, can be made available to community groups, empowering them to understand the challenges and potentials facing their neighborhoods. In this way, the high-tech world of the Internet, and the tools to analyze and display data, serve to further the core mission of planners: *to help improve the communities they serve.*

Maria Yen and Grace York, "Information from Secondary Sources," *Planner's Use of Information*, ed. Hemalata Dandekar, pp. 80-88. Copyright © 2003 by Taylor & Francis Group. Reprinted with permission.

Thanks to the expanding number of organizations collecting planning data, coupled with the Internet as an entry point to search for data, people and organizations at the smallest geographic level are gaining access to valuable information that they can use to t plan for their communities. At the same time, local; challenges often have global implications. Revitalizing a downtown business district dependent on garment manufacturing requires access to information on the links of this industry to overseas manufacturers, and on its dependence on international migrant workers, many of whom are women. Searching for low-cost and efficient alternatives to subways will lead transportation planners to seek information from cities across the globe that are designing their own creative mass-transit solutions.

This chapter focuses on the substantial amount of information directly relevant to local planning that has already been collected by local and state governments, federal agencies, professional organizations, private businesses, international organizations and nonprofit groups. This information can often be found in published form or on computer databases at public or university libraries, in the files and records of private businesses and public agencies, or on Web pages identified through Internet search engines. Finding and using secondary sources of information enable a planner to quickly develop relatively inexpensive background information and analyses on particular planning issues and sections of the city.

While more organizations form to provide planning information, and while planners and the public can access this information more easily today, challenges do exist in finding and using secondary sources. First, information has usually been collected for some purpose other than the needs of the local planning office. For example, a city transportation planner may be excited to learn that the Federal Highway Administration (FHA) publishes data on fatal accidents, including information on the vehicle, type of crash, persons involved and other key variables down to the place level of census geography.

However, the excitement may fade when the planner realizes the data have been collected only for highway fatalities, and cannot help in designating those city intersections that have been the scenes of repeated deadly accidents. While the city's police department may not yet have data for fatal accidents on the Internet, it may be the most reliable source in finding information about this problem. In addition, an organization that in the past has collected information useful for planners may simply cease collecting and publishing the information, making plans based on trend analysis far more challenging. This happens frequently in government agencies where funding priorities may shift under different political administrations.

A second challenge is created by the enormous diversity in types and sources of information that exist. A small-town planner wants to determine how much local retail business is being lost to a neighboring large city. Should he or she turn to sales tax receipts from his or her town or the big city, U.S. Census data on the town's total size, a study undertaken by a university's extension program or some other source? An overview of major types of information, along with some planning scenarios, are presented here to assist planners facing these types of choices.

The third challenge arises in assessing the quality of information found on the Internet. The Internet makes available information from sources at all geographic levels and across a stunning array of topics relevant to planning. For example, planners interested in data on crimes can use the World Wide Web to find information from local sources such as neighborhood watch groups, national sources such as the

INCREASING RANGE AND AVAILABILITY OF SECONDARY SOURCES OF INFORMATION

Geographic Information System mapping and analysis programs, virtual reality software and other technologies for generating, storing, analyzing and displaying spatial data have become accessible to trained planners as well as community members. Combining these tools with access to information can democratize the planning process by bringing on board those who will be affected by land use, economic development and other decisions that affect the local quality of life.

There is a growing movement among community-based nonprofit organizations, local governments and educational institutions around the world to develop electronic community networks that provide the public with access to useful information across a range of topics. Some of these networks also provide the technologies to visualize and analyze communities using programs for mapping and computer animation.

Community groups and individuals can use the tools and data made available on community networks in many ways to improve the local quality of life. For example, residents in the City of Los Angeles, concerned about a saturation of abandoned and neglected structures in their neighborhood, can access data on property tax delinquencies from the Neighborhood Knowledge Los Angeles (NKLA) Web site. Here, residents can create maps that depict the spatial distribution of these properties and link these to census data, showing a disproportionate number of abandoned structures in low-income or minority communities.

In another case, a group of entrepreneurs in Jefferson County, Missouri can use the Jefferson County Online Information Network (JOIN-N) to get information on business licenses, economic development plans and delays due to road construction that might affect the opening of a new enterprise. The following selected Web sites illustrate this movement to democratize data and put the tools to analyze local information in the hands of communities.

Boulder Community Network
bcn.boulder.co.us

> Users can click on several resource "centers" to get access to information such as a sample lease agreement for landlords and renters, the latest minutes from city council meetings and an extensive list of community groups serving the Boulder County area.

InfoResources West Philadelphia
westphillydata.library.upenn.edu

(Continued)

Residents of West Philadelphia can find useful information about their local quality of life, including data on public health issues, housing and total population in their neighborhoods, zip codes or census tracts. They can visualize the spatial distribution of this data through maps. The University of Pennsylvania's Department of City and Regional Planning developed this site.

Jefferson County, Missouri Online Information Network (JOIN-N) www.join-n.org

JOIN-N is a community network that strives to provide access to a vast array of community-oriented groups, both governmental and nongovernmental, and the information they possess. Users can find tax forms, voter information, business license forms and instructions, information on local road construction plans, links to human service organizations and many other useful links.

Neighborhood Knowledge Los Angeles (NKLA) nkla.ucla.edu

Proclaiming on its home page that "Neighborhood Improvement and Recovery is Not Just for the Experts," NKLA's Web site (developed at the University of California at Los Angeles) provides access to information on conditions such as tax delinquencies, nuisance properties, code violations and other indicators that can serve as early warnings of neighborhood decline. Users can create maps with this information, along with demographic data from the U.S. Census Bureau, to visualize the needs and potential of their neighborhoods.

Shaping Dane Project
www.lic.wisc.edu/shapingdane

The "Shaping Dane" pilot project, run by Dane County, Wisconsin, seeks to involve citizens in evaluating the land use choices facing their area. The challenge of accommodating growth while preserving the area's character and quality of life provides the background for this project, which is centered in the town of Verona. Residents can use the site to create maps depicting how much land is being used in Dane County and for what purposes, and to consider alternative plans for their communities.

(Continued)

> Woodberry Down Regeneration Team (WDRT)
> of Hackney Council, United Kingdom
> www.casa.ucl.ac.uk/woodberry
>
> WDRT's Web site was developed by the Centre for Advanced Spatial Analysis, University College London, to communicate the redevelopment of some 2,500 housing units in Woodberry Down, London to its local residents. Residents who visit the site can take a virtual tour of the plans for their housing estate, "stepping inside" certain parts of the neighborhood for a closer look. This tour allows them to visualize alternative scenarios, on which they can comment and vote over the Web.

Federal Bureau of Investigation (FBI), and global sources such as the International Criminal Police Organization (INTERPOL).

Careful searches allow access to records once only available from numerous treks to city clerks' offices and local libraries. However, while the World Wide Web offers the potential for quicker and more comprehensive searches of secondary source information, access to greater quantities of information does not necessarily translate into higher quality data for planning purposes. Not all data presented on the Web are accurate, updated and thorough. Given the time and effort needed to keep updated records on the Internet, some organizations simply allow their Web sites to languish, leading to stale information that should not be used in constructing fresh planning initiatives.

If planners seek to compare local information from different geographic areas or over different time periods, they may run into trouble with Web-based sources since the quality and currency of organizations' data can vary so drastically. It is a good idea to review the quality of information from any source before relying on it (see the sidebar entitled "Evaluating the Quality of the Data"). This is especially true for Internet sources.

The best technique for finding planning information may remain old-fashioned, human contact. Knowledgeable employees of local organizations can point planners in the right direction; sometimes a simple phone call will do the trick. At other times, a trip to the library is a good way to begin a secondary source information search. Most libraries have a password to the Online Computer Library Center World Catalog, so they can identify the location of material they may not own and borrow it for you.

The Internet can serve as a sort of high-tech "Yellow Pages" for enterprising planners—a place where they can search out human contacts in local agencies and libraries, who can then direct them to both hard-copy and computer-based secondary sources. Using the Internet can also help planners network across agencies. (A sample of Internet Web sites useful to planners is listed in the "Bibliography.") It is likely that some will change their address or their Uniform Resource Locator (URL). You can often identify

THE PLANNER FINDS INFORMATION

While dealing with the problem of the Main Street trash receptacles in Middlesville, Assistant Planner is asked to get background information on another issue that had been brewing for a while in another neighborhood of Middlesville: the need to develop a plan to revitalize Walnut Hill Park.

A few miles east of Main Street is the Walnut Hill neighborhood. Once a district of fine homes for the city's elite, the past decade has seen the flight of wealthier residents to the suburbs. While no longer a high-income enclave, Walnut Hill is a lively and bustling community whose population has grown due to a surge of immigration from Latin America. Houses that once held single families have been converted to apartments; schools that once were threatened with closure are now bursting with pupils.

Walnut Hill Park, however, is one city amenity that is not keeping up with this surge in growth and activity. Planned in the 1950s, the park contains playground equipment, a few deteriorating picnic tables and a large baseball diamond. In such a busy community, the parks and recreation department is surprised to find minimal park usage. The baseball field—once the center of neighborhood life in the summer evenings—is mainly deserted. The picnic tables and playground equipment are in dire need of replacement It is obvious that few families spend time in Walnut Hill Park.

Assistant Planner knows that observations using field methods, interviews and surveys will provide valuable primary, firsthand information on the community's recreation needs. However, he also knows that basic background information might be available from secondary sources. Finding this information could put the issue of the park's low usage in context and help to identify the kind of additional information needed to remedy the situation.

Assistant Planner devises a quick strategy to guide his search:

- *Problem:* Walnut Hill Park has become run down and underutilized.
- *Approach:* Compile information on the area and write a recreation needs assessment to see how the park can better fit neighborhood needs.
- *Information:* Demographic, recreation and education information is required.

Assistant Planner's first stop is the U.S. Census Bureau's Web site at www.census.gov, where he can gather basic background data on the people of Walnut Hill. He is initially overwhelmed by the amount of available information in the American Community Survey on this neighborhood, but decides to focus solely on race, place of birth, year of migration, age and sex.

(Continued)

> From this data, he does a quick analysis and discovers that 85% of the neighborhood population consists of people who are Latinos of various races, and 60% have migrated to Walnut Hill directly from various Latin American countries within the past five years. He works up an age/sex pyramid and notes that the population has a large group of children who are under five years old. Projecting 10 years ahead, he realizes that this group will be a major presence in the local primary and middle schools in the near future.
>
> This leads Assistant Planner to call the Middlesville school board. His contact there confirms his assessment, provides more recent data on the school population in Walnut Hill and suggests he talk to the neighborhood elementary school principal. The principal expresses concern that the park, while bordering the school grounds, is run down and barely used. At the same time, the school's own recreation spaces are insufficient. "The children are forced to play soccer in the streets or in narrow spaces between houses," she tells Assistant Planner. "Soccer has really become the primary sport in this neighborhood; few are interested in baseball."
>
> Assistant Planner realizes that the 1950's design of the park does not reflect or respond to the culture and preferences of the new residents in Walnut Hill. On the advice of the city's parks and recreation department head, Assistant Planner visits the National Recreation and Park Association Web site, where he orders a handbook on designing parks in urban areas. A search on the Internet also reveals a nonprofit organization, the Hiatonka Outdoor Enthusiasts, which is accepting proposals for park improvement schemes. Worthy groups will be granted $ 10,000 to improve neighborhood parks.
>
> Before writing his background analysis and coming up with a proposal. Assistant Planner must carry out more field research and perhaps a survey of neighborhood children. However, this first hunt for secondary source material has already given him a preliminary understanding of the changing recreation needs in Walnut Hill.

the new URL by shortening the address or by using an Internet search engine. Some Web sites will change their information content or fade away over time while newer, improved versions may be developed.

This chapter begins by introducing the granddaddy of all planning-related secondary sources in the United States: the Censuses of Population and Housing. The U.S. Census provides comprehensive and reliable information for planners interested in creating a demographic portrait of their local areas. The sections that follow are organized by planning issue:

- population and demographics
- housing and construction
- economics
- transportation
- health and welfare
- education
- environment, natural resources and recreation
- crime

THE PLANNER'S USE OF INFORMATION

- governmental activities
- laws, legislation and regulations

Two final sections deal specifically with resources at the federal, state and local levels. Wherever possible, the sections list public agency, private business and nonprofit sources of planning information across geographical levels (local, regional, state, national and, where relevant, international). Not all planning issues are covered by all types of organizations (public, private and nonprofit) and not all planning issues lend themselves to analysis at every geographic level. Moreover, it is inevitable that the reader will come across useful sources that are not mentioned in this chapter.

Since considerable variability exists among the types of information gathered and published by agencies at the local, state and national levels, the reader should check with the relevant agency to see if the information described in this chapter is, in fact, available in their locality of interest. The reader will note that some sources make appearances in several sections (e.g., local school boards are mentioned both in the section on education and on demographics). Since school boards sometimes provide updated counts of neighborhood school-aged children, planners can use this information to describe general community demographics when U.S. Census data are unavailable or old.

U.S. CENSUSES OF POPULATION AND HOUSING

The most comprehensive source of data on people and their communities is the United States Census. The U.S. Census Bureau conducts three major counts: the Censuses of Population and Housing, the Economic Census and the American Community Survey.

- The Census of Population and Housing collects data every 10 years, in the years ending with a zero, on population and housing characteristics from the national to the county, city and neighborhood levels.
- The Economic Census collects data every five years on every business establishment in the U.S. (see also the section in this chapter entitled Local Information Sources").
- The American Community Survey collects policy-relevant population and housing data on selected communities every three or five years, depending on the size of the community. When fully implemented in 2003, it is expected to provide neighborhood (or census tract) data similar to the Decennial Census. It may replace the long (sample) census form in 2010.

The Censuses of Population and Housing that are collected every 10 years gather information on a limited number of questions asked of every person and housing unit existing in the U.S. These questions make up the short form—or "100% characteristics"—since they cover 100% of all respondents. (Of course, not 100% of all people in America respond to the census.) In addition, a more detailed set of questions is asked of a sample of people (generally one in six) and housing units. This more detailed questionnaire makes up the long form—or "sample characteristics." (See the sidebar entitled "The Censuses of Population and Housing.") Actual questions that are contained on the short-or long-form questionnaires can vary from census to census, making comparability across time challenging. For example, the 2000 census was the first that permitted people to identify themselves as multiracial. As a result, racial data in 2000 is not entirely comparable with earlier years.

Census geography is not necessarily intuitive, as Figure 1 (a diagram constructed by the Census

Bureau to represent census geographic entities in the year 2000) illustrates. Census geography contains confusingly similar entities such as urban areas (cities defined by total population and density of settlement) and places (cities defined as political entities).

For the local area planner, the most useful approach to understanding U.S. Census geography, beyond reading the many online guides available on the Census Bureau's Web site and from the sources listed in the annotated bibliography, is to see it from the neighborhood level on up. As Figure 2 (a diagram produced by the Census Bureau) shows, the smallest geographic unit for which the Census Bureau tabulates data is the *block* (lower left-hand corner of the diagram).

Blocks are generally bounded by streets or other distinguishing features and contain about 85 people—similar to the neighborhood concept in city planning. Up from the block is the *block group* (a collection of census blocks sharing identifying numerical codes and containing an average of 1,000 people). Block groups together make up *census tracts* (averaging about 4,000 people). They tend to have stable boundaries, although there is variation over time, especially in fast-growing cities.

Up from census tracts are *places* (incorporated geographic entities with concentrations of people and legally prescribed boundaries, powers and functions).

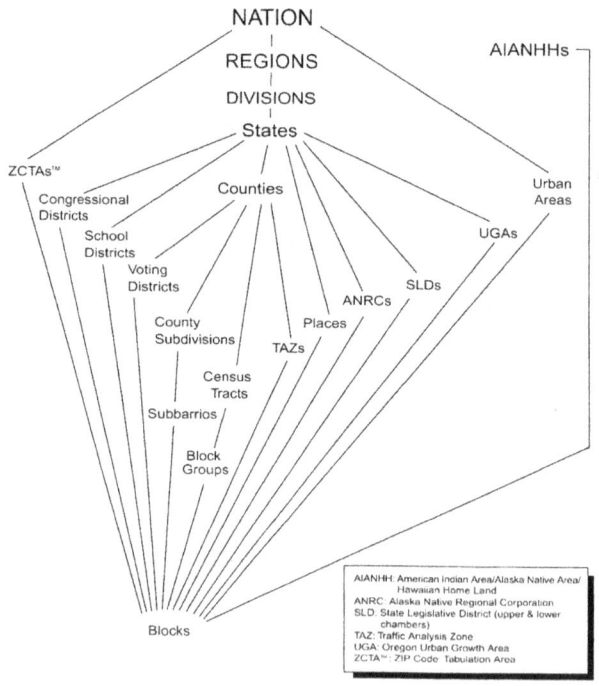

Figure 1 Standard hierarchy of census geographic entities

THE CENSUSES OF POPULATION AND HOUSING

Short-form Questions (100% characteristics) from Census 2000

- household relationship
- sex
- age
- Hispanic or Latino origin
- race
- tenure (whether home is owned or rented)
- vacancy characteristics

Long-form Questions (sample characteristics) from Census 2000

POPULATION

- marital status
- place of birth, citizenship and year of entry
- school enrollment and educational attainment
- ancestry
- migration (residence in 1995)
- language spoken at home and ability to speak English
- veteran status
- disability
- grandparents as caregivers
- labor force status
- place of work and journey to work
- occupation, industry and class of worker
- work status in 1999
- income in 1999

HOUSING

- value of home or monthly rent paid
- units in structure
- year structure built
- number of rooms and number of bedrooms
- year moved into residence
- plumbing and kitchen facilities
- telephone service
- vehicles available
- heating fuel
- farm residence
- utilities, mortgage, taxes, insurance and fuel costs

THE LIVING LANDSCAPE

INTRODUCTION

BY FREDERICK STEINER

Conventionally the planning process is presented as a linear progression of activities. Decision making, like other human behavior, seldom occurs in such a linear, rational manner. Still, it is a logical sequence of activities and presents a convenient organizational framework. The common steps in the process include the identification of problems and opportunities; the establishment of goals; inventory and analysis of the biophysical environment, ideally at several scales; human community inventory and analysis; detailed studies like suitability analysis; the development of concepts and the selection of options; the adoption of a plan; community involvement and education; detailed design; plan implementation; and plan administration. This book is organized around these conventional topics—but with an ecological perspective. The chapters that follow cover most of the steps in the process.

Each chapter includes a "how-to" section for accomplishing the pertinent step, and a few examples where such activities have been successfully undertaken. For many of the chapters, various planning efforts undertaken in northern Phoenix, Arizona, are used to illustrate each step. The author has been involved in the Phoenix planning work for the past decade. Because this work is largely on the suburban fringe, and because ecological planning is also useful for more urban and rural areas, several additional prototypical efforts have been selected to illustrate the principles described and to compare them with the more conventional approaches to planning.

Before discussing each step, it will be helpful to first define a few key terms. It will then be necessary to provide a brief overview of traditional planning in the United States. The ecological planning method, the subject of this

Frederick Steiner, "Introduction," *The Living Landscape: An Ecological Approach to Landscape Planning*, pp. 3-24, 439-457. Copyright © 2008 by Island Press. Reprinted with permission.

book, can then be described and the difference of its approach better understood.

BASIC CONCEPTS

Planning has been defined as the use of scientific, technical, and other organized knowledge to provide options for decision making as well as a process for considering and reaching consensus on a range of choices. As John Friedmann (1973) has succinctly put it, planning links knowledge to action. There is a difference between project planning and comprehensive planning. *Project planning* involves designing a specific object such as a dam, highway, harbor, or an individual building or group of buildings. *Comprehensive planning* involves a broad range of choices relating to all the functions of an area. Resolution of conflicts, often through compromises, is the inherent purpose of comprehensive planning. *Environment* refers to our surroundings. *Environmental planning* is "the initiation and operation of activities to manage the acquisition, transformation, distribution, and disposal of resources in a manner capable of sustaining human activities, with a minimum distribution of physical, ecological, and social processes" (Soesilo and Pijawka 1998, 2072).

Management has been defined as the judicious use of means to accomplish a desired end. It involves working with people to accomplish organizational goals. For practical purposes, many see the distinction between planning and management as largely semantic. The management of resources, such as land, may be a goal of a planning process. Conversely, planning may be a means of management. *Ecosystem management* is the deliberate process of understanding and structuring an entire region with the intention of maintaining sustainability and integrity (Slocombe 1998a, 1998b).

Land use is a self-defining term. One can debate whether a harbor involves land use or water use, but "land" generally refers to all parts of the surface of the earth, wet and dry. The same area of that surface may be used for a variety of human activities. A harbor, for instance, may have commercial, industrial, and recreational purposes. A farm field may be used for speculation and recreation as well as for agriculture. All human activity is in one way or another connected with land.

Landscape is related to land use. The composite features of one part of the surface of the earth that distinguish it from another area is a *landscape*. It is, then, a combination of elements—fields, buildings, hills, forests, deserts, water bodies, and settlements. The landscape encompasses the uses of land—housing, transportation, agriculture, recreation, and natural areas—and is a composite of those uses. A landscape is more than a picturesque view; it is the sum of the parts that can be seen, the layers and intersections of time and culture that comprise a place—a natural *and* cultural palimpsest.

The English word *ecology* is derived from the Greek word for house, *oikos*. The expanded definition is the study of the reciprocal relationships of all organisms to each other and to their biotic and physical environments (Ricklefs 1973). Obviously, humans are organisms and thus are engaged in ecological relationships.

The use of ecological information for planning has been a national policy since late 1969, when the U.S. Congress, through the National Environmental Policy Act (NEPA), required all agencies of the federal government to "initiate and utilize ecological information in the planning and development of resource oriented projects." The act, signed into law by President Richard Nixon on January 1, 1970, is a relatively recent development in American planning. In spite of NEPA and other laws, ecological information has not yet been adequately integrated into the planning process. Although much more work will still be necessary to realize an ecological approach to planning, NEPA represents an important step. To begin to understand its importance, it is useful to quickly review the status of American planning.

THE TRADITIONAL FRAMEWORK OF PLANNING IN THE UNITED STATES

The function of land-use planning in the United States has been the subject of much debate. There are diverse opinions about the purpose of planning; that is, whether it is to achieve a specific physical project, or comprehensive social, economic, or environmental goals. The traditional role of planning in the United States is responsible for many of these divisions. In England, for instance, planning is undertaken as a result of strong statutes. Statutory planning gives English planners considerable authority in the decision-making process. In contrast, American planners generally have more limited statutory power than in England and other European nations.

There are several reasons for the differences between European and American planning. First, land is recognized as a scarce commodity in Europe and in many other parts of the world. In land-hungry Europe over the last century, public officials have been granted increasing planning powers over use of land (and other resources) through the governing process. In Europe, there is much concern about the quality of the environment, both in the older democracies of the European Union and the emerging democracies of Central and Eastern Europe. This concern has resulted in complex systems of planning that address a broad range of issues, including

Landscape is the sum of the parts that can be seen with the eye. (David C. Flaherty, Washington State University College of Engineering and Architecture)

housing, recreation, aesthetics, open space, and transportation.

Another reason emerges from the origins of the United States. Thomas Jefferson and the other founding fathers were influenced strongly by John Locke, who viewed the chief end of establishing a government as the preservation of property. Locke, in his *Two Treatises of Government*, defined property as "lives, liberties, and estates" (Laslett 1988). Elsewhere, Locke wrote of the "pursuit of happiness." It was Jefferson who combined Locke's terms, "life, liberty, and the pursuit of happiness." But it has been the view of property as possession, rather than Locke's predominant version—life, liberty, and estate—that has prevailed. The constitution of the Commonwealth of Pennsylvania states in Article 1, Section 1, that "all … men have certain inherent and indefeasible rights, among which are those of enjoying and defending life and liberty, of acquiring, possessing and protecting property." And the Fifth Amendment of the U.S. Constitution contains this clause: "No person shall … be deprived of life, liberty, or property, without due process of law; nor shall private property be taken for public use without just compensation." To those in the new republic, who had fought against the landed elite of the mother country, property rights were seen as a fundamental freedom.

The Bill of Rights institutionalized the founding fathers' concern about private property rights. Their "Bill of Rights included no fewer than four separate provisions aimed specifically at protecting private interests in property," observes John Humbach (1989, 337). However, Humbach also notes that "private property exists to serve the public good" (1989, 345). The influential British utilitarian philosopher Jeremy Bentham declared that "before laws were made, there was no property; take away laws and property ceases" (1887, 113). As a result, according to Humbach (and other legal scholars), "Property rights are a creation of laws, and the law of property must, like all other law, serve a public purpose" (1989, 345).

The initial public purpose for the new nation was the settlement, or the resettlement by mostly European immigrants, of the American subcontinent (Opie 1998). However, when Jefferson (who had written the Declaration of Independence) and the others who authored the Constitution rode to Philadelphia on horseback or in carriages from their Virginia estates, their Pennsylvania farms, or their New England towns, they traveled through a seemingly endless expanse of woodlands, rich farmlands, and rolling pastures graced by fresh, clear creeks and rivers, abundant game, and pristine coastlines. In Philadelphia they were concerned foremost with protecting human rights and freedoms. Even the most foresighted of the framers of the Constitution could not have envisioned the environmental and social crises that subsequently accompanied the industrialization and urbanization of America.

The U.S. Constitution, however, does give the states and their political subdivisions the power of regulation. Police powers, which provide the basis for state and local regulation, were derived by the states from the Tenth Amendment, which reads: "The powers not delegated to the United States by the Constitution, nor prohibited by it to the States, are reserved to the States respectively, or to the people."

The states, in the use of police powers, must consider the Fifth Amendment because the U.S. Supreme Court has held that the "taking clause" is embodied in the due process clause of the Fourteenth Amendment and hence applies to the states. In addition, state constitutions contain taking clauses, some with rather interesting twists. For instance, Article 1, Section 16 (the Ninth Amendment) of the Washington State Constitution states: "No private property shall be taken *or damaged* for public *or private use* without just compensation having first been made" [emphasis added]. A person's private use of property cannot damage the property of another person in Washington State.

Given this constitutional backdrop, the federal and several state legislatures have slowly but steadily increased statutory authority for planning. In addition, the courts have consistently upheld land-use regulations that do not go "too far" and thus constitute a taking. In addition, courts have supported some restrictions on the use of environmentally sensitive areas, such as wetlands, floodplains, and the habitats of endangered species. However, planning remains a fragmented effort in the United States, undertaken primarily by powerful vested business interests and sometimes by consent. Planning by consent, which depends largely on an individual's persuasive power, has caused several adaptations on the part of American planners. These adaptations can be broken down into two broad categories: *administrative* and *adversary.*

Administrative planners are realists who respond directly to governmental programs either as bureaucrats in a city or regional planning agency or as consultants. Successful administrative planners build political power in the city or metropolitan region where they work. They administer programs for voluntary community organizations and health, education, and welfare associations designed to support the political-economic structure of the nation-state. They may also administer transportation or utility programs deemed necessary by the same structure. By building political power, administrative planners serve the power structure of the city or region. The result is that often the unempowered groups in an area suffer. Poor people suffer the most, bearing the brunt of the social costs, when planners and others administer the programs of the status quo.

Adversary planners are idealists and respond to issues, such as those resulting from social or environmental concerns, often as advocates for a certain position. They usually work outside the power structure, forming new coalitions among the previously unorganized in order to mobilize support for their cause. Often advocacy planners work for veto groups—ad hoc organizations opposed to a controversial project or proposal such as a highway, a high-density housing complex, a factory, or a landfill. Advocacy planners also work for nongovernmental organizations (NGOs), neighborhood planning committees, and community associations.

The rights of people have a deep-seated heritage in American history, from the Declaration of Independence, the Constitution, and the Bill of Rights through the Thirteenth and Nineteenth Amendments and to the labor, civil rights, and women's movements. Human rights have been the important issue for one group of advocacy planners called by various terms including *community organizers, adversary planners,* and *change agents.* In *Reveille for Radicals,* Saul Alinsky (1946) best articulated the philosophy for the latest crest of this movement, which began to ebb when Richard Nixon cut off funding for a variety of programs created during the 1960s. Many of the social programs created during the 1960s were concerned with making basic changes in the urban power structure. The programs were a result of the civil rights movement and the attention brought to the poor living conditions in urban ghettos by the riots that occurred there. The withdrawal of the federal commitment to domestic human rights programs begun by

President Nixon continued through most of the 1970s, except during the presidency of Jimmy Carter. During the Ronald Reagan administration, the social programs that had been created during the 1960s were almost completely dismantled. The emphasis on "privatization" and "state and local control" for addressing social issues continued during the 1990s in the United States, as well as in some European nations.

With the passage of the NEPA, the Congress of the United States put into motion the machinery for the protection of the environment by setting forth certain general aims of federal activity in the environmental field, establishing the Council on Environmental Quality (CEQ), and instructing all federal agencies to include an impact statement as part of future reports or recommendations on actions significantly affecting the quality of the human environment. Subsequent regional, state, and federal actions—such as state environmental policy acts, land-use legislation, and the Coastal Zone Management Act (CZMA)—have furthered this commitment.

As with the heritage for human rights, these environmental measures are deeply rooted in the American tradition. Laced throughout the social criticism of Henry David Thoreau, the novels of Mark Twain, the poetry of Walt Whitman, the photography of Ansel Adams, the films of John Ford, the art of Georgia O'Keeffe, and the music of Woody Guthrie is the love for nature.

Even before the recent governmental action, both administrative and adversary planners had been concerned with degradation of the environment. In the nineteenth century, the young Frederick Law Olmsted traveled to England where he witnessed the efforts of reformers to use techniques of the English landscape garden tradition to relieve the pressures of urban blight brought on by the Industrial Revolution. The resulting public parks were viewed as natural refuges from the evils of the surrounding industrial city. Public parks in English cities were pastoral retreats and escapes from urban congestion and pollution. Olmsted and American reformers adopted the idea. Their first creation was Central Park in New York City, planned and built between 1857 and 1861. Eventually, these efforts led to the City Beautiful Movement, after the World's Columbian Exposition of 1893 in Chicago. The City Beautiful Movement resulted in numerous parks and public facilities being built in the early twentieth century.

During the late nineteenth and early twentieth centuries a great national parks system took form and blossomed under the leadership of President Theodore Roosevelt. Also in the late nineteenth century, the use of river drainage basins or watersheds as the basic geographical unit for planning was initiated. The humanist engineer Arthur Morgan, an advocate of the watershed conservancy idea, helped organize the Miami Conservancy District in and around Dayton, Ohio, and later directed the Tennessee Valley Authority. During the New Deal, greenbelt new towns—new satellite communities surrounded by parks and accessible to cities by automobile—were created by economist Rexford Tugwell and other leaders. Urban parks, national parks, watershed conservancies, greenbelt new towns—each was a response designed to maintain some portion of the natural environment during periods of increased human settlement.

Ian McHarg (1969) was Saul Alinsky's environmentalist counterpart and the author of a manifesto for ecological planning similar to the one Alinsky wrote for community advocacy. Although social activism and environmentalism are separate (and sometimes conflicting) American traditions, they share common problems. Environmental programs were as vulnerable in the 1980s as social programs were a decade earlier. Ronald Reagan chose not to enforce many environmental laws enacted during the 1970s. He appointed people to key positions in environmental and natural resource management agencies who were opposed to the conservation missions of those agencies. Legally established environmental goals will not be achieved unless governmental enforcement is supported by the public. In spite of actions of the Reagan administration, the American public has generally continued to favor the protection of water, air, and land resources. In addition, President Reagan's successor, George H. W. Bush, declared himself an environmentalist, and when presenting Ian McHarg with the National Medal of Art in 1992, he stated, "It is my hope that the art of the twenty-first century will be devoted to restoring the earth" (McHarg 1997a, 331). Furthermore, former vice president Al Gore is an avowed environmentalist (see Gore 1992). The Clinton–Gore administration established the influential President's Council on Sustainable Development (1996) and generally emphasized more environmentally sensitive policies for the federal government. However, even the Clinton-Gore approach was not as "green" as those taken by many other nations.

Neither administrative nor advocacy planners have been totally effective. While administrative planners may be able to get things done, unempowered groups often suffer. While advocacy planners may win important civil rights struggles or stop flagrant abuse of the natural environment, overall problems persist and people remain poor—frequently poorer—and environmental degradation continues, too often at a more rapid rate.

A NEW APPROACH

There is a need for a common language, a common method among all those concerned about social equity and ecological parity. This method must be able to transcend disciplinary territorialism and be applicable to all levels of government. And it is imperative that this approach incorporate both social and environmental concerns. As the poet Wendell Berry has observed, "The mentality that destroys a watershed and then panics at the threat of flood is the same mentality that gives institutionalized insult to black people [and] then panics at the prospect of race riots" (1972, 73).

What is needed is an approach that can assist planners in analyzing the problems of a region as they relate to each other, to the landscape, and to the national and local political economic structure. This might be called an *applied human ecology*, or simply *ecological planning*. Each problem is linked to the community in one or more specific ways. Banking is related to real estate which is related to development pressure which is related to schools which is related to a rising tax base which is related to retirees organizing against increasing property taxes. This approach identifies how people are affected by these chain reactions and presents options for the future based on those impacts.

University of Wisconsin wildlife biologist Aldo Leopold was perhaps the first person to advocate an "ecological ethic" for planning, doing so in the 1930s (1933, 1949). He was subsequently joined by such individuals as Lewis Mumford (1944, 1961) and Benton MacKaye (1940). Mumford and Mac-Kaye were strongly influenced by the Scottish biologist and town planner Patrick Geddes and the English garden city advocate Ebenezer Howard. Others who have proposed or developed ecological approaches for planning include the Canadian forester G. Angus Hills (1961); the Israeli architect and town planner Artur Glikson (1971); the American landscape architects Philip Lewis (1969), Ian McHarg (1969, 1996, with Steiner

1998), Anne Spirn (1984), Rob Thayer (1994), and John Lyle (1994); the Canadian landscape architect Michael Hough (1995); the American planners Jon Berger (with Sinton 1985), Randall Arendt (1996), and Tim Beatley (with Manning 1997); the French geographer and planner Jean Tarlet (1985, 1997); the Italian planners Enzo Scandurra and Silvia Macchi (1995); and the American architects Sim Van der Ryn (with Cowan 1996) and Peter Calthorpe (1993). Daniel Smith and Paul Helmund (1993) present a wonderful guide for applying ecology to the planning of greenways, while the Italian planner Danilo Palazzo (1997) provides a comprehensive overview of the development of ecological planning in the United States.

ECOLOGICAL PLANNING METHOD

What is meant by *ecological planning? Planning* is a process that uses scientific and technical information for considering and reaching consensus on a range of choices. *Ecology* is the study of the relationship of all living things, including people, to their biological and physical environments. *Ecological planning* then may be defined as the use of biophysical and sociocultural information to suggest opportunities and constraints for decision making about the use of the landscape. Or, as defined by Ian McHarg, it is the approach "whereby a region is understood as a biophysical and social process comprehensible through the operation of laws and time. This can be reinterpreted as having explicit opportunities and constraints for any particular human use. A survey will reveal the most fit locations and processes" (1997a, 321).

McHarg has summarized a framework for ecological planning in the following way:

All systems aspire to survival and success. This state can be described as synthropic-fitness-health. Its antithesis is entropic-misfitness-morbidity. To achieve the first state requires systems to find the fittest environment, adapt it and themselves. Fitness of an environment for a system is defined as that requiring the minimum of work and adaptation. Fitness and fitting are indications of health and the process of fitness is health giving. The quest for fitness is entitled adaptation. Of all the instrumentalities available for man for successful adaptation, cultural adaptation in general and planning in particular, appear to be the most direct and efficacious for maintaining and enhancing human health and wellbeing (1981, 112–113).

Arthur Johnson explained the central principle of this theory in the following way: "The fittest environment for any organism, artifact, natural and social ecosystem, is that environment which provides the [energy] needed to sustain the health or wellbeing of the organism/artifact/ecosystem. Such an approach is not limited by scale. It may be applied to locating plants within a garden as well as to the development of a nation" (1981, 107).

The ecological planning method is primarily a procedure for studying the biophysical and sociocultural systems of a place to reveal where specific land uses may be best practiced. As Ian McHarg has summarized repeatedly in his writings and in many public presentations: "The method defines the best areas for a potential land use at the convergence of all or most of the factors deemed propitious for the use in the absence of all or most detrimental conditions. Areas meeting this standard are deemed intrinsically suitable for the land use under consideration."

As presented in Figure 1, there are 11 interacting steps. An issue or group of related issues is identified by a community—that is, some collection of people—in Step 1. These issues are problematic or present an opportunity to the people or the environment of an area. A goal(s) is then established in Step 2 to address the problem(s). Next, in Steps 3 and 4, inventories and analyses of biophysical and sociocultural processes are conducted, first at a larger level, such as a river drainage basin or an appropriate regional unit of government, and second at a more specific level, such as a small watershed or a local government.

In Step 5, detailed studies are made that link the inventory and analysis information to the problem(s) and goal(s). Suitability analyses are one such type of detailed study. Step 6 involves the development of concepts and options. A landscape plan is then derived from these concepts in Step 7. Throughout the process, a systematic educational and citizen involvement effort occurs. Such involvement is important in each step but especially so in Step 8, when the plan is explained to the affected public. In Step 9, detailed designs are explored that are specific at the individual land-user or site level. These designs and the plan are implemented in Step 10. In Step 11, the plan is administered.

The heavier arrows in Figure 1 indicate the flow from Step 1 to Step 11. Smaller arrows between each step suggest a feedback system whereby each step can modify the previous step and, in turn, change from the subsequent step. The smaller indicate other possible modifications through the process. For instance, detailed

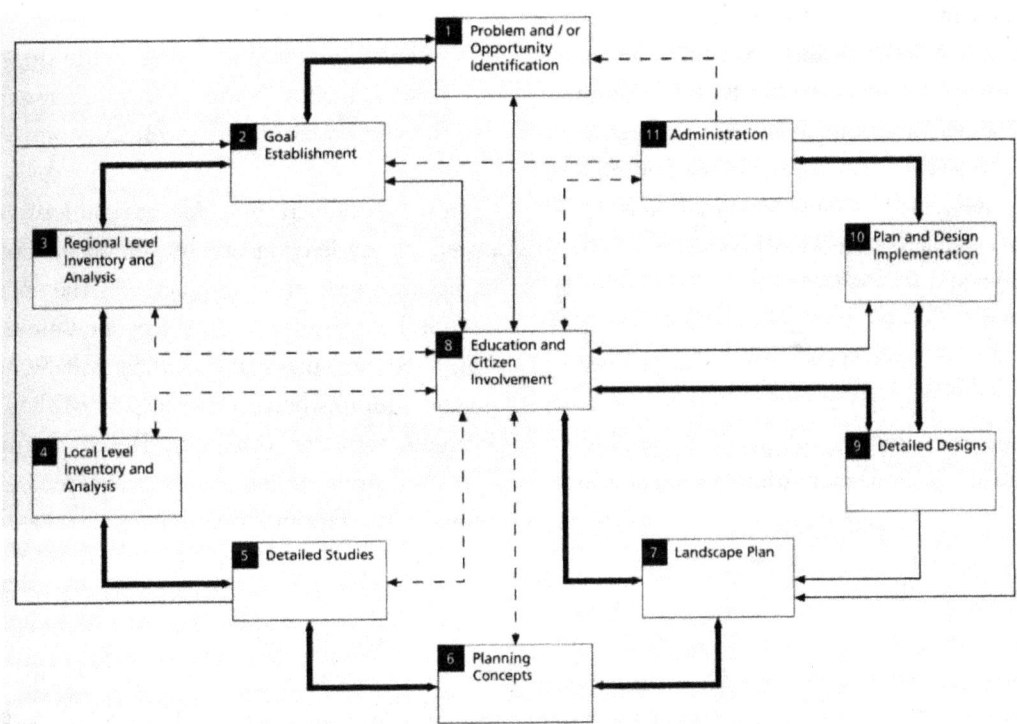

Figure 1. Ecological planning model.

studies of a planning area (Step 5) may lead to the identification of new problems or opportunities or the amendment of goals (Steps 1 and 2). Design explorations (Step 9) may change the landscape plan, and so on. Once the process is complete and the plan is being administered and monitored (Step 11), the view of the problems and opportunities facing the region and the goals to address these problems and opportunities may be altered, as is indicated by the dashed lines in Figure 1.

This process is adapted from the conventional planning process and its many variations (see, for instance, Hall 1975; Roberts 1979; McDowell 1986; Moore 1988; and Stokes et al. 1989, 1997), as well as those suggested specifically for landscape planning (Lovejoy 1973; Fabos 1979; Zube 1980; Marsh 1983; and Duchhart 1989). Unlike some of these other planning processes, design plays an important role in this method. Each step in the process contributes to and is affected by a plan and implementing measures, which may be the official controls of the planning area. The plan and implementing measures may be viewed as the results of the process, although products may be generated from each step.

The approach to ecological planning developed by Ian McHarg at the University of Pennsylvania differs slightly from the one presented here. The Pennsylvania, or McHarg, model places a greater emphasis on inventory, analysis, and synthesis. This one places more emphasis on the establishment of goals, implementation, administration, and public participation, yet does attempt to do so in an ecologically sound manner.

Ecological planning is fundamental for *sustainable development*. The best-known definition of sustainable development was promulgated by the World Commission on Environment and Development (WCED), known as the Bruntland Commission, as that which "meets the needs of the present without compromising the ability of future generations to meet their own needs" (WCED 1987, 8). A more recent definition was provided by the National Commission on the Environment, which has defined sustainable development as

> a strategy for improving the quality of life while preserving the environmental potential for the future, of living off interest rather than consuming natural capital. Sustainable development mandates that the present generation must not narrow the choices of future generations but must strive to expand them by passing on an environment and an accumulation of resources that will allow its children to live at least as well as, and preferably better than, people today. Sustainable development is premised on living within the Earth's means (National Commission on the Environment 1993, 2).

Enzo Scandurra and Alberto Budoni have stated the underlying premise for sustainability especially well and succinctly: "The planet cannot be considered as a gigantic source of unlimited raw materials, neither, equally, as a gigantic dump where we can dispose of all waste from our activities" (1997, 2). The environment is both a source and a sink, but its capacities to provide resources and to assimilate wastes are not limitless.

Timothy Beatley and Kristy Manning (1997) relate sustainable development to ecological planning. They note that "McHargian-style environmental analysis ... [has] become a commonplace methodological step in undertaking almost any form of local planning" (Beatley and

Manning 1997, 86). They also note, however, that although such analyses are "extremely important, ... a more comprehensive and holistic approach is required" (Beatley and Manning 1997, 86). The steps that follow attempt to provide a more comprehensive approach.

STEP 1: IDENTIFICATION OF PLANNING PROBLEMS AND OPPORTUNITIES

Human societies face many social, economic, political, and environmental problems and opportunities. Since a landscape is the interface between social and environmental processes, landscape planning addresses those issues that concern the interrelationship between people and nature. The planet presents many opportunities for people, and there is no shortage of environmental problems.

Problems and opportunities lead to specific planning issues. For instance, suburban development often occurs on prime agricultural land, a circumstance that local officials tend to view as a problem. A number of issues arise involving land-use conflicts between the new suburban residents and the farmers—such as who will pay the costs of public services for the newly developed areas. Another example is an area like an ocean beach or mountain town with the opportunity for new development because of its scenic beauty and recreational amenities. A key challenge would be that of accommodating the new growth while protecting the natural resources that are attracting people to the place.

STEP 2: ESTABLISHMENT OF PLANNING GOALS

In a democracy, the people of a region establish goals through the political process. Elected representatives will identify a particular issue affecting their region—a steel plant is closing, suburban sprawl threatens agricultural land, or a new power plant is creating a housing boom. After issues have been identified, goals are established to address the problem. Such goals should provide the basis for the planning process.

Goals articulate an idealized future situation. In the context of this method, it is assumed that once goals have been established there will be a commitment by some group to address the problem or opportunity identified in Step 1. Problems and opportunities can be identified at various levels. Local people can recognize a problem or opportunity and then set a goal to address it. As well, issues can be national, international, or global in scope. Problem solving, of which goal setting is a part, may occur at many levels or combinations of levels. Although goal setting is obviously dependent on the cultural-political system, the people affected by a goal should be involved in its establishment.

Goal-oriented planning has long been advocated by many community planners. Such an approach has been summarized by Herbert Gans:

> The basic idea behind goal-oriented planning is simple: that planners must begin with the goals of the

Residents and community leaders can help to identify local environmental issues that require future planning.

community—and of its people—and then develop those programs which constitute the best means for achieving the community's goals, taking care that the consequences of these programs do not result in undesirable behavioral or cost consequences (1968, 53).

There are some good examples of goal-oriented planning, such as Oregon's mandatory land-use law (see, for instance, Pease 1984; Eber 1984; DeGrove 1992; and Kelly 1993). However, although locally generated goals are the ideal, too often goals are established by a higher level of government. Many federal and state laws have mandated planning goals for local government, often resulting in the creation of new administrative regions to respond to a particular federal program. These regional agencies must respond to wide-ranging issues that generate specific goals for water and air quality, resource management, energy conservation, transportation, and housing. No matter at what level of government goals are established, information must be collected to help elected representatives resolve underlying issues. Many goals, those which are the focus of this book, require an understanding of biophysical processes.

STEP 3: LANDSCAPE ANALYSIS, REGIONAL LEVEL

This step and the next one involve interrelated scale levels. The method addresses three scale levels: region, locality, and specific site (with an emphasis on the local). The use of different scales is consistent with the concept of levels-of-organization used by ecologists. According to this concept, each level of organization has special properties. Novikoff observed, "What were wholes on one level become parts on a higher one" (1945; as quoted by Quinby 1988). Watersheds have been identified as one level of organization to provide boundaries for landscape and ecosystem analysis. Drainage basins and watersheds have often been advocated as useful levels of analysis for landscape planning and natural resource management (Doornkamp 1982; Young et al. 1983; Steiner 1983; Dickert and Olshansky 1986; Easter et al. 1986; Fox 1987; Erickson 1995; Smith et al. 1997; and Golley 1998). Dunne and Leopold provide a useful explanation of watersheds and drainage basins for ecological planning. They state that the term *drainage basin*

> is synonymous with *watershed* in American usage and with *catchment* in most other countries. The boundary of a *drainage basin* is known as the drainage divide in the United States and as the *watershed* in other countries. Thus the term watershed can mean an area or a line. The drainage basin can vary in size from that of the Amazon River to one of a few square meters drainage into the head of a gully. Any number of drainage basins can be defined in a landscape ... depending on the location of the drainage outlet on some watercourse (Dunne and Leopold 1978, 495).

Essentially, drainage basins and watersheds are the same thing (catchment areas), but in practical use, especially in the United States, the term *drainage basin* is generally used to refer to a larger region and the term *watershed* to a more specific area. Drainage basins cover a river and all of its tributaries, while watersheds generally encompass a single river or stream.

A major aim of landscape analysis is to obtain insight about natural processes. (A. E. Bye)

Richard Lowrance and his colleagues (1986), who have developed a hierarchial approach for agricultural planning, refer to watersheds as the landscape system, or ecologic level, and the larger unit as the regional system, or macroeconomic level. In the Lowrance et al. hierarchy, the two smallest units are the *farm system,* or *microeconomic level,* and *field system,* or *agronomic level.* The analysis at the regional drainage-basin level provides insight into how the landscape functions at the more specific local scale.

Drainage basins and watersheds, however, are seldom practical boundaries for American planners. Political boundaries frequently do not neatly conform with river catchments, and planners commonly work for political entities. There are certainly many examples of plans that are based on drainage basins, such as water quality and erosion control plans. Several federal agencies, such as the U.S. Forest Service (USFS) and the U.S. Natural Resources Conservation Service (NRCS, formerly known as the Soil Conservation Service or SCS), regularly use watersheds as planning units. Planners who work for cities or counties are less likely to be hydrologically bound.

STEP 4: LANDSCAPE ANALYSIS, LOCAL LEVEL

During Step 4, processes taking place in the more specific planning area are studied. The major aim of local-level analysis is to obtain insight about the natural processes and human plans and activities. Such processes can be viewed as the elements of a system, with the landscape a visual expression of the system.

This step in the ecological planning process, like the previous one, involves the collection of information concerning the appropriate physical, biological, and social elements that constitute the planning area. Since cost and time are important factors in many planning processes, existing published and mapped information is the easiest and fastest to gather. If budget and time allow, the inventory and analysis step may be best accomplished by an interdisciplinary team collecting new information. In either case, this step is an interdisciplinary collection effort that involves search, accumulation, field checking, and mapping of data.

Ian McHarg and his collaborators have developed a layer-cake model (Figure 2) that provides a central group of biophysical elements for the inventory or chorography of the place. Categories include the earth, the surface terrain, groundwater, surface water, soils, climate, vegetation, wildlife, and people (Table 1). UNESCO, in its Man and the Biosphere Programme, has developed a more exhaustive list of possible inventory elements (Table 2).

Land classification systems are valuable for analysis at this stage because they may allow the planner to aggregate specific information into general groupings. Such systems are based on inventoried data and on needs for analysis. Many government agencies in the United States and elsewhere have developed land classification systems that are helpful. The NRCS, USFS, the

ESSENTIAL READINGS IN URBAN PLANNING

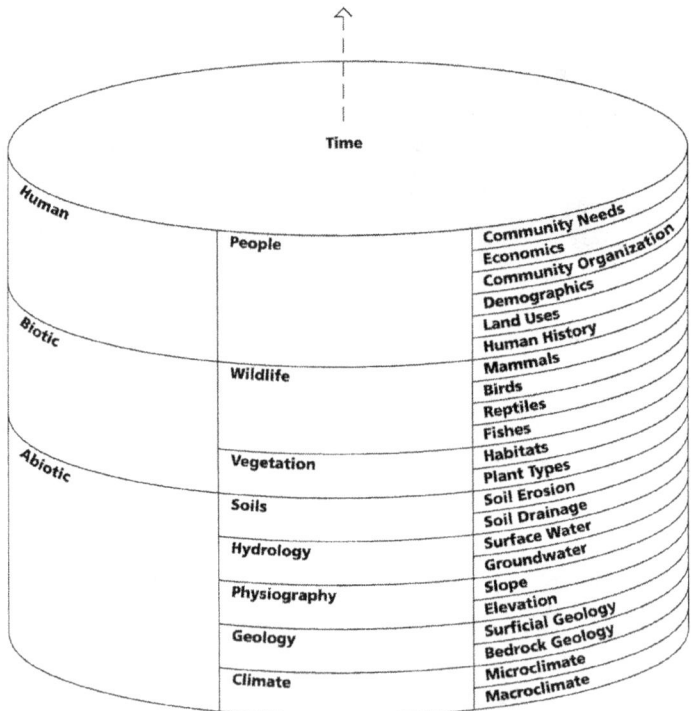

Figure 2. Layer-cake model. (Source: Adapted from Ian McHarg and drawn by Mookesh Patel)

Table 1. Baseline Natural Resource
Data Necessary for Ecological Planning

The following natural resource factors are likely to be of significance in planning. Clearly the region under study will determine the relevant factors, but many are likely to occur in all studies.

CLIMATE. Temperature, humidity, precipitation, wind velocity, wind direction, wind duration, first and last frosts, snow, frost, fog, inversions, hurricanes, tornadoes, tsunamis, typhoons, Chinook winds

GEOLOGY. Rocks, ages, formations, plans, sections, properties, seismic activity, earthquakes, rock slides, mud slides, subsidence

SURFICIAL GEOLOGY. Karnes, kettles, eskers, moraines, drift and till

GROUNDWATER HYDROLOGY. Geological formations interpreted as aquifers with well locations, well logs, water quantity and quality, water table

PHYSIOGRAPHY. Physiographic regions, subregions, features, contours, sections, slopes, aspect, insolation, digital terrain model(s)

SURFICIAL HYDROLOGY. Oceans, lakes, deltas, rivers, streams, creeks, marshes, swamps, wetlands, stream orders, density, discharges, gauges, water quality, floodplains

SOILS. Soil associations, soil series, properties, depth to seasonal high water table, depth to bedrock, shrink-swell, compressive strength, cation and anion exchange, acidity-alkalinity

VEGETATION. Associations, communities, species, composition, distribution, age and conditions, visual quality, species number, rare and endangered species, fire history, successional history

WILDLIFE. Habitats, animal populations, census data, rare and endangered species, scientific and educational value

HUMAN. Ethnographic history, settlement patterns, existing land use, existing infrastructure, economic activities, population characteristics

Source: Adapted from McHarg 1997b.

Table 2. UNESCO Total Environmental Checklist: Components and Processes

Natural Environment—Components

Soil	Energy resources		
Water	Fauna		
Atmosphere	Flora		
Mineral resources	Microorganisms		

Natural Environment—Processes

Biogeochemical cycles	Fluctuations in animal and plant growth
Irradiation	Changes in soil fertility, salinity, alkalinity
Climatic processes	
Photosynthesis	
Animal and plant growth	Host/parasite interactions, and epidemic processes

Human Population—Demographic Aspects

Population structure:	Population size
• Age	Population density
• Ethnicity	Fertility and mortality rates
• Economic	Health statistics
• Education	
• Occupation	

Human Activities and the Use of Machines

Migratory movements	Mining
Daily mobility	Industrial activities
Decision making	Commercial activities
Exercise and distribution of authority	Military activities
Administration	Transportation
Farming, fishing	Recreational activities
	Crime rates

Societal Groupings

Governmental groupings	Information media
Industrial groupings	Law-keeping media
Commercial groupings	Health services
Political groupings	Community groupings
Religious groupings	
Educational groupings	Family groupings

Products of Labor

The built-up environment:	Food
• Buildings	Pharmaceutical products
• Roads	
• Railways	Machines
• Parks	Other commodities

Culture

Values	Technology
Beliefs	Literature
Attitudes	Laws
Knowledge	Economic system
Information	

Source: Boyden 1979.

U.S. Fish and Wildlife Service (USFWS), and the U.S. Geological Survey (USGS) are agencies that have been notably active in land classification systems. However, there is not a consistency of data sources even in the United States. In urban areas, a planner may be overwhelmed with data for inventory and analysis. In remote rural areas, on the other hand, even a Natural Resources Conservation Service survey may not exist, or the survey may be old and unusable. An even larger problem is that there is little or no consistency in scale or in the terminology used among various agencies. A recommendation of the National Agricultural Lands Study (1981) was that a statistical protocol for federal agencies concerning land resource information be developed and led by the Office of Federal Statistical Policy and Standards. One helpful system that has been developed for land classification is the USGS Land-Use and Land-Cover Classification System (Table 3).

The ability of the landscape planner and ecosystem manager to inventory biophysical processes may be uneven, but it is far better than their capability to assess human ecosystems. An understanding of human ecology may provide a key to sociocultural inventory and analysis. Since humans are living things, *human ecology* may be thought of as an expansion of ecology—of how humans interact with each other and their environments. Interaction then is used as both a basic concept and an explanatory device. As

Table 3. U.S. Geological Survey Land-Use and Land-Cover Classification System for Use with Remote Sensor Data

Level I	Level II
1 Urban or built-up land	11 Residential
	12 Commercial and services
	13 Industrial
	14 Transportation, communications, and services
	15 Industrial and commercial complexes
	16 Mixed urban or built-up land
	17 Other urban or built-up land
2 Agricultural land	21 Cropland and pasture
	22 Orchards, groves, vineyards, nurseries, and ornamental horticultural
	23 Confined feeding operations
	24 Other agricultural land
3 Rangeland	31 Herbaceous rangeland
	32 Shrub and brush rangeland
	33 Mixed rangeland
4 Forestland	41 Deciduous forestland
	42 Evergreen forestland
	43 Mixed forestland
5 Water	51 Streams and canals
	52 Lakes
	53 Reservoirs
	54 Bays and estuaries
6 Wetland	61 Forested wetland
	62 Nonforested wetland
7 Barren land	71 Dry salt flats
	72 Beaches
	73 Sandy areas other than beaches
	74 Bare exposed rocks
	75 Strip mines, quarries, and gravel pits
	76 Transitional areas
	77 Mixed barren land
8 Tundra	81 Shrub and brush tundra
	82 Herbaceous tundra
	83 Bare ground
	84 Mixed tundra
9 Perennial snow ice	91 Perennial snowfields
	92 Glaciers

Source: Anderson et al. 1976.

Gerald Young (1974, 1978, 1983, 1989), who has illustrated the pan-disciplinary scope of human ecology, noted:

> In human ecology, the way people interact with each other and with the environment is definitive of a number of basic relationships. Interaction provides a measure of belonging, it affects identity versus alienation, including alienation from the environment. The system of obligation, responsibility and liability is defined through interaction. The process has become definitive of the public interest as opposed to private interests which prosper in the spirit of independence (1976, 294).

STEP 5: DETAILED STUDIES

Detailed studies link the inventory and analysis information to the problem(s) and goal(s). One example of such studies is *suitability analysis*. As explained by Ian McHarg (1969), suitability analyses can be used to determine the fitness of a specific place for a variety of land uses based on thorough ecological inventories and on the values of land users. The basic purpose of the detailed studies is to gain an understanding about the complex relationships between human values, environmental opportunities and constraints, and the issues being addressed. To accomplish this, it is crucial to link the studies to the local situation. As a result, a variety of scales may be used to explore linkages.

A simplified suitability analysis process is provided in Figure 3. There are several techniques that may be used to accomplish suitability analysis. Again, it was McHarg who popularized the "overlay technique" (1969). This technique involves maps of inventory

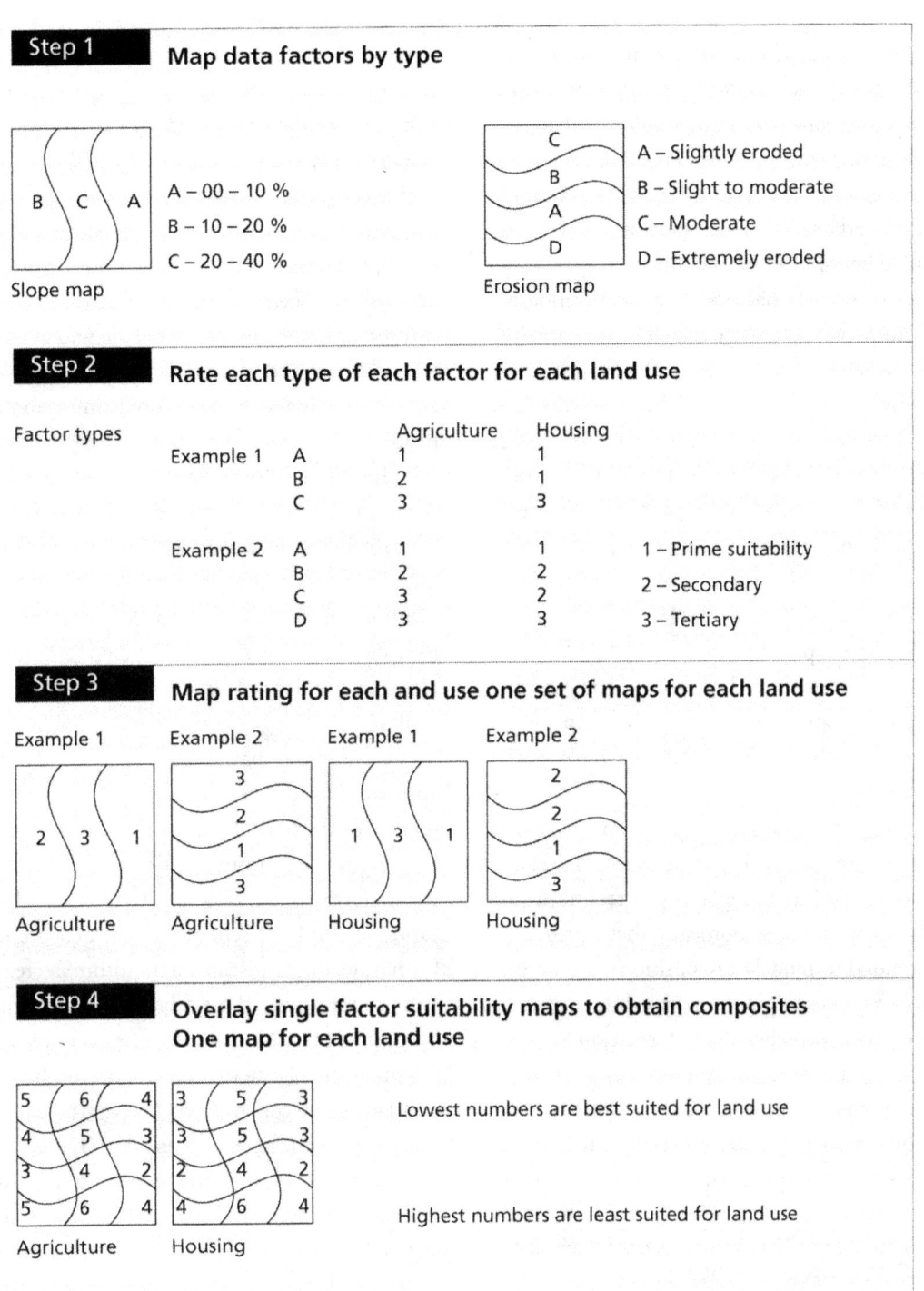

Figure 3. Suitability analysis procedure.

information superimposed on one another to identify areas that provide, first, opportunities for particular land uses and, second, constraints (Johnson, Berger, and McHarg 1979). Bruce MacDougall (1975) has criticized the accuracy of map overlays and made suggestions on how they may be made more accurate.

Although there has been a general tendency away from hand-drawn overlays, there are still occasions when they may be useful. For instance, they may be helpful for small study sites within a larger region or for certain scales of project planning. It is important to realize the limitations of hand-drawn overlays. As an example, after more than three or four overlays, they may become opaque; there are the accuracy problems identified by MacDougall (1975) and others that become especially acute with hand-drawn maps; and there are limitations for weighting various values represented by map units. Computer technology may help to overcome these limitations.

Numerous computer program systems, called *geographic information systems* (GIS), have been developed that replace the technique of hand-drawn overlays. Some of these programs are intended to model only positions of environmental processes or phenomena, while others are designed as comprehensive information storage, retrieval, and evaluation systems. These systems are intended to improve efficiency and economy in information handling, especially for large or complex planning projects.

STEP 6: PLANNING AREA CONCEPTS, OPTIONS, AND CHOICES

This step involves the development of concepts for the planning area. These concepts can be viewed as options for the future based on the suitabilities for the use(s) that give a general conceptual model or scenario of how problems may be solved. This model should be presented in such a way that the goals will be achieved. Often more than one scenario has to be made. These concepts are based on a logical and imaginative combination of the information gathered through the inventory and analysis steps. The conceptual model shows allocations of uses and actions. The scenarios set possible directions for future management of the area and therefore should be viewed as a basis for discussion where choices are made by the community about its future.

Choices should be based on the goals of the planning effort. For example, if it is the goal to protect agricultural land, yet allow some low-density housing to develop, different organizations of the environment for those two land uses should be developed. Different schemes for realizing the desired preferences also need to be explored.

The Dutch have devised an interesting approach to developing planning options for their agricultural land reallocation projects. Four land-use options are developed, each with the preferred scheme for a certain point of view. Optional land-use schemes of the area are made for nature and landscape, agriculture, recreation, and urbanization. These schemes are constructed by groups of citizens working with government scientists and planners. To illustrate, for the nature and landscape scheme, landscape architects and ecologists from the *Staatsbosbeheer* (Dutch Forest Service) work with citizen environmental action groups. For agriculture, local extension agents and soil scientists work with farm commodity organizations and farmer cooperatives. Similar coalitions are formed for recreation and urbanization. What John Friedmann (1973) calls a *dialogue process* begins at the point where each of the individual schemes is constructed. The groups come together for mutual learning so that a consensus of opinion can be reached through debate and discussion.

Various options for implementation also need to be explored, which must relate to the goal of the planning effort. If, for example, the planning is being conducted for a jurisdiction trying to protect its agricultural land resources, then it is necessary not only to identify lands that should be protected but also the implementation options that might be employed to achieve the farmland protection goal.

STEP 7: LANDSCAPE PLAN

The preferred concepts and options are brought together in a landscape plan. The plan gives a strategy for development at the local scale. The plan provides flexible guidelines for policymakers, land managers, and land users on how to conserve, rehabilitate, or develop an area. In such a plan, enough freedom should be left so that local officials and land users can adjust their practices to new economic demands or social changes.

This step represents a key decision-making point in the planning process. Responsible officials, such as county commissioners or city council members, are often required by law to adopt a plan. The rules for adoption and forms that the plans may take vary widely. Commonly in the United States, planning commissions recommend a plan for adoption to the legislative body after a series of public hearings. Such plans are called *comprehensive plans* in much of the United States but are referred to as *general plans* in Arizona, California, and Utah. In some states (like Oregon) there are specific, detailed elements that local governments are required to include in such plans. Other states permit much flexibility to local officials for the contents of these plans. On public lands, various federal agencies, including the USFS, the U.S. National Park Service (NPS), and the U.S. Bureau of Land Management (BLM), have specific statutory requirement for land management plans.

The term *landscape plan* is used here to emphasize that such plans should incorporate natural and social considerations. A landscape plan is more than a land-use plan because it addresses the overlap and integration of land uses. A landscape plan may involve the formal recognition of previous elements in the planning process, such as the adoption of policy goals. The plan should include written statements about policies and implementation strategies as well as a map showing the spatial organization of the landscape.

STEP 8: CONTINUED CITIZEN INVOLVEMENT AND COMMUNITY EDUCATION

In Step 8, the plan is explained to the affected public through education and information dissemination. Actually, such interaction occurs throughout the planning process, beginning with the identification of issues. Public involvement is especially crucial as the landscape plan is developed, because it is important to ensure that the goals established by the community will be achieved in the plan.

The success of a plan depends largely on how much people affected by the plan have been involved in its determination. There are numerous examples of both government agencies and private businesses suddenly announcing a plan for a project that will dramatically impact people, without first having consulted those individuals. The result is predictable—the people will rise in opposition against the project. The alternative is to involve people in the planning process, soliciting their ideas and incorporating those ideas into the plan. Doing so may require a longer time to develop a plan, but local citizens will be more likely to support it than to oppose it and will often monitor its execution.

STEP 9: DESIGN EXPLORATIONS

To design is to give form and to arrange elements spatially. By making specific designs based on the landscape plan, planners can help decision makers visualize the consequences of their policies. Carrying policies through to arranging the physical environment gives meaning to the process by actually conceiving change in the spatial organization of a place. Designs represent a synthesis of all the previous planning studies. During the design step, the short-term benefits for the land users or individual citizen have to be combined with the long-term economic and ecological goals for the whole area.

Since the middle 1980s, several architects have called for a return to traditional principles in community design. These "neotraditionals" or "new urbanists" include Peter Calthorpe, Elizabeth Plater-Zyberk, Andres Duany, Elizabeth Moule, and Stefanos Polyzoides. Meanwhile, other architects and landscape architects have advocated more ecological, more sustainable design; these include John Lyle, Robert Thayer, Sim Van der Ryn, Carol Franklin, Colin Franklin, Leslie Jones Sauer, Rolf Sauer, and Pliny Fisk. Michael and Judith Corbett with others helped merge these two strains in the Ahwahnee Principles (Local Government Commission 1991; Calthorpe et al. 1998). (See Table 4.)

Ecological design, according to David Orr, is "the capacity to understand the ecological context in which humans live, to recognize limits, and to get the scale of things right" (1994, 2). Or, as Sim Van der Ryn and Stuart Cowan note, ecological design seeks to "make nature visible" (1996, 16). These principles provide clear guidance for ecological design (see also Grant et al. 1996, Beatley and Manning 1997). While some designers and planners might object to the placement of design within the planning process, in an ecological perspective such placement helps to connect design with more comprehensive social actions and policies.

STEP 10: PLAN AND DESIGN IMPLEMENTATION

Implementation is the employment of various strategies, tactics, and procedures to realize the goals and policies adopted in the landscape plan. The Ahwahnee Principles provide guidelines for implementation (Table 4). On the local level, several different mechanisms have been developed to control the use of land and other resources. These techniques include voluntary covenants, easements, land purchase, transfer of development rights, zoning, utility extension policies, and performance standards. The preference selected should be appropriate for the region. For instance, in urban areas like King County, Washington, and Suffolk County, New York, traditional zoning has not proved effective for protecting farmland. The citizens of these counties have therefore elected to tax themselves to purchase farmland preservation easements from farmers. In more rural counties like Whitman County, Washington, and Black Hawk County, Iowa, local leaders have found traditional zoning effective.

One implementation technique especially well suited for ecological planning is the use of performance standards. Like many other planning implementation measures, *performance standards* is a general term that has been defined and applied in several different ways. Basically, performance standards, or criteria, are established and must be met before a certain use will be permitted. These criteria usually involve a combination of economic, environmental, and social factors. This technique lends itself to ecological planning because criteria for specific land uses can be based on suitability analysis.

Table 4. The Ahwahnee Principles

Preamble:
Existing patterns of urban and suburban development seriously impair our quality of life. The symptoms are: more congestion and air pollution resulting from our increased dependence on automobiles, the loss of precious open space, the need for costly improvements to roads and public services, the inequitable distribution of economic resources, and the loss of a sense of community. By drawing upon the best from the past and the present, we can plan communities that will more successfully serve the needs of those who live and work within them. Such planning should adhere to certain fundamental principles.

Community Principles:
1. All planning should be in the form of complete and integrated communities containing housing, shops, work places, schools, parks, and civic facilities essential to the daily life of the residents.
2. Community size should be designed so that housing, jobs, daily needs, and other activities are within easy walking distance of each other.
3. As many activities as possible should be located within easy walking distance of transit stops.
4. A community should contain a diversity of housing types to enable citizens from a wide range of economic levels and age groups to live within its boundaries.
5. Businesses within the community should provide a range of job types for the community's residents.
6. The location and character of the community should be consistent with a larger transit network.
7. The community should have a center focus that combines commercial, civic, cultural, and recreational uses.
8. The community should contain an ample supply of specialized open space in the form of squares, greens, and parks whose frequent use is encouraged through placement and design.
9. Public spaces should be designed to encourage the attention and presence of people at all hours of the day and night.
10. Each community or cluster of communities should have a well defined edge, such as agricultural greenbelts or wildlife corridors, permanently protected from development.
11. Streets, pedestrian paths, and bike paths should contribute to a system of fully-connected and interesting routes to all destinations. Their design should encourage pedestrian and bicycle use by being small and spatially defined by buildings, trees and lighting; and by discouraging high-speed traffic.

Regional Principles:
1. The regional structure should be integrated within a larger transportation network built around transit rather than freeways.
2. Regions should be bounded by and provide a continuous system of greenbelt/wildlife corridors to be determined by natural conditions.
3. Regional institutions and services (government, stadiums, museums, etc.) should be located within the urban core.

Implementation Strategies:
1. The general plan should be updated to incorporate the above principles.
2. Rather than allowing for developer-initiated, piecemeal development, a local government should initiate the planning of new and changing communities within its jurisdiction through an open planning process.
3. Prior to any development, a specific plan should be used to define communities where new growth, infill, or redevelopment would be allowed to occur. With the adoption of specific plans, complying projects can proceed with minimal delay.
4. Plans should be developed through an open process and in the process should be provided illustrated models of the proposed design.

Source: Calthorpe et al. 1998.

STEP 11: ADMINISTRATION

In this final step, the plan is administered. *Administration* involves monitoring and evaluating how the plan is implemented on an ongoing basis. Amendments or adjustments to the plan will no doubt be necessary because of changing conditions or new information. To achieve the goals established for the process, planners should pay special attention to the design of regulation review procedures and of the management of the decision-making process.

Administration may be accomplished by a commission comprising citizens with or without the support of a professional staff. Citizens should play an important role in administering local planning through commissions and review boards that oversee local ordinances. To a large degree, the success of citizens' boards and commissions depends on the extent of their involvement in the development of the plans that they manage. Again, Oregon provides an excellent example of the use of citizens to administer a plan. The Land Conservation and Development Commission (LCDC), comprising seven members who are appointed by the governor and supported by its professional staff, is responsible for overseeing the implementation of the state land-use planning law. Another group of citizens, 1000 Friends of Oregon, monitors the administration of the law. The support that the law has received from the public is evidenced by the defeat of several attempts to abolish mandatory statewide land-use planning in Oregon. However, as Department of Land Conservation and Development (DLCD) staff member Ron Eber observes, "It is a myth that planning is easy in Oregon—it is a battle every day!" (personal communication 1999). For example, in the early 1990s, a counterforce to 1000 Friends of Oregon was organized; "Oregonians in Action" is a property-rights group that is opposed to the progressive statewide planning program.

WORKING PLANS

A method is necessary as an organizational framework for landscape planners. Also, a relatively standard method presents the opportunity to compare and analyze case studies. To adequately fulfill responsibilities to protect the public health, safety, and welfare, the actions of planners should be based on a knowledge of what has and has not worked in other settings and situations. A large body of case study results can provide an empirical foundation for planners. A common method is helpful for both practicing planners and scholars who should probe and criticize the nuances of such a method in order to expand and improve its utility.

The following chapters are organized roughly parallel to the method. The identification of planning problems and opportunities is not discussed independently because it is assumed that once an issue has been defined, a process such as the one described here will be triggered. In addition, many of the techniques described in the next chapter can be used to both define issues and establish goals. Also, there are no separate discussions of regional- and local-level ecological inventories (Steps 3 and 4) because the techniques used are similar. Instead, there are separate detailed descriptions of inventories and analyses of the biophysical environment and the human community.

The approach suggested here should be viewed as a working method. The pioneering forester Gifford Pinchot advocated a conservation approach to the planning of the national forests. His approach was both utilitarian and protectionist, and he believed "wise use and preservation of all forest resources were compatible" (Wilkinson and Anderson 1985, 22). To implement this philosophy, Pinchot in his position as chief of the U.S. Forest Service required "working plans." Such plans recognized the dynamic, living nature of forests. In the same vein, the methods used to develop plans should be viewed as a living process. However, this is not meant to imply that there should be no structure to planning methods. Rather, working planning methods should be viewed as something analogous to a jazz composition: not a fixed score but a palette that invites improvisation.

The method offered here has a landscape ecological—specifically, human ecological—bias. As noted by the geographer Donald W. Meinig, "Environment sustains us as creatures; landscape displays us as cultures" (1979, 3). As an artifact of culture, landscapes are an appropriate focus of planners faced with land-use and environmental management issues. Ecology provides insight into landscape patterns, processes, and interactions. An understanding of ecology reveals how we interact with each other and our natural and built environments. What we know of such relationships is still relatively limited, but it is expanding all the time. As Ilya Prigogine and Isabelle Stengers have observed, "Nature speaks in a thousand voices, and we have only begun to listen" (1984, 77).

REFERENCES

Alinsky, Saul D. 1946. Reveille for radicals. Chicago, Illinois: University of Chicago Press.

Arendt, Randall G. 1996. Conservation design for subdivisions: a practical guide to creating open space networks. Washington, D.C.: Island Press.

Beatley, Timothy, and Kristy Manning. 1997. The ecology of place: planning for environment, economy, and community. Washington, D.C.: Island Press.

Bentham, Jeremy. 1887. Theory of legislation (5th ed.).

Berger, Jonathan, and John W. Sinton. 1985. Water, earth, and fire. Baltimore, Maryland: Johns Hopkins University Press.

Berry, Wendell. 1972. A continuous harmony, essays cultural and agricultural. New York: Harcourt Brace Jovanovich.

Calthorpe, Peter. 1993. The next American metropolis: ecology, community and the American dream. Princeton, New Jersey: Princeton Architectural Press.

Calthorpe, Peter, Michael Corbett, Andres Duany, Elizabeth Plater-Zyberk, Stefanos Polyzoides, Elizabeth Moule with Judy Corbett, Peter Katz, and Steve Weissman. 1998. "The Ahwahnee Principles." In Creating sustainable places symposium, Audrey Brichetto Morris ed., pp. 3–6. Tempe, Arizona: Herberger Center for Design Excellence, Arizona State University.

DeGrove, John M., 1992. The new state frontier for land-use policy: planning and growth management in the States. Cambridge: Massachusetts: Lincoln Institute of Land Policy.

Dickert, Thomas, and Robert B. Olshansky. 1986. "Evaluating erosion susceptibility for land- use planning in coastal watersheds." Coastal Zone Management 13(3⁄4): 309–333.

Doornkamp, John C. 1982. "The physical basis for planning in the Third World, IV: regional planning." Third World Planning Review 4(2):111–118.

Duchhart, Ingrid. 1989. Manual on environment and urban development. Nairobi, Kenya: Ministry of Local Government and Physical Planning.

Dunne, Thomas, and Luna B. Leopold. 1978. Water in environmental planning. New York: W. H. Freeman.

Easter, William K., John A. Dixon, and Maynard M. Hufschmidt (eds.). 1986. Watershed resource management. Boulder, Colorado: Westview Press.

Eber, Ronald. 1984. "Oregon's agricultural land protection program." In Protecting farmlands, Frederick R. Steiner and John E. Theilacker eds., pp. 161–171. Westport, Connecticut: AVI Publishing Company.

Eber, Ronald. 1999. (Telephone interview, 13 January.) Salem, Oregon: Department of Land Conservation and Development.

Erickson, Donna L. 1995. "Rural land- use and land-cover change: implications for local planning in the River Raisin watershed (USA)." Land Use Policy 12:223–236.

Fabos, Julius Gy., 1979. Planning the total landscape. Boulder, Colorado: Westview Press.

Friedmann, John. 1973. Retracking America. Garden City, New York: Anchor Press/Doubleday.

Fox, Jeff. 1987. "Two roles for natural scientists in the management of tropical watersheds: examples from Nepal and Indonesia." Environmental Professional 9:59–66.

Friedmann, John. 1973. Retracking America. Garden City, New York: Anchor Press/Doubleday.

Gans, Herbert J., 1968. People and plans. New York: Basic Books.

Glikson, Artur. 1971. The ecological basis of planning. The Hague, The Netherlands: Matinus Nijhoff.

Golley, Frank B. 1998. A primer for environmental literacy. New Haven, Connecticut: Yale University Press.

Gore, Al. 1992. Earth in the balance: ecology and the human spirit. New York: Houghton Mifflin Company.

Grant, Jill, Patricia Manuel, and Darrell Joudrey. 1996. "A framework for planning sustainable residential landscapes." Journal of the American Planning Association 62(3):331–344.

Hall, Peter. 1975. Urban and regional planning. New York: Halsted Press/John Wiley & Sons.

Hills, G. A. 1961. The ecological basis for land- use planning (Research Report No. 46). Toronto, Ontario: Ontario Department of Lands and Forests.

Hough, Michael. 1995. Cities and natural processes. London and New York: Routledge.

Humbach, John A. 1989. "Law and a new land ethic." Minnesota Law Review 74:339–370.

Johnson, Arthur H. 1981. "Guest editorial: human ecological planning—methods and studies." Landscape Planning 8:107–108.

Johnson, Arthur H., Jonathan Berger, and Ian L. McHarg. 1979. "A case study in ecological planning: the Woodlands, Texas." In Planning the uses and management of land, Marvin T. Beatty, Gary W. Petersen, and Lester D. Swindale eds., pp. 935–955. Madison, Wisconsin: American Society of Agronomy, Crop Science Society of America, and Soil Science Society of America.

Kelly, Eric Damian. 1993. Managing community growth: policies, techniques and impacts. Westport, Connecticut: Praeger.

Laslett, Peter (ed.). 1988. John Locke: two treatises of government (student ed.). Cambridge, England: Cambridge University Press.

Leopold, Aldo. 1933. "The conservation ethic." The Journal of Forestry 31(6):634–643.

Leopold, Aldo. 1949. A Sand County almanac and sketches here and there. New York: Oxford.

Lewis, Philip H. 1969. "The inland water tree." American Institute of Architects Journal 51(6):59–63.

Local Government Commission. 1991. The Ahwahnee principles. Sacramento, California.

Lovejoy, Derek (ed.). 1973. Land use and landscape planning. New York: Barnes & Noble.

Lowrance, Richard, Paul F. Hendrix, and Eugene P. Odum. 1986. "A hierarchical approach to sustainable agriculture." American Journal of Alternative Agriculture 1(4):169–173.

Lyle, John Tillman. 1994. Regenerative design for sustainable development. New York: John Wiley & Sons.

MacKaye, Benton. 1940. "Regional planning and ecology." Ecological Monographs 10(3):349–353.

Marsh, William M. 1983. Landscape Planning. Reading: Massachusetts: Addison-Wesley.

McDowell, Bruce D. 1986. "Approaches to planning." In The practice of state and regional planning, Frank S. So, Irving Hand, and Bruce D. McDowell eds., pp. 3–22. Chicago, Illinois: American Planning Association.

McHarg, Ian L. 1968. "A comprehensive highway routesection method." Highway Research Record 246:1–15.

McHarg, Ian L. 1969. Design with nature. Garden City, New York: Doubleday/The Natural History Press. (1992. 2nd ed.) New York: John Wiley & Sons.

McHarg, Ian L. 1981. "Human ecological planning at Pennsylvania." Landscape Planning 8:109–120.

McHarg, Ian L. 1996. A quest for life. New York: John Wiley & Sons.

McHarg, Ian L. 1997a. "Ecology and design." In Ecological design and planning, George F. Thompson and Frederick Steiner eds., pp. 321–332. New York: John Wiley & Sons.

McHarg, Ian L. 1997b. "Natural factors in planning." Journal of Soil and Water Conservation 52(1):13–17.

McHarg, Ian L., and Frederick R. Steiner (eds.). 1998. To heal the earth: selected writings of Ian L. McHarg. Washington, D.C.: Island Press.

Meinig, D. W. 1979. "Introduction." In The interpretation of ordinary landscapes, D. W. Meinig ed., pp. 1–7. New York: Oxford University.

Moore, Terry. 1988. "Planning without preliminaries." Journal of the American Planning Association 54(4):525–528.

Mumford, Lewis. 1944. The condition of man. New York: Harcourt, Brace and Company.

Mumford, Lewis. 1961. The city in history: its origins, its transformations and its prospects. New York: Harcourt, Brace, and World.

National Agricultural Lands Study. 1981. Final report. Washington, D.C.: U.S. Department of Agriculture and Council on Environmental Quality.

National Commission on the Environment. 1993. Choosing a sustainable future. Washington, D.C.: Island Press.

Novikoff, A. B. 1945. "The concept of integrative levels and biology." Science 101:209–215.

Opie, John. 1998. Nature's nation: an environmental history of the United States. Fort Worth, Texas: Harcourt Brace & Company.

Palazzo, Danilo. 1997. Sulle spalle di giganti. Le matrici della pianificazione ambientale negli Stati Uniti. Milano, Italy: FrancoAngeli/DST.

Orr, David W. 1994. Earth in mind: on education, environment, and the human prospect. Washington, D.C.: Island Press.

Pease, James R. 1984. "Oregon's land conservation and development program." In Planning for the conservation and development of land resources, Frederick R. Steiner and Hubert N. van Lier eds., pp. 253–271. Amsterdam, The Netherlands: Elsevier Scientific Publishing.

President's Council on Sustainable Development. 1996. Sustainable America: a new consensus for prosperity, opportunity, and a healthy environment for the future Washington, D.C.: U.S. Government Printing Office.

Prigogine, Ilya, and Isabelle Stengers. 1984. Order out of chaos. New York: Bantam Books.

Ricklefs, Robert E. 1973. Ecology. Newton, Massachusetts: Chiron Press.

Roberts, John C. 1979. "Principles of land use planning." In Planning the uses and management of land, Marvin T. Beatty, Gary W. Petersen, and Lester D. Swindale eds., pp. 47–63. Madison, Wisconsin: American Society of Agronomy, Crop Science Society of America, and Soil Science Society of America.

Scandurra, Enzo, and Silvia Macchi (eds.). 1995. Ambiente e pianificazione: lessico per le scienze urbane e territoriali. Rome, Italy: Etas Libri.

Scandurra, Enzo, and Alberto Budoni. 1997. "For a critical revision of the concept of sustainable development: ten years after the Brundtland report." Paper presented to the 20th Annual Meeting, 30 May- 1 June, Northeast Regional Science Association, Boston, Massachusetts.

Slocombe, D. Scott. 1998a. "Lessons from experience with ecosystem-based management." Landscape and Urban Planning 40:31–39.

Smith, Daniel S., and Paul Cawood Helmund (eds.). 1993. Ecology of greenways: design and function of linear conservation areas. Minneapolis, Minnesota: University of Minnesota Press.

Smith, Tony, Brian Trushinski, Jim Willis, and Gord Lemon. 1997. The Laurel Creek watershed study. Waterloo, Ontario: Grand River Conservation Authority, and City of Waterloo.

Soesilo, Andy J., and K. David Pijawka. 1998. "Hazardous waste planning." In Encyclopedia of environmental analysis and remediation, Robert A. Meyers ed., pp. 2072–2090. New York: John Wiley & Sons.

Spirn, Anne Whiston. 1984. The granite garden. New York: Basic Books.

Steiner, Frederick. 1983. "Resource suitability: methods for analyses." Environmental Management 7(5):401–420.

Stokes, Samuel N., A. Elizabeth Watson, Genevieve P. Keller, and J. Timothy Keller. 1989. Saving America's countryside. Baltimore, Maryland: Johns Hopkins University Press.

Stokes, Samuel N., A. Elizabeth Watson, and Shelley Mastran. 1997. Saving America's countryside: a guide to rural conservation (2d ed.). Baltimore, Maryland: Johns Hopkins University Press.

Tarlet, Jean. 1985. La planification écologique: méthodes et techniques. Paris: Economica.

Tarlet, Jean. 1997. Intégration des données de l'environnement naturel dans l'aménagement et la gestion de l'espace par la méthode de planification écologique. Aix Marseille, France: Université de Provence.

Thayer, Robert L., Jr. 1994. Gray world, green heart: technology, nature, and the sustainable landscape. New York: John Wiley & Sons.

Van der Ryn, Sim, and Stuart Cowan. 1996. Ecological design. Washington, D.C.: Island Press.

Wilkinson, Charles F., and H. Michael Anderson. 1985. "Land and resource planning in national forests." Oregon Law Review 64(1 & 2):1–373.

Young, Gerald L. 1974. "Human ecology as an interdisciplinary concept: a critical inquiry." Advances in Ecological Research 8:1–105.

Young, Gerald L. 1976. "Environmental law: perspectives from human ecology." Environmental Law 6(2):289–307.

Young, Gerald L. 1978. Human ecology as an interdisciplinary domain: an epistemological bibliography. Monticello, Illinois: Vance Bibliographies.

Young, Gerald L. 1989. "A conceptual framework for an interdisciplinary human ecology." Acta Oecologiae Hominis 1:1–136.

Young, Gerald L. (ed.). 1983. Origins of human ecology. Stroudsburg, Pennsylvania: Hutchinson Ross Publishing. Young, Gerald L., Frederick Steiner, Kenneth Brooks, and Kenneth Struckmeyer. 1983. "Determining the regional context for landscape planning." Landscape Planning 10(4):269–296.

Zube, Ervin H. 1980. Environmental evaluation. Monterey, California: Brooks/Cole.

DESIGN WITH NATURE

CHAPTER 13: *The Metropolitan Region*

BY IAN L. MCHARG

A city occupies an area of land and operates a form of government; the metropolitan area also occupies an area of land but constitutes the sum of many levels and forms of government. It is united neither by government, planning nor the expression of these. While the name has been coined to describe the enlargement of the older city, it is appropriate to observe that this is more a convenience for cartographers than a social organism. Yet the coalescence of sepia blotches exists, encircling the city.

The American dream envisioned only the single-family house, the smiling wife and healthy children, the two-car garage, eye- level oven, foundation planting and lawn, the school nearby and the church of your choice. It did not see that a subdivision is not a community, that the sum of subdivisions that make a suburb is not a community, that the sum of suburbs that compose the metropolitan fringe of the city does not constitute community nor does a metropolitan region. It did not see that the nature that awaited the subdivider was vastly different from the pock-marked landscape of ranch and split-level houses.

And so the transformation from city to metropolitan area contains all the thwarted hopes of those who fled the old city in search of clean government, better schools, a more beneficent, healthy and safe environment, those who sought to escape slums, congestion, crime, violence and disease.

There are many problems caused by the form of metropolitan growth—the lack of institution which diminishes the power to effect even local decisions, the trauma that is the journey to work,

---

Ian L. McHarg, "The Metropolitan Region," *Design with Nature*, pp. 153-161. Copyright © 1991 by John Wiley & Sons, Inc. Reprinted with permission.

the increasingly difficult problem of providing community facilities. Perhaps the most serious is the degree to which the subdivision, the suburb and the metropolitan area deny the dream and have failed to provide the smiling image of the advertisements. The hucksters made the dream into a cheap thing, subdivided we fell, and the instinct to find more natural environments became the impulse that destroyed nature, an important ingredient in the social objective of this greatest of all population migrations.

Let us address ourselves to this problem. In earlier studies we saw that certain types of land are of such intrinsic value, or perform work for man best in a natural condition or, finally, contain such hazards to development that they should not be urbanized. Similarly, there are other areas that, for perfectly specific reasons, are intrinsically suitable for urban uses. This method has been applied to the Potomac River Basin, its constituent physiographic regions: there is no good reason why it should not be applicable to the metropolitan region of Washington.

Thus we can state as a proposition that certain lands are unsuitable for urbanization and others are intrinsically suitable. If our hearts are pure and our instincts good, then the lands that best perform work for man in a natural condition will not be those that are most suitable for urbanization. And because we are not necessarily pure or good, but lucky, it transpires, as we have seen before, that if one selects eight natural features, and ranks them in order of value to the operation of natural process, then that group reversed will constitute a gross order of suitability for urbanization. These are: surface water, floodplains, marshes, aquifer recharge areas, aquifers, steep slopes, forests and woodlands, unforested land. As was discussed in the study of metropolitan open space, natural features can absorb degrees of development—ports, harbors, marinas, water-related and water-using industries must be in riparian land and may occupy floodplains. Surface water, floodplains and marshes may be used for recreation, agriculture and forestry. The aquifer recharge areas may absorb development in a way that does not seriously diminish percolation or pollute groundwater resources. Steep slopes, when forested, may absorb housing of not more than one house per three acres, while forests on relatively flat land may support a density of development up to one-acre clusters.

We can expect that there will be regional and subregional variation in intrinsic suitabilities. After all, this region includes parts of the Coastal Plain and the Piedmont; within the latter there is the important Triassic subprovince. Indeed, topographic variation is least in the Triassic area and greatest in the crystalline Piedmont. Stream dissection, and thus steep slopes, are greatest in the Piedmont, followed by deposits of the Lower Cretaceous. Streams are all but absent in the Triassic area, but abundant in the remainder of the Piedmont—less so in the Coastal Plain. Aquifers are concentrated in the Triassic area and Coastal Plain, but absent in the remaining Piedmont.

This being so, there are revealed areas that are intrinsically unsuitable for urbanization, and these are shown. We can now plot the reverse, and indicate the areas that are suitable for urban uses. Here is the obverse of the first, and what is revealed is the regionally of urban suitability: a broad swath of land running parallel to the Triassic formation is shown to be the most suitable area, with a greater opportunity north of the Potomac than south of it. Lesser areas are visible in the Coastal Plain.

When an uncontrolled growth model is projected, it is seen that development bears no relation either to definitions of natural process

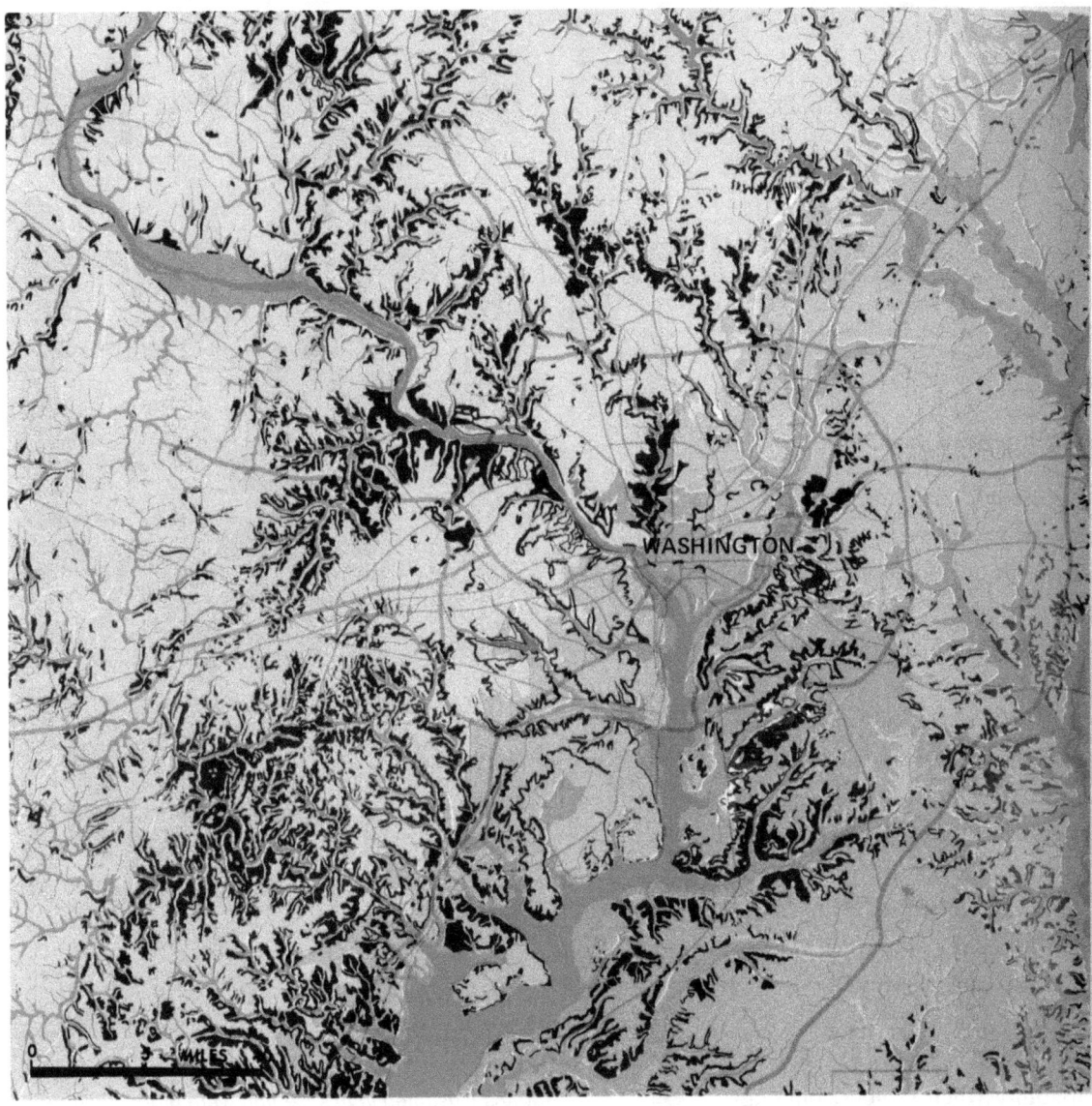

values or to intrinsic suitability. Indeed, when the Year 2000 Plan developed for Washington, is examined against these factors, it is seen that it is almost as oblivious as is unplanned growth.

It is most disconcerting to conclude that not only does uncontrolled growth fail to recognize intrinsic suitabilities and unsuitabilities for urban growth, but that the formal planning process is almost as culpable.

We require more precise information on which to base our decisions. It is not enough to describe land as unforested: one must examine its agricultural value, factors of foundations, suitability of soils for septic tanks and their susceptibility to erosion and the relative values of groundwater resources. To this end, a sector of the metropolitan region has been examined more specifically. It extends north and west from the Capitol to enclose an area of almost four hundred square miles, reaching out to the rural perimeter, including both Dulles Airport and the new town of Reston.

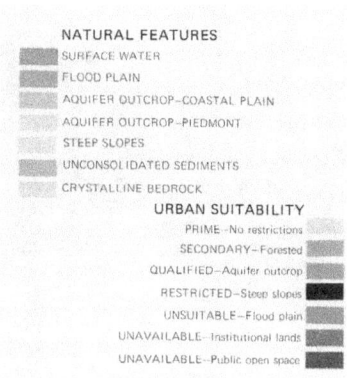

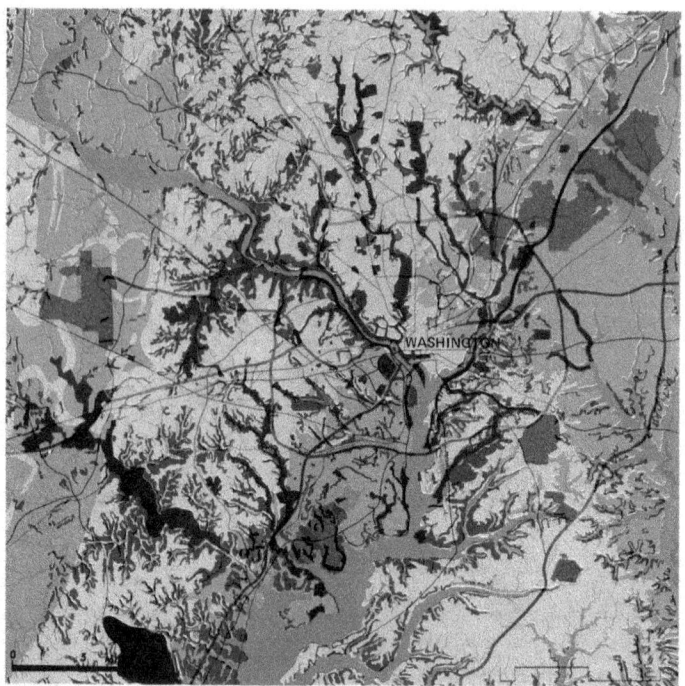

THE QUADRANT

The method has now been used repeatedly and follows the familiar litany of historical geology, physiography, hydrology, and so on, and thereafter interprets these data to reveal intrinsic suitabilities. In this exercise the major prospective land use is urban; it is this that the method seeks to select. There is also an effort made to relate the density of prospective development, not only to the characteristics of the land, but also to its carrying capacity.

The area under study reveals both its characteristics and its variability when geology, physiography, hydrology, soils and slopes are examined. The major divisions of the Triassic Piedmont, the crystalline Piedmont and the Coastal Plain are immediately evident. In the Triassic formation the area is quite flat, streams are few and show little dissection, floodplains are absent, the substructure is limestone—it is associated with an important deep aquifer—and the soils are rich.

In the crystalline Piedmont there are two subdivisions which are roughly divided by the Potomac. In the southern section the slope map most clearly reveals the fissures of streams and the

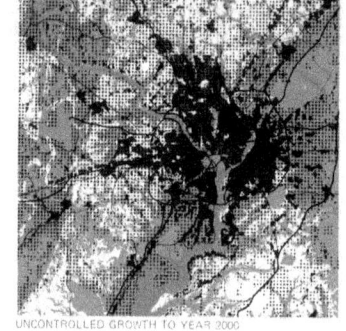
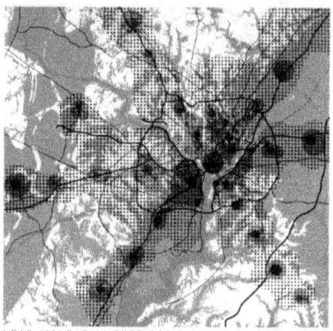

Maps Illustrated in this section were produced for the AIA Task Force on the Potomac by Wallace, McHarg, Roberts and Todd. The work was under the direction of Dr. David A. Wallace, was supervised by Mr. Narendra Juneja and performed by Messrs. Bradford, Bachelor, De Boer and Drummond.

marked dissection that accompanies them. The study area reveals the greatest topographic variety, which is displayed by the entire Piedmont. The landscape is folded, small in scale, and soils are variable in response to topographic change and conditions of slope and exposure. There is little groundwater.

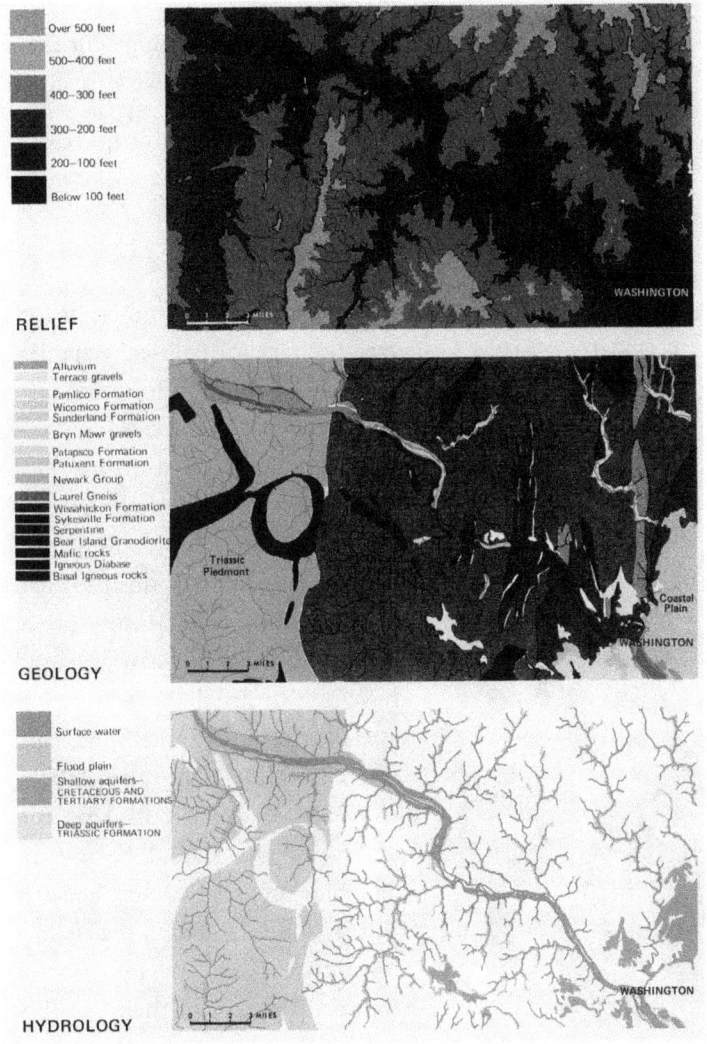

RELIEF

GEOLOGY

HYDROLOGY

and the productive soils of the Triassic formation represent an important value and thus a constraint. Dulles Airport now withdraws 1000 gallons per minute from this groundwater. The southern section of the Piedmont is broadly unsuitable because of the abundance of steep slopes and the absence of large areas of relatively flat land. The northern section of this region has the fewest constraints and offers the greatest opportunity for urbanization. The Coastal Plain does contain aquifers, floodplains and marshes, but also areas of land that impose few constraints.

Existing woodlands persist as residues of earlier and larger forests or as areas of farmland that have been abandoned and have returned to forest. Because of their value in diminishing runoff, reducing erosion and sedimentation and sustaining wildlife—in addition to their scenic and recreational uses—it was decided that in this study, such woodlands should be considered a value and thus only marginally capable of accepting urbanization.

The presence of Dulles International Airport exerts a significant influence upon land uses in the area—mainly detrimental. The zones of 90 and 80 decibels have been identified—this sound level is equivalent to an average machine shop or the noisiest street corner in New York City. For this reason, the F.H.A. has refused to insure loans on residential construction within these zones. They are, therefore, considered unsuitable for urban development.

The Coastal Plain is generally 200 feet lower than the adjacent Piedmont and the change occurs in the Fall zone. The topography of the Coastal Plain is flat, but it is distinguishable from the Triassic formation by the pattern of streams, their floodplains, and the associated dissection. There are several elements unique to this region—escarpments and terraces, the marshes and bays and the estuarine aspect which the Potomac assumes in this region.

When this area is considered in terms of the incidence of factors that render it unsuitable for urbanization, it is seen that the major aquifer

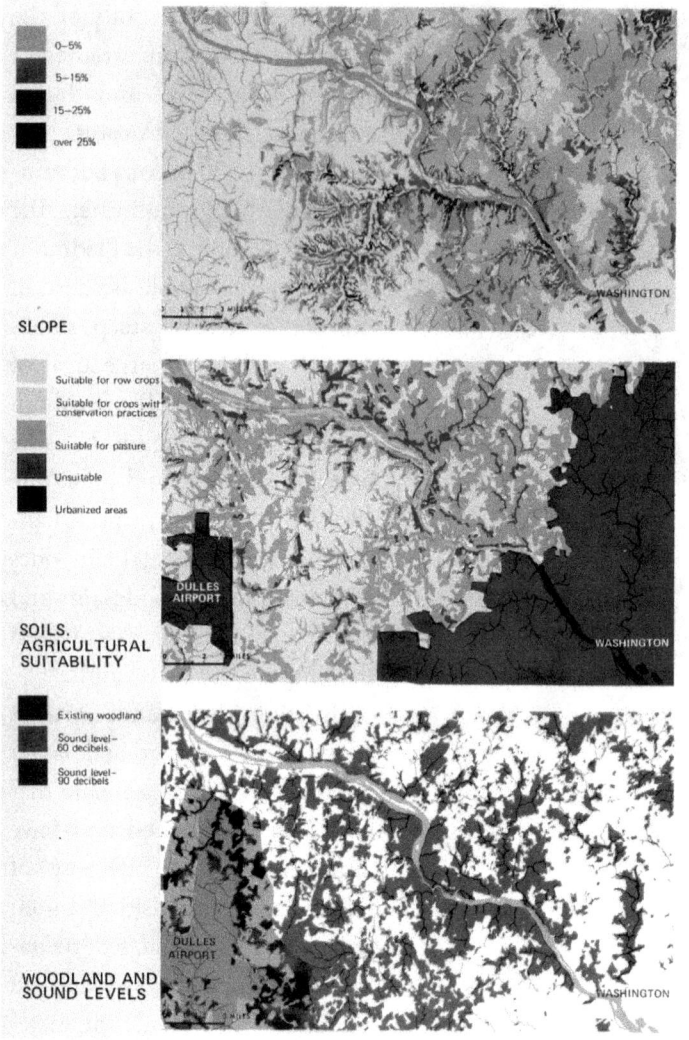

In this study it is assumed that given the possibility of choice, prime agricultural land should not be employed for urban land uses on the grounds that this sterilizes an irreplaceable resource, all but irreversibly. For this reason, soils were identified in terms of four grades of agricultural potential production—row-cropland, cropland, pasture and permanent woodland to diminish erosion on susceptible soils or excessive slope.

From the foregoing information, certain lands were selected as unsuitable for urbanization. These included row-cropland and cropland, floodplains, slopes in excess of fifteen per cent, areas which (for reasons of erosion due to slope or soils) should be in forest cover, major aquifer recharges, forests and noise zones. The areas suitable for urbanization in this initial examination were the least productive agricultural soils—mainly pasture land. Examination quickly revealed that this provided inadequate space for future urban growth and that other lands would have to be utilized.

Clearly some agricultural land will be absorbed by urbanization. It was decided that both cropland and woodland should be investigated for urban suitability, but that this should be based on the characteristics of soils for the provision of foundations and for their usability for septic tanks, and that these qualifications would determine which of the cropland should be designated as suitable for urban development. The same analysis was accorded to forest.

The highest category of suitability in this analysis is noncropland with a capacity to bear foundations of high-density construction. The second category is identical to the first, save that it is cropland. The next category consists of low-bearing-capacity soils that are incapable of supporting septic tanks. These, it was thought, would be suitable for medium-density

DESIGN WITH NATURE

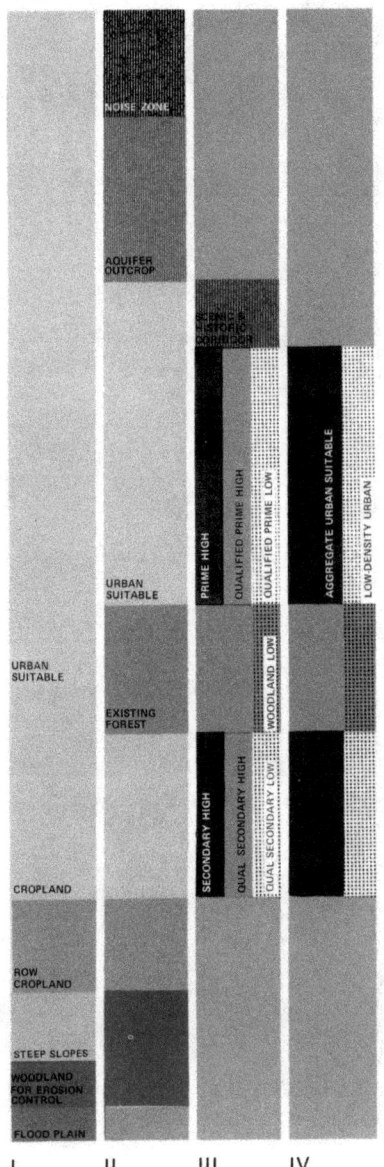

Urban suitability selection process

development, served by sewers. The next category was identical to the preceding, save that it involved the employment of cropland. A further category included poor-bearing-capacity soils that were capable of supporting septic tanks and thus could be used for low-density development. This condition, where cropland is lost, constitutes the next category.

The aggregate of these conclusions is a discrimination system whereby the propensity of the region to support urban land uses is disclosed. It selects surface water and floodplains, steep slopes (over fifteen per cent), major aquifer recharges, noise zones and soils susceptible to erosion from which it is recommended that development be excluded.

Agricultural land is examined in detail, pasture land is identified as the least sacrifice of agricultural land for urban use, cropland is divided into categories of suitability, for foundations and septic tanks. Those forests able to support septic tanks are indicated for low-density development.

As cities are not composed entirely of buildings, and countryside is not entirely without them, the entire area has been examined to find large blocks of land that are preponderantly suitable for urban uses. The study of the enlarged metropolitan region and that of the Quadrant

PHASE I: Exclusion of flood plains, woodlands for erosion control, steep slopes, row-cropland, cropland.

PHASE II: Exclusion in addition to Phase I of aquifer outcrops, noise zones, existing forest cover.

PHASE III: Exclusion in addition to Phases I and II of scenic and historic corridors. Ranking of urban suitability based upon bearing capacities of soils and suitability for septic tanks.

PHASE IV: Identification of aggregations of urban suitable land.

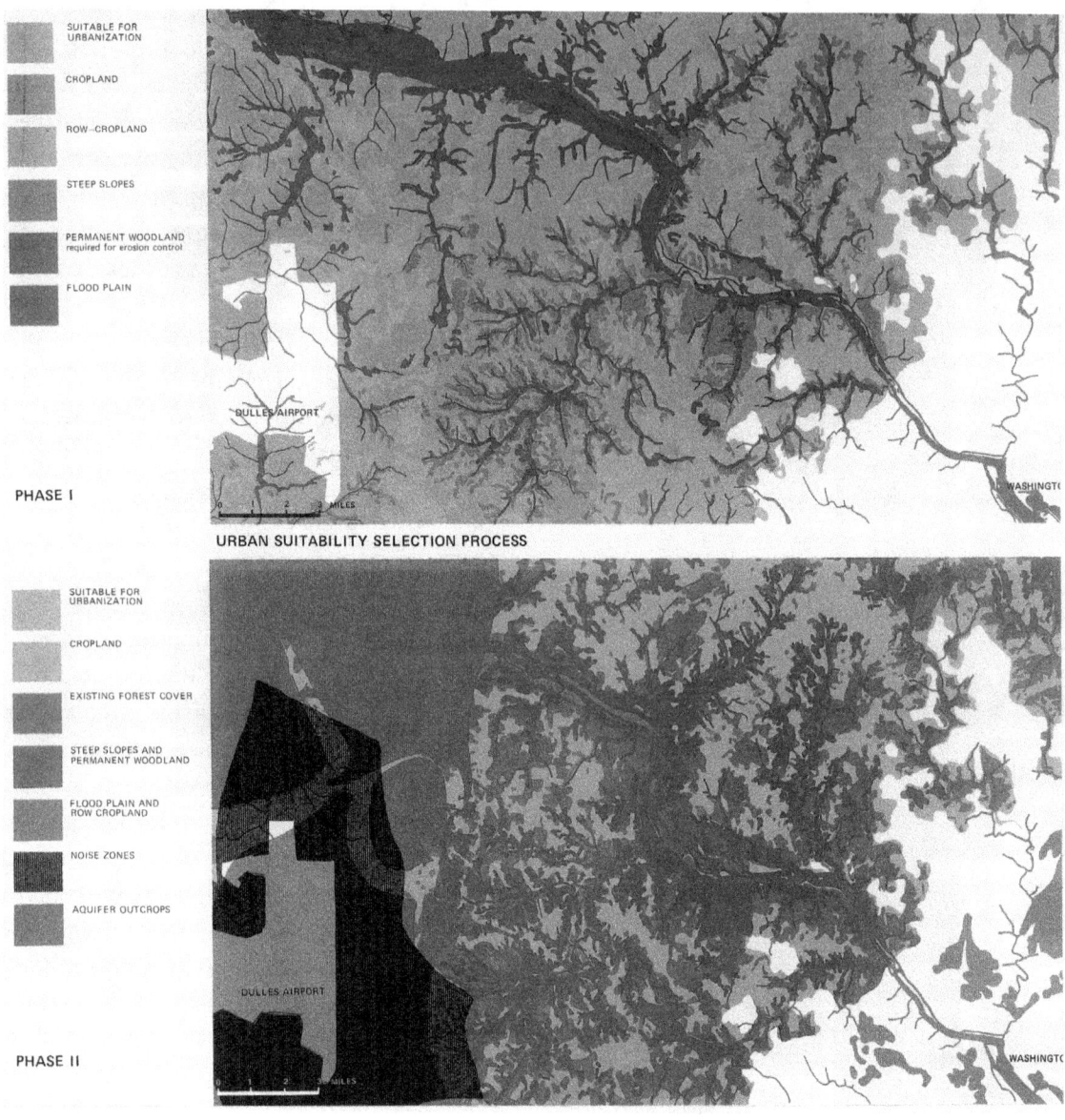

PHASE I

URBAN SUITABILITY SELECTION PROCESS

PHASE II

revealed the propensity of the land itself to support urbanization and showed the resulting system of both open space and urban structure that would result if this method were employed. The most arresting fact is the regional variability and the abundance of land available for prospective metropolitan growth. It is clear that many alternative patterns could be employed within any conscious plan.

This, of course, is not a plan. It merely shows the implications that the land and its processes display for prospective development and its form. The plan can be developed only when there is adequate information on the nature of demand, its locational and resource characteristics, the capacities to realize objectives and, indeed, the social goals of the community. It is enough to say here that—whatever the

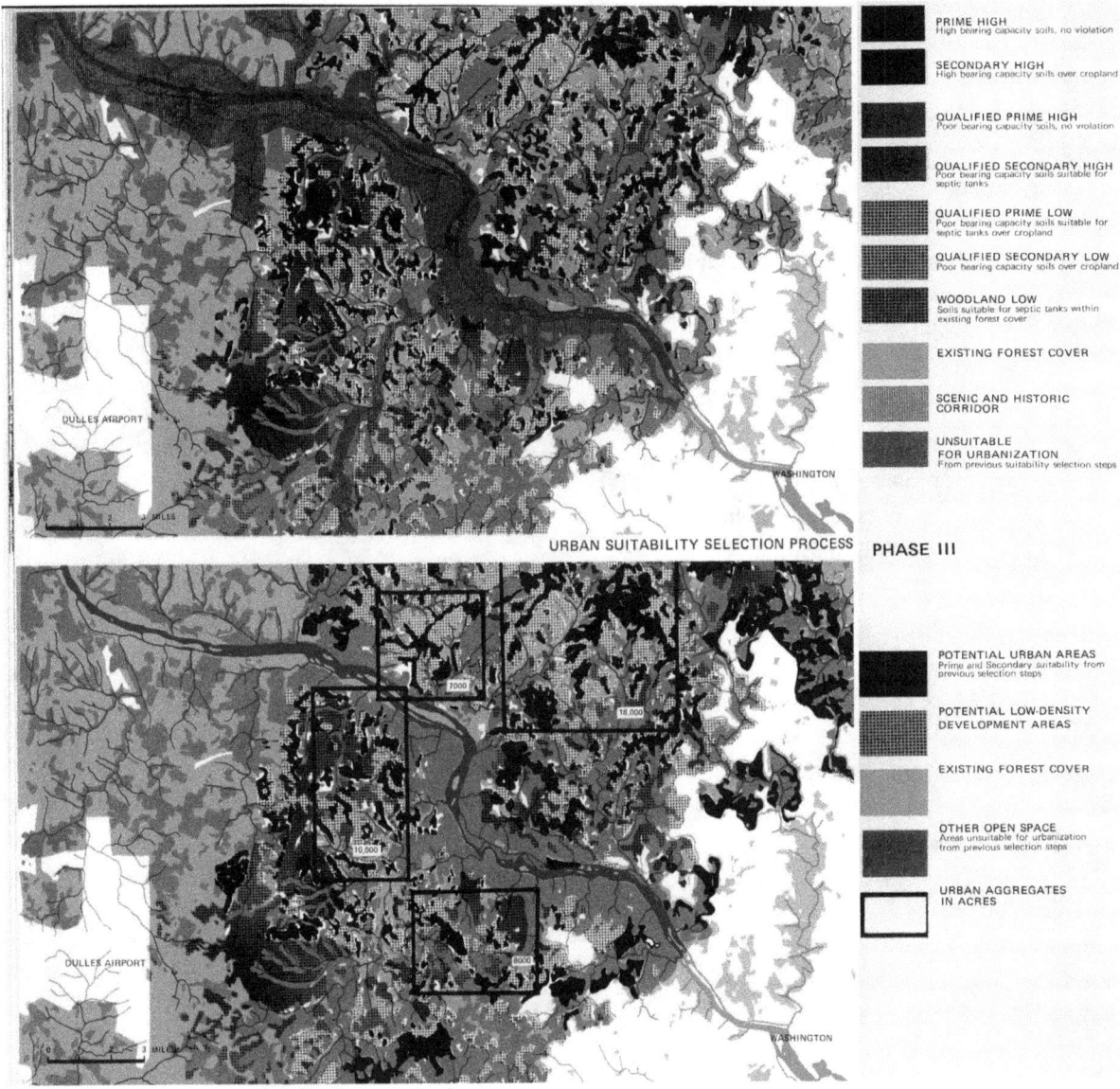

characteristics of demand—the formulation of a plan for the metropolitan region should respond to an understanding of natural processes. It must plan with nature.

Finally, this investigation is concerned with the matter of form. If growth responds to natural processes, it will be clearly visible in the pattern and distribution of development—and, indeed, in its density. But the formal investigation, it must be admitted, is not at a very high level. By responding to nature, one only avoids the allegation of ignorance, stupidity and carelessness. When we can demonstrate this elementary level of intelligence and perception, then we may aspire to more elevated objectives; but that is clearly premature.

At the moment, much of the area is unaffected by planning. Where planning does occur, its single instrument is zoning and by this device political subdivisions are allocated densities irrespective of geology, physiography, hydrology, soils, vegetation, scenery or historic beauty. The adoption of the ecological method would at least produce the negative value of a structure of open space wherein nature performed work for man, or wherein development was dangerous. It would canalize development to areas that were propitious. Positively, it can be employed to find the morphology of man- nature-Washington.

THE NORMAL FATE OF THE LAND

The Quadrant study was a part of the Potomac River Basin Study undertaken by graduate students of Landscape Architecture of the University of Pennsylvania during the 1965–66 academic year. The students responsible for the Quadrant study were Messrs. Bradford, Chitty, Meyers and Sinatra.

GROWING COOLER: EVIDENCE ON URBAN DEVELOPMENT AND CLIMATE CHANGE

CHAPTER 9: *Policy and Program Recommendations*

BY REID EWING, KEITH BARTHOLOMEW, STEVE WINKLEMAN, JERRY WALTERS, AND DON CHEN

Climate stabilization will require the United States to reduce greenhouse gas (GHG) emissions by 60 to 80 percent below 1990 levels by 2050. To keep the nation moving along that critical path, our GHG emissions will need to be well below 1990 levels by 2030, and leading analysts believe we have less than ten years, and possibly less than five years, to get on track (Bierbaum 2006). In the transportation sector, progress will be required on all three legs of the policy stool: vehicle efficiency, fuel content, and vehicle miles traveled (VMT). The national policy discussion on vehicles and fuels is mature and active, and a variety of proposals would have the automobile and oil industries take responsibility for their contributions to GHG. Thus far, however, no one has been put in charge of reducing the GHG impacts of VMT growth.

In this chapter, we aim to identify the roles and responsibilities of different levels of government to meet the climate challenge. Civic leaders,

---

Reid Ewing, Keith Bartholomew, Steve Winkleman, Jerry Walters, and Don Chen, "Policy and Program Recommendations," *Growing Cooler: Evidence on Urban Development and Climate Change*, pp. 129-154. Copyright © 2008 by Urban Land Institute. Reprinted with permission.

consumers, businesses, and other stakeholders also can make substantial contributions to this effort.

The key to making substantial GHG reductions is to get *all policies and practices, funding and spending, incentives, and rules and regulations pointing in the same direction,* toward smart growth and away from sprawl. Currently, most of these instruments are pointed toward sprawl, creating conditions that lead to ever-increasing GHG emissions. One example is the link between federal transportation funding and VMT levels, which rewards states for VMT growth (FHWA 2006). Another example is the low-density zoning that keeps localities dependent on cars, undermining public expenditures on transit, pedestrian, and bicycling facilities.

Our recommendations draw on the analyses in earlier chapters, most notably Chapter 4. That chapter makes clear the priority order of development if GHG emissions are to be substantially reduced. From a climate perspective, the best development is highly accessible to existing urban centers, served by transit, and dense, diverse, and well-designed. Such development has all 5D variables (discussed in Chapter 4) going for it. The next most climate-friendly development is highly accessible to existing urban centers and transit, but lacks one or more of the other Ds.

With 120 million additional Americans projected for 2050, it is not realistic to expect all development and redevelopment to take one of these forms. Inevitably, greenfield development will continue in suburban settings. But this development need not take the form of suburban sprawl. It can be dense, diverse, and well designed. Even in the absence of transit, it can be walkable, and can render many automobile trips much shorter than those in suburbia today.

FEDERAL POLICY RECOMMENDATIONS

The federal government plays a powerful role in shaping growth patterns and travel choices through regulations, funding, tax credits, technical assistance, and other policies. To accomplish the emissions reductions discussed in this book, we recommend the implementation of the following major federal policies.

A MIGHTY CHALLENGE

The current mismatch between what exists and what is necessary to achieve meaningful VMT and GHG reductions highlights the enormity of the challenge and focuses attention on the need for bold initiatives. Incremental policy changes will not suffice. Only profound, systemic change will do. "Make no little plans" Daniel Burnham admonished a century ago. "They have no magic to stir humanity's blood and probably themselves will not be realized" (Moore 1921). Burnham's advice could not be more appropriate to the task at hand.

ADOPT A "GREEN-TEA" FEDERAL TRANSPORTATION ACT

Approximately every six years, Congress reauthorizes the nation's federal transportation planning and funding legislation. One advantage of having to reauthorize transportation statutes so frequently is that each reauthorization has the potential to match the needs of the nation at that time. Past transportation statutes have focused on linking the nation with interstate highways (1956), providing for mass transit (1964), facilitating metropolitan planning (1973), and promoting system efficiency (1991) (Weiner 1999).

In 1991, Congress began the process of policy change by adopting the Inter modal Surface Transportation Efficiency Act (ISTEA), altering the ways that transportation planning and funding would occur in this country. Although these changes were largely carried forward in subsequent legislation—1998's Transportation Equity Act for the 21st Century (TEA-21) and 2005's Safe, Accountable, Flexible, Efficient Transportation Equity Act: A Legacy for Users (SAFETEA-LU)—the latter statutes did not build on the foundation laid by ISTEA.

As outlined in this book, the most pressing current need is to stabilize the climate for the future economic and environmental well-being, not only of this country, but of the entire planet. With the reauthorization of SAFETEA-LU slated for 2009, the time has come for the next transformation in how we think about, plan for, and fund the nation's surface transportation system. The reauthorization will allocate approximately $300 billion, representing by far the largest category of federal infrastructure spending. How this spending is allocated, and what planning requirements accompany it, will have a profound impact on the nation's future VMT and GHG emissions. In a very real sense, transportation policy *is* climate policy. To meet the current need for VMT and GHG reductions, we suggest that the next surface transportation act build on the acronyms of the previous two statutes and be dubbed "Green-TEA" (Center for Clean Air Policy 2007). We further suggest that this new statute incorporate the following changes in law.

Establish National Goals for Transportation

Traditionally, federal transportation legislation has parceled out federal dollars to the states. Planning came late to the system, with the first mandates for long-range planning in metropolitan areas appearing in 1962; parallel requirements for states did not exist until 1991 (Weiner 1999). Even then, the emphasis was, and remains, on planning procedures, not outcomes. States and metropolitan planning organizations (MPOs) are required to incorporate certain "planning factors" into analyses used to develop long-range plans, but the requirement is couched in permissive language: states/MPOs must *consider the* specified factors. No particular result must be achieved or standard attained. The reality—that these planning factors are mere suggestions—is further cemented by language barring anyone from suing a state or MPO for failing to consider the factors (23 U.S.C. §§ 134(h), 135(d)). States and MPOs must certify to the U.S. Department of Transportation (USDOT) that they considered the planning factors, but oversight and enforcement of even this modest requirement are weak.

Given that most other federal programs that allocate funds to state or local governments—including those for education, public housing, and welfare—contain performance-based requirements, it is rather remarkable that transportation funding (with some exceptions) is more or less a blank check. It is time for transportation to incorporate performance standards as well. Performance- or goal-based planning is not new.

Land use planning statutes in many states contain substantive standards that local plans must meet. In one of the better-known examples, the state of Oregon has articulated 19 goals that cities and counties must advance through their comprehensive land use plans (Oregon Department of Land Conservation and Development 2007).

A similar structure should be included in Green-TEA. The statute should articulate a national vision for transportation—one based on climate stability—and define a set of national goals and objectives. To ensure attainment of these goals and objectives, Green-TEA should require that all planning documents—including state and MPO long-range plans and transportation improvement programs, project-level environmental impact statements, and MPO certifications—demonstrate compliance with these goals and objectives. The U.S. Environmental Protection Agency (EPA), in consultation with the USDOT, should be put in charge of reviewing planning documents for compliance and should be given the enforcement tools necessary to guarantee compliance.

There are many goals that could be incorporated into a performance-based transportation planning system. Naturally, a planning system that has climate stability as its main goal should give highest priority to reductions in GHG emissions and VMT. Additional goals would prioritize repair and rehabilitation over new construction ("fix-it-first"), ensure seamless intermodal transfers, and provide for "complete streets" (see "Adopt a Statewide Complete Streets Policy and Funding Program" later in this chapter). Further goals are suggested by current metropolitan and state planning factors: economic vitality, safety, security, accessibility, mobility, environmental enhancement, energy conservation, operation and management efficiency, and system preservation (23 U.S.C. §§ 134(h), 135(d)).

Use Funding Formulas that Provide Incentives for VMT Reduction

Discussions of transportation policy frequently focus on the need for additional revenues to meet growing needs. Rarely is the alternative of balancing resources and needs by reducing demand seriously considered. This alternative can and should be pursued through Green-TEA.

For many decades, transportation funds have been allocated to states based, in large part, on VMT, fuel use, and lane miles (Federal Highway Administration 2006). The more of each factor a state can demonstrate, the more funding the state will receive, thereby allowing the state to build more lane miles, which in turn encourages more VMT (see Chapter 6). More VMT results in increased state gas tax revenues, further exacerbating the perverse spiral of revenue generation, facility expansion, and VMT growth. Obviously, one of the results is ever-increasing GHG emissions.

Funding allocation systems need to stop rewarding VMT growth and start rewarding measures that reduce travel demand and emissions. The original ISTEA legislation, as passed by the Senate in 1991—far ahead of its time—offers a model of how federal funding could be transformed to a performance-based system (S. 1204 § 106(b), June 19, 1991). This legislation would have created an Energy Conservation, Congestion Mitigation, and Clean Air Act Bonus program. A state's funding allocation would have been reduced if it showed a 10 percent or greater increase in VMT per person over an established base year. The withheld funds would have been pooled to provide bonuses to states achieving a 10 percent or greater decrease in VMT per person. Such a program could be administered either through state allocations and metropolitan suballocations or, better still, through direct allocations to MPOs (as described below).

Level the Playing Field for Transportation Choices

Prior to the passage of ISTEA, funding and planning processes essentially tipped the decision-making scales in favor of new road projects. Faced with a given transportation need, state and metropolitan decision makers could choose to address that need with new or expanded roads, which would receive 80 or 90 percent funding from the federal government, or they could address the need with transit, which would receive far less federal funding, often as little as 50 percent. Although ISTEA allowed for the equalizing of federal funding between highway and transit projects, it did not mandate it. The actual practice of the USDOT has largely maintained conditions as they existed prior to ISTEA. Transit projects rarely receive more than 50 percent federal funding, while highway projects frequently receive 80 percent (Beimborn & Puentes 2003).

Moreover, a series of procedural hurdles gives highways an additional edge. Virtually all major (and many minor) transit capital projects must go through a "new starts" application process that requires them to meet standards for cost effectiveness, operational efficiency, mobility improvement, environmental benefit, and supportive land uses—criteria that highways do not have to meet. In addition, funds are allocated to project applicants in very different ways under highway and transit programs. Highway capital funds are distributed to state DOTs via entitlement formulas, while transit capital funds are distributed through a highly competitive discretionary grant program. Finally, unlike highway projects, transit projects are subject to intense federal oversight and postcompletion evaluation.

Of course, there are at least two ways to level the transit/highway playing field: either make transit funding conform to highway procedures or vice versa. While most commentators suggest equalizing federal funding shares at 80 percent, many point to the project selection process and criteria currently used for transit as the basis for good transportation decision making. In other words, rather than "dumbing down" transit to highway funding procedures, we could make highways "smarten up" by applying the same rigorous qualification standards and evaluation processes to highways as we do to transit (Beimborn and Puentes 2003; Katz, Puentes, and Bernstein 2003). This would not only give transit a fair shake, but would ensure that road projects meet basic efficiency and effectiveness standards.

Provide Funding Directly to MPOs

ISTEA gave MPOs new planning authority and responsibilities. It also required state DOTs to provide MPOs for large metropolitan areas with a minimum suballocation of project funds. Under the current transportation law, SAFETEA-LU, that amount is approximately 5 percent of a state's federal highway allocation (Wolf et al. 2007). As important as these changes were, they have hardly made a dent in what is an increasingly inequitable distribution of transportation dollars. Metropolitan areas contain more than 80 percent of the nation's population and 85 percent of its economic output (Puentes and Bailey 2005). Investment by state DOTs in metropolitan areas lags far behind these percentages (Hill et al. 2005).

The issue, however, is not just the *amount* of funding; it is also the authority to decide *how* the money is spent. More than one-third of the states that receive funds from the federal Congestion Mitigation Air Quality Program—funds that by definition are to be used in MPO areas—do not suballocate those funds to their respective MPOs. Only 12 states suballocate federal Transportation Enhancement Program dollars to MPOs. The other states decide how these funds are to be spent. Even among the

5 percent of funds that are required to be suballocated to MPOs, many MPO staff members report that state DOTs wield substantial influence (Puentes and Bailey 2005).

What is necessary to remedy the long history of structural and institutional inequities is a new system of allocating federal transportation funds directly to metropolitan areas. Instead of sending federal allocations to the states and expecting the states to "do the right thing" for metropolitan areas, future federal legislation should provide for the direct allocation of project funds to MPOs, without filtering these funds through state DOTs. Moreover, the amount of the allocation should be closely linked to the proportion of an MPO's population and economic activity compared to other MPOs and non-MPO areas in the same state. Because different states have different needs for rural and interstate facilities, this formula could be adjusted on a state-by-state basis.

Direct MPO funding likely would require significant institutional changes within many MPOs, so that boards and staff will be equipped to deal with new authority and responsibility, and will be held accountable for system performance and new GHG reduction requirements. California's MPOs, such as those in the Sacramento and Bay Area regions, have significant decision-making authority and are developing GHG reduction plans to comply with state GHG mandates. They will provide important lessons for other MPOs around the country.

Require Land Use/Transportation Scenario Planning

Good planning is critical to land use and transportation reforms at the regional level. The metropolitan planning sections of Green-TEA should require integrated land use/transportation scenario analyses (as described in "Regional Growth Simulations" in Chapter 4) for all regional transportation plans. Current law requires alternatives analyses for specific large projects. However, it does not require alternatives analyses for long-range plans or improvement programs. More importantly, current law does not require consideration of alternative land use patterns or plans.

As emphasized throughout this book, land use and transportation define each other; neither can be fully understood or rationalized in isolation. The costs and benefits of alternative land use patterns and transportation investments cannot be fully appreciated on a project-by-project basis. Because both sectors—land use and transportation—function in an integrated fashion at a regional level, intelligent analysis and policymaking must occur at that level. More detailed alternatives analyses still would occur at the project level, but would be tiered, to account for plan and program analyses of regional-scale impacts. Both levels of analysis would incorporate the performance goals described above. Recognizing that this level of analysis would require more resources than most states and MPOs currently invest in planning processes, Green-TEA should substantially increase funding for regional and state planning. Funding emphasis should be given to enhancements of land use and travel data, transportation models, scenario planning tools, visioning processes, and public engagement.

Establish a National Transportation System Administration

A half-century ago, Congress adopted the Federal-Aid Highway Act of 1956, launching the Interstate Highway System, an unprecedented engineering project that quickly changed everything about the way Americans traveled and built communities. During the same period, the nation developed and implemented a national aviation system, stitching together state and municipally owned airports into a seamless, efficient network. The nation's freight systems already were largely in place. Notably absent from the nation's transportation system is high-quality intercity passenger rail.

Passenger rail, once the exclusive purview of private railroad companies, is now the responsibility of Amtrak, the semipublic national rail agency. Aside from the northeast corridor—which extends from Washington, D.C., to Boston—Amtrak does not own the tracks on which it runs, but must purchase track rights from freight railroads. This effectively forecloses the possibility of significant upgrades to passenger rail service, especially in the critically important area of increased operating speeds. As the nation's airports become ever more congested, the price of oil continues to rise, and the climate impacts of airline travel become more apparent, it is time to get serious about a national high-speed passenger rail network.

To carry out this task, Green-TEA should create a new federal agency within the USDOT and charge it with building and operating a national passenger rail system. Ideally, the new agency would be in charge of all nationally operated passenger systems—aviation as well as rail—to ensure intermodal integration and policy consistency. Creating an effective high-speed passenger rail system would reinforce the other land use and transportation initiatives outlined in this book. It would strengthen central cities and sub-regional centers, further encouraging compact, infill development and discouraging sprawl. Directly and indirectly, such a system would increase transit usage and bicycle and pedestrian travel, further reducing GHG emissions.

REQUIRE TRANSPORTATION CONFORMITY FOR GHGS

In *Massachusetts* v. *EPA*, the U.S. Supreme Court affirmed the EPA's authority to regulate GHG emissions under the current federal Clean Air Act, and its duty to do so unless it found that such emissions were not harmful to public health and welfare—an impossibility, given the scientific evidence reviewed in Chapter 3. The obvious and best way for the EPA to respond is to extend transportation conformity requirements from criteria pollutants to GHGs (see "What is Conformity?" on the following page).

Under such a system, state and local governments would be required to adopt mobile source GHG emission reduction budgets (like the emissions budgets for other pollutants) that demonstrate reasonable progress in limiting emissions. Currently, regions that fail to develop transportation plans consistent with "reasonable further progress" goals risk curbs on federal transportation funds. Withheld funds could be used to reward states and MPOs that effectively reduce per capita VMT.

Although we acknowledge that, to date, land use and transportation demand management (TDM) policies generally have not played a significant role in meeting regional conformity requirements,[1] we believe that comprehensive strategies aimed at GHG reductions would be more successful and less easily circumvented. Responsibility should be "nested" so that the federal government is responsible for the GHG impacts of federal transportation spending and state and local governments bear responsibility for the GHG impacts of their transportation spending.

WHAT IS CONFORMITY?

Under Section 110 of the Clean Air Act (42 U.S.C. § 7506(c)), states develop and implement air pollution control plans called state implementation plans (SIPs) to demonstrate attainment with national ambient air quality standards (NAAQS) set by the EPA at levels deemed necessary to protect public health and welfare. The Clean Air Act Amendments of 1990, along with subsequent transportation legislation, required air quality and transportation officials to work together through a process known as conformity. A metropolitan region that has exceeded the emission standards for one or more pollutants must show that the region's transportation plan will conform to applicable SIPs and contribute to timely attainment of the NAAQS. According to the regulations, a proposed project or program must not produce new air quality violations, worsen existing violations, or delay timely attainment of the NAAQS (62 Fed. Reg. 43780). Metropolitan planning organizations must demonstrate this conformity through their long-range transportation plans and transportation improvement programs (TIPs). Projects that do not conform cannot be approved, funded, or advanced through the planning process, nor can they be implemented unless the emissions budget in the SIP is revised.

Under such circumstances, if an MPO fails to adopt a new TIP that stays within the motor vehicle emissions budget in the SIP, the area faces what is known as a conformity lapse. During this period, the MPO cannot approve funding for new transportation projects or new phases of previously funded transportation projects except for those projects that are adopted as transportation control measures in the SIP or are otherwise exempt from conformity as air quality—neutral activities.

If an area fails to submit a required SIP by a deadline, it may face a "conformity freeze," in which it cannot approve any new projects until this deficiency is remedied. If this failure is prolonged, the area can face the ultimate sanction of losing federal transportation funding. For some metropolitan areas, this potential loss of transportation funds could amount to more than $100 million per year. While 63 U.S. areas have suffered conformity lapses, no state or region has ever lost federal transportation funds as a result of a conformity lapse, freeze, or sanctions (Center for Clean Air Policy 2004b).

USE A CAP-AND-TRADE SYSTEM TO PROMOTE SMART GROWTH

Many Congressional proposals for climate stabilization would authorize a national cap-and-trade market system similar to those in Europe and under development in several states. By placing a price on GHG emissions, a cap-and-trade system can send the right signal for reducing the emissions associated with vehicle travel (Winkelman, Hargrave, and Vanderlan 2000). Moreover, regulated parties such as oil companies will have an incentive to support policies that slow VMT growth, because actions that increase VMT will make carbon emission allowances more costly.

Investment of Cap-and-Trade Revenues

Under recent Congressional cap-and-trade proposals, carbon allowances will be worth an estimated $50 billion to $300 billion per year by 2020. A portion of these revenues could be used to support smart growth. We identify a few worthwhile uses of such funds:

- **Technical Assistance for Smart Growth Planning.** Most state and local governments have very limited capacity to implement smart growth. A portion of carbon allowance revenue could support technical assistance to MPOs and to state and local governments for improvements in planning data, models, and scenario planning tools.
- **Smart Location Tax Credits.** The federal government and many state governments currently provide tax credits for hybrid vehicles, solar technology, and other technologies that reduce energy use. The same could be done for smart growth projects that will reduce regional VMT. The federal government could direct states and MPOs to identify smart locations based on the "five D" performance criteria—density, diversity, design, destination accessibility, and distance to transit—discussed in this book. Developers of new for-sale or rental units within the most efficient locations could qualify for a federal smart location tax credit. A portion of the incentive could be used to finance affordable housing units.
- **Increased Support for Travel Alternatives.** Efficient land use patterns and rich transportation choices go hand in hand. A portion of carbon allowance value could support transit, cycling, and pedestrian infrastructure that complement compact development.
- **National Infrastructure Bank.** Infill development and redevelopment in already built-up areas is one of the most effective strategies for reducing VMT and GHG emissions. The infrastructure in many central cities and older suburbs, however, is obsolete and in need of expensive upgrades and rehabilitation. Because many of these cities lack the tax base to adequately fund such projects, national resources are needed. Senator Christopher Dodd (D, Connecticut) has introduced legislation that would provide such funding through a national infrastructure bank, which would help fund improvements in transit systems, public housing, roads, bridges, drinking water systems, and wastewater systems (S. 1926, 2007).

Smart Growth Offset Projects

In a cap-and-trade system, regulated industries—like electric power generation—would be subject to emission limits and could sell any unused emission capacity below those limits to other emitters. Although land development is unlikely to become a regulated activity, it might have a role to play in offset markets.

Offsets are projects that can demonstrate quantifiable emission reductions compared to some "business as usual" baseline. Purchasers of offsets might be regulated industries that need offsets to help them meet their emission obligations, or other interested parties, acting voluntarily, who wish to help reduce GHG emissions. Examples of this latter group include companies such as HSBC, an international banking and financial services organization, that want to become carbon-neutral for business and product-differentiation reasons; airline passengers who want to offset the carbon emitted by their travel; and organizations such as FIFA, the international soccer federation, that want to offset the carbon emissions associated with specific events such as the 2010 World Cup (Bayon, Hawn, and Hamilton 2007).

As this book documents, smart growth can substantially reduce GHG emissions compared to business as usual. As such, it should be considered as a project category in offset markets. Land development projects might be assumed to generate a certain level of GHGs under normal circumstances, but emit substantially less because of their higher density, better land use mix, or more central location. Developers could sell the difference in emissions as an offset.

One of the hurdles that will need to be overcome for this to work is the issue of bundling. Given the prevailing price per ton of carbon on most of the world's carbon exchanges, the emission reductions associated with the typical land development project are probably too small to justify the associated market transaction costs. Several projects bundled together, however, could make such a deal worth the effort. This is, after all, what happens with individual home mortgages—they are bundled into larger packages that can be bought and sold in secondary markets. The metropolitan region is probably the most appropriate scale for bundling. If a region were to outperform its GHG conformity target, it could sell its excess reductions as an offset to another region.

The rules governing cap-and-trade systems are very specific about how regulated entities can demonstrate compliance, including what types of offsets can be counted toward compliance. While those voluntarily seeking to reduce their carbon emissions are not affected by such restrictions, the effective elimination of the compliance-bound entities would substantially undercut the marketability of a particular offset type. Granted, the smart growth offset market is untested, but so are many of the other components of cap-and-trade systems. As Congress and various states consider adopting cap-and-trade systems, they should avoid restrictions that would preclude the use of smart growth projects as offsets.

PLACE MORE HOUSING WITHIN REACH

In general, the cost of housing declines with distance from job centers and other desired destinations. When the cost of gasoline was low, this led many households to seek housing far away from where they ideally would have lived, driving until they qualified for mortgages. With rising gasoline costs, however, the financial tradeoff between a longer commute and cheaper housing is changing (Lipman 2006). Living in a convenient location with transportation choices is becoming a more important aspect of affordability (Bernstein, Makarewicz, and McCarty 2005). Much of the need for housing during the next 30 years can be met within walking distance of the nation's 4,000 transit stations (Center for Transit-Oriented Development 2004). The challenge is to match affordable housing with transit availability.

Federal housing programs need to be better targeted. Take the Low Income Housing Tax Credit (LIHTC), the country's largest rental housing assistance program (U.S. Department of Housing and Urban Development 2008). The criteria governing the location for LIHTC-supported projects do not include access to transit (Gustafson and Walker 2002). In Washington, D.C., for example, only 6 percent of LIHTC housing units are located within walking distance of Metrorail stations (Rube 2008). With transportation costs now consuming more than 40 percent of income for households in the lowest-income quintile (Bureau of Labor Statistics 2001), proximity to high—quality transit needs to become a major factor in LIHTC allocations.

STATE POLICY RECOMMENDATIONS

Traditionally, major U.S. public policy initiatives have originated at the federal level, with states and local governments providing implementation muscle and expertise. This has been especially true in the areas of environmental protection and public health. With respect to climate change, however, the federal government has chosen not to take a leadership role, effectively ceding that role to states and localities. More than half of the states—29 at last count—are filling this vacuum by creating their own plans to reduce GHG emissions. One-third of the states have set GHG reduction targets, and many more are in the process of doing so. Some states have taken the additional step of banding together in multistate compacts to create cap-and-trade programs (Regional Greenhouse Gas Initiative 2005; Western Climate Initiative 2008).

State climate control plans in New York, Connecticut, and Massachusetts include comprehensive VMT-reduction recommendations, although their experiences in implementing these plans have been mixed (Center for Clean Air Policy 2003, 2004a). The state of New York requires MPOs to report the GHG impacts of federally required transportation improvement programs and long-range transportation plans (ICF Consulting 2005). Connecticut created an Office of Responsible Growth to promote transit-oriented development, provide transit alternatives, encourage walkable communities, and target state funding to support development in designated "responsible growth" areas (Rell 2006). In California, a working group created by the state energy commission has established a set of policy recommendations on land use and climate change based on a comprehensive review of state and local efforts (California Energy Commission 2007).

Our recommendations for state policies build on many of these programs, focusing on land use strategies to reduce VMT and GHG emissions. As formulated, they can either stand alone or be integrated with future federal climate policies, such as those outlined in the preceding section. We recommend that states pursue all of the following policy changes.

ESTABLISH GHG PLANS THAT INCLUDE TARGETS FOR VMT REDUCTIONS

Regardless of whether the federal government acts to reduce GHG emissions, states can and should develop GHG reduction plans that include targets for reducing vehicular travel (VMT). To be effective, these VMT targets need to be suballocated among regions and localities within the state. Metropolitan planning organizations and local governments then would develop plans to achieve the targets, using strategies that best fit their communities. The state would review and rate the regional and local plans for compliance with overall state goals and suballocated targets.

The Washington State Commute Trip Reduction program provides an example of how this system might work. The program, which is focused on reducing single-occupant vehicle commutes and GHG emissions, sets targets for reductions in single-occupant vehicle commutes and VMT per commuter. Local jurisdictions then must set goals that are at least equal to the state goals and create plans for achieving the target measures (Washington Administrative Code 468-63-030). Another example is New Mexico's recent requirement that state-funded comprehensive plans include an analysis of and a reduction plan for GHG emissions related to land use, economic development, housing, and transportation patterns.

ALIGN STATE SPENDING WITH CLIMATE GOALS AND PLANS

Once local and regional VMT reduction plans are approved, states should align spending programs to support plans and reward successful local implementation efforts. All discretionary spending programs, whether funded directly by the state or through federal grants, would be considered in this realignment. Particularly important are programs with direct ties to land development, including those in housing, economic development, infrastructure, water and sewer systems, schools, transportation, and recreation.

Once identified and pooled, these discretionary funds could provide a significant incentive for counties and municipalities. When Massachusetts adopted this approach for its Commonwealth Capital funding program, discretionary funds totaled roughly $500 million within an annual state budget of $27 billion. To allocate these funds, Massachusetts uses a scorecard system to assess the consistency of local policies and implementation actions with state sustainable development goals. This incentive has led to hundreds of changes in local plans and zoning ordinances statewide.

In addition to its capital funding program, Massachusetts provides financial incentives for the establishment of smart growth zoning districts. To qualify, an area must meet certain minimum density, affordability, and location requirements. The program tightly links spending with results: communities get some funding when they make initial zoning changes, and additional funding when smart new development projects are built. A companion statute guarantees that the state will cover any additional costs incurred by a local school system as a result of housing construction in a smart growth zoning district.

The California Infrastructure and Economic Development Bank's Infrastructure State Revolving Fund Program uses a similar state scorecard system. This program rates applications on a 200-point scale. Preference is given to projects that are in or adjacent to already developed areas or areas with high unemployment, and to projects that contribute to public transit use and downtown revitalization.

One of the most comprehensive structures for aligning state spending with smart growth goals is Maryland's Smart Growth Funding Areas system. Enacted in 1997, the system restricts development-related state expenditures to designated priority funding areas (PFAs), which were defined to include all municipalities as well as unincorporated areas served by water and sewer services. Areas outside the PFAs are ineligible for state funding of infrastructure or economic development. A recent report by the National Center for Smart Growth suggests the need to carefully track spending under such as system, and illustrates the implementation failures that can occur if this is not done (Knaap and Lewis 2007).

In Illinois, the Business Location Efficiency Incentive Act, passed in 2005, gives companies a small additional corporate income tax credit if a new job site is accessible by public transportation or located near affordable workforce housing. Companies seeking the credit at sites that do not initially qualify can qualify later with a site remediation plan that provides employer-assisted housing, shuttle services, pre-tax transit passes, or carpooling assistance.

REDUCE "FISCALIZATION OF LAND USES"

Local governments rely upon a variety of development-related revenue streams to fund public services. However, not all types of development generate the same amount of revenue or the same degree of service demands. There is a fiscal incentive to limit low-revenue/high-demand land uses, such as workforce housing, in favor of high-revenue/low-demand uses, such as big-box retail. Competition among localities for high-revenue/low-demand uses is fierce, often leading jurisdictions to offer large economic inducements to commercial developers. Local governments that succeed at this competition frequently fail to provide sufficient land for low-revenue/high-demand uses, effectively exporting them to neighboring jurisdictions. The result is that people must travel longer distances between affordable workforce housing and job centers, shopping, and other important services (Thomas 2006).

Local governments in a few metropolitan areas—including Minneapolis/St. Paul; Charlottesville and Albemarle County, Virginia; Davis and Yolo County, California; and the New Jersey Meadowlands—have developed pacts to dampen these fiscal incentives and deter intraregional competition by sharing tax bases. Such arrangements often require state authorizing legislation. In California, authorization was provided recently through a ballot initiative.

There are other ways states can reduce perverse local fiscal incentives. In parts of the West where property tax caps are more common, sales taxes can be a driver of land use decisions, and reform efforts must focus on this dynamic. In Arizona, local government retail incentive packages became so large and so common that the state passed a law prohibiting them in the Phoenix metropolitan area. In many New England states, property taxes are the dominant funding source, and property tax reform is seen as a potential solution. Massachusetts now provides towns with a hold-harmless guarantee: if education costs rise because certain smart growth zoning regulations lead to an influx of families with school-age children, the state makes up the difference.

ADOPT A STATEWIDE COMPLETE STREETS POLICY AND FUNDING PROGRAM

With approximately 50 percent of trips in the United States less than three miles in length (USDOT 2001), walking and bicycling can and should provide alternatives to the automobile for many daily trips. Even for more distant destinations, walking and bicycling have a role to play as the first and last segments of transit trips. Yet, streets and highways all across America lack basic facilities for pedestrians and bicyclists. Many lack sidewalks, have lanes that are too narrow for bicycles, are dangerous to cross, lack comfortable transit stops, and are inaccessible to people with disabilities. According to a national survey of pedestrians and bicyclists, 25 percent of walking trips occur on roads without sidewalks or shoulders; only 5 percent of bike trips occur on roads with bike lanes (National Highway Traffic Safety Administration and Bureau of Transportation Statistics 2003). In short, public streets and roads are hostile environments for travelers who are not inside cars. To make other modes of transportation viable, a network of complete streets and highways is needed.

A complete streets policy would require that pedestrian and bicycle facilities be provided on all new and reconstructed streets and highways, and that pedestrians' and bicyclists' needs be considered in routine roadway operation and maintenance. For more than 35 years, the Oregon Bike Bill has done just that, requiring state and local governments to provide "[f]ootpaths and bicycle trails … wherever a highway, road or street is being constructed, reconstructed or relocated" (Oregon Revised

Statute (ORS) 316.514(1)). Instead of using permissive language that would allow the inclusion of pedestrian and bicycle facilities, the Oregon bill mandates that inclusion, with narrowly defined exceptions. More than 50 jurisdictions at all levels of government have adopted complete streets policies in the last few years. The National Complete Streets Coalition (2005) has developed a nine-point program for complete streets, which should be the minimum standard in all states.

To create "complete communities," a complete streets policy could mandate that new streets be interconnected and culs-de-sac be discouraged so that travel distances for pedestrians and bicyclists are minimized. Again, Oregon provides useful examples. The state's Transportation Planning Rule requires all local and regional governments to adopt standards for the layout of local streets (Oregon Administrative Rule 660-12-0020(2)(b)). These standards must provide "reasonably direct routes for bicycle and pedestrian travel." Portland Metro, the Portland-area regional government, has interpreted this state provision as requiring local street plans that limit the use of cul-de-sacs and dead ends, create direct travel routes, and provide full intersections at least every 530 feet and pedestrian/bicycle accessways every 330 feet (Metro 2004, pp. 6-15-6-17). The state of Virginia is considering a similar requirement for all subdivision streets under its jurisdiction, but with specific performance standards for street connectivity.

The third component of a complete streets policy is adequate state-level funding. Oregon's Bike Bill requires both state and local governments to set aside at least 1 percent of state highway funds for pedestrian and bicycle facilities (ORS 366.514(3)). While this is a commendable base, it would be better to set funding levels commensurate with actual or desired mode shares. Approximately 10 percent of trips currently are made by bicycling or walking (USDOT 2001). A reasonable objective for 2030 is to double that percentage. To stand a chance of meeting this objective, state funding levels for pedestrian and bicycle facilities will have to be commensurate. Funding should be provided to retrofit all existing "incomplete" streets that present barriers to bicycling, walking, and transit use.

REQUIRE ANALYSIS OF GHG EMISSIONS AS PART OF PLANNING APPROVALS

Following Congress's adoption of the National Environmental Policy Act (NEPA) in 1969, 13 states and the District of Columbia passed state-level "mini-NEPAs," requiring assessments of state and local actions in a manner similar to NEPA. The actions covered by these mini-NEPAs vary from state to state. In some states, such as Connecticut, the mini-NEPA affects only state agency activities. In others, such as New York, actions by local governments, including land use permitting, are covered. Although the specifics vary, all of the mini-NEPAs mandate some level of analysis and, in some cases, mitigation of actions that have significant impacts on the environment. The attorney general of California has interpreted that state's mini-NEPA—the California Environmental Quality Act (CEQA)—as applicable to GHG emissions. In a celebrated lawsuit against San Bernardino County, the attorney general asserted that CEQA required the county to assess and mitigate GHG emission impacts associated with an update of the county's general plan (see "Smart Growth and Climate Change Policy in California" on the following page).

In California, Assembly Bill 32 contains a legislative declaration that "[g]lobal warming poses a serious threat to … the environment of California." This declaration provides the basis

SMART GROWTH AND CLIMATE CHANGE POLICY IN CALIFORNIA

California must address VMT growth if the state is to meet its GHG reduction target pursuant to Assembly Bill 32 (AB 32), the Global Warming Solutions Act of 2006. California state agencies are working hard on a recipe for comprehensive policy changes to advance smart growth, cut VMT, and reduce GHG emissions. They have a rich set of ingredients with which to work, including a statewide climate target (AB 32), Blueprint Planning Grants to promote integrated regional transportation and land use planning, climate change impact assessment guidelines under the California Environmental Quality Act (CEQA), proposed legislation (SB 375) to provide incentives for smart growth planning and implementation, and some $40 billion in infrastructure bonds that could be "green-leveraged" to encourage climate-friendly development patterns. State, regional, and local officials, as well as environmental advocates and developers, are working out the details of policy design issues, including how to set and meet regional VMT/GHG targets, how to address GHGs in project and plan environmental impact reports (EIRs), and how to ensure that bond funds advance sustainable communities and GHG reduction goals.

In setting regional VMT or GHG targets, the twin challenges are to ensure that 1) regional VMT targets, in aggregate, are sufficient to help meet state GHG goals, and 2) targets are feasible in light of the unique conditions of each region, including population growth, demographic and economic trends, development patterns, and transportation infrastructure. There is an emerging sense—but no consensus—that it may be best to start with voluntary regional targets and support their implementation via technical assistance and planning support (for data and model improvements, and for scenario planning tools). As the regions' expertise and experience grows, these could evolve over time into mandatory targets, with incentives offered by attaching VMT/GHG performance conditions to allocation of transportation and other infrastructure funding.

The state already has established a precedent for requiring GHG reduction goals in regional and local plans. Last year, California Attorney General Jerry Brown, Jr., sued San Bernardino County on grounds that the county violated CEQA by not adequately addressing climate change impacts in its general plan update EIR. The parties subsequently reached a settlement wherein the county agreed to prepare a plan that will include a GHG emissions inventory and emissions reduction targets. Although it is temporarily barred from filing further lawsuits until the state provides more direction on climate change impact assessment in its CEQA guidelines (to become effective January 1, 2010), the attorney general's office continues to comment on general plan, regional plan, and development project EIRs, recommending further analysis and specific impact mitigations.

Today, all eyes are on California. Smart growth and climate change policy development in this state will offer important insights and models for other states and the federal government.

for enforcement action under CEQA. Yet, even without similar legislative pronouncements in other mini-NEPA states, the scientific evidence regarding GHG emissions and climate change—much of which is summarized in Chapter 3—argues for environmental assessments of GHG emissions.

While generally positive, mini-NEPA compliance can be costly. In states where a mini-NEPA covers private land development activities, the cost of compliance can negatively affect housing affordability. California is now considering legislation (Senate Bill 375) that would provide partial or full exemptions from CEQA compliance for compact development meeting specified standards. This combination of policies—generally requiring GHG assessments for development proposals, while exempting qualified compact developments—would give compact developments a significant edge in the real estate market. It is a model that could be duplicated in other mini-NEPA states.

REGIONAL POLICY RECOMMENDATIONS

Success in meeting our climate challenge will require cooperation across state and city boundaries. Minnesota's Twin Cities and their suburbs provide an example of regional coordination to tackle regional problems. When the state legislature created the Metropolitan Council in 1967, the region—which had 272 separate local units of government—was plagued by inadequately treated sewage, a deteriorating bus system, and rapid loss of open spaces. Making the situation worse, many communities lacked the funding to tackle these problems (Metropolitan Council 2004). Since its creation, the Metropolitan Council has contributed to the Twin Cities's reputation as a green, livable, vibrant region. This regional approach is now helping the Twin Cities reduce global warming pollution.

Although regional agencies like the Metropolitan Council are still rare in the United States, every medium and large metropolitan area has an MPO. Congress required the establishment of MPOs in the 1970s as a condition of federal transportation funding. These agencies often are also councils of governments (regional councils) that coordinate and assist their local cities and counties in addressing regional concerns. In some states, MPOs are now involved in land planning as well as transportation planning. MPOs are the logical entities to carry out many of the policies recommended in this section. They will need to be given enhanced powers and resources, consistent with the new duties assigned to them, and become more accountable for regional outcomes. Their governing bodies will need to be representative of the regions they serve, with cities and suburbs represented according to population. It would be best if MPOs operated as part of broad-based, multiservice regional councils.

INCLUDE CLIMATE GOALS IN REGIONAL TRANSPORTATION PLANS

Regional long-range transportation plans are the blueprints that guide investment in a region's transportation system. Including GHG and VMT reduction targets in these plans will help ensure that transportation investments contribute to climate protection. In California, MPOs, state agencies, and the state legislature currently are considering incorporating GHG reduction targets into long-range transportation plans to comply with AB 32, the California Global Warming Solutions Act of 2006.

GIVE FUNDING PRIORITY TO COMPACT, TRANSIT-SERVED AREAS

Metropolitan planning organizations could give funding priority to compact, transit-served areas where development will help reduce GHG emissions. In concert with local governments, MPOs would designate "priority funding areas" where local governments have planned for compact development.

In the Twin Cities, the Metropolitan Council's 2030 Regional Development Framework seeks to encourage infill of "developed communities," those in which more than 85 percent of the land is developed and infrastructure is well established. To advance this goal, the Metropolitan Council administers the Livable Communities Act (LCA), which underwrites grants for brownfields cleanup, affordable housing, and mixed-use projects, and is funded through a metro-area property tax (EPA 2003). This voluntary program has engaged more than 100 communities in the seven-county metropolitan area, leveraging billions of dollars in private investments as well as additional public investments.

The San Diego Association of Governments (SANDAG) has developed a smart growth concept map in concert with local governments. For a share of incentive funding, local governments have been willing to designate smart growth areas and accept more growth and density. Incentive funds will amount to $240 million through the year 2040. To be designated, an area must currently meet minimum density and transit service standards, or have planning and zoning in place that will lead to such densities. Because funds for the program come from a regional sales tax, qualifying areas can use the money for a wide range of improvements, not just those directly related to transportation. Areas that do not yet have the necessary planning and zoning in place can apply for planning grants to complete plan and code changes that would qualify them for infrastructure funding (SANDAG 2006).

Similar programs are in place in the San Francisco Bay Area, the Sacramento area, and Portland, Oregon. In these regions, however, because federal transportation funds are used (primarily CMAQ and enhancement funds), qualifying projects have to be transportation related.

REDIRECT TRANSPORTATION FUNDS FROM ROAD EXPANSION TO TRANSIT AND BIKE/PEDESTRIAN FACILITIES

Metropolitan planning organizations should redirect transportation resources in order to develop top-notch infrastructure for nonauto travel modes. Shifting investment away from road expansion toward transit, bicycling, and walking facilities can lead to better climate outcomes, not only by encouraging the use of alternative modes of transportation but by moderating induced traffic and induced development (see Chapter 6).

The Sacramento Area Council of Governments (SACOG), which is responsible for coordinating the planning of 22 cities and six counties in the Sacramento area, was dissatisfied with the projected outcomes of its 2025 Transportation Plan. Under the plan, it was projected that VMT would continue to outpace population growth, transit ridership would increase only marginally, and the nonmotorized (walking and bicycling) mode share would decline.

The SACOG 2035 Plan sought to reverse these trends. It focused on four performance indicators: VMT, congestion and delay, transit ridership, and nonmotorized travel mode share (SACOG 2007). Out of a total spending package of $41.7 billion, the 2035 Plan earmarks $14.3 billion for transit and $1.4 billion for bicycle and pedestrian projects.

Projections show that VMT growth through 2035 will fall from its historic growth rate of 2.5 percent per year to 1.4 percent per year. The VMT growth rate is projected to be lower than the population growth rate of 1.6 percent (SACOG 2007, p. 4–4). This plan also will save money. A recent SACOG study found that infrastructure costs an average of $20,000 less per housing unit for compact development than for sprawl.

USE LAND USE/TRANSPORTATION SCENARIO PLANNING TO EVALUATE GROWTH OPTIONS

Land use/transportation scenario planning, once considered "state-of-the-art," should become state-of-the-practice everywhere. In regional scenario planning, one future scenario represents "business as usual" or a continuation of current growth trends, usually some variant of sprawl. Other scenarios usually represent more compact and transit-oriented development patterns. Scenarios are run through regional travel models and other performance assessments. Scenario planning helps clarify the costs and benefits of alternative development patterns. It helps identify options available to communities in the region, the different investments they will require, and the tradeoffs involved.

Scenario planning has been conducted all over the country (see "Regional Growth Simulations" in Chapter 4). One of the best examples is the Sacramento Region Blueprint Transportation-Land Use Study, which used an extensive public outreach process, cutting-edge Internet-accessible planning software, and a detailed business-as-usual baseline growth forecast to help participants explore alternative growth scenarios through 2050. The "preferred scenario," ultimately adopted, features infill development and transportation investments that will produce 12.3 fewer daily VMT per household by 2050, a 26 percent reduction below the baseline (SACOG 2005).

Other well-known scenario planning studies include Portland Metro's Region 2040, which began in 1992 and was the first large-scale scenario planning exercise in the nation (Metro 2000), and Louisiana Speaks (2007), which was launched to help coastal communities craft redevelopment plans after Hurricanes Katrina and Rita. There are numerous examples of visioning and scenario planning that have not led to changes in development patterns (Bartholomew 2007). Those that have been successful were backed by political will and the resources required to continue the process after the initial public participation is complete.

Under a GHG conformity requirement (see "Require Transportation Conformity for GHGs" earlier in this chapter), regions such as Sacramento and Portland would be able to use their interactive transportation and land use models to develop land use and transportation scenarios that achieve VMT reduction targets, and limit investment to transportation projects that comply with the "constrained" plan. Coordination will be more difficult in the many regions without integrated land use and transportation models.

ESTABLISH A REGIONAL TRANSFER OF DEVELOPMENT RIGHTS PROGRAM

Transfer of development rights (TDR) programs enable landowners to sell their development rights to other landowners through a market-based system. Such programs have long been used to help protect farmland and open space by shifting development rights from such lands to areas designated for higher-density development. Effectively crafted, TDR programs can help reduce VMT by directing growth to compact, transit-served areas and away from low-density greenfield sites, thus reducing the need for long-distance travel.

Taxpayers benefit from TDR programs because they cost less than outright government purchase of open space or farmland. The programs also are generally popular with citizens in rural areas because they compensate rural landowners for the development potential of their land. While TDR programs typically are administered by local governments, a regional TDR program could have greater impact because it would encompass more rural and urban areas than a local program. Montgomery County, Maryland, located just north of Washington, D.C., has a large subregional TDR program that has protected nearly 51,000 acres of farmland in the past 25 years. Regional TDR programs exist in the New Jersey Pinelands and the Lake Tahoe area.

CREATE A CARBON IMPACT FEE FOR NEW DEVELOPMENT

Cheap land and subsidized infrastructure make suburban and exurban development less expensive than urban infill. Regulatory reforms alone cannot overcome this advantage. For decades, governments have charged impact fees on new development to offset the costs of schools, libraries, sewers, parks, and transportation. Creating and implementing a regional Co_2 emissions impact fee would internalize carbon impacts into development costs, thereby rewarding best development practices and raising the price of carbon-inefficient development. Coupled with a TDR program as described above, an impact fee would require exurban landowners who developed their land to pay, while exurban landowners who stewarded their land would get paid. Fee revenues could be used to help fund transit, bicycling facilities, sidewalks and other pedestrian amenities, and other smart growth projects in compact areas.

Although novel, such a fee would not be the first instance of an emissions-based development impact fee. The San Joaquin Valley Air Pollution Control District in the Fresno, California, area imposes a fee on new development to fund mitigation of several transportation-related air pollutants and to encourage developers to build projects that minimize emissions. The program, which applies to all development above a minimum size, assesses fees for the estimated ten-year total emissions associated with the development. The fees, which in 2007 were $7,100 per ton for NOx and $5,594 per ton for PM 10, are based on the cost of offsetting emission reduction strategies.

The incentive part of the San Joaquin program provides fee reductions for project features that will reduce transportation-related emission rates below base levels. These features include proximity to retail, a balance of jobs and housing, proximity to transit services, high intersection density, and the provision of sidewalks, bicycle lanes, and long-term bicycle parking. In 2006/2007, the district collected nearly $13 million in fees and spent more than $9.5 million on emission reduction projects. These projects resulted in emission reductions of 824 tons of NOx and 34 tons of PM 10 (SJVAPCD 2007).

The San Joaquin program could be adapted for Co_2 emissions. Using the project-level simulation techniques outlined in Chapter 4 and borrowing elasticities from disaggregate travel studies discussed there, policy makers could craft a reasonable system for calculating project-level Co_2 emissions.

ENHANCE REGIONAL TRAVEL MODELS TO ACCOUNT FOR LAND USE/TRAVEL INTERACTIONS

Conventional regional travel models used in long-range transportation planning are unable to access the full impacts of the development patterns advocated in this book. They cannot account for the effects of density, diversity, or design on travel distance or mode choice. Most models disregard the possibility of walking or bicycle use on short trips, assuming instead that all trips are by motor vehicle. They predict travel between "traffic analysis zones," which usually are based on divisions of census tracts, leaving intrazonal travel poorly represented. As a consequence, these models underestimate the potential of smart growth to reduce VMT and GHG emissions.

Some MPOs have developed more advanced travel models that overcome these limitations. The Metropolitan Transportation Commission (MTC), the MPO for the San Francisco Bay Area, includes both walk and bicycle modes in its model, basing projections for these modes on such factors as travel time and employment density (for work trips). The MTC model also includes a wider variety of trip purposes than the typical travel model. Montgomery County, Maryland; Portland, Oregon; and Sacramento also are among the handful of regions with enhanced models. Planners in leading regions are beginning to use a new generation of activity-based travel models that simulate the travel of individual households. These microsimulation models overcome the limitations of travel analysis zones and also provide improved accounting of VMT and congestion.

ASSIST LOCAL GOVERNMENTS WITH LAND DEVELOPMENT REFORMS

Rewriting local land development codes to encourage more climate-friendly growth requires significant expertise and funding, which many communities lack. The EPA Smart Growth program, which runs a technical assistance program for localities, receives more than 60 applications a year for five or six grants. Regional governments as well as states should take the lead in helping communities bring their development regulations into the 21st century.

In the Bay Area, the MTC provides $7.5 million in Transportation for Livable Communities planning grants for local governments to plan and zone for transit-oriented development. The program provides grants of up to $750,000 to fund transit station area plans, zoning ordinances, and other land development guides designed to boost transit ridership and reduce VMT (MTC n.d.). The MTC also provides funding for capital improvements and may expand eligibility to include such unconventional projects as land banking for affordable housing. The Sacramento MPO, SACOG, has a similar program.

LOCAL POLICY RECOMMENDATIONS

More than 780 U.S. mayors are signatories to the U.S. Conference of Mayors Climate Protection Agreement (Mayors Climate Protection Center 2007), and about 600 have signed on as "Cool Mayors" with the Mayors for Climate Protection program (2008). Both programs commit cities to meeting the Kyoto target of emissions 7 percent lower than 1990 levels by the year 2012. Counties, too, are taking action under a "Cool Counties" campaign launched by the Sierra Club in partnership with King County, Washington; Fairfax County, Virginia; and Nassau County, New York. Concrete actions that localities can take are outlined in this section.

DEVELOP A LOCAL CLIMATE ACTION PLAN

To meet these commitments, many cities and counties are developing climate action plans. The best of these plans create a baseline inventory of GHG emissions from various sources, such as transportation, land use, energy use, and solid waste; identify actions and policies needed to reduce emissions from each source;

set reduction targets, with benchmarks along the way to track progress; create a budget for what is needed to achieve the reductions; and identify potential funding sources to pay for improvements.

The Seattle Climate Action Plan (2007) has all these elements. With GHG emissions from transportation making up about 60 percent of the total, the city sees transportation as its biggest challenge. The city's plan incorporates transit service expansion, a complete streets ordinance, bicycle and pedestrian master plans, a commercial parking tax, a traffic calming program, and a "center city strategy" that promotes growth in the downtown and adjacent neighborhoods. The plan's well-defined benchmarks and reporting requirements help to hold city government accountable. Charlotte, North Carolina, has a Transportation Action Plan with essentially the same elements.

PlaNYC: GREENING THE CITY

The average American is responsible for annual emissions of 24.5 metric tons of CO_2. Residents of New York City, however, are responsible for only 7.1 metric tons of CO_2 per year, less than one-third the national average. New York City is more energy efficient for two key reasons: a more efficient transportation system and more efficient buildings. Two-thirds of New Yorkers take transit or walk to work; fewer than 5 percent drive to work in the central business district. And almost no one drives to the store to pick up a quart of milk or to the gym to ride a stationary bicycle. The city's multifamily, mixed-use buildings share walls and use less energy than freestanding structures.

New York City's savings opportunities are not maxed out. Building upon an already efficient footprint, PlaNYC sets a goal of reducing citywide carbon emissions by 30 percent below 2005 levels. An annual GHG emissions inventory will track progress toward this goal. The city will address growing congestion on roadways and transit lines by expanding transit services, improving cycling and pedestrian infrastructure, and significantly increasing the availability of affordable housing near workplaces. The proposed revenue-raising mechanism, a congestion pricing program, would cut traffic and air pollution by more than 10 percent, while raising some $400 million to $500 million per year to be invested in transit. If this congestion pricing plan is approved by the city council and the state legislature, New York City will receive $350 million through an Urban Partnership Agreement with the U.S. Department of Transportation. Importantly, the city has attracted a dream team of experts and advisers from the private, public, and nonprofit sectors to develop, market, and implement the plan.

CHANGE THE RULES OF DEVELOPMENT

Some of the biggest impacts on VMT can be achieved through changes to local land development policies. Many communities have not overhauled their zoning and subdivision ordinances since they were created in the 1950s or 1960s, when they were designed to separate land uses, maintain low densities and large setbacks, ensure plentiful parking, keep streets wide, and save money by limiting sidewalks. Communities need to examine their development rules to determine if and how these rules should be changed to meet GHG reduction targets. They should include in their review the following items:

- zoning codes;
- subdivision regulations;
- street design standards;
- parking standards;
- annexation rules; and
- design guidelines.

Tools such as scorecards and zoning code audits are available to help in this review process (Smart Growth Leadership Institute 2006). New models such as form-based codes and smart codes are readily adaptable from other localities or from national models.

FAVOR SMART GROWTH PROJECTS IN THE APPROVAL PROCESS

Once communities have reformed their codes to allow smart growth, they should make it easier for such projects to gain approval. Predictability in the approval process is valuable to everyone concerned, including local government, citizens, and developers, for whom time is money. Laying out the guidelines and rules for what local government seeks in the way of development makes the process more predictable and fair, as does defining the benefits developers will derive from meeting or exceeding a community's VMT reduction targets.

One way to favor compact development is to provide incentives. If development projects meet or exceed a community's targets, developers can be rewarded with, for example, density bonuses that allow them to build more or permitting fee waivers that allow them to pay less. Alternatively, local governments can calculate the traffic reduction benefits of compact development and reduce, accordingly, the amount of exactions or fees for which developers are responsible.

Another way to favor compact development is to offer streamlined permitting for projects that meet specified community targets. Of course, the process still must include opportunities for meaningful public input and ensure compliance with public safety and environmental safeguards. Nevertheless, because less time spent negotiating approval processes can translate into significant cost savings for developers, the promise of faster permitting can be an effective incentive for smart growth. Orlando, Florida, has provided all of these incentives for traditional urban development in the city's southeast sector.

ADOPT PEDESTRIAN-FRIENDLY SITE AND BUILDING DESIGN STANDARDS

Site and building design standards, especially for commercial and institutional uses, need to provide for a comfortable and attractive environment at the sidewalk. The regional transportation plan adopted by Portland Metro requires new retail, office, and institutional buildings at major transit stops to be located no farther than 20 feet from the stop or, alternatively, to provide a pedestrian plaza at the stop with a direct pedestrian connection to the building entrance (Metro 2004, p. 6–23). The city of Portland went a step further, requiring that all new multifamily residential, commercial, and institutional structures along transit-served streets be located within 20 feet of the sidewalk. The city also banned off-street parking from the front of buildings, requiring it to be located at the side or the back of a structure (Portland Code 33.266.130). Facilitating these changes in site design are off-street parking standards that reduce the minimum amount of parking required—in some cases eliminating it entirely—and establish a maximum amount that will be allowed (Metro Code 3.07.210-3.07.220).

The Local Government Commission (2003), a California-based nonprofit, has compiled a comprehensive catalog of additional design strategies, drawn in part from the Sacramento city code and recommendations from the U.S. Department of Housing and Urban Development (HUD).

PROVIDE FOR WORKFORCE HOUSING NEAR JOBS

Two leading planning researchers recently asked, "which reduces vehicle travel more, jobs/housing balance or retail/housing mixing?" (Cervero and Duncan 2006). The answer—surprisingly, since work trips represent less than 20 percent of all trips—was jobs/housing balance. In most metropolitan areas, the cost of housing declines with distance from job centers and other desired destinations, while the cost of transportation increases. Without workforce housing, people have to drive until they qualify for a mortgage or else live in substandard housing. They also have to drive until they find decent schools for their kids. With rising gasoline prices, the financial tradeoff between a longer commute and less expensive housing is changing, and the potential savings from living in a convenient location with transportation choices is becoming a larger part of affordability.

Local governments have many options for promoting workforce housing (Haughey 2007):

- allowing accessory apartments on single-family house lots;
- enacting inclusionary zoning requirements that affordable homes be built along with market-rate housing;
- enacting linkage requirements that workforce housing be provided in return for approval of offices or industrial facilities;
- offering density bonuses in return for affordable units;
- donating or selling municipal lands with workforce housing requirements; and
- creating housing trust funds that earmark revenue from multiple sources for a community's housing needs.

INVEST IN CIVIC ENGAGEMENT AND EDUCATION

Successful planning requires the meaningful engagement of people who live and work in the affected community. Meaningful public engagement requires that planners and decision makers actively seek out public input early in the planning process, well before threshold questions are framed or alternatives crafted. When residents are engaged in the planning process from the beginning and know that their concerns and ideas are being considered, they are more likely to support new development. Visioning processes and design charrettes are two popular techniques that localities have used in recent years to engage citizens.

One example comes from Davidson, North Carolina, where the town's planning ordinance requires developers to hold design charrettes. Involving the public at this early stage can make the approval process smoother for developers, offsetting any added costs they may incur by involving the public.

DEVELOPING A COMPREHENSIVE POLICY PACKAGE

Such a comprehensive overhaul of America's development processes will be a mighty challenge. But it is on the same ambitious scale as other proposals that are being considered in the climate change debate, including efforts to switch to renewable fuels, dramatically increase vehicle efficiency, end oil imports from hostile nations, and renew investments in nuclear power.

The fact is, no huge amount of reduction will come easily, and few strategies are likely to take advantage of consumer demand as well as those discussed in this book. Most communities that have adopted land development reforms have done so for self-interested reasons, such as traffic management or fiscal health, and not because they wished to reduce greenhouse gas emissions. We are confident that these improvements to the built environment can offer win-win benefits, for communities and the global climate.

ENVIRONMENTAL PLANNING HANDBOOK FOR SUSTAINABLE COMMUNITIES AND REGIONS

TAKING STOCK OF THE ENVIRONMENT AND CREATING ENVIRONMENTAL PLANS

BY TOM DANIELS

If we cannot imagine a healthy, bountiful, and sustaining environment today, it will elude us tomorrow.

—Mark Dowie[1]

Planning is about organizing resources and making choices to achieve goals and objectives. Rachel Carson first used the term "environment" in her book *Silent Spring* to refer to natural places and processes as well as the condition of human settlements. *Environmental planning* explains how governments, businesses, and households decide how to use natural resources, financial capital, and human resources to solve problems in natural areas, rural working landscapes, and the built environments of cities, suburbs, and towns. Governments can use laws, regulations, taxation, infrastructure spending, and financial incentives to encourage environmentally friendly business practices

Tom Daniels, "Taking Stock of the Environment and Creating Environmental Plans," *The Environmental Planning Handbook for Sustainable Communities and Regions*, pp. 3-40. Copyright © 2014 by Taylor & Francis Group. Reprinted with permission.

and household lifestyles. Businesses seek to sell goods and services and earn a profit for their owners or shareholders. Businesses are finding that they can reduce costs by cutting waste and energy consumption and also increase profits by offering environmentally responsible goods and services to consumers and other businesses. Households provide labor for government and businesses and are consumers of goods and services. Household choices of what to buy, where to live, and how to live (i.e., recycling efforts) directly affect the quality of the environment.

Planning also involves anticipating problems before they happen. Environmental planning can help communities to avoid or minimize air and water pollution, loss of wildlife, the conversion of farm and forest lands, and degradation of the built environment.

The environment in general consists of air, water, and three main land uses:

1. *Natural areas* are undeveloped lands and waters that provide an array of environmental services, such as water supply, water recharge and filtration, fish and wildlife habitats, air filtration, and recreation. Natural areas also include natural hazards that pose environmental constraints, such as floodplains, wetlands, and steep slopes.
2. *Working landscapes* of farms, rangeland, forests, mines, and commercial recreation areas provide food, fiber, lumber, minerals, and energy and contribute to the health of rural and metropolitan economies.
3. *Built environments* of cities, suburbs, and towns involve the design and siting of buildings, transportation systems, sewer and water facilities, and public spaces and parkland.

How these three land uses interact with one another affect a community's appearance, size, operations, richness of ecosystem services, and overall environmental quality. Deciding how, when, and where these land uses should or should not change is a fundamental challenge of environmental planning. Yet in the past few decades, the overarching challenge that has arisen is global climate change (see Chapter 4). Climate change has raised air and ocean temperatures and is expected to produce more frequent and severe storms and droughts. Climate change also increases vulnerability to invasive species, wildfires, coastal storms, and rising sea levels. Mitigating emissions of greenhouse gases that contribute to climate change have become central goals of climate change have become central goals of environmental planning.

This book emphasizes how planners, elected officials, and the public-at-large can add environmental planning to the comprehensive plan, land-use regulations, building codes, and infrastructure spending programs. Chapters 3 through 20 each contain examples of how to add environmental planning to the comprehensive plan and how to achieve environmental goals and objectives through an Environmental Action Plan of innovative zoning and subdivision regulations and capital improvements programs (CIPs). It is important to consult your state's planning and zoning-enabling legislation to determine which land-use regulatory tools and financial incentives are allowed in your state. Finally, each chapter contains a discussion of what a planning staff or planning commission should look for in reviewing a development proposal in order to minimize environmental impacts.

1.1: ADDING ENVIRONMENTAL PLANNING TO THE COMPREHENSIVE PLANNING PROCESS

Public environmental planning is put into practice through federal, state, and local government

BOX 1. THE ROLE OF THE PLANNER IN ENVIRONMENTAL PLANNING

Planning is central to any government policy or business decision. Elected leaders and citizens rely on public plans to guide budgets and financial investments, make land-use regulations, and adopt infrastructure spending programs. Local government decisions about public infrastructure investment influence private development decisions. Both public and private developments have major outcomes on transportation systems, development patterns, the mix of land uses, and air, water, and ecosystem quality. Planners need to bring a long-range perspective to the planning process, particularly the cumulative impacts of development projects on the environment.

Planners play a variety of roles in environmental planning: educator, communicator, negotiator, facilitator, enabler, data manager, and expert.

Planners who work for local governments serve as staff to a city or county planning commission. Public planners can help to educate the planning commission about best planning practices for development and environmental protection. Planners also provide data and analysis of development proposals and recommend how these proposals could be improved. In short, planners enable the planning commission to make more informed recommendations to the elected officials about development proposals and changes to the local comprehensive plan, zoning and subdivision regulations, and capital improvements programs. The elected officials make the legally binding decisions about whether to approve development proposals and changes to local regulations and infrastructure programs. Public planners also work directly with the elected officials, keeping them apprised of land-use and environmental matters and helping them respond to public inquiries and requests for action.

Planners must be able to communicate effectively with the public about the purpose of planning for the environment and how different planning tools work. One way local government planners have done this is by offering special evening courses for interested citizens. Another way is to use Internet websites, wikis, and social media to make communication more convenient for the public.

Planners must work with the public to build a consensus on a vision for the community—that is, a direction to work toward. Planners need to explain the importance of the environment to the community as well as the benefits of new planning programs and the costs of inaction. This is especially important when planners are promoting a new comprehensive plan, zoning ordinance, or infrastructure spending program. But communication is not just one way; ideally, planners must involve a variety of stakeholders in the community and broad citizen participation to create active discussions and explorations of a variety of possible planning actions and tools to make the desired changes. In short, planners should not assume that they have all the answers and should be willing to learn what the public wants and how planning can achieve those desired outcomes. A planner who communicates well can garner public support, which can attract the attention and support of the planning commission and elected officials.

(Continued)

Public planners also need to have good negotiation skills for interacting with the public, developers, landowners, the planning commission, and the elected officials. Planning is a political process as well as a legal process, and politics often involves compromise through negotiation.

Planners can facilitate public meetings about planning and can explain to landowners and developers how the comprehensive plan and land-use regulations affect their development proposals. In this way, planners can promote the certain types of development and redevelopment, well-designed developments, and developments in desired locations while protecting environmentally sensitive lands, such as steep slopes, wetlands, and floodplains.

Planners who work for private sector clients should keep in mind that the American Institute of Certified Planners (AICP) code of ethics emphasizes the public interest over private gain. So a planner with a private client should try to promote decisions that are profitable for the client as well as beneficial to the public-at-large. Here, the planner as educator and enabler can help the client understand why a more environmentally friendly development design can be more profitable because it will gain a quicker approval and less public opposition than a poorly designed project. Finally, private sector planners are legitimate experts. They may testify on land-use and environmental planning cases in court.

laws, regulations, tax policy, and spending programs that discourage, encourage, or require certain actions by companies, individuals, and governments. Federal laws set national standards to protect public health and wildlife and compel improvements in air and water quality and the clean-up of hazardous waste sites. State governments have environmental agencies that coordinate compliance with federal laws and regulations and in some cases set their own environmental standards. Private businesses, households, and nonprofit organizations also do environmental planning to guide their actions that influence environmental quality. But the focus of this book is mainly on environmental planning by cities, towns, and counties. The day-to-day decisions of America's 39,000 local governments about the siting and types of private development and public infrastructure arguably have the greatest consequences for the national environment.

Municipal and county governments have primary responsibility for planning the use of the natural and built environments, although local comprehensive plans and regulations may be influenced by federal and state laws, requirements, and guidelines. The main purposes of local comprehensive planning process are to

1. decide on the appropriate uses of land and the spatial pattern of development;
2. identify lands with development constraints, such as floodplains, wetlands, steep slopes, and shallow depth to bedrock, as well as lack of central water and sewage service;
3. regulate the location, timing, and design of development; and
4. invest in gray infrastructure, such as sewer and water facilities, public buildings, roads, and transit, and in green infrastructure, such as parks, tree planting, green streets, and green roofs, to address current needs and to

influence the siting, design, intensity, and sustainability of future development.

THE COMPREHENSIVE PLAN

The comprehensive plan establishes the traditional foundation for local and regional planning. The plan sets forth a vision of how a community or region should look, function, and grow over the next 10 to 20 years and sometimes longer. The plan provides direction for public and private sector decision makers through an inventory of current conditions and the identification of future needs. The plan expresses goals and objectives for housing, the economic base, public facilities and services, transportation, land use, parks and recreation, and the environment.

A crucial part of the comprehensive plan is a projection of population change. More people bring greater demands for housing, jobs, water, sewage treatment, and land for development. On the other hand, some communities may be losing population or experiencing little population change, but population shifts and new developments within such communities can still affect environmental quality. For example, sprawling development can occur even when there is little population growth and result in more vehicle miles traveled and air pollution emissions.

Particularly important is the comprehensive plan's future land-use map, which details the location of desired land uses and lays the foundation for the zoning map. Planners, public officials, and the general public should evaluate private development proposals and public infrastructure programs according to the goals and objectives of the comprehensive plan as well as the future land-use map.

A fundamental reason to emphasize environmental planning within the comprehensive plan is that it provides a legal basis for the zoning ordinance and subdivision regulations that, along with the CIP and design guidelines, put the comprehensive plan into action. Consistency among the comprehensive plan, implementing regulations, and spending programs is essential. A lack of consistency creates confusion for landowners, developers, elected officials, and the public about the purpose of the plan, the legality and fairness of the regulations, and the need for infrastructure spending.

Also, environmental planning—like a comprehensive plan—should be holistic because, as the second law of ecology states, "everything is connected to everything else."[2] Planning for one aspect of the environment, such as water quality, without recognizing the impacts of other activities (such as air pollution degrading water quality) will result in less effective plans, less accurate regulations, and less successful incentives to maintain or improve environmental quality.

Traditional city or county comprehensive plans often have several shortcomings for sustainable environmental planning. First, the traditional plan usually emphasizes economic development, transportation, and housing and does not place a high priority on environmental quality. It is not uncommon to find comprehensive plans that have little to say about the development capabilities and constraints of the natural environment. This is frequently the case with larger cities that have small amounts of open, developable land as well as rural communities that are hungry for economic activity. Communities on the metropolitan fringe often designate their remaining farmland as "vacant" in the comprehensive plan, as if the land has no legitimate current use and is just waiting to be developed. Many smaller communities try to save time and money by drafting a "policy plan" that does not include an inventory of facts or an analysis of environmental conditions. As a result, policy recommendations often sound like nothing more than a wish list.

A weakness of the traditional comprehensive plan is that it lists several goals and objectives that are often difficult for planners and local governments to prioritize. Is an affordable housing goal more important than a water supply goal? Or, how does an objective to purchase 10 natural gas–powered buses compare with an objective to add 30 acres of parkland?

Many communities have comprehensive plans that are more than 10 years old and no longer reflect the community's conditions or goals and objectives for growth, development, or environmental quality. All too frequently, planning commissions and planning staff find themselves overwhelmed with reviewing development proposals and have little or no time to devote to updating the comprehensive plan, the zoning and subdivision regulations, or the CIP.

Another common problem is that the comprehensive plan of a single community or county may not recognize the environmental impacts of its land-use and development activities on neighboring jurisdictions or vice versa. For instance, the destruction of wetlands upstream will create more flooding downstream. Most land-use and environmental problems are regional, not local. Yet local governments usually try to address these problems by themselves rather than through regional cooperation.

To promote environmental planning, planners would be wise to cite the importance of a quality environment in the economic development chapter of the comprehensive plan. Two of the largest economic sectors in America are high technology and tourism. High technology includes computer-related businesses, health care, biotech, optics, and aerospace, among others. High-tech companies are footloose; they can locate just about anywhere. Moreover, they employ well-paid and highly educated workers who value a healthy environment and an overall good quality of life. Attractive cities, towns, and villages with good air and water quality and access to open space are competitive for high-tech businesses and their workers.

Tourists are looking for unique and enjoyable sights and activities. Scenic vistas, wildlife, recreation areas, clean air and water, historic sites and buildings, and good places to eat, shop, and spend the night all contribute to positive experiences in places that can be visited again and again. This is not to say that everyone should be employed in writing computer software or in hotels. Heavy manufacturing is still important to many communities, as are retail trades, finance, energy production, agriculture, and a variety of service and government-related jobs. But there is a close link between sustainable economic activity and a sustainable environment.

FUNCTIONAL AND AREA PLANS

Local governments have a choice of whether to emphasize environmental issues within a comprehensive plan or to create separate strategic plans. Strategic plans fall into two categories: (1) functional plans and (2) area plans.

A functional plan goes into more detail on a particular topic in a comprehensive plan. For example, many local governments have adopted a functional park-and-recreation plan in addition to the community facilities section of the comprehensive plan. An area plan focuses on a certain geographic location, such as a neighborhood, a transportation corridor, or part of a county. Functional plans and area plans can help to expand on the inventory and analysis of data and the goals and objectives contained in the comprehensive plan. For instance, a hazard mitigation plan is an area plan with elements of a functional plan that expand on the land use and natural resources inventory sections of a comprehensive plan. Planners use a comprehensive plan to note the location of places that are vulnerable to natural hazards. But a comprehensive plan is not a substitute for a detailed hazard mitigation plan.

Local functional environmental plans often include a park and open space plan, water supply plan, Energy Plan, Heritage Area Plan, transportation plan, stormwater management plan, and a hazard mitigation plan. These and other plans are explored in greater depth in the chapters that follow.

In recent years, several local governments have added a separate green infrastructure plan, which applies to particular areas and expands on the land use and natural resources inventory sections of the comprehensive plan. Climate action plans are also hybrids of functional and area plans. More than 100 local governments have drafted climate action plans to provide guidance on how to reduce greenhouse gas emissions, especially from transportation and buildings, as well as how to adapt to warmer temperatures, more frequent storm events, and rising sea levels.

A small but growing number of local governments have drafted sustainability plans that express the interconnected long-range goals of a sustainable economy, environment, and society. These plans strive for the long-term health of the natural environment, productive working landscapes, efficient public investments, a durable built environment, economic prosperity, and access to a quality environment for all income groups.

Separate functional and area plans can be much more *strategic* than a comprehensive plan. A comprehensive plan asks the general question: "What kind of community do we *want* to have in 20 years?" A strategic plan asks a very different question: "What do we have to do to be the community we *need* to be in 20 years?" Many comprehensive plans fail to come to life because they do not have an action plan element to implement them. A strategic plan more often lays out the regulations, incentives, and investments that a local government and the private sector need to make in order to achieve a level of environmental quality within a set time frame. Strategic plans often include quantifiable goals, such as a 20 percent reduction in greenhouse gases by 2025, or 10 miles of greenways and trails by 2020, or 25 more miles of light rail by 2030.

Whether in a comprehensive plan or a strategic plan, environmental planning must be economically and technologically feasible. It makes little sense to advocate tax policies, capital spending programs, or technologies that a community, region, businesses, or households cannot afford. A plan alone will not guarantee long-term progress toward greater sustainability and quality of life. The key factors are the political will of elected officials; the mix of regulations, incentives, and investments to implement the plan; and the support of the general public for their communities.

By referencing a functional plan or an area plan, the comprehensive plan can effectively make these strategic plans part of the comprehensive plan. As long as the functional and area plans are formally adopted by the elected officials as part of the comprehensive plan, they will have the same legal authority as a traditional comprehensive plan in setting a basis for zoning and subdivision regulations and in guiding capital investments. In short, a modern comprehensive plan is connected to a network of supporting functional and area plans. This network of plans is especially important for including detailed environmental data, analysis, policies, and action strategies to implement the comprehensive plan and the related functional and area plans.

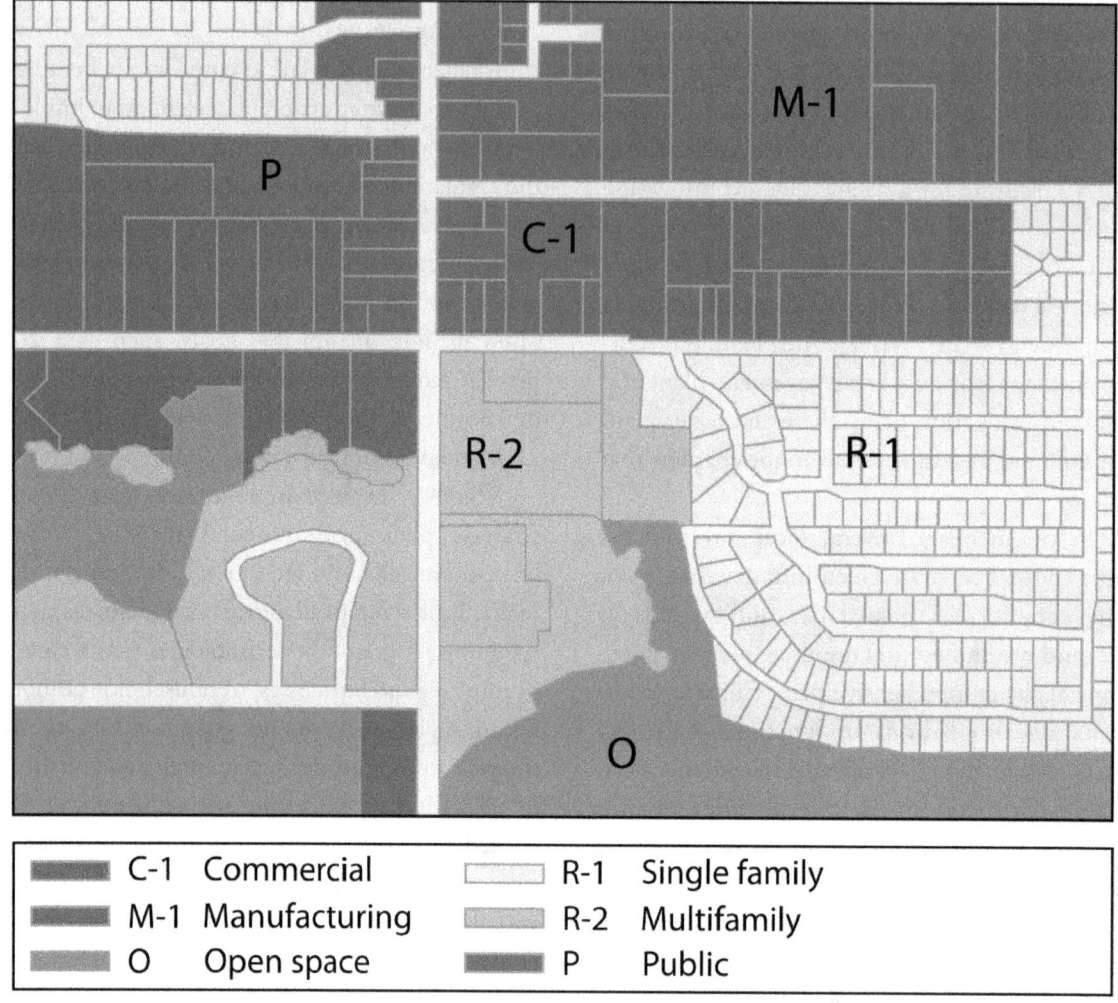

Figure 1. General Zoning Map

ZONING

Zoning is the most widely used land-use control in the U.S. to guide the future growth and development of a municipality or county. The traditional zoning ordinance consists of two parts: a text describing the rules for each zoning district (Residential, R-1 Single Family, R-2 Multifamily, Commercial C-1, Manufacturing M-1, etc.) and a map showing the location and boundaries of the zoning districts (see Figure 1).

Zoning has several purposes. First, it serves to implement the goals and objectives of the comprehensive plan and, in particular, the plan's future land-use map. Thus the zoning ordinance should be consistent with the comprehensive plan. In some states, a zoning ordinance that is not consistent with the comprehensive plan could be ruled invalid in a court of law.

Another purpose of zoning is to separate potentially conflicting land uses—such as keeping a steel factory away from single-family homes—to protect public health, safety, and welfare. Each zoning district has different rules for permitted uses, special exceptions, and conditional uses. Permitted uses are normally allowed outright after a review by planning commission staff. Special exceptions are usually reviewed by the zoning board (also called the zoning board of adjustment) after a public hearing, while conditional uses are typically reviewed by the planning commission and the elected governing body after public hearings. Each zoning district also has specific regulations on lot size, height of buildings, building setbacks from property lines, lot coverage (i.e., how much of a site can be covered with impervious surfaces), and may include other requirements.

One of the most common uses of zoning in environmental planning is the *overlay zone*. An overlay zone creates a double-zone where a landowner or developer must meet the standards of both the underlying zone (such as R-1 Residential Single Family) and the overlay zone (such as a Floodplain Zone). Planners employ overlay zones to protect the public health, safety, and welfare in sensitive environmental areas. For instance, overlay zones include floodplain overlays, aquifer overlays, and steep slope overlays, among others.

Zoning regulations must not remove all economic use of a private property. Otherwise the zoning will violate the takings test of the Fifth Amendment to the U.S. Constitution (see Chapter 2). Zoning must also be reasonable. The reasonableness test is largely a matter of common sense, based on land-use capabilities and constraints. But there should be a clear link between the goals of the comprehensive plan and what the zoning ordinance requires. Zoning, for example, can be used to protect natural areas from intense development; but the importance of the protection of natural areas, such as wetlands, should be described as a goal in the comprehensive plan for environmental, fiscal, aesthetic, and economic reasons.

A valid criticism of traditional zoning is that it often separates commercial and residential land uses and forces people to travel by car from where they live to where they work and shop. This separation of land uses causes more energy consumption, air pollution, and sprawling development. The zoning ordinances of many cities and suburbs have only recently begun to allow for the mixing of commercial and residential uses. A number of commercial and residential uses can be safely combined in a mixed-use zone of small shops, houses, offices, and apartments to create a more attractive, compact, and pedestrian-friendly built environment.

Another criticism of zoning is that it tends to be rigid, resulting in "cookie cutter" housing developments with uniform rectangular lots. Also, local governments may poorly administer their zoning by frequently granting use variances and rezonings for other land uses that defeat the development goals and objectives of the comprehensive plan.

Because of the lack of guidance for the design of buildings in the traditional zoning ordinance, more than 300 cities in the U.S. have adopted a form-based code, at least for specific parts of the city, such as a downtown or a transit corridor. Other cities have incorporated elements of form-based codes into their traditional zoning ordinance to create what is known as a parallel code. A form-based code regulates the design and appearance of buildings more so than land uses. A form-based code emphasizes the importance of the public realm and how private and public buildings influence the public realm in terms of the building height and bulk, building façades, orientation to the street, and parking requirements. Local governments can implement a form-based code by adopting a regulating plan for a part of the city or even the entire city, as Miami has done. The regulating plan includes a combination of street and building standards and may include architectural standards as well.

It is far easier to create mixed-use buildings and developments with a form-based code than the traditional zoning ordinance. Thus a form-based code may prove to be more effective in producing walkable mixed-use areas with sufficient density to make mass transit service feasible.³

Communities can use *performance zoning* to regulate the potential impacts of land uses rather than limiting land uses to those generally thought to be compatible with the area. Typically, performance zoning relies on buffers in the form of berms, vegetation, and setbacks to minimize noise and light that would spill over from one property to another. If a landowner can demonstrate that a proposed land use in a certain location will not adversely affect traffic, water quality, or other environmental features, then the proposed land use will be allowed. Performance zoning depends on adequate and trained planning staff to implement and enforce it. We do not recommend performance zoning in rural areas with few planning staff or little planning expertise.

Local governments have all too often based their zoning ordinances and rezoning decisions on the hunt for new development to expand the property tax base. As a result, planning and zoning decisions have tended to downplay topography, hydrology, soils, wildlife habitat, or the availability of adequate infrastructure to support new development. Many communities allow commercial, industrial, and large-lot residential development that will increase the property tax base but openly discourage multi-family housing for fear of a greater property tax burden. This practice—known as "fiscal zoning"—zones out low-income households and promotes both large-lot residential sprawl and arterial commercial sprawl instead of compact, mixed-use developments.

Finally, many zoning ordinances are long, dry texts. It is a good idea to place drawings or photos depicting correct zoning practices in the zoning text. These illustrations will help landowners, developers, elected officials, and concerned citizens to better understand the zoning concepts and implement them in new developments.

Subdivision and Land-Development Regulations

The subdivision and land-development ordinance establishes rules for the design and layout of lots, necessary roads and sidewalks, sewage disposal, drinking water supplies, and stormwater drainage, as well as the retention of open space and vegetation. In some states or communities, the subdivision ordinance may require an environmental impact assessment for all major subdivisions and land-development plans.

The subdivision and land-development process requires the planning commission to review and approve a development proposal in three stages: the sketch plan, the preliminary plat, and the final plat. In the sketch plan stage, the developer presents a conceptual layout of the proposal. This is a brainstorming and negotiation process between the developer and the planning commission or staff rather than a rigorous review of requirements. The planning commission or staff recommends ways to improve the proposal, and the developer then prepares a preliminary plat.

The preliminary plat shows a considerable amount of information about the proposed development, including planned lot configurations, building locations, streets, utilities, neighboring landowners and land uses, and environmental features such as streams, slopes, and vegetation. The planning commission and staff review the proposed development according to the subdivision and land-development regulations and provide an opportunity for the public to comment. The planning commission may approve the preliminary plat, approve it with conditions, or deny it. Most often, the planning commission imposes conditions to ensure that the proposed development meets the standards of the subdivision ordinance. The developer may be required to put up a bond for installing streets, sidewalks, and utilities for the development to ensure that adequate funding for installing the infrastructure will be provided, even if the developer does not perform the installation.

Once the planning commission approves the preliminary plat, there is little the public can do to change the proposed development. The developer responds to the conditions attached to the preliminary plat approval and then submits a final plat for approval. At this stage, the municipality or county determines whether the developer has met the conditions attached to the preliminary plat, and if so, the chair of the elected officials signs the final plat and it is recorded with the recorder of deeds at the county courthouse. Then the land may legally be subdivided or developed.

From the date the final plat is approved, the developer usually has up to three years to commence the project and five years to complete it. If the project is not begun within the three years or completed within five years, the final plat is null and void and a new application for a subdivision is required. Exceptions may be granted for large developments that are phased in over time, such as for some planned unit developments that can take several years to complete. Time limits for most types of development are a good idea because environmental and other factors can change. In several western states, there is no time limit for starting or completing new construction. For instance, in the real estate boom of the early 2000s, many subdivisions were laid out, legally approved, and then never developed. A large number of these "zombie subdivisions" are still sitting empty. Also, some local governments have mistakenly approved substandard lots in quickly laid out subdivisions that are often constrained by small lot sizes, steep slopes, lack of road access, and lack of water. These substandard lots cannot be developed.

In many suburban communities, subdivision regulations together with rigid zoning ordinances have produced cookie-cutter residential layouts, varied only by the use of road loops and cul-de-sac "lollipops." Curvilinear street patterns that maximize driving and disorientation are all too common. Any open space that is preserved is typically fragmented and often not useful for recreation, wildlife habitat, or other purposes.

The subdivision review process should require developers to present detailed studies of the likely environmental impacts of their proposed projects. Developers may be asked to consider alternative project designs that may be more compatible with the environment. For instance, local subdivision and land-development regulations may require developers to mitigate stormwater runoff through a limit on impervious surface coverage, grass swales, retention of vegetation, and by avoiding construction on steep slopes.

THE CAPITAL IMPROVEMENTS PROGRAM (CIP)

Public roads, mass transit systems, schools, parks, sewer and water facilities, and police and fire stations have a powerful influence on where development occurs, when it occurs, and the type of development. A CIP describes (1) what public infrastructure a community will build, repair, or replace; (2) where these services are or will be located; (3) when construction, repair, or replacement will happen; and (4) how these infrastructure projects will be funded. Local governments typically use a CIP to budget 5 to 10 years into the future, but this may vary according to a community's estimates of future population growth and service needs.

The purpose of the CIP is to anticipate the location, type, and amount of public service needs and to provide adequate services at a reasonable cost. The CIP can help coordinate projects and avoid mismanagement, such as paving a street one year and tearing it up the next to install a sewer line.

A CIP commonly includes public investments in roads and bridges, mass transit, school buildings, sewer and water treatment plants and lines, municipal buildings, and solid waste disposal sites. These public facilities are also known as "gray infrastructure." A CIP should also include "green infrastructure" projects, such as parks, trails, purchases of land and conservation easements, green roofs on public buildings, and financial incentives to encourage private landowners to install green roofs, rain gardens, and swales to reduce stormwater runoff. The CIP should contain detailed information on the capacity of current facilities, the projected future demand for public services, and estimated future costs and financing arrangements in relation to expected municipal or county revenues and operating budgets.

Local officials and planners need to coordinate the CIP with the comprehensive plan and the zoning ordinance. *Concurrency* is a policy that requires infrastructure to be in place before public or private development can begin. Local governments can adopt an adequate public facilities ordinance (APFO) or add a concurrency policy into the subdivision and land-development regulations to ensure that new development will not exceed infrastructure capacity or impose an unreasonable tax burden on the community. Concurrency and APFOs are a good way to promote compact phased growth. The State of Washington requires local governments to practice concurrency as part of its 1990 State Growth Management Act. Many local governments in other states have adopted APFOs. Communities may choose to allow privately financed infrastructure to meet concurrency requirements. But it is important to note that a concurrency policy on public infrastructure may not stop the construction of buildings in areas that rely on private wells and individual on-site septic systems.

Many extensions of central water and sewer by municipalities, authorities, and private developers have resulted in leapfrog development and the premature conversion of farmland, forests, wildlife habitats, and open space. Sewer line extensions mean local water bodies will be receiving more treated effluent. More highways and wider roads generate more traffic, air pollution, wildlife fatalities, and storm-water runoff into waterways. The construction of public buildings, such as the city hall, post office, and schools, outside of downtowns and on arterial strips promotes automobile dependence, energy consumption, air pollution, and sprawling development patterns.

One of the most successful uses of CIPs with zoning is an urban growth boundary. The growth boundary is a limit of urban services, such as central sewer and water, agreed on by a city and its one or more surrounding counties. Inside the growth boundary, there should be sufficient land to accommodate development for 20 years. Outside the boundary, the land is primary in farm or forest uses. The idea of a growth boundary is to promote compact development that can gradually expand over time and thus minimize sprawl and the loss of open space.

1.2: THE ENVIRONMENTAL PLANNING PROCESS

A good way to make the comprehensive plan a "living document" that people use is by communities and counties adopting an Environmental Action Plan. Local governments can use an Environmental Action Plan to implement goals and objectives from several parts of the comprehensive plan, especially the natural resources inventory, economic base, land use, and community facilities sections. In addition, the Environmental Action Plan can draw on planning strategies and tools in the functional and area plans that are connected to the comprehensive plan. The Environmental Action Plan can recommend regulations, financial incentives, infrastructure spending programs, and other actions toward promoting a sustainable environment. Finally, the Environmental Action Plan can list short-term, medium-term, and long-term actions; funding sources; and who will be responsible for carrying out the actions and when.

STEPS IN THE ENVIRONMENTAL PLANNING PROCESS

The environmental planning process has eight main steps, most of which contain a mix of technical planning and political "selling" of the benefits of environmental planning (see Table 1).

Recognizing the Need for Environmental Planning

To start the environmental planning process, elected officials must be convinced that certain environmental problems exist or could pose threats to public health, safety, and welfare. It helps if interest groups, business leaders, and the general public recognize the need for environmental planning and voice their concerns to the elected officials. Recognizing the need for environmental planning may result from a study done by the local government, such as a water supply plan. Similarly, a partnership of citizens and local government may do a study that alerts public officials about environmental needs and compels them to act. Elected officials are more likely to adopt an Environmental Action Plan

Table 1. Eight Steps in Creating an Environmental Action Plan

1.	The public and elected officials recognize the need for environmental planning.
2.	Officials then commit people and funding to the environmental planning effort and appoint an environmental advisory committee to assist the planning commission.
3.	The planning commission, staff, and the environmental advisory committee conduct an Environmental Needs Assessment Survey and solicit public input.
4.	The planning commission, staff, and the environmental advisory committee develop a factual base of environmental conditions and analyze the information.
5.	The planning commission, staff, and the environmental advisory committee review the community's comprehensive plan to revise the vision statement, broad goals, and specific objectives to incorporate environmental data and needs over the next 20 years or more.
6.	The planning commission, staff, and the environmental advisory committee draft an Environmental Action Plan to articulate a set of land-use controls, financial incentives, infrastructure spending, tax programs, and building design regulations that will put the environmental goals and objectives of the comprehensive plan into practice.
7.	Elected officials solicit public input and adopt the Environmental Action Plan.
8.	The planning commission and elected officials implement, monitor, and evaluate the performance of the Environmental Action Plan through an annual review of progress toward benchmarks and then make revisions and updates as needed.

and support specific actions if they receive credit for their support.

Committing People and Money to the Environmental Planning Effort

Elected officials can either give the planning commission and staff the task of drafting an Environmental Action Plan or hire a professional planning consultant to do the job. A wise move is for the elected officials or planning commission to appoint an environmental advisory committee to help with drafting the action plan. Many communities in the northeastern states have appointed a standing local conservation commission to assist the planning commission and elected officials in drafting the environmental elements of the comprehensive plan. The conservation commission can also review and comment on the potential environmental impacts of proposed developments. A local conservation commission or environmental advisory committee should ideally have between 8 and 12 members, and include people from a range of backgrounds, such as business, a local university, environmental groups, local planning, any adjacent municipality that may share a natural resource such as a river, and citizens from different areas of the community. For technical expertise, it is a good idea to include a biologist and an engineer on the committee.

Some communities may want to hire a consultant to help with the Environmental Action Plan. Make sure the consultant is willing to tailor the action plan to the needs and desires of the community. A pitfall to avoid is allowing a consultant to present a "boiler plate plan" used by several communities, an all-too-common practice among consultants. Spell out in a contract what is expected of the consultant, when the work is due, the amount of the consultant's fee, and payment dates.

The Environmental Action Plan should include an acknowledgment of all public and private sources of funding for the plan as well as the major participants, including the planning commission, any advisory committees and volunteers, any consultants, and, of course, the elected officials who will be asked to adopt the plan.

Surveys and Soliciting Public Input

An Environmental Action Plan must involve broad and meaningful participation from the public and a variety of interest groups. A good way for the planning commission and advisory committee to involve the public in the planning process is to conduct an *Environmental Needs Assessment Survey*. The survey gives people in the community the opportunity to voice their opinions about environmental conditions and needed improvements. The survey can ask specific questions about a range of environmental issues, as well as include open-ended questions about what improvements are needed. Other questions might ask for levels of willingness to pay for new environmental services such as additional parks or upgraded water treatment facilities.

Surveys may be distributed in a variety of ways. One way is to mail a survey to a sample of households in the community. Surveys that are clear and short and include a self-addressed stamped envelope and cut-off date for responses often have good return rates. Another way is to post the survey on the community's website. The survey responses will indicate issues of concern in the community or county and will help the advisory committee and planning commission in revising the comprehensive plan. This may include redrafting the vision statement, gathering and analyzing additional environment-related data, and formulating general environmental goals and specific objectives for the community or county.

Community or neighborhood public meetings, newsletters, and notices in the local media are also helpful in publicizing the needs assessment effort and eliciting public comments. Two sets of meetings are recommended. The first set is to solicit input from the public. The advisory committee and planning commission members should ask people to identify the important environmental aspects of their communities and improvements they would like to see. This can be done effectively in small-group brainstorming sessions (known as focus groups) to draw people out and hear from everyone. It is helpful to have maps of the community or county on hand.

After the surveys and informational meetings have been completed and incorporated into a draft of the action plan, the planning commission and advisory committee should present their findings and recommendations at a second set of public meetings to get feedback from the public. Does the action plan reflect a public consensus? Keep in mind that a consensus does not mean 100 percent support—there will always be some opposition. Are there important environmental issues or strategies that were left out? Taking the extra time to involve the public and make changes to the Environmental Action Plan will pay dividends in the long run. The public will appreciate the opportunity to voice concerns and opinions and will gain a better understanding of what the Environmental Action Plan is trying to do. Additionally, public support is crucial for convincing elected officials to adopt the Environmental Action Plan.

Gathering Data About Environmental Conditions and Analyzing the Data

Studies of the natural and built environments, including projected future impacts of population on environmental resources, create a factual base. The factual base in a comprehensive plan should include (1) a natural resources inventory of air, land, water, and wildlife resources and (2) a built environment inventory of buildings and gray infrastructure. These studies should present accurate, unbiased information on the current condition of the local or regional environment.

The factual base will help to answer a variety of questions, such as the following: What is the quality of the community's air and water? What type of wildlife and wildlife habitats exist? What is the condition of the sewage treatment plants? What is the suitability of lands and water resources in the community for different types of development? Federal, state, regional, and local governments are good sources of information. Local and state universities and environmental nonprofit organizations may also be helpful. Private consultants may be useful for specific tasks. Some of this information may be available from the community's current comprehensive plan.

Natural Resources Inventory

Natural resources include air, water, soils, geologic formations, farmland, forests, minerals, wetlands, and plant and animal species. In the inventory, planners should identify the location, quantity, and quality of these resources as well as their suitability for development, development constraints such as steep slopes and floodplains, and vulnerability to pollution or natural hazards.

A frequent challenge in putting together a natural resources inventory is that a community's political boundaries may differ from geologic or ecological boundaries. For example, the community may be part of a river basin or wildlife migration route. A community may need to consult with neighboring communities, counties, and regional planning agencies to gather complete inventory data. Dutchess County, New York, adopted a natural resources inventory in 2010 to serve as an information source for individual towns as they create comprehensive plans and make day-to-day decisions on the location of new development.[4] The natural resources section of the Port Washington, Wisconsin, comprehensive plan states, "Approximately 25.8 percent of the City of Port Washington planning area is covered

ESSENTIAL READINGS IN URBAN PLANNING

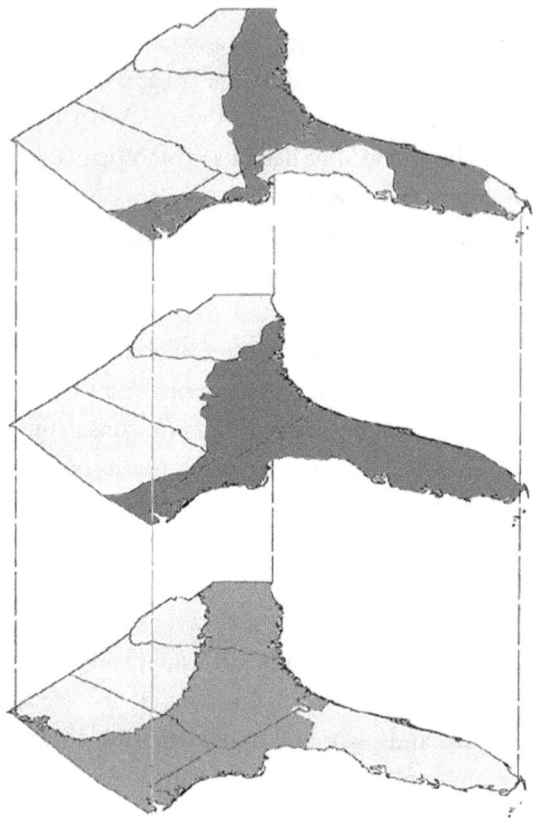

Figure 2. Geographic Information System Database Layers: Aquifer Systems of the Southeastern United States

Green: *surficial aquifer system; orange: Floridian aquifer system; blue: Southeastern Coastal Plains aquifer system.*

Source: Adapted from U.S. Geological Survey, *Ground Water Atlas of the United States*, HA-730-G, Figures 8, 10, and 11, 2009. http://pubs.usgs.gov/ha/ha730/ch_g/jpeg/G009.jpeg.

by hydric soils (about 2,531 acres), generally associated with stream beds and wetland areas. Although hydric soils are generally unsuitable for development, they may serve as important locations for the restoration of wetlands, as wildlife habitat, and for stormwater detention."[5]

Resource maps are very useful, and a composite map of natural resource layers, generated by a geographic information system (GIS) is highly recommended (see Figure 2). Several states have GIS databases accessible online. If available, remote sensing information may also be helpful, especially for regional maps. Topographic maps from the U.S. Geological Survey (USGS) display elevations, roads, water bodies, and settlements. Other USGS maps can help to identify historic, current, and projected community land-use patterns. Aerial photos of the community or region can be especially helpful in showing the pattern of development (whether sprawled or compact), the amount of built-up area and undeveloped land, and where future development might best be accommodated.[6] Orthophotos are computerized aerial photographs that are scale-corrected and distortion free. They are available from most local offices of the Natural Resources Conservation Service (NRCS). Digitized property tax maps showing property boundaries and land parcel patterns can be overlaid on top of the orthophotos. Planners can then add GIS data layers from the natural resources inventory maps (see Table 2) and built environment maps (roads, sewer and water lines, schools, hospitals, and other buildings). Planners can identify land parcels from local tax maps. Areas with many small parcels will not be suitable for development that requires large acreages, such as industrial parks. Areas with large parcels have better potential for natural resource uses, such as farming, forestry, or mining. Combining parcel patterns with soils, topography, and proximity to sewer, water, and major roads provides a picture of

Table 2. Environmental Features to Show on the Natural Resources Inventory Maps

Natural Environmental Features

1.	Soils, geology, and topography
2.	Watersheds, streams, water bodies, floodplains, and wetlands
3.	Aquifer recharge areas and delineated wellhead areas
4.	Wildlife habitat
5.	Vegetation (forest cover, cropland, pasture, prairie, etc.)

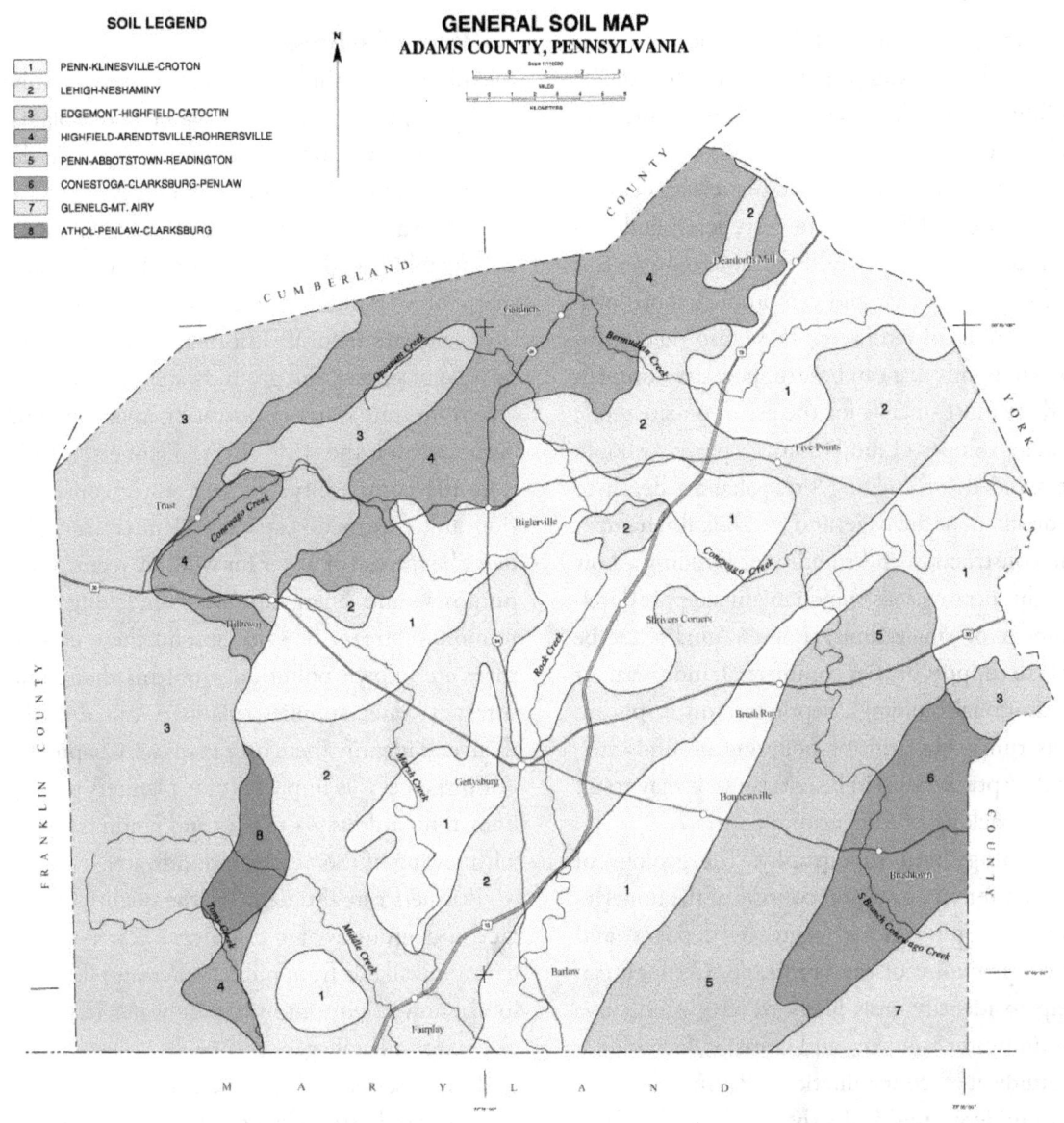

Figure 3. Map of Soil Types from the Adams County, Pennsylvania, Soil Survey.
Source: Natural Resources Conservation Service (NRCS).

development potential for specific sites. It is also important to identify any lands owned by federal, state, or county governments, which are generally off-limits to development.

Planners can include discussions of the following natural resources in a natural resources inventory: soils, geography and topography, water resources, wildlife habitat, vegetation, and air quality.

Soils. Soils information can include slope, erosion potential, wetness, strength, depth to bedrock, frost action, shrink-swell, prime agricultural soils, forest soils, and suitability for on-site septic systems. County soil surveys produced by the NRCS provide all this information as well as general soils maps (see Figure 3). In many counties, soil surveys have been digitized for GIS applications. Soils information indicates the ability of an area or parcel of land to support buildings, absorb water, and grow plants (see Table 1 in Chapter 14).

Soils with high productive capability for agriculture and forestry are deep, level, and well drained; contain a wealth of micro-organisms and organic matter; and can produce crops with a minimum of fertilizers. These also tend to be the same soils that can best support development and are most suitable for the use of on-site septic systems. Slopes of more than 15 percent should be avoided for building sites. Shallow depth to bedrock, poor drainage, and wet soils also hamper the construction and stability of buildings. Low weight–bearing soils, which might support development of single-family houses, might not be able to support heavier commercial, industrial, or institutional buildings. Septic systems in porous soils run a high risk of polluting groundwater, while septic systems in heavy clay soils may result in the back up of effluent to the surface.

Geology and Topography. The geology of the community or region consists of the underlying rocks, mineral and aggregate deposits, and the topography of the landscape. Geology can help to identify areas likely to have productive groundwater aquifers and areas vulnerable to groundwater contamination. Planners should map underground faults that could lead to land subsidence, landslides, or earthquakes. There may also be unique geological features such as caves, mesas, and rock outcroppings that planners should note. Topographic maps will show ridges and steep slopes (Figure 4) and reveal stormwater drainage patterns. A study of topography will also be helpful in viewshed analysis, with an eye toward protecting outstanding vistas. Planners can obtain data on geology and topography from the USGS, the state environmental agency, and the state land grant university.

Water Resources. Important water resources include groundwater and surface water, public water supplies, wetlands, and floodplains. Planners should obtain or draft maps on the location and extent of water resources as well as watershed and aquifer boundaries (see Chapter 5). Topographic quadrant maps from the USGS and maps of wetlands from the national wetlands inventory are helpful. Information on the flow or yield of surface and groundwater may be available from state water resources or environmental agencies and the U.S. EPA. Planners should note the community's present water consumption and treatment capacity. Planners can also describe the use of water for wildlife, recreational purposes, and energy production, along with minimum stream flows to sustain these uses. If there are known pollution problems that could threaten water supplies, planners can describe them and identify them on a map (see Chapter 6). For instance, it is important for planners to map known hazardous waste sites and landfills, along with testing of the nearby groundwater.

Planners can also describe the quality of surface and groundwater resources. Water-quality data are available from public water suppliers, the local municipality, and the state water resources or environmental agency.

It is essential for planners to identify and map wetlands (see Chapter 11). Good sources of information include the national wetlands inventory from the U.S. Fish and Wildlife Agency and state-level wetlands maps from the state environmental agency. The county soil survey has maps that identify the location of wet or hydric soils, although not all hydric soils are considered wetlands.

Identifying floodplains is important to avoid construction in these dangerous areas (see Chapter 13). The Federal Emergency Management Agency (FEMA) publishes floodplain maps

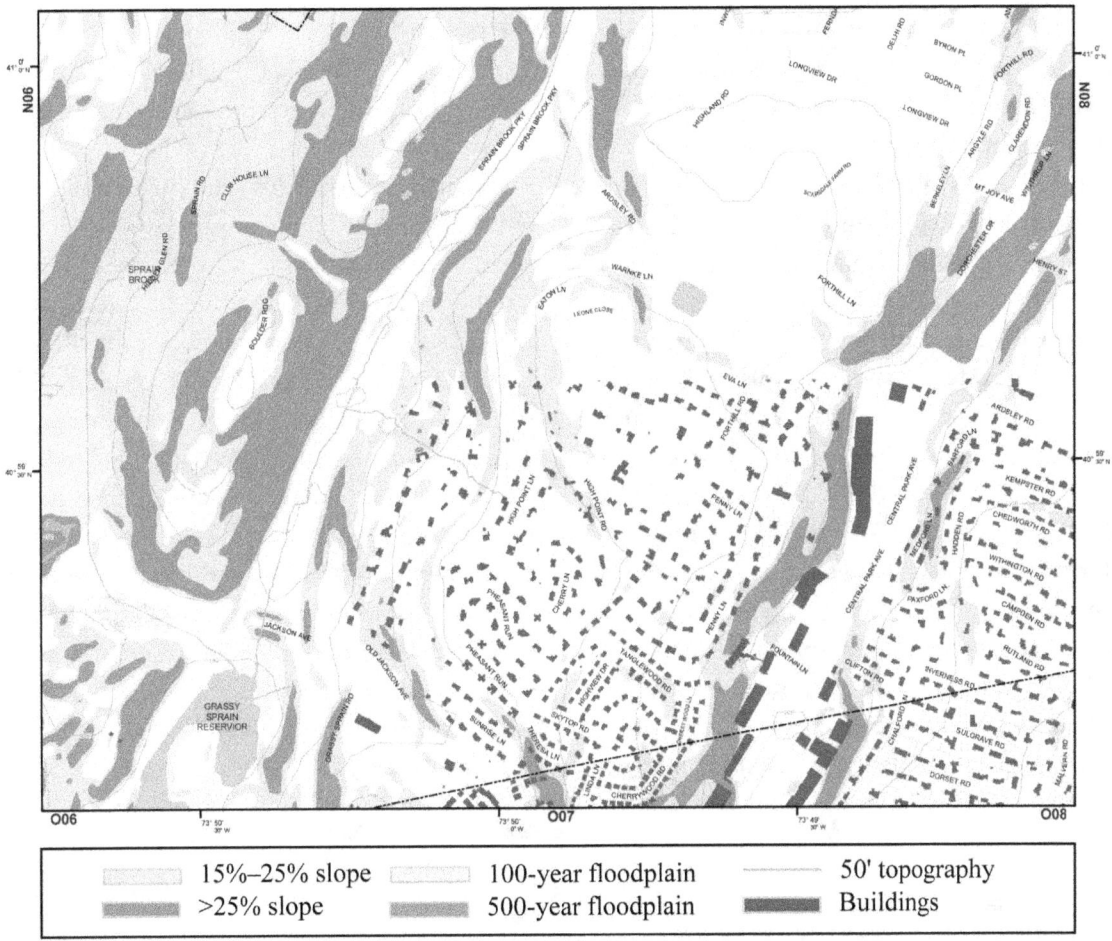

Figure 4. Map Identifying Steep Slopes for the Natural Resources Inventory, Yonkers, New York.
Source: Westchester County, NY, GIS Department.

nationwide. While much of the mapping is old, FEMA has updated maps for many communities. Additional information may be available from the state environmental or water resources agency.

Wildlife Habitat. Planners should describe and map significant wildlife habitat, nesting areas, migration routes, fish spawning grounds, and feeding spots. Wildlife habitat can be identified by knowledgeable local volunteers, conservation groups, and personnel from the state land grant university and state fish and wildlife department. Habitats can be rated for importance and vulnerability. Planners can identify in a general way any threatened and endangered plant and animal habitats so as to protect species from possible poaching or habitat destruction (see Chapter 10). But state environmental agencies are often reluctant to give out specific information on the location of threatened or endangered species habitat.

Vegetation. Planners can list and map lands in forest cover, farm use, or other type of vegetation. Sources of information include satellite imagery and aerial photos. Planners can digitize this information into a GIS database and combine it with the wildlife habitat map.

Air Quality. An inventory of air quality includes measurements of carbon monoxide, particulates, nitrogen dioxide, lead, ozone, and sulfur oxides, which are the main air pollutants identified by the federal government under the Clean Air Act Amendments of 1970 (see Chapter 3). Planners can note how many days each year the air quality fails to meet one or more of the standards for these six pollutants. Carbon dioxide emissions are also important to determine, though this information may be more difficult to find. Carbon dioxide was ruled a pollutant by the U.S. Supreme Court in 2007, and as of 2014, the EPA had not yet adopted broad regulations on carbon dioxide emissions, which contribute to climate change (see Chapter 4). Information on air quality is available from the state environmental agency and from the regional office of the EPA. Local air quality is typically described but not mapped. Regional air-quality maps are more common.

A Built Environment Inventory

A built environment inventory can show the location, number, age, and condition of the housing stock, commercial and industrial buildings, parks, and public buildings. The inventory can also include the location and condition of public infrastructure, including roads, sewer and water lines, schools, landfills, and police and fire stations. The built environment has important connections with the natural environment. The amount of developed land, land with development potential, and the location of different land uses have implications for stormwater management, transportation and energy use, air and water quality, and exposure to natural hazards. For example, the Town of Dennis, Massachusetts, included a section on Human/Built Systems in a draft of their 2012 comprehensive plan.

The section includes the following four topics: (1) a housing inventory, (2) cultural and historic resources, (3) public services and facilities, and (4) transportation.[7]

Planners can identify and map buildings and neighborhoods with historic and cultural value, public buildings and spaces, streetscapes, and blighted areas. These are all areas with potential for improving the quality of life for residents in the neighborhood. Historic buildings and streetscapes have been key assets in the redevelopment of many cities and towns across America. Public buildings and spaces draw people together and create a sense of community. Open spaces and green-ways offer parkland and wildlife habitat, filter runoff, and buffer watercourses. Information on the built environment can be found through the state historic preservation office and city and county planning offices.

Analysis of the Natural Resources Inventory and Built Environment Inventory

The analysis of the natural resources inventory and the built environment inventory consists of three parts: a land and water suitability analysis, an environmental quality analysis, and a current trends analysis.

Land and Water Suitability Analysis. A key product of the natural resources inventory is a *land and water suitability analysis*, which identifies those areas of the community that are appropriate for development, places that have moderate limitations for most developments, and areas that should be protected in their natural state because of severe environmental constraints and natural hazards. Planners can show the suitability analysis for the community on one or more GIS maps with several layers of environmental information (see Table 2). The analysis should also denote land with particular capabilities, such as productive farm and forest soils, as well as areas that will maintain critical natural processes such as wetlands and aquifer recharge areas. Overall, the land and water suitability analysis can provide important information on the *carrying capacity* of the community—that is, how many people and how much development the community can sustainably support before serious negative environmental impacts occur. In short, the land and water suitability analysis is a primary building block of the comprehensive plan and any sustainability plan. For example, Lancaster County, Virginia, located in the eastern Tidewater area, identified two types of rural areas in its efforts to protect the water quality of the Chesapeake Bay: (1) Resource Protection Areas and (2) Resource Management Areas. The Resource Protection Areas are lands that directly affect water quality, such as tidal wetlands, shorelands, and buffer lands. The Resource Management Areas are lands that, if improperly managed, could degrade water quality. Development on these lands is subject to standards and permit requirements to ensure minimum impact.[8]

Rating Natural Resources and Development Suitability. The land and water suitability analysis should contain a method to rate or classify the development potential of different lands. For instance, planners can identify development constraints and natural hazards with a color code on GIS maps (red for severe limitations, orange for moderate limitations, yellow for few limitations) or a numerical points system with developable lands receiving higher points than lands with development limitations.

Planners can depict natural resources worthy of protection by using a separate color code, such as shades of green. For instance, prime farmland could be shown in dark green and farmland with more than 15 percent slope in light green.

Planners can prioritize natural resources for protection according to

1. whether the resource is renewable or irreplaceable—if irreplaceable, the resource is more valuable;
2. the rarity of the site—the less common, the more valuable the resource, particularly in the case of habitats of threatened and endangered plant and wildlife species;
3. the size of the site—generally, the larger the site, the more important it is;
4. the diversity of plants, wildlife, scenic views, and other natural features—the greater the diversity the more important the site is; and
5. the fragility of the site, including the quality of the undisturbed site and human threats to the site.

Planners can create a rating system for development potential that is clear and understandable to nonexperts. The rating system and maps will help planners in creating the future land-use map and zoning map, as well as in the day-to-day development review process.

Environmental Quality Analysis. Planners can perform an environmental quality analysis to compare state and federal environmental standards with actual conditions in the community. For example, planners can compare local air and water quality against federal air and water pollution standards. This analysis provides baseline information that can help a community identify environmental quality problems, evaluate alternative solutions, rank its natural resources for protection, and set priorities for action. Planners can use the baseline information to set environmental quality targets, which can be readily updated to document progress toward environmental quality benchmarks.

Current Trends Analysis. Recent trends in population growth, acreage developed, acreage in public parks, vehicle miles traveled, waste recycling, loss of threatened or endangered plant and animal species, air and water quality, and water use give indications of the direction of environmental quality. In the current trends analysis, planners ask the following questions: Where are we going in terms of population growth, land development, and environmental quality? Are these trends sustainable? What will be the environmental costs if these trends continue? What will be the economic costs and social impacts? Planners can project recent environmental trends to help answer these questions.

In the current trends analysis, planners can discuss the indicators of environmental strengths, weaknesses, opportunities, and threats to the community or region based on the information provided in the Natural Resources and Built Environment Inventories together with population projections. Strengths for a particular community might include a pleasant setting with scenic views, good-quality water, and a collection of solid historic buildings. Weaknesses might feature poor air quality and a lack of public transportation. Opportunities might exist for creating a greenway along a riverfront and rehabilitating historic buildings for commercial purposes in the downtown. Threats might involve flooding, sprawling suburbs, and a loss of open space. The current trends analysis will be useful in revising the community's comprehensive plan, especially the vision statement and the broad goals and specific objectives to achieve that vision. A major purpose of a comprehensive plan is to influence current trends to produce better outcomes.

The Vision Statement, Broad Goals, and Specific Objectives

The planning commission and environmental advisory committee combine input from the public Environmental Needs Assessment Survey and the data and analysis of the built and natural environments into a *vision statement* for the community or region. The vision statement describes what the quality of the natural, working, and built environments of the community or region should be over the next 20 or more years. The vision statement serves as an overall policy directive for the local government, as well as the foundation for the environmental goals, objectives, and the Environmental Action Plan. The vision statement typically advocates four outcomes: compliance with state and federal environmental standards; a healthy, sustainable environment; a sustainable economy; and a good quality of life for all citizens.

Next, the planning commission and advisory committee can articulate environmental goals and objectives that not only reflect community desires and priorities but also provide direction for elected officials on public spending, taxation, and land-use regulation. This is the first step in making the environmental vision a reality. The goals and objectives must be based on a solid technical analysis of the natural and built environments, realistic costs, and an understanding of relevant state and federal environmental programs. A common problem is that a goal or objective may be rejected for being "politically not feasible," even though it would significantly improve or protect environmental quality. Goals and objectives should address the full range of environmental issues facing the community or region and should build on strengths (such as a good water supply), address weaknesses (lack of park land), opportunities (ecotourism), and threats (groundwater pollution).

Setting Goals and Objectives

Goals. Goals are broad statements that reflect a community's values and desires. Goals provide direction to local officials in their decision making and should be clear and decisive. Sample environmental goals might include the following:

1. Ensure compliance with state and federal environmental standards for air and water quality.
2. Increase the recycling of solid waste into useful products.
3. Conserve on the amount of land used for development by promoting compact, mixed-use development.
4. Expand mass transit to reduce reliance on the automobile and reduce air pollution.
5. Increase the amount of public park land.
6. Reduce the emission of greenhouse gases.

Objectives. Objectives spell out specific ways to attain goals. Each goal usually depends on achieving more than one objective. The following sample objectives would help meet each of the preceding goals:

a. Adopt a wellhead protection ordinance to limit development near public water supplies.
b. Contract with a private recycling firm to increase the amount of solid waste recycled.
c. Revise the zoning ordinance to allow smaller minimum lot sizes and a mix of commercial and residential uses.
d. Explore funding for additional buses or the construction of a commuter light-rail system.
e. Revise the subdivision ordinance to require mandatory dedication of park land or fees in lieu thereof.
f. Add bicycle lanes to promote cycling as an alternative to driving.

It is very important for planners and elected officials to coordinate the goals and objectives of the comprehensive plan. A major problem with many traditional comprehensive plans is that they have several conflicting goals and objectives that may create confusion and effectively cancel each other out. The common theme of sustainability should link the goals and objectives. Communities and planners will find it useful to prioritize environmental goals and objectives, especially in relation to housing, transportation, community facilities, and economic development goals.

The Environmental Action Plan

The chief reason so many comprehensive plans end up sitting on a shelf is that they do not include a detailed action strategy. Planners can establish indicators of success in the Environmental Action Plan along with annual benchmarks for progress toward short-term and long-term outcomes or targets. For instance, Marin County, California, did this in their 2007 Countywide Plan. Then planners can report on progress toward the targets in periodic reports, ideally each year. For example, New York City produced reports in 2011 and 2012 to measure the success of its 2007 PlaNYC.

The Environmental Action Plan articulates a set of land-use regulations, infrastructure spending, tax and incentive programs, and building codes that will put the comprehensive plan into practice (see Table 3). These recommended actions should be consistent with the plan's objectives. The action plan lists proposed activities, who is expected to do the work, funding options, and timelines for completion and is laid out in an easy-to-read table format. A clearly presented action plan will keep the comprehensive plan alive in the minds of the public and local government and help toward its full implementation. Ideally, the local elected officials will adopt the Environmental Action Plan as part of the comprehensive plan.

Table 3. Innovative Techniques to Implement an Environmental Action Plan

Zoning

1. Special overlay zones protect sensitive resources, such as wildlife areas, steep slopes, wellhead protection areas, floodplains, and wetlands.
2. Performance zoning regulates impacts rather than uses.
3. A community and the federal government can designate historic districts to help protect historic areas and make property owners eligible for federal (and possibly state) investment tax credits (see Chapter 19).
4. Bonus density or an increased height bonus is available for environmentally sensitive building design or use of green roofs.
5. Form-based codes regulate the appearance of development rather than uses.
6. Large minimum lot-size zoning protects farmland, forestland, and conservation areas.

Subdivision Regulations

1. To evaluate the potential impacts of development, especially for a large development, a local government's subdivision ordinance can require a developer to conduct a local environmental impact assessment.
2. Vegetation requirements can include buffers between properties and the replacement of trees and vegetation removed in the development process.

Capital Improvements Programs

1. Urban or village growth boundaries link capital improvements with zoning. They also provide a way to resolve annexation disputes, identify urban service areas for public sewer and water service, and separate developed areas from rural areas (see Chapters 14 and 20).
2. A policy of concurrency linked to an adequate public facilities ordinance can promote phased growth.
3. Impact fees and exactions require developers to pay for the cost of the development of public services, such as parkland and traffic improvements (see Chapter 20).
4. Property tax incentives in the form of reductions in property tax assessments for farm and forest lands or historic properties can provide an incentive not to convert property from these uses (see Chapters 14, 15, and 19).
5. Fee simple land acquisition, the purchase of development rights, and the transfer of development rights are techniques to keep land open. The public purchase of land in fee simple gives the public ownership of the land, such as in the case of purchasing land for a park. In a purchase of development rights program, a landowner voluntarily sells to the public the right to develop his or her land; the landowner still owns the land but can only use it for farming, forestry, or open space purposes. A transfer of development rights program to protect farmland and open space areas or historic structures allows landowners to sell transferable development rights to developers who transfer the development rights to properties they are then allowed to develop more intensively (see Chapters 9, 14, and 15).

Other Regulations

1. Building codes are standards for the construction of new buildings and renovations and can address energy conservation, as well as safety (Chapter 19).
2. Nuisance ordinances can regulate light and noise pollution.

Note: Planners may want to seek legal advice about how to implement these tools and techniques and whether they are legally allowed in their particular state or community.

Plan Implementation, Monitoring, and Evaluation

A plan is only meaningful if it is implemented. As the City of San Francisco said in its 1997 sustainability plan, "The only goal of producing this plan is to begin implementing it."[9] The successful implementation of an Environmental Action Plan involves the use of effective spending programs, incentives, and environmental and land-use regulations. Above all, it requires cooperation among government, businesses, citizens groups, and households.

Monitoring of the implementation efforts is essential for identifying successes and shortcomings and can provide information for recommending changes to existing programs as well as opportunities to use new environmental planning techniques. To monitor the progress of the Environmental Action Plan and to keep the local government accountable, planners can

---

BOX 2. THE PRIVATE SECTOR AND ENVIRONMENTAL PLANNING

One of the most important trends since 1970 is the growth in private sector environmental planning. To comply with government regulations, businesses have formed environmental management units. Moreover, in working to reduce the costs of environmental compliance, businesses have been challenged to operate more responsibly and sustainably. New technologies are enabling businesses to reduce waste and toxic substances, save energy and water, and produce more durable products. These trends are encouraging because they show that businesses can be both environmentally friendly and profitable.[10]

In several states and many communities, land developers have had to address a wide range of questions about the impacts of their proposed developments on the natural and built environments, from air and water quality to transportation and aesthetics. Some developers have abandoned the uniform "cookie-cutter" designs of residential subdivisions in favor of mixed-use residential and commercial projects that emphasize pedestrian access over motor vehicles. The trend toward urban redevelopment after the housing crash and Great Recession of 2007–2009 has highlighted the principles of new urbanism, which takes as its model the village—designed to be compact and walkable, with mixed uses at a human scale, and a vibrant public realm.

The private nonprofit sector has taken on a rapidly expanding role in environmental planning, especially in the protection of natural areas, wildlife habitat, waterways, working landscapes, and historic buildings. The number, size, and importance of land trusts, conservancies, watershed associations, and citizens groups have grown impressively over the past 30 years. No longer is environmental planning conducted solely by governments. The result has been an increasing number of public-private partnerships in local and regional planning, land preservation, watershed protection, and redevelopment efforts.

use benchmarking. Benchmarks are measurable targets, such as acquisition of a certain number of acres of park land, improvements in water quality from Class C (impaired) to Class A (swimmable and fishable), or adding 10 miles of track to a light-rail system. Each year, the planning commission or elected officials can set targets tied to specific objectives in the action plan. The planning commission can then assess the progress toward the benchmarks and publish an annual Environmental Action Report. The report can indicate which benchmarks were met and which were not and then suggest needed adjustments in policy priorities, regulations, and spending programs. Above all, benchmarking and the annual Environmental Action Report keep the Environmental Action Plan and the comprehensive plan in front of the public, businesses, and elected officials. Finally, the planning commission should review and update the action plan every three to five years to reflect changes in community desires and priorities, to keep the plan responsive to changes in environmental quality, and to keep the community on course toward long-range sustainability goals.

1.3: A FURTHER LOOK AT FUNCTIONAL AND AREA ENVIRONMENTAL PLANS

Many local governments have adopted one or more environmentally oriented functional or area plans in addition to their comprehensive plan. The purpose of these special plans is to focus attention on one or more environmental problems and to create a strategic course of action. Ideally, these plans should be made part of the comprehensive plan because the comprehensive plan provides the legal basis for zoning and subdivision regulations and guides CIPs.

CLIMATE ACTION PLAN

The lack of federal policies and actions to curb greenhouse gas emissions has compelled more than 120 American cities to draft climate action plans to mitigate and adapt to climate change.[11] These cities recognized that local decisions about land use, transportation, building design, and energy consumption can have not just local impacts but global impacts as well. The first step in creating a climate action plan is to estimate the greenhouse gas emissions in a baseline year from the community's energy consumption and waste generation.

Next, a forecast is made of future emission levels based on current trends. Then greenhouse gas reduction targets are established according to a timeline.[12] The city drafts an action plan to implement changes to land-use regulations, infrastructure investment, building codes, and public education to achieve the greenhouse reduction targets. The city must then monitor progress toward the reduction targets and make adjustments in its climate action programs as needed.

Albany, California's 2010 climate action plan (see Chapter 4) features three strategies that have the greatest potential to reduce greenhouse gas emissions:[13]

1. Increased energy efficiency in buildings, including zero emissions city buildings by 2015; enhanced energy efficiency standards for new construction, increased use of renewable energy, and improved energy management in homes and businesses
2. Reduced automobile emissions through improving pedestrian and bicycle infrastructure, improving public transit service, promoting pedestrian-and transit-oriented development, and improving the energy efficiency of the city's vehicle fleet
3. Increasing recycling and composting through educating residents

GREEN INFRASTRUCTURE PLAN

The term "green infrastructure" covers a range of open space and stormwater management investment projects. At the site level in cities, green infrastructure in the form of green roofs, rain gardens, bioswales, and street trees have proven effective in capturing, retaining, and infiltrating stormwater. At the regional or landscape scale, green infrastructure can link open spaces, providing recreation and a variety of ecosystems services (see Box 3).

Benedict and McMahon define green infrastructure as "a strategically planned and managed network of wilderness, parks, green-ways, conservation easements, and working lands with conservation value that supports native species, maintains natural ecological processes, sustains air and water resources, and contributes to the health and quality of life for America's communities and people."[14]

In most cities and counties, the CIP emphasizes the construction, repair, and maintenance of "gray infrastructure," such as roads, bridges, public sewer and water facilities, schools, municipal buildings, and police and fire equipment. Yet cities and counties can include "green infrastructure" investments in parks, greenways, trails, stormwater management, and farmland and forestland preservation in their CIPs. Like gray infrastructure, green infrastructure usually involves long-term investments and annual operating costs that require careful consideration of financing arrangements and project priorities.

One goal of green infrastructure is to maximize ecosystem services. There are four general categories of ecosystem services: provisioning, regulating, cultural, and supporting.[15] Provisioning services produce food, fiber, and energy for humans, plants, and animals. Regulating services affect climate, air quality, waste treatment, and water quality and supplies. Cultural services refer to opportunities for recreation, education, and spiritual or aesthetic enjoyment from contact with nature. Supporting services underlie the others with basic natural processes such as photosynthesis and nutrient cycling. Different types of green spaces provide different arrays of services. Thus communities and regions need a variety of green infrastructure to provide a range of ecosystem services, from provisioning (farms and forests), to regulating (forest and wildlife preserves), to cultural (parks and green-ways), and supporting (open space). A green infrastructure project can provide multiple ecosystem services. For example, greenways often buffer water bodies; intercept, infiltrate, and filter pollutants; and provide recreational trails and wildlife migration corridors.

Green infrastructure plans embody six design characteristics:

1. Multifunctionality
2. Connectivity
3. Habitability
4. Resiliency
5. Identity
6. Return on investment[16]

A key goal of any green infrastructure plan is connectivity.[17] Isolated strips of open land do not provide as rich ecosystem services (air and water filters, wildlife and plant habitat) as a connected network of green spaces. The connected green infrastructure is also more resilient to natural events, such as rainstorms and flooding. Finally, connected green infrastructure can help create regional networks of trails that tie cities and suburbs with the countryside.

Lancaster County, Pennsylvania, adopted its green infrastructure plan, *Greenscapes*, in 2009. The plan has four main themes: (1) the preservation of outstanding natural resources, such as pristine streams and interior forests; (2) the conservation and stewardship of important natural resources, including floodplains, steep slopes, and wetlands; (3) the restoration of degraded ecosystems, and improvement of air and water quality; and (4) recreation as a way to improve public health.[18] The plan first presents an analysis of existing conditions: land use, demographics, natural vegetation, steep slopes and highly erodible soils, unique geological features, watersheds, water quality, air quality, biodiversity, interior forests, priority plant and animal habitat, parks and recreation areas, and trails. The plan then lays out the desired green infrastructure system of open-space hubs and greenways and smaller open-space nodes and links in a series of maps based on the pattern in Figure 5.

Each of the four goals in Greenscapes is supported by objectives and strategies to achieve those goals. The plan describes a variety of tools that local governments can use, including land-use, transportation, watershed, and open space policies and plans; zoning and subdivision regulations; investments in green infrastructure to acquire land or permanent conservation easements; and education and partnerships with landowners and nonprofit organizations.

ENVIRONMENTAL POLICY PLAN

A policy plan is a set of desired outcomes and recommendations to achieve those outcomes. Typically, however, a policy plan lacks the detailed facts and careful analysis found in a comprehensive plan or a future land-use map on which to base the zoning map. In many cases, a policy plan appears to be a wish list, which may or may not realistically reflect the community's ability to make recommended changes.

In 2007, New York City adopted *PlaNYC 2030: A Greener, Greater New York*, which can be thought of as a hybrid between a comprehensive plan and an environmental policy plan.[19] The plan differs from a comprehensive plan in three main ways. First, the plan was drafted by the city with input from 25 city agencies rather than broad public input. Second, the city's economic and social issues were not explored in depth. PlaNYC strongly implies, however, that environmental improvement, both in the natural and built environments, will strengthen the resilience of the economy and promote social harmony. Third, PlaNYC does not contain a future land-use map on which to base the zoning map.

PlaNYC addressed New York City's need to accommodate an expected increase of one million residents by 2030 while advocating for improvements to the city's built and natural environments. The plan focused on six issues: land (housing, open space, and brownfields), water quality and supply, transportation congestion and repair, energy, air quality, and climate change. For each issue, the plan spelled out

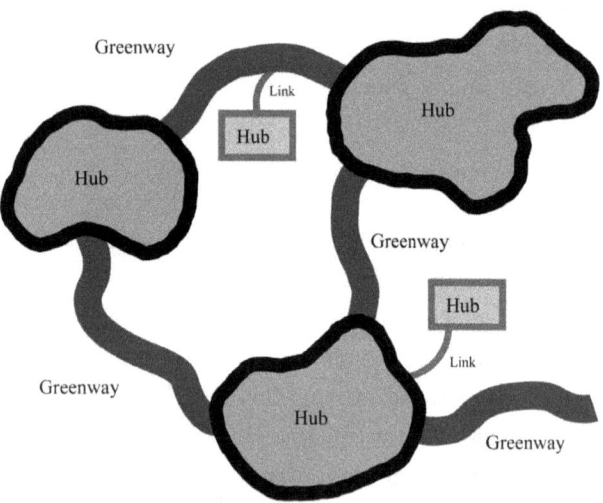

Figure 5. Hub and Greenway, Node and Link Patterns for Connected Green Infrastructure
Source: Lancaster County, PA, Planning Commission, *Greenscapes*, 2009, p. 78.

goals and objectives. In total, the plan listed 127 objectives or initiatives for the city. Like a comprehensive plan, the goals and objectives were tied to a new vision for New York:

> It is a vision of providing New Yorkers with the cleanest air of any big city in the nation; of maintaining the purity of our drinking water and opening more of our rivers and creeks and coastal waters to recreation; of producing more energy more cleanly and more reliably, and offering more choices on how to travel quickly and efficiently across our city. It is a vision where contaminated land is reclaimed and restored to communities; where every family lives near a park or playground; where housing is sustainable and available to New Yorkers from every background, reflecting the diversity that has defined our city for centuries.[20]

In 2011 and 2012, the City of New York released updates to PlaNYC, reporting on progress toward the goals and objectives of the 2007 plan. Achievements included stricter energy efficiency regulations for buildings, more than 200 acres of new parkland, the planting of nearly half a million trees, and a 13 percent reduction in greenhouse gas emissions from 2005 to 2011.[21] This kind of benchmarking and monitoring is essential for keeping a plan alive in the minds of elected officials and the general public. The goals of the 2011 update include the following:

1. Create homes for almost a million more New Yorkers while making housing and neighborhoods more affordable and sustainable.
2. Ensure all New Yorkers live within a 10-minute walk of a park.
3. Clean up all contaminated land in New York City.
4. Improve the quality of our waterways to increase opportunities for recreation and restore coastal ecosystems.
5. Ensure the high quality and reliability of our water supply system.
6. Expand sustainable transportation choices and ensure the reliability and high quality of our transportation network.
7. Reduce energy consumption and make our energy systems cleaner and more reliable.
8. Achieve the cleanest air quality of any big U.S. city.
9. Divert 75 percent of our solid waste from landfills.
10. Reduce greenhouse gas emissions by more than 30 percent by 2030.
11. Increase the resilience of our communities, natural systems, and infrastructure to climate risks.[22]

New York City has succeeded in creating a plan that provides direction for action by the city government, businesses, and households. The benchmarking and monitoring has helped to keep the plan a living document. In short, PlaNYC has established a model for an environmental policy plan that other large cities can look to as they forge goals, objectives, and actions to improve their natural and built environments.

SUSTAINABILITY PLAN

A true sustainability plan must address the long-term durability of the natural and built environments, the local economy, and social equity.

In 2010, the City of Grand Rapids, Michigan, approved a sustainability plan for the

ESSENTIAL READINGS IN URBAN PLANNING

next five years with the subtitle *Managing the Economic, Social, and Environmental Resources of the City through a Framework of Sustainability Outcomes and Targets.*[23] The city established a planning process based on a variety of local plans that city departments could use to achieve targets and outcomes by specific deadlines (see Figure 6). Each department submits a quarterly report on progress, which is summarized in a gap analysis, documenting the difference between progress and the targets. The city then can amend the sustainability plan to better focus resources on outcomes and targets that are proving more difficult to meet.

The elements of the sustainability plan include the following:

Economic Sustainability
1. A strong economy
2. Diverse supplier base
3. Employment and workforce training
4. Financial management/sustainability
5. Enhanced customer service
6. Vital business districts

Social Sustainability
1. Great neighborhoods
2. Strong education, arts, and community

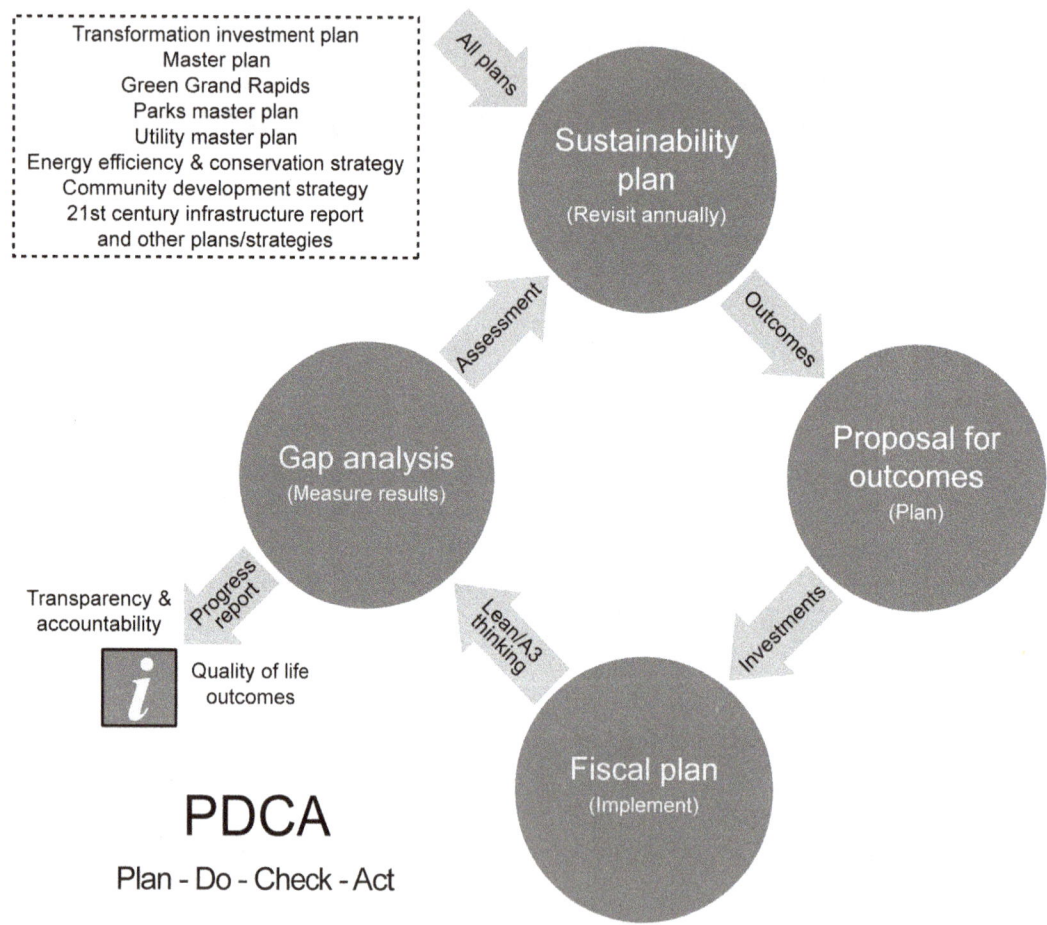

Figure 6. City of Grand Rapids Sustainability Plan: Plan-Do-Check-Act Process

3. Civic engagement
4. Healthy lifestyles and healthy environments
5. Public safety

Environmental Sustainability
1. Energy and climate protection
2. Environmental quality and natural systems
3. Land use and development

The following are specific desired environmental outcomes:

A. Maintain an adequate and safe water supply.
B. Improve the quality of the Grand River and its tributaries.
C. Protect and maintain healthy ecosystems and habitats.
D. Reuse and recycle; and reduce waste sent to landfills.
E. Ensure that sound land uses enhance the natural environment.
F. Ensure quality design and construction of the built environment in accordance with the City's Master Plan and Zoning Ordinance.
G. Ensure access to parks and open spaces for all citizens.
H. Reduce greenhouse gas emissions (carbon footprint) and impact on climate change.[24]

These principles speak to the importance of the triple bottom line of environmental, economic, and social sustainability. The challenge, of course, is to implement the plan and move toward greater sustainability over time.

STATE AND REGIONAL ENVIRONMENTAL PLANS

States and regional governments have crafted a number of environmental plans to guide decision making. For instance, California, Georgia, Hawaii, New Mexico, Pennsylvania, and Texas have state water management plans. Thirty-three states have source water protection plans to protect surface and groundwater used by rural residents.[25] Every state has a wildlife action plan to protect land and water bodies that provide wildlife habitat. The 2008 Farm Bill required every state to conduct an assessment of their forests and devise ways to respond to threats and improve forest health. These plans, known as Forest Action Plans, also identify priority forest landscapes for long-term protection and preservation. Each state has a State Comprehensive Outdoor Recreation Plan, which is required for eligibility to obtain funding for recreation projects from the federal Land and Water Conservation Fund. All states have a State Implementation Plan to improve air quality to meet federal air-quality standards.

There are four main types of regional environmental plans: (1) plans that protect special environmental regions and resources, (2) river basin plans, (3) metropolitan transportation plans, and (4) growth management plans that aim to balance environmental protection with economic growth. The Adirondack Park Plan in upstate New York, the Pinelands Plan in New Jersey, and the Lake Tahoe Regional Plan spanning parts of California and Nevada are examples of plans that were created to protect special fragile ecological regions from excessive development.[26] The comprehensive plan of the Delaware River Basin Commission directs the decisions of staff and representatives from four states (Delaware, New Jersey, New York, and Pennsylvania) and the U.S. Army Corps of Engineers.[27] The Delaware River watershed provides water to more than 15 million people. The commission, created in 1961, has responsibilities for water-quality protection, water withdrawals, issuing permits for natural gas wells, drought management, flood management, and recreation. Transportation plans for metropolitan areas were required under the Intermodal Surface Transportation Efficiency Act (ISTEA) of 1991. ISTEA mandated that a metro area have a transportation plan in order to qualify for federal transportation funds (see Chapter 18). A metro area drafts a 20-year regional transportation plan, a three- to five-year Transportation Improvement Program, and a list of desired transportation projects. Furthermore, the metro plans must be consistent with the State Implementation Plan for achieving compliance with the federal air-quality standards under the Clean Air Act.

Envision Utah, a public-private partnership of business and civic leaders and elected officials, was formed in 1997 and has advocated that communities and regions pursue a quality growth strategy for a strong economy, environment, and quality of life.[28] Envision Utah first focused on the Greater Wasatch region around Salt Lake City, where population growth, water supply, air quality, transportation systems, and affordable housing are key issues. The Greater Wasatch region is expected to grow from 1.6 million people in 1995 to 5 million in 2050. The region has 10 counties and 91 cities and towns. Envision Utah decided to use *scenario planning* to form their regional plan. With plenty of public input, Envision Utah then developed four alternative growth scenarios. The first scenario continued the sprawling low-density, automobile-oriented development patterns. The second scenario was only a little less sprawling, based on current local land-use plans. The third scenario emphasized more compact and walkable development, some of which would be placed within existing urban areas. House-lot sizes would average slightly more than a quarter of an acre. The fourth scenario would put nearly half of all new development in existing urban areas and accommodate most of the remaining growth in compact new towns. The transit system would be greatly expanded. After a broad public outreach campaign, a public survey showed a preference for the fourth scenario. TRAX, the light-rail system around Greater Salt Lake City, opened in 1999 and has grown to three lines, 41 stations, and 20 miles of track with more expansions planned by 2015.[29] The light-rail system helps to implement the compact development and investment in urban areas called for in the fourth scenario. One example is the new town of Daybreak, which began construction in 2004. When Daybreak is fully built out by 2024, it is expected to have 20,000 residential units and 9.1 million square feet of commercial space. Already, Daybreak is connected by the TRAX light-rail system to Greater Salt Lake City.[30]

The Metropolitan Area Planning Council (MAPC) of Greater Boston used scenario planning in creating their 2008 MetroFuture plan, a 30-year plan for managing growth.[31] The first scenario showed a projection of trends based on current development (see Figure 7a). The purpose of a plan is to change negative trends and support positive trends. In this case, the MAPC wanted to enable economic growth while reducing the amount of open space lost to development. The MAPC then tested a number of alternative scenarios using different assumptions about future development. From the several alternative scenarios, a preferred scenario was selected (see Figure 7b). The preferred scenario would reduce the loss of open space by 115,000 acres between 2000 and 2030.

1.4: DAY-TO-DAY PLANNING DECISIONS: REVIEW OF DEVELOPMENT PROPOSALS

The day-to-day implementation of the comprehensive plan and other environmental plans

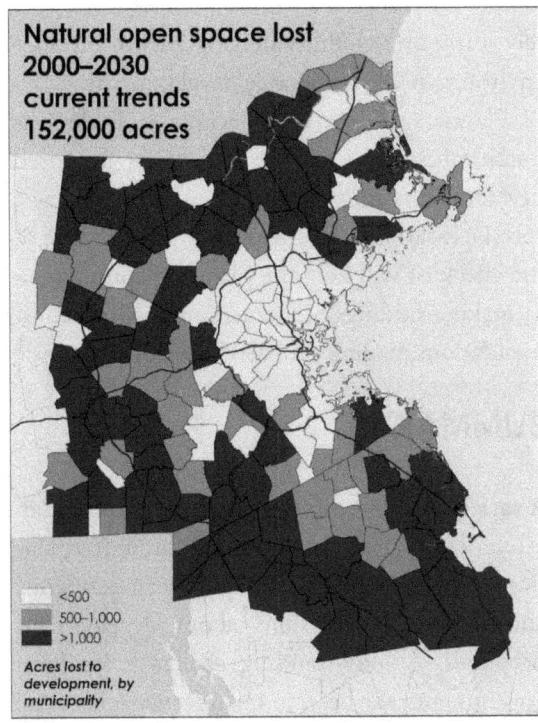

Figure 7a. Scenario A: Expected Loss of Open Space in Greater Boston, 2000–2030, if Current Development Trends Continue (152,000 Acres)

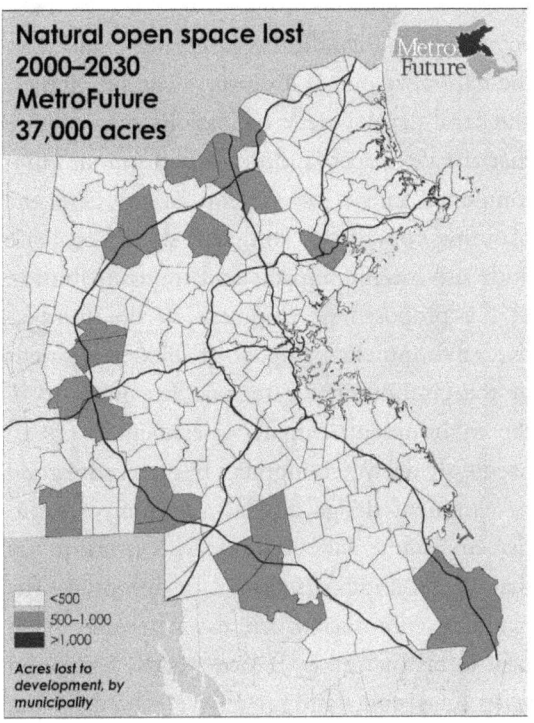

Figure 7b. Scenario B: Expected Loss Under the MetroFuture Plan (37,000 Acres)
Source: Metropolitan Area Planning Council, *MetroFuture Plan*, 2008, p. 21.

occurs through the recommendations and decisions made by planning commissions, zoning boards, zoning officers, and elected officials as they review proposed development projects for consistency with the plans, the zoning ordinance, subdivision regulations, CIPs, and other local standards.

When a development proposal is submitted to the planning commission, the commission should make an assessment of the potential environmental impacts. First, the commission should refer to any state or federal requirements. For example, if federal funds or approvals are involved in a proposed project, the developer must follow the federal environmental impact statement (EIS) procedures according to the National Environmental Policy Act (NEPA; see Chapter 2). If there is a State Environmental Policy Act, its rules may affect the proposed development project. Air and water quality, water withdrawals, wetlands, and threatened and endangered species are examples of environmental issues that might require a review and approval from a federal or state agency.

The planning commission should next refer to the local plans and zoning and subdivision regulations in reviewing a development proposal. For instance, if the natural resources inventory of the comprehensive plan has been properly used for drafting the future land-use map, zoning map, and ordinance language, then development will tend to be guided toward the most appropriate locations and inappropriate development proposals will be rare. The subdivision and land-development regulations should require developers to provide information about on-site environmental conditions in greater detail than the natural resources inventory. The subdivision and land-development regulations may require that the developer/landowner perform an environmental impact assessment. In any case, the planning commission and staff should evaluate both site-specific impacts and the contribution of the proposed development to the cumulative environmental impact of all development in the community or region. The purpose of the environmental impact assessment is not to needlessly delay development but to ensure good development design and a minimum of negative environmental outcomes. This is not to say that all developments should be approved. The planning commission can also determine what new infrastructure is needed (roads, sewer and water lines, police and fire service, schools), what infrastructure the developer must provide, and what the local government will supply. Finally, it is important to note that often a development will be approved subject to conditions—for example, actions a developer is required to make, such as planting trees and vegetation to reduce stormwater runoff—to improve the design and environmental performance of the proposed development. Whenever a development is approved with conditions, the local government will need to monitor the development to ensure that the developer met the conditions or else compel the developer to make the required changes.

Development review is a case-by-case process that depends on the size, location, and design of the proposed project as well as the current environmental conditions. Small developments, often referred to as minor subdivisions of three or fewer lots, should have a more streamlined review than major subdivisions. Though some flexibility in development projects can be allowed, planners and elected officials should not rely solely on voluntary negotiations to produce environmentally acceptable developments.

Planners can use the checklist in Table 4 as a guide for reviewing the impacts of proposed developments on the natural environment at a specific location. The answers to the questions in the checklist will help the planning commission in making findings of fact to support its recommendations about a proposed development.

SUMMARY

A variety of environmental plans exist, but a plan is useful only if it is implemented through regulations, incentives, public and private investments, and day-to-day decisions about development proposals. A long-standing challenge for local governments has been to include environmental issues in the traditional comprehensive plan. One way to do this is to put environmentally oriented goals and objectives in the comprehensive plan. But it is vitally important to emphasize the implementation of these environmental goals and objectives through an action plan of regulations, incentives, and infrastructure investments. Several local governments have adopted special environmental plans both to give environmental issues priority and to spell out specific strategies. These special plans include climate action plans, green infrastructure plans, environmental policy plans, and sustainability plans. It is a good idea to tie these plans to the comprehensive plan, which is the legal basis for zoning and subdivision regulations. States have created environmental plans for wildlife, water management, forests, and outdoor recreation. Regional environmental plans feature special protection plans for fragile ecological areas, river basin plans, metropolitan transportation plans, and growth management plans.

Table 4. Environmental Impact Checklist for Reviewing Proposed Development Projects

1.	Is the proposed development consistent with the goals and objectives of the comprehensive plan and the future land-use map?
2.	Is the proposed development consistent with the zoning ordinance or is a rezoning requested?
3.	Is the proposed development consistent with the subdivision and land-development regulations?
4.	Is the proposed development consistent with the CIP?
5.	What use or uses are proposed in the development?
6.	What is the size of the proposed development, including buildings, acreage, and lot coverage (impervious surface) by buildings, roads, driveways, and sidewalks?
7.	Can the development be considered a "development of regional impact"?
8.	Could the development have an impact on groundwater supplies or quality?
9.	Could the development have an impact on the water quality of or supply of water in a lake, pond, stream, or wetland?
10.	What will the source of water be? If on-site water is proposed, is there sufficient water to accommodate the use? Is there a possibility the proposed water source could be contaminated from nearby landfills or commercial or industrial uses? Could the on-site use of water adversely affect existing water availability to adjoining properties?
11.	Could the development change stormwater drainage patterns or increase runoff off-site?
12.	Could the development produce significant soil erosion and sedimentation?
13.	How will sewage be disposed of? If on-site sewage disposal is proposed, are soils appropriate and is the lot large enough to provide an adequate absorption field?
14.	How will the development affect air quality?
15.	How will the development affect transportation use and patterns?
16.	How will solid waste, including any toxic substances, from the development be disposed of?
17.	What kind of energy will the development use and where will it come from?
18.	Could the development affect any threatened or endangered plant or animal species, sensitive wildlife habitat, or hunting and fishing areas?
19.	Is the development proposed for an area with known natural hazards, especially floodplains and steep slopes?
20.	Would the development affect any scenic views or unique land forms?
21.	Could the development adversely affect nearby agricultural land or forest land operations?
22.	How will the development fit in with the existing built environment in terms of scale, use, and aesthetics?
23.	Will the development spur additional development in the vicinity?
24.	Will the development affect any known archaeological or historic sites or historic buildings?
25.	Will the development generate unreasonable noise, odors, glare, or other off-site impacts that might be considered a nuisance?
26.	What state and federal reviews and permits are needed for approval of the proposed development and have they been obtained?

NOTES

1. Dowie, M. *Losing Ground: American Environmentalism at the Close of the Twentieth Century.* Cambridge, MA: MIT Press, 1995, p. 7.
2. Commoner, B., quoted in Egan, M. *Barry Commoner and the Science of Survival: The Remaking of American Environmentalism.* Cambridge, MA: MIT Press, 2007, p. 126.
3. For example, see the SmartCode at SmartCode Central. Home page. http://smartcodecentral.org.
4. Dutchess County, NY. *Dutchess County Natural Resources Inventory.* 2010. http://www.co.dutchess.ny.us/CountyGov/Departments/Planning/16138.htm. Retrieved September 10, 2012.
5. Port Washington, WI. *A Comprehensive Plan for the City of Port Washington: 2035.* Chapter 3: Inventory of Agricultural, Natural, and Cultural Resources. 2009. http://www.cityofportwashington.com/compPlan.html. Retrieved May 22, 2014.
6. Humstone, E., J. Campoli, and A. McLean. *Above and Beyond: Visualizing Change in Small Towns and Rural Areas.* Chicago: Planners Press, American Planning Association, 2001.
7. Town of Dennis, MA. *Draft Local Comprehensive Plan: Human/Built Systems.* 2012. http://dennismalocalcomprehensiveplan.wordpress.com/humanbuilt-systems. Retrieved September 10, 2012.
8. Lancaster County, VA. *Lancaster County Comprehensive Plan.* Chapter 2: Suitability of Land for Development. 2012. http://www.lancova.com/comp_plan_ch2.pdf. Retrieved September 10, 2012.
9. City of San Francisco. *Sustainability Plan, 1997.* http://www.sustainable.org/creating-community/community-visioning/717-the-sustainability-plan-for-the-city-of-san-francisco. Retrieved September 10, 2012.
10. See Hawken, P., A. Lovins, and H. Lovins. *Natural Capitalism: Creating the Next Industrial Revolution.* Boston: Little, Brown, 1999.
11. Henderson, H. "Planners Library: Keeping It Local." Review of *Local Climate Action Planning,* by M. Boswell, A. Grieve, and T. Seale. *Planning,* February 2012, p. 45.
12. See City of Albany, CA, and ICLEI. *Baseline Greenhouse Gas Emissions Inventory Report.* Albany, CA: City of Albany, 2006.
13. City of Albany, CA. *Climate Action Plan, 2010.* http://www.albanyca.org/index.aspx?page=256. Retrieved May 16, 2012.
14. Benedict, M., and E. McMahon. *Green Infrastructure: Linking Landscapes and Communities.* Washington, DC: Island Press, 2006. Quoted in Rouse, D., and I. Bunster-Ossa. *Green Infrastructure: A Landscape Approach.* Planning Advisory Report Number 571. Chicago: American Planning Association, 2013, p. 10.
15. Millennium Ecosystem Assessment. *Ecosystems and Human Well-Being: Synthesis.* Washington, DC: Island Press, 2005. http://www.millenniumassessment.org/documents/document.356.aspx.pdf. Retrieved June 6, 2013.
16. Rouse, D., and I. Bunster-Ossa. *Green Infrastructure: A Landscape Approach.* Planning Advisory Report Number 571. Chicago: American Planning Association, 2013, p. 18.
17. See Benedict, M., and E. McMahon. *Green Infrastructure: Linking Landscapes and Communities.* Washington, DC: Island Press, 2006.
18. Lancaster County, PA, Planning Commission. *Greenscapes: The Green Infrastructure Element.* Lancaster, PA: Lancaster County Planning

Commission, 2009. http://www.lancastercountyplanning.org/134/Greenscapes. Retrieved May 22, 2014.
19. City of New York. *PlaNYC 2030: A Greener, Greater New York*. New York: City of New York, 2007. http://nytelecom.vo.llnwd.net/o15/agencies/planyc2030/pdf/full_report_2007.pdf. Retrieved May 17, 2012.
20. Ibid., p. 141.
21. City of New York. *PlaNYC 2030: A Greener, Greater New York*. Update April 2011, pp. 3, 12. http://nytelecom.vo.llnwd.net/o15/agencies/planyc2030/pdf/planyc_2011_planyc_full_report.pdf. Retrieved May 17, 2012.
22. Ibid., p. 15.
23. City of Grand Rapids, MI. *Sustainability Plan, FY 2010-FY 2015: Managing the Economic, Social, and Environmental Resources of the City through a Framework of Sustainability Outcomes and Targets*. Grand Rapids, MI: City of Grand Rapids, 2011. http://www.grand-rapids.mi.us/enterprise-services/officeofenergyandsustainability/Documents/Sust%20Plan%20as%20amended%206-21-11.pdf. Retrieved May 22, 2014.
24. Ibid., pp. 27–31.
25. U.S. Department of Agriculture, Farm Service Agency. "Source Water Protection Program." http://www.fsa.usda.gov/FSA/webapp?area=home&subject=copr&topic=swp. Retrieved May 17, 2012.
26. See Lapping, M., and O. Furuseth, eds. *Big Places, Big Plans: Large-Scale Regional Planning in North America*. Hampshire, UK: Ashgate, 2004.
27. Delaware River Basin Commission. *Comprehensive Plan, 2001*. http://www.state.nj.us/drbc/library/documents/comprehensive_plan.pdf. Retrieved May 20, 2012.
28. Envision Utah. *The History of Envision Utah, 2003*. http://envisionutah.org/about/mission-history. Retrieved May 18, 2014.
29. Utah Transit Authority. *Trax Fact Sheet, 2012*. http://www.rideuta.com/uploads/FactSheets_TRAX_2012.pdf. Retrieved May 21, 2012.
30. Daybreak, Utah. Home page. http://www.Daybreakutah.com.
31. Metropolitan Area Planning Council. *MetroFuture Plan, 2008*. http://www.metrofuture.org. Retrieved May 21, 2012.

PLANNING FOR COMMUNITY RESILIENCE

WHAT IS RESILIENCE?

BY JAMIE HICKS MASTERSON ET AL.

To begin tackling the problem of increased vulnerability to natural disasters, we must understand what we are trying to achieve. In recent years, the term *resilience* has gained popularity, but it is used in widely varying ways. All communities should strive for resilience, but what does it mean? Resilience has different definitions arising from a range of disciplines that use the concept, including natural hazard management, ecology, psychology, sociology, geography, psychiatry, and public health.[1] These different perspectives mean that *resilience* is a widely used term that can take on different meanings in different contexts. The following is an in-depth look at the ecological and social aspects of resilience as defined in various fields of research.

BIOPHYSICAL SYSTEMS AND COMMUNITY SYSTEMS

Perhaps the definition of *resilience* most relevant to disaster management comes from the field of ecology. Ecology's well-defined concept of resilience has evolved over the years (see box 1). A number of common elements emerge from these definitions. First, the unit of analysis is generally an ecosystem. Second, there is a notion of resilience being defined as either the ability of systems to absorb changes and yet maintain themselves or the ability to rapidly bounce back from some form of impact. These two notions suggest that resilience may be measured by the amount of shock a system is able to absorb and the rapidity with which it rebounds after the

Jamie Hicks Masterson et al., "What Is Resilience?," *Planning for Community Resilience: A Handbook for Reducing Vulnerability to Disasters*, pp. 25-40. Copyright © 2014 by Island Press. Reprinted with permission.

BOX 1. DEFINITIONS OF RESILIENCE FROM ECOLOGY

"An ecosystem is the measure of the ability of an ecosystem to absorb changes and still persist." Holling, 1973[a]

"The speed with which a system returns to its original state following a perturbation." Pimm, 1984[b]

"A buffer capacity or ability of a system to absorb perturbation, or the magnitude of the disturbance that can be absorbed before a system changes its structure by changing the variables and processes that control behavior." Holling, 1995[c]

"The potential of a particular configuration of a system to maintain its structure/ function in the face of disturbance, and the ability of the system to re-organize following disturbance-driven change and measured by size of stability domain." Lebel, 2001[d]

"A potential of a system to remain in a particular configuration and to maintain its feedbacks and functions, and involves the ability of the system to reorganize following the disturbance driven change." Walker et al., 2002[e]

"Resilience for social–ecological systems is related to three different characteristics: (a) the magnitude of shock that the system can absorb and remain in within a given state; (b) the degree to which the system is capable of self-organization, and (c) the degree to which the system can build capacity for learning and adaptation." Folke et al., 2002[f]

"The capacity of a system to absorb disturbances, to undergo changes, and still retain essentially the same function, structure, and feedbacks." Walker and Salt, 2006[g]

"Ecosystem resilience is the capacity of an ecosystem to tolerate disturbance without collapsing into a qualitatively different state that is controlled by a different set of processes. Thus, a resilient ecosystem can withstand shocks and rebuild itself when necessary. Resilience in coupled social-ecological systems, the social systems have the added capacity of humans to learn from experience and anticipate and plan for the future." Resilience Alliance, 2007[h]

a. Holling, C. S. "Resilience and Stability of Ecological Systems." *Annual Review of Ecology and Systematics* 4 (1973): 1–23.
b. Pimm, S. L. "The Complexity and Stability of Ecosystems." *Nature* 1984: 321–6.
c. Holling, C. S. "What Barriers? What Bridges?" In *Barriers and Bridges to the Renewal of Ecosystems and Institutions*, edited by L. H. Gunderson, C. S. Holling, and S. S. Light, 3–34. New York: Columbia University Press, 1995.
d. Lebel, L. "Resilience and Sustainability of Landscapes." *ASB Partnership* 2001. http://www.asb.cgiar.org/docs (accessed August 5, 2007).
e. Walker, B., et al. "Resilience Management in Social–Ecological Systems: A Working Hypothesis for a Participatory Approach." *Conservation Ecology* 2002.
f. Folke, C., S. R. Carpenter, T. Elmqvist, L. Gunderson, C. S. Holling, and B. Walker. "Resilience and Sustainable Development: Building Adaptive Capacity in a World of Transformations." *Ambio* 31 (2002): 437–40.
g. Walker, B., and D. Salt. Resilience Thinking: Sustaining Ecosystems and People in a Changing World. Washington, DC: Island Press, 2006.
h. Resilience Alliance. *Assessing and Managing Resilience in Social–Ecological Systems: A Practitioner's Workbook.* Stockholm: Author, 2007.

shock. From these perspectives, a more resilient system is one that can absorb larger shocks and bounce back in a shorter period of time. A third theme emerging from these definitions is a subtle shift focusing on the capacities of a system to resist or absorb impacts and its ability to maintain or return to largely the same form, function, structure, or qualitative state. So a resilient system not only has the ability to resist impact, but when impacted it can return to its previous state, and the focus is on the capacities of systems that provide the abilities to absorb, resist, and bounce back.

More recently, the ecological literature has sought to expand its notion of a system to include coupled social-ecological systems (SESs). The addition of social systems adds an important new dimension in that now a resilient system is a system that has the ability to learn from experiences and adapt (see box 2). Thus, the idea is

BOX 2. DEFINITIONS OF RESILIENCE WITH A SOCIAL SYSTEM PERSPECTIVE

"The measure of a system's or part of the system's capacity to absorb and recover from occurrence of a hazardous event." Timmerman, 1981[a]

"The capacity to cope with unanticipated dangers after they have become manifest, learning to bounce back." Wildavsky, 1991[b]

"The capacity that people or groups may possess to withstand or recover from the emergencies and which can stand as a counterbalance to vulnerability." Buckle, 2000[c]

"A measure of how quickly a system recovers from failures." FEMA, 1998[d]

"Local resiliency means that a locale is able to withstand an extreme natural event without suffering devastating losses, damage, diminished productivity, or quality of life without a large amount of assistance from outside the community." Mileti, 1999[e]

"The capacity to adapt existing resources and skills to new systems and operating conditions." Comfort et al., 1999[f]

"Social resilience is the ability of groups or communities to cope with external stresses and disturbances as a result of social, political, and environmental change." Adger, 2000[g]

"The qualities of people, communities, agencies, and infrastructure that reduce vulnerability. Not just the absence of vulnerability rather the capacity to prevent or mitigate loss and then secondly, if damage does occur to maintain normal condition as far as possible, and thirdly to manage recovery from the impact." Buckle et al., 2000[h]

"The amount of disturbance a system can absorb and still remain within the same state ... the degree to which the system is capable of self-organization ... the degree to which the system can build and increase the capacity for learning and adaptation." Klein et al., 2003[i]

"The ability of social units (organizations, communities) to mitigate hazards, contain the effects of disasters when they occur, and carry out recovery activities in ways that minimize social disruption and

(Continued)

mitigate the effects of future earthquakes. Characteristics of a resilient system: 1) Reduced failure probabilities; 2) Reduced consequences from failures, in terms of lives lost, damage and negative economic and social consequences; and 3) Reduced time to recovery (restoration of a specific system or set of systems to their 'normal' level of performance)." Bruneau et al., 2003[j]

"Resilience is the capacity to survive, adapt and recover from a natural disaster. Resilience relies on understanding the nature of possible natural disasters and taking steps to reduce risk before an event as well as providing for quick recovery when a natural disaster occurs. These activities necessitate institutionalized planning and response networks to minimize diminished productivity, devastating losses and decreased quality of life in the event of a disaster." Walter, 2004[k]

"The capacity of a system, community or society potentially exposed to hazards to adapt, by resisting or changing in order to reach and maintain an acceptable level of functioning and structure. This is determined by the degree to which the social system is capable of organizing itself to increase this capacity for learning from past disasters for better future protection and to improve risk reduction measures." UN/ISDR, 2005[l]

"Resilience is a measure of how well people and societies can adapt to a changed reality and capitalize on the new possibilities offered." Paton and Johnston, 2006[m]

"The ability to survive future natural disasters with minimum loss of life and property, as well as the ability to create a greater sense of place among residents; a stronger, more diverse economy; and a more economically integrated and diverse population. … Applies to the process of recovery planning in which all affected stakeholders—rather than just a powerful few—have a voice in how their community is to be rebuilt." Berke and Campanella, 2006[n]

"Social resilience is the capacity of a social entity e.g. group or community to bounce back or respond positively to adversity. Social resilience has three major properties, resistance, recovery, and creativity." Maguire and Hagan, 2007[o]

"A community that anticipates problems, opportunities, and potentials for surviving; reduces vulnerabilities related to development paths, socioeconomic conditions, and sensitivities to possible threats; responds effectively, fairly, and legitimately in the event of an emergency; and recovers rapidly, better, safer, and fairer." Wilbanks, 2008[p]

"The ability of social systems, be they the constituent element of a community or society, along with the bio-physical systems upon which they depend, to resist or absorb the impacts (deaths, damage, losses, etc.) of natural hazards, to rapidly recover from those impacts and to reduce future vulnerabilities through adaptive strategies." Peacock et al., 2008[q]

a. Timmerman, P. "Vulnerability, Resilience and the Collapse of Society." *Environmental Monograph 1* (Institute for Environmental Studies, University of Toronto), 1981.
b. Wildavsky, A. *Searching for Safety.* New Brunswick, NJ: Transaction, 1991.
c. Buckle, P. "Re-defining Community and Vulnerability in the Context of Emergency Management." *Australian Journal of Emergency Management*, 2000: 8–14.
d. Federal Emergency Management Agency (FEMA). *Homeowner's Guide to Retrofitting: Six Ways to Protect Your House from Flooding.* Washington, DC: Author, 1998.

e. Mileti, D. S. *Disasters by Design: A Reassessment of Natural Hazards in the United States.* Washington, DC: Joseph Henry Press, 1999.
f. Comfort, L., et al. "Reframing Disaster Policy: The Global Evolution of Vulnerable Communities." *Environmental Hazards* 1, no. 1 (1999): 39–44.
g. Adger, W. N. "Social and Ecological Resilience: Are They Related?" *Progress in Human Geography* 24, no. 3 (2000): 347–64.
h. Buckle, P., G. Mars, and S. Smale. "New Approaches to Assessing Vulnerability and Resilience." *Australian Journal of Emergency Management* 15, no. 2 (2000): 8–15.
i. Klein, Richard J. T., Robert J. Nicholls, and Frank Thomalla. "Resilience to Natural Hazards: How Useful Is This Concept?" *Environmental Hazards*, 2003: 35–45.
j. Bruneau, M., et al. "A Framework to Quantitatively Assess and Enhance the Seismic Resilience of Communities." *Earthquake Spectra* 19, no. 4 (November 2003): 733–52.
k. Walter, C. "Community Building Practice." In *Community Organizing and Community Building for Health*, edited by M. Minkler. New Brunswick, NJ: Rutgers University Press, 2004.
l. United Nations Office for Disaster Risk Reduction (UN/ISDR). "Hyogo Framework for 2005–2015: Building the Resilience of the Nations and Communities to Disasters." 2005. www.unisdr.org/wcdr/intergover/official-docs/Hyogo-framework-action-english.pdf (accessed January 4, 2007).
m. Paton, D., and D. M. Johnston. *Disaster Resilience.* Springfield, IL: Charles C. Thomas, 2006.
n. Berke, P. R., and T. J. Campanella. "Planning for Postdisaster Resiliency." *Annals of the American Academy of Political and Social Science* 604, no. 1 (2006): 192–207.
o. Maguire, B., and P. Hagan. "Disasters and Communities: Understanding Social Resilience." *Australian Journal of Emergency Management* 22 (2007): 16–20.
p. Wilbanks, T. J. "Enhancing the Resilience of Communities to Natural and Other Hazards: What We Know and What We Can Do." *Natural Hazards Observer* 32 (2008): 10–11.
q. Peacock, W. G., H. Kunreuther, W. H. Hooke, S. L. Cutter, S. E. Chang, and P. R. Berke. *Toward a Resiliency and Vulnerability Observatory Network: RAVON.* HRRC reports: 08-02R, 2008.

that systems can modify themselves in response to impacts and thereby become more resistant to future impacts.

There is much to be gained from the applications of these definitions to the study of social systems and the hazard context. However, we must also be wary about the simple application of these definitions or approaches to social systems. For example, the notion of bouncing back to roughly the same form or state as before a disaster event may not be necessarily advantageous or desired. The analysis of disasters often finds that disasters themselves represent failures of social systems to properly adapt to the biophysical environment, inappropriate development, and land use patterns and that systemic weaknesses in the form of social vulnerabilities are often generated by the systems themselves.[2] Returning or bouncing back to the predisaster state is not necessarily resilient or adaptive but rather lays the seeds for future disasters. Nevertheless, these definitions help us to understand the nature of resilience and what it might mean for disaster management.

DIMENSIONS OF RESILIENCE

Our definition, which draws from various disciplines and takes a more holistic and interdependent approach, suggests that "resilience is the ability of a community and the biophysical systems upon which they depend, to:

- Resist or absorb the impacts (deaths, damage, losses, etc.) of natural hazards;
- Rapidly recover from those impacts; and
- Reduce future vulnerabilities through adaptive strategies."[3]

More recently there has been increasing emphasis on more formally identifying these dimensions of resilience. For example, it has been suggested that addressing the ability of a system to absorb, deflect, or resist potential disaster impacts implies a reduction or diminishing of impacts, a reduction of failure probabilities, or reducing the consequences of failures. Some researchers use the terms *resistance* or *robustness* for this dimension of resilience.[4] The bounceback after being impacted is of course associated with restoration and recovery or some notion of reducing the time to restore or return to "normal" functioning. This time dimension is sometimes called rapidity, and it is associated with the slope of the trajectory of recovery: how quickly the social system returns to normal. Furthermore, the trajectory of recovery may stabilize (i.e., flatten out) at a point short of the predisaster trajectory or surpass it.

The potential for surpassing the original (predisaster) trajectory suggests the ability to increase resiliency through system learning or adaptation. This potential is often a critical element in notions of resilience in the disaster literature.[5] Communities that stress learning and adapting in response to disasters have the potential to build capacity, become more sustainable, and develop higher states of resiliency. Common themes are improving a system's mitigation status, enhancing robustness, and reducing future loss potential or failure probabilities; reducing preexisting physical and social vulnerabilities; and promoting sustainable disaster recovery by increasing economic, ecological, and social sustainability.

Figure 1 captures these resiliency themes drawn from the literature and our working definition of resilience. System resiliency implies robustness, rapidity, and enhancement in response to natural disasters. A resilient system is, relatively speaking, robust with respect to its ability to absorb and resist the impacts of a hazard agent, implying a reduction in potential disaster impacts. Furthermore, having experienced a disaster, a resilient system is able to bounce back quickly, reaching restoration levels in rapid fashion, relatively speaking. Finally, as part of the recovery process, a resilient system enhances its capacities by improving its mitigation status, reducing preexisting vulnerabilities, and improving its sustainability. Enhancements may include adaptations that acknowledge the community's cultural and natural attributes and symbolize its endurance in the face of disasters.

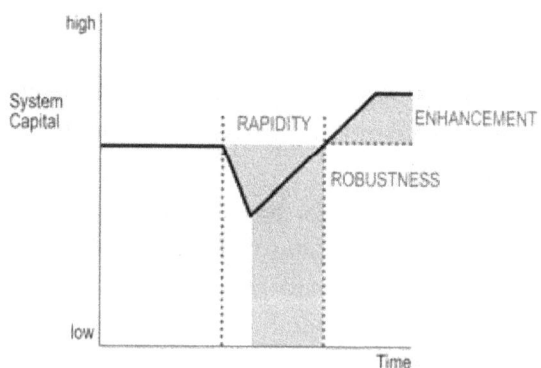

Figure 2.1. Critical dimensions of resilience. Resilience implies system robustness, or the ability to withstand potential hazard impacts; rapidity, or how quickly restoration or recovery levels are achieved; and enhancement, or the quality of recovery processes in terms of learning and adapting. (Adapted from Bruneau et al., 2003)

Box 3 describes how citizens in Galveston used their skills to transform the landscape and adapt and embrace their new community after the disaster.

WE NEED AN INCLUSIVE EFFORT

Disasters are not one-time events. Although certainly some communities are more vulnerable than others, disasters are not a matter of if;

BOX 3. SYMBOLS OF RESILIENCE

Before Hurricane Ike, one of Galveston's most notable environmental features was the Broadway Avenue esplanade of live oak trees that welcomed visitors to the city and led them to the island's Gulf Coast beaches. It also created a stately backdrop for the city's unparalleled-in-the-state stock of historic Victorian homes. The saltwater incursion that accompanied Ike's surge killed the trees, destroying more than 75 percent of the island's tree canopy and destroying the natural habitat for migratory birds that have used the island as a winter destination.

The loss of the trees dealt a psychological blow to island residents. They were irreplaceable, and their loss changed the face of the island. Although tree-planting campaigns initiated a decades-long road to recovery, the dead trees stood as a reminder of all that had been lost.

Rather than take the trees out, community members elected to create sculptures from them (figure 2). Up and down Broadway Avenue, and in the blocks off of it that make up the historic district and beyond, tree sculptures now stand where dead trees once did. The initiative to create the tree sculptures was a spontaneous, grassroots effort led by the Galveston Island Tree Conservancy. The range of sculptures is impressive, and many of the images represent the island's culture and natural attributes, including pelicans, mermaids, dolphins, and more (figure 3). Some are simple, some are very elaborate. Many were created by professional artists, but others were created by property owners themselves. The result is a touching and spontaneous but lasting testament to the resilience of the people and the place.

Figure 2. Seventy-five percent of the 100-year-old tree canopy on Galveston Island was lost after Hurricane Ike. Today, you can find the remnants of the beautiful trees that have been transformed into art. (Credit: Dustin Henry.)

Figure 3. Birds carved from the trees that did not survive the surge waters and salt intrusion. (Credit: Dustin Henry.)

The tree sculptures remind us that resilience is not about a return to prestorm conditions. It is about adapting to circumstances as they arise, working with what you have, appreciating the change in situation, celebrating the essence and way of life of the community, and creating strength and beauty in unexpected places.

they are a matter of when and what. Planning for hazards cannot and should not be the sole responsibility of emergency managers. Emergency managers are well equipped to address preparedness and response functions, but they are ill equipped for mitigation and recovery, the other two stages of disaster management, and the ones that take place between disasters. When they occur, disasters magnify and accelerate processes already taking place in our communities.[6] Treating them as unpredictable, improbable, and unique events takes the responsibility for mitigation out of the hands of community members and decision makers. Resilient communities will be those that incorporate disaster planning and management into everyday actions, taking care to move people out of harm's way and create capacity and networks that allow community members to respond quickly and effectively. Research and experience have shown that the key to community resilience is a strong community fabric, where citizens and organizations with a stake in reducing the impact of disasters are acting in concert. Therefore, planners must be skilled in designing and executing inclusive planning programs. By involving citizen and organizational stakeholders in determining community land use patterns and maximizing adaptive community capacity in the implementation of land use strategies, planners play a significant role in increasing community resilience.

THE IMPORTANCE OF PUBLIC PARTICIPATION

Citizen participation begins with community building, or the work of organizing people with common interests and focusing their efforts to achieve common goals. True community building takes place when all are informed, included, and respected.[7] In addition, there are a range of choices planners can make to influence this participation.[8] These choices can yield authentic dialogue, for example, which in turn motivates and empowers all to change the future for the interest of the whole.[9] Therefore, community building is key to planning processes. However, promoting citizen participation programs can be messy and result in unintended negative consequences if it is not done well. The benefits of community hazard planning include the following:

- Increasing public awareness and understanding of vulnerabilities
- Building partnerships with diverse stakeholders, increasing opportunities to leverage data and resources in reducing workloads
- Expanding understanding of potential risk reduction measures
- Informing development, prioritization, and implementation of mitigation projects
- Unifying and coordinating with other community plans, such as comprehensive plans, transportation plans, parks and recreation plans, school district strategic plans, and county strategic plans
- Expediting the delivery of internal and external support before and after disasters

Two months after Hurricane Ike, the Galveston City Council began the process of appointing a Long-Term Recovery Committee. Initially, the thirty-member steering committee for the underway comprehensive plan update was selected. However, there was great interest from the community to participate in the recovery process. Over the next six weeks, the Long-Term Recovery Committee expanded to include 330 Galveston residents. Because of the large size of the committee, significant coordination was needed to manage the multiple topics being considered for the recovery plan. The committee was assisted in this process by city staff and the FEMA Long Term Community Recovery Team (Emergency Support Function 14 [ESF-14]).

One of the first actions of the steering committee was to develop a communication subcommittee to ensure that citizens had an opportunity to contribute to the development of the recovery plan. To gain more input and participation from Galveston residents, ten open houses were held in the last two weeks of January 2009 (4 months after the storm), including off-island locations for displaced citizens. More than 800 people attended these open houses and provided more than 2,700 comments to consider in the recovery planning process. There was also substantial outreach by electronic communication, primarily through e-mail and on the city's website. A dedicated website was also developed to serve as a source for recovery information and to share information with the public about the committee's planning activities.

After the primary public outreach efforts, the steering committee met from February 2 to March 23, 2009 for three hours every Monday night. The public was invited to all steering committee meetings and were given the opportunity to speak to the committee formally at the beginning of each meeting or to participate informally in the smaller group work sessions. This large-scale planning effort totaled more than 4,200 volunteer hours to create the Recovery Plan.

The steering committee determined to focus on six recovery areas: the environment, economic development, housing and community character, health and education, transportation and infrastructure, and disaster planning.

Over the six-week planning process, the committee developed a vision and goals and identified forty-two projects that would lead the recovery process for the city. The Long Term Community Recovery Plan was presented to the public at a community open house at the end of March 2009 and to the Galveston City Council on April 9, 2009. Ultimately, the responsibility for completion of these projects was assigned to various organizations throughout the community, with the City of Galveston taking the lead on numerous recovery initiatives. Many of these initiatives were incorporated into two significant planning projects: the Hazard Mitigation Plan and the Comprehensive Plan. No one in Galveston will forget the 330 citizen committee members and the countless hours to improve and transform their community. This example of citizen engagement promotes collaborative governance and yields community members who support and seek to follow through on implementation and action.

TAPPING INTO COMMUNITY CAPACITIES

Another component to consider when planners set out to engage the community is tapping into community capacities that often go unnoticed or underused but are critical. *Capacity* generally denotes notions of containing or storing and of ability, talent, competence, or experience.[10] *Community capacity* therefore refers to the sum of individual and organizational capacities within a community and, more specifically, the extent to which individual and organizational capacity is aligned to achieve community goals. In recent years the major forms of capital (social, economic, physical, and human) have been recognized as important factors in building community capacities to deal with disasters.[11] The hazard literature suggests that the sustainability and resilience of a community depend on its ability to access and use the major forms of capital.[12] The following discussion summarizes the four major forms of capital and how they can contribute to building community disaster resilience.

SOCIAL CAPITAL

Many definitions of *social capital* exist in the literature.[13] Social capital has been defined as the features of social organization such as networks, norms, and social trust that facilitate coordination and cooperation for mutual benefit. Although social capital has been defined in a variety of ways, there is a common emphasis on the aspect of social structure, trust, norms, and social networks that facilitate collective actions.[14] In the context of community disaster resilience, social capital reflects social cooperation or community connectedness, which provides an informal safety net during disasters and often helps people access resources.[15] For instance, community ties and networks are beneficial in building disaster resilience because they allow people to draw on the social resources in their communities and increase the likelihood that such communities will be able to adequately address their disaster concerns.[16] Similarly, social networks such as friends, relatives, and coworkers are important in building disaster resilience because they provide resources that can assist households during disaster response and recovery.[17] Also, social bonds have been shown to influence adoption and implementation of hazard adjustment.[18] Furthermore, research has demonstrated that, in circumstances where characteristics of social capital or connectedness are lacking in a community, members of that community tend to have less capacity in terms of networks for dealing with disasters.[19] With regard to organizations, ties are linkages between the organizations and individuals, other local organizations, and government agencies such as social services, public health, emergency management, and community development. These local or internal networks enable communities to act collectively for mutual benefit and adapt to change in disasters.[20] Furthermore, community linkages to external capacity through federal and state agencies and nongovernmental organizations that deal with disaster relief (e.g., Red Cross, philanthropic organizations, and faith-based organizations) and development (Department of Housing and Urban Development, Habitat for Humanity, and the Small Business Administration) can facilitate the delivery of external support when necessary.[21] Therefore, the work of assessing, cultivating, and coordinating the human and social capital in a community is fundamental to increasing community resilience.

ECONOMIC CAPITAL

Fundamentally, *economic capital* is the financial resources people use to support their livelihoods.[22] It includes savings, income, investments or businesses, and credit. The importance of economic capital in building community disaster resilience is perhaps straightforward in the sense that economic resources increase the ability and capacity of individuals, groups, and communities to absorb disaster impacts and speed up the recovery process. People with access to financial resources recover more quickly from disasters.[23] Also, access to credit and hazard insurance are associated with the level of household preparedness and ability to take protective measures.[24] The hazard literature suggests that a more stable and growing economy will generally increase community disaster resilience, whereas an unhealthy or declining economy is an indication of increasing vulnerability.[25] Furthermore, the planning literature clearly suggests that economic resources can be critical for effective hazard mitigation planning.[26]

PHYSICAL CAPITAL

Physical capital refers to the built environment, which includes residential housing, commercial and industrial buildings, public buildings, and dams and levees. It also includes lifelines such as electricity, water, sewer, transportation, telecommunication facilities, and critical facilities such as hospitals, schools, fire and police stations, and nursing homes.[27] The hazard literature suggests that physical capital is one of the most important resources in building a disaster-resilient community. A primary element of this capital is housing,[28] of course, but other features of a community's physical infrastructure, such as roads, bridges, dams, levees, and communication systems, are essential elements for proper functioning of a community.[29] Furthermore, critical facilities play an important role in ensuring that people have resources and support arrangements during disaster response and recovery. In general, lack of physical infrastructure or critical facilities may have a direct negative impact on a community's capacity to prepare for, respond to, and recover from disasters.

HUMAN CAPITAL

Economists have defined *human capital* as the capabilities embodied in the working-age population that allow it to work productively with other forms of capital to sustain economic production.[30] Sometimes human capital is simply called the labor force or the ability to work. However, two main components of human capital are frequently mentioned in the literature: education and health of the working population group.[31] Education, which includes knowledge and skills that are accumulated through forms of educational attainment, training, and experience, is an essential component of human capital. Health of the working-age population is another important component of human capital. Health is considered a critical component of human capital because an unhealthy population may not be able to harness other forms of capital.[32] As a result, a community cannot fully engage in the process of building disaster resilience without human capital. For instance, knowledge and skills of local people on types of hazards, hazard history, and hazard risk in their community can be an important asset in building community disaster resilience. An individual's access to resources—whether financial, political, or logistical—or ability to move out of harm's way can determine his or her level of disaster resilience.[33] In general, the literature suggests that human capital in the form of knowledge, skills, health, and physical ability determines a person's level of disaster resilience more than other types of capital.[34] Likewise, when networks of individuals and organizations pool their collective human capital, it can have a positive effect on community disaster resilience.

CONCLUSION: PULLING THE PIECES TOGETHER

The consensus of the scientific community is that natural disasters are not wholly "natural" events but rather the outcome of the interaction between biophysical systems, human systems, and their built environment.[35] Furthermore, they are in large measure a function of human action or, very often, failure to act. Many of our nation's communities continue to develop and expand into high-hazard areas, contributing to increased hazard exposure. So not only are the number and severity of disasters increasing, but our exposure to them is also increasing, making our communities less resilient. Therefore, it is important to understand that social and ecological systems play a part in absorbing and deflecting impact, in rapidly recovering from those impacts, and in providing flexibility to adapt, learn, and ultimately enhance previous conditions.

Research and experience are starting to show that, by engaging the public and understanding the various interests, abilities, knowledge, and resources in a community, planners can make themselves and their communities better able to manage all phases of disaster management. Unfortunately, although many local planners and aid providers are well intentioned, they often have limited capacity of their own to design and manage inclusive citizen participation programs, which could exacerbate the effect of the existing limited capacity of communities to cope with losses.[36]

The ability of a community to withstand, absorb, and bounce back from a disaster depends on the capacity of that community to act at each phase of disaster to mitigate, anticipate, protect, respond, deflect, and recover. Capacities may be understood as capital assets (social, human, economic, and physical) that are needed to mobilize the necessary resources. The next chapter describes the disaster phases through the lens of capital assets.

EXERCISE 1. PEELING BACK THE LAYERS OF YOUR COMMUNITY

Now that you've read chapter 2, take a moment to answer these questions. They are intended to be used as brainstorming questions to begin thinking about your community's resilience.

1. What characteristics embody an ideal resilient community? First, imagine what makes a strong community. Elicit answers from your work group on flip charts or through a focus group. After the group completes their responses, take a moment to reflect. Are there themes that emerge? Are any of these characteristics missing from your community? *Example: Where folks know their neighbors.*

2. Do characteristics refer to ecological systems or social systems? Second, evaluate the responses to determine whether your answers address social systems or ecological systems. If your list is not balanced, take a moment to identify a few more characteristics or ideas of community resilience. Take a moment to reflect on how your own idea of resilience might have changed. *Example: Social system.*

3. Which characteristics identified increase robustness, rapidity, or enhancement? Third, knowing that there are three dimensions of resilience, determine whether the responses could provide robustness, foster rapidity, or promote enhancement. Which dimension is missing most from your list? If your list is not balanced, meaning you do not have an equal number of characteristics that address all three dimensions, take a moment to add additional elements to create a more balanced list. *Example: Rapidity: One may recover more quickly if he or she can connect to people with other resources.*

4. Are there groups or organizations that could participate? Fourth, we should consider not only social and ecological systems and the robustness, rapidity, and enhancement of each but also whether there are groups that can participate in building a resilient community. Look back at your list of the elements you feel contribute to a resilient community. Are there groups or stakeholders associated with each element that could participate, engage, or collaborate to increase resilience? *Example: Homeowners' associations, neighborhood groups, school district, Adopt-a-Highway, churches, local bowling league.*

5. Which provide human, physical, social, or economic capital? Fifth, which characteristics are associated with the four possible community capital resources (human, social, physical, and economic)? You may find that multiple capital assets apply to each characteristic. Which capital assets are recurring more often, and which are not? Are there other components of resilience you haven't addressed or included yet? If your list is not balanced, think about what other characteristics of a resilient community could be included. *Example: Social capital.*

6. Which apply to your community (strong, need work, weak, nonexistent)? Lastly, look at the first list one more time. Which of your ideal community characteristics pertain to your community? Identify the elements your community is currently strong in, needs work on, or is weak in. Remember, your list is only a fraction of the components that could be added to increase resilience. Do you see how complex this is becoming? *Example: Weak: I occasionally see my neighbors when I get the mail.*

REFERENCES

1. Klein, R. J. T., R. J. Nicholls, and F. Thomalla, "Resilience to Natural Hazards: How Useful Is This Concept?" *Environmental Hazards* 2003: 35–45; Manyena, S. B., "The Concept of Resilience Revisited," *Disasters* 30, no. 4 (December 2006): 434–50; Norris, F. H., S. P. Stevens, B. Pfefferbaum, K. F. Wyche, and R. L. Pfefferbaum, "Community Resilience as a Metaphor, Theory, Set of Capacities, and Strategy for Disaster Readiness," *American Journal of Community Psychology* 41, no. 1–2 (March 2008): 127–50.
2. Bates, F. L., and W. G. Peacock, *Living Conditions, Disasters, and Development: An Approach to Cross-Cultural Comparisons*, Athens: University of Georgia Press, 2008.
3. Peacock, W. G., H. Kunreuther, W. H. Hooke, S. L. Cutter, S. E. Chang, and P. R. Berke, *Toward a Resiliency and Vulnerability Observatory Network: RAVON*, HRRC reports: 08-02R, 2008.
4. Bruneau, M., et al., "A Framework to Quantitatively Assess and Enhance the Seismic Resilience of Communities," *Earthquake Spectra* 19, no. 4 (November 2003): 733–52.
5. Comfort, L., et al., "Reframing Disaster Policy: The Global Evolution of Vulnerable Communities," *Environmental Hazards* 1, no. 1 (1999): 39–44; Maguire, B., and P. Hagan, "Disasters and Communities: Understanding Social Resilience," *Australian Journal of Emergency Management* 22 (2007): 16–20; Bates and Peacock, *Living Conditions, Disasters, and Development*; Berke, P. R., and T. J. Campanella, "Planning for Postdisaster Resiliency," *Annals of the American Academy of Political and Social Science* 604, no. 1 (2006): 192–207; Smith, G., and D. Wenger, "Sustainable Disaster Recovery: Operationalizing an Existing Agenda," in *Handbook of Disaster Research*, edited by H. Rodriguez, E. Quarantelli, and R. Dynes, New York: Springer, 2006; Wilbanks, T. J., "Enhancing the Resilience of Communities to Natural and Other Hazards: What We Know and What We Can Do," *Natural Hazards Observer* 32 (2008): 10–11; Peacock et al., *Toward a Resiliency and Vulnerability Observatory Network*.
6. Olshansky, R., L. Hopkins, and L. Johnson, "Disaster and Recovery: Processes Compressed in Time," *Natural Hazards Review* 13, no. 3 (2012): 173–78.
7. Innes, J. E., and D. E. Booher, "Reframing Public Participation: Strategies for the 21st Century," *Planning Theory & Practice* 5, no. 4 (2004): 419–36.
8. Burby, R. J., R. E. Deyle, D. R. Godschalk, and R. B. Olshansky, "Creating Hazard Resilient Communities through Land-Use Planning," *Natural Hazards Review*, 2000: 99–106.
9. Innes and Booher, "Reframing Public Participation."
10. Chaskin, R. J., "Defining Community Capacity: A Framework and Implications from a Comprehensive Community Initiative," *Urban Affairs Association Annual Meeting*, Chicago: The Chapin Hall Center for Children at the University of Chicago, 1999.
11. Callaghan, E. G., and J. Colton, "Building Sustainable & Resilient Communities: A Balancing of Community Capital," *Environmental Development Sustainability* 10 (2008): 931–42; Dynes, R. R., "Finding Order in Disorder: Continuities in the 9/11 Response," *Mid-South Sociological Society*, October 18, 2002: 1–22; Haque, C. E., and D. Etkin, "People and Community as Constituent Parts of Hazards: The Significance of Societal

Dimensions in Hazards Analysis," *Natural Hazards* 41 (2007): 271–82; Walter, C., "Community Building Practice," in *Community Organizing and Community Building for Health*, edited by M. Minkler, New Brunswick, NJ: Rutgers University Press, 2004.

12. Beeton, R. J. S., *Society's Forms of Capital: A Framework for Renewing Our Thinking*, Canberra: Department of the Environment and Heritage, Australian State of the Environment Committee, 2006; Walter, "Community Building Practice."

13. See, for example, Bourdieu, P., "The Forms of Capital," in *Handbook of Theory and Research for the Sociology of Education*, edited by J. G. Richardson, 110–20, New York: Greenwood, 1986; Coleman, J. S., *Foundations of Social Theory*, Cambridge, MA: Harvard University Press, 1990; Putnam, R. D., "Bowling Alone: America's Declining Social Capital," *Journal of Democracy*, 1995: 65–78; Putnam, R. D., *Bowling Alone: The Collapse and Revival of American Community*, New York: Simon and Schuster Paperbacks, 2000.

14. Green, G. P., and A. Haines, *Asset Building and Community Development*, Thousand Oaks, CA: Sage Publications, 2002.

15. Walter, "Community Building Practice."

16. Dynes, "Finding Order in Disorder"; Walter, "Community Building Practice."

17. Dynes, "Finding Order in Disorder"; Lindell, M. K., and C. S. Prater, "Assessing Community Impacts of Natural Disasters," *Natural Hazards Review* 4, no. 4 (2003): 176–85.

18. Mileti, D. S., *Disasters by Design: A Reassessment of Natural Hazards in the United States*, Washington, DC: Joseph Henry Press, 1999.

19. National Research Council (NRC), *Facing Hazards and Disasters: Understanding Human Dimensions*, Washington, DC: National Academies Press, 2006; Walter, "Community Building Practice."

20. Dynes, "Finding Order in Disorder."

21. Berke, P. R., J. Kartez, and D. Wenger, "Recovery after Disaster: Achieving Sustainable Development, Mitigation and Equity," *Disasters*, 1993: 93–109.

22. Department for International Development (DFID), *Sustainable Livelihoods and Poverty Elimination*, London: Author, 1999; Smith, R., C. Simard, and A. Sharpe, *A Proposed Approach to Environment and Sustainable Development Indicators Based on Capital*, Ottawa, ON: The National Round Table on the Environment and the Economy's Environment and Sustainable Development Indicators Initiative, 2001.

23. Mileti, *Disasters by Design*; Walter, "Community Building Practice."

24. Lindell and Prater, "Assessing Community Impacts of Natural Disasters."

25. Buckle, P., G. Mars, and S. Smale, "New Approaches to Assessing Vulnerability and Resilience," *Australian Journal of Emergency Management* 15, no. 2 (2000): 8–15; Walter, "Community Building Practice."

26. Burby, R. J., *Cooperating with Nature: Confronting Natural Hazards with Land-Use Planning for Sustainable Communities*, Washington, DC: Joseph Henry Press, 1998; Godschalk, D. R., T. Beatley, P. Berke, D. Brower, and E. Kaiser, *Natural Hazard Mitigation: Recasting Disaster Policy and Planning*, Washington, DC: Island Press, 1999.

27. DFID, *Sustainable Livelihoods and Poverty Elimination*; Walter, "Community Building Practice."

28. Bates and Peacock, *Living Conditions, Disasters, and Development*; Peacock, W. G., D. Dash,

and Y. Zhang, "Shelter and Housing Recovery Following Disaster," in *The Handbook of Disaster Research*, edited by H. Rodriquez, E. L. Quarantelli, and R. Dynes, 258–74, New York: Springer, 2006; Zhang, Y., and W. G. Peacock, "Planning for Housing Recovery?" *Journal of the American Planning Association* 76, no. 1 (2010): 5–24.

29. Walter, "Community Building Practice."
30. Smith, R., C. Simard, and A. Sharpe, *A Proposed Approach to Environment and Sustainable Development Indicators*.
31. DFID, *Sustainable Livelihoods and Poverty Elimination*; Smith, Simard, and Sharpe, *A Proposed Approach to Environment and Sustainable Development Indicators*; Walter, "Community Building Practice."
32. Smith, Simard, and Sharpe, *A Proposed Approach to Environment and Sustainable Development Indicators*.
33. Burby, R. J. *Cooperating with Nature*; Godschalk et al., *Natural Hazard Mitigation*; Walter, "Community Building Practice."
34. Walter, "Community Building Practice"; Burby, R. J., *Cooperating with Nature*; Godschalk et al., *Natural Hazard Mitigation*.
35. Mileti, *Disasters by Design*.
36. Berke, P. R., and T. Beatley, *After the Hurricane: Linking Recovery to Sustainable Development in the Caribbean*, Baltimore, MD: Johns Hopkins University Press, 1997; NRC, *Facing Hazards and Disasters*.

BIBLIOGRAPHY

Adger, W. N. "Social and Ecological Resilience: Are They Related?" *Progress in Human Geography* 24, 3 (2000): 347–64.

Bates, F. L., and W. G. Peacock. *Living Con… and Development: An Approach… Comparisons*. Athens: Universi… 2008.

Beeton, R. J. S. *Society's Fo… for Renewing Our Th…* the Environment and Heritage, Australian State of the Environment Committee, 2006.

Berke, P. R., and T. Beatley. *After the Hurricane: Linking Recovery to Sustainable Development in the Caribbean*. Baltimore, MD: Johns Hopkins University Press, 1997.

Berke, P. R., and T. J. Campanella. "Planning for Postdisaster Resiliency." *Annals of the American Academy of Political and Social Science* 604, no. 1 (2006): 192–207.

Berke, P. R., J. Kartez, and D. Wenger. "Recovery after Disaster: Achieving Sustainable Development, Mitigation and Equity." *Disasters*, 1993: 93–109.

Bourdieu, P. "The Forms of Capital." In *Handbook of Theory and Research for the Sociology of Education*, edited by J. G. Richardson, 110–20. New York: Greenwood, 1986.

Bruneau, Michel, Stephanie E. Chang, Ronald T. Eguchi, George C. Lee, Thomas D. O'Rourke, Andrei M. Reinhorn, Masanobu Shinozuka, Kathleen Tierney, William A. Wallace, and Detlof von Winterfeldt. "A Framework to Quantitatively Assess and Enhance the Seismic Resilience of Communities," *Earthquake Spectra* 19, no. 4 (November 2003): 733–52; Tierney, K., and M. Bruneau, "Conceptualizing and Measuring Resilience," *Transportation News*, May–June 2007: 14–17.

Buckle, P. "Re-defining Community and Vulnerability in the Context of Emergency Management." *Australian Journal of Emergency Management*, 2000: 8–14.

Buckle, P., G. Mars, and S. Smale. "New Approaches to Assessing Vulnerability and Resilience." *Australian Journal of Emergency Management* 15, no. 2 (2000): 8–15.

Burby, Raymond J. *Cooperating with Nature: Confronting Natural Hazards with Land-Use Planning for Sustainable Communities*. Washington, DC: Joseph Henry Press, 1998.

Burby, R. J., R. E. Deyle, D. R. Godschalk, and R. B. Olshansky. "Creating Hazard Resilient Communities through Land-Use Planning." *Natural Hazards Review*, 2000: 99–106.

Callaghan, E. G., and J. Colton. "Building Sustainable & Resilient Communities: A Balancing of Community Capital." *Environmental Development Sustainability* 10 (2008): 931–42.

Chaskin, R. J. "Defining Community Capacity: A Framework and Implications from a Comprehensive Community Initiative." *Urban Affairs Association Annual Meeting*. Chicago: The Chapin Hall Center for Children at the University of Chicago, 1999.

Coleman, J. S. *Foundations of Social Theory*. Cambridge, MA: Harvard University Press, 1990.

…fort, L., et al. "Reframing Disaster Policy: The Global …lution of Vulnerable Communities." *Environmental …zards* 1, no. 1 (1999): 39–44.

Department for International Development (DFID). *Sustainable Livelihoods and Poverty Elimination.* London: Author, 1999.

Dynes, R. R. "Finding Order in Disorder: Continuities in the 9/11 Response." *Mid-South Sociological Society*, October 18, 2002: 1–22.

Federal Emergency Management Agency (FEMA). "Homeowner's Guide to Retrofitting: Six Ways to Protect Your House from Flooding." Washington, DC: Author, 1998.

Folke, C., S. R. Carpenter, T. Elmqvist, L. Gunderson, C. S. Holling, and B. Walker. "Resilience and Sustainable Development: Building Adaptive Capacity in a World of Transformations." *Ambio* 31 (2002): 437–40.

Godschalk, D. R., T. Beatley, P. Berke, D. Brower, and E. Kaiser. *Natural Hazard Mitigation: Recasting Disaster Policy and Planning.* Washington, DC: Island Press, 1999.

Green, G. P., and A. Haines. *Asset Building and Community Development.* Thousand Oaks: Sage Publications, 2002.

Haque, C. E., and D. Etkin. "People and Community as Constituent Parts of Hazards: The Significance of Societal Dimensions in Hazards Analysis." *Natural Hazards* 41 (2007): 271–82.

Holling, C. S. "Resilience and Stability of Ecological Systems." *Annual Review of Ecology and Systematics* 4 (1973): 1–23.

Holling, C. S. "What Barriers? What Bridges?" In *Barriers and Bridges to the Renewal of Ecosystems and Institutions*, edited by L. H. Gunderson, C. S. Holling, and S. S. Light, 3–34. New York: Columbia University Press, 1995.

Innes, Judith E., and David E. Booher. "Reframing Public Participation: Strategies for the 21st Century." *Planning Theory & Practice* 5, no. 4 (2004): 419–36.

Klein, Richard J. T., Robert J. Nicholls, and Frank Thomalla. "Resilience To Natural Hazards: How Useful Is This Concept?" *Environmental Hazards*, 2003: 35–45.

Lebel, L. "Resilience and Sustainability of Landscapes." *ASB Partnership*, 2001. http://www.asb.cgiar.org/docs (accessed August 5, 2007).

Lindell, M. K., and C. S. Prater. "Assessing Community Impacts of Natural Disasters." *Natural Hazards Review* 4, no. 4 (2003): 176–85.

Maguire, B., and P. Hagan. "Disasters and Communities: Understanding Social Resilience." *Australian Journal of Emergency Management* 22 (2007): 16–20.

Manyena, Siambabala Bernard. "The Concept of Resilience Revisited." *Disasters* 30, no. 4 (December 2006): 434–50.

Mileti, D. S. *Disasters by Design: A Reassessment of Natural Hazards in the United States.* Washington, DC: Joseph Henry Press, 1999.

National Research Council (NRC). *Facing Hazards and Disasters: Understanding Human Dimensions.* Washington, DC: National Academies Press, 2006.

Norris, F. H., S. P. Stevens, B. Pfefferbaum, K. F. Wyche, and R. L. Pfefferbaum. "Community Resilience as a Metaphor, Theory, Set of Capacities, and Strategy for Disaster Readiness." *American Journal of Community Psychology* 41, no. 1–2 (March 2008): 127–50.

Olshansky, R., L. Hopkins, and L. Johnson. "Disaster and Recovery: Processes Compressed in Time." *Natural Hazards Review* 13, no. 3 (2012): 173–78.

Paton, D., and D. M. Johnston. *Disaster Resilience.* Springfield, IL: Charles C. Thomas, 2006.

Peacock, W. G., D. Dash, and Y. Zhang. "Shelter and Housing Recovery Following Disaster." In *The Handbook of Disaster Research*, edited by H. Rodriquez, E. L. Quarantelli, and R. Dynes, 258–74. New York: Springer, 2006.

Peacock, W. G., H. Kunreuther, W. H. Hooke, S. L. Cutter, S. E. Chang, and P. R. Berke. *Toward a Resiliency and Vulnerability Observatory Network: RAVON.* HRRC reports: 08-02R, 2008.

Pimm, S. L. "The Complexity and Stability of Ecosystems." *Nature*, 1984: 321–26.

Putnam, R. D. "Bowling Alone: America's Declining Social Capital." *Journal of Democracy*, 1995: 65–78.

Putnam, R. D. *Bowling Alone: The Collapse and Revival of American Community.* New York: Simon and Schuster Paperbacks, 2000.

Resilience Alliance. *Assessing and Managing Resilience in Social-Ecological Systems: A Practitioners Workbook.* Stockholm: Author, 2007.

Smith, G., and D. Wenger. "Sustainable Disaster Recovery: Operationalizing an Existing Agenda." In *Handbook of Disaster Research*, edited by H. Rodriguez, E. Quarantelli, and R. Dynes, 234–57. New York: Springer, 2006.

Smith, Robert, Claude Simard, and Andrew Sharpe. *A Proposed Approach to Environment and Sustainable Development Indicators Based on Capital.* Ottawa, ON: The National Round Table on the Environment and the Economy's Environment and Sustainable Development Indicators Initiative, 2001.

Timmerman, P. "Vulnerability, Resilience and the Collapse of Society." *Environmental Monograph 1* (Institute For Environmental Studies, University of Toronto), 1981.

United Nations Office for Disaster Risk Reduction (UN/ISDR). "Hyogo Framework for 2005–2015: Building the Resilience of the Nations and Communities to Disasters," 2005. www.unisdr.org/wcdr/intergover/official-docs/Hyogo-framework-action-english.pdf (accessed January 4, 2007).

Walker, B., and D. Salt. *Resilience Thinking: Sustaining Ecosystems and People in a Changing World.* Washington, DC: Island Press, 2006.

Walker, B., et al. "Resilience Management in Social–Ecological Systems: A Working Hypothesis for a Participatory Approach." *Conservation Ecology*, 2002.

Walter, C. "Community Building Practice." In *Community Organizing and Community Building for Health*, edited by M. Minkler. New Brunswick, NJ: Rutgers University Press, 2004.

Wilbanks, T. J. "Enhancing the Resilience of Communities to Natural and Other Hazards: What We Know and What We Can Do." *Natural Hazards Observer* 32 (2008): 10–11.

Wildavsky, A. *Searching for Safety*. New Brunswick, NJ: Transaction, 1991.

Zhang, Y., and W. G. Peacock. "Planning for Housing Recovery? Lessons Learned from Hurricane Andrew." *Journal of the American Planning Association* 76, no. 1 (2010): 5–24.

SITE PLANNING: INTERNATIONAL PRACTICE

INFRASTRUCTURE SYSTEMS

BY GARY HACK

Developing a site usually requires installing infrastructure both within its boundaries and beyond. On greenfield sites, roadways, sewer and water lines, and communications infrastructure may need to be extended out to a site, and drainage courses may need to be modified to transport runoff away from it. If the site is large, there is usually the option of creating freestanding infrastructure systems that serve just the site, but small sites need to rely on larger public systems. The need for infrastructure may be minimized by creative site design that reduces runoff, reuses water, keeps the size of roadways to a minimum, and lowers site maintenance through the use of indigenous vegetation. Local engineering standards usually spell out what is normally permitted, and exceptions will need to be negotiated.

INFRASTRUCTURE INVESTMENTS

The cost of installing infrastructure is a significant financial hurdle, often equaling or exceeding the cost of acquiring a site. Who pays for the infrastructure is a matter of local convention. In many places, the developer must install all infrastructure, designed to meet government standards, prior to transferring land to those who will occupy it. In other places, sewer, water, roadways, parks and open spaces, and other essential services are installed by local governments and paid for out of fees charged to the site developer, or through bonded capital raised by the local government, repaid from taxes or user fees. In some places, electrical and telephone lines are installed by the local service companies, with

Gary Hack, "Infrastructure Systems," *Site Planning: International Practice*, pp. 254-264. Copyright © 2018 by MIT Press. Reprinted with permission.

costs charged to the developer or covered as part of the utility's rate base. If infrastructure beyond the site—such as sewer treatment facilities or water treatment plants or arterial roads—must be expanded, frequently the local government or utility company will do so, charging the site developer for the incremental costs. Off-site systems may have been oversized in anticipation of a site's development, with the developer reimbursing the local government for its fair share of earlier investments.

Regardless of who pays for it, infrastructure always implies two types of costs: immediate capital costs to construct or install it, and long-term operating and maintenance costs incurred over its life. There are often tradeoffs between the two. Placing electrical lines on poles may be far less costly than installing them in trenches below ground, but maintenance and replacement costs will be higher, especially in locations with high winds and freezing rain, not to mention the intangible value of avoiding unsightly poles and lines above ground. Transporting water away from roads in large storm pipes is far more costly than creating swales on the sides of roadways, but the latter may require more land to be devoted to rights-of-way and will necessitate regular maintenance. When alternatives are considered, they should be analyzed in terms of life cycle costs:

LCC = IC + PV(AM) + PV(RC)
where
LCC = life cycle costs,
IC = initial capital costs,
PV = present value discounted at borrowing cost rate,
AM = annual maintenance costs,
RC = replacement costs.

The lifetime to be valued should equal the expected life of the most durable component, although as a practical matter the present value

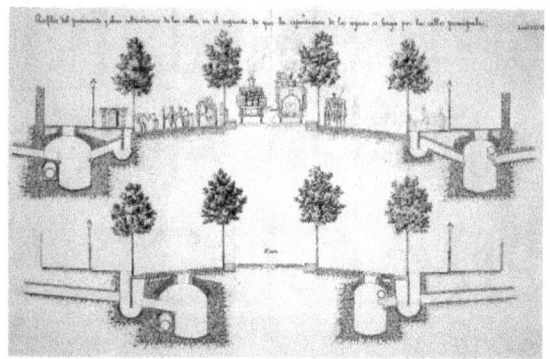

Figure 1. Underground sewers proposed in 1865 by Ildefons Cerdà for l'Eixample (the expansion) of Barcelona, one of the earliest examples of planning Infrastructure in advance of development. (Ildefons Cerdà)

Figure 2. Sewers, water, drainage, and sidewalks being Installed in Rio de Janeiro's hillside favela. (Gary Hack)

of expenditures required 50–75 years into the future is very small.

In situations with very low resources available, such as rapidly urbanizing areas of developing countries, infrastructure may need to be created over time as resources permit rather than at the outset of the development. Initially, only the rights-of-way may be established, then overhead electrical lines installed, with other infrastructure added later. Most North American cities were developed in this way: in residential areas, gravel roads lined by ditches, wooden sidewalks, overhead electric and telephone lines, and minimal underground water lines were installed in most cities in the nineteenth century, replaced later by paved streets, underground storm drains, concrete sidewalks, larger-diameter water mains with hydrants for firefighting, and, sometimes, underground electric and telephone lines. This process of upgrading, common today in many barrios and favelas, is a practical way to provide services without excluding low-income people from urban areas.

RIGHTS-OF-WAY FOR INFRASTRUCTURE

Infrastructure is usually installed in a public right-of-way, usually a street, although it may cross private lands where easements have been granted for access, maintenance, and replacement. Since many types of infrastructure must share the right-of-way, it is essential that the location of infrastructure—above, on, and below ground—be carefully organized, keeping in mind that most systems will require regular maintenance. Most cities have conventions for the precise location of each infrastructure system. Water pipes are typically located on the opposite side of the street from the electrical and telecommunications lines, to avoid damage in the case of a water line break. Storm and sanitary sewer lines, usually the largest and most costly systems, are generally in the center of the street, where they can easily serve inlets from either side. Underground lines are generally spaced away from tree roots that can easily damage them. Cities provide infrastructure planners with standard street profiles that they are obliged to follow, making it easy for emergency workers to quickly locate a line that needs to be repaired.

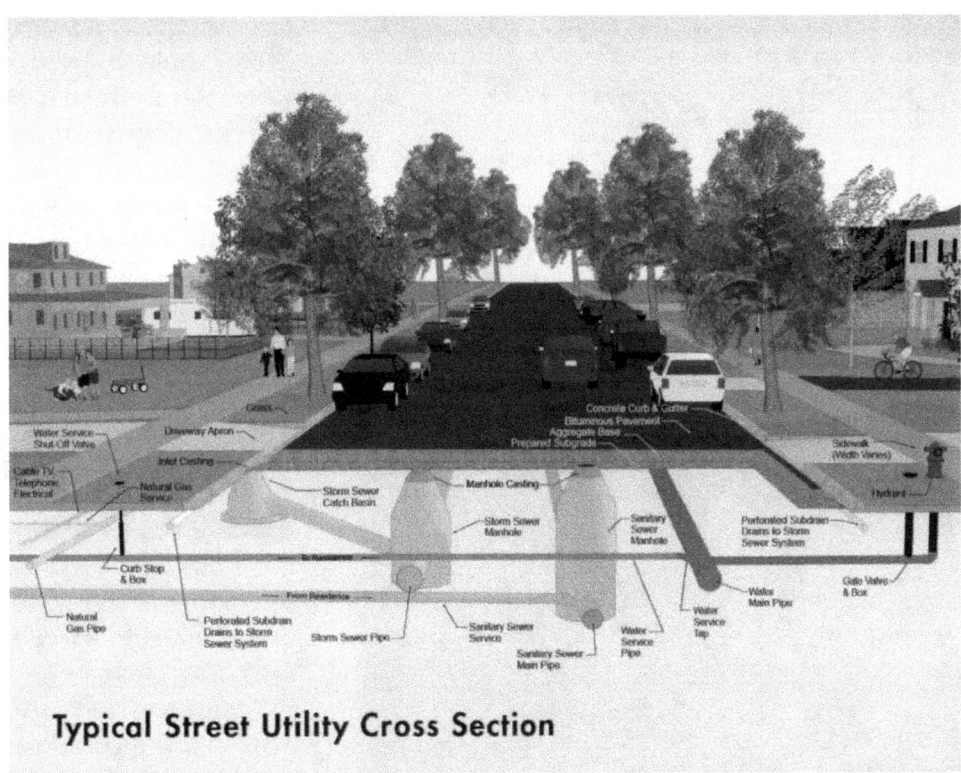

Figure 3. Typical low-density suburban street cross section, with conventional infrastructure. (Courtesy of Bolton & Menk, Inc.)

Street profiles in rapidly urbanizing countries reflect the necessity of using less costly infrastructure systems. Many cities use combined sewer systems that are less costly to install, collecting sewage in drainage trenches located below sidewalks or at the edges of properties, rather than providing individual building hookups to the sewer lines. Where storm drainage systems are in place, they customarily are limited to roadway runoff.

Historically, the width of a street right-of-way has been largely determined by the number of lanes required to move traffic and accommodate parked vehicles, but other factors also play a role. The desire to introduce landscape to absorb runoff, provide shade, or simply to add beauty to the street can add to its width, as can the need for generous sidewalks in dense urban areas. The disruption of digging up streets has led to the installation of common utility boxes or trenches in some dense urban areas, sometimes located below sidewalks, but other times occupying a separate portion of the right-of-way width. Wide rights-of-way may also reflect the desire to maintain flexibility for the future, keeping the option open to add dedicated mass transit lanes along a street, or to expand the moving lanes as traffic grows in an area. Such possibilities should be carefully scrutinized, however, since overly wide streets can discourage walkability and waste scarce land resources.

Rights-of-way in US and European cities typically occupy 20–30% of the land resources of a city, while in dense older areas of Asian cities they may only occupy half that amount or less (Vasconcellos 2001). As income rises in

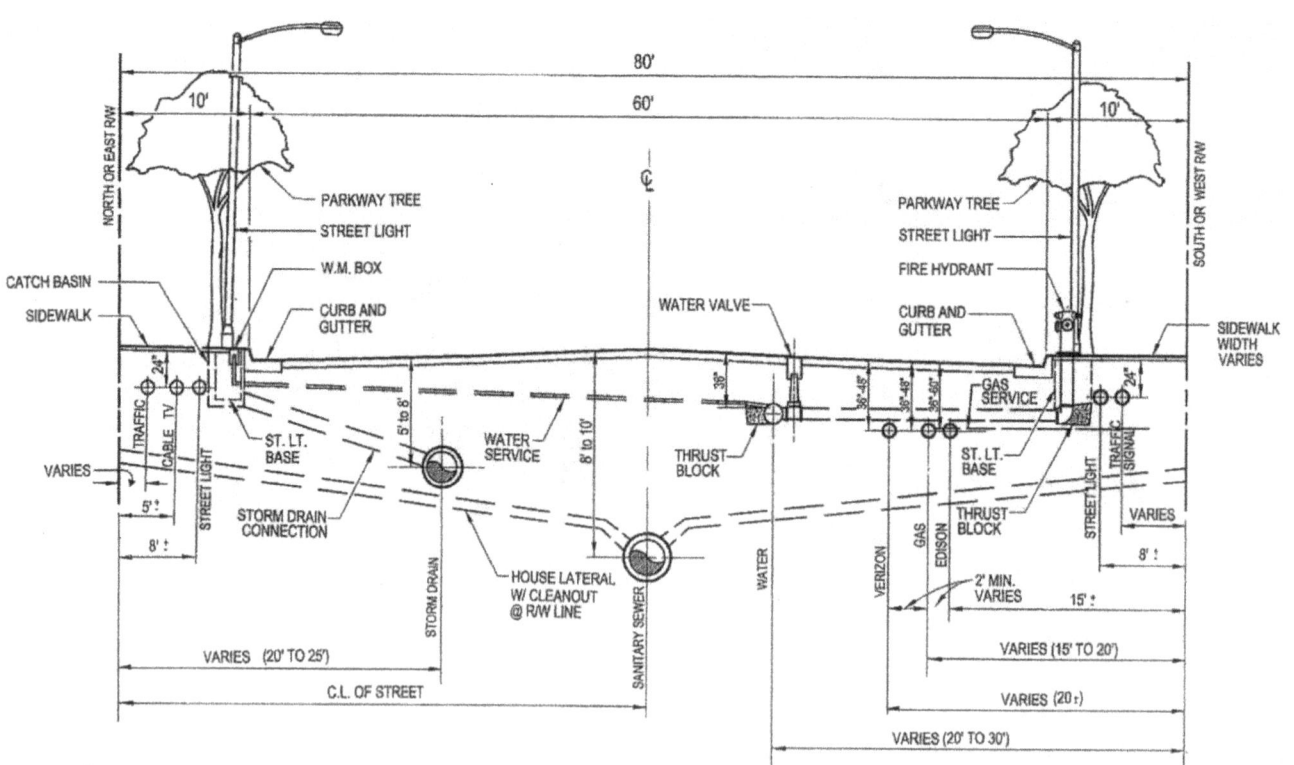

Figure 4. Standard cross section with location of infrastructure, Santa Monica, California. (City of Santa Monica)

SITE PLANNING: INTERNATIONAL PRACTICE

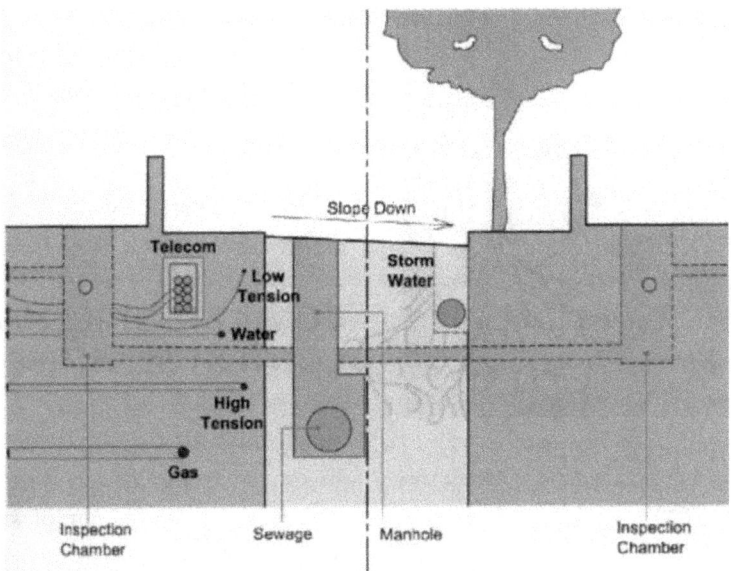

Figure 5. Recommended street cross section in India, relying on utility trenches for collection of wastes. (Courtesy of Environmental Planning Collaborative/Institute for Transport and Development Policy)

a country, automobile ownership rates increase, and there is a corresponding rise in the amount of land devoted to roadways. One study suggests that the elasticity is 1: for every 1% increase in national income, the length of roadways (and area occupied by them) rises by 1% (Ingram and Liu 1997). Nonetheless, limiting the area devoted to rights-of-way to less than 20% of the land available is a reasonable target, requiring ingenuity on the part of the site planner.

Since roadways are generally laid out first on a site, there is a tendency to err on the side of making rights-of-way overly generous. Most of Manhattan was developed with 60 ft (18 m) rights of way on east-west streets and 100 ft (30 m) on north-south avenues and major crosstown streets. It has evolved from a city of townhouses to one where tall apartments and office buildings predominate, but continues to exist comfortably at high densities within its original framework. Streets in New York represent over 26% of the surface area of the city. Many of Philadelphia's charming "alley streets" are as narrow as 30 ft (9 m). At the other extreme, new Chinese cities are commonly built with rights-of-way of 80 to 150 m (262–492 ft) for major arterials, and 18 m (60 ft) for local streets. These streets are excessively wide for the number of vehicles

Figure 6. Use of a common trench for the diverse and constantly changing telecommunications technology simplifies the replacement costs. (Gary Hack)

409

Figure 7. Streets of 60 ft (18 m) laid out in Manhattan for townhouses. (Gary Hack)

Figure 8. Streets of 60 ft (18 m) continue to function for high-density office uses. (Gary Hack)

Figure 9. Philadelphia alley street with 30 ft (9 m) right-of-way. (Gary Hack)

currently using them, and planners justify them through future projections of traffic and vehicle ownership, which may or may not materialize. Residential subdivisions in the US often require 60 ft (18 m) street widths, even in the lowest-density areas, also far in excess of what is required.

COMPLETE STREETS AND CONTEXT-SENSITIVE DESIGN

Since much of the infrastructure is housed in streets, we typically begin site planning with their design. The layout of streets and rights-of-way is often seen strictly as an engineering problem of how to most effectively organize infrastructure to minimize installation costs and operating problems. Each system is optimized within the available right-of-way, and conventions have evolved for typical types of streets. A better approach, however, begins with a list of the human needs to be served by the channels being constructed. The list might include:

Moving autos, buses, and trucks,
Space for children to play,
Access to frontages,
Space for pedestrians to walk,
Parking space for cars,
Shade for pedestrians,
Safe bicycle travel,
Allowing pedestrians to cross streets safely,
Potable water,
Mail delivery,
Water for firefighting,
Incorporating ornamental landscape,
Piped natural gas,
Absorbing most runoff to support landscape,
Electrical service,
Draining excessive storm runoff,
Cable service for TV and telephones,
Accommodating snow removal and storage,

Figure 10. Arterial street, 80 m (260 ft) In width, Qun Li New Town, Harbin, China. (Gary Hack)

Figure 11. Example of a complete street proposed for Redmond, Washington, balancing the needs of motorists, transit riders, pedestrians, cyclists, and adjoining properties. (Courtesy of Crandall Arambula PC)

Safe bus stops,
Street sweeping and cleaning,
Lighting for pedestrian safety.

Satisfying all these demands may create conflicts, particularly in dense urban situations with constrained rights-of-way. Thus it is important to get priorities straight in order to guide tradeoffs. New York City has publicized its priorities for traffic moving over city streets: (1) pedestrians, (2) bicyclists, (3) bus riders, and (4) motorists (New York City Department of Transportation 2009). Other conventions hinge on safety issues, such as allowing adequate space between sewer and water lines or between gas and electric lines. Unfortunately, issues of aesthetics and use, such as where trees can be planted or whether sidewalks are widened at intersections, are hamstrung by a host of engineering decisions.

The *complete streets* movement has emerged as an effort at rebalancing the use of streets to better reflect the needs of a diverse set of users. It is also rooted in considerations of public health and the realization that the decline of walking and cycling is in part a result of inhospitable streets (Seskin and McCann 2012; Seskin et al. 2012). Typically, the objectives of a complete streets program are "to ensure that the safety and convenience of all users of the transportation system are accommodated, including pedestrians, bicyclists, users of mass transit, people with disabilities, the elderly, motorists, freight providers, emergency responders and adjacent land users ..." (Bloomington, Indiana, MPO 2009). Most complete streets programs only deal with organizing the surface of the street—the moving and parking lanes, pedestrian walks, crosswalks, medians, and landscaped areas of the street. A truly comprehensive street program would, of course, take into account what occurs below and above ground as well.

Complete streets encourage safe walking and cycling, even if doing so reduces vehicle capacity or speeds or requires a reduction of on-street parking. In the US, half the trips in metropolitan areas are of three miles or less, and 20% are of one mile or less, yet the vast majority of trips are taken by automobile (Federal Highway Administration 2008). Shifting short-distance trips to walking or cycling, or longer-distance trips to transit, can more than offset any delays that may occur as a result of devoting a greater share of the roadway corridor to pedestrian, bicycle, or bus usage. Better pedestrian facilities can also promote safety: over 40% of pedestrian fatalities occurred on roads where no crosswalks were available, with more than half occurring on fast-moving arterial roads (Ernst and Shoup 2009). The most vulnerable groups are those who have no options for travel, including many of the elderly, children, and people with disabilities. European countries have generally adopted a more balanced approach to the use of street space, and comparative studies have shown that pedestrian death rates in Germany and the Netherlands are typically half to one-sixth the rates in the US per km traveled (Jacobsen 2003).

European cities have pioneered many complete streets solutions, particularly in integrating safe bicycle and pedestrian ways, dedicated or shared transit routes, and vehicular traffic in streets. Hundreds of US cities have adopted complete streets strategies, converting existing streets and revising standards and prototypical layouts of new rights-of-way. A common theme is revisiting standards to offer the flexibility needed to respond to the varying needs of streets. Traffic planners have pursued a parallel approach, seeking *context-sensitive solutions* that differentiate design standards based on their location (Institute of Transportation Engineers 2006). Many of these approaches have been integrated in the chapters that follow.

Surprisingly, there has been less innovation in below-ground infrastructure. Streets continue to need constant excavation to add new lines, replace obsolete ones, and repair breaks and damages. The evolution of telecommunications technologies has required many streets to be dug up for installation of cable, fiber optic, and other data conduits. Underground pipes are subject to routine blockages, although the problem is slowly being reduced by the use of curved pipes and continuous conduit. Nonetheless, underground infrastructure remains vulnerable to damage by tree roots, high water tables, poorly planned excavations, and other hazards. Some of this can be solved by intelligent organization of underground infrastructure.

One approach is limiting the area of disruption through the use of *common trenches* for certain infrastructure elements. On newly planned sites, common trenches are often located between the public right-of-way and the building face in a public *utility easement*, and are generally at least 0.5 m (18 in) wide and 1.4 m (54 in) deep. Accommodating half a dozen lines in this area requires careful planning, to allow subsequent access for upgrades or repairs. Trenches are filled as lines are added with fine-grain backfill material, often sand, that is nonabrasive and easily excavated. A common trench may contain some combination of cables for gas, TV, fiber optic, telephone, primary and secondary electric, and street lighting. Some cities limit what can be included in common trenches by requiring a minimum of 1 m (3 ft) horizontal spacing between gas, domestic sewer, storm sewer, and water lines.

In dense urban complexes, or areas undergoing rapid development, it may be worthwhile to take the next step of creating a continuous utility tunnel below ground, where infrastructure can be organized and worked on without disrupting the surface. Dense development may also necessitate large vaults below ground for switching, telephone connections, and transformers, fed by the utility tunnel. In addition to traditional infrastructure, steam, hot water, and chilled water lines may run through such utility tunnels. Medical complexes and universities often expand utility tunnels so that they are capable of serving as underground passageways for building services (removal of wastes, transporting goods received) or even as internal passageways for patients and professionals. If planned in advance,

SITE PLANNING: INTERNATIONAL PRACTICE

Figure 12. Common utility trench, Prince William Street, St. John, New Brunswick, Canada, combining all electrical and telecommunication conduits. (Courtesy of A. J. Good/Streetscape Canada)

the climate, thereby reducing the need for air conditioning. All of these moves need to be considered as a system of *green infrastructure*, such passageways could be located either above ground or below.

GREEN INFRASTRUCTURE

Cables, pipes, moving-vehicle lanes, lighting, and walkways are the infrastructure we are most familiar with. However, natural processes can provide an alternative for some forms of infrastructure. Runoff can be accommodated on a site through *rain gardens* or *rainwater detention areas,* rather than transported away in large pipes. *Solar panels* or *wind turbines* can generate electricity locally, powering buildings or streetlights, rather than relying on large amounts of electrical power generated remotely. *Composting* and *recycling* at the scale of a site can reduce the transport of wastes to landfills, and on large sites waste may provide the raw materials for energy generation. Water used on a site can be recycled for landscape irrigation (as *gray water*) or purified for reuse. Trees and other landscape elements can absorb greenhouse gases, humidify the air, and temper

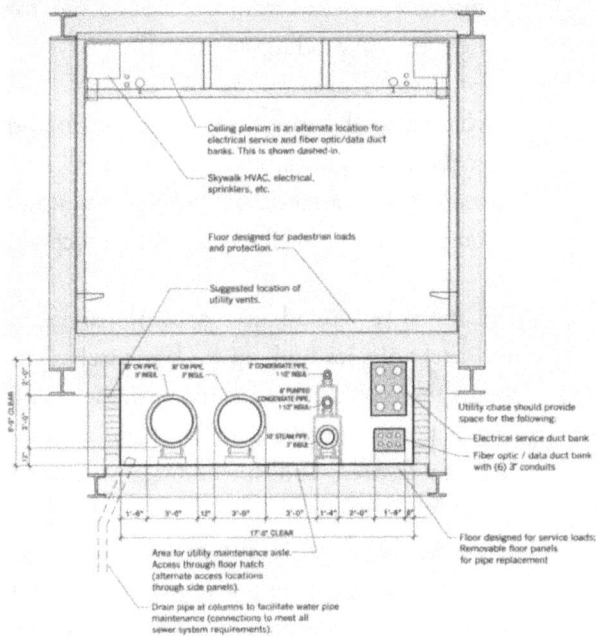

Figure 13. Utility tunnel, Gujarat International Finance Tec-City (GIFT), India, with ample room for expansion as the city grows. (Atul Tegar/Wikimedia Commons)

Figure 14. Proposed skywalk with utilities, Texas Medical Center, Houston. (Courtesy of Skidmore, Owings and Merrill/Texas Medical Center)

which can complement or displace the need for *gray infrastructure* on a site.

An essential idea behind green infrastructure planning is creating *closed loops* on a site. Resources consumed on a site are reused or returned to a usable state on site, thereby minimizing the impact of the site on its larger environment. An excellent example is the new community of Hammarby Sjöstad in Stockholm, which serves as a model for integrating a range of green environment systems (see chapter 40). The essential loops in a community include:

- *Water loops*—for domestic consumption, wastewater, storm runoff, irrigation, use in production, use in tempering outdoor spaces;
- *Energy loops*—for heating and cooling, for movement to and from and around site, for lighting, for production;
- *Carbon loops*—consumption of resources, discharges to the atmosphere, absorption and sequestration of carbon;
- *Materials loops*—products for use in homes and businesses, recycling processes, reuse processes.

Hammarby Sjöstad uses a combination of green technologies and up-to-date mechanical systems that serve the residents, businesses, and industries of the new district. The results are constantly monitored, and operations are adjusted to remedy problems.

Among the closed-loop systems, water loops are among the easiest to put in place on almost any site. In most places, water is too valuable a resource to use only once, and a combination of conservation and recycling is needed. There is a long history of harvesting rainwater for purposes of supporting landscape, reprocessing water for reuse, using water for recreation, and celebrating water through fountains and water bodies.

Today, carbon loops are at least as important, requiring low-carbon strategies and sequestering carbon emissions. And green infrastructure often serves several purposes. Large groves of trees can improve both water and carbon loops while improving local climate, creating a more attractive place to live, and offering recreation opportunities.

Green infrastructure has potential at all scales, from whole communities to individual sites. High-performance buildings such as the Visionaire in Battery Park City, New York reduce the dependence on public infrastructure by generating significant quantities of energy within the structure, harvesting rainwater, recycling a large fraction of the domestic water used in the building, and reducing energy consumption through the building's skin and systems. At lower densities, absorbing all the rainwater on a site can obviate the need for major storm sewers, at significant savings of infrastructure costs. Often, however, the savings flow to others or to the broader public. Charging the owners of buildings and sites for water discharged into storm sewers is one way to create an incentive to invest in retention infrastructure.

INTELLIGENT INFRASTRUCTURE

The technology of infrastructure has changed slowly over the past century, and many of the systems in the ground today are only slight improvements over systems installed many decades ago. Roadways today are only subtly different from what they were half a century ago; storm sewer technology may now use precast elements rather than clay or steel pipes but has improved very little. Regulations have stalled innovation in infrastructure, and there is little incentive for governments to try new

SITE PLANNING: INTERNATIONAL PRACTICE

arrangements that may fail. However, new technologies and materials offer the potential of adding intelligence to public services in urban areas. The innovations include new sensing and control devices, self-adapting systems, robotic maintenance equipment, real-time information systems, wireless communication systems, GPS technologies, new transmission and conduit materials, and sophisticated human-systems interfaces. The addition of new software is making it possible to change the hardware.

The chapters that follow outline some of the potentials on the horizon for the individual components of site infrastructure. Taken as a whole, they have as objectives:

More effective use of fixed resources—better utilization of roadways through improved flows of vehicles, diverting traffic in the case of breakdowns, better scheduling of public facilities, demand-sensitive routing of buses, managing distributed parking inventories, and car-sharing systems;

Load balancing—balancing energy loads across a network, shifting the sources of district heating over the day and year, and managing stormwater flows to reduce their effects;

Better predictions of failure—systems monitoring to detect potential failures, and rerouting around failures;

Improving safety—collision avoidance systems, automated vehicles, and surveillance systems to prevent crime;

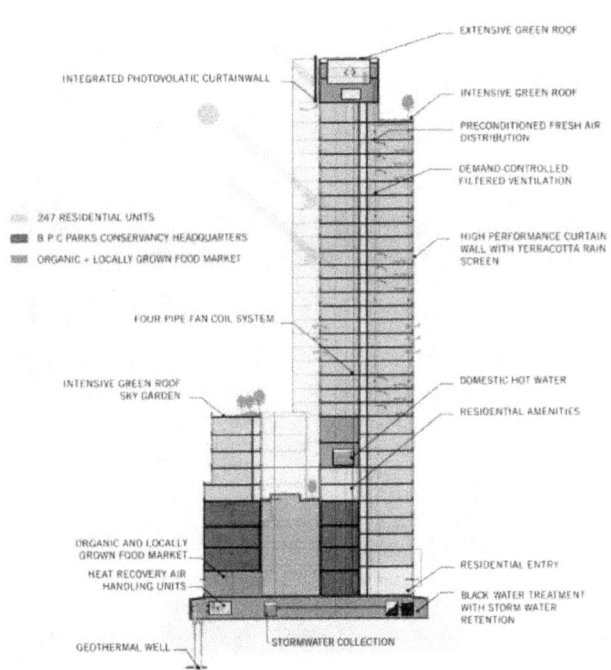

Figure 15. The Visionaire, a high-efficiency residential building, Battery Park City, New York. (© Jeff Goldberg/Esto)

Figure 16. Sustainability systems in the Visionaire, Battery Park City, New York. (The Albanese Organization/Pelli Clarke Pelli)

415

Improving information for personal decisions—telepresence systems that help avoid travel, real-time transport information systems, location reports, and rerouting algorithms on personal devices;

Reducing maintenance and operating costs—automated reading of meters, detection systems for waste disposal needs, and robotic maintenance systems.

Intelligent environments depend upon wired or wireless communications that link displays with sensors, and sophisticated software and hardware to store data and make estimates of the future. Every major systems corporation has produced its image of how intelligent cities should be organized, favoring of course devices and programs where they have a comparative advantage. It will take a while for experience to guide standardization, and in the meantime many thousands of partial solutions are being implemented. The chapters that follow discuss approaches to intelligent infrastructure in greater detail.

Most intelligent infrastructure systems also require people inhabiting sites to change their everyday patterns. A car-sharing system can significantly reduce the need for parking spaces and stretch roadway capacity, but also requires individuals to change their habits of car use. A distributed energy generation system which employs arrays of panels on individual houses requires individuals to participate in the maintenance of the system. Nonetheless, intelligent systems offer plenty of benefits to compensate, and infrastructure offers plenty of scope for technological development, large and small.

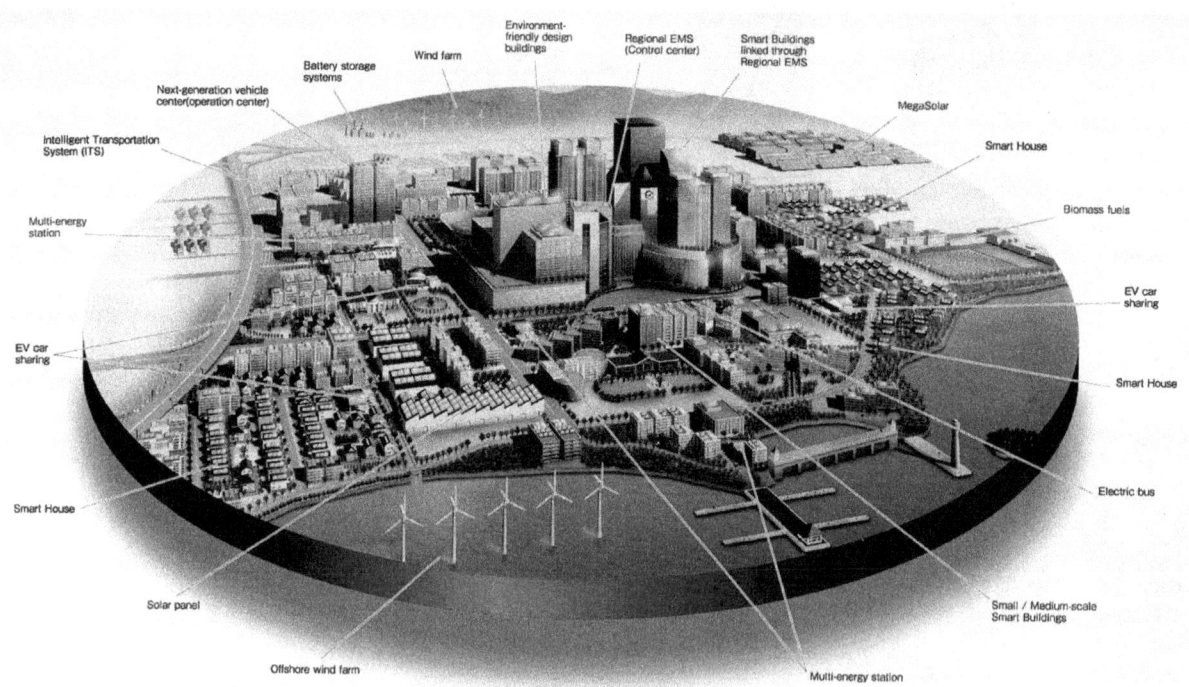

Figure 17. Emerging intelligent city components. (Ministry of Urban Development, India)

*Figure 18. City operation center, Rio de Janeiro.
(Gary Hack)*

HAZARD MITIGATION AND PREPAREDNESS

CHAPTER 2: *Preparedness, Hazard Mitigation, and Climate Change Adaptation: An Overview*

BY ANNA K. SCHWAB, DYLAN SANDLER, AND DAVID J. BROWER

WHAT YOU'LL LEARN

- Phases of the comprehensive emergency management cycle
- Differences between preparedness and hazard mitigation
- The link between natural hazards and climate change
- Characteristics of sustainable and resilient communities

GOALS AND OUTCOMES

- Assess the value of hazard mitigation and preparedness
- Identify hazard mitigation and adaptation strategies
- Explore the links between climate change adaptation and hazard mitigation
- Describe the timing of hazard mitigation and preparedness relative to disasters
- Understand the connection among hazard mitigation, resilience, and sustainability

2.1 INTRODUCTION

As we learned in Chapter 1, we cannot stop most natural hazards from happening, nor can we prevent many human-made hazards from threatening communities. But we *can* take action to reduce the impacts of these hazards so that the damage is less extensive and recovery can take place quickly. This chapter introduces the concepts of hazard mitigation and preparedness as important pieces of the emergency management system in the United States. The chapter also lays the groundwork for a basic understanding of

Anna K. Schwab, Dylan Sandler, and David J. Brower, "Preparedness, Hazard Mitigation, and Climate Change Adaptation: An Overview," *Hazard Mitigation and Preparedness*, pp. 23-45. Copyright © 2017 by Taylor & Francis Group. Reprinted with permission.

adaptation in the context of climate change and natural hazards. In addition to describing hazard mitigation, preparedness, and adaptation, we also discuss some of the primary types of tools and processes that can help reduce hazard risk. This chapter then explains how actions taken to lower disaster risk can ultimately help communities reduce losses and become more environmentally, economically, and socially stable.

2.2 THE EMERGENCY MANAGEMENT CYCLE

Comprehensive emergency management is a widely used approach at the local, state, and federal levels to deal with the inevitability of natural hazards and the possibility of human-made hazards and their potential to cause disasters in a community. The four traditional phases of a comprehensive emergency management system are **Preparedness, Response, Recovery,** and **Mitigation.** A fifth phase, **Prevention** is occasionally included in the description of the emergency management system, primarily in the context of human-made hazards and public health threats. Table 1 outlines each of these phases.

Although other models of emergency management are used as well, the four traditional phases of comprehensive emergency management are

Table 1. Phases of Comprehensive Emergency Management

Preparedness	• Activities to improve the ability to respond quickly in the immediate aftermath of an incident • Includes development of response procedures, design and installation of warning systems, evacuation planning, exercises to test emergency operations, and training of emergency personnel
Response	• Activities during or immediately following a disaster to meet the urgent needs of disaster victims • Involves mobilizing and positioning emergency equipment and personnel; includes time-sensitive operations such as search and rescue, evacuation, emergency medical care, food and shelter programs, and bringing damaged services and systems back online
Recovery	• Actions that begin after the disaster, when the most urgent needs have been met. Recovery actions are designed to put the community back together • Includes repairs to roads, bridges, and other public facilities, restoration of power, water, and other municipal services, and other activities to help restore normal operations to a community
Hazard mitigation	• Activities that prevent a disaster, reduce the chance of a disaster happening, or lessen the damaging effects of unavoidable disasters and emergencies • Includes engineering solutions such as dams and levees; land use planning to prevent development in hazardous areas; protecting structures through sound building practices and retrofitting; acquiring and relocating damaged structures; preserving the natural environment to serve as a buffer against hazard impacts; insurance, such as flood insurance, to protect homeowner's investment and lessen the financial impact on individuals, families, communities, and society as a whole; and educating the public about hazards and ways to reduce risk
Prevention	• Countermeasure activities such as heightened inspections, improved surveillance, and security operations to determine the full nature and source of the threat • Law enforcement activities aimed at deterring, preempting, interdicting, or disrupting illegal activity • Public health activities to detect and prevent pandemic, such as surveillance, testing, mass immunization, isolation, and quarantine

HAZARD MITIGATION AND PREPAREDNESS

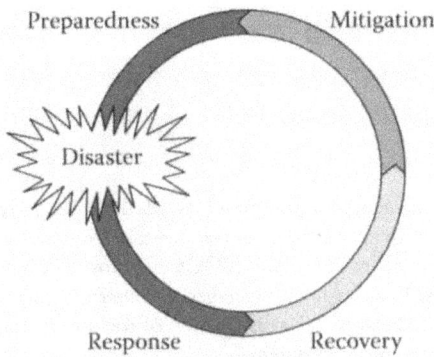

Figure 1. The emergency management cycle consists of preparedness, response, recovery, and mitigation. While these are distinct phases in the diagram, the reality is that these phases often run together, and actions taken in one phase may significantly affect other phases of the emergency management cycle.

often illustrated in a circular pattern, signifying its cyclical nature (see Figure 1). We prepare for disasters before they occur. When a disaster happens, a community must first respond to that particular event and soon thereafter begin recovery. But even while the community is still recovering from one disaster, it must begin the process of mitigating the impacts of the next disaster.

Also known as the **disaster life cycle,** this system describes the process through which emergency managers prepare for emergencies and disasters, respond to them when they occur, help people and institutions recover from them, and continually take actions to mitigate the effects of disasters on communities.

We are *always* preparing for and mitigating the impacts of disasters. These two phases are the building blocks for creating more resilient communities—communities that anticipate hazards and plan ahead to reduce losses. Interestingly, the period of recovery following a hazard event often provides unique opportunities to rebuild in a way that incorporates mitigation concepts into the redevelopment of a damaged community. In fact, the availability of government funding to carry out mitigation plans and projects has historically been highest during the recovery phase of the disaster life cycle. New emphasis is being placed on pre-disaster mitigation activity, but the post-disaster environment continues to be one of significant increases in funding availability. The level of technical expertise to carry out hazard mitigation activities also tends to surge in the aftermath of a disaster, so communities that are aware can often find advantage in the midst of adversity.

2.2.1 PREPAREDNESS

Preparedness ensures that if a disaster occurs, people are ready to get through it safely and respond to it effectively. Preparedness can he characterized as a "state of readiness" to respond to any emergency or disaster. It involves anticipating what might happen during different sorts of hazard events and developing plans to deal with those possibilities. Preparedness also involves carrying out exercises, evaluating plans for shortfalls, and training and education. Although emergency managers must remain flexible and able to adapt their plans to meet immediate needs as the situation warrants, a plan or established protocol for dealing with disasters and emergencies of all sorts is crucial to a successful response. We will discuss preparedness in more detail in Chapter 11, but for now, the activities listed in Table 2 will give you some idea of the range of actions an emergency manager can expect to carry out prior to disaster to help citizens get ready for any type of emergency.

Table 2. Examples of Preparedness Activities

PREPAREDNESS ACTIVITY	DESCRIPTION
Planning	All 56 U.S. states and territories prepare emergency operations plans (EOPs). The EOP establishes a chain of command, designates responsible parties, provides for continuity of government functions, establishes an emergency operations center (EOC), and provides a road map for decision making during emergencies. Evacuation and emergency sheltering are also an important planning function of the preparedness phase, as is creation of back-up lifeline services such as power, water, sewage, and communication systems
Training	Emergency managers, first responders, and public officials take classes in emergency planning, disaster management, hazardous materials response, fire service management, etc.
Exercises and drills	From "tabletop" discussions of a specific problem to full-scale exercises that involve detailed disaster scenarios that unfold over several days, exercise events bring together every agency and volunteer organization that would respond in a real disaster
Emergency awareness and education	Educational messages include teaching children how to make a 911 call, reminding parents to keep emergency supplies on hand, showing homeowners how to make their homes more hazard proof, distributing disaster specific messages to areas at risk, and so forth
Warning	Warning activities include development of warning systems, emergency alert systems, and coordination of sirens and other emergency notification methods. Regular testing of warning and notification devices is critical

2.2.2 FEDERAL PREPAREDNESS PROGRAMS

Preparedness activities are one element of a broader national preparedness system led by the Federal Emergency Management Agency (FEMA). The **National Preparedness Directorate** was established in 2007 following Hurricane Katrina. It provides policy and planning guidance to build prevention, protection, response and recovery capabilities for states and local governments nationwide, including many of the strategies that enable professional First Responders to carry out their preparedness duties. You can find out more about the Directorate at www.fema.gov/national-preparedness-directorate.

FEMA's public engagement and awareness campaign, Ready.gov provides a wealth of information, in both English and Spanish to empower Americans to prepare for and respond to emergencies, including natural and man-made disasters. The goal of the campaign is to get the public involved and ultimately to increase the level of basic preparedness across the nation. Ready.gov urges individuals to do three things

1. Build an emergency supply kit
2. Make a family emergency plan
3. Be informed about the different types of emergencies that can occur and their appropriate response

TURN AROUND DON'T DROWN

An example of a very successful warning system is the placement of road signs to alert drivers to dangerous flood hazards. According to the National Weather Service (NWS), almost half of all flood fatalities occur in vehicles. Local storms can quickly fill underpasses and cover bridges, and as little as two feet of water can cause a vehicle to float, even a large SUV or truck. If the water is moving, vehicles can be swept away. Driving at night during a local flood can be especially hazardous. To increase awareness of the dangers of shallow flooding, the NWS has initiated the "Turn Around Don't Drown" program to help communities educate residents about the dangers of walking or driving in floodwaters (see Figure 2).

Figure 2. "Turn Around Don't Drown" is a National Weather Service campaign which promotes preparedness by warning people of the hazards of walking or driving through flood waters.

Ready.gov/business is an extension of the Ready program that focuses on business preparedness, while Ready.gov/kids provides tools, including interactive games, accessible information, and planning templates for educators and parents to teach children in grades 8 through 12 about emergencies and how to prepare for them in a nonthreatening, age appropriate way.

TRAINING AND EXERCISES: DISASTER CITY

While it is important to have a well-informed and prepared citizenry, the skills of professional first responders are essential in any large-scale emergency or disaster. A critical element of a successful preparedness program relies on frequent training and exercises for first responders. There are many training facilities throughout the United States, but one of the oldest and best known is located near Texas A&M University in College Station, Texas. The 52-acre training campus, known as Disaster City, includes a wide variety of emergency scenarios, complete with full-scale props such as derailed trains, collapsed buildings, leaking hazmat tanks, and other realistic disaster situations. There is even a portion of a WWII battle ship to simulate the experience of fires and other emergencies that can occur aboard large oil and gas tankers and drilling platforms. Experienced facilitators expose fire fighters, law enforcement, emergency medical technicians (EMTs), emergency managers, industrial workers, and others responsible for public and worker safety to rigorous training "in the field." For more information, visit the Texas A&M Engineering Extension Service at http://www.teex.com (Figure 3a and b).

Figure 3. (a) Each year, thousands of first responders from around the globe receive intensive hands-one scenario-based training at the "Disaster City" training ground at Texas A&M University. (b) A simulated train wreck is used to teach emergency workers how to respond quickly and effectively in potentially dangerous conditions. (Courtesy of Anna Schwab.)

2.2.3 HAZARD MITIGATION

Hazard Mitigation is defined as "any sustained action to reduce or eliminate long-term risk to people and property from hazards and their effects." This definition highlights the long-term benefits that effective mitigation can have. This definition also emphasizes that mitigation is an ongoing effort that communities must make on a continuous basis. Mitigation involves planning, strategizing, and implementing action ideas in advance of a hazard event. The ultimate purpose of mitigation plans, strategies, and actions is to avoid placing people and property in harm's way and to make structures safer and stronger when avoidance is impossible or impractical.

2.2.4 THE DIFFERENCE BETWEEN PREPAREDNESS AND MITIGATION

Preparedness involves the functional, logistical, and operational elements of emergency management. Although preparedness activities are carried out in advance of a hazard event, they are directed to the response and, to a lesser degree, the recovery phases of the emergency management cycle. During preparedness, we gather our supplies and make our plans for what to do when the disaster hits.

Preparedness can be visualized as the phase in which we pose a series of "what if" questions, and seek to find the answers before they become reality. For instance, an emergency manager may consider various worst-case scenarios, such as the following:

- What if the power goes out? Do we have generators and a supply of fuel? What about telecommunications, water, and sewer service?
- What if the roads are blocked? How will we deliver needed supplies and medical services to impacted populations?
- What if our food supplies are cut off? Do we have access to water, ice, Meals-Ready-to-Eat? Where are these supplies stored, and how quickly can they become available?
- What if there are multiple injuries? Who are our medical contacts? Will they need transportation, supplies, a power source, blood?
- What if residents have to leave their homes quickly? Is an evacuation plan in place? Does it account for fluctuations in populations, such as the tourist season in a resort community? What about people who do not own cars or are not independently mobile? How do we handle residents who are disabled, ill, old, young, and illiterate?
- Are community buildings ready to serve as shelters? Are their locations clearly identified and accessible? Who opens the shelters? Are pets provided for as well?
- Are first responders ready to carry out search and rescue missions? Have they been trained to serve in disaster conditions? How will they communicate with one another?

These are the types of issues that the preparedness phase attempts to address before emergency conditions render the situation unmanageable.

Hazard mitigation, in contrast, is the ongoing effort to lessen the impacts of disasters on people and property through pre-disaster activities. Mitigation can take place months, years, and even decades before a hazard event and continues after a disaster occurs with an eye to the future. Mitigation differs from the other phases of emergency management in that it looks for long-term solutions to reduce hazards. Hazard mitigation involves a different thought process and a different skill set, one that is oriented toward long-range policy and decision-making processes.

One of the primary differences between hazard mitigation and preparedness is the visibility of the respective results. The benefits of mitigation often are not realized for some time—months or even years after being implemented. Success is measured by what does *not* occur, or "losses avoided." Avoidance and prevention are the outcomes of mitigation done well, outcomes that can be difficult to quantify. As a result, communities have often favored highly visible, results-oriented action in preparation for the immediacy of an emergency situation over the more deliberate, process-oriented strategy of hazard mitigation.

Unfortunately, hazard mitigation is often neglected until after a disaster actually occurs.

REBUILDING THE JERSEY SHORE

When Hurricane Sandy came ashore in October of 2012, tens of thousands of families living along the New Jersey shoreline were displaced, and the $16 billion Jersey Shore tourism industry, crucial to the state economy, ground to a halt. In the weeks and months following the storm there was intense pressure on political leaders—from the local town mayor up to the Governor—to rebuild immediately, so that businesses could reopen in time for the busy summer season. But despite the rush to rebuild, some Sandy-impacted communities are taking a more deliberate approach, realizing that another intense storm may come ashore again, and that the constantly changing climate must be considered as part of a long-range approach to planning for the future (see Figure 4).

Figure 4. Following Hurricane Sandy, several businesses along the Jersey Shore were open for business in time for the busy summer season. Many more, however, will take much longer to recover, if in fact they are rebuilt at all. (Official White House photo by Sonya Herbert.)

> **SELF-CHECK**
>
> - List the four stages of the comprehensive emergency management cycle.
> - Discuss the difference between preparedness and mitigation.
> - Describe the primary preparedness tasks that Ready.gov encourages citizens to carry out.

In the case of natural disasters, history is filled with examples of communities that rebuild in the same places, in the same manner as previously, only to suffer the same perils when the hazard event recurs. It's natural and expected for people whose homes and businesses have been destroyed by a hurricane, tornado, or flood to want to get their lives back to normal—and they want that to happen as quickly as possible. But sometimes rebuilding too quickly means opportunities to build back *smarter* may be missed. Hazard mitigation seeks to consciously break the cycle of destruction and reconstruction that accompanies repeat disasters by adapting human settlement patterns and construction techniques to reflect the threat posed by future hazards.[1]

2.3 CLIMATE CHANGE ADAPTATION[1]

As we will explore further in later chapters, climate change has a direct and causal effect on many of the natural hazards we deal with today. As climate continues to change, the frequency, intensity, spatial extent, duration, and timing of extreme weather will change and may result in unprecedented extreme weather and climate events. Events that occurred only once every 30 years on average may begin occurring every 4–5 years in the future.

There is little that can be done to prevent this increase in extremes, but there are opportunities to decrease community vulnerability and climate impacts, and in doing so, decrease losses from current and future disasters. While climate change may increase the frequency and intensity of hazards, the damage caused by those hazards cannot be attributed to climate change alone—good policy can reduce risk today and in the future.

2.3.1 WHAT CAN BE DONE?

Responses to climate change are generally divided into two categories: **mitigation** efforts that address the "cause" of human-induced climate change—this typically involves attempts to reduce greenhouse gas emissions that cause warming of the Earth's atmosphere; and **adaptation** efforts to address the "symptoms" of climate change. Neither of these efforts pursued alone can help us avoid all climate change impacts, rather, mitigation and adaptation complement each other, and if pursued together, can significantly reduce the results of climate change.[2]

---

[1] The sections in this chapter and throughout the book that focus on climate change are largely adopted from Woodruff, S. C. et al. 2013. *Adapting to Climate Change: A Handbook for Local Governments in North Carolina.* Chapel Hill, NC: Coastal Hazards Center at the University of North Carolina at Chapel Hill. Available online at coastalhazardscenter.org/adapt.

> ## HAZARD MITIGATION, CLIMATE MITIGATION, AND CLIMATE ADAPTATION: CONFUSING TERMS!
>
> Climate mitigation aims to reduce the forcing that causes climate change while adaptation aims at reducing vulnerability to climate change. Hazard mitigation, focused on reducing vulnerability to natural hazards, shares many of the same characteristics of climate adaptation. Both are focused on identifying vulnerability to natural hazards and developing strategies to reduce that vulnerability; in fact, many of the strategies used for both hazard mitigation and climate mitigation overlap. So what's the difference? Although both take the long view, climate adaptation in general requires a longer time frame and broader approach than is incorporated into the typical hazard mitigation plan, which tends to have a 5–15 year planning horizon.

2.3.2 THE CASE FOR ADAPTATION

Even if carbon dioxide emissions stopped today, we know that we are already committed to some warming of global temperatures, and that this warming will affect many of the critical services and functions that governments provide, especially at the local level. Some communities are already feeling the effects of climate change in the form of frequent flooding, long-lasting drought, changing fauna and flora, and higher disaster costs. However, the high cost and damage of climate change are not inevitable. Adaptation provides an opportunity to reduce these risks.

The good news is that many adaptation actions have obvious immediate benefits as well as long-term advantages for the community and are worth pursuing in and of themselves. Adaptation strategies are generally consistent with sound environmental practice, by improving resource use and preserving natural features.

> ## ROOFTOP GARDENING IS COOL!
>
> Many adaptation actions also reduce greenhouse gas (GHG) emissions. Green roofs (see Figure 5), or rooftop gardens, cool cities, helping to adapt to the "heat island" effect of urban areas (*adaptation*). These vegetated roofs also retain water during storms and reduce the amount of runoff that comes from impervious surfaces (*hazard mitigation*); at the same time, green roofs also increase the energy efficiency of buildings, resulting in lower demand for fossil fuels and lower emission of greenhouse gases (*climate mitigation*).

HAZARD MITIGATION AND PREPAREDNESS

Figure 5. Green roofs, like this one on City hall in Chicago, are good examples of multiobjective building techniques, by serving both natural hazard mitigation as well as climate change mitigation purposes. The vegetation captures excess rainwater while also cooling the building, thereby reducing the building's energy consumption.

SELF-CHECK

- Describe the relationship among hazard mitigation, climate mitigation, and adaptation.
- Explain why climate change adaptation is important even if steps are taken to reduce greenhouse gas emissions.

2.4 HAZARD MITIGATION AND ADAPTATION STRATEGIES[3]

There is a wide variety of tools and techniques that a community can use to reduce the impacts of hazards on people and property, while also adapting to climate change. Although every community is unique in terms of its hazards and individual level of risk, some of the possible options available to reduce that risk may include the following categories of hazard mitigation and adaptation actions.

Infrastructure strategies involve changes or modifications of the basic physical systems of society to make both infrastructure itself, and the community that depends on it, more resilient to natural hazards and climate change impacts. Examples of this type of strategy include construction of new water storage systems, increased street maintenance, and raising waste-water treatment plants above flood levels and more.

Land use strategies guide development and people out of harm's way, as well as improve design and location of development to better respond to hazard risks. Land use includes restrictions on development in flood zones, low impact design to improve management of storm water, and urban landscaping to reduce summer temperatures.

Natural resource strategies reduce consumption of raw resources and protect ecosystems that provide essential services. For example, techniques to reduce fresh water consumption and measures to protect coastal marshes that limit storm damage would both be considered natural resource strategies.

Education strategies disseminate information to the general public and businesses about climate change and natural hazard impacts, along with information about adaption and mitigation measures. The success of many of the above strategies relies on the willing participation of community members; thus education strategies are central to effective risk reduction.

Each of these types of strategies seeks to reduce the vulnerability of the built environment to the impacts of hazards (see Figure 6). Many communities use a combination of strategies to meet their risk reduction needs. See Chapter 12 for a more detailed discussion of hazard mitigation tools and techniques.

2.4.1 RISK ASSESSMENT AND MAPPING

Before a community can implement any of its hazard mitigation or climate change adaptation strategies, it must have a clear picture of the types of hazards that pose a threat and how those hazards may impact people and property. Hazard identification is the necessary first step to reducing vulnerability; it involves a process of culling

Figure 6. Sea Bright, New Jersey: Construction crews are elevating this house damaged during Hurricane Sandy. Elevation, or raising the base floor above expected flood heights, is one way to mitigate flooding for a home situated in a flood zone.

information about the community's hazard history, profiling various hazard events, and making predictions about the possibility of future hazards. The community must also determine what assets and populations are vulnerable to the hazards that have been identified, including analysis of land use patterns, growth potential, and development trends to evaluate what may be at risk in the future. Maps are an important component of a community **risk assessment,** as they can be used to illustrate where hazards intersect with the built environment in a graphic and visual way. The analysis and maps produced during a risk assessment can help a community make important decisions about how to protect local assets and vulnerable populations against likely hazards. See Chapter 10 for a more in-depth discussion about community risk assessment.

Many communities in the United States have an official flood insurance rate map, or FIRM, that shows the location of flood-prone areas throughout the jurisdiction. These maps indicate the likelihood that a particular home, street or business could be flooded during the next 100-year flood (a flood that has a 1% chance of occurring during a given year). These maps also contain visual information about the frequencies of other flooding events. These maps are used as the basis for developing ordinances that regulate the types of structures that are allowed in the community's floodplain and specify how structures must be protected to mitigate the impacts of various levels of flooding.

2.4.2 MANAGING COMMUNITY GROWTH AND DEVELOPMENT

One of the most effective approaches to hazard mitigation and climate change adaptation involves managing community growth and development through land use planning and regulations, as well as controlling the quality of structures that are built through building standards and code requirements. Local governments can use zoning and subdivision ordinances to steer development away from hazardous locations such as floodplains, seismic risk areas, landslide-prone sites, and wildfire areas. Local governments can also install infrastructure such as roads, utility lines, water and sewage treatment facilities, and other public services to avoid hazardous areas. By making hazardous areas less attractive for development though strategic investment in capital improvements, communities can discourage building on inappropriate sites.

The choices we make regarding where and how we build determine our level of vulnerability to many natural and human-made hazards. Hazard mitigation should not be seen as an impediment to growth and development of a community. On the contrary, incorporating hazard mitigation into decisions related to a community's growth can result in a safer, more resilient community and one that is more attractive to new families and businesses.

RISK REDUCTION REQUIRES POLICY IMPLEMENTATION

A thoughtful risk assessment will provide good information that identifies potential hazards and illustrates the impact those hazards are likely to have on the community. However, a viable risk reduction strategy relies on more than the production of colorful maps, no matter how detailed they are. Instead, decision makers must use the information gathered during the risk assessment to develop sound policies that specifically address the identified threats. But even that step is not going far enough—it is not until the policies are implemented will changes take place that reduce the level of risk. Unfortunately, all too often this final "action" step does not take place, and local residents remain vulnerable, despite the knowledge that danger lurks.

Tragically, this seems to be the case in Oso, Washington, where on March 22, 2014 a very large, rapidly moving landslide killed approximately 39 people, many of whom were in their homes when a wall of mud rushed down a steep slope, engulfing an entire neighborhood in a suffocating mix of earth, stones, tree trunks and other debris. Aerial photography clearly showed the occurrence of previous landslides (an indication that future landslides were possible), Identifying the area as a very high landslide risk zone. The county had considered buying up and emptying property later wiped out in the mudslide but decided instead to stabilize the base of the slope and leave residents where they were. Additionally, there were few restrictions on new construction in the area. If more stringent development guidelines had been implemented to limit residents' exposure to the landslide risk, the tragedy in Oso may have been avoided.

SELF-CHECK

- List four major categories of hazard mitigation strategies that can also be used for climate change adaptation.
- Describe how risk assessment and mapping help inform the hazard mitigation strategy process.
- How can land use planning contribute to a community's overall risk reduction strategy?

2.5 THE VALUE OF HAZARD MITIGATION AND PREPAREDNESS

We have learned that the goal of mitigation is to save lives and reduce property damage by encouraging long-term reduction of hazard vulnerability (see Table 3). Hazard mitigation can be accomplished through cost-effective and environmentally sound actions which, in turn, can reduce the enormous cost of disasters to property owners, businesses, and all levels of government. In addition, hazard mitigation can protect critical community facilities, reduce exposure to liability, and minimize community disruption. At the same time, preparedness saves lives and property, and facilitates response operations through pre-disaster plans, training, and exercises.

2.5.1 HAZARD MITIGATION PAYS OFF

A fundamental premise of mitigation is that current dollars invested in hazard mitigation will significantly reduce the demand for future dollars by reducing the amount needed for emergency response, recovery, repair, and reconstruction following a disaster. By protecting its investment in infrastructure and capital assets, a community will enjoy cost savings over the long term. Hazard mitigation, therefore, is a fiscally responsible activity for a community to pursue. The benefits of mitigation and preparedness likewise accrue to business, industry, and other members of the private sector. By reducing risk to hazard losses, companies can protect their employees, their income stream, and company assets, and they are better equipped to maintain fiscal solvency and economic viability even after a disaster. See Chapter 9 for a discussion of private sector mitigation and preparedness activities.

Table 3. Benefits of Mitigation and Preparedness

MITIGATION AND PREPAREDNESS BENEFIT	DESCRIPTION
Reduces loss of life and damage to property	Communities can save lives and reduce property damage from hazards through mitigation actions, such as moving families and their homes out of harm's way. Mitigation and preparedness also reduce the risk to emergency workers who must rescue people and pets during a disaster
Reduces vulnerability to future hazards	By having mitigation and preparedness plans in place, a community is able to take steps to permanently reduce the risk of future losses
Saves money	A community will experience cost savings by not having to provide emergency services, rescue operations, or recovery efforts. Communities also avoid costly repairs or replacement of buildings and infrastructure
Speeds response and recovery	By considering mitigation and preparation in advance, a community can identify post-disaster opportunities before a disaster occurs. A strategy that is thought out prior to a disaster allows the community to react quickly when the time comes
Demonstrates commitment to community health and safety	A mitigation and preparedness strategy demonstrates the community's commitment to safeguarding its citizens and protecting its economic, social, and environmental well-being

> ### A DOLLAR FOR HAZARD MITIGATION SAVES FOUR!
>
> Several programs authorize the use of federal funds to mitigate the impacts of natural hazards on American communities. Between mid-1993 and mid-2003, more than $3.5 billion of federal, state, and local funds were spent to reduce flood, windstorm, and earthquake risk. In light of those expenditures, the U.S. Congress directed the FEMA to fund an independent study to assess future savings resulting from hazard mitigation activities. The study analyzed the costs and benefits of nearly 5500 mitigation grants for earthquake, flood, and wind hazards. The results indicate that the overall benefit-cost ratio for FEMA mitigation grants is about 4:1, meaning that for every dollar spent in hazard mitigation activities, an average of four dollars is saved over time because of reduced or avoided losses from future disasters.[4]

2.6 SUSTAINABILITY AND DISASTER RESILIENCE

As hazard mitigation serves to protect the environment and reduce disaster-related costs, it can contribute to the community's long-term sustainability, supporting economic vitality, environmental health, and quality of life for the community as a whole. Climate change adaptation takes this one step further, by factoring future climate conditions into decisions made today. Sustainability is attained when decisions made by the present generation do not reduce the options of future generations. **Sustainable development** is development that "meets the needs of the present without compromising the ability of future generations to meet their own needs."[2] Building in a way that reduces or avoids the impacts of disasters is an essential characteristic of a sustainable community.

Sustainability is a concept that can help communities of all sizes and in all locations make decisions that will lead to a better quality of life for all of their members, now and in the future. The principles of sustainability also apply to communities that find they must recover and rebuild in the after-math of a disaster. The goal of sustainable development (and redevelopment) is to create and maintain safe, lasting communities through the protection of life, property, the natural environment, and the economy. Hazard mitigation and climate change adaptation activities are a very important part of any effort to become more sustainable.

The guiding principles of sustainable development are intended to provide a sense of direction to decision makers for ensuring the quality of development. Sustainability recognizes that the economy and the environment are not in conflict, but are intricately intertwined. These principles are not an impediment to growth; instead, sustainable development fosters smart growth.

Embracing hazard mitigation and climate change adaptation is also a key component of disaster resilience. A **disaster resilient community** is a

---

** This is the definition of "sustainable development" developed by the Brundtland Commission in 1987, World Commission on Environment and Development, Our Common Future 43. 1987.

HAZARD MITIGATION AND PREPAREDNESS

community or region developed or redeveloped to minimize the social, environmental, and economic losses and disruption caused by disasters. A resilient community understands natural systems and realizes that appropriate siting, design, and construction of the built environment are essential to advances in disaster prevention.[5] Resilient communities are towns, cities, counties, and states that prepare and plan for, recover from, and more successfully adapt to adverse events.[6] Actions to prepare for natural and human-made hazards and mitigate the impacts of these hazards are essential components of resilience. See Chapter 13 for further discussion of the role of mitigation and preparedness in building community sustainability and resilience.

Hurricane Sandy Recovery: Promoting Resilience through Innovative Planning and Design

When Hurricane Sandy devastated communities in the region, we were reminded of the importance that climate change will have in all development and planning for our communities to become more resilient and sustainable.

Shaun Donovan
U.S. Secretary of Housing and Urban Development (HUD)

Hurricane Sandy was unlike any storm before it. The unprecedented damage revealed the true threat that weather events pose to our communities, states and greater region, and marked a new era of public awareness that we must change our practices and thinking and way of living to address climate change and sea level rise. While everyone affected by the storm continues to push forward with the recovery process, it is clear that we cannot simply rebuild what existed before. We need to think differently this time around, making sure the region is resilient enough to rebound from future storms.

To address these challenges, in June 2013, Secretary Donovan launched Rebuild by Design, a multistage design competition to develop innovative, implementable proposals to promote resilience in the Sandy-affected region. To read more about the Rebuild by Design initiative, visit http://www.rebuildbydesign.org.

SELF-CHECK

- Describe four benefits of hazard mitigation and preparedness.
- Explain how hazard mitigation and preparedness are connected to sustainable development.

CHAPTER SUMMARY

Hazard mitigation and preparedness activities help communities become more resilient to the impacts of hazards, and climate change adaptation gives communities a running start to deal with the impacts of natural hazards in the future. Disaster costs continue to escalate in the United States, and we must increase our efforts to keep property out of vulnerable locations through implementation of long-lasting and forward-thinking mitigation strategies such as natural resource protection and land use regulations to keep development out of hazard areas, and building codes to strengthen homes and businesses against hazard impacts. We have much to do in terms of preparedness as well. The loss of life and property during Hurricanes Sandy and Katrina, and other recent catastrophic events, highlights the need for vast improvements in our ability to evacuate, shelter, and administer emergency aid to disaster victims. These areas of improvement should serve as a catalyst for further research and study into the most effective means of preventing disasters so that community resilience becomes reality. These issues are explored in detail in Chapters 10 through 12.

KEY TERMS

Adaptation	The process of adjustment to the actual or expected climate and its effects, in order to moderate harm or exploit beneficial opportunities.
Comprehensive emergency management	Approach used to deal with natural hazards and human-caused hazards and their potential to cause disasters in a community.
Disaster life cycle	The cycle of the four phases of the comprehensive emergency management system as it interacts with a disaster event.
Disaster resilient community	A community or region developed or redeveloped to minimize the human, environmental, and property losses and the social and economic disruption caused by disasters. A resilient community understands natural systems and realizes that appropriate siting, design, and construction of the built environment are essential to advances in disaster prevention.
Hazard mitigation	Any sustained action to reduce or eliminate longterm risk to people and property from hazards and their effects.
National Preparedness Directorate	Within FEMA, the National Preparedness Directorate provides strategy, policy and planning guidance to build prevention, protection, response, and recovery capabilities for states and local governments nationwide. You can find out more about the Directorate at www.fema.gov/national-preparedness-directorate.
Preparedness	A state of readiness to respond to any emergency or disaster.
Ready.gov	FEMA's public outreach and education program that helps communities, businesses, families, and individuals learn about steps they can take to be prepared for any emergency.

Recovery	Phase in the emergency management cycle that involves actions that begin after a disaster to rebuild the community; examples include road and bridge repairs and restoration of power.
Response	Phase in the emergency management cycle that involves activities to meet the urgent needs of victims during or immediately following a disaster; examples include sheltering, evacuation, search and rescue, and delivery of emergency supplies.
Risk assessment	The process or methodology used to evaluate risk.
Sustainable development	Development that meets the needs of the present without compromising the ability of future generations to meet their own needs.

ASSESS YOUR UNDERSTANDING

SUMMARY QUESTIONS

1. Hazard mitigation can only be carried out during or after a disaster takes place. True or False?
2. Exercises and drills are a valuable component of disaster preparedness. True or False?
3. Which of the following websites is not part of FEMA's public engagement and awareness campaign?
   a. Ready.gov
   b. Ready.gov/kids
   c. Ready.gov/business
   d. Ready.gov/homeowners
4. Because residents want to recover from disasters as quickly as possible, planners and emergency managers should always make speed their only recovery goal. True or False?
5. Installing air conditioning to better cope with heat waves is a form of climate change mitigation. True or False?
6. Some climate change adaptation strategies may have immediate benefits and cost savings. True or False?
7. A resilient community is a community that prevents hazards from happening. True or False?
8. Preparedness involves anticipating what might happen during different types of hazard events. True or False?
9. Which of the following is an example of preparedness measures?
   a. Rebuilding water-supply systems
   b. Conserving floodplains
   c. Training those involved in emergency situations
   d. Road repairs
10. The period following a disaster is a valuable time for implementing mitigation measures. True or False?
11. Mitigation is a way to save communities money. True or False?

REVIEW QUESTIONS

1. What stages of the emergency management cycle do resilient communities use to try to limit the long-term impact of a disaster?
2. Citing examples, explain the difference between preparedness and hazard mitigation.
3. A comprehensive emergency management system follows four stages. Name the stages.
4. Hazard mitigation should be considered a wise investment for a community. Explain why.

5. How does hazard mitigation affect a community's decisions regarding growth and development?
6. Describe the results of research analyzing the overall return on investment for money spent on hazard mitigation.
7. Explain the difference between climate change mitigation and climate change adaptation.

APPLYING THIS CHAPTER

1. Compare how a town in northern Minnesota would prepare for hazards versus a town in Arizona. Which measures are consistent?
2. As the chief emergency manager in your town, you must present a proposal to the local governing board about a new state program that requires local governments to engage in hazard mitigation activities. How will you describe what a resilient community is? What will you include in your presentation about the benefits of hazard mitigation? How will you convince the board to authorize spending local resources to reduce the impacts of hazards?
3. Explain how hazard mitigation and climate change adaptation are similar.

YOU TRY IT

Tracking a Hurricane

As an official with your local government, you have a responsibility to ensure the safety of those who live in your town. You haven't experienced a serious hurricane in decades, but one changed its track last year and narrowly missed your town. Assume that hurricane season is approaching, and outline a public announcement that will update residents about what your town has done to prepare for this year's season. The National Oceanic and Atmospheric Administration (NOAA) hurricane tracking website (www.nhc.noaa.gov) is an excellent resource.

JUDGING RESILIENCY

Assume you are an emergency manager in a flood-prone community. What factors will you look at to determine how resilient your community is to this hazard? How can you determine whether your community will experience a natural hazard event, so that damage is minimal and people are safe, or whether your community will suffer a disaster?

REFERENCES

1. Blanchard, W. 1997. *Emergency Management USA: Student Manual.* FEMA Emergency Management Institute, Emmitsburg, MD.
2. Bernstein, L., R. K. Pachauri, and A. Reisinger, 2008. *Climate Change 2007: Synthesis Report.* Geneva, Switzerland: IPCC, in Woodruff.
3. Woodruff, S.C. et al. 2013. *Adapting to Climate Change: A Handbook for Local Governments in North Carolina.* Chapel Hill, NC: Coast Hazards Center at the University of North Carolina at Chapel Hill.
4. Rose, A. et al. 2007. Benefit-cost analysis of FEMA hazard mitigation grants. *Nat. Hazards Rev.,* (American Society of Civil Engineers) 8(4): 97–111.
5. The H. John Heinz III Center for Science, Economics and the Environment. 2000. *The Hidden Costs of Coastal Hazards: Implications for Risk Assessment and Mitigation.* Washington, DC: Island Press.
6. National Research Council. 2012. *Disaster Resilience: A National Imperative.* Washington, DC: The National Academies Press.

THE TRANSPORTATION PLANNING HANDBOOK

The Transportation Planning Process

Transportation System Characteristics & Urban Travel Characteristics

BY MICHAEL D. MEYER

III. THE TRANSPORTATION PLANNING PROCESS

Transportation planning is often portrayed as an orderly and rational process of steps that logically follow one another. In reality, planning and project development are much more complex, often with many different activities occurring concurrently. Shown in Figure 1, the planning process starts with understanding the problems facing a community and ending with a solution to identified problems (projects programmed and designed). In a typical planning context, many of these steps may have already occurred and therefore are not relevant to a particular planning effort. For example, metropolitan planning organizations (MPOs) in the United States have been developing transportation plans for decades, and as a result, a typical planning effort might simply be updating an existing transportation plan. In the context of Figure 1, the development of goals, objectives and performance measures might consist of validating those that were developed for the prior version of the plan. Even with these caveats, the planning process shown in Figure 1 helps identify important components of the planning process and how they relate to one another. The planning process in Figure 1 will be referenced throughout this handbook.

A. MAJOR STEPS IN TRANSPORTATION PLANNING

The planning process begins with an *understanding of the socio-demographic, land-use, and*

Michael D. Meyer, "The Transportation Process and Changing Context for Transportation Planning and Transportation System Characteristics & Urban Travel Characteristics," *Transportation Planning Handbook*, pp. 3-12, 16-34. Copyright © 2016 by John Wiley & Sons, Inc. Reprinted with permission.

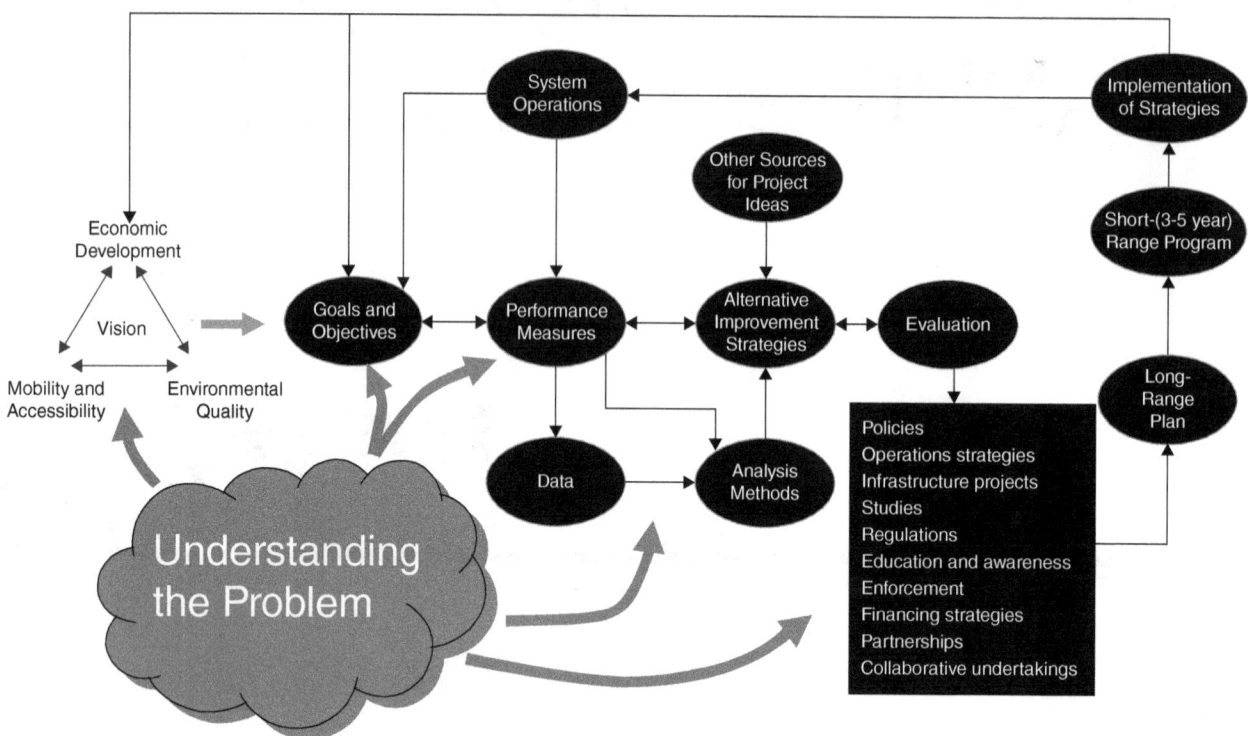

Figure 1. Conceptual Framework for Transportation Planning
Source: Adapted from Meyer and Miller, 2014, Reproduced with permission of M. Meyer.

economic context within which a transportation system operates. This is followed by becoming aware of the problems, challenges, opportunities, and deficiencies of transportation system performance within this context, be it a state, province, region, or community. This usually entails some form of analysis and assessment of the changing context of transportation system performance and an examination of both the existing and expected challenges facing the transportation system. This initial step is important because a planning agency usually begins a planning study based on the planning and analysis that has preceded it. More often, a transportation plan is being updated, or some specific problems have been identified that require a planning effort to be undertaken. Understanding the nature of the challenges facing a community thus becomes an important starting point for the planning steps that follow.

The next step is *developing a community or study area vision*. The dimensions of the vision portrayed in Figure 1 reflect the interaction among desired states of economic prosperity, environmental quality, and social equity/ community quality of life. These three factors have been chosen purposely as defining a vision because they are often considered to be the three major elements of sustainable development; a concept well-developed and accepted in recent years (see chapter 3). The vision can consist of general statements of desired end states or can be as specific as a defined land-use scenario. The visioning process often relies on extensive public outreach and is considered one of the most community-interactive steps of the planning process.

Once a vision has been defined, the next step is to *acquire more specific information* about what the vision means. What is the desired performance of the transportation system? What characteristics of community life can be most positively affected by transportation improvements? This more specific definition of a community's future is usually accomplished by *defining goals and objectives* that provide overall direction to the planning process. These goals and objectives not only help define the purposes of the planning process for the public, but can also help identify criteria to evaluate different transportation system options and alternatives.

Goals and objectives can also lead to the identification of *system performance measures*. Using measures to monitor the performance of the transportation system and the progress of transportation plans and programs is relatively new to the transportation field (see, for example, the performance management requirements of the 2012 U.S. federal transportation law—Moving Ahead for Progress in the 21st Century (MAP-21)). The primary purpose of collecting data on key system performance characteristics is to provide information to decision makers on the aspects of performance that are most important to them. Performance measures can be used to monitor whether congestion, average speeds, system reliability, and mobility options have changed over time. Many planning programs have also developed performance measures relating to such things as environmental quality, economic development, and quality of life. In these cases, transportation is just one factor that contributes to achieving overall community goals.

Collecting and analyzing data, the next step of the planning process, is key to understanding the problems and potential challenges facing the transportation system and the surrounding community. This analysis process primarily focuses on understanding how a transportation system and its components work and how changes to the system will alter its performance. A large part of the analysis step is identifying the current status of system performance. Analysis also includes identifying alternative strategies or projects that meet the objectives of the study. Analysis tools, ranging from simple data analysis to more complex simulation models, are used to produce the information that feeds the next step of the process, which is evaluation.

Evaluation is the process of synthesizing the information produced during the analysis step (for example, the benefits, costs, and impacts of different alternatives) so that judgments can be made concerning the relative merits of different actions. As noted by Meyer and Miller [2014], evaluation should incorporate the following characteristics:

- Focus on the decisions being faced by decision makers.
- Relate the consequences of alternatives to goals and objectives.
- Determine how different groups are affected by transportation proposals.
- Be sensitive to the time period in which project impacts are likely to occur.
- In the case of regional transportation planning, aggregate information in a way that allows planners to assess the likely effects of alternatives at varying levels.
- Analyze the implementation requirements of each alternative.
- Assess the financial feasibility of plan recommendations.
- Provide information on the value of alternatives in a readily understandable form and timely fashion for decision makers.

One of the most common ways to ensure that the results of the evaluation process are linked closely to decision making is through the evaluation criteria used to assess the cost-effectiveness of individual alternatives or strategies and that reflect important decision-making concerns. These criteria provide important guidance to planners and engineers on the type of data and analysis tools to be used in producing the desired information.

Note in Figure 1 that planning can result in many different products. Studies can recommend the pursuit of specific transportation projects or services; they can recommend changes to institutional structures or funding programs that would make the management of the transportation system more effective. Some studies might recommend specific policy changes, such as how land-use and development plans should be linked to the transportation plan. In the United States, one of the most important products of the statewide and metropolitan transportation planning process is the development of a transportation plan. Much of what is covered in this handbook focuses on the steps necessary to develop such a plan. However, it is important to recognize that the ongoing planning process actually results in many different products aimed at improving the performance of the transportation system and in enhancing the economy and quality of life of the community it serves.

The actual program of action—in the United States called the transportation improvement program (TIP) for a metropolitan area or a state transportation improvement program (STIP) for a state—is connected to the plan through a process called *programming*. Programming matches the most desirable actions that have surfaced through the evaluation process with available funds. Priorities must be set when there are insufficient funds to satisfy all of the funding needs. This process can take many forms, ranging from political considerations to the use of systems analysis tools to assign priorities to different projects or alternatives.

Once a project or action has been programmed for implementation, its design and operation must be further refined, and likely impacts further explored. This process of refinement is called *project development*. Project development takes various forms, depending on the scope and magnitude of the project and the expected effects. Three major steps in project development include: developing project concepts, planning the project in finer detail than typically occurs in systems planning, and preliminary/final engineering. When significant environmental impacts are expected, the project development process will usually (depending on federal and state laws) include an environmental analysis process whose steps are well laid out in rules and regulations.

The final component of the framework is *system monitoring*. Note in Figure 1 that system monitoring provides feedback to the definition of goals and objectives and the use of performance measures. Poor system performance can lead to further planning analysis to better understand the dynamics of the underlying problem, or it might very well lead to the identification of new goals and objectives.

The planning process shown in Figure 1 is very different from more traditional constructs. First and perhaps most significantly, system planning as shown encompasses a broad set of planning steps. Many books on transportation planning have focused almost exclusively on analysis and evaluation, with the visioning process, program and/or project implementation, and system monitoring occurring outside the planners' purview. The approach toward planning in this handbook adopts a much broader perspective to transportation planning.

Second, the use of performance measures is a relatively new addition to systems planning, and as shown in Figure 1, is a central concept to the overall process. Given the important linkage between planning and decision making that serves as the core concept in the definition of planning used in this handbook, performance measures should focus on the information of greatest concern to decision makers. Performance measures not only help define data requirements and influence the development of analytical methods, but also become a critical way of providing feedback to the decision-making process on the results of previous decisions.

Third, a major purpose of planning is to identify and analyze alternative improvement strategies and projects, which could include traditional infrastructure projects, but also actions to influence travel behavior and system performance. For example, travel demand management (TDM) strategies, such as variable work hours, rideshare programs, and parking pricing, have become important options in many metropolitan areas for reducing demand for transportation. Likewise, many intelligent transportation system (ITS) actions are not really projects as much as they are efforts to better improve transportation system performance through the use of technology. The planning process in Figure 1 provides for a much wider consideration of actions and strategies than what is usually considered part of the transportation planning process.

Figure 1 was presented primarily as a structure for planning in the United States. Other countries have their own requirements for transportation planning, or in the case of developing countries, they often follow the guidance of international lending institutions, such as the World Bank. However, although the goals and objectives, models and analysis tools, and strategies might be different from those found in the United States, the overall approach to planning in other countries is still similar to what is shown in Figure 1.

A final characteristic of planning proposed here is the periodic feedback provided to the original vision definition, goals statement, and identification of performance measures through system management and operations. System management and operations serves as a major source of information on transportation system performance and thus is an important indicator of system deficiencies or opportunities for improvement.

One of the useful aspects of the process shown in Figure 1 is that it provides a framework for assessing how comprehensive a planning process is for addressing specific issues. For example, Table 1, structured from Figure 1, is an example of how to assess the effectiveness of a transportation planning process with respect to safety issues. Similar constructs could be developed for almost any issue of concern to a community.

B. LINKAGE TO POLICY AND OTHER PLANNING EFFORTS

Because much of transportation planning has developed in response to the needs of a nation, individual states or provinces and municipalities, a great deal of what a transportation professional does is defined by law. In the United States, for example, the Constitution establishes the structure of government and the powers, responsibilities, and limits of the different branches and levels of government. Those powers vested in the federal government take precedence over the actions and authority of state and local governments. Thus, although state departments of transportation (DOTs) and MPOs focus on state and metropolitan/local issues, respectively, federal law often requires that certain actions be taken. For example, federal law requires that each state and metropolitan area have its own transportation plan. Federal law, interpreted through regulations, requires that the process for developing these plans must have certain characteristics, such as an effective public participation process. In those areas that have not attained air-quality standards as set forth in federal regulations, the transportation system plan, improvement program and selected projects must be found to be in conformance to the adopted air quality plan. It is beyond the scope of this chapter to identify all of the U.S. federal requirements that influence transportation planning; however, some additional description of key laws that transportation planners in the United States will be exposed to is important (for more a more exhaustive presentation of relevant federal laws see [Gayle, 2009; Meyer and Miller, 2014]).

Federal guidance on transportation planning is justified by the importance of transportation to the nation—the economy, national security, and health and welfare of its citizens. It is this national purpose that generates the need for an informed and consistent approach to transportation investment across the nation, especially where federal funds are involved. Congress first established a federal requirement for metropolitan transportation planning in the Federal-Aid Highway Act of 1962. To receive federal transportation funds, this law required urbanized areas with a population greater than 50,000 to develop a *continuing, comprehensive* transportation plan that was a *cooperative* venture with state and local governments. This requirement, known as the 3C planning process, still serves as the foundation of today's transportation plans.

Table 1. Assessing the Consideration of Safety in the Transportation Planning Process

Vision

- Is safety incorporated into the current vision statement of the jurisdiction's transportation plan? If not, why not?
- Is safety an important part of the mandates and enabling legislation of key agency participants in the planning process?
- Is safety an important concern to the general public and planning stakeholders? If not, should it be?
- How is safety defined by the community?
- What type of information is necessary and desired to educate the community on the importance of a safe transportation system?

Goals and Objectives

- Is safety incorporated into the current goals and objectives set of the jurisdiction's transportation plan? If not, why not? If so, what, if anything, needs to be changed in the way safety is represented?
- How does the safety goal relate to the community understanding of safety as discovered through the vision development process?
- Does the safety goal lead only to recommended project construction and facility operating strategies, or does it also relate to strategies for enforcement, education, and emergency service provision?
- Does the safety goal reflect the safety challenge of all modes of transportation, that is, is it defined in a multimodal way?
- Are there goal-related objectives that provide more specific directions on how the goal is going to be achieved? Are these objectives measurable?
- Do the objectives reflect the most important safety-related issues facing a jurisdiction?
- Can the desired safety-related characteristic of the transportation system be forecast or predicted? If not, is there a surrogate measure or characteristic that will permit one to determine future safety performance?

- What type of information is necessary and desired to educate the community on the importance of a safe transportation system as it relates to planning goals and objectives?
- If target values are defined in objective statements (for example, fatal crashes will be reduced by 20 percent), have these targets been vetted through a technical process that shows that the target value can be reached?

Performance Measures

- What are the most important safety-related characteristics of the transportation system that have resulted from community outreach efforts to date? If performance measures are used, are these characteristics reflected in the articulated set of performance measures?
- Will the safety performance of the transportation system (as defined in the performance measures) likely respond to the types of strategies and projects that will result from the planning process? That is, are the performance measures sensitive enough to discern changes in performance that will occur after program implementation?
- Are the number of safety performance measures sufficient to address the safety concerns identified in the planning process? Alternatively, are there too many safety measures that could possibly "confuse" one's interpretation of whether safety is improving?
- Does the capability exist to collect the data that are related to the safety performance measures? Is there a high degree of confidence that the data and the data collection techniques will produce valid indicators of safety performance? Who will be responsible for data collection and interpretation?
- Can the safety performance measures link to the evaluation criteria that will be used later in the planning process to assess the relative benefits of one project or strategy over others? If so, can the safety performance measures be forecast or predicted for future years?

Analysis—Data

- Given the definition of safety that resulted from the visioning and goals/objectives phases of the planning process, what types of data are needed to support the safety desires of the community?
- Are these data available currently? If not, who should collect these data? Are there ways of collecting these data, or are there surrogate data items that can be used to reduce the cost and burdens of data collection?
- Does the state (or region) have a systematic process or program for collecting safety-related data? If not, who should be responsible for developing one?
- Is there a quality assurance/quality control strategy in place to assure the validity of the data collected? If not, who should develop one?
- Are there opportunities to incorporate data collection technologies into new infrastructure projects or vehicle purchases (for example, surveillance cameras or speed sensors)?
- Does the safety database include safety data for all modes of transportation that are relevant to the planning process (for example, pedestrians, bicyclists, transit, intermodal collisions, etc.)? If not, what is the strategy for collecting such data? Who should be responsible?
- What types of database management or data analysis tools are available to best use the data (for example, a geographic information system)? Are such tools available to produce the type of information desired by transportation decision makers?
- Are there other sources of data in your state or region that might have relevant data for safety-related planning (for example, insurance records, hospital admissions, nonprofit organizations, etc.)? If yes, who should approach these groups to negotiate the sharing of data?
- Are there any liability risks associated with the collection and/or reporting of crash data? If so, how can your agency be protected against such risk?

Analysis—Tools

- What is the scale of the safety problem being faced? Regional? Corridor? Site-specific? Are tools available that analyze safety problems at the same scale of analysis?

Source: Washington, Meyer, et al. 2006. Permission granted by the Transportation Research Board.

The 1973 Federal-Aid Highway Act and subsequent FHWA-Urban Mass Transportation Administration (UMTA) Joint Regulations on Transportation Planning had a profound impact on the institutional responsibilities for transportation planning. For the first time, federally supported urban transportation planning was funded separately: half of 1 percent of all federal-aid funds were designated for this purpose and apportioned to the states on the basis of urbanized area population. These funds were to be made available to "metropolitan planning organizations (MPOs) responsible for comprehensive transportation planning in urban areas." The Joint Planning regulations thus required that an entity called the metropolitan planning organization be established in every urbanized area with a population of more than 50,000.

A multiyear prospectus and annual unified work program had to be submitted specifying all transportation-related planning activities for an urban area as a condition for receiving federal planning funds. The urban transportation planning process was required to produce a long-range transportation plan, which had to be reviewed annually to confirm its validity. The transportation plan had to contain a long-range element and a shorter-range "transportation systems management element" (TSME) for improving the operation of existing transportation systems without new facilities. A multiyear "transportation improvement program" (TIP) also had to be developed consistent with the transportation plan. The TIP had to include all highway and transit projects to be implemented within the coming five years. The TIP had to contain an "annual element" that would be the basis for the federal funding decisions on projects for the coming year. The consequences of these requirements were that they changed the emphasis from long-term planning to shorter range transportation system management, and provided a stronger linkage between planning and programming. [Weiner, 1992, 2008] Most of these requirements, except the TSME of the long-range transportation plan, are still operative today.

In 1991, the Intermodal Surface Transportation Efficiency Act (ISTEA) ushered in what many saw as a new era for transportation planning in the United States at both the metropolitan and statewide levels. This law fully established MPOs as the central forum for making transportation planning and investment decisions in metropolitan areas; it required a robust public involvement process, and it provided new flexibility in the use of federal capital program funds so that MPOs and states could find the best solutions to their transportation problems, rather than funding projects that fit the eligibility requirements of specific categorical funding programs. Different planning factors were to be addressed in the transportation planning process, including the need for the plan to be multimodal and intermodal, and to better understand the linkage between land use and transportation. ISTEA also required that both the plan and the TIP be fiscally constrained to only those projects that had a reasonable expectation of funding.

Prior to ISTEA, there was no federal requirement for statewide transportation planning, although many states do such planning. Along with the new requirements for metropolitan planning, ISTEA required states to create a planning process that would produce a long-range, intermodal statewide transportation plan and a short-range program of projects. While the process and content of the statewide plan did not have to be as rigorous as the MPO plan, Congress did include a list of planning factors that states were to consider.

The Moving Ahead for Progress in the 21st Century Act (MAP-21) passed in 2012 consolidated numerous categorical funding programs into a much smaller number of programs. For transportation planning, its biggest impact was in its requirement for state DOTs and MPOs to adopt performance measures. [FHWA, 2014a] The U.S. DOT was required to establish performance measures for safety, pavement conditions, bridge conditions, operational performance of the Interstate, operational performance of the non-interstates on the National Highway System (NHS), freight movements, mobile source emissions, and congestion. For transit, the U.S. DOT must "establish a national transit asset management system and performance measures for keeping transit in a state of good repair." States and MPOs were to establish targets for each performance measure, and adopt a "performance-based approach" in planning and programming transportation projects. This performance-based planning and programming approach was more than just imposing performance measures on states and MPOs; it also required MPOs to measure and report on the outcome of investments from the TIP/STIP as they affected the travelling public. [FHWA, 2014a]

In recognition of the important role that freight plays in the national, state, and regional economies, MAP-21 required the U.S. DOT to report biennially on the conditions and performance of the "national freight network," and to develop tools for "an outcome-oriented, performance-based approach to evaluate proposed freight-related and other transportation projects." The transportation goals specified in this law for the federal highway programs included:

- "*Safety*—To achieve a significant reduction in traffic fatalities and serious injuries on all public roads.

- *Infrastructure Condition*—To maintain the highway infrastructure asset system in a state of good repair.
- *Congestion Reduction*—To achieve a significant reduction in congestion on the National Highway System.
- *System Reliability*—To improve the efficiency of the surface transportation system.
- *Freight Movement and Economic Vitality*—To improve the national freight network, strengthen the ability of rural communities to access national and international trade markets, and support regional economic development.
- *Environmental Sustainability*—To enhance the performance of the transportation system while protecting and enhancing the natural environment.
- *Reduced Project Delivery Delays*—To reduce project costs, promote jobs and the economy, and expedite the movement of people and goods by accelerating project completion through eliminating delays in the project development and delivery process, including reducing regulatory burdens and improving agencies' work practices." [FHWA, 2014b]

The most recent federal transportation legislation (as of the date of publication of this handbook) is the Fixing America's Surface Transportation (FAST) Act. This law reaffirmed the planning requirements of MAP-21 and added the following requirements to the metropolitan planning process.

- "Continue to require metropolitan transportation plans and transportation improvement programs (TIPs) to provide for facilities that enable an intermodal transportation system, including pedestrian and bicycle facilities. It adds to this list other facilities that support

intercity transportation (including intercity buses, intercity bus facilities, and commuter vanpool providers).
- Expand the scope of consideration of the metropolitan planning process to include: improving transportation system resiliency and reliability; reducing (or mitigating) the stormwater impacts of surface transportation; and enhancing travel and tourism. Specifically, it required the consideration of strategies to reduce the vulnerability of existing transportation infrastructure to natural disasters. [FHWA, 2016]
- Add public ports and certain private providers of transportation, including intercity bus operators and employer-based commuting programs to the list of interested parties that an MPO must provide with reasonable opportunity to comment on the transportation plan."

Given that transportation plays such a critical role in a nation's economy and in promoting the well-being of its citizens, it should be no surprise that transportation is part of many other legislative initiatives aimed at achieving nontransportation goals such as economic development and environmental quality. Again, it is beyond the scope of this handbook to identify all such laws. In terms of impact on transportation planning and project development, the most notable are the National Environmental Policy Act (NEPA), the Clean Air Act (and its amendments), and the Americans With Disabilities Act (ADA). [Gayle, 2009] Chapter 4 on environmental considerations in the planning process discusses these and other laws and regulations relating to environmental factors; chapter 12 and chapter 13 on transit planning and pedestrian and bicycle planning, respectively, describe ADA requirements for transit and pedestrian facilities; and chapter 15 and chapter 16 discuss the laws and regulations relating specifically to statewide and metropolitan transportation, respectively.

State governments also create and enforce laws relating to transportation (where not superseded by federal law). For example, a state can pass laws regulating the licensing and operations of trucks or other vehicles moving freight, but state laws cannot impede interstate commerce, which is protected by the Constitution. State laws are important in transportation for several reasons. First, they create the institutional structure for transportation planning at the state and, in many cases, metropolitan levels. That is, state DOTs and their roles and responsibilities are defined in state statutes, as are the roles and responsibilities of MPOs. Second, local units of government such as cities and counties are created by state governments. These local governments often cannot adopt laws and policies or raise taxes without enabling legislation from the state legislature. For example, in most states, a city cannot adopt a sales tax for transportation purposes without approval from the state. Third, state governments pass laws that can have significant impact on transportation planning. In Washington state and California, for example, state environmental laws require that statewide and metropolitan transportation plans undergo an environmental review to determine potential environmental consequences of the plan's proposed investment strategy. Finally, state governments establish their own sources of funding for transportation investment, which are even more important than federal sources for supporting a state's transportation system.

Similar to federal laws that recognize transportation's influential role in achieving nontransportation goals, other types of state-mandated planning often include transportation as a means of accomplishing program goals and objectives. Some examples of the linkage between transportation planning and other planning efforts are provided below to illustrate how transportation planning influences, and is influenced by, other planning activities.

Oregon: In many states, land use planning is the responsibility of local governments with only minimal guidance from state law. In 1973, the state of Oregon established the Land Conservation and Development Commission along with fairly rigorous (at least by the standards of most states) policy requirements for local planning. Subsequent goals adopted by the commission, which by reference have the force of law, cover numerous topics including the relationship between transportation and urbanization. The adopted transportation goal spells out the required content of transportation plans, while the urbanization goal includes adopting urban growth boundaries. In Oregon, state law clearly influences the range of actions to be considered in the transportation planning process. [Abbot, 2014]

New Hampshire: Transportation plans often demonstrate the need for future travel corridors in a metropolitan area or state, whether highway or transit. However, once a corridor is designated in a plan, developers may see it as a preferred development site because of improved access. If future rights of way are built upon, the construction of the planned facility will be more expensive because of higher land acquisition cost. The New Hampshire legislature passed a law permitting the commissioner of transportation to designate corridors for planning purposes that provides both funding flexibility and land use protection (called corridor preservation). [New Hampshire Statutes, 1993]

Georgia: Many states require local jurisdictions to conduct comprehensive planning and to prepare plans that foster orderly growth. Georgia's local comprehensive planning law requires the evaluation of the following transportation assets as part of a community's comprehensive plan. [Georgia DCA, 2013]

- Road network: Roads, highways, and bridges.
- Alternative modes: Bicycle, pedestrian facilities, public transportation, or other services for populations without automobiles.
- Parking: Areas with insufficient parking or inadequate parking facilities.
- Railroads, trucking, port facilities, and airports.
- Transportation policies, programs, and projects and their alignment with local land use development policies.

Many states have passed smart growth legislation whose purpose is to guide development in the state and in communities where transportation or other infrastructure already exists or where it can be provided through developer contributions. Chapter 3 describes smart growth efforts in more detail.

Local governments, such as counties, cities, towns, and municipalities, also pass laws to protect the health, safety, and general welfare of their citizens. Local governments can influence transportation planning through their control of local street systems as well as their legal responsibilities for land-use zoning. Zoning ordinances empower local governments to take actions that protect the health, safety, and general welfare of their populace. These local policy and regulatory roles are critical to metropolitan transportation planning because of the close linkage between transportation and land use. As comprehensive plans and zoning codes define the location of different land uses and the density of development, they create over time an urban form that places demands and constraints on the transportation system. In addition, the provision or improvements to the transportation system can influence where development occurs. If both do not proceed in a coordinated fashion, the respective decisions may not always be compatible.

Local governments use a number of legal tools to address traffic impacts, including access management regulations, Complete Street requirements, impact fees and adequate public facilities ordinances. Some notable examples include:

- *Access management* is a strategy to reduce the number of conflict points on arterial streets, thereby increasing both capacity and safety. It is applied primarily where there is continuous retail and commercial development along an arterial road, where the tendency is for each site to have its own driveway access points.
- *Adequate public facilities ordinances* were developed in response to the need for public agencies to provide infrastructure to accommodate the needs of private development. Such ordinances are used to assure that public schools, roads, sewers, police and rescue response times, and/or other infrastructure or services are "adequate" to support proposed new development. For example, large subdivisions were often built with the developer providing only the internal infrastructure. The presumption was that the local government, pleased with the addition to its property tax base, would solve any resulting problems of traffic congestion, overcrowded schools, lack of public parks, demands on sanitary sewers and treatment plants, and so forth. Local governments in growing regions came to understand that the cost of providing all of the supporting infrastructure and services could outweigh the tax benefits of the development. The response was adopted ordinances requiring developers either to demonstrate the availability of adequate public facilities or to build whatever may be necessary to accommodate the needs of the new residents.
- *Traffic or transportation impact fees* are used by governments to internalize the cost of transportation improvements associated with development proposals. Such fees are typically enabled by state law and created by local government ordinance. The revenue generated by the fee is used by the local government to defray the cost of off-site transportation improvements. This model is most often used in high-growth areas as a way to capture the cumulative impact of numerous individual site developments.

More is said about the tools available to local communities and their impact on transportation planning in chapter 3 on land use.

The preceding discussion focused on the U.S. policy and legal context for transportation planning. Other countries have similar structures establishing the legal foundation for planning activities (countries in the British Commonwealth, for example, have a long legacy of comprehensive planning legislation that has included transportation in significant ways). Transportation planning, no matter where practiced, reflects the institutional structure for such planning established by national, state/provincial, and local governments. In addition, transportation planning is influenced by the societal, economic, and technological factors that define the context within which transportation planning occurs. As such, it is important for transportation planners to think about those trends and the likely characteristics of the future that will influence the use and performance of the transportation system.

II. TRANSPORTATION SYSTEM CHARACTERISTICS

Several characteristics of the transportation system are measured and used in almost every transportation planning process. This section discusses five of these characteristics: functional classification, system extent, system usage, system performance/capacity, and system condition.

A. FUNCTIONAL CLASSIFICATION

Transportation system data are categorized in a variety of ways to allow transportation professionals to understand the performance of different components of the system for which they are responsible. System-level measures, such as crash rates, pavement condition levels and average travel time, provide a broad overview of how the system is performing, and provide a context for strategic decisions about where additional investment at the program level might be necessary. A more detailed examination of the data, however, could be useful in understanding where problems exist and what types of strategies might be appropriate. For example, crash rates and the types of crashes occurring on interstate highways are very different from those occurring on rural two-lane highways. Performance characteristics for bus services are very different from those for rail lines. To provide more useful information about transportation system performance, transportation engineers and planners categorize data using different classification schemes.

A basic characterization of the road network used in many parts of the world is to describe different road segments by the function they serve in the network. Roads that are high on the

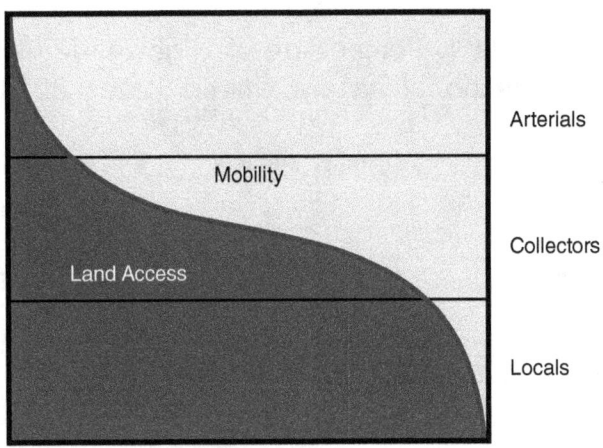

Figure 2. Relationship Between Road Classification and Road Function.
Source: Federal Highway Administration, *Our Nation's Highways 2011* http://www.fhwa.dot.gov/policyinformation/pubs/hf/pl11028/onh2011.pdf

functional classification scale provide mobility, while roads with lower classifications serve an accessibility role (see Figure 1). Typical road functional classifications include:

Interstates are highest level of arterials with the longest uninterrupted distances and the highest speeds.

Other Arterials include other forms of limited access roads as well as connections to major urbanized areas and tie the national defense system (the interstates) to the cities and industrial centers.

Collectors involve both land access and traffic circulation. They link local roads to arterials and are generally lower-speed facilities.

Local Roads primarily serve the adjacent land use with access to higher-order roads.

In 2013, there were just over 4 million miles of road in the United States. [BTS, 2015] The availability and use of these roads are shown by functional class in Table 1. As can be seen, the

Table 1. Percentage of Highway Miles, Bridges, and Vehicle Miles Traveled by Functional System, United States, 2013 (2015 for Bridges)

Functional System	Miles	Vehicle Miles Traveled	Bridges
Rural Areas			
Interstate	0.7%	7.8%	4.1%
Other freeway and expressway	0.1	0.7	NA[a]
Other principal arterial	2.2	6.5	6.0
Minor arterial	3.2	4.8	6.2
Major collector	10.1	5.6	15.1
Minor collector	6.4	1.8	7.8
Local	48.7	4.3	33.2
Subtotal Rural	71.4	31.5	72.4
Urban Areas			
Interstate	0.4%	16.9%	5.2%
Other freeway and expressway	0.3	7.5	3.4
Other principal arterial	1.6	15.5	4.8
Minor arterial	2.7	12.8	5.0
Major collector	2.9	6.1	3.7
Minor collector	0.1	0.2	NA[a]
Local	20.6	9.5	5.5
Subtotal urban	28.6	68.5	27.6
Total	100.0	100.0	100.0

[a] Bridges on rural other freeway and expressway included under rural other principal arterial; bridges on urban minor collector included under urban major collector

Source: FHWA, 2015

higher classified roads, that is, the interstates and arterials, constitute 11.2 percent of the nation's road mileage, but 71.9 percent of the vehicle miles traveled (out of a total 2.97 trillion miles).

It should be noted that this traditional way of classifying the role of transportation facilities has been criticized because of its focus on the role of individual facilities in the transportation system, rather than the role they play in the surrounding community. This concept has also been found in design approaches called *context-sensitive solutions (CSS)* and *Complete Streets*, which encourage road designs that better "fit" into the community and natural environment. Chapter 3 on land use and urban design and chapter 9 on road and highway planning discuss both concepts in more detail.

B. SYSTEM EXTENT

The extent of a transportation system relates to the size or number of assets that compose that system. For example, a state or metropolitan

Table 2. Extent of the U.S. Transportation System

Mode	Components
Highway	
Public road miles (as of 2013)	4,115,462
Public road lane–miles (as of 2013)	8,656,070
Bridges (as of 2014)	610,749
Air (as of 2014)	
Total number of airports	19,299
General aviation airports	18,762
Rail (as of 2014)	
Class I freight railroad track miles[a]	95,235
Amtrak (passenger) track miles[b]	21,356
Public transit (as of 2013)	
Commuter rail track miles	7,731
Heavy rail track miles	1,622
Light rail track miles[c]	1,836
Water (as of 2013)	
Miles of navigable waterways	25,000
Pipeline	
Miles of gas pipeline	2,149,299
Miles of oil pipeline	19,417
Trade Gateways	
Number of gateways handling $50 billion or more of international trade	21

[a] Includes 561 miles of the U.S. Class I freight railroad system owned by Canadian railroads.
[b] Approximately 97 percent of the trackage on which Amtrak operates is owned by other railroads.
[c] Includes directional route-miles on exclusive right-of-way, controlled right-of-way, and mixed traffic.

Source: Bureau of Transportation Statistics. 2015b.

area might have *x* miles of interstate highways, *y* number of transit vehicles, and *z* number of airports. This information, which is often incorporated into an *inventory* database, is used to compare one system to another and to calculate productivity factors for agency operations (such as dollars expended per lane-mile of major arterial road or per bus seat-mile). The inventory is also used to define ownership of the different transportation assets. Table 2 shows the extent of the U.S. transportation system.

Statistics on the extent of state road networks can be found in the Federal Highway Administration's (FHWA) *Highway Statistics* series. Similar types of information for transit systems can be found in the Federal Transit Administration's (FTA) National Transit Database (NTD). Other statistics on the U.S. transportation system can be found at the Bureau of

Transportation Statistics (BTS) website, www.bts.gov, and in Canada at the website for Statistics Canada, http://www5.statcan.gc.ca/subject-sujet/theme-theme.action?pid=4006&lang=eng&more=0.

C. SYSTEM USE

An important indicator of the value of a transportation system is how much it is used. Existing usage is also the baseline for predicting future system use. Thus, transportation planners spend considerable effort in determining the current travel volumes on transportation systems. Such use is particularly impressive for the U.S. road network. In 2013 an estimated 2.9 trillion vehicle-miles were traveled on the U.S. road network. [BTS, 2015a] This was an approximate 38 percent increase from the level estimated in 1990. The data show that urban vehicle-miles traveled (VMT) outpaced those for rural highways, which is a result of both the substantial growth in urban population during this time period and the redesignation of urban area boundaries to place more road mileage within urban areas. However, since the early 2000s, the national VMT has declined and stabilized, as shown in Figure 2. The reasons for this include the dampening effect on travel of a national economic recession, more efficient travel patterns, and more urban travelers who use either other modes or have shorter trips. For a good discussion of the impact of an economic recession on travel, see [BTS, 2015b].

With regard to passenger trips, over 4.9 trillion passenger-miles (a person traveling one mile on a mode of transportation) occurred in 2013 on the U.S. transportation network: 4 billion by cars and trucks, 590 billion via airplane, 56.5 billion via passenger transit and intercity bus systems and 7.3 billion on Amtrak (the U.S. national rail service). [BTS, 2015b] Approximately 5.9 trillion ton-miles of freight (one ton moving one mile) moved on the U.S. freight system in 2011, with 2.6 trillion moving by truck, 1.7 trillion by rail, 1 trillion by pipeline, 500 billion by domestic water transportation, and 12 billion ton-miles by aviation. [BTS, 2015b]

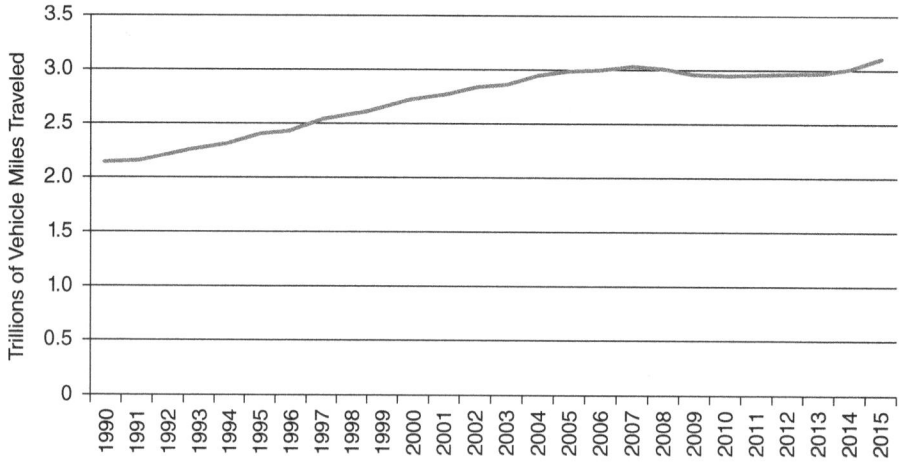

Figure 2. Highway Travel in the United States, 1990–2015
Source: BTS, 2015a

Figure 3 shows the number of unlinked transit trips in the United States from 1970 to 2012. (Unlinked trips are individual trips on a trip segment. For example, a bus trip that transfers to another bus or a rail trip would be two unlinked trips). As seen in this figure, beginning in the mid-1990s, transit ridership in the United States has begun to increase after years of declining or relatively flat growth. From 1995 to 2009, the percent of U.S. daily trips occurring on bus transit rose from 3.0 percent to 3.3 percent, with rail staying at 0.6 percent (motor vehicle trips accounted for 83.4 percent of daily travel). [BTS, 2015] With respect to walking and bicycling, the percent of U.S. daily travel for these modes rose from 5.5 percent in 1995 to 10.4 percent in 2009 for walking and from 0.9 percent to 1.0 percent for bicycling over the same time period.

The percent of daily travel by mode will vary by trip purpose and by time of day. Figure 4 shows the U.S. mode share for commute trips in 2013. As can be seen, the mode share percentages for the commute trip are different than that described above for all trips taken during the day.

D. SYSTEM PERFORMANCE

Transportation system performance is one of the most visible and important transportation system characteristics to local decision makers and the general public. Traffic congestion and traffic delays have engaged—and will likely continue to involve—transportation planners and engineers in discussions and debates about how transportation problems can be solved. Several characteristics of system performance, including mobility and accessibility, are key decision criteria and are evaluated and monitored by transportation agencies.

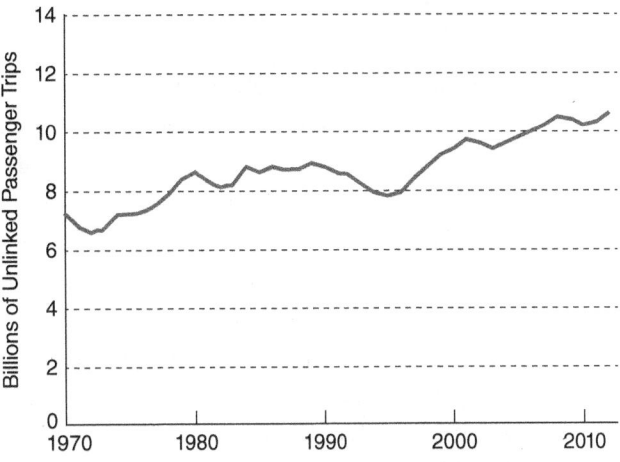

Figure 3. Unlinked Passenger Transit Trips, United States, 1970–2012
Source: BTS, 2015

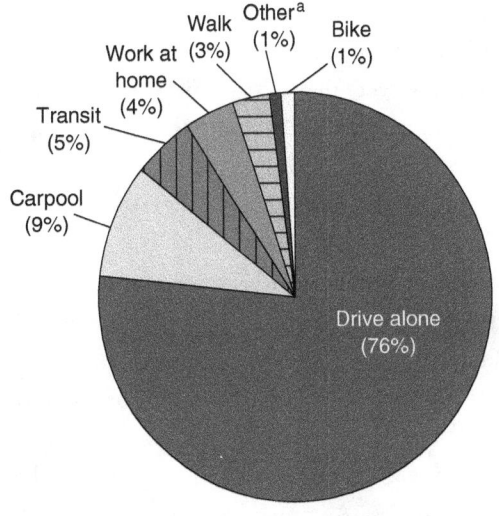

Figure 4. Commute Mode Share, United States, 2013

[a] Includes motorcycle, taxi, and other means

Notes: Percents do not add up to 100 due to rounding. The *American Community Survey* asks for the mode usually used by the respondents to get to work.

For more than one mode of transportation, respondents select the mode used for most of the distance.

Source: U.S. Department of Commerce, U.S. Census Bureau, American Community Survey, 1-Year Estimates, available at www.census.gov/acs as of September 2014.

1. MOBILITY

Mobility reflects those travel conditions associated with the ability to travel, such as average speed, delay, congestion levels, and the availability of modal options. Mobility is provided by multiple modes, including many trips that require the use of more than one. For example, driving a car to a work place or school usually includes a walk trip at either end. Many transit trips also include not only walk trips but often transfers to other transit modes. Mobility is thus inherently a part of a multimodal measure of system performance. However, there are very few instances in practice where multimodal measures of mobility have been developed; instead, measures of the individual modal components of a trip are usually reported by planners, for example, levels of congestion on the road network or transit line. The following sections discuss system performance from a modal perspective. The reader should be aware, however, that a true measure of system performance should include the performance contribution from multiple modes.

Road Mobility. The Texas A&M Transportation Institute (TTI) and INRIX produce information biennially on levels of congestion on the U.S. road system. An interesting aspect of the *Urban Mobility Report* is that it represents a combination of data sources, including INRIX data, which are collected via global positioning system (GPS) probe vehicles. As noted in the preface to the report, this represents, "hundreds of speed data points on almost every mile of major road in urban America for almost every 15-minute period of the average day of the week. For the congestion analyst, this means 900 million speeds on 1.3 million miles of U.S. streets and highways."

Figure 5 shows data from the Institute's *Urban Mobility Report 2015*. [Schrank et al., 2015] According to the report, "average daily

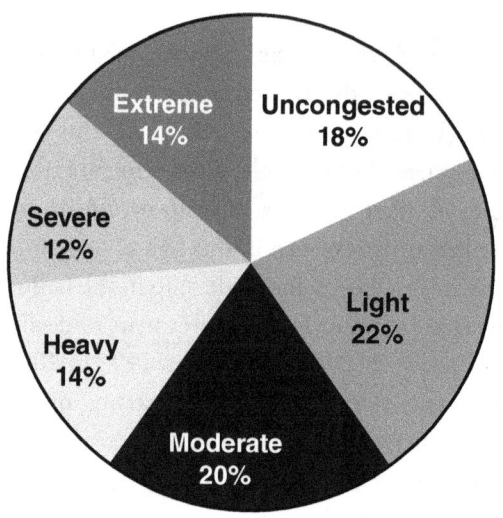

Figure 5. Vehicle Travel in Congestion Conditions, United States, 2014
Source: Schrank et al., 2015, Reproduced with permission of the Texas A&M Transportation Institute.

percent of vehicle miles traveled (VMT) under congested conditions" is an indicator of the portion of daily traffic on freeways and other principal arterials in an urbanized area that moves at less than free-flow speeds. As shown in the figure, approximately 40 percent of urban travel in the United States in 2014 occurred in extreme, severe, or heavy congested conditions.

Figure 6 shows that the change in the hours of delay per automobile commuter has varied by urbanized area size. In areas with over one million persons, 2014 auto commuters experienced an average of 63 hours of extra travel time, a road network that was congested for 6 hours of the average weekday, and experienced an average congestion "cost" of $1,440 (primarily the value of time lost). Even in small and medium-sized urbanized areas, the hours of delay have increased (small urbanized areas are those with a population less than 500,000; medium areas have a population between 500,000 and 999,999; large areas have a population between 1 and 3 million; and very large areas have above 3 million in population). Of course, individual urbanized areas will experience different trends. It is interesting to note that while the hours of delay per automobile commuter increased from 18 to 37 hours between 1982 to 2000, the period from 2000 to 2014 saw this average stabilizing between 40 and 42 hours, primarily due to the impact of an economic recession. [Schrank et al., 2015, Exhibit 2] The cost of congestion, estimated as part of the TTI *Urban Mobility* report, consists primarily of travel time delays, crashes, and fuel. This estimated cost rose from a national total of $24.4 billion in 1982 to $160 billion in 2014 (in $2014).

The *Urban Mobility Report* also measures the *Travel Time Index (TTI)*, a common metric for congested networks used in many planning studies, especially in larger urban areas. The TTI is the ratio of existing motor vehicle trip travel time to the travel time under free-flow conditions. Thus, a TTI value of 1.18 means that travelers take 18 percent (1.18–1.00) more time to travel than a similar trip with no delays. The national TTI value has increased from 1.07 in 1982 to 1.22 in 2014. Not surprisingly, TTI values in 2014 varied by urban area size: very large urban areas (15 total), 1.32; large urban areas (31 total), 1.23; 33 medium urban areas, 1.18; and small urban areas (22 total), 1.14. [Schrank et al., 2015]

Although travel time has historically been the measure of most interest to transportation planners and system operators, there has been a recent shift in interest from absolute travel time toward travel time reliability. The 2015 *Urban Mobility Report* reported on a measure of reliability called the *Planning Time Index (PTI)*. The PTI is "based on the idea that travelers would want to be on time for an important trip 19 out of 20 times; so one would be late only one day per month (on time for 19 out of 20 work days each month)." [Schrank et al., 2015] A PTI value

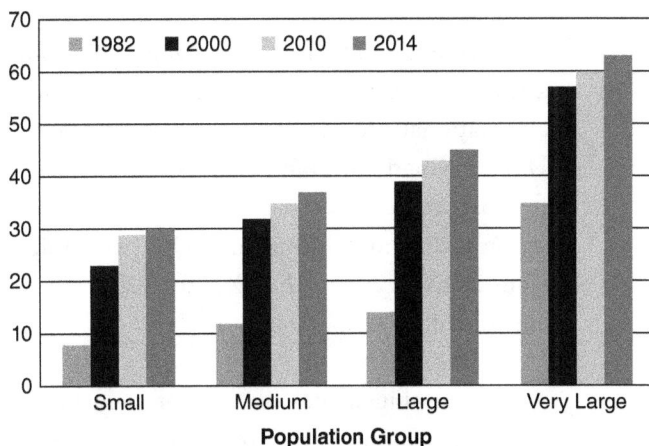

Small = less than 500,000
Medium = 500,000 to 1 million
Large = 1 million to 3 million
Very Large = more than 3 million

Figure 6. U.S. Congestion Conditions by Year, by Metropolitan Area Size
Source: Schrank et al., 2015, Reproduced with permission of the Texas A&M Transportation Institute.

of 3.00 indicates that a traveler should allow 60 minutes to make an important trip that takes 20 minutes in uncongested traffic (3 × 20). In essence, the 19th worst commute is affected by crashes, weather, special events, and other causes of unreliable travel and can be improved by a range of transportation improvement strategies. Similar to the TTI, the values of PTI vary by size of urban area. Very large urban area freeways had an average PTI value of 3.06 (top three areas were Los Angeles 3.75; Washington, D.C. 3.48; and Seattle 3.41); large urban area freeways had an average of 2.46 (top three areas were Portland, Oregon, 3.27; San Jose, California, 3.24; and Riverside/San Bernardino, California, 3.21); medium-sized urban area freeways had an average of 2.08 (top three areas were New Orleans, 3.46; Bridgeport/Stamford, Connecticut, 3.32; and Baton Rouge, Louisiana, 2.80); and small urban area freeways had an average of 1.76 (top three areas were Boulder, Colorado, 2.48; Stockton, California, 2.27; and Anchorage, Alaska, 2.26).

A recent study forecasts congestion and associated costs for individual households and national economies in the United States, United Kingdom, France, and Germany. The forecasts were based on forecasted levels of urbanization and increased GDP per capita from 2013 to 2030. [INRIX, 2015] The study concluded:

- The combined annual cost of congestion in these countries is expected to increase to $293.1 billion by 2030, an estimated 50 percent increase from 2013.
- The cumulative cost of congestion for the countries combined is estimated to be $4.4 trillion.
- The overall economic impact is greatest in the United States where the estimated cumulative cost of traffic congestion by 2030 is $2.8 trillion.
- The UK (at 66 percent) and London (at 71 percent) will see the greatest annual rise in the cost of congestion by 2030, mainly as a result of seeing the highest increase in urbanization.
- Traffic congestion costs drivers $1,740 in 2014 on average across the four countries. This number is expected to grow more than 60 percent to $2,902 annually by 2030.

Transit Mobility. Data relating to transit system performance in the United States are collected by transit agencies and reported to the National Transit Database (NTD), which is managed by the U.S. Federal Transit Administration (FTA). Average transit vehicle operating speed, an approximate measure of the speed experienced by transit riders, varies by transit mode. In 2010, the average operating speed for heavy rail was 20.2 mph (32.5 kph); for light rail, 15.0 mph (24.1 kph); and for bus, 12.5 mph (20.1 kph). [FHWA, 2013] According to the 2009 National Household Travel Survey (NHTS), 49 percent of all passengers who ride transit wait for 5 minutes or less for a vehicle to arrive, and 75 percent wait 10 minutes or less.

In Canada, the average transit commute travel time by public transit is 44 minutes, varying from 39 minutes in Montreal to 49 minutes in Toronto. Not surprisingly, commute times for public transit for commute trips varies significantly by the residential density of the workers' home neighborhood. ... 51 minutes for the lowest residential density to 36 minutes for the highest residential density. [Turcotte, 2011]

More meaningful transit performance data is collected by transit agencies so as to provide the best service to their customers. For example, on-time performance is a widely used metric that provides customers with a sense of service reliability. Other measures such as dollar expended per revenue mile, farebox recovery, and percent of the population within 1/2 mile of transit service are used to provide a broader perspective on the effectiveness of the transit system overall. Additional information on transit system performance is provided in chapter 12 on transit planning.

2. ACCESSIBILITY

Whereas mobility performance reflects the ease with which travelers can make a trip, accessibility relates to a traveler's ability to reach a destination, and includes such measures as percent of employment within a certain distance of a transit station. In broad terms, mobility is more directly influenced by physical characteristics of the infrastructure and operating characteristics of the system. For example, an interstate highway may provide great mobility, but limited accessibility to adjacent land uses, while a driveway to an office building provides excellent accessibility to that facility, but limited mobility. Accessibility is a function of how a transportation network is structured, but it also depends on land use patterns, available modes, and geographic area. When land is developed with greater density and multiple land uses are clustered together, accessibility to goods and services may be enhanced. In a suburban setting, a combination of walking, driving, riding transit, and using parking facilities may be needed to accomplish a set of tasks or errands. In a dense urban environment with mixed land uses clustered together, it might be possible to reach all of the desired destinations by walking or riding a bus (see chapter 19 on site planning and traffic impact analysis).

Moving people is an important goal of most transportation agencies. In an urban environment, however, restricting access to individual properties may be necessary to allow for the smooth, uninterrupted flow of traffic on the adjacent roads (called access management, see chapters 3 and 19). Accessibility determines the adequacy of the transportation system and the value to related activities, such as commerce, employment, recreation, and overall quality of life. A balance between mobility and accessibility is often necessary to achieve community goals.

3. SAFETY

Transportation safety is often identified as the most important goal of transportation agencies. Therefore, it is monitored by agencies at the national, state/provincial, and local levels. Four important measures are often used to monitor the trends in transportation safety: number of fatalities, number of injuries, fatalities per100 million vehicle miles traveled (MVMT), and injuries per 100 million vehicle miles traveled. The latter two are called fatality and injury rates, and reflect the amount of exposure travelers will have to the transportation system itself. Note that in some cases, the measures could lead to different conclusions. For example, the number of fatal crashes might increase over a particular time period, but because the number of vehicle miles traveled increased at a proportionately higher percentage, the fatality rate might decrease. So, one indicator suggests that the safety problem has become worse, and the other shows improvement.

Table 3 shows the change in crash and injury statistics in the United States from 2002 to 2013. As shown, the trend in every category (except in public transit, motorcyclists, and pedacyclists) has been to fewer fatalities. With respect to injuries, the largest increases have occurred for motorcyclists and transit rail (most likely because of the opening of new services).

Road Safety. As noted earlier, there is a difference between fatalities and injuries and fatality and injury rates. Just as the number of fatalities and injuries has declined over the past 10 years, so too has the fatality rate. In 1995, the fatality rate per 100 million VMT was 1.73, which dropped to 1.09 in 2013. [Insurance Institute for Highway Safety, 2015] This decrease in rate was due to an increase in VMT as well as an increase in seatbelt use and vehicle safety improvements. Fatality rates are generally lower in urban areas than rural areas and for higher functional systems than lower functional systems. For example in 2010, the fatality rate per 100 million vehicle miles traveled was 2.5 times higher in rural areas than in urban areas (1.83 and 0.73, respectively).

Chapter 23 on safety provides more information on the current performance of the transportation system. From a planning perspective, it is important to note where crashes occur (for example, approximately 40 percent of the total number of crashes in any given year occur at intersections), who is involved in crashes (for example, males aged 20–24 and 85 and older had the highest rates of crash deaths), and the cause of crashes (for example, speeding has been

Table 3. Transportation Fatalities and Injuries, United States, 2002 and 2013

	2002		2013	
Mode	Fatalities	Injuries	Fatalities	Injuries
Aviation	616	337	429	250
Highway	43,005	2,925,758	32,719	2,313,000
Car occupants	20,569	1,804,788	11,977	1,296,000
Motorcyclists	3,270	64,713	4,668	88,000
Light truck occupants	12,274	879,338	9,155	750,000
Heavy truck occupants	689	26,242	691	24,000
Bus occupants	45	18,819	48	13,000
Pedestrians	4,851	70,664	4,735	66,000
Pedacyclists	665	48,011	743	48,000
Other	642	13,182	702	16,000
Rail Crashes With Cars				
Highway/road crossings	357	999	231	972
Transit (as of 2012)				
Bus	78	11,995	97	11,872
Light rail	13	557	45	888
Heavy rail	73	4,806	102	7,212
Commuter rail	116	1,483	112	1,575
Water	863	4,856	642	3,432

Source: BTS, 2015b

a factor in about 30 percent of crash deaths since 2004).

Good sources for transportation safety statistics include:

- Insurance Institute for Highway Safety (http://www.iihs.org/iihs/topics/t/general-statistics/fatalityfacts/overview-of-fatality-facts/2013#Trends).
- National Highway Traffic Safety Administration (http://www.nhtsa.gov/NCSA).
- U.S. Census (http://www.census.gov/compendia/statab/cats/transportation/motor_vehicle_accidents_and_fatalities.html).

Transit Safety. For transit systems, the number of fatalities increased from 280 in 2002 to 356 in 2012, and fell from 0.66 per 100 million person-miles traveled (PMT) in 2002 to 0.54 per 100 million PMT in 2012. Fatalities, weighted by PMT, are lowest for motorbuses and heavy rail systems. Fatality rates for commuter and light rail are, on average, higher than fatality rates for heavy rail, most likely because of the at-grade road crossings that often characterize these services. Incidents (safety and security combined) and injuries per 100 million PMT declined for all transit modes from 2002 to 2012. Incidents and injuries, when weighted by PMT, are consistently lowest for commuter rail and highest for demand-responsive systems.

Other Countries. Countries with different legal requirements and enforcement strategies have a very different safety record than the United States. Countries like Australia, Denmark, England, and Sweden have applied very aggressive enforcement strategies and as a result have reduced their fatality levels by more than 50 percent. In contrast, many developing countries experience skyrocketing fatality rates as automobile ownership increases dramatically and as motor vehicle–based mobility has replaced slower modes of transportation. See chapter 23 for further discussion on transportation safety.

4. SYSTEM CONDITION

A deteriorating physical condition of transportation system assets is one of the significant challenges facing transportation systems in many countries. In many developed countries, for example, much of the highway and transit infrastructure was built 40 to 50 years ago and is nearing the end of its useful life. Most of the transportation plans in U.S. metropolitan areas have the majority of investment targeted at preserving infrastructure. Data on the condition of transportation infrastructure are critical for identifying investment priorities, such as needs related to deteriorating pavement and bridge conditions (see chapter 9 on road and highway planning).

Figure 7 shows the percentage of VMT on the National Highway System (higher functionally classified roads) by pavement rated as "good," "acceptable," and "not acceptable" from 2002 to 2010. As seen, the percent of VMT with "good" ride quality increased between 2002 and 2010, primarily because of improved pavements on rural interstates. For urban areas, the percent of "good" ride quality road miles declined, in this case primarily because of deteriorating pavement conditions on lower functionally classified roads. When weighted by VMT, the percentage of roads with "good" ride quality increased in both urban and rural areas, again because of pavement improvements in the higher functionally classified roads that carry more traffic.

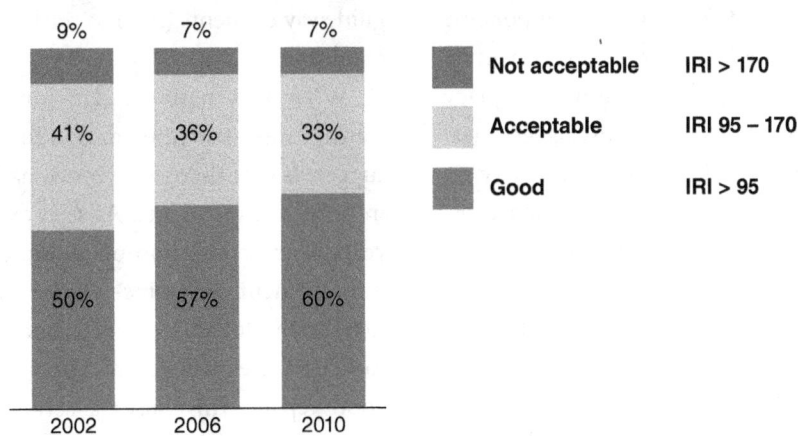

Figure 7. Pavement Condition on the National Highway System, United States, 2002–2010
Source: FHWA, 2013a

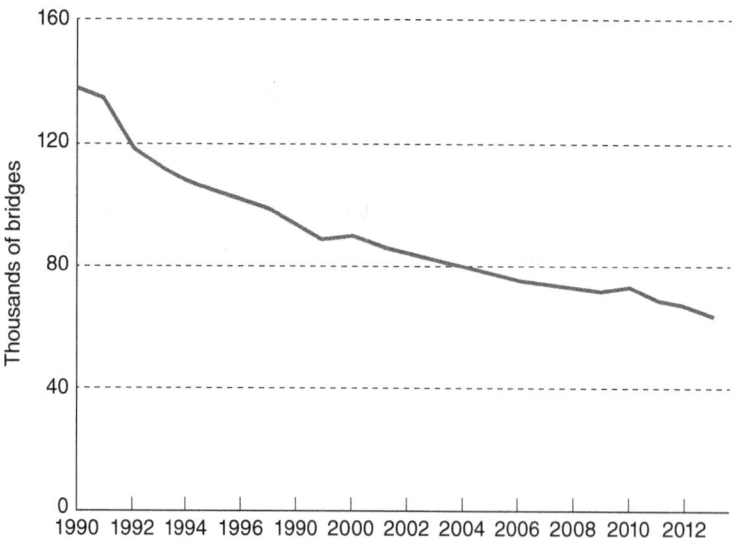

Figure 8. Structurally Deficient Bridges, United States, 1990–2013
Source: FHWA, 2013a

Figure 8 shows the change in structurally deficient bridges in the United States between 1990 and 2013. The bridge assessment process (that is, identifying those bridges that are structurally deficient and/or functionally obsolete) is based on load-carrying capacity, deck geometry, clearances, waterway adequacy, and approach roadway alignment. As noted by FHWA, "structural assessments" together with ratings of the physical condition of key bridge components determine whether a bridge should be classified as "structurally deficient." Functional adequacy is assessed by comparing the existing geometric configurations and design load-carrying capacities to current standards and demands. Disparities between the actual and preferred configurations are used to determine whether a bridge should be classified as "functionally obsolete" (see chapter 9 on road and highway planning). [FHWA, 2013a]

With respect to transit, according to the U. S. DOT's *2013 Condition and Performance Report to Congress*, the condition of the nation's urban bus fleet was at the bottom of the "adequate" rating in 2010, with an average vehicle age of 6.1 years. The average condition of rail vehicles was slightly better, but with an average age of 18.9 years. Of some concern, close to 2,000 rail vehicles exceeded 35 years in age. The report also noted that 19 percent of train communications systems, train control systems, and traction power systems were in "poor" condition, and 17 percent of rail guideway elements (such as track) were in "poor" condition.

What this national data on highway and transit infrastructure and vehicle condition suggest is that there is a serious national backlog in needed investments. As seen over the past 10 years in transportation plans and transportation improvement programs, a large share of future investment dollars is going to be allocated simply to keep the existing infrastructure in a state-of-good repair. This raises a serious question of where the dollars are going to come from to invest in new projects (see chapter 5 on transportation finance and funding).

III. URBAN TRAVEL CHARACTERISTICS

Urban travel and trip patterns are influenced by numerous factors. The most important patterns relate to the availability and costs (real and perceived) of different modes of transportation. Thus, for example, if a traveler has an option of reaching a destination by driving, taking a bus, or ridesharing, the decision of which to choose depends on that traveler's perception of how much time each will take, how much it costs, how comfortable and safe it is, and what other activities the traveler might want to accomplish during the trip. The trip patterns resulting from the collective trip-making decisions of an urban area's population are also influenced by population demographics, land-use patterns in the metropolitan area, and the travel options that are available for each type of land use.

Table 4 shows how some of the key factors that influence travel behavior have changed since 1969. Each of these factors is an important predictor of some aspect of travel behavior. The following sections present data on these and other characteristics of urban travel and the factors influencing it. It should be noted that much of this data was obtained years ago; for example, much of the travel behavior data is collected by the decennial census, thus reflecting travel behavior and transportation system performance and cost characteristics facing travelers at that point in time. Alan Pisarski has developed a report over the past two decades entitled, *Commuting in America*, largely based on an analysis of the latest Census information. This report series has become an important "big picture" study of the factors that affect commuting in the United States—see http://traveltrends.transportation.org/Pages/default.aspx for the most up-to-date information. Much of the information found in the following sections comes from this document.

Although these data are important for understanding historic patterns in travel behavior, they should not necessarily be viewed as a picture of what behavior might be today or certainly what future behavior might look like. Fuel cost, for example, has been historically low in the United States, which has undoubtedly contributed to the high automobile mode share seen in U.S. urban areas. If fuel costs were to increase significantly, it is likely that some travel behavior would change, and if the cost of energy continued to stay high over the longer term, land-use patterns (and the corresponding effect on travel) might also

Table 4. Change in Factors Influencing Vehicle Travel, United States, 1969–2009

	1969	2009
Total number of drivers	100 million	200 million
Average vehicles per licensed driver	0.7	1.1
Average daily vehicle trips per driver	2.3	3.3
Average daily person miles per household	61.6	95.5
Average daily vehicle miles per household	34.0	58.1
Average household size	3.2	2.6
Percent single-person households	13%	27%

Source: FHWA, 2013b

change. Economic conditions are another strong influence on travel behavior—during economic recessions, traveling declines as more people are without jobs and fewer discretionary trips are taken in order to minimize household costs.

A. POPULATION CHARACTERISTICS

Urban travel is heavily influenced by the demographic characteristics of the traveling population. Thus, not surprisingly, transportation planning relies heavily on credible population and employment forecasts. Fifty years ago, the average U.S. household consisted of two young to middle-aged, English-speaking parents, two children, a single wage earner, and minimal disposable income. Today, U.S. households exhibit a range of characteristics, including single adults with no children, many non-English-speaking adults, many older heads of household, and many two-career households of younger adults with substantial disposable income. These characteristics strongly influence where people live, the types of jobs they have, and how time is spent outside the household. All of these activities affect travel behavior.

In the United States and in many other countries, the census is a major source of data on population characteristics. The U.S. Census Bureau provides numerous single-variable tables at different geographic levels, and as well provides special tabulations of key variable relationships (see http://factfinder.census.gov). For many planning efforts, such as establishing the relationships among the variables that influence travel decisions, the Bureau provides public use microdata sample (PUMS) datasets. According to Tierney, PUMS is used by many state DOTs and MPOs for the following reasons:

1. Developing cross-tabulations of variables not readily available from for other sources especially analyses that examine population characteristics of special subpopulations (for example, members of ethnic groups, people of certain ancestries, group quarters residents, or bicycle commuters).
2. Developing cross-tabulations of variables that might already be available to transportation planners, but can now be done with more currency. PUMS data are available on an ongoing basis and thus the most recent data can be used for cross tabulations.
3. Conducting disaggregate analyses at the household- or person-level to develop models relying on the inter-relationships among household and person characteristics. PUMS allows the planner to identify variable relationships at the housing unit and person level.
4. Comparing different jurisdictions and regions, PUMS provides common data sets for all regions of the country, which thus allows consistent comparisons.
5. Comparing relationships over time—PUMS data can be used to track changes in housing and person characteristics and changes in the interrelationships between these characteristics over time.
6. Validating other data sources—PUMS data can be used to check relationships based on other data sources, such as travel surveys, demographic estimates, and modeling results. [Tierney, 2012]

The census is an important source of demographic and household data and thus transportation planners should be familiar with how such data is accessed and utilized.

1. Population Growth

Estimating the number of people who will be living, shopping, or working in a study area, usually at some target year (for example, 25 years from today), is often a starting point for many planning studies. The census in most countries is an excellent source of socio-demographic statistics describing national, state, and metropolitan area trends (for the United States, see www.census.gov).

At a national level, the U.S. population is expected to grow over the next 50 years. The current U.S. population is just over 320 million (2015), with a growth of approximately 25 to 30 million each decade. Over the past two decades, substantial immigration to the United States, which is expected to continue albeit at slower rates than historically, has significantly increased the population beyond what would have occurred through natural birth/death rates. Many of these immigrants are 25 to 45 years old and seek jobs, thus immediately becoming part of the commute travel market. Although the U.S. population as a whole is increasing, some regions or communities are expected to grow, while others are expected to lose population. Thus, it is important for every transportation planning study to obtain the latest information on expected population growth or decline in the study area.

The level of population growth is not the only population-related variable used by transportation planners. Another important characteristic is the age distribution of this population. For example, between 2000 and 2010, those older than 55 continuing to work grew by more than 60.8 percent, while the actual numbers of individuals over 55 grew by only 12 percent. This is an important phenomenon because the number of individuals 55 or older will be 28.7 percent of the population by 2020. The number of individuals in the labor force who are 65 years or older is expected to grow 75 percent by 2020, while the number of individuals in the workforce who are 25 to 54 is only expected to grow by 2 percent. In 2016, one-third of the total U.S. workforce is 50 years or older—a group that may number 115 million by 2020. The extent to which many in this age group continue to work will have important implications for transportation.

2. Household Characteristics and Vehicle Availability

The household is an important variable in transportation planning because many modeling tools use household characteristics to predict future travel. For example, households with different numbers of workers, automobiles, and/or children will exhibit differences in daily travel behavior. Many data sources, such as those from the U.S. Census, produce and report their information based on households.

As indicated in Table 4, the number of persons per household has declined dramatically since 1960, while at the same time the number of households has greatly increased. The number of households has grown at twice the rate of population during the past 40 years, with many of these households being single adults, single parents, elderly, or young childless couples.

Figure 9 shows the relationship between households and automobile ownership; the largest shares of households without cars are renters. Figure 9 suggests that the percentage of households having a set number of vehicles seems to have stabilized with approximately 38 percent of the U.S. households having two cars, 35 percent having one, 17 percent having three or more, and 10 percent having no vehicles (New York City accounts for 20 percent of the U.S. households without vehicles).

Figure 10 illustrates two characteristics of the U.S. population that have an important influence on mode choice. First, the percentage of older Americans having a driver's license has historically been much lower than that for those younger. This, however, is likely to

ESSENTIAL READINGS IN URBAN PLANNING

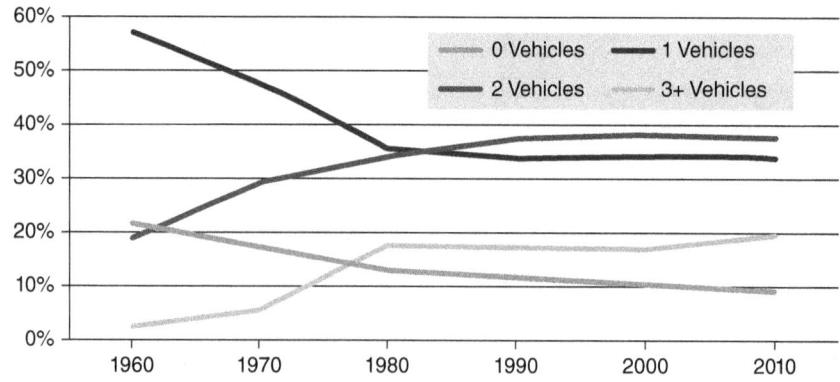

Figure 9. Percentage of Households by Number of Vehicles Owned, United States, 1960 to 2010
Source: AASHTO, 2013a, Reproduced with permission of AASHTO.

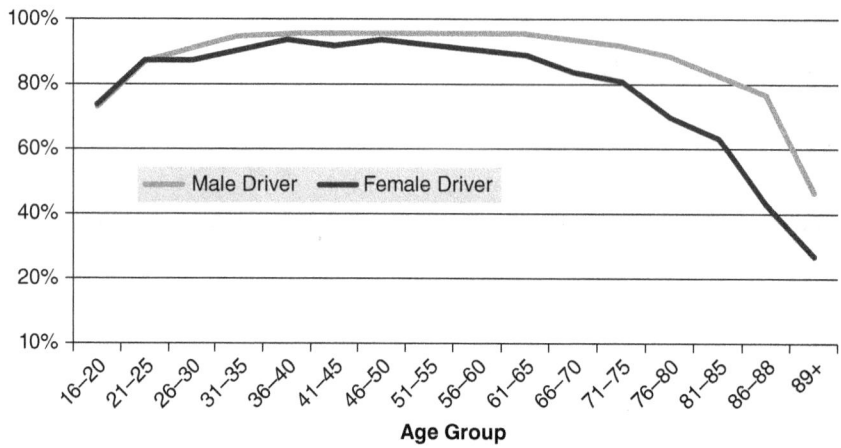

Figure 10. Persons Ages 16+ with Driver's Licenses, United States
Source: AASHTO, 2013a, Reproduced with permission of AASHTO.

change over time as the younger drivers grow older. Second, most Americans in the 16 to 50 age group have a driver's license, although male drivers have a higher rate of licensure than females.

3. Spatial Distribution of Growth

More than 200 regions in the United States are classified as large metropolitan statistical areas (MSAs). These represent the largest of the nation's urban areas and have populations exceeding 250,000. From 2000 to 2010, the rate of growth in MSAs was mostly in the double digits, with many areas experiencing growth exceeding 20 percent. Some achieved growth rates in excess of 50 percent (see the U.S. Bureau of the Census website for current growth rate data for MSAs, www.census.gov).

One of the defining trends during the past 50 years in the United States and in many other countries has been the rapid population and employment growth in the suburbs. Prior to 1960, the majority of the U.S. population lived in nonmetropolitan areas with the suburbs of metropolitan areas having the smallest percentage of the population. By 2000 this ratio was reversed, with approximately 50 percent of the U.S. population living in the suburbs.

THE TRANSPORTATION PLANNING HANDBOOK

Table 5. U.S. Population Trends by Geographic Area

	1990			2000			2010		
	Count (millions)	% of U.S. Total	% of Metro Total	Count (millions)	% of U.S. Total	% of Metro Total	Count (millions)	% of U.S. Total	% of Metro Total
Total Population	248.7	-	-	281.4	-	-	308.7	-	-
Living in Metro Areas	198.2	79.7%	-	232.6	82.7%	-	262.5	85.0%	-
Living in Central Cities	65.8	26.5%	33.2%	70.3	25.0%	30.2%	75.3	24.4%	28.7%
Living in Other Principal Cities	12.9	5.2%	6.5%	23.6	8.4%	10.1%	24.1	7.8%	9.2%
Living Outside Principal Cities (Suburbs)	119.5	48.0%	60.3%	138.7	49.3%	59.6%	163.1	52.8%	62.1%
Living Outside of Metro Areas	50.5	20.3%	-	48.8	17.3%	-	46.2	15.0%	-

Source: AASHTO, 2013b, Reproduced with permission of AASHTO.

Table 5 shows the trend in the United States from 1990 to 2010. In 2010, the percentage of the U.S. population residing in MSAs increased to approximately 85 percent. What is interesting about this table is the growth in central city population during this period (indicated in gray areas), although on a percentage of the region basis, the proportion of central city population declined over the 20-year period. Some U.S. cities, such as Atlanta, Phoenix, Denver, and Tampa, saw much greater migration to the central city from domestic origins than from immigrants. In the Atlanta metropolitan area, for example, the last 20 years have seen a movement of population back into the central urban area. The increase in growth rates above might suggest that this is occurring in other parts of the country as well.

One can also see from Table 5 the increase on a percentage basis (also shown in gray) of those living in the suburbs, and a corresponding decline in the percentage of U.S. residents living outside metropolitan areas. Table 6 shows that metropolitan and nonmetropolitan areas had different growth rates (or decline) in population between 2000 and 2010: [AASHTO, 2013b]

The growth in metropolitan areas exceeding 5 million population is slightly misleading, because only 8 million of this population increase was actual new growth. The remaining 24 million in growth resulted from different U.S. metropolitan areas being combined by the Census (such as Baltimore and Washington, DC), thus putting this combined area into the 5 million population range. As of 2010, there were 8 metropolitan

Table 6. Metropolitan Area Growth Rates, by Size, United States, 2000 to 2010

Metropolitan Area Population	Growth Rate
>5 million	26.6%
2.5 to 5 million	18.8
1 to 2.5 million	6.5
0.5 to 1 million	34.4
250,000 to 500,000	−18.8
100,000 to 250,000	−21.0
50,000 to 100,000	−10.0
All metropolitan areas	12.8
Nonmetropolitan areas	−5.2

Source: AASHTO, 2013b, Reproduced with permission of AASHTO.

areas with populations exceeding 5 million and 52 metropolitan areas with populations over 1 million in the United States.

The implication of this population trend toward urban areas is that many of the future mobility and accessibility challenges in the United States (and in other countries) will be primarily urban in nature.

B. TRAVEL CHARACTERISTICS

Whereas the previous sections focused on the characteristics of travelers, transportation planners also use data on the trip itself, such as trip purpose, mode choice, time of travel, and so forth. This section discusses the trip characteristics that are most important to the transportation planning process.

1. Trip Purpose

Travel demand is considered a *derived demand*, meaning that trips are taken to achieve some purpose at a destination. For transportation analysis purposes, therefore, it is important to know why trips are being made. This is referred to as *trip purpose*. Although traditionally many transportation studies have focused on the commute or work trip, in reality the greatest increase in trip-making during the past two decades has been for other trip purposes, especially in family/personal business and social/recreational trips. Figure 11 shows the relative magnitude of commute travel as it has changed over time. As shown, work travel has declined as a percentage of total travel as reflected in several different performance measures. Figure 12 shows how the number of trips per day for different trip purposes has changed from 1977 to 2009. Note in Figure 12 that trip purpose has been aggregated to five major types—work, family/personal business, school/church, social/recreational, and other. In many transportation studies, additional trip purposes are added to the study, depending on the types of trips that need to be examined (such as airport trips) and the availability of data. As an example, the 2009 National Household Travel Survey listed 36 different trip purposes in its survey form.

Multipurpose single trips are another important phenomenon that has occurred with increasing frequency over the past several decades. Known as *trip chaining*, this travel characteristic presented challenges to transportation analysts who had traditionally based trip modeling on a single-purpose trip. According to Pisarski [2006], the attributes of trip chains include:

- Trips to work with stops are increasing, both in number of workers making stops and number of stops per worker.
- Persons with stops take longer in miles and minutes than they did in 1995 and are longer than those not making any stops.
- People who make stops tend to be those that live a greater distance from work.

THE TRANSPORTATION PLANNING HANDBOOK

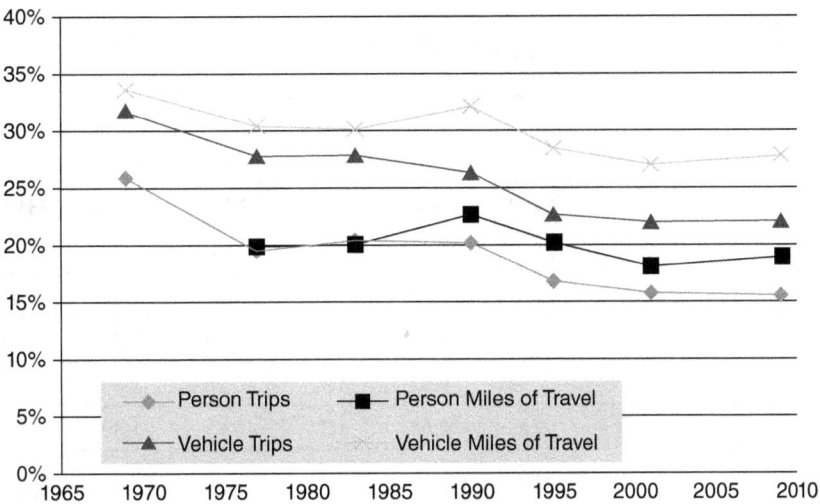

Figure 11. Work Travel as a Percentage of Total Travel Using Key Travel Measures, United States
Source: AASHTO, 2013b, Reproduced with permission of AASHTO.

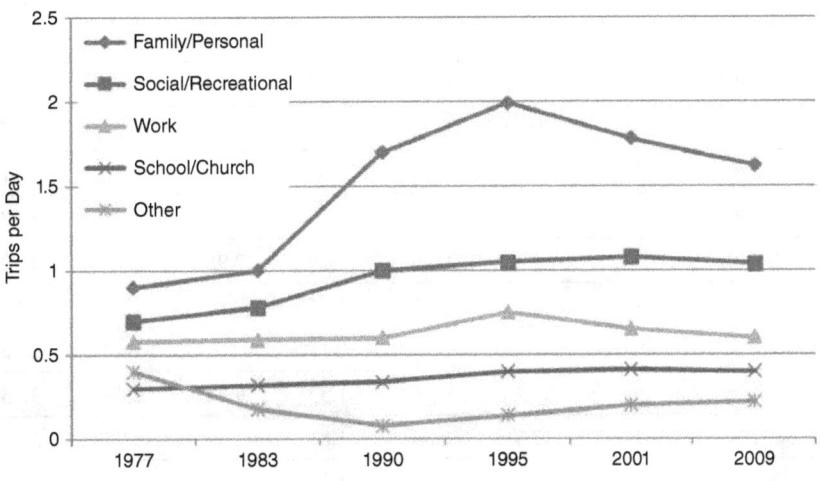

Figure 12. Change in Trip Purpose, United States, (Trips/Day), 1977–2009
Source: AASHTO, 2013a, Reproduced with permission of AASHTO.

- Suburbanites make more stops than urban dwellers.
- Stops are increasing for men as well as for women.
- Women still make the greater number of stops in both work and home directions.
- The greater increase has been by men in the work-bound direction, often just for coffee.
- Use of nonvehicular and nonpersonal auto modes drops sharply for those making stops.

Another qualifier often attached to "trip purpose" is whether one end of the trip occurs at the traveler's home. Thus, transportation planners often use terms such as home-based work, home-based shopping, home-based other, and non-home-based other to describe different types of trips made in a study area. Table 7 shows the percentage of these different types of trip purposes found in travel surveys undertaken in the 1990s in the United States. Although somewhat dated,

469

Table 7. Trips by Trip Purpose, Selected U.S. Metropolitan Areas, Most Recent Survey

City	% Trips by Type			Daily Trip Rate per Person			Daily Trip Rate per Household		
	HBW	HBO	NHB	HBW	HBO	NHB	HBW	HBO	NHB
Albuquerque, NM	17.7%	53.9%	28.4%				1.70	5.20	2.80
Amarillo, TX	18.1	49.5	32.4	0.72	1.93	1.26	1.86	5.00	3.26
Atlanta, GA	21.6	51.3	27.1	0.71	1.68	0.89	1.83	4.33	3.20
Baltimore, MD	22.1	50.3	27.6	0.62	1.42	0.78	1.69	3.84	2.10
Brownsville, TX	15.2	57.2	27.6	0.48	1.74	0.85	1.80	6.51	3.17
Cincinnati, OH	18.1	51.6	29.7						
Dallas, TX				0.75	1.65	0.84	1.94	4.30	2.18
Eugene, OR	15.6	57.6	26.8	0.76	2.82	1.32	1.80	6.70	3.10
Ft. Collins, CO	13.0	60.0	27.0	0.55	2.55	1.15	1.39	6.40	2.88
Houston, TX	19.8	52.3	27.9				1.79	4.75	2.53
Las Vegas, NV	25.8	42.0	32.2				2.15	3.49	2.68
Los Angeles, CA	19.3	52.1	28.6	0.60	1.62	0.89	1.78	4.80	2.64
Madison, WI	19.6	36.6	19.0	0.75	1.40	0.73	1.91	3.57	1.85
Minn/St. Paul, MN	14.3	52.8	32.8	0.56	2.03	1.28	1.45	5.31	3.36
Phoenix, AZ	22.8	48.0	29.2				1.86	3.97	2.33
Reno, NV	28.1	40.8	31.1	0.89	1.29	0.98	2.15	3.12	2.37
San Antonio, TX	26.9	41.9	31.2	0.67	1.66	0.91	1.95	4.81	2.63
San Diego, CA							1.20	2.40	
San Francisco, CA	25.2	46.4	28.4	0.76	1.39	0.85	2.03	3.73	2.29
Seattle, WA	22.9	44.3	32.8	0.94	1.81	1.34	1.99	3.85	2.85
St. Louis, MO				0.64	1.73	1.04	1.70	4.58	2.77
Tucson, AZ	17.6	56.5	25.9	0.60	1.94	0.89	1.53	4.92	2.25
Wilmington, DE	32.1	49.6	18.3	0.71	1.11	0.39	1.82	2.89	1.02

HBW = Home-based work; HBO = Home-based other; NHB = Non-home-based

Source: Reno, Kuzmyak and Douglas, 2002. Reproduced with permission of the Transportation Research Board.

the general percentages as shown for different trip types are similar to what is found today. (Note that travel demand modeling is evolving to a new form called activity-based modeling that no longer relies on such a distinction on individual trips. See chapter 6 on travel demand modeling.)

2. Travel Patterns

Transportation planners are very interested in travel patterns because to a large extent these patterns suggest what is needed with respect to transportation infrastructure and services. Alternatively, transportation officials can influence these patterns through public policies intended to affect land use and household/employment location decisions. Similar to the trend of increasing suburbanization of population and employment during the past 50 years, the greatest growth in urban travel patterns has been in the suburb-to-suburb trip. Suburb-to-suburb commute travel accounts for 46 percent of metropolitan commuting activity, with only 19 percent of the typical metropolitan area commuting following the suburb-to-central city pattern. Commuting within the central city constitutes approximately 25 percent, and the reverse commute—from central city to suburb—accounts for 9 percent. Not surprisingly given these trip patterns, suburbs account for 53 million of the 107 million job destinations within U.S. metropolitan areas.

The percentage of the commute trips destined outside of the worker's home county is another characteristic of the growing trend in inter-suburban trips (note that this statistic will vary in different parts of the United States due to the size of counties). During 2006 to 2010, more than a quarter (27.4 percent) of U.S. workers traveled outside of their home county for the work trip. [McKenzie, 2013] In comparison, in 1960, approximately 15 percent of commuting included a work destination outside of the worker's resident county. Between 1990 and 2000, 51 percent of the new workers added to metropolitan areas worked outside of their home county. This longer distance travel has resulted in an increasing average commute trip length.

Average commute travel time has also increased due to longer trip distances and, more importantly, to the level of congestion faced during the trip. In the United States, the average commute travel time in 2011 was 38.0 minutes (measured over 498 urbanized areas), with 47 percent of workers traveling less than 20 minutes and 8 percent traveling more than 60 minutes. With longer trip distances and longer travel times, it is not surprising that average speed has declined as well (see Figure 13).

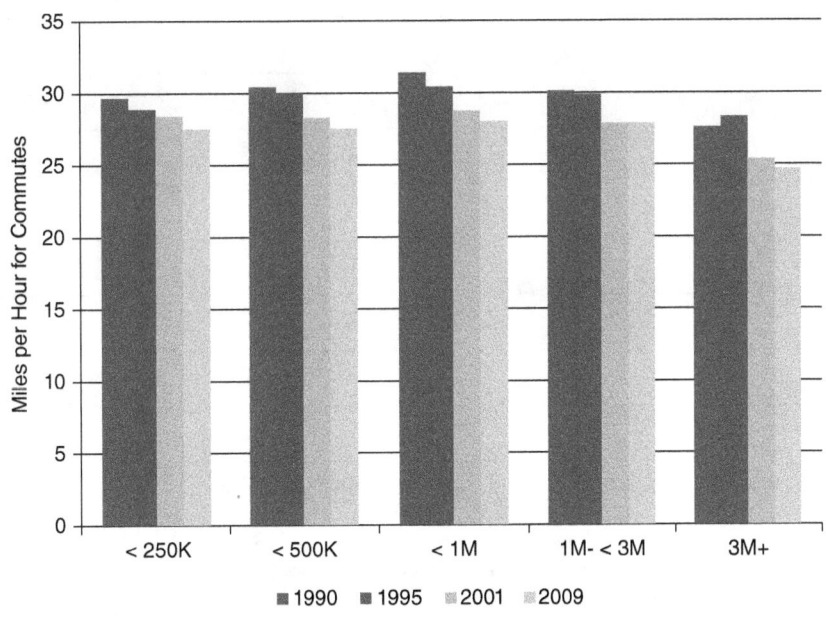

Figure 13. Change in Average Commute Speed, United States, 1990–2009 (mph)
Source: Santos et al., 2011

3. Temporal Distribution

The time of day when trips occur is another important characteristic of urban travel patterns, one that leads to system congestion when many of these trips occur in the same time periods. In most cases, system capacity is available to handle daily trips; if trips were spread evenly over the 12 hours of daytime, there would be no traffic congestion. However, the trip peaking phenomenon reflects individual travelers' combined desires of being places more or less at the same time. Figure 14 shows data from the 2009 National Household Travel Survey, indicating the concentration of person trip-making during the daytime. Because of the limited capacity of transportation systems to handle the peak loads, many metropolitan areas have found that travel is beginning to spread out into the very early hours or after the main peak is over.

Figure 15 shows the percentage of a day's total delay that occurs by hour of the day. As can be seen, the afternoon peak period experiences the most delay of the day.

Unlike commuter trips, which generally peak between 7:00 to 9:00 a.m. and 4:00 to 7:00 p.m., truck trips tend to be at their highest levels between 10:00 a.m. and 4:00 p.m.

4. Mode Usage

The likelihood of individuals choosing one mode over another for different trip purposes depends on a variety of factors, many of which are often masked when using national data. For example, many urban corridors and activity centers show significant transit ridership, even though the metropolitan area average for transit mode share could be quite small. Thus, the following data

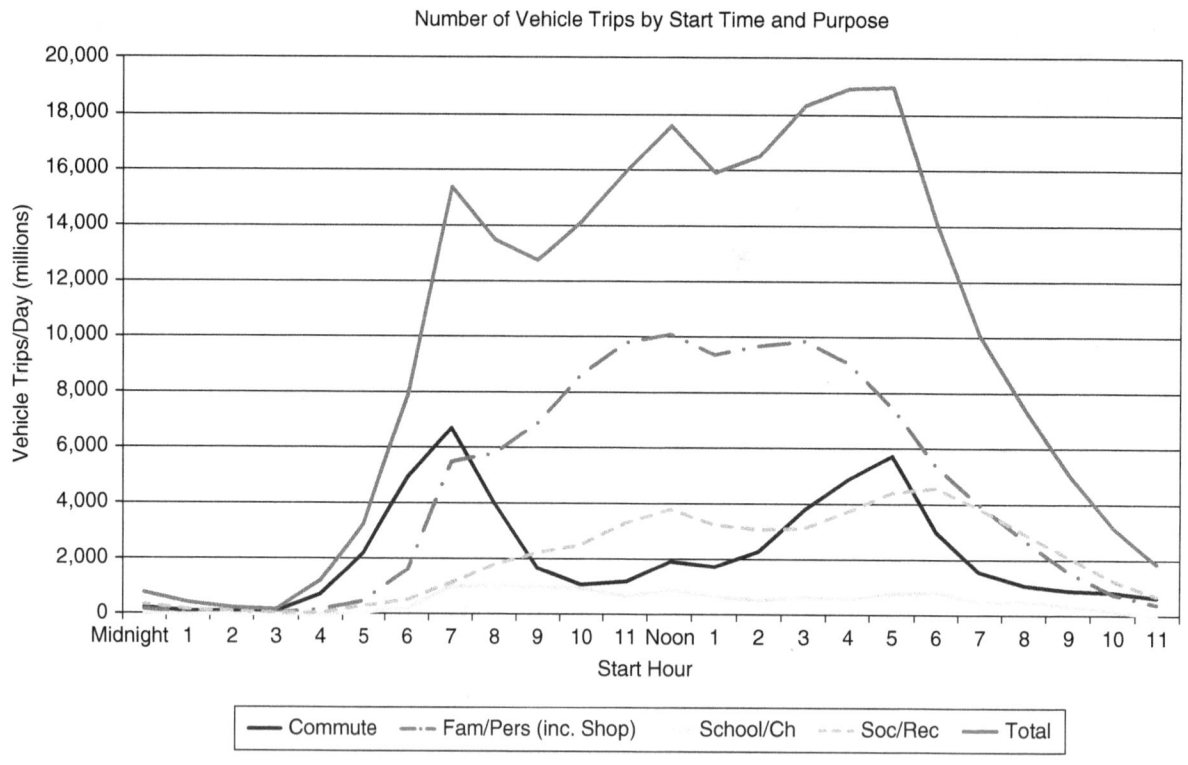

Figure 14. Typical Percent of Daily Trips by Time Period
Source: Santos et al., 2011

should be viewed with an understanding that they represent national numbers, reflecting many different types of transportation contexts.

Both the number and the percentage of urban travelers driving a car have increased significantly since the 1950s. For example, the percentage of U.S. commute trips made in a single-occupant vehicle as compared to all other modes was 64.4 percent in 1980 and increased to 76.1 percent in 2009. Carpool and transit use has slightly increased in absolute number of trips but has declined in market share. Many of the differences in mode use seen historically have lessened somewhat during the past 30 years; however, there are still important differences that can affect transportation service:

- Women still have a higher propensity to use transit than men and use carpools almost the same amount as men.
- Working at home and walking are important transportation modes in higher age groups.
- Higher age groups tend to use transit less than younger age groups, particularly buses and the subway.
- Minority populations tend to use transit much more than Caucasians (African Americans have transit use levels four times that of Caucasians; Hispanics use transit at more than twice the level of nonHispanics).
- Carpooling by Hispanics is double that of nonHispanics (23 percent to 11 percent).
- The higher the household income, the less likely one is to use transit or carpool, until the highest incomes are reached and then the transit share increases (most likely due to increased commuter rail and ferry use). Lower-income households have a much higher use of transit, biking, walking, and taxicabs.
- As metropolitan size increases, transit use increases in both central cities and suburbs;

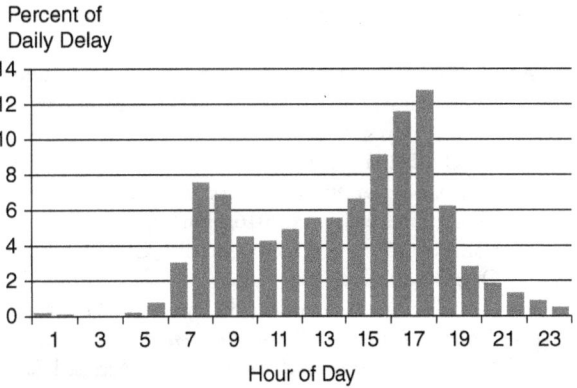

Figure 15. Percentage of Daily Delay by Time of Day, United States
Source: Schrank, D., B. Eisele, and T. Lomax. 2015, Reproduced with permission of Texas A&M Transportation Institute.

carpool rates are much more stable across different metropolitan area sizes.
- Nonmotorized travel averaged about 14.6 percent of all trips nationally in 2009, which is a decrease in market share from 1990 but represents a larger number of trips than taken in 1990.
- Those who have resided in the United States for only a short period of time tend to use transit (13 percent market share), carpools (almost 26 percent), and walking (6.8 percent) at much higher rates than those who have lived in the United States for a longer time.

Much of urban transportation policy during the last 30 years has focused on increasing the mode share for nonsingle occupant vehicle modes, primarily transit. Understanding the socio-demographic characteristics of those who ride transit and perhaps more importantly those who do not becomes an important foundation for planning studies aimed at enhancing transit ridership. Many transportation plans outline a long list of policies and program initiatives aimed at increasing transit market share; transportation planners need to understand the behavioral aspects of encouraging more people to do so.

VIII. REFERENCES

Atlanta Regional Commission. 2005. "Selected Measures for Measuring Peer States." Memorandum from Bomar, M. to J. Hayes, Atlanta, GA.

AASHTO. 2013a. *Commuting in America 2013, The National Report on Commuting, Brief 2. Patterns and Trends*, Accessed Jan. 19, 2016, from http://traveltrends.transportation.org/Documents/B2_CIA_Role%20Overall%20Travel_web_2.pdf.

———. 2013b. Commuting in America 2013, *The National Report on Commuting Patterns and Trends, Brief 3. Population and Worker Trends*. Accessed Jan. 19, 2016, from http://traveltrends.transportation.org/Documents/B3_Population%20and%20Worker%20Trends_CA03-4_web.pdf.

———. 2013c. *Commuting in America 2013, The National Report on Commuting Patterns and Trends, Brief 7. Vehicle and Transit Availability*. Accessed Jan. 14, 2016, from http://traveltrends.transportation.org/Documents/B7_Vehicle%20and%20Transit%20Availability_CA07-4_web.pdf.

Bureau of Transportation Statistics (BTS). 2015a. *Public Road and Street Mileage in the United States by Type of Surface*. Washington DC: U.S. Department of Transportation. Accessed Feb. 8, 2016, from http://www.rita.dot.gov/bts/sites/rita.dot.gov.bts/files/publications/national_transportation_statistics/html/table_01_04.html.

———. 2015b. National Transportation Statistics. Washington, DC, USA: USDOT, Research and Innovative Technology Administration. Accessed Feb. 9, 2016, from http://www.rita.dot.gov/bts/sites/rita.dot.gov.bts/files/publications/national_transportation_statistics/index.html.

City of Ames. 2014. *Ames Area MPO 2014 Regional Travel Survey*. Survey conducted by ETC, Inc. for Department of Public Works, Ames, IA. Accessed Jan. 31, 2016, from http://www.amesmobility2040.com/files/3914/1866/7185/ETC_TravelSurvey_Ames2014LRTP_Report_12-11-14.pdf

City of Redmond Public Works Department. 2009. *Annual Traffic Growth at Screenlines*. Redmond, WA.

Federal Highway Administration (FHWA). 2001. *Guide for Estimating Urban Vehicle Classification and Occupancy*. Washington, DC: Federal Highway Administration (FHWA).

———. 2010. *Travel Survey Manual, Chapter 2, The Generic Travel Survey Process*. Accessed Feb. 13, 2016, from http://www.travelsurveymanual.org/Chapter-2-1.html.

———. 2013a. *2013 Status of the Nation's Highways, Bridges, and Transit: Conditions & Performance*, Report to Congress. Accessed Feb. 14, 2016, from http://www.fhwa.dot.gov/policy/2013cpr/index.htm.

———. 2013c. *Traffic Monitoring Guide*. Washington, DC: Office of Highway Policy Information. Accessed Feb. 19, 2016, from http://www.fhwa.dot.gov/policyinformation/tmguide.

———. 2014. *Highway Performance Monitoring System, Field Manual*, Office of Highway Policy Information, Washington D.C. Accessed Feb. 18, 2016, from https://www.fhwa.dot.gov/policyinformation/hpms/fieldmanual/chapter2.cfm#chapt2_2_2.

———. 2015. *Highway Statistics 2013*. Office of Highway Policy Information, Washington DC. Accessed Feb. 8, 2016, from, https://www.fhwa.dot.gov/policyinformation/statistics/2013/.

Georgia Department of Transportation, 2015. *Regional Traffic Operations Program Spring 2015 Executive Report*. Report by Arcadis and Westat. Atlanta, GA.

Hallenbeck, M. E., and L. A. Bowman. 1984. *Development of a Statewide Traffic Counting Program Based on the Highway Performance Monitoring System*. Washington, DC: U.S. DOT, FHWA.

Holguin Veras, J., M. Jaller, I. Sanchez-Diaz, J. Wojtowicz, S. Campbell, H. Levinson, C.Lawson, E. Levine Powers, and L. Tavasszy. 2012. *Freight Trip Generation and Land Use*. NCFRP Report 19 and NCHRP Report 739, Transportation Research Board, Washington DC: Accessed Jan. 19, 2016, from http://onlinepubs.trb.org/onlinepubs/ncfrp/ncfrp_rpt_019.pdf

INRIX. 2015. *Economic and Environmental Impact of Traffic Congestion in Europe and the US*. Website. Accessed Feb. 5, 2016, from http://inrix.com/economic-environment-cost-congestion.

Institute of Transportation Engineers (ITE). 2010. *Manual of Transportation Engineering Studies*. 2nd Edition. Washington, DC: Institute of Transportation Engineers.

———. 2012. *Trip Generation*, 9th Edition. Washington, DC: Institute of Transportation Engineers.

Insurance Institute for Highway Safety. 2015. *Crash Statistics*, Accessed Feb., 4, 2016, from http://www.iihs.org/iihs/topics/t/general-statistics/fatalityfacts/overview-of-fatality-facts/2013.

Kittleson, Inc. 2005. *Downtown Portland On-street Parking Study, Lloyd District*. In City of Portland, Parking Study, Appendix B. Portland, OR. Accessed Jan. 30, 2016, from https://www.portlandoregon.gov/transportation/article/224787.

Lomax, T., et al. 1997. *Quantifying Congestion, Volume 1*, National Cooperative Highway Research Program Report 398, Final Report. Transportation Research Board, Washington, D.C. Accessed Jan. 31, 2016, from http://onlinepubs.trb.org/onlinepubs/nchrp/nchrp_rpt_398.pdf.

Massachusetts DOT. 2012. Massachusetts Travel Survey. Boston, MA. Accessed Jan. 30, 2016, from http://www.massdot.state.ma.us/Portals/17/docs/TravelSurvey/MTSFinalReport.pdf.

McKenzie, B. 2013. "County-to-County Commuting Flows: 2006-10," Accessed Feb. 4, 2016, from http://www.census.gov/hhes/commuting.

McKenzie, B. 2014. "Modes Less Traveled—Bicycling and Walking to Work in the United States: 2008–2012," American Community Survey Report 25, May. Accessed Feb. 2, 2016, from http://www.census.gov/hhes/commuting/files/2014/acs-25.pdf.

New York State DOT. 2011. *2011 Traffic Data Report for New York State*. Albany, NY. Accessed Jan. 19, 2016, from https://www.dot.ny.gov/divisions/engineering/technical-services/hds-respository/Traffic%20Data%20Report%202011%20Introduction.pdf.

Pisarski, A. 2006. *Commuting in America III*. NCHRP Report 550/TCRP Report 110: Washington DC: Transportation Research Board.

Reno, A., R. Kuzmyak, and B. Douglas. 2002. *Characteristics of Urban Travel Demand*, Transit Cooperative Research Program Report 73. Transportation Research Board, Washington, DC. Accessed Jan. 31, 2016, from http://www.tcrponline.org/ PDFDocuments/TCRP_RPT_73a.pdf.

Rhodes, S., M. Berndt, P. Bingham, J. Bryan, T. Cherrett, P. Plumeau, and R. Weisbrod. 2012. *Guidebook for Understanding Urban Goods Movement*. NCFRP Report 14. Transportation Research Board. Accessed Jan. 19, 2016, from http://onlinepubs.trb.org/onlinepubs/ncfrp/ncfrp_rpt_014.pdf.

Santa Clara Valley Transportation Authority. 2009. *Comprehensive Operations Analysis*, Presentation by Michael Burns, General Manager. Accessed Jan. 19, 2016, from http://www.mtc.ca.gov/planning/tsp/Comprehensive_Operations_Analysis.pdf.

Santos, A., N. McGuckin, H. Y. Nakamoto, D. Gray, and S. Liss. 2011. *Summary of Travel Trends: 2009 National Household Travel Survey*. Report FHWA-PL-ll-022. Washington D.C., Accessed Feb. 19, 2016, from http://nhts.ornl.gov/2009/pub/stt.pdf.

Schrank, David, Bill Eisele, Tim Lomax, and Jim Bak. 2015. 2015 *Urban Mobility Scorecard*. Published by The Texas A&M Transportation Institute and INRIX. Aug. Accessed Jan. 28, 2016, from http://mobility.tamu.edu.

Stopher, P., et al. 2008. *Standardized Procedures for Personal Travel Surveys*, National Cooperative Highway Research Program Report 571. Transportation Research Board, Washington, DC. Accessed Jan. 31, 2016, from http://onlinepubs.trb.org/onlinepubs/nchrp/nchrp_rpt_571.pdf.

Tierney, K. 2012. *Use of the U.S. Census Bureau's Public Use Microdata Sample (PUMS) by State Departments of Transportation and Metropolitan Planning Organizations*. NCHRP Synthesis 43. Washington DC: Transportation Research Board. Accessed March 2, 2016, from http://onlinepubs.trb.org/onlinepubs/nchrp/nchrp_syn_434.pdf

Turcotte, M. 2011. *Commuting to work: Results of the 2010 General Social Survey, Component of Statistics Canada Catalogue no. 11-008-X*, Canadian Social Trends, Statistics Canada, August 24. Accessed Feb. 5, 2016, from http://www.statcan.gc.ca/pub/11-008-x/2011002/article/11531-eng.pdf.

Urban Mass Transportation Administration (UMTA). 1985. *Transit Data Collection Design Manual, Final Report*. Washington, DC: UMTA.

Washington, S., M. Karlaftis and F. Mannering. 2003. *Statistical and Econometric Methods for Transportation Data Analysis*. Boca Raton, FL: Chapman Hall/CRC Press.

Westat, Inc. 2014. *Mid-Region Council of Governments 2013 Household Travel Survey*, Final Report. Albuquerque, NM.

THE ETHICAL PLANNER

INTERPRETATIONS AND CONCLUSIONS

BY JERRY WEITZ

In this final part, I suggest some interpretations of the AICP Code and offer conclusions.

SUGGESTED INTERPRETATIONS OF THE CODE

The code includes a number of key phrases but does not provide definitions except for "serious crime." The decision not to provide definitions in the AICP Code is, for the most part, intentional, because definitions and interpretations—of "the public interest," for example—will depend on the specific context and will most likely change from one context to another, as well as evolve over time. Listed in this section are several instances where the AICP Code, strictly construed, limits significantly the context in which the rule applies. The ethical planning practitioner will examine ways in which a rule of conduct might be deemed applicable even if a plausible argument could be made that a strict interpretation of the rule would render it inapplicable.

ACCEPT AN ASSIGNMENT

This phrase in the AICP Code—used in principle 2.c and rules of conduct 2 and 3, and its variation, "accept work," as used in rule 16, should be broadly construed to mean not only accepting an assignment but also "continuing an assignment." A planner may have already been engaged in a given assignment when an ethical issue arises. The ethical planning practitioner will not continue working on an assignment that requires actions inconsistent with the AICP Code.

ADEQUATE INFORMATION

The aspiration to provide adequate information (principle 1.d and rule of conduct 1) should be interpreted as an aspiration to provide "complete" information, with no omissions. Deliberately omitting information could be considered a violation of rule of conduct 1 and aspirational principle 1.d, even though the term "complete" does not appear in the applicable code provisions. Exclusion of certain information should be considered inconsistent with these code provisions, in my view.

AUTHORITY TO MAKE A BINDING, FINAL DETERMINATION

A planner who has authority to make a formal recommendation should construe rule of conduct 8 to be applicable, even though the strict context would suggest that a formal recommendation is clearly not a "binding, final determination."

DECISION MAKERS

The provision of rule of conduct 19 that planners shall not engage in discussions with "decision makers" in a manner prohibited by rules, procedures, or custom might be broadened to include private discussions with certain groups. To exclude private groups from this code construct would assume that they have no power to make relevant decisions or at least no ability to influence such decisions.

EMPLOYMENT

When considering whether a given action or activity is a conflict of interest, interpret the term "employment," as used in rule of conduct 4, to include elected positions. Further, it may be extended to appointed positions, even if they do not come with remuneration. Also, rule 4, which applies to "salaried" employees, should be considered more broadly applicable to any "contracted" employee or consultant. Moreover, in other places, the AICP Code uses broader terms—"professional services we perform" (2.b) and "services to be performed" (rule 2)—which may be applied in additional contexts.

OTHER PROFESSIONALS

"Other professionals," as used in rule of conduct 10, should be interpreted to include planning professionals and participants in all other professions.

PLANNING ISSUES

The phrase "planning issues" appears in rule of conduct 1. Planners engaged in administrative decision making on a zoning recommendation or grant proposal may conclude that such activities are not "planning issues." "Planning issues" are broad and should be interpreted to include instances outside the periphery of actual planning processes. The spirit of the AICP Code, in my view, would suggest that this rule of conduct should be applied broadly and thoroughly.

PLANNING PROCESS

This phrase appears in principle 1.h and rules of conduct 8, 9, and 19. Zoning and development code administration, as well as other facets of planners' work, should be broadly interpreted to be within the realm of a "planning process" for purposes of the AICP Code's rules of conduct. Similarly, "planning process participants" should, by extension, be broadly construed to apply to people making decisions involving administrative discretion as well as anyone engaged in any other activities that involve planners but lie outside the mainstream of planning processes. The context of the "planning process" might even be broadened to include personnel matters. Also, litigation after a rezoning decision could conceivably be considered a continuation of the planning process. The ethical planning practitioner will critically contemplate when the planning process starts and ends, extending the timing beyond the strict situation at hand. Hearings and debates on a zoning decision could reasonably be considered a planning process, in my view. I foresee circumstances where it could be appropriate to extend the term "planning process" even to a decision about whether to attend a training event. Finally, how does one treat an action by a certified planner that technically falls outside the traditionally accepted notion of a "planning process"—for example, that takes place in the political environment of an elected official?

SOLICIT PROSPECTIVE CLIENTS OR EMPLOYMENT

This provision in rule of conduct 11 should be interpreted as applying not only to private planning consultants but to public- and nonprofit-sector planners who are trying to conduct consulting assignments or seek other gain.

CONCLUSIONS

This book, which focuses on the applicability of the AICP Code of Ethics and Professional Conduct, approaches questions of ethics in planning practice using a mostly "legalistic" approach, at least initially. My central conclusion is this: Practicing planners will almost always gain a satisfactory answer to an ethics question by applying a legalistic perspective—that is, by systematically examining the AICP Code and applicable laws and rules. The ethical planning practitioner achieves this by rigorously analyzing how each and every aspirational principle and rule of conduct, as well as applicable laws and rules, may apply to a given ethics question.

Many planners take a legalistic approach to ethics at the outset. After all, when we act, the greatest threat is that our activities may be illegal according to local or state laws. One of the first questions a planner is likely to ask is whether his or her activities broke the law. Close behind that first question, the ethical planning practitioner will ask if there is a rule of conduct in the AICP Code that governs the matter or specifically indicates whether an activity is unethical and thus disallowed.

Every AICP planner should want to stay out of trouble with the law and avoid behaving in an unethical way that is subject to scrutiny by the professional institute's enforcement arm. A legalistic approach is a safe and practical way to achieve those goals and is perhaps the best place for planners to start. Taking a legalistic approach helps us to meet the biggest need of all planners: to protect our livelihoods—that is, self-interest—while doing our jobs ethically.

There are limits to a purely legalistic approach to ethics, and therefore, there are some clear limits to the narrow focus on the AICP Code in this book. Laws cannot cover every type of misbehavior that may be contemplated. Enforceable rules of conduct must maintain some general applicability and therefore must sometimes be vague in practical application. This is evident in the prior section, which shows how there is much room for planners to interpret the strict dictates of the AICP Code.

A potential big danger of the legalistic approach to ethics is that it could lead to narrow, impoverished views of ethics in planning (Howe 1994). The fact that an action is legal does not mean it is morally permissible to take that action (Barrett 2001). In other words, laws do not include moral and ethical statements. Bolan (1983) makes a similar point in his observation that codes of conduct "offer a false sense of security and obscure the subtle, tacit and unstated norms that are often instrumental in guiding action."

I have distilled some key points from Howe (1994) and my own thoughts into this set of suggested best practices:

Extend ethical values to non-AICP members. Do not discard a given ethical issue simply because the person acting unethically is not an AICP member. APA Ethical Principles in Planning (1992) apply to all planners, whether they are members of APA or not. And those principles are, in many ways, similar to the content of the AICP Code.

Rely on public processes to infuse legitimacy. Planners should consider how open a process is in arriving at a public decision. Accountability should take precedence over a planner's own idea of the public interest if the decision is made in an open process. Do not substitute your own conception of the public interest for a notion of the public interest that is arrived at through an open and fair public process. Actions that would violate duties of justice should be resisted and should not be justified by appeals to serving the public interest (Howe 1994).

Be wary of perceptions of special advantage. Be wary of situations where others could perceive that you are obtaining a special advantage from a position or appointment. Think more deeply about how conflicts of interest could surface. Anticipate conflicts and responses, and write them into a conflict-of-interest management plan.

Do not condone the conflicts of interest of others. Do not acquiesce to another person's conflict of interest, because knowingly letting such a conflict continue without dissenting is inconsistent with the AICP Code. Acquiescence means you are tacitly confirming and condoning that unethical behavior by another person.

Consider the consequences of dissent and covert action. Consider whether your ethical principles and your cause are worth the fight, and whether it is prudent for you to rock the boat. Consider whether letting the issue slide will allow you more influence in the long run. The option of acting covertly should be viewed with suspicion. Go underground only if you are prepared to face the consequences.

Disseminate information widely. If information is appropriate for dissemination to one person or group of persons, then it is appropriate to distribute it broadly to others, even if they are not sympathetic to your cause.

Employ avoidance strategies. To relieve political pressure, sidestep any discussions with elected officials outside the public planning and public hearing processes, if possible. Ask that elected officials raise issues in public forums, rather than privately and individually with you.

Act on opportunities to pursue social goals. Recognize, and act on, opportunities to advance social justice.

When in doubt, seek permission. When in doubt or in an ethical gray area, seek permission to engage in the contemplated activity.

Be careful where you choose to invest. Avoid investment opportunities that have even a remote relation to your official position or are within the jurisdiction in which you work.

Treat younger planners with delicacy. If you are a director, when a junior planner disagrees with your position, spend time educating the younger planner on why you have arrived at your decision. Make sure you can prove any allegations of misconduct against a younger planner. Help young planners understand their errors and forgive them for first offenses.

THE ETHICAL PLANNING PRACTITIONER

Building on Steinberg and Austern (1990) and Barrett (2001), I suggest that the discernible traits of the ethical planner are as follows:

1. The ethical planning practitioner is a respectable professional who:
    - knows what the laws require and obeys them
    - does not commit unethical acts
    - seeks to avoid doing bad things
    - is guided by integrity and a sense of what is right
    - embraces obligations to others
    - acts with due regard for individual and societal freedoms
    - extends obligations beyond legal compliance
    - assumes an attitude of stewardship and responsibility for protection and enhancement of human and natural resources

2. The ethical planning practitioner is a scholar of the AICP Code who:
    - reads and rereads the AICP Code frequently, or at least every time an ethics question manifests
    - monitors the professional institute for changes to, and interpretations of, the AICP Code, including any enforcement actions
    - knows the AICP Code in the same way a zoning administrator knows a locality's zoning code
    - applies the AICP Code with strict construction but also expands the narrow contexts of the rules of conduct to the broadest reasonable contexts
    - respects the aspirational principles and never discards them as unenforceable
    - attends continuing education sessions about ethics, and absorbs and applies the information gleaned
    - recognizes that conflicts exist among principles, among rules of conduct, and between the principles and rules of conduct of the AICP Code
    - is willing to seek advice from AICP's Ethics Officer

3. The ethical planning practitioner is a conscientious deliberator and prudent decision maker who:
    - corrects his or her perspective, or that of another person, when thought processes are leading to the rationalization of a choice that the planner or the other person wants to make
    - chooses the best approach when none of the available approaches will provide the ideal result
    - resolves personal value conflicts ethically and legally, without sacrificing integrity
    - adjusts his or her behavior in response to new information
    - recognizes errors in judgment, including ethical mishaps
    - recognizes that inaction, including omission, is a choice with ethical implications
    - develops the capacity to meet ethical crises and prevent them before they arise

4. The ethical planning practitioner is an inspirational, professional role model who:

- sets the standard for normal conduct of planning and agency business
- is the epitome of integrity
- says "no" to all requests to do something unethical or illegal
- does not excuse others for unethical or illegal acts
- sees to it that those failing to serve the public office are removed from public service if they don't change their ways
- engages in preventive avoidance, such as keeping social distance from influential people, to reduce pressure for favoritism
- maintains and fosters open and honest communication
- devotes time generously to groups that need assistance, especially disadvantaged persons
- commits to serving the public interest and acts in accordance with the public interest
- exercises administrative discretion responsibly and consistently
- provides ways to ensure accountability of action and responsibility for actions
- finds ways to advance the public's positive association with the work of planners, not just to preserve the status quo of the profession in the public eye
- finds ways to positively reward others for their ethical behavior

REFERENCES

American Institute of Certified Planners. 2009. Rev. ed. AICP Code of Ethics and Professional Conduct. Available at www.planning.org/ethics/ethicscode.htm.

American Planning Association. 1992. Ethical Principles in Planning. Adopted by the APA Board of Directors, May.

Barrett, Carol. 2002. *Everyday Ethics for Practicing Planners*. Chicago: APA Planners Press.

Bolan, Richard S. 1983. "The Structure of Ethical Choice in Planning Practice." *Journal of Planning Education and Research* 3: 23–34.

Howe, Elizabeth. 1994. Acting on Ethics in City Planning. New Brunswick, N.J.: Center for Urban Policy Research, Rutgers University.

Steinberg, Sheldon S., and David T. Austern. 1990. *Government, Ethics, and Managers: A Guide to Solving Ethical Dilemmas in the Public Sector*. Westport, Conn.: Quorum Books.

CPSIA information can be obtained
at www.ICGtesting.com
Printed in the USA
FSHW021707030820
72661FS